a complete repertoire based on Nc3 and Nc6

Cyrus Lakdawala

a ferocious opening repertoire

Christoph Wisnewski

play 1...Nc6!

a complete chess opening repertoire for Black

EVERYMAN CHESS

www.everymanchess.com

A Ferocious Opening Repertoire
First published 2011 by Gloucester Publishers Ltd, London.
Copyright © 2011 Cyrus Lakdawala

Play 1...Nc6
First published 2007 by Gloucester Publishers Ltd, London.
Copyright © 2007 Christof Scheerer

This edition first published in 2019 by Gloucester Publishers Ltd.

British Library Cataloguing-in-Publication Data
A catalogue record for this book is available from the British Library.

ISBN: 978-1-78194-495-0

Distributed in North America by National Book Network,
15200 NBN Way, Blue Ridge Summit, PA 17214. Ph: 717.794.3800

Distributed in Europe by Central Books Ltd.,
50 Freshwater Road, Chadwell Heath, London, RM8 1RX Ph: 44(0)845 458 9911

All other sales enquiries should be directed to Everyman Chess:
Email: info@everymanchess.com; Website www.Everymanchess.com

Everyman is the registered trade mark of Random House Inc. and is used in this work under license from Random House Inc.

EVERYMAN CHESS SERIES
Chief Advisor: Byron Jacobs
Cover Design: Horacio Monteverde

Printed and bound in the UK by TJ International Ltd, Padstow, Cornwall.

Contents

Bibliography   4

Introduction   5

1   The Veresov: 3...♘bd7 4 f3!?   10

2   The Veresov: 3...♘bd7 4 ♕d3   45

3   The Veresov: Other Defences   71

4   Veresov versus French: Lines with ...♘f6   109

5   Veresov versus French: Lines without ...♘f6   130

6   1 d4 d5 2 ♘c3: Second-Move Alternatives   163

7   Veresov versus Caro-Kann   188

8   Veresov versus Dutch   208

9   Modern, Pirc and Philidor   233

10   Schmid Benoni and Czech Benoni   263

11   1...♘c6 and Owen's Defence   280

Index of Variations   298

Index of Games   302

Bibliography

Dangerous Weapons: The French, John Watson (Everyman Chess 2007)
Dangerous Weapons: The Pirc and Modern, Richard Palliser (Everyman Chess 2009)
Dealing with d4 Deviations, John Cox (Everyman Chess 2005)
Fighting the Anti-King's Indians, Yelena Dembo (Everyman Chess 2008)
French: Advance and Other Lines, Steffen Pedersen (Gambit 2005)
How to Play Against 1 e4, Neil McDonald (Everyman Chess 2008)
Pirc Alert!, Lev Alburt and Alex Chernin (Chess Info. and Research Centre 2001)
Play 1...b6, Christian Bauer (Everyman Chess 2005)
Play 1...♘c6, Christoph Wisnewski (Everyman Chess 2007)
Play the Dutch, Neil McDonald (Everyman Chess 2010)
Play the French, John Watson (Everyman Chess 2003)
Starting Out: d-pawn Attacks, Richard Palliser (Everyman Chess 2008)
Starting Out: The Modern, Nigel Davies (Everyman Chess 2008)
Starting Out: The Pirc/Modern, Joe Gallagher (Everyman Chess 2003)
The Black Lion, Jerry van Rekom and Leo Jansen (New in Chess 2008)
The Flexible French, Viktor Moskalenko (New In Chess 2008)
The French, Viacheslav Eingorn and Valentin Bogdanov (Gambit 2008)
The French Defense, Svetozar Gligoric and Wolfgang Uhlmann (RHM Press 1975)
The Lion, Jerry van Rekom and Leo Janssen (Uitgeverij Schaaknieuws 2001)
The Pirc Defense, Alex Chernin and Jan Cartier (Hays 1997)
The Richter-Veresov System: The Chameleon Chess Repertoire, Eduard Gufeld and Oleg Stetsko (Thinker's Press 1999)
The Ultimate Pirc, John Nunn and Colin McNab (Batsford 1998)
The Veresov, Nigel Davies (Everyman Chess 2003)
The Veresov Attack, Ken Smith and John Hall (Chess Digest 1994)
Tiger's Modern, Tiger Hillarp Persson (Quality Chess 2005)
Win with the London System, Sverre Johnsen and Vlatko Kovacevic (Gambit 2005)

I also referred to material from ChessPublishing.com

Introduction:
The Veresov

This book is really the result of a happy accident. I had just finished my first book for Everyman Chess on the London System, when John Emms asked if I wanted to do a second book – on the Veresov. Apparently he had seen several of my games with the Veresov in the database. There was only one problem: John had been looking at my younger brother Jimmy's games! The database had inadvertently posted many of Jimmy's games under my name. Jimmy had played the Veresov in the 80's and had long since retired from tournament play to become a captain of industry, running our family business. I, on the other hand, had not played a single Veresov in my life. After confessing this to John he gave me the go ahead anyway. Perhaps John thought Veresov was in the Lakdawala family genes!

The book constituted a real challenge, and the irony of a London-loving chess chicken like me writing a book on one of the most bloodthirsty openings in chess was not lost on me. I had al-ways considered the Veresov an opening of dubious lineage. After all, with 1 d4 and 2 ♘c3 White violates one of the biggest taboos in chess, which is don't block your c-pawn with your knight in a Queen's Pawn opening. What never occurs to Veresov naysayers is the fact that White isn't trying for c4, but instead plays for e4! Diehard Veresovers like Jimmy knew better. He would heap poetic praises upon his beloved opening. Not wishing to hurt the lad's feelings, I indulged him by nodding politely, coughing, looking up at the ceiling and whistling through my teeth, holding back any criticism of his favourite opening. Now, having thoroughly studied the opening, I can state with confidence that Jimmy was right and I was wrong. The Veresov is completely playable, and if you are a tactician and attacking player, it tends to suck your opponent into your realm of power. Nobody bothers to study the line as Black. So the greatest strength of the Veresov is its own dubious reputation!

Profile of a Veresover

Jimmy was born to play the Veresov:

1. He was incredibly lazy about opening study. In fact, he reached an impressive US Chess Federation rating just over 2400 without ever studying a single chess book! A feat only the young Capa matched. The opening is easy to learn because you play d4, ♘c3, ♗g5 and often f3 against just about everything. The idea behind the opening is incredibly simple: force e4! no matter how Black responds. This one guiding principle makes your opening choices easy.

2. He was lopsided in his chess abilities. I would estimate his strategic understanding at the level of a typical kindergartener, while his tactical and calculation abilities were right in the neighbourhood of *Rybka*! Once at a family birthday party I was playing GM Kaidanov in a 5-0 game on the ICC. Jimmy came in late, looked at the position for about 20 seconds and stopped me from making the move I was going to play. He reeled off a long variation with a cheapo at the end and insisted I play it. Kaidanov walked right into it!

3. Jimmy was happiest when the position was a mess. The more unclear the position, the better. And with the Veresov that's what you get.

So if you have any of the following similar traits, then the Veresov is a perfect opening choice: you don't have much time or inclination for study; you are a natural tactician; and you revel in chaotic positions.

A History of the Veresov

Besides Jimmy, the other founding fathers of the opening were Savielly Tartakower, who invented the line in the 1920's and played it his entire life; Kurt Richter, who played it mostly in the 30's; and Gavril Veresov, who played it from the 30's to the mid-70's. Gavril Veresov must have had the better press agent for the opening to be named after him. Its pedigree includes four World Champions who employed it: Smyslov, Tal, Spassky and Karpov. The top GMs who play it today are Hector and Khachian.

Here is an early game in the Veresov. Note the utter confusion the opening inflicts on Black!

Game 1
K.Richter-G.Rogmann
Berlin 1937

1 d4 ♘f6 2 ♘c3 d5 3 ♗g5 c6 4 f3 ♕b6

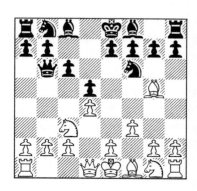

Logical. Black hits the sore spot on b2 before White gets into his groove with ♕d2 and 0-0-0.

5 e4!?

White can also take the milquetoast route with 5 ♖b1, but any red-blooded Veresover would hang his head down in shame if this were played!

5...♕xb2 6 ♘ge2 e6

Choosing to keep the game closed to protect himself from White's development lead. Instead, 6...dxe4!? 7 fxe4 ♕a3 8 e5 ♘d5 9 ♗d2 ♗g4 10 ♘xd5 cxd5 11 ♕b1! gives White enough for the pawn.

7 e5 ♘fd7 8 ♖b1 ♕a3 9 ♖b3 ♕a5 10 ♗d2 ♕c7 11 ♘f4 a6!

It is too soon for 11...c5?! 12 ♘b5 ♕c6 13 c4! dxc4 14 ♗xc4 cxd4 15 ♕e2 when the game has blasted open and White holds a massive development lead.

12 ♗d3?

His d-pawn required support with 12 ♘ce2 c5 13 c3.

12...♗e7?

I just don't buy that White has full compensation for the piece if Black strikes with 12...c5! 13 ♘cxd5 (what else?) 13...exd5 14 ♘xd5 ♕d8 15 e6 fxe6 16 ♕e2 ♔f7 17 ♘f4 ♘b6. Moreover, Black's failure to counter in the centre results in a massive build-up against his king later in the game.

13 0-0 0-0

This time the central counter entails risk: 13...c5!? 14 ♘cxd5 exd5 15 ♘xd5 ♕d8 16 c3 ♘c6 17 ♗e3 cxd4 18 cxd4 0-0 19 ♘xe7+ ♕xe7 20 ♕b1 and White has only one pawn for the piece, but

may still have adequate compensation. He enjoys plenty of extra space and the bishop pair, not to mention that his pieces are aimed at Black's king and he might begin a giant pawn roller, starting with f4.

14 ♕e1 ♖e8

Black's position falls apart after the mistimed 14...c5? 15 ♘cxd5! exd5 16 ♘xd5 ♕d8 17 ♗a5! b6 18 ♕e4! g6 19 ♖xb6!.

15 ♕g3 ♘f8?!

15...c5! 16 ♘cxd5! exd5 17 ♘xd5 ♕d8 is messy but probably still in Black's favour.

16 ♘h5 ♘g6 17 f4 ♗d8?!

Black just doesn't believe in countering wing attacks with central counters! He had to plunge into the craziness of 17...c5 18 f5!.

18 ♕h3 b5?!

On his tombstone, Rogmann should have had the undertaker inscribe: "I wish I had played ...c5!" Even here, 18...c5 19 f5 exf5 20 ♘xd5 leads to a typical Veresov mess.

19 g4! ♕e7

For the love of God, man, ...c5! But maybe now it is too late. Also, please note how kind I am in awarding most of Black's non-...c5 moves '?!' instead of the full '?' that they deserve.

Here after 19...c5 20 f5 exf5 21 gxf5 c4 22 ♘xg7! White has a crushing attack.

20 g5!

Planning to entomb Black's king with a knight sac on f6.

20...♗b6 21 ♘e2 c5!

Hooray! Perhaps this move should be awarded a '!!'. Unfortunately, it arrives too late.

22 ♘f6+!

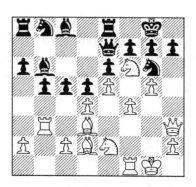

The original maestro of the Veresov (the Richter-Veresov?) goes on to give a beautiful demonstration in the art of attack.

22...gxf6 23 gxf6 ♕f8 24 ♔h1 cxd4

The force of White's kingside build-up is revealed in the lines: 24...c4?? 25 ♗b4! which traps the queen, and 24...♘c6 25 f5 exf5 26 ♗h6 f4 27 ♕h5.

25 ♖g1 ♘d7 26 ♕h5 ♘xf6 27 exf6 ♖a7 28 ♗b4!

Deflecting a key defender.

28...♗c5 29 ♗xc5 ♕xc5 30 ♗xg6 fxg6 31 ♖xg6+!

Obvious but still pretty.

31...♔h8

Black's king is utterly overwhelmed. This is how Napoleon must have felt near the end of the Battle of Waterloo! If 31...hxg6 32 ♕xg6+ ♔f8 33 ♖g3 and mate next move.

32 f7! 1-0

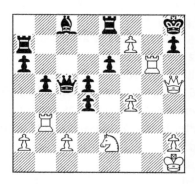

Black can't deal with the double threats of 33 fxe8(Q+) and 33 ♕e5+.

Summary

...c5 was required! Defensive technique has come a long way since 1937. Today, most club players would reflexively counter in the centre at the first sign of a white attack, but one thing remains constant: the Veresov continues to confuse Black.

The Tone of this Book

I hope the reader will forgive my occasional overly-goofy tone. In the middle of a chapter, I may suddenly engage you in a conversation about the Borg Collective and go on to confess impure thoughts towards space goddess Sevenofnine! The idea is to recreate the casual atmosphere of chess lessons at my home rather than that of a professor in a lecture hall. It's actually a mystery to me why most chess books are so formally written, as if readers are Amish elders rather than the goofs and nerds most of us are! Besides, I can't help it. The dangerous combination of Jimi Hendrix and Buddhist chants blasting away on the CD player while I write induces such outbursts! I hope the reader gets as much enjoyment reading this book as I did writing it.

Acknowledgments

No project this large gets produced by a single individual without the helping kindness of others. I would like to thank John Emms for his Capa-like clarity with the chapter outlines, and also for allowing me to write the book the way I did. Thanks to Richard Palliser for his final edit of the book. Thanks to my friends Dave Hart and Peter Graves for their helpful discussions and suggestions while the book was in progress. Thanks to proof-reader-in-chief Nancy, and to computer wiz Timothy (I would like to add that any lingering resentment over the fact that the damned fool accidentally deleted a full day's work in Chapter Six has dissolved in the fog of time!).

Cyrus Lakdawala,
San Diego,
November 2010

Chapter One
The Veresov: 3...♘bd7 4 f3!?

1 d4 ♘f6 2 ♘c3 d5 3 ♗g5 ♘bd7 4 f3!?

If you decide to play the 4 f3!? Veresov, be prepared to enter the rabbit hole. The lines in this chapter are the craziest and some would claim most unsound of the entire Veresov. And indeed, there are several lines which are flat out unsound. I tried to weed these out and place them at a safe distance in the notes! Don't worry though. If you don't like the positions from this chapter, you always have the

option of skipping the lines here and heading to the solidity of 4 ♕d3 in Chapter Two.

Key ideas to remember

1. The first two games deal with Black's worst option, which is the French-like situations arising from the ...e6 lines. The trouble for Black is that he already committed his knight to d7, and everyone knows that the b8-knight should be developed to c6 in a French.

2. Khachian-Donchenko is an example of the ...c5 lines, usually played on Black's fourth move. Here I recommend taking on c5 and holding on for dear life, usually with b4. Black normally regains the pawn due to his development lead and the arising positions are interesting battles between White's big queenside pawn majority and Black's central advance.

3. The diagram below reveals the

big problem with playing 4 f3. The recipe for Black (often given as a refutation of the Veresov itself) is the set-up ...♘bd7, ...c6, and when White plays e4, capture on e4 and hit back with a timely ...e5!.

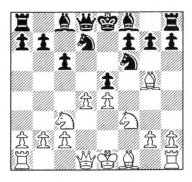

Structurally White remains pretty shaky in these lines and he is often forced to part with his powerful dark-squared bishop. I tried to thread the needle, and feel that the lines recommended here are the only playable options for White who gets activity, a development lead and attacking chances to compensate for some of his positional failings. Yilmazyerli-Song is a good example of White's explosive potential in this line.

4. Warning: This line is reserved for the very bravest of you out there! The 7 ♘f3 line, as in the above diagram, is your wildest option in the whole 4 f3 Veresov. White gives up structure, taking on an isolani on e4, and sometimes even gives up his b-pawn to boot. But don't despair. You get quite a bit in return in the form of tremendous piece

activity, open files and real attacking chances. Here you just plunge into the ocean and either get the pearl or drown!

Game 2
R.Réti-S.Tartakower
Vienna 1919

1 d4 d5 2 ♘c3 ♘f6 3 ♗g5 ♘bd7 4 f3

Who would have guessed that it was Réti, godfather of the hypermoderns, who employed the very first pure Veresov?

4...h6 5 ♗h4

I recently tested the rarely-played 5 ♗f4!? in an ICC blitz game, which continued 5...c5 6 e4 cxd4 7 ♕xd4 e5?! (unsound, but very difficult to meet in a blitz game) 8 ♗xe5 ♗c5 9 ♗xf6 gxf6 10 ♕xd5 (the safer 10 ♕d2!? also denies Black full compensation since 10...♕b6? is met by the simple 11 ♘a4!) 10...♕b6 11 ♘ge2? (11 0-0-0!! refutes Black's sac after 11...♗xg1 12 ♗b5 ♗e3+ 13 ♔b1 0-0 14 ♗xd7 ♖d8 15 ♗xc8!! ♖xd5 16 ♘xd5 ♕c5 17 ♗xb7 ♖f8 18 ♘xf6+ and

White's knight, rook and four pawns outweigh Black's lone queen) 11...♗f2+ 12 ♔d1 0-0 and in C.Lakdawala-'Zq', Internet blitz 2010, Black had full compensation in the form of his lead in development, White's harassed king, and his domination of the dark squares.

5...e6 6 e4 ♗e7?!

This move is played all the time by Black, but it simply leads to a rotten French Defence, with his knight misplaced on d7. Perhaps Black should risk 6...dxe4!? 7 fxe4 ♗b4 8 e5 g5 9 ♗g3 ♘d5 10 ♘ge2 c5 11 a3 ♗xc3+ 12 ♘xc3 ♘e3 13 ♕d2 cxd4 14 ♘b5 ♕b6 15 ♘d6+ ♔f8 and now, instead of 16 ♖c1!? as in F.Cottegnie-R.Cardoso, correspondence 2004, White might play the safer 16 c3! dxc3 17 ♕xc3 ♘d5 18 ♕d2 ♕e3+ 19 ♕xe3 ♘xe3 20 ♖c1 when his development lead and open files give him more than enough compensation for the pawn in the queenless middlegame.

7 e5 ♘h5

7...♘g8 8 ♗f2 ♗b4 9 f4 ♘e7 10 ♘f3 leaves Black tangled.

8 ♗xe7 ♕xe7 9 g3

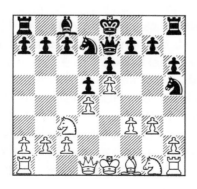

Preparing to build his centre with f4. Meanwhile, Black's knight floats in outer space on h5.

9...0-0 10 f4 g6 11 ♕d2

White has achieved a wonderful version of the French Defence.

11...♘g7 12 ♘f3 c5 13 ♗h3

Playing for the f5 pawn break.

13...♔h7 14 0-0

14 0-0-0! and then continuing as he did in the game looks grim for Black.

14...cxd4 15 ♘xd4 a6 16 ♖ae1 b5

16...h5 only stalls White's plan of g4: 17 ♗g2 b5 18 h3 and g4 follows.

17 g4!

The breakthrough f5 is coming.

17...♗b7 18 f5 ♕g5?!

Fearing for his king, Black bails out into a rancid ending. He probably should have taken his chances in the line 18...♕h4 19 ♖f3 gxf5 20 gxf5 ♖g8 21 ♔h1 ♘c5. Even here though, White's attacking chances clearly trump Black's ability to counterattack against the somewhat exposed position of White's king.

19 ♕xg5 hxg5 20 f6 ♘e8 21 ♖e3 ♖h8

22 ♖d1

Retaining the bind over the materialistic 22 ♘f3!? ♔g8 23 ♘xg5 d4 24 ♖d3 ♘xe5 25 ♖xd4 ♖c8 which offers Black some counterplay for the pawn.

22...♔g8 23 a3??

Careless. 23 ♗f1 keeps Black totally tied up.

23...♖c8??

Laissez faire? Both Grandmasters overlook the simple 23...♘xe5! 24 ♖xe5 ♖xh3 which leaves White down a pawn and overextended.

24 ♗f1!

Now he sees the threat.

24...♘exf6!

A temporary piece sac to mix it up. Possibly Réti, a habitual time trouble addict, may have been low on the clock at this point. Tartakower's sac gives him practical chances.

25 exf6 e5 26 ♘f3!

26 ♘dxb5?! allows Black back into the game after 26...axb5 27 ♗xb5 ♘xf6 28 ♖xe5 ♖h4! and Black is still kicking.

26...d4 27 ♘xd4?

27 ♘xe5! ♘xe5 28 ♖xe5 dxc3 29 bxc3 ♗f3 30 ♖d6 ♖xc3 31 ♗d3 ♖xa3 32 ♗xg6! and *Fritz* announces a forced mate in 21 moves, while *Rybka* disputes this and claims a mate in 10. Obviously someone is not telling the truth here!

27...exd4 28 ♖xd4 ♘xf6 29 h3 ♔g7 30 ♗g2?!

30 a4! was White's last chance to continue the pressure.

30...♗xg2 31 ♔xg2 ♖hd8 ½-½

A lucky escape for Black.

Summary

One of the great trade secrets of Veresov practitioners is to con unsuspecting opponents into bad versions of the French Defence. You will see this pattern over and over again in this book.

Game 3
M.Khachian-A.Kostin
Pardubice 1996

1 d4 ♘f6 2 ♘c3

My friend GM Melik Khachiyan and I have had many interesting battles over the years. He is one of the few grandmasters who regularly employs the Veresov.

2...d5 3 ♗g5 ♘bd7 4 f3 h6 5 ♗h4 e6?! 6 e4 ♗e7 7 e5 ♘h5 8 ♗xe7 ♕xe7 9 ♘h3!

Possibly even stronger than 9 g3 which Réti used in the very first Veresov. White threatens to trap the wayward h5-knight with g4. But the question remains: is g4 really a threat?

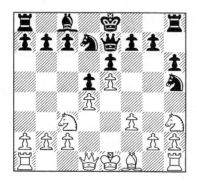

9...c5?!

Allowing the trap. Black sacs a piece to destroy the white centre, but just doesn't get enough for it. He probably couldn't, though, stomach the position after 9...g5 10 g3 ♘g7 11 ♕d2 a6 12 ♘d1 c5 13 c3 f6 14 f4.

10 g4!

The answer is: Yes, g4! is a real threat.

10...♕h4+ 11 ♔e2

Welcome to a typical Veresov position! The situation looks irrational and possibly very dangerous for White, but Khachian shows deep understanding of his lines and demonstrates that the position is clearly in White's favour, if not winning.

11...cxd4 12 ♕xd4 f6

He can't extricate the knight with 12...g6?? 13 ♘b5! (hitting c7, and also covering White's queen on d4) 13...0-0 14 gxh5.

13 ♕f2!

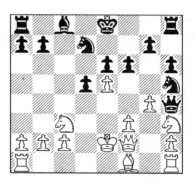

The power of preparation. What first looked like a dangerous black attack is now an arrow shot with the strength of a child. Black would have decent compensation if he could keep the queens on the board. Unfortunately for him, they come off and he just doesn't have enough against accurate defence.

13...♕xf2+ 14 ♔xf2 fxe5 15 gxh5 0-0 16 ♔g2 ♘f6?!

16...♖f5 puts up more resistance, but still fails to 17 ♗d3 ♖xh5 18 ♗g6 ♖h4 19 ♖he1 b6 20 ♘f2 ♗b7 21 ♘d3 e4 22 ♔g3! (certainly not 22 fxe4?? ♖g4+) 22...♘f8 23 ♘e5 ♘xg6 24 ♘xg6 ♖h5 25 h4! ♔h7 26 ♘f4 ♖e5 27 fxe4 dxe4 28 ♖ad1 and White wins without trouble.

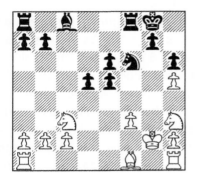

17 ♖e1 e4 18 fxe4 d4 19 ♘d1 e5

19...♘xh5 20 ♗e2 ♘f6 21 e5 is also quite joyless for Black.

20 ♗e2 ♗e6 21 ♘df2 ♖ac8 22 ♖c1 ♗f7 23 ♖hf1 ♘xh5 24 ♗xh5 ♗xh5 25 ♘d3 ♖fe8 26 ♘g1!

Preparing to hit the e5-pawn a second time with ♘f3 and also denying Black even a trace of counterplay like in the line 26 ♖f5? ♗g6 27 ♖xe5 ♖xe5 28 ♘xe5 ♗xe4+ 29 ♔g3 ♗xc2 when Black is still busted but at least has some hope.

26...♖c7 27 ♘f3 ♖ec8

Passive defence with 27...♖ce7 28 c3 ♗g6 29 ♖fe1 doesn't improve matters.

28 ♖f2 ♗g6 29 ♖e2 ♗f7 30 a3

The e5-pawn is not running away.

30...♗c4 31 ♘fxe5 ♗b5 32 ♖d2 ♖e8 33 ♖e1 ♖ce7 34 ♘f3 ♖xe4 35 ♖xe4 ♖xe4 36 ♘f2! 1-0

Summary

White has a wealth of good moves in this line on move nine, including 9 ♘h3!.

1 d4 ♘f6 2 ♘c3 d5 3 ♗g5 ♘bd7 4 f3 h6!?

Tossing in this move and chasing the bishop from g5 actually may help White over the normal lines.

5 ♗h4

Alternatively 5 ♗f4 c6 6 e4 ♕b6 and now:

a) White obtains a clear advantage after 7 e5! ♘h5 8 ♗c1 g6 9 f4 thanks to his huge space advantage, while every developed black piece looks misplaced.

b) However, Jimmy Lakdawala, unlike his timid older brother, rarely backed down from semi-sound sacs, so J.Lakdawala-L.Shamkovich, US Open 1987, continued 7 ♕d2?! dxe4!? (if Black is going to allow White a Blackmar-Diemer Gambit then his queen is misplaced on b6; 7...♕xb2 looks quite reasonable since the position remains closed for the time being, and the onus is on White to prove he has enough compensation for the pawn) 8 0-0-0 e3!? (chickening out! I would still accept with 8...exf3) 9 ♗xe3 ♕a5 10 ♗c4 ♘b6 11 ♗b3 ♘fd5 12 ♘xd5 ♕xd2+ 13 ♗xd2 cxd5 with an equal ending.

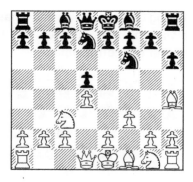

5...c6

The lines involving 4...c6 and 5...c6 are clearly the biggest headache for White in the 4 f3 Veresov.

6 ♕d2!?

A move like this may transpose to 4 ♕d2 lines.

6 e4 is also fine here as long as White is willing to sac the b2-pawn: 6...dxe4 7 fxe4 (7 ♗c4!? is a Blackmar-

Diemer Gambit) 7...♕b6!? (7...e5?! doesn't make as much sense when the white bishop has been chased away from g5) 8 dxe5 ♘xe5 (the problem is that Black doesn't have the normal ...♕a5 in this line since there is no hanging bishop on g5) 8 ♗c4 ♕xb2 9 ♘ge2 ♕b4 10 ♕d3 ♘b6 11 ♗b3 g5 12 ♗g3 was G.Portisch-M.Hell, St Ingbert 1997, when White had great compensation for the pawn:

1. A development lead;

2. Control over the centre;

3. The open b- and f-files for his rooks; and

4. Black's ...g5!? makes it easier for White to prise open the kingside.

6...e5 7 e3

Very flexible. White doesn't have to achieve e4 in every single Veresov.

7...exd4 8 exd4

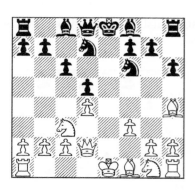

We reach an opposite-wing attacking version of an Exchange line of the French Defence. Let's assess:

1. Black weakened her king's cover with ...h6;

2. White may take advantage of this

with a quick g4-g5, opening lines quickly against Black's king;

3. White's bishop on h4 is in the way of the h-pawn and slows his attack;

4. White must also be on the lookout for tactics based on the loose bishop with ...♘e4 tricks; and

5. White's king doesn't exactly have a safe haven on the queenside and Black's attack develops quickly there too.

Conclusion: the chances are dynamically balanced.

8...♗e7 9 0-0-0 0-0

Accepting the challenge. Another plan is to be uncooperative and try to castle queenside with 9...♘f8!?. The obvious trouble with this plan is that it is slow.

10 g4 b5

Both sides go after each other with great abandon!

11 ♘h3!?

He wants to achieve g5 as quickly as possible. Another plan would be to clear the way for his h-pawn and control b8 with 11 ♗g3 ♘b6 12 h4 ♘c4. Now White can choose between:

a) 13 ♕f2 ♕a5 14 ♗xc4 dxc4 15 g5 ♘d5 16 ♘xd5 cxd5 17 ♔b1 h5 and the player with the superior attacking skills will probably win this one.

b) 13 ♗xc4 bxc4 14 g5 ♘h5 15 ♗e5 f6 16 gxf6 ♗xf6 17 ♘ge2 with mutual chances.

11...♘b6 12 ♖g1 b4 13 ♘b1

13 ♘e2!? leads to a mess after 13...♘c4 14 ♕d3 a5 15 g5 hxg5 16

♗xg5 a4 17 ♗h6 ♘g4! 18 ♗xg7 ♔xg7 19 fxg4 a3 20 b3 ♘b2 21 ♕d2 ♘xd1 22 ♔xd1. For the exchange White gets a pawn, the safer king and attacking ideas like ♘ef4 and ♘h5+, although I'm not sure if this fully compensates him for his material and weakness on the dark squares.

13...♘c4 14 ♕e1!

Walking into a combination which gives up the queen for activity and sufficient material. Other moves fall short:

a) 14 ♗xc4?! dxc4 15 ♗xf6 ♗xf6 16 ♕xb4 ♗xd4 17 ♖ge1 c5 18 ♕xc4 ♗e6 when Black seizes the initiative and may even soon regain her missing pawn.

b) 14 ♕f2?! ♖e8 15 g5 ♘h7 16 f4 ♗xh3 17 ♗xh3 hxg5 18 fxg5 ♗xg5+ 19 ♗xg5 ♘xg5 and Black remains up a pawn with some initiative, while White does not have enough time to organize an attack down the g-file.

14...♖e8 15 ♘d2 b3!

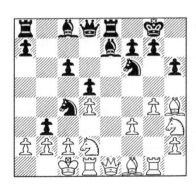

16 axb3 ♗b4 17 ♕xe8+! ♕xe8 18 bxc4 ♕e7

Alternatively 18...♕e3 and:

a) 19 ♗f2! ♗xd2+ 20 ♖xd2 ♕xf3 21 ♖d3 ♕e4 22 ♖e3 ♕h7 (22...♕g6 23 ♘f4 ♕g5 24 ♘h3 is a draw by repetition) 23 ♗d3 ♘e4 24 ♗g3! and White achieves counterplay based on the sorry position of Black's queen, which is sinking in quicksand on h7.

b) 19 ♗xf6?! (tempting, but White must keep some control over the dark squares; the damage inflicted to Black's structure is insufficient reason to take the knight) 19...gxf6 20 f4 ♕xd4 21 cxd5 cxd5 22 ♘b3 ♕b6 and Black soon organizes an attack based on ...a5 and ...a4.

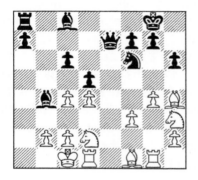

19 c5! ♕b7 20 ♘f2!

The knight scurries to defend b2. Notice how White avoids ♗xf6?!, which weakens the dark squares.

20...♗a5 21 ♘d3 ♗c7 22 ♗g3 ♗xg3 23 hxg3 a5 24 c3 ♘e8 25 ♔c2 ♘c7 26 ♖a1 a4 27 ♗e2 ♘b5 28 ♖ge1 a3 29 b3 f5?

Abrahamyan will come to regret this rash move which gives up control over e5. Black is under the false impression that she is winning, when in reality the situation remains unclear... until now!

30 ♘e5 fxg4 31 fxg4 ♗e6 32 ♗d3 ♖e8 33 ♖e3 ♖a8 34 g5!

Black's attack is at a dead end, while White's is just beginning.

34...h5

34...hxg5?! 35 ♘df3 feeds White's attack.

35 ♘g6 ♖e8?!

A self-pin. Black had to try 35...♗g4.

36 ♖ae1 ♕d7 37 ♘f4

Black can't survive after 37 g4! h4 38 ♘xh4 ♗f7 39 ♖xe8+ ♗xe8 40 ♘f5.

37...♗f7!?

Sac'ing a piece in an attempt at counterplay. It is also unlikely Black can hold things together in the line 37...♘c7 38 ♖e5 ♗g4 39 ♖xe8+ ♘xe8 40 ♘g6 ♘c7 41 ♘e5.

38 g6 ♖xe3 39 gxf7+ ♕xf7 40 ♖xe3 a2 41 ♖e1 g5 42 ♘g6

Although White has the advantage, his position is very difficult to play. He must worry about tricks with Black's advanced a-pawn, the fact that he has multiple pawn targets for Black's queen and perpetual checks.

42...♕f2 43 ♖e8+ ♔g7 44 ♖a8 h4 45

gxh4 gxh4 46 ♘xh4!

Offering a knight for the dangerous passer is a bargain.

46...♕xh4 47 ♖xa2 ♘c7?

Passive defence loses. Perhaps another piece sac was in order to attempt to expose White's king to perpetual check threats with 47...♘xd4+! 48 cxd4 ♕xd4 49 ♖a5 ♕b4 50 ♖a7+ ♔f6 51 ♖a4 ♕xc5+ 52 ♖c4! ♕b6 53 ♖f4+ ♔e7 and conversion will not be an easy task for White.

48 ♖a7 ♕h2 49 ♖b7!

There is no defence to 50 ♖b6 when c6 and then d5 will fall. Black's position is a decaying old house on the verge of collapse.

49...♔f7 50 ♖b6

White begins to pluck pawns.

50...♘e6 51 ♖xc6 ♘f4 52 ♗f1 ♘e6 53 ♖d6 ♘g5

Threatening ...♘e4.

54 ♔d1! ♕f2

54...♕h1 doesn't cover the pawn since White can take it anyway with 55 ♖xd5! exploiting the pin on the a2-g8 diagonal.

55 ♖xd5 ♘e4 56 ♘xe4 ♕xf1+

A strange situation, indeed, when the lioness faces a hungry pack of Hyenas and is overwhelmed by sheer numbers.

57 ♔d2 ♕g2+ 58 ♔e3 ♕g1+ 59 ♔f4 ♕h2+ 1-0

Possibly Black lost on time. If she resigned, it was probably premature since White must observe vigilance not to walk into perpetual checks.

Summary

When Black plays a quick ...e5 you have an option to respond with e3, turning the game into a super-sharp, opposite-wings attack version of an Exchange French.

Game 5
H.Nakamura-J.Becerra Rivero
US Online League 2009

1 d4 d5 2 ♘c3 ♘f6 3 ♗g5 ♘bd7 4 f3 e6

This is quite common, but again I'm convinced it's just an inferior French for Black, who must now deal with a misplaced knight on d7 instead of the normal c6-square.

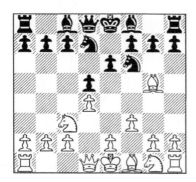

5 e4 ♗e7

Alternatively:

a) 5...dxe4 6 fxe4 h6 7 ♗h4 ♗b4 8 e5 g5 9 ♗f2 ♘e4 10 ♕d3 ♘xf2 11 ♔xf2 also favours White, who is in a position to exploit Black's ragged pawn structure and the e4-square.

b) 5...h6 6 ♗f4!? ♗b4 7 e5 ♗xc3+ 8 bxc3 ♘g8 9 c4 ♘e7 10 ♕d2 and White's bishop pair and space give him a clear advantage, R.Saptarshi-E.Haak, Vlissingen 2006.

6 e5 ♘g8 7 ♗e3

Following the principle which states: avoid exchanges when your opponent is cramped.

7 ♗xe7 ♘xe7 8 f4 also looks promising for White, who has space and the good bishop.

7...a6?!

He should hit the centre immediately, before White can back up the d4 point with a pawn: 7...c5! 8 f4 ♘h6 9 ♘f3 ♘f5 10 ♗f2 a6 11 ♗d3 cxd4 12

♘xd4 ♘xd4 13 ♗xd4 ♘c5 and Black was only slightly worse in J.Bathke-W.Vandrey, Hamburg 1997.

8 ♘ce2!

Ensuring a large space advantage, since White backs up the d4 point with c3.

8...b6 9 ♕d2 c5 10 c3 a5!

The dormant bishop comes to life on a6.

11 a3 ♗a6 12 h4!

Offering a pawn to open the h-file.

I can tell you from experience that Hikaru Nakamura is one of the most intimidating players I have ever faced. In our game at the 2005 US Championship he had the disconcerting habit of staring at the sky instead of the board when it was his move! I found what I believed to be a long combination at one point in the game. I checked, re-checked and re-rechecked the line for 45 minutes before plunging in. Nakamura looked at the ceiling for about five minutes, made his move, and saw one ply further, upon which my position disintegrated and I promptly received a sharp kick to the gluteal region!

12...♝f8?!

No, thank you! But this is not the most efficient way to develop:

a) 12...♝xh4+?! 13 g3 ♝e7 14 ♞h3 cxd4 15 cxd4 ♜c8 16 ♞hf4 offers White huge compensation for the pawn. Black is handcuffed on the kingside and it isn't clear how he completes development;

b) 12...h5! stakes out much-needed kingside space and intends to develop with ...♞h6.

13 h5!

Now Black is denied ...h5 and White's kingside territorial advantage takes on alarming proportions.

13...h6 14 f4 ♞e7 15 ♞f3 ♛c7 16 g4 a4

Black has ideas of ...♞c6 and ...♞a5, where the knight threatens to invade on c4 and b3.

17 ♝h3 ♞c6 18 f5 ♝e7

18...♞a5?! 19 fxe6 fxe6 20 ♛c2! is a very efficient move which attacks the a4-pawn, evades Black's threat to fork on b3 and threatens a check on g6.

19 fxe6 fxe6 20 ♛c2! ♞f8

Protecting the a4-pawn is out of the question: 20...♝b5?? 21 ♛g6+ ♚f8 22 ♞f4 ♞d8 23 ♛xe6! is crushing.

21 ♞f4?!

It feels a little strange to criticize the normally-explosive Nakamura for overcaution! There is no reason to refrain from the pawn grab on a4. He should plunge in: 21 ♛xa4! b5 22 ♛c2 b4 23 cxb4 cxb4 24 ♞f4 bxa3 25 bxa3 ♝c4 26

♚f2 with complications in White's favour.

21...♛d7 22 ♚f2 ♞a5 23 ♞g6 ♜g8 24 ♚g3 ♞b3 25 ♜ae1 0-0-0

Seeking refuge for his king on the queenside where the extra space should protect him. The trouble is White continues to press on the kingside.

26 ♞d2

White has a better line in 26 ♞xe7+! ♛xe7 27 g5! g6 28 ♚h2! and then:

a) 28...gxh5? 29 gxh6 ♞h7 30 ♜hg1 when White has multiple advantages: a surprisingly safe king, a powerful passed pawn on h6, the bishop pair and control over the kingside dark squares.

b) 28...hxg5! 29 ♝xg5 ♛f7 30 ♝xd8 ♛f4+ 31 ♚g1 gxh5+ 32 ♝g2 ♚xd8 and Black has some but probably not enough play for the exchange.

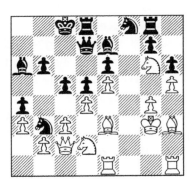

26...♞xd2 27 ♝xd2

Black gets dangerous chances against White's king in the line 27 ♞xe7+!? ♛xe7 28 ♝xd2 ♛e8! 29 ♝e3 g6 30 hxg6 ♞xg6 31 ♝g2 ♞e7.

27...♞xg6 28 ♕xg6 ♔b8 29 g5 ♗c8 30 ♗f1 ♖df8 31 ♗d3 c4!?

Locking the queenside.

32 ♗b1 ♕b5 33 ♗c1 ♗xg5

33...hxg5 34 ♖e2 regains the pawn.

34 ♗xg5 hxg5

34...♕xb2?! looks like a fishy sac: 35 ♗e3 ♕xc3 36 ♕g4 ♕xa3 37 ♗h7 ♖h8 38 ♕xg7 b5 39 ♖h2 b4 40 ♕e7! halting the avalanche whereupon White's extra piece should prevail.

35 ♖e2 ♕d7 36 ♕xg5 ♕f7 37 ♕g4

Let's take stock of the position:

1. Black is stuck with pawns on the same colour of his remaining bishop;

2. Despite appearances, White's king is quite safe because Black has no entry points; and

3. White has chances to apply pressure on g7, or play h6 at an appropriate time, giving him a superior ending.

37...♕e7 38 ♗h7 ♖h8 39 ♗g6 ♔c7 40 ♖f2 ♖xf2 41 ♔xf2 ♗d7 42 ♔e2 ♔d8 43 ♖f1 ♖f8 44 ♖g1 ♗e8 45 ♔d1

45 ♗xe8?! ♕xe8 46 ♕g5+ ♔c8 47 ♕g6 ♕f7 48 ♕xf7 ♖xf7 49 ♖g6 ♔d7 50 h6 gxh6 51 ♖xh6 ♖g7 is drawn.

45...♗xg6 46 ♕xg6 ♖f7

46...♖f5 47 ♔c2 ♕f7?? 48 ♕xg7 ♕xg7 49 ♖xg7 ♖xh5 50 ♖b7 and White picks off both the b- and a-pawns.

47 h6

Nakamura dissolves Black's weakness in an attempt to open lines to Black's king.

47...gxh6 48 ♕xh6 ♔d7 49 ♔c1

Intending to hide the king on a2. The difference in king safety is Black's main worry.

49...♖h7 50 ♕d2 ♕f7 51 ♔b1 ♕f3 52 ♔a2 ♕e4 53 ♕f2!

Threatening ♕f8.

53...♕f5!

Excellent defence. Black should draw the rook ending.

54 ♕xf5!?

White still has practical chances if he keeps queens on the board with 54 ♕g2 ♕f7 55 ♖f1 ♕g7 56 ♕c2 b5, although even here it isn't clear how he makes progress.

54...exf5 55 ♖g6 ♔e7?!

55...♔c7! 56 ♖f6 ♖h5 and White can't make progress: for example, 57 ♖d6 f4 58 ♖xd5?? f3 and it is Black who promotes.

56 ♖xb6 ♖h1 57 ♖f6

White doesn't have time for 57 ♖d6 f4! when he can't take the d5-pawn.

57...♖f1?

Placing the rook in front of his passed pawn loses. The counterintuitive lateral defence plan holds after 57...♖h5!. If White tries to make progress with 58 ♔b1 ♖h1+ 59 ♔c2 ♖h2+

60 ♔c1 ♖h1+ 61 ♔d2 ♖h2+ 62 ♔e3 then 62...♖xb2 63 ♖a6 ♖b3 64 ♖xa4 ♖xc3+ 65 ♔f4 ♖d3 66 ♖a7+ ♔e6 67 ♖a6+ with a draw.

58 ♖d6! f4 59 ♖xd5 ♔e6

59...f3 60 ♖d6 f2 61 ♖f6 ♔d7 62 d5 ♖d1 63 ♖xf2 ♖xd5 64 ♖f7+ ♔c6 65 ♖a7 ♖xe5 66 ♖xa4 wins too. White must simply be careful not to swap his b-pawn for Black's c-pawn, which would lead to a theoretical draw.

60 ♖d6+ ♔f5 61 ♖f6+ ♔g4 62 e6 ♖e1 63 d5 ♔g5 64 ♖f7 ♖e5 65 e7 1-0

65...♔g6 66 ♖xf4 is hopeless.

Summary

This was another example of Black landing in an inferior French due to the unfortunate placement of his d7-knight.

Game 6
M.Khachian-A.Donchenko
Moscow 1995

1 d4 d5 2 ♘c3 ♘f6 3 ♗g5 ♘bd7 4 f3 c5

5 dxc5

If you are the more bloodthirsty type, you can go for a reversed Albin Counter-Gambit with 5 e4 and then:

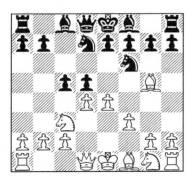

a) 5...dxe4 6 d5 exf3 7 ♘xf3 g6 8 ♕d2 ♗g7 9 0-0-0 when White's development lead and the cramping effect of the d5-pawn gave him reasonable compensation for his pawn in G.Mateuta-B.Istrate, Baile Tusnad 1999.

b) 5...cxd4 6 ♗xf6 exf6 7 ♕xd4 ♗c5 8 ♕d2 0-0 (8...♕b6? 9 ♘a4 is a trick you need to be familiar with: 9...♗e3 10 ♘xb6 ♗xd2+ 11 ♔xd2 ♘xb6 12 exd5 ♘xd5 and White's healthy queenside pawn majority gives him a nagging edge in the endgame) 9 ♘xd5 was R.Saptarshi-V.Goswami, Hyderabad 2006, when Black had compensation for the pawn with:

1. The bishop pair;
2. A lead in development;
3. Control over the dark squares;
4. The open c-file for his attack.

5...e6 6 b4

He is not going to make it easy for Black to recapture the lost pawn.

6...♗e7 7 ♖b1 a5 8 a3 b6!

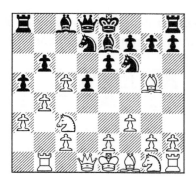

Logical. Black challenges the white pawns while he leads in development.

9 c6 ♘e5 10 b5 ♗xa3

Let's assess:

1. Black has regained his pawn;

2. White establishes a powerful and cramping passed pawn on c6;

3. Black gets good counterplay on the dark squares; and

4. Black controls the greater share of the centre.

Overall, the position looks interesting but hard to assess.

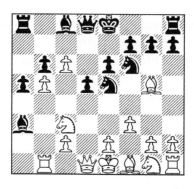

11 e4!? ♗b4 12 ♗d2 dxe4 13 ♘a4!

A strong pawn sac. He blockades Black's passed a-pawn and also applies pressure to b6. White's king doesn't look so healthy in the line 13 fxe4?! 0-0 14 ♘f3 ♘fg4 15 h3 ♘xf3+ 16 ♕xf3 ♘e5 17 ♕g3 ♕d4 18 ♖d1 f5!.

13...♘d5 14 c3 ♗d6 15 f4!

The careless 15 fxe4?? loses instantly to 15...♕h4+.

15...♘g6 16 g3 e3!?

16...0-0 17 c4 ♘b4 18 ♗e3 e5! 19 f5 ♗xf5 20 ♘xb6 ♖b8 21 c5 and White's queenside pawns look rather scary.

17 ♗c1 ♘gxf4! 18 c4!

Also, 18 ♘f3! ♘h5 19 ♗g2 gives White full compensation for his missing two pawns.

18...♕f6 19 ♘f3

19 gxf4!? leads to total chaos after 19...♕h4+ 20 ♔e2 e5! 21 ♗xe3 ♗g4+ 22 ♘f3 e4 23 ♕xd5 ♗xf3+ 24 ♔d2 ♖d8 25 ♔c2 ♗xf4 26 c7! ♖xd5 27 c8♕+ ♖d8 28 ♕c6+ ♔e7 29 ♗xb6 ♗xh1 30 ♗c5+ when *Rybka* helpfully claims the game is dead even in this totally irrational position.

19...e2?

Losing his sense of direction in the storm. Black should go in for 19...♗b4+! 20 ♖xb4 ♘c3! 21 ♕c2 axb4 22 ♘xc3 ♘g6 23 ♘e4 ♕xf3 24 ♗g2 ♕h5 25 ♗xe3 ♖a1+ 26 ♔f2 ♖xh1 27 ♗xh1 ♕xh2+ 28 ♗g2 0-0 and once again the position is very difficult to assess as White picks off b6 with three passed pawns close to touchdown, while Black goes after White's king, possibly with plans like ...♘e5 and ...♘g4, or ...f5, ...e5 and ...f4.

20 ♗xe2 ♘xe2 21 ♔xe2!

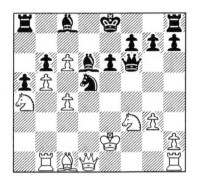

Black has trouble due to the pile-up of pieces on the d-file.

21...0-0!

He doesn't get enough compensation for the piece after this, but it is a superior practical choice over the unpleasant ending arising from 21...♕f5 22 ♕d3 ♕xd3+ 23 ♔xd3 ♘b4+ 24 ♔c3 ♘a2+ 25 ♔d2 ♖b8 26 ♗b2 0-0 27 ♗d4 ♗c7 28 c5 when Black's chances look slim.

22 cxd5 exd5 23 ♔f2 ♗g4 24 ♖b3 ♖fe8 25 h3

Or 25 ♗e3 ♖e6 26 ♗xb6 ♖ae8 27 ♖f1 ♗h3 28 ♔g1 ♗xf1 29 ♕xf1 when White's position stabilized and his two queenside passers should carry the day.

25...♗f5 26 ♗f4?!

26 ♖e3! ♗e4 27 ♘xb6 wins.

26...♖e4 27 ♘c3?!

A second inaccuracy. Best is 27 ♖e3! ♗xf4 28 gxf4 ♖xf4.

27...♗c5+ 28 ♔g2 a4 29 ♘xd5 ♕e6 30 ♖b2 a3?

Missing an opportunity to crawl back into the game with 30...♖d8! 31 c7

♖xd5 32 c8♕+ ♕xc8 33 ♕xd5 ♕e8 34 ♕d1 a3 35 ♖d2 ♕xb5 and the situation is not so clear, despite White's extra rook for only three pawns. Black's passed pawns and bishop pair give him reasonable chances in the ensuing fight.

31 ♖d2 a2 32 ♘c7! a1♕ 33 ♖d8+?

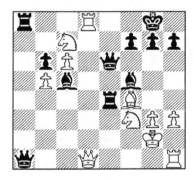

Please don't adjust your TV screen! The diagram is correct and there are queens everywhere. However, White should forgo the check and take immediately on e6: 33 ♘xe6! ♕xd1 34 ♖hxd1 ♖xe6 35 ♖d8+ ♖e8 36 c7 ♗e7 37 ♖xe8+ ♖xe8 38 ♗e3 is hopeless for Black.

33...♗f8 34 ♘xe6 ♖a2+?

The final error. Black is still in trouble, but kicking after 34...♕a2+! 35 ♖d2 ♕xe6 36 ♘g5 ♕c4 37 ♘xe4 ♗xe4+ 38 ♔h2 g5! 39 ♗e3! ♗xh1 40 ♕xh1.

35 ♘d2! ♖xd2+

The alternatives are also hopeless as can easily be seen.

a) 35...♕xd1?? 36 ♖xf8 mate.

b) 35...♖xe6 36 ♕xa1 ♖xa1 37 ♖xa1.

36 ♕xd2 ♕xh1+ 37 ♔xh1 ♖xe6 38 ♖xf8+ 1-0

Summary

This is the Veresov at its chaotic best. Even *Rybka* became disoriented analysing this one and requested a cold compress for a headache!

Game 7
T.Nabaty-K.Lerner
Elkana 2007

---

1 d4 ♘f6 2 ♘c3 d5 3 ♗g5 ♘bd7 4 f3 c5 5 dxc5 e6 6 b4

A move which warms the greedy hearts of all Slav players. We Slavazoids love to gobble the opponent's c-pawn and then protect the extra pawn with a timely push of the b-pawn.

An alternative is to fight back in the centre with 6 e4 ♕a5 7 ♗b5 dxe4 8 ♕d2 ♗xc5 9 ♗xf6 gxf6 10 0-0-0 when the game ended abruptly after Black's next move: 10...♔e7?? (10...0-0 11 ♕f4! ♘e5 12 ♕xf6 ♘g6 13 fxe4 ♗e7 and despite the damaged pawns on the kingside, Black looks fine due to the usual dark-square influence) 11 ♘d5+

1-0 E.Hasanova-T.Fodor, Budapest 2005.

6...♗e7

Black is in no rush to regain the lost pawn and calmly completes his development.

7 e4 0-0 8 ♗b5 a5 9 a3 axb4 10 axb4 ♖xa1 11 ♕xa1 dxe4 12 fxe4 ♘xe4! 13 ♘xe4

Avoiding 13 ♗xe7? ♕xe7 14 ♘xe4 ♕h4+ 15 ♔f1 ♕xe4.

13...♗xg5 14 ♘f3 ♗e7 15 0-0

I prefer White for four reasons:

1 White's advanced queenside pawns cramp Black;

2. White's queenside majority looks faster than Black's kingside pawn majority;

3. White leads in development; and

4 White's centralized knights are active and stand their ground against Black's bishop pair.

15...♘f6 16 ♘xf6+

16 ♘f2!? is an idea, since d5 is not a secure spot for Black's knight.

16...♗xf6 17 ♕d1?!

After this inaccuracy, Black should

hold the draw. Correct was 17 ♕c1! ♗c3 18 ♖d1 ♕c7 19 ♕a3 ♗f6 20 c4 e5 21 ♕e3 and White relies on his faster pawn majority for an edge.

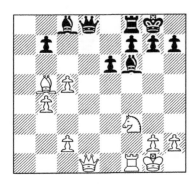

17...♗c3! 18 ♕xd8 ♖xd8 19 ♖b1 ♗f6?

Missing an opportunity to roll his majority forward with 19...e5! 20 ♗c4 (or 20 ♖b3 ♗a1 21 ♖a3 ♗b2 22 ♖b3 ♗a1 with a draw by repetition) 20...♗f5 21 ♖b3 ♗d4+ 22 ♘xd4 ♖xd4 23 ♖c3 ♔f8 24 b5 ♔e7.

20 ♔f2 g5 21 ♔e2 ♔f8 22 ♘d2 ♗e5 23 ♘f3 ♗f6 24 ♘d2 ♗e5 25 h3!?

White is not satisfied with a draw by repetition against his higher-rated opponent.

25...♔e7 26 ♘c4 ♗c7 27 ♖a1 e5?!

Weakening d5. White has the slightly better chances after the more accurate 27...f5 28 ♖a7 ♗b8 29 ♖a8 ♗c7 30 c6!? bxc6 31 ♗xc6 ♖d4! 32 ♘e3 ♗d7 33 ♗xd7 ♖xd7 34 b5 because his passers look more formidable than Black's on the other wing.

28 ♘e3 e4 29 c4 ♗e5 30 ♖a7

Threatening c6.

30...♔f8

Passive. I would have moved the king forward with 30...♔f6.

31 c6

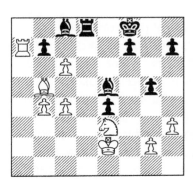

Creating two connected passed pawns.

31...bxc6 32 ♗xc6 ♗e6

An unfortunate necessity since 32...f5? is met by 33 ♘xf5! ♗xf5 34 ♖a5 ♗xh3 35 ♖xe5 ♗xg2 36 ♖xg5 ♗f3+ 37 ♔e3 ♖d3+ 38 ♔f4 ♖b3 39 b5 when Black is busted, as the e-pawn is a goner and White has much the better king position. Moreover, White's queenside passers move much faster than Black's pip-squeak of an h-pawn.

33 ♗xe4 ♖d4 34 ♗d3 h5 35 ♖a5 ♗f4 36 ♘f5 ♖d8 37 g4!

Nullifying Black's 3-versus-2 pawn majority. In essence White is up two clean pawns.

37...hxg4 38 hxg4 ♖b8 39 ♖a4 ♗d7 40 b5 ♖e8+ 41 ♔f3 ♗xf5

Black's best shot at saving the game is opposite-coloured bishops.

42 ♗xf5 ♖e3+ 43 ♔f2 ♖b3 44 ♔e2 ♗e3 45 ♗c2 ♖c3 46 ♗d3 ♗d4 47 ♖a6 ♔e7 48 ♖c6!

Black can't stop both the c5 and b5 pawn advances.

48...♖b3

48...♔d7? 49 ♗f5+ ♔e7 50 b6 is just a waste of time for Black.

49 c5 ♖c3 50 b6! ♖xc5 51 b7 ♖e5+ 52 ♔d2 ♗e3+ 53 ♔c2 ♗a7 54 ♖a6?

This innocent-looking move throws away a hard-earned victory, which was there after 54 ♖c8! ♔d6 55 ♖a8 ♔c7 56 ♖xa7 ♔b8 57 ♖a6 ♔xb7 58 ♖f6.

54...♗b8 55 ♖a8 ♖c5+ 56 ♔b1

56 ♔d1 ♖d5! 57 ♔e2 ♖d8! 58 ♗f5 ♔d6 59 ♗c8 ♔c7 and Black should hold the draw.

56...♖d5!!

57 ♖xb8

The only real try for a win lies in 57 ♔c2 ♖d8 58 ♗e4.

57...♖xd3 58 ♖e8+ ♔xe8 59 b8♕+

White gets a queen but not the win. Black creates an impregnable fortress.

59...♖d8 60 ♕e5+ ♔f8 61 ♕c5+ ♔e8 62 ♕e5+ ♔f8 63 ♕c5+ ♔e8 64 ♕b5+ ♔f8 65 ♕xg5 ♖e8! 66 ♔c2 ♖e6!

Lazarus rises! Despite *Rybka*'s optimistic assessment of +4.48 for White,

the position is a dead draw. The white king can't break through the barrier of the third rank.

67 ♔d3 ♖g6 68 ♕f5 ♔g8 69 ♔e4 ♔g7 70 ♕e5+ ♔g8 71 ♔f5 ♔h7 72 ♕e8 ♔g7 73 g5 ♖e6

Black is happy to go into a drawn king and pawn ending should White get dramatic and sac his queen for rook and pawn.

74 ♕d7 ♖g6 75 ♔g4 ♖e6 76 ♕d4+ ♔g8 77 ♔f5 ♖g6 ½-½

Summary

This game is a good example of how to push forward the queenside super-pawn majority.

1 d4 ♘f6 2 ♘c3 d5 3 ♗g5 ♘bd7 4 f3 c5 5 dxc5 ♕a5

Black avoids 5...e6 6 b4 and ensures the recapture of the lost pawn.

6 ♕d2

6 ♗xf6?! wins a pawn, but is not recommended since White gives up all control over the dark squares and has thrown in the weakening f3 to boot. Black also has a substantial lead in development, as was graphically highlighted by 6...♘xf6 7 ♕d4 e5! 8 ♕xe5+ ♗e6 9 e4 0-0-0 10 c6 ♗d6 11 ♕d4 dxe4 12 ♕a4 ♕g5 13 ♗a6 ♗c5 14 ♘d1 ♕xg2 15 ♗xb7+ ♔b8 16 ♗a8 ♖xd1+! and 0-1 in N.Dobrev-D.Howell, Marseille 2006.

6...e6 7 e4

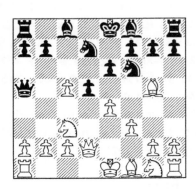

7...♗xc5

Black is prepared to sac his d-pawn later for the bishop pair. After the

7...dxe4 8 ♘b5! ♕xd2+ 9 ♗xd2 ♖b8 of C.Scholz-H.Emunds, Senden 2001, the cramping effect of the c5-pawn gives White an edge with 10 b4! a6 11 ♘c3.

8 exd5 exd5 9 ♘ge2 0-0 10 0-0-0 d4! 11 ♗xf6 ♘xf6 12 ♘xd4

12...♗b6

Other options are:

a) 12...♖d8?! 13 ♘b3! ♖xd2 14 ♘xa5 ♖xd1+ 15 ♘xd1 and it's doubtful that Black has full compensation for the pawn, despite his bishop pair and development lead in the ending.

b) 12...♗b4 13 ♘b3 ♕c7 14 ♕d4 ♗xc3 15 ♕xc3 ♕xc3 16 bxc3 ♗e6 17 ♘d4!? (17 c4! hangs on to the extra pawn and may give White a slight pull) 17...♗xa2 18 c4 ♖ac8 19 ♘f5 ♖c5 20 ♘d6 ♖d8?! 21 ♘xb7 ♖xd1+ 22 ♔xd1 ♖c7 23 ♘a5 ♖c5 24 ♘b3 ♗xb3 25 cxb3 ♖a5 26 ♔d2 ♖a1 27 g3! and White managed to convert the extra pawn in A.Allahverdiev-N.Umudova, Baku 2006.

13 ♘b3

13 ♕f4! ♗c7 14 ♕h4 ♗e5 15 ♔b1 ♖d8 16 ♗c4 holds on to the extra pawn.

13...♕h5 14 ♗c4 ♕h4 15 ♘d4!?

Very brave, but Black can't exploit the pin in any effective way. Still, such heroics are not necessary when the simple 15 g4! denies Black's bishop the f5-square and prepares to roll forward on the kingside.

15...♖d8 16 ♘ce2 ♕f2 17 ♔b1 h6

17...♕xg2? 18 ♖hg1 ♕xh2 19 ♖xg7+! ♔xg7 20 ♕g5+ ♔f8 21 ♕xf6 ♕c7 22 ♗b3 nets White a winning attack.

18 ♕d3 ♗e6?!

18...♖d6 19 ♖hf1 ♕h4 (once again – as you may suspect – it is ridiculous to take the g2-pawn: 19...♕xg2?? 20 ♖g1 ♕xh2 21 ♕g6!) 20 ♕b3! escapes the pin through tactics. For example, 20...♗xd4? 21 ♘xd4 ♖xd4?? 22 g3! ♖xd1+ 23 ♖xd1 ♕h3 24 ♖d8+ ♔h7 25 ♗d3+ ♗f5 26 ♖xa8.

19 ♗xe6 fxe6 20 ♕c4 ♗xd4 21 ♘xd4

21...♕xg2?

There is a saying which goes: "When you are in a hole, stop digging!"

Black succumbs to the temptation to equalize material and accepts the taboo pawn. Instead, 21...♖d6! 22 ♘xe6 ♖c6 23 ♕b3 ♖b6 24 ♖hf1! ♕xg2 25 ♕c4 ♖c6 26 ♖g1 ♕f2 27 ♕b3 ♖b6 28 ♕d3 ♖xe6 29 ♕g6 ♖e7 30 ♕xf6 ♖c7 leaves White up a pawn, but the full point is a long way away.

22 ♖dg1 ♕f2 23 ♘xe6 ♖dc8 24 ♘c7+ ♔h8 25 ♕f7!

Black can resign after this move. White wins heavy material.

25...♘h5

25...♖xc7 26 ♕xc7 ♖g8 27 ♕xb7 is also curtains for Black.

26 ♘xa8 ♕xc2+ 27 ♔a1 ♕c5 28 ♕xb7 g6 29 a3 ♘f4 30 ♖c1 ♕xc1+ 31 ♖xc1 ♖xc1+ 32 ♔a2 g5 33 ♘c7 ♖e1 34 ♕c6 ♘e2 35 ♕xh6+ ♔g8 36 ♕xg5+ ♔f7 37 a4 a5 38 ♕h5+ ♔g7 39 ♘e6+ ♔f6 40 ♕h4+ ♔xe6 1-0

Black resigns just in time before White takes all the pieces with ♕xe1 followed by ♕xe2!

Summary

5...♕a5 regains the c-pawn and the game takes an Open Sicilian flavour after 6 ♕d2 and 7 e4.

Game 9
T.Vogler-A.Balzar
German League 1991

1 d4 d5 2 ♘c3 ♘f6 3 ♗g5 ♘bd7 4 f3 c6
A critical test of the 4 f3 Veresov.

5 e4 dxe4 6 fxe4 e5
Alternatives for Black are:

a) 6...♕b6, although if you are on a pawn-grabbing adventure perhaps Morozevich is not the most suitable opponent to face when doing so! The game A.Morozevich-V.Lazarev, Alushta 1993, continued 7 ♘f3 e5!? 8 dxe5 ♘g4 9 ♕d2 ♘dxe5? (Black's position is getting hard to navigate, and he goes astray; 9...♘gxe5 is correct) 10 h3! ♘xf3+ 11 gxf3 ♘e5 12 0-0-0 and Black fell dangerously behind in development.

However, I have never quite understood the psychology behind playing ...♕b6 and then *not* taking on b2. Here 7...♕xb2 forces the white bishop to retreat after 8 ♗d2 ♕a3 9 e5 ♘d5 10 ♘xd5 cxd5 11 ♗d3, although for the

pawn White has:

1. A cramping space advantage;

2. A big lead in development;

3. Attacking chances down the open f-file; and

4. Black has no safe spot for his king, because he faces the open b-file on the queenside.

b) 6...♕a5 7 e5 ♘e4 (7...♘xe5?? drops a piece to 8 ♗xf6) 8 ♗d2! (GM Davies thinks this is White's best line; also playable is 8 ♘f3!? increasing the development lead) 8...♘xd2 9 ♕xd2 e6 10 ♘f3 ♗b4 11 a3 c5 12 ♖b1 ♗xc3 13 bxc3 ♕xa3 14 ♗d3 was I.Miladinovic-P.Charbonneau, Montreal 2002, when White had full compensation for the pawn thanks to his space advantage with the cramping pawn on e5 and lead in development. Again he also enjoys excellent attacking chances no matter which side Black castles due to the open a-, b- and f-files.

7 dxe5
An ambitious alternative is 7 ♘f3!?, as we'll see later in the chapter.

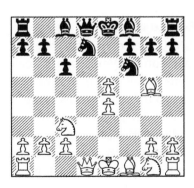

7...♕a5!

Black gets buffeted around after 7...♘xe5?! 8 ♕xd8+ ♔xd8 9 0-0-0+ ♔e8 10 ♘f3 ♘xf3 11 gxf3 ♗e6 12 f4 ♗g4 13 ♖d3 ♖d8 when White had several advantages in C.Lakdawala-'Dinochess', Internet blitz 2010:

1. A strong pawn centre;

2. Black can't castle and has problems with lines of communications with his h-rook; and

3. White still leads in development.

8 ♗xf6!

Grabbing a pawn with 8 exf6?! is too risky: 8...♕xg5 9 fxg7 ♗xg7 10 ♕d2 ♕xd2+ 11 ♔xd2 ♘c5 and Black's bishop pair, dark-square control and development lead gave him more than enough compensation for the pawn in L.Alburt-M.Tal, USSR Championship, Baku 1972.

8...gxf6 9 e6!

Loosening up the pawn front in front of Black's king is much better than capturing on f6: 9 exf6? ♗a3! 10 ♕c1 ♘xf6 and White was fighting for survival in C.Brauer-M.Crosa Coll, Mendoza 2004.

9...fxe6 10 ♕g4!

GM Davies gives this move a '?!' in his book on the Veresov, but I believe it is White's only move, and recommend this as your choice in this position. The more natural 10 ♗c4? leads to immediate difficulties after 10...♗a3! 11 ♕b1 ♘c5 12 ♔f1 with a wretched position for White, A.Dries-H.De Jong, correspondence 1981.

10...♘b6

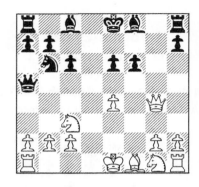

Resisting the temptation to post a knight on e5 at the cost of allowing a queen check on h5.

11 0-0-0

11 ♗e2?! is toothless: 11...♗d7 12 ♕h5+ ♕xh5 13 ♗xh5+ ♔e7 and in T.Vogler-W.Ebert, Wiesbaden 1993, Black already stood better in the ending due to his bishop pair, dark-square control and centralized king.

11...♗d7 12 ♕f4!

White must fight for e5. This may be an improvement over 12 ♕h4 0-0-0 13 ♘f3 (13 ♕xf6 ♖g8 with ...♗g7 to follow gives Black a lot of play for the pawn) 13...♗g7 14 ♔b1 f5 when White must defend accurately. Good thing this was a correspondence game. Nothing like having *Rybka* and *Fritz* to do the heavy lifting! Indeed, after 15 ♖d3 c5 16 e5! (it is crucial to plug the a1-h8 long diagonal) 16...♕b4 17 ♕e7 ♘c4 18 ♘d1 ♗xe5 somehow White managed to hold the draw in F.Cottegnie-G.Feldmann, correspondence 2003.

12...0-0-0

After 12...♕g5!? 13 ♕xg5 fxg5 14

♘f3 ♗e7 15 ♗e2 White has a decent game, with plans like ♘e5, or h4, or e5.

13 ♗d3

If White tries 13 ♕xf6?! in an attempt to clear the e5-square, once again Black gets promising play for the pawn with 13...♖g8 followed by ...♗g7.

13...♖g8 14 ♘ge2?!

Better is 14 g3!.

14...♗e7?!

He should continue to open the position for his bishops with 14...♖xg2! 15 ♕xf6 ♗g7 with an edge for Black.

15 g3 h5 16 ♔b1 ♘a4?!

16...e5 takes control over d4 and f4: 17 ♕h6! ♖h8 18 ♕g7 ♖de8 19 ♘c1 and White has a few kingside pawn targets and the f5-square, while Black should try and whip up an attack on the queenside.

17 ♘xa4 ♕xa4 18 e5!

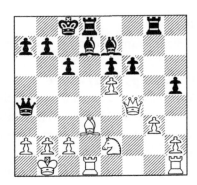

Forcing a slightly superior ending.

18...♕xf4 19 ♘xf4 fxe5 20 ♘g6 ♗c5?!

Black can improve over the game continuation with 20...♗d6! 21 ♖he1 e4! 22 ♗xe4 ♔c7 and the e6-pawn is safer than in the game.

21 ♘xe5 ♗e8?

Now e6 falls. He should try 21...♔c7.

22 ♗c4 ♖xd1+ 23 ♖xd1 ♖f8 24 ♗xe6+ ♔c7 25 ♘d7!?

Black also should save the game in the lines:

a) 25 ♗d7 ♗d6 26 ♗xe8 ♗xe5! 27 ♗xh5 ♖h8 28 g4 ♗xh2.

b) White can try to avoid the opposite-coloured bishops with 25 ♘d3 ♗d6, but even here Black's bishop pair should save him.

25...♗xd7 26 ♖xd7+ ♔b6 27 ♗f7 ♗g1 28 h3 ♗h2 29 g4 hxg4 30 hxg4 ♗f4 31 c3 ♖h8 32 ♖d1 ♖h2 33 ♗e6 ♖f2 34 a3 a5 35 a4 ♔c5 36 ♔a2 b5 37 axb5 cxb5 38 ♖d5+

38...♔b6?!

Black holds the draw quite easily after 38...♔c6! (the threat is 39...♗c1) 39 ♖f5 ♗e3.

39 ♗d7! b4 40 ♖b5+ ♔c7 41 ♗f5 ♗c1??

Too fancy. The straightforward 41...bxc3 42 ♖c5+ ♔d6 43 ♖xc3 ♗e5 44 ♖b3 ♔c5 holds the draw without any trouble.

42 cxb4!

Winning a second pawn.

42...♗xb2

Realizing that 42...♖xb2+?? 43 ♔a1 ♔d6 44 ♖c5 drops a piece.

43 bxa5 ♗d4+ 44 ♔b3 ♖f4

If Black eliminates rooks with 44...♖b2+ 45 ♔c4 ♖xb5 46 ♔xb5 ♔b8 47 g5 ♔a7 48 g6 ♗g7 49 ♗d3 ♗c3 50 ♔c6 ♔b8 51 ♔d7 ♔a7 52 ♔e7 ♔b8 53 ♔f7 ♔a7 54 g7 ♗xg7 55 ♔xg7 the trouble is White has the correct coloured bishop and wins.

45 ♖b4 ♔d6 46 a6 ♖f3+ 47 ♔c4 ♗c5 48 ♖b3! ♖f4+ 49 ♔b5 ♗f2 50 ♖d3+ ♔e5

Or 50...♔c7 51 ♖d7+ ♔b8 52 ♗e6 ♖e4 53 ♖b7+ ♔a8 54 ♗d5 and wins.

51 ♖a3 ♗a7 52 ♔c6 ♖b4 53 ♖a5+ ♔f4 54 ♖b5!

Continuing to exploit the fact that Black cannot trade rooks.

54...♖a4 55 ♔b7 ♗d4 56 ♗d7 ♖a3 57 ♖b4 ♔e5 58 ♖xd4!

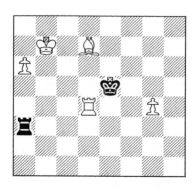

The simplification sac clears the way for the passed a-pawn.

58...♔xd4 59 a7 ♖b3+ 60 ♔c6 ♖a3 61 ♔b6 ♔e5 62 ♗b5!

Threatening a roadblock with ♗a6.

62...♔d6 63 ♔b7

Even better was 63 ♗a6! ♖b3+ 64 ♔a5 ♖a3+ 65 ♔b5 ♖b3+ 66 ♔a4.

63...♖b3 1-0

Summary

In my opinion 10 ♕g4! is one of the only lines for White which avoids reaching an inferior position. Although Black gets the bishop pair and dark-square control, White has a lead in development and attacking chances to keep the balance.

Game 10
F.Cottegnie-A.Scarani
correspondence 2002

1 ♘c3

This is an interesting way to reach the Veresov.

1...d5

If Black wants to dodge the Veresov then he should try 1...e5 or 1...c5.

2 d4 ♘f6 3 ♗g5 ♘bd7 4 f3 c6

After 4...h6 5 ♗h4 c6 6 e4, just as in London, Torre and Trompowsky, I absolutely love it when opponents lash out with the 'active' ...h6 and ...g5, here with 6...g5?!. Black's kingside pawns become a big bull's eye target for White later on: 7 ♗f2 dxe4 8 fxe4 ♘b6 9 ♘f3 ♗g7 10 ♕d2 ♗e6 11 0-0-0 0-0 (Black can't try and castle queenside since 11...♕c7? is met by 12 ♗g3) 12 h4 disturbing the pawn front around Black's king, F.Eid-P.Van Hoolandt,

Turin Olympiad 2006.

5 e4 dxe4 6 fxe4 e5 7 dxe5 ♕a5 8 ♗xf6 gxf6 9 e6 fxe6 10 ♕g4 ♕g5!?

A tricky idea suggested by *Rybka*.

11 ♕xg5

You can also take on e6. 11 ♕xe6+ ♗e7 and now there is only one good plan for White:

a) 12 ♕f5! ♕xf5 13 exf5 ♘e5 14 0-0-0 ♗xf5 15 ♘ge2 when Black's bishop pair compensates him for the slightly weakened structure.

b) 12 ♘f3? ♕e3+ 13 ♗e2 ♘e5 14 ♕b3 ♘xf3+ 15 gxf3 f5! 16 h4? ♗xh4+! and White's king is in big trouble.

c) 12 ♕c4? ♘e5 13 ♕e2 ♗g4 14 ♕d2 ♕xd2+ 15 ♔xd2 0-0-0+ and for the pawn, Black has too much for White to deal with:

1. A massive development lead;

2. An attack, despite queens being off the board;

3. The bishop pair in a wide open position; and

4. As always, dark-square control.

11...fxg5 12 ♗e2 ♗g7 13 h4!

Activating the sleeping rook on h1

and creating a target of Black's h-pawn. 13 ♗h5+?! is just a waste of time and only helps Black after 13...♔e7.

13...gxh4

13...h6 14 hxg5 hxg5 15 ♖xh8+ ♗xh8 16 ♘f3 ♗f6 is equal.

14 ♖xh4 ♘f8

After 14...♗xc3+ 15 bxc3 ♘c5 16 ♘f3 ♖g8 17 ♔f2 ♗d7 18 e5 0-0-0 19 ♖d1 ♗e8 20 ♖xd8+ ♔xd8 21 ♗d3 ♗g6 22 ♗xg6 hxg6 23 ♔e3 White's strong piece activity and advanced king give him a micro-edge, despite his shattered queenside pawn structure.

15 ♘f3 e5

If he avoids plugging up the e5-square with a pawn with 15...♘g6 16 ♖h1 ♘e5 then after 17 0-0-0 ♘xf3 18 gxf3 h5 19 f4! ♗h6?! 20 ♖df1 Black begins to overextend.

16 ♖h5 ♘g6 17 ♘d1!

Now f5 and c4 are possible destinations.

17...♘f4 18 ♖h2 ♘xe2!?

I'm not so sure this is a good decision.

19 ♔xe2 ♗e6 20 ♘e3

The position is deceptive. Most players would take Black, but White's knights more than hold their own against Black's bishops in this unbalanced ending because the pawn structure is fixed on the kingside and centre. Also, White controls the f5-square, a nasty outpost for a knight.

20...0-0-0 21 ♘g5 ♗g8 22 g4!

A knight on f5 will rule.

22...♖d7 23 ♖ah1 h6 24 ♘f3 ♗h7 25 ♘f5 ♖e8 26 ♖d1?!

White wants to swap a pair of rooks to lower the chances of a sudden black attack down the d-file. However, a better way to seal the d-file is 26 ♘e1! ♗g6 27 ♘d3 ♗f8 28 ♔e3 h5! 29 g5! keeping a grip on the position.

26...♖xd1 27 ♔xd1 ♗f8 28 ♔e2 ♔c7 29 a3 ♗g6 30 c3 ♖e6!

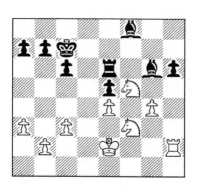

A clever plan. Black finds counterplay by playing ...c5 and swinging the rook to either b6 or a6 to harass White's queenside pawns.

31 b4 c5! 32 ♔e3 ♖a6 33 ♘xe5 ♗xf5 34 gxf5 ♖xa3 35 ♘g6! ♖xc3+ 36 ♔f4

Numbers don't matter. All that counts is that White's central pawns are faster than Black's queenside pawns.

36...♗g7 37 e5 ♖c4+ 38 ♔g3

38 ♔e3! cxb4 39 f6 ♖g4 40 ♘f4 ♗f8 41 ♘e6+ wins even faster.

38...cxb4 39 f6 ♖c6 40 ♘e7! ♖c3+ 41 ♔g4 ♗f8

41...♖c4+ 42 ♔f5 ♗f8 43 ♘g6 ♗c5 44 e6 wins.

42 ♘d5+ ♔d7 43 ♘xc3 1-0

After 43...bxc3, 44 ♔f5 secures e6 when there is no stopping the pawns.

Summary

The ending after 11 ♕xg5 is dynamically balanced. White's active pieces compensate for Black's bishop pair.

Game 11
M.Yilmazyerli-R.Song
Singapore 2007

1 d4 ♘f6 2 ♘c3 d5 3 ♗g5 ♘bd7 4 f3 c6 5 e4 dxe4 6 fxe4 e5 7 dxe5 ♕a5 8 ♗xf6 gxf6 9 e6 fxe6 10 ♕g4 ♘e5

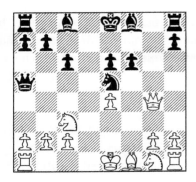

Black will not be denied the beautiful square for his knight. The price is the temporary discomfort of his king.

11 ♕h5+ ♚d8

Alternatively, 11...♚e7!? (intending 12...♘d3+) 12 ♗e2 (or 12 ♕h3 ♗g7 13 ♘f3 ♗d7 14 0-0-0 with a Sicilian-like position with mutual chances) 12...b6?! (the beginning of a bad plan; better was 12...♗d7 13 0-0-0 ♖d8) 13 0-0-0 ♗a6?! 14 ♚b1 ♗xe2 15 ♘gxe2 (all Black has achieved with his plan is to aid White's development, and weaken both c6 and e6) 15...♘c4 16 ♕h3! (gunning for e6) 16...♕e5 17 ♕d3! ♘d6 18 ♘d4 ♖c8 19 ♘f3! ♕c5 20 e5! fxe5 21 ♘g5 and White's attack is decisive, C.Broeker-W.Eisenmann, correspondence 2000.

12 0-0-0+ ♚c7 13 ♕h4 ♗e7 14 ♚b1 ♗d7 15 ♘f3 ♖ad8?

Allowing White an interference sac. Instead 15...♖ae8! 16 ♗e2 looks dynamically balanced. White has a lot of pawn targets (h7, f6 and e6), but Black has the bishop pair and dark-square control to compensate. Black looks like

he holds all the positional trumps and his cup runneth over after his last move. What could possibly go wrong?

16 ♘b5+!

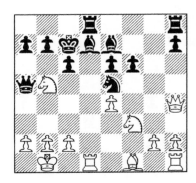

A right hook which disconnects Black's queen's coverage of e5 to pull off a disrupting tactic.

16...cxb5 17 ♘xe5 ♗c8 18 ♖xd8 ♖xd8

If 18...♗xd8? 19 ♘f7 ♖f8 20 ♘xd8 ♖xd8 21 ♗d3 and Black will drop at least one pawn.

19 ♗d3 ♖e8 20 ♘g4

Or 20 ♕h5! ♖d8 21 ♕xh7 ♕b4 22 a3 ♕c5 23 ♘g6 ♖d7 24 ♘xe7 ♖xe7 25 ♕g6 ♕e5 26 ♖f1 f5 27 g3 when White has the initiative, the superior structure and an extra pawn.

20...e5 21 ♘xf6!

Oh, I like it! Licking honey off a razor blade! Surprisingly there is no way for Black to exploit the pin due to knight checks on e8 and d5.

21...♗e6! 22 b3!

There is no good reason to allow complications with 22 ♘xe8+?! ♚d8 23 ♕g3 ♕xa2+ 24 ♚c1 ♕a1+ 25 ♚d2 ♕xh1 26 ♗xb5.

22...♔b8?

A blunder in a lost position. Of course, 22...♖f8?? fails miserably to 23 ♘d5+, but 22...♔b6 23 ♕h6 ♗xf6 24 ♕xf6 ♕c3 was the only way to continue the game.

23 ♕h5!

Kids rarely miss tactical tricks: e8 and e5 are hit simultaneously.

23...♖f8 24 ♘d7+!

Eliminating Black's last chance, his dark-squared bishop.

24...♗xd7

24...♔c7? 25 ♘xf8 ♗xf8 26 ♕xe5+ ♔d7 27 ♕xb5+ ends any attacking dreams Black may have had.

25 ♕xe5+ ♔c7 26 ♕xe7 ♖c8 27 ♕xh7

Now White has two connected passed pawns on the g- and h-files.

27...a5 28 ♕g7 a4 29 h4

The simple plan is to promote on h8 while avoiding mate.

29...♕d6 30 h5 ♗e6 31 h6!

Ignoring Black's threat.

31...axb3 32 axb3 ♗xb3

General Custer's last stand!

33 h7 ♕b4 34 ♕b2! 1-0

Summary

10...♘e5 plants the knight on its best square. The natural drawback is that it allows White the disrupting check on h5.

> ### Game 12
> ### D.Berges-A.Delorme
> Fouesnant 1999

1 d4 d5 2 ♘c3 ♘f6 3 ♗g5 ♘bd7 4 f3 c6 5 e4 dxe4 6 fxe4 e5 7 ♘f3

This is a radical option which may appeal to the true red-blooded Veresov player. Compare our line to the Fantasy Variation of the Caro-Kann: 1 e4 c6 2 d4 d5 3 f3 dxe4 4 fxe4 e5 5 ♘f3. Let's see what White gets and what he must give up in the 7 ♘f3 line of the Veresov:

1. White allows damage to his pawn structure, isolating his e-pawn and creating a hole on e5.

2. White often must sac his b-pawn to some form of ...♕b6 and ...♕xb2.

3. White gets the open f-file for his attack. This in conjunction with ♗c4

and a timely e5 could be deadly for Black, who could implode on f7.

4. White in general gets great piece activity, with a powerful bishop on c4, potentials of ♘d4 and ♘f5, and play along the f-file, d-file or b-file if White has sac'ed his b-pawn.

5. You will probably lose most endings if you get there without doing some damage to Black but as Tarrasch once said: "Before the endgame the gods have placed the middlegame!"

7...♕a5

Several of my students suggested 7...♗d6 to fortify e5 and play the same strategy Black uses against the Fantasy line of the Caro-Kann: 8 ♕d2 (not 8 dxe5?! ♘xe5 and Black already stood better, K.Nickl-H.Heimsoth, Dortmund 1989) 8...h6 9 ♗h4 ♕e7 10 0-0-0 0-0 11 ♗e2 ♖e8 (11...b5? is well met by 12 d5! b4 13 dxc6! with a clear advantage to White) 12 ♖hf1 and I like the look of White's position:

1. At some point we will play dxe5 and ♘d4, heading for f5;

2. We have pressure down the f-file;

3. At any point ...b5?! is conveniently met by d5!.

8 ♗c4

Worthy of consideration is 8 ♗xf6 ♘xf6 9 ♘xe5 ♘xe4 10 ♕f3 ♘d6 11 0-0-0 f6 12 ♖e1! ♔d8 13 ♘c4 when White's safer king is more meaningful than Black's bishop pair, Lim Yee Weng-W.Jordan, Melbourne 2004.

8...♗b4

Nobody yet has had the nerve to en-

ter 8...♗a3!? 9 ♗d2 ♗xb2 10 ♘b5 ♕b6 11 ♘d6+ ♔e7 12 ♖b1! ♔xd6 13 dxe5+ ♔c7 14 exf6 gxf6 15 c3! when I prefer White in the complications.

9 0-0 exd4

9...♗xc3?! 10 bxc3 ♕xc3 11 ♕e2 0-0 12 ♖ad1 offers White excellent compensation for the pawn. He has a big attack coming on the kingside.

10 e5!

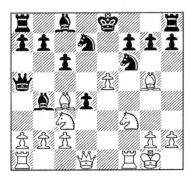

In King's Gambit style. There is no turning back or hesitation now. Lines must be prised open quickly.

10...dxc3 11 exf6 0-0

Alternatively, 11...gxf6 12 ♖e1+ ♗e7 13 ♕e2 0-0 14 ♕xe7 cxb2 15 ♗xf6! bxa1♕ (15...♘xf6? 16 ♖ab1 threatens ♕xf6 and ♖e5 among other things) 16 ♗xa1 ♕c5+ 17 ♕xc5 ♘xc5 18 ♖e5 ♘e6 19 ♗xe6 fxe6 20 ♖g5+ ♔f7 21 ♖g7+ ♔e8 22 ♘g5 and Black is up a full exchange and a pawn in the endgame, but has to fight for the draw!

12 fxg7 ♔xg7 13 ♕d4+ ♔g8!

Black gets toasted after 13...f6? 14 ♕g4! cxb2 15 ♖ad1 fxg5 16 ♘xg5.

14 ♕h4 ♖e8?!

14...cxb2 15 ♖ad1 ♗c3 16 ♗e7! also wins for White.

15 ♗xf7+!

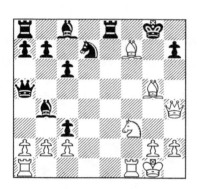

Black's king is now a small child abandoned in the dark forest.

15...♔xf7 16 ♕xh7+ ♔e6 17 ♖ad1!

The first rule of a king-hunt is to avoid blindly chasing the opponent's king. Instead, the key is to cut off escape routes.

17...♗c5+ 18 ♔h1 1-0

White threatens both 19 ♖fe1+ and 19 ♕g6+, obliterating Black.

Summary

The 7 ♘f3 line can pay off big time if Black allows your piece activity to get out of control as it did in this game.

Game 13
N.Nestorovic-S.Pezelj
Zlatibor 2007

1 e4 c6 2 d4 d6

Patience please, we will soon reach our position.

3 ♘c3 ♘f6 4 ♗g5 ♘bd7 5 f4 e5 6 fxe5 dxe5 7 ♘f3 h6

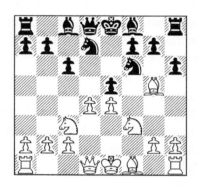

Wow, what a funky transposition into a Veresov via the Pirc!

The idea behind throwing in ...h6 is to chase the bishop to h4, denying White ♗d2 ideas. Black can also just play the immediate 7...exd4 8 ♕xd4 ♕b6 and now:

a) 9 ♕d2 ♕xb2 10 ♖b1 ♕a3 11 e5 ♘d5 12 ♘xd5 cxd5 13 ♗b5 was Zhang Pengxiang-J.Benjamin, Cap d'Agde (rapid) 2000. White has excellent chances for his pawn(s), depending on how greedy Black gets. Benjamin, perhaps not liking his position, made a shaky piece sac with 13...♗c5?!. This really should not work, although one must also factor in the practical worth of such a sac. After 14 ♕xd5 0-0 15 ♗xd7 ♗xd7 16 ♕xd7 ♕xa2 White went passive with 17 ♕d1?! and allowed Black's attack to flare up. I am skeptical about Black's compensation after the superior 17 ♕b5!.

The problem with this line is 9...♗b4! (instead of Benjamin's

9...♕xb2) which was suggested by one of my students, Tom Nelson. Here 10 ♗d3 0-0 11 0-0-0 ♕a5 12 a3 ♗xc3 13 ♕xc3 ♕xc3 14 bxc3 ♖e8 looks unappetizing for White.

b) In view of this, perhaps White should play 9 0-0-0 instead of 9 ♕d2, with similar play to the main game.

8 ♗h4 exd4 9 ♕xd4

I can't find a single game with 9 ♘xd4 in my databases, yet the move may be playable if White is brave enough! Indeed, after 9...♕b6 10 ♕d2 ♕xb2 11 ♖b1 ♕a3 12 ♘f5 g6 13 e5! ♕a5 14 exf6 ♕xf5 15 ♗d3 ♕e6+ 16 ♘e4 ♗c5 White has compensation for the pawn:

1. Black can't castle;

2. Black is behind in development; and

3. The pawn on f6 has a choking effect on Black.

Overall, chances look approximately even.

9...♕b6

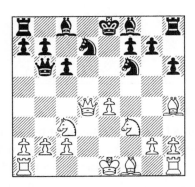

9...♗c5 10 ♕d2 ♕e7 11 0-0-0 0-0 is an option for Black, who keeps his grip

on e5, but has yet to solve the problem of the pin on the f6-knight.

10 0-0-0!

White's activity sustains him even after queens come off the board. Backing down with 10 ♕d2?! looks too passive after 10...♗b4 11 0-0-0 0-0, C.Haller-G.Gal, Balatonbereny 1995.

10...♕xd4

White would be happy to be chased with 10...♗c5?! 11 ♕c4 threatening 12 e5.

11 ♘xd4 g5?!

Not a good idea. He weakens himself along the f-file and gives up the f5-square. Black should play 11...♗b4 12 ♘f5 0-0 13 ♘d6 ♘e5 14 ♗g3 when White's superior activity compensates for his inferior pawn structure.

12 ♗g3 ♘c5 13 ♗e5 ♘cd7 14 ♗g3 ♘c5 15 ♖e1

I don't see why the pawn needed protection. He should increase his lead in development with 15 ♗c4!.

15...♘h5 16 ♗f2 ♗d7 17 e5 0-0-0 18 ♗c4 ♖h7

After 18...♘f4 19 g3 ♘fe6 20 ♘xe6 ♗xe6 21 ♗xe6+ fxe6 22 ♖hf1 White still has the edge due to the extra space provided by the e5-pawn.

19 a3

19 g3! leaves Black's knight dangling on the periphery.

19...a5 20 a4 ♘f4 21 g3 ♘g6 22 e6 fxe6 23 ♘xe6 ♘xe6 24 ♗xe6 ♗d6 25 ♗xd7+ ♖hxd7?

Black held things together from a slightly inferior position until his last move. The game would head for a draw after the correct 25...♔xd7! covering e6. **26 ♖e6!**

26...♘e5

Now a pawn falls by force. However, 26...♖g8 27 ♘e4 ♗e7 28 ♗b6 ♖d5 29 ♖e1 leaves Black tied up.

27 ♗b6 ♖f8 28 ♖e1 ♘f7 29 ♗xa5 ♗c7 30 ♗xc7 ♔xc7 31 a5 g4 32 ♘a4 ♘g5 33 ♘c5!

Or 33 ♖xh6 ♖f2 34 ♘b6 ♖dd2 35 ♔b1! and the c2-pawn is untouchable due to Black's insecure king position.

33...♖df7

33...♖f5 34 ♘xd7 ♘xe6 35 ♖xe6 ♔xd7 36 ♖xh6 ♖xa5 37 ♖h7+ ♔c8 38

♔d2 is also a bust for Black, who is a pawn down with an imprisoned king on the last rank.

34 ♖xh6 b6 35 axb6+ ♔xb6 36 ♘d3 ♘f3 37 ♖e4 ♖a8 38 b3 ♖g7 39 ♔b2 ♖d8 40 ♖b4+ ♔c7 41 ♘c5 1-0

Summary

White's initiative sustains you even into an ending in this line.

Game 14
K.Krug-C.Tiemann
Dresden 2008

1 d4 ♘f6 2 ♘c3 d5 3 ♗g5 ♘bd7 4 f3 c6 5 e4 dxe4 6 fxe4 e5 7 ♘f3 ♕b6

Striking at White's soft spots. Black simultaneously hits b2 and d4.

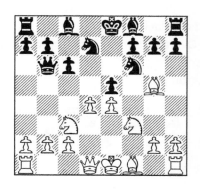

8 ♕d2

It is thematic to sac your b-pawn for development and an open file in this line. You should avoid the gimmicky 8 a3?! exd4 (White's idea is found in the silly line 8...♕xb2?? 9 ♘a4 when he wins material) 9 ♘xd4 ♗c5 10 ♗e3

♕c7 and White has not made anything of his initiative, leaving Black closer to consolidating his structural edge, D.Berges-D.Primel, Sautron 2001.

8...exd4

After 8...♕xb2? 9 ♖b1 ♕a3 10 dxe5 ♘g4 11 h3! Black is in big trouble.

9 ♘xd4 ♗b4 10 ♘f5 0-0

Black can also take the bait with 10...♘xe4 when 11 ♕e2 ♘df6 12 ♘d6+! ♗xd6 13 ♗xf6 gxf6 14 ♘xe4 ♕a5+ 15 c3 ♗e5 16 ♘xf6+ ♔f8 17 ♕f3 ♗f5 18 ♗e2 ♗xf6 19 0-0 ♖e8 20 ♗d3! Is sharp.

11 ♗d3 ♖e8 12 0-0-0 ♘xe4!?

A risky pawn grab when behind in development. Instead, 12...♕a5! 13 ♖hf1 ♘g4 (13...♘xe4? 14 ♕f4! ♘xc3? 15 ♘h6+! ♔h8 16 ♘xf7+ ♔g8 17 ♗c4 wins) 14 h3 ♘ge5 15 ♕f4? (15 a3! ♗xc3 16 ♕xc3 ♕xc3 17 bxc3 and White's activity again compensates for his wretched pawn structure) 15...♘b6? (White doesn't have enough if Black calls his bluff with 15...♗xc3!) 16 ♘xg7! and Black's king cover was stripped in K.Krug-F.Bracker, Willingen 2006.

13 ♗xe4 ♖xe4 14 ♖he1

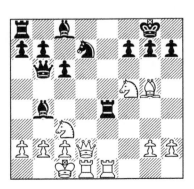

Black has fallen behind and his pieces remain dormant on the queenside.

14...♖xe1 15 ♖xe1

15...♘f8?

Alternatively, 15...f6 16 ♖e8+ and now:

a) 16...♔f7 17 ♕e2 ♘e5 18 ♕h5+ ♘g6 19 ♖xc8! ♖xc8 20 ♕xh7 ♗xc3 21 bxc3 ♕g1+ 22 ♔b2 ♕b6+ is drawn by perpetual check.

b) 16...♘f8? 17 ♗e3 ♕a5 18 ♘d6 wins.

16 ♘xg7!

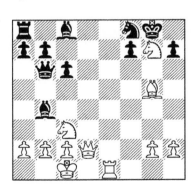

Delivering a left cross on g7!

16...♗g4

The knight has immunity: 16...♔xg7?? 17 ♗h6+ ♔h8 18 ♕f4 ♕d8 19 ♕xf7 ♕d4 20 ♗g5! wins.

17 ♘e8!

Threatening a devastating check on f6. Black has no recourse but to give up material.

17...♖xe8 18 ♖xe8 ♕g1+ 19 ♖e1 ♕xh2 20 ♗f6 ♘e6 21 a3 ♗d6 22 ♔b1 h6 23 ♖e4 ♗f4

23...♗f5 24 ♖h4 ♕g1+ 25 ♔a2 ♗f8 26 ♘e4 is also hopeless.

24 ♕d7

Infiltration.

24...♕h1+ 25 ♔a2 ♕h5 26 ♕xb7

Well, okay, but White had a quicker win with 26 ♖xf4! ♘xf4 27 ♕e8+ ♔h7 28 ♕h8+ ♔g6 29 ♕g7+ ♔f5 30 ♗d4!.

26...♕f5 27 ♕c8+ ♔h7 28 ♕h8+ ♔g6 29 ♗e5 ♗g5

It's just a matter of technique after 29...♗xe5 30 ♕xe5 ♕xe5 31 ♖xe5 ♘f4

32 g3 ♘h5 33 ♖e3.

30 ♕g8+ ♔h5 31 ♖e1! 1-0

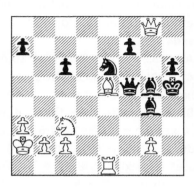

Black's king is led to the slaughter along the h-file.

Summary

If you like to play in the romantic style of the old greats, then the 7 ♘f3 line should be your choice in this chapter. I would bet that Morphy would give this line two enthusiastic thumbs up!

Chapter Two
The Veresov: 3...♞bd7 4 ♛d3

1 d4 ♞f6 2 ♞c3 d5 3 ♗g5 ♞bd7 4 ♛d3

This is a sounder alternative to the chaos of 4 f3 from the first chapter.

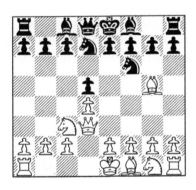

In this chapter, we deal with:

a) 4...c6 from which you get mostly Caro-Kann style positions;

b) 4...e6 where you deal with French positions;

c) 4...h6?! usually leads to inferior French positions;

d) 4...g6 leads to a hybrid Caro/Pirc position; and

e) 4...c5 when Black will capture on d4 with greater central control, but your development lead in the open position could make life tough for Black.

Game 15
Z.Kozul-A.Brkic
Zagreb 2006

1 d4 ♞f6 2 ♞c3 d5 3 ♗g5 ♞bd7 4 ♛d3 c6 5 ♞f3

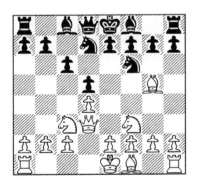

GM Prié considers this the mainline of the 4 ♕d3 Veresov. White takes a wait-and-see approach and refrains from an immediate e4. One drawback is that White loses the option of slowly building his centre with f3 and e4.

5...b5

Blind ambition! Black launches an attack even before White commits his king to the queenside. Instead, after 5...g6 6 e4 dxe4 7 ♘xe4 ♗g7 (the game looks like it arose from some kind of Gurgenidze Pirc) 8 ♗e2 h6 9 ♘xf6+ ♘xf6 10 ♗f4 White has a little extra space but Black stands solidly, A.Zubov-N.Papenin, Simferopol 2003.

6 a3!

White remains flexible, changes gears and plans to castle kingside.

6...a5!?

If you are brave and stubborn enough, you can actually still castle queenside: for example, 6...h6 7 ♗h4 e6 8 e4 dxe4 9 ♘xe4 ♗e7 10 ♘xf6+ ♘xf6 11 0-0-0!? 0-0 12 ♘e5 (the key for White is central play, since he is slower if he begins to attack Black's king) 12...♗b7 13 ♗e2 a5 14 ♗f3 ♘d5?! (14...b4!) 15 ♗xe7 ♕xe7 16 ♗xd5 cxd5 17 ♕xb5! ♖fc8?! 18 ♕d7! and White was up a pawn in the ending but later botched it, M.Pogromsky-A.Pugachov, Internet 2004.

7 e4 b4!?

Or 7...♗a6 8 b4 axb4 9 axb4 dxe4 10 ♘xe4 ♗b7 11 ♖b1 e6 12 ♗e2 with an interesting position where White stands just a shade better. Black controls d5 for

his pieces while White owns c5.

8 axb4 ♗a6 9 b5!

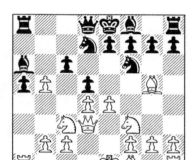

9...cxb5?

After this Black experiences serious difficulties. He should enter the line 9...♗xb5! 10 ♘xb5 dxe4 11 ♕e3! cxb5 (11...exf3?? 12 ♘d6 mate would be a pleasant surprise for White) 12 ♘d2 ♕b6 13 ♘xe4 ♘d5 14 ♕d3 e6 when White stands a tad better due to his bishop pair, but Black's queenside play gives him counterplay.

10 ♘xd5 ♘xd5 11 exd5 b4 12 ♕b3 ♗xf1 13 ♔xf1 ♕b6

Brkic had probably intended 13...♘b6?! 14 c4! bxc3 15 bxc3, but then realized that he couldn't recapture: 15...♘xd5?? 16 ♘e5! and Black is helpless to stop ♕b5+ or ♕a4+.

14 ♕a4!

Pinning the knight and preparing c4.

14...f6 15 ♗d2 ♖c8 16 ♔e2!

Very brave. He sees that d1 is actually a secure spot for the king. Black simply doesn't have the attackers to do the job. An alternative plan is to play h3 and walk the king to h2.

The opening has been a disaster for Black. Let's assess:

1. He is down a pawn;

2. Not only is Black behind in development, but the d5-pawn clogs Black's even further;

3. White's king is safe and comfortable in the middle since Black doesn't have enough attackers;

4. The a5-pawn is weak and hanging; and

5. Black is stuck in an annoying pin on the a4-e8 diagonal.

16...g5 17 c3 ♕a6+ 18 ♔d1 bxc3 19 bxc3 ♕d3 20 ♕xa5 ♖b8 21 ♕a2! ♕f5 22 h3 ♖g8 23 c4 g4 24 hxg4 ♖xg4

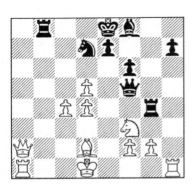

After 24...♕xg4 25 ♖h2 everything is covered and White remains two pawns in the plus column.

25 ♕c2!

Simplifying into an easily won endgame. Black can't dodge the trade.

25...♕xc2+ 26 ♔xc2 ♖xg2 27 ♗e3 f5?

27...♖c8 28 ♔d3 ♘b6 29 ♘d2 is also hopeless.

28 ♘h4 1-0

Summary

White takes a waiting approach with 5 ♘f3. He eventually plays for e4 no matter how Black responds.

Game 16
J.Bosch-A.Kabatianski
Dutch League 2009

1 d4 ♘f6 2 ♘c3 d5 3 ♗g5 ♘bd7 4 ♕d3 c6 5 ♘f3 g6

A more sober approach than 5...b5.

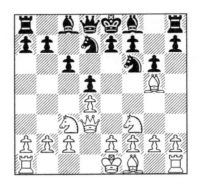

6 e4 dxe4 7 ♘xe4 ♗g7 8 0-0-0 0-0 9 ♔b1

Moving the king to b1 is almost a

reflex in such positions, but in opposite-wing attacks every tempo counts. Perhaps White should continue with the immediate 9 h4! h6 10 ♗xf6 ♘xf6 11 ♘xf6+ ♗xf6 12 h5 ♕a5? (reckless; he should play the saner move 12...g5) 13 hxg6 ♗f5 14 gxf7+ ♖xf7 15 ♕b3 ♗e4 16 ♗c4 ♗g5+ 17 ♘xg5 ♕xg5+ 18 ♔b1 ♗d5 19 ♖h3! and White had a material advantage as well as an attack, R.Barhudarian-Y.Nikolaev, St Petersburg 2008.

9...a5

Black is first to begin to attack, but one advantage in White's favour is extra space, which keeps his king safer. It was Steinitz who first advised against attacking if you control less territory than your opponent.

10 ♘g3

Putting a stop to ...♗f5 ideas and also preparing h4-h5.

10...♘b6!?

Going for piece play over a traditional pawn storm. A more normal approach would be 10...b5 11 h4 ♘g4 12 ♕d2 h6 13 ♗f4 h5 14 ♘e4 ♘b6 15 ♘fg5 ♘d5 16 ♗g3 ♗f5 17 ♖e1 ♕b6 18 f3 ♘gf6 19 c3 ♖fd8 20 ♔a1 b4 21 c4 ♘c7 22 c5 when the chances look balanced.

11 c4!?

Taking control over d5 at the cost of undermining support for his d-pawn.

11...♗e6

Traditionally in such structures, Black tries to eliminate his light-squared bishop for a knight. However,

after 11...♗g4 12 ♗e2 a4 13 h3 ♗xf3 14 ♗xf3 a3 15 b3 White's space and bishop pair give him a clear edge and help keep his king safe.

12 ♕c2 ♘bd7

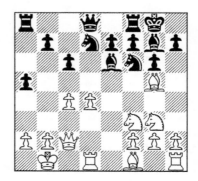

The work is done on b6 and he prepares ...b5.

13 h4 b5

Black can also try to halt the advance of White's h-pawn: 13...h5!? 14 ♖e1! (an exchange sac on e6 will be strategically devastating to Black) 14...♗g4 15 ♘h2! (threat: 16 f3) 15...♖e8 16 f3 ♕c7! 17 ♘xg4 ♕xg3 18 ♘f2 a4 19 ♖h3 ♕c7 20 g4 a3 21 b3 and White's attack looks a bit faster, but his structure is also more shaky. Perhaps chances are balanced.

14 h5 bxc4 15 hxg6 hxg6 16 ♗xc4

Or 16 ♖e1!? (contemplating an exchange sac on e6) 16...♗d5 17 ♗xc4 ♘b6 18 ♗xd5 ♘bxd5 19 ♘e4 and White's knights will attain powerful outposts on c5 and e5. Black has the open b-file and chances against White's king, but I give White a slight edge.

16...♗xc4 17 ♕xc4 ♕b6 18 ♗h6 ♗xh6?

There was no reason for Black to give White a free move to double on the h-file. He should play 18...♖fb8! 19 ♕c1 ♗h8.

19 ♖xh6 ♔g7 20 ♖dh1?

A critical moment in the game. White's move allows Black to challenge the h-file with his rooks. White missed the more subtle 20 ♕c1! and Black must be very careful. For example:

a) 20...♖h8?? 21 ♘f5+! mates.

b) 20...♖fb8?? 21 ♘f5+! and once again White mates in five.

c) 20...♖g8! (the only move) 21 ♘e5 ♔f8 22 ♘xd7+ ♘xd7 23 ♘e4 ♖b8 24 ♖h7 and Black's king is in a precarious situation; ♘g5 is in the air.

20...♕b5!

A terrific defensive move. Black covers the critical f5-square and deprives his opponent of opportunities to sac on f5. This allows Black time to challenge the h-file with equality.

21 ♕c1 ♖h8

No more ♘f5+ tricks, so Black confronts White on the h-file.

22 a3 ♖ab8 23 ♔a1 ♘g4 24 ♖xh8 ♖xh8 25 ♖e1 e6 26 ♕d2 ♘gf6

Black has equalized. The mutual weaknesses on d4 and c6 cancel each other out.

27 ♘e5?!

His d-pawn needs support: 27 ♖c1 c5 28 ♕c3 cxd4 29 ♕xd4 e5 30 ♕c4 ♕xc4 31 ♖xc4 is balanced but still sharp due to the opposite-wing pawn majorities.

27...♕d5 28 f3 ♘c5

Threatening to land on b3, but this isn't the strongest move. Black should go for 28...c5! 29 ♕xa5 ♖a8 30 ♕b5 ♕xd4 31 ♘xd7 ♘xd7 (threatening to take on a3) 32 ♕b3 ♖b8 33 ♕c2 ♘e5 with the initiative.

29 ♔b1 ♘b3

30 ♕e3?

Meekly submitting to the loss of a pawn. White misses an opportunity to counterattack and target f7 with the line 30 ♕f4! ♕xd4 (Black is in big trouble after 30...♘xd4? 31 ♘e4 ♘f5 32 g4 ♖h4 33 ♘g5) 31 ♘e4! ♘d2+! 32 ♕xd2 ♕xe5 33 ♘xf6 ♕xf6 34 ♕xa5, which regains the lost pawn with equality.

30...♘xd4 31 ♖c1 ♖h2 32 ♘e2 ♘b3 33 ♘c3 ♕d2 34 ♕xd2 ♘xd2+ 35 ♔a2 ♖xg2 36 ♘a4

The pure pawn race favours Black: 36 ♘xc6 ♘xf3 37 ♘xa5 ♘e5 38 a4 g5 39 ♘b7 ♘c4 40 ♘d1 ♖g4 and now 41 a5?? isn't possible due to 41...♘xa5! 42 ♘xa5 ♖a4+.

36...♘d5 37 ♖xc6 ♖g5! 38 ♘g4 ♖f5 39 ♘c5 ♘xf3 40 ♖a6 ♘d2?

Black wins easily after 40...♘c3+! 41 bxc3 ♖xc5 42 ♔b3 g5 when his three connected passers carry the day.

41 ♖a7 ♔f8?

There was no need to defend the threat on e6. Indeed, Black once again misses 41...♘c3+! 42 bxc3 ♖xc5.

42 ♘d7+ ♔e8 43 ♘de5 ♘f3 44 ♖a8+ ♔e7 45 ♘c6+ ♔d6 46 ♘xa5

Black is still winning, but one gets the sense that he is in the process of botching things!

46...♖f4 47 ♘h6 g5 48 ♘b7+ ♔c7?

He should move closer to his pawns with 48...♔e5!.

49 ♘d8!

49...♘e5?

Yet another missed opportunity. It's like a once-powerful wizard whose magic has drained away. Black should play the superior 49...♘b6!, but White still has a problem-like draw with 50 ♘hxf7 ♘xa8 51 ♘xe6+ ♔d7 52 ♘xf4 gxf4 53 ♘h6 ♘e5 54 ♔b3 ♔e6 55 ♔c3 ♘b6 56 ♔d4 f3 57 ♔e3 ♘bc4+ 58 ♔f2 ♘xb2 59 ♘g4 ♘bd3+ 60 ♔e3 ♔f5 61 ♘h2 f2 62 ♘f1 ♔g4 63 ♔e2 ♔h3 64 ♘e3 ♘g4 65 ♘d1! eliminating f2 and drawing the game.

50 ♘hxf7! ♘xf7 51 ♘xe6+ ♔d6 52 ♘xf4 gxf4

All White has to do is sac his rook for the pawn to seal the draw.

53 ♖g8 ♘e3 54 ♔b3

54 ♖g1 also gets in range to sac: 54...f3 (or 54...♘e5 55 ♖h1 f3 56 ♖h2 ♘5g4 57 ♖h3 f2 58 ♖f3) 55 ♖g6+ ♔e5 56 ♖g3 f2! 57 ♖f3! reaches the target.

54...f3 55 ♖g6+ ♔e7 56 ♖g3!

The f-pawn is worth more than the rook! White finally engineers a position where the pawn cannot escape the sac.

56...♘e5 57 ♖xf3! ♘xf3 58 ♔c3 ♔d6 59

b4 ♔d5 60 a4 ♘e5 61 b5 ♔c5 62 a5 ♘d5+ 63 ♔d2 ♔xb5 64 a6 ♔xa6 65 ♔e2 ½-½

Phew! A close call for White, who was on life support for a long time before his miraculous recovery. I was sure *Rybka* and *Fritz* would be fooled and erroneously claim Black is up +6 at the end, but they both saw the light and had it almost at dead even. I am very sorry to have to report that *Crafty*, their naive cousin, has Black winning here. Well, nobody's perfect!

Summary

5...g6 is a good way to respond to the 5 ♘f3 line. Black should equalize with correct play.

Game 17
M.Khachian-I.Miller
US Open, Los Angeles 2003

1 d4 ♘f6 2 ♘c3 d5 3 ♗g5 ♘bd7 4 ♕d3 c6 5 e4

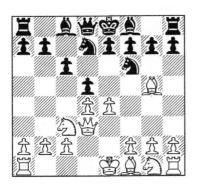

5...dxe4 6 ♘xe4

Now we get a ...♘d7 Caro-Kann with two key differences:

1 White's bishop is committed to g5. Black may make use of this to engineer a freeing swap later on.

2. White's queen is on d3. This may help, since the queen can later go to g3 or h3, targeting Black's kingside. In some cases White may even manage ♕e4 and ♗d3, ganging up on h7.

6...e6

Khachian also had this position against one of my students: 6...♘xe4 7 ♕xe4 ♕a5+ 8 ♗d2 ♕d5 9 ♕h4 (9 ♕e3 is covered next game) 9...♘f6 (blasting free with 9...e5!? may not be wise: 10 ♘f3 ♗e7 11 ♕g3 exd4 12 ♕xg7 ♗f6 13 ♕h6 ♕e4+ 14 ♔d1 ♕g6 15 ♗d3 ♕xh6 16 ♖e1+ ♔d8 17 ♗xh6 favours White since he has the better pawn structure) 10 c4 ♕e4+ 11 ♕xe4 ♘xe4 12 ♗e3 with just an edge to White, who has space, but will have a tough time making anything of it because Black stands solidly, M.Khachian-E.Liu, Los Angeles 2003.

7 ♘f3 ♗e7 8 ♘xf6+ ♗xf6 9 h4 h6!?

He doesn't want the annoying bishop to sit on g5 forever. However, if Black now castles kingside, the h6-pawn is a ripe sac target, and White has the simple plan of h4 and g4-g5, prising things open.

10 ♗e3 ♕e7 11 0-0-0 e5!

Probably the best choice in a difficult situation. Black frees himself, despite his lag in development.

In other lines, Black faces a dilemma of where to place his king:

a) Let's say he goes queenside with 11...b6?! 12 ♕e4 ♗b7 13 ♗f4 0-0-0 then 14 ♗g3! threatens 15 ♕f4 and after 14...g5 15 ♗a6! ♘b8 16 ♗xb7+ ♕xb7 17 ♘e5 Black scrambles to cover his multiple weaknesses.

b) The kingside looks even worse: 11...0-0? 12 ♕e4! ♖d8 13 ♗d3 ♘f8 14 g4 and Black will not survive.

c) 11...c5?! 12 dxc5 ♘xc5 13 ♕b5+ ♘d7 and Black has opened the position while dangerously behind in development.

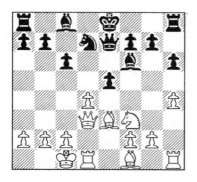

12 ♕e4!

White foresees a superior ending.

12...exd4 13 ♕xe7+ ♔xe7

Black can also give up a pawn in the hope of a draw after 13...♗xe7 14 ♘xd4 ♘b6 15 ♖e1! and then:

a) After 15...0-0 16 ♗xh6 ♗f6 17 ♗e3 ♘d5 18 c3 ♘xe3 19 ♖xe3 ♗xd4 20 cxd4 ♗e6 21 b3 ♖fd8 22 ♖e4 ♖d6 23 ♗c4 White begins to consolidate his extra pawn.

b) 15...♘d5? 16 ♗c4 ♘xe3 17 ♖xe3 ♔d8 18 ♖d1 and Black's king is caught in traffic.

14 ♘xd4 ♘e5 15 ♗e2 ♖d8

15...♘g4? would be similar to the game: 16 ♘xc6+! bxc6 17 ♗c5+ ♔e8 18 ♖he1 ♘e5 19 ♗f3 ♗b7 20 ♗d4 wins.

16 f4!

This looks like a strategic blunder by White, who gives up the g4-square. But beware: when a GM plays such a move, there is usually a very good reason!

16...♘g4?

A trusting soul. Black jumps into g4 and also into a trap. He had to play 16...♘g6 17 g3, but even here White's space and slight development lead put him in control.

17 ♘xc6+!!

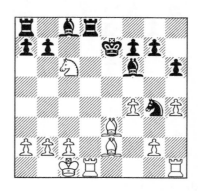

A bolt of lightning from a blue, summer sky! Black's king is a lot less safe than he believed.

17...bxc6 18 ♗c5+ ♔e8 19 ♖de1!

A sting at the end. Black has no choice but to return the piece to get out of the crossfire.

19...♔d7?

After 19...♖d5! 20 ♗xg4+ ♔d8 21 ♗xc8 ♖xc5 22 ♗g4 the factor of opposite-coloured bishops gives Black some hope of survival.

20 ♗xg4+ ♔c7 21 ♗xc8 ♖axc8 22 ♗e7!

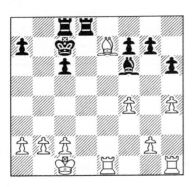

22...♖d7!?

Deliberately allowing his pawns to sustain damage, but banking on counterplay down the g-file. Black should lose the rook ending after 22...♗xe7 23 ♖xe7+ ♖d7 24 ♖xd7+ ♔xd7 25 ♖e1 ♖b8, since White is up a clear pawn and has multiple targets: a7, c6 and possibly even g7 with the plan ♖e3, h5 and ♖g3.

23 ♗xf6 gxf6 24 g3 h5 25 ♖e3 ♖g8 26 ♖d1 1-0

The five isolanis are driftwood scattered along a beach. Black is only one pawn down, but the damage to his structure is too much to overcome.

Summary

Be prepared to go into an odd, Smyslov line of the Caro if you choose to play a quick e4 against 4...c6.

Game 18
M.Khachian-I.Koniushkov
Moscow 1996

1 d4 d5 2 ♘c3 ♘f6 3 ♗g5 ♘bd7 4 ♕d3 c6 5 e4

If you castle, you can sometimes transpose to the 4...g6 line: 5 0-0-0 g6 6 f3 ♗g7 7 e4 dxe4 8 fxe4 ♕a5 9 e5 ♘d5 10 ♘xd5 cxd5 11 ♕b3 sees White lead in development and space, J.Hector-H.Olsen, Swedish Team Championship 2006.

5...♘xe4 6 ♘xe4 dxe4 7 ♕xe4 ♕a5+

This is an annoying manoeuvre borrowed from the Caro, which forces White to back off for a few moves.

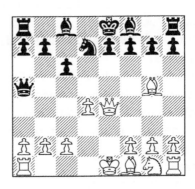

8 ♗d2 ♕d5 9 ♕e3

Nothing but nyet! The side with extra space should avoid trades.

9...♘f6 10 ♘f3 ♗f5 11 c4 ♕e4

Also borrowed from the Caro. The removal of queens minimizes Black's disadvantage.

12 ♘e5 ♖d8 13 ♕xe4 ♘xe4 14 ♗e3 f6 15 ♘f3?!

White loses his edge after this inaccuracy. Instead, 15 ♘d3! covers e5 and d5, and prepares to eject the intruder from e4, which makes more sense.

15...e6

15...g5! takes away ♘h4 ideas and seizes some space of his own.

16 0-0-0

White doesn't get any advantage going after the bishop immediately: 16 ♘h4?! ♗b4+ 17 ♔e2 ♘d6 18 a3 ♗a5 19 c5 g5! 20 ♘xf5 (or 20 cxd6?! gxh4 21 ♗f4 ♗b6 22 ♖d1 c5 23 dxc5 ♗xc5 24 b4 ♗b6 25 g3 and White's d6-pawn may later fall) 20...♘xf5 21 ♖d1 ♗c7 22 g3 e5 with equality.

16...♔f7!?

Black can also be reasonably happy with the outcome of the opening after 16...g5 17 ♗d3.

17 ♘h4 ♘d6 18 c5 g5 19 ♘xf5 ♘xf5 20 ♗c4 ♘xe3?

Black picks a bad plan. He has an excellent position if he redeploys his knight to d5: 20...♘e7! 21 ♖he1 ♘d5. I often get such positions out of the Slav and prefer Black.

21 fxe3

White's advantages:

1. The opposite-coloured bishops

favour White, whose bishop aims at the key e6- and d5-squares;

2. White may build space on the queenside with b4 and possibly b5 later; and

3. White can play for e4 and possibly d5.

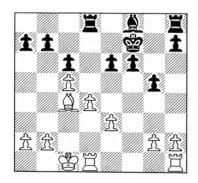

21...f5 22 ♔c2 h5 23 b4 a6 24 e4!

This break gives Black problems.

24...fxe4

He can't bypass and allow 24...f4? 25 d5 ♗g7 (even worse is the line 25...cxd5? 26 exd5 e5 27 ♖he1 ♗g7 28 d6+) 26 dxc6 bxc6 27 ♗xa6.

25 ♖hf1+ ♔e7 26 ♖fe1 ♖h6 27 ♖xe4 ♗g7 28 d5!

Ridding himself of his weak pawn and creating a second target on b7.

28...cxd5 29 ♖xd5 e5

Perhaps the time has come to give up a pawn to activate his remaining pieces with 29...g4 30 ♖xd8 ♔xd8 31 ♗xe6 ♖f6 32 ♖e2.

30 a4 ♖f8 31 ♖d2

Clearing d5 for his bishop.

31...b6!?

Desperation. Passive defence fails: 31...♖c6 32 ♔b3 ♖c7 33 ♖d6 ♖f2 34 ♖e6+ ♔d8 35 ♖e2 ♖xe2 36 ♗xe2 g4 37 ♗d3 and Black can't hold the game. For instance, 37...♖e7 38 ♖xe7 ♔xe7 39 ♗e4 or 37...a5 38 bxa5 ♖xc5 39 ♗b5!.

32 ♗xa6 bxc5 33 b5?

White couldn't resist the temptation to grab two connected passers, but this gives Black drawing chances. White should win with good technique in the line 33 ♗b5! cxb4 34 ♖d7+ ♔f6 35 ♖xb4.

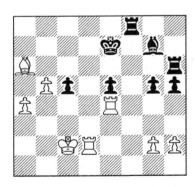

33...♖d6 34 a5 ♖xd2+ 35 ♔xd2 ♖f2+ 36 ♖e2 ♖xe2+ 37 ♔xe2 ♔d6 38 ♗b7 e4??

The wrong pawn! Black just barely draws if he pushes the c-pawn to clear c5 for his king: 38...c4! 39 ♗e4 ♔c5!. Now, getting the White passers to move forward is like herding cats! 40 a6 (the crucial point is that 40 b6 ♗f8! stops White's pawns and holds the draw) 40...♔b6 41 ♔d2 g4 42 ♔c3 ♗h6 43 ♔xc4 h4 44 ♗f5 ♗f4 45 ♗xg4 ♗xh2 with a dead draw.

39 b6!

Slamming the door in the face of Black's king, who is helpless to prevent the march of the a-pawn.

39...c4 40 a6 1-0

Summary

15 ♘d3! is an improvement which gets you a slightly better Caro ending.

Game 19
J.Hector-H.Koneru
Wijk aan Zee 2003

1 d4 d5 2 ♘c3 ♘f6 3 ♗g5 ♘bd7 4 ♕d3 e6

Black wants to go with a Rubinstein French set-up with White's queen committed to d3.

5 e4 dxe4 6 ♘xe4 ♗e7 7 ♘xf6+ ♗xf6

By recapturing with the bishop Black keeps control over the e5-square.

8 ♗xf6 ♕xf6 9 ♘f3 0-0 10 ♕e3!

There is a thin line between compromise and being compromised! This is a key move to remember. White wisely invests a tempo to prevent the freeing break ...e5. As we shall see, the ...c5 break is not so equal.

Instead, 10 0-0-0 e5! 11 ♕e3 exd4 12 ♖xd4 ♘c5 13 ♖f4 ♕h6 14 g4!? ♕b6 leads to a sharp game with equal chances, K.Shirazi-M.Quinteros, Jakarta 1978.

10...c5?

Believe it or not, this natural freeing move is an error because it violates the principle stating: don't open the position when behind in development. Black should be okay if she unravels slowly with 10...b6! 11 0-0-0 ♗b7.

11 0-0-0 b6

Alternatively, 11...cxd4 12 ♖xd4 ♘c5 13 ♘e5 and then:

a) 13...a5 14 ♖d6! ♘a6 15 ♗c4 ♘c7

16 ♖hd1 b5 17 ♗e2 ♘d5?? (Black's position was bad anyway, but this certainly doesn't help his cause!) 18 ♖1xd5 1-0 J.Hector-M.Fraser, St Helier 2005.

b) After the more natural 13...b6, White keeps the advantage if he plays boldly with 14 b4! ♘b7 15 c3! a5 16 ♔b2 ♕e7 17 ♗d3. Despite the opening of the a-file, White's attack is far more dangerous than Black's for three reasons:

1. White is better developed;

2. Black is tangled; and

3. Black's pieces are posted too passively to mount a serious queenside assault.

12 ♗b5!

Black is behind in development and his pieces are in a bit of a knot.

12...cxd4 13 ♖xd4 ♕e7

After 13...♘c5 White keeps the grip with 14 ♘e5. Now 15 b4 is a serious strategic threat, but 14...a5 is well met by 15 ♖d6 ♖b8 16 ♖hd1.

14 ♗c6! ♖b8 15 ♖hd1 ♘f6 16 ♕e5

16 ♘e5 also keeps Black tied up.

16...♗a6

16...♗b7? 17 ♖d7! ♘xd7 18 ♖xd7 loses two pieces for the rook.

17 ♖a4! ♖bc8 18 ♘d4

The edifice begins to crack.

18...♘g4

8...♕c5? just drops a clean pawn: 19 ♕xc5 bxc5 20 ♖xa6 cxd4 21 ♖xd4.

19 ♕f4!

Both sides have loose pieces, but the difference is White's work together beautifully, although he had to avoid 19 ♕g3? e5 20 ♘f5 ♕g5+ 21 ♘e3 ♖xc6 22 ♖xa6 h5 23 h3 f5!.

19...h5

19...e5?? loses on the spot to 20 ♘f5!.

20 ♖xa6 e5 21 ♘f5 ♕f6 22 ♕f3 ♖xc6

No better is 22...♘xh2 23 ♕xh5 ♖xc6 24 ♖h1! ♖fc8 25 c3 and the h-file becomes the gateway to pain for Black.

23 ♕xc6!

This small combination picks off the exchange.

23...♕xf5 24 ♕f3 ♕g5+ 25 ♔b1 ♘xh2 26 ♕g3 ♘g4

Or 26...♕xg3 27 fxg3 e4 28 ♖xa7 e3 29 ♖e7 ♘g4 30 c4 and Black's passers

have been neutralized, while White is just beginning on the queenside.

27 f3 ♖d8

Also hopeless is 27...♕e3 28 ♖e1 ♖d8 29 a4 ♕f2 30 ♕xf2 ♘xf2 31 ♖xe5.

28 ♖xd8+?

The simple 28 ♖c1! wins the pinned knight.

28...♕xd8 29 ♕e1 ♘f6 30 ♖xa7 e4 31 fxe4 ♘xe4

Black is trying to make a race of it and plans to push on the kingside. White's plan is to pick off b6 and then queen first.

32 a4 f5 33 ♕e2 ♕g5 34 ♖b7 ♕g6 35 ♕b5!

35...♕g4

35...♕xg2?? isn't much of a pawn grab after 36 ♕e8+ ♔h7 37 ♕xh5+ ♔g8 38 ♖b8 mate.

36 ♖xb6 h4 37 a5 ♘d2+ 38 ♔a2 ♘c4

She can't go after White's king because hers falls first: 38...♕d1?? 39 ♕e8+ ♔h7 40 ♕g6+ ♔g8 41 ♖b8 mate. Nor can she take on g2: 38...♕xg2?? 39 ♕e8+ ♔h7 40 ♕h5+ ♔g8 41 ♖b8 mate.

39 ♖c6 ♘e3 40 a6 ♕d4 41 c3 1-0

Summary

By playing 4...e6 in response to 4 ♕d3, Black gets a Rubinstein French where White's queen is committed to the d3-square. If you remember to play the key move ♕e3! just before Black unravels with ...e5, you may still get an edge.

Game 20
S.Conquest-A.Sokolov
Portuguese Team
Championship 2006

1 d4 ♘f6 2 ♘c3 d5 3 ♗g5 ♘bd7 4 ♕d3 h6

Let's see how things work out if Black tosses in this move.

5 ♗h4 e6?!

The ...e6 lines don't work so well for Black if he throws in the weakening ...h6. Better was 5...c5.

6 e4 dxe4 7 ♘xe4 ♗e7 8 ♘xf6+ ♗xf6

Alternatively, 8...♘xf6 9 0-0-0 0-0 10 ♘f3 b6 11 ♘e5 ♗b7 12 ♖g1! (the not-so-subtle plan of g4-g5 is still very effective) 12...♕d5 13 c4 ♕a5?! (after

13...♕e4! 14 ♕xe4 ♗xe4 15 f3 White's central space gives him a small edge) 14 a3 ♖fd8 15 g4! (ignoring the threats to his d-pawn) 15...c5 16 d5 exd5 17 ♕h3! d4 (closing the centre always helps the attacker, but the alternative 17...dxc4? 18 ♗xc4 is even worse for Black) 18 g5 and White had a winning attack in J.Hall-R.Jones, Gothenburg 2005.

9 ♗xf6 ♕xf6 10 ♘f3 0-0 11 ♕e3!

Remember: don't allow ...e5!

11...c5 12 0-0-0 b6 13 ♗b5! cxd4 14 ♖xd4 ♕e7

So we have the exact position as Hector-Koneru, with the inclusion of the move ...h6.

15 g4!

It becomes obvious that extra move ...h6 is not so great for Black. White's clear plan of g5 to prise open the g-file is hard to meet.

15...♘f6?

Handing over matches to the kid who loves to start fires! Now White's attack accelerates at an alarming rate. Sokolov had to try 15...♘c5 16 g5 hxg5

17 ♘xg5 f6 18 ♘e4 e5 19 ♘xc5 bxc5
(but not 19...♕xc5?? 20 ♗c4+ ♔h7 21
♖h4+ ♔g6 22 ♕g3+ ♔f5 23 ♕g4 mate)
20 ♖d5 ♗e6 21 ♕xc5 ♕f7 22 ♖d6 ♖fc8
23 ♖c6 when White's extra pawn may
not be easy to convert since he has isolanis on the f- and h-files.

16 g5 hxg5 17 ♕xg5 ♗b7 18 ♖g1 g6

19 ♖d7?!

This trick which wins Black's queen
is not the best move. Black gets crushed
if White plays directly for mate with 19
♘e5! ♖ac8 20 ♗d3 ♖c7 21 ♕h6! and
Black can resign since he has no defence to 22 ♖h4.

19...♕xd7 20 ♗xd7 ♘xd7 21 ♘h4!

Target: g6.

**21...♗e4 22 ♖g4 ♗f5 23 ♘xf5 exf5 24
♕xf5**

A pawn falls and Black's king remains in trouble.

24...♖ad8 25 ♕g5

Black is totally busted:

1. He has only rook and knight versus White's queen and pawn;

2. White has the attacking idea ♖h4
and ♕h6, not to mention that of h4-h5.

25...♘c5 26 ♖h4 ♖fe8

Threatening mate.

27 b3

Well, that was easy!

**27...♔g7 28 ♕h6+ ♔f6 29 ♖f4+ ♔e6 30
♕g7 ♖f8 31 ♖f6+ ♔e7 32 ♖xg6**

Leaching away the vitality and life-
blood of Black's kingside.

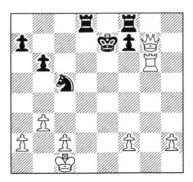

**32...♘e6 33 ♕f6+ ♔e8 34 ♖g4 ♖d5 35
h4 1-0**

Summary

Getting the 'free' move ...h6 is no picnic
for Black. White simply uses this as a
launching pad for attacks based on the
simple plan of ♖g1!, g4 and g5.

Game 21
J.Hector-J.Sprenger
Hamburg 2003

1 d4 d5 2 ♘c3 ♘f6 3 ♗g5 ♘bd7 4 ♕d3 e6 5 e4 dxe4 6 ♘xe4 ♗e7 7 ♘xf6+ ♘xf6 8 ♘f3 0-0 9 0-0-0 b6?!

Black plays very sensibly, delaying ...c5, which opens the game when he is lagging in development. Nevertheless, ...c5 should be played here, as 9...b6 is just too slow and allows White to whip up an attack without being bothered in the centre.

Instead, 9...c5!? 10 dxc5 ♕a5 11 ♕b5 ♕xb5 12 ♗xb5 ♗xc5 and now, instead of the lame 13 ♖hf1 from O.Rodriguez Vargas-S.Cacho Reigadas, Spanish Team Championship 1993, White could try 13 ♗xf6! gxf6 14 ♖d2 to unbalance the game. White's lead in development looks more meaningful than Black's bishop pair.

10 ♘e5 ♗b7 11 ♕h3!

The queen is well posted on h3, where it eyes mating attacks along the

h-file and also potential knight sacs on f7, followed by ♕xe6.

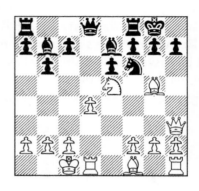

11...♘e4

Alternatively, 11...♘d7 12 ♗e3 ♗e4 and then:

a) 13 ♗d3?! ♗xd3 14 ♖xd3 ♘xe5 15 dxe5 ♕e8 16 ♕g3 and the cramping e5-pawn still gives White a tiny edge, but my feeling is it isn't enough and Black should draw, K.Lie-E.Moskow, Gausdal 2007.

b) 13 f3! is an improvement, after which Black is in danger: 13...♗b7 14 ♗d3 g6 15 ♕g3! when sacs loom over g6 and White also has the simple plan of prising open the kingside with h4 and h5.

12 ♗e3 f5!?

It is hard to blame Black for lashing out with this committal move which keeps his king safer, but weakens e6. His position remains passive if he avoids such a move: for instance, 12...♗d6 13 f3 ♘f6 14 ♗d3 c5 15 ♕h4 cxd4 16 ♗xd4 doesn't look very tempting. White has an obvious attack in the works while Black has not made the slightest headway against White's king.

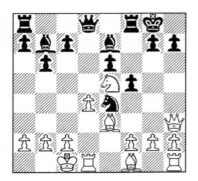

13 f3 ♘d6 14 ♗d3 ♕e8 15 ♖he1 b5 16 g4 ♗d5 17 ♔b1 a5 18 gxf5 exf5!

Black finds himself in serious difficulties if he captures with a piece on f5: 18...♘xf5? 19 ♖g1 ♗d6 20 ♗h6! and Black drops at least an exchange.

19 ♖g1 ♖f6?

A superior defensive plan would be to hunker down and defend g7 with everything he has after 19...♗f6 20 ♗h6 c6! 21 ♖de1 ♖a7!.

20 ♗g5 ♖e6

It is too late to back down now. Black will not survive 20...♖f8? 21 ♕h4! ♗xg5 22 ♖xg5.

21 ♗xf5 ♘xf5 22 ♕xf5

White has picked up a pawn and his attack continues.

22...c6 23 f4

The f-pawn supports the outpost on e5 and gets ready to enter the attack with future plans of f5 and f6.

23...♗d6 24 ♕g4 ♗xe5

The dismal alternative would be 24...♖a7 25 f5 ♖xe5 26 dxe5 ♗xe5 27

♖de1 ♕b8.

25 dxe5

The two pawns surge forward like a wave against Black's king.

25...♖a7 26 ♗f6 ♕g6 27 f5

A practical decision. White can also keep queens on the board with 27 ♕h3 ♕e8 28 ♕h6.

27...♕xg4 28 ♖xg4 ♖e8 29 ♖dg1

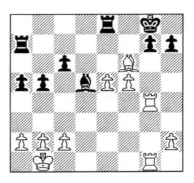

Now g7 is an open wound and the attack continues into the endgame.

29...g6 30 fxg6

The opposite-coloured bishops can't save Black.

30...♔f8 31 ♖h4! ♗g8

31...hxg6?? drops a rook after 32 ♖h8+ ♔f7 (or 32...♗g8 33 ♖xg6 ♔f7 34 ♖g7+) 33 ♖h7+ ♔e6 34 ♖xa7.

32 gxh7 ♖xh7 33 ♖xh7 ♗xh7 34 ♖g7 ♗e4 35 h4!

With a rather simple plan of heading for the promotion square.

35...♖e6

35...♖d8 36 ♔c1 ♗f3 37 b4! ♖d1+ 38 ♔b2 axb4 39 e6 ♗d5 40 ♖d7! either mates or wins a rook.

36 h5 1-0

Summary

Black has a tough choice in such positions:

1. Play ...c5 and risk opening the game prematurely.

2. Play ...b6 when Black's non-confrontational strategy gives White a free hand to launch a kingside attack without central distractions.

Also, remember the move ♕h3!. It crops up a lot in this line.

Game 22
J.Hector-K.Moberg
Swedish Team
Championship 2001

---

1 d4 ♘f6 2 ♘c3 d5 3 ♗g5 ♘bd7 4 ♕d3 g6 5 f3

I prefer this slower build-up to other moves in this position.

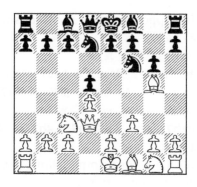

5...♗g7 6 e4 dxe4

The most accurate move. Many games see Black forgoing the trade and getting squeezed.

7 fxe4 0-0

After 7...c6 8 ♘f3 h6 9 ♗e3 ♘g4 10 ♗g1 e5 11 d5 0-0 12 0-0-0 I prefer White, mainly because his extra space should make his king safer than Black's, J.Hector-J.Ingbrandt, Malmo 2005.

8 e5 ♘e8 9 h4!?

Not all Swedish GMs play like Ulf Andersson! This hyper-aggressive move borrowed from the Austrian attack line of the Pirc is an attempt to intimidate. A more positionally-minded player would have played the calmer 9 ♘f3.

9...c5 10 ♘d5!?

Instead, 10 ♘f3! cxd4 11 ♕xd4 ♘c7 12 0-0-0 ♘e6 13 ♕b4 puts pressure on Black.

10...f6 11 ♕b3! e6!

The gullible piece grab 11...fxg5?? loses to 12 ♘xe7+ ♔h8 13 ♘xg6+! hxg6 14 hxg5+ ♗h6 15 ♖xh6+ ♔g7 16 ♗d3.

12 ♘xf6+ ♘dxf6 13 0-0-0 ♕b6

Alternatively, 13...cxd4! 14 ♘f3 ♕b6 15 exf6 ♘xf6 and then:

a) 16 ♖xd4! ♘d5 17 ♖d1 and the e6 isolani gives White some hope for an advantage.

b) However, Black holds his own in the line 16 ♗c4 ♕xb3 17 ♗xb3 ♘d5 18 ♘xd4 h6! 19 ♗xd5 exd5 20 ♗e3 ♗g4.

14 exf6 ♘xf6 15 dxc5 ♕xc5 16 ♗c4 ♔h8

Black can try to offer a pawn to take the sting out of White's initiative with 16...♘d5?! 17 ♗xd5 exd5 18 ♖xd5 ♕b6 19 ♖b5+ ♕e6 20 ♘f3, but his bishops don't provide full compensation for the investment.

17 ♘f3 b5!?

18 ♗e2

The human move. The counterintuitive and very greedy *Rybka* suggestion 18 ♕xb5! actually works, though: 18...♕xb5 19 ♗xb5 ♖b8 20 a4 ♘d5 (20...a6? 21 ♗f4! ♖b6 22 ♗c7 ♖b7 23 ♗d6 axb5 24 ♗xf8 ♗xf8 25 ♖d8 wins material) 21 c3 a6 22 ♗d3 and Black doesn't get enough compensation for the pawn.

18...e5?!

Better was 18...♗b7.

19 ♕xb5!

Now the pawn is quite safe to eat since Black blocked his own bishop's path to b2.

19...♕xb5 20 ♗xb5 ♗f5 21 ♖he1 ♖ac8 22 ♗a4

Black's initiative is not enough to make up for the missing pawn.

22...♘e4 23 ♗e7! ♖f7 24 ♖d8+

Swapping off an attacker.

24...♖xd8 25 ♗xd8 ♘c5 26 ♗c6!?

He wants to hang on to his bishops. White has a simpler technical win with 26 ♗b3! ♘xb3+ 27 axb3 e4 28 ♘g5 ♖d7 29 ♗a5 ♗h6 30 ♗d2 ♗xg5 31 hxg5 ♔g8 32 ♗e3 when Black's passed e-pawn is locked on e4 and White is in essence two pawns up. Conversion is simply a matter of carefully creating passed pawns on the queenside.

26...e4 27 ♘g5 ♖f8 28 b4!?

After 28 ♗a5 ♖c8 29 ♗b5 ♘d3+ 30 ♗xd3 exd3 31 c3 White should win by blockading with his king on d2 and slowly pushing on the queenside.

28...♖xd8?

A faulty combination. Black believes he is sac'ing an exchange for a pawn. He can offer maximum resistance with 28...♗c3! 29 ♖e3 ♗d4 30 ♖e2 ♗d7! 31 ♗d5 ♖f1+ 32 ♔d2 ♗g4 33 ♘xe4 ♘xe4+! 34 ♗xe4 (34 ♖xe4?? ♖d1 mate would be embarrassing) 34...♗xe2 35 ♔xe2 when White's two pawns for the exchange should still win, although not without technical problems.

29 ♘f7+ ♔g8 30 ♘xd8 ♗c3 31 ♖e3 ♗xb4 32 ♗d5+!

A little celebratory gunfire before his big finish. White clears c6 for the knight.

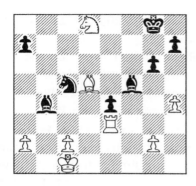

32...♔g7 33 ♘c6! 1-0

Trapping the bishop on an open board.

Summary

5 f3, planning to build with e4, is a good reaction to the 4...g6 line.

1 d4 ♘f6 2 ♘c3 d5 3 ♗g5 ♘bd7 4 ♕d3 g6 5 f3 ♗g7 6 e4 h6

Black can also try the plan of capturing on e4 and then countering with ...e5: 6...dxe4! 7 fxe4 h6 (better to forgo this move and just castle, planning either ...e5 or ...c5) 8 ♗f4?! ♘h5?! (missing a perfect chance to strike back in the centre with 8...e5!) 9 ♗e3 e5 10 0-0-0 exd4 11 ♗xd4 0-0 12 ♗xg7 ♘xg7? 13 ♘f3 c6?! 14 ♕d2! and Black was forced to give up a key pawn with 14...♘e6 in P.Kolognat-N.Ravic, Mataruska Banja 2007, since 14...♔h7? is

met by 15 ♘e5!, winning the exchange.

7 ♗h4 ♘b6?!

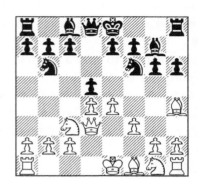

Black has problems generating any counterplay after this move. He should trade on e4.

8 e5 ♘h7

White's attack is faster if Black allows 8...♘fd7?! 9 e6 ♘f6 10 exf7+ ♔xf7 11 0-0-0.

9 0-0-0 ♗f5 10 ♕d2 g5?!

A poor decision. Black weakens to make room for the bishop. Instead, he should do everything in his power to stop g4 by playing 10...h5!.

11 ♗f2 ♘f8

It was high time to make preparations to castle queenside. Better was 11...♕d7 12 g4 ♗g6 13 h4 gxh4 14 ♗xh4 0-0-0 15 f4 f5 16 ♗d3 and White's advantage is not as large as in the game. However, it is too late for 11...h5?! 12 h4! as Black is not ready for such line-openings on the king's wing.

12 g4 ♗g6 13 h4 gxh4?

After 13...♘e6! 14 ♘h3 ♕d7 15 f4 gxf4 16 ♘xf4 ♘xf4 17 ♕xf4 h5! 18 g5 0-0-0 White has a big space advantage, but at least Black's position remains solid. White will play for ♘e2 and ♘f4, while Black reroutes with ...e6, ...♗f8 and plays for the ...c5 break.

14 f4

The steamroller moves forward with Black's pieces in its path.

14...f5 15 ♗d3

Also very tempting is the line 15 exf6 ♗xf6 16 f5 ♗f7 17 ♗xh4 e6 18 ♘f3 when the h6-pawn is doomed and Black still hasn't found shelter for his king.

15...♕d7

He has trouble castling if he tries to maintain the f5 point: 15...e6 16 gxf5 ♗xf5 17 ♗xf5 exf5 18 ♗xh4 ♕d7 19 ♕g2 ♕f7 20 ♖h3 ♔d7 21 ♖g3 ♖h7 and Black is still in a terrible tangle.

16 ♗xh4 fxg4

Black cannot castle out of his problems: 16...0-0-0 17 e6! ♕xe6 18 ♖e1 ♕g8 19 gxf5 ♗h7 20 ♖xe7 and Black is busted. For example, 20...♗xd4? 21 ♘b5 or 20...♘fd7 21 ♘f3 ♗f6 22 ♗xf6 ♘xf6 23 ♘e5 ♖e8 24 ♖xe8+ ♕xe8 25 ♖xh6.

17 e6!

The steamroller continues forward.

17...♕d8

He can't accept the offer:

a) 17...♕d6? 18 f5 ♗h7 19 ♘b5 ♕c6 20 ♕b4 ♘c8 21 ♗g3 and now 21...♘d6?? fails miserably to 22 ♘xd6+! cxd6 23 ♗b5.

b) 17...♕xe6?? 18 ♖e1 ♕f7 19 ♖xe7+.

18 f5 ♗h7

The f8-knight and the h7-bishop have been placed in custody and behind bars.

19 ♗g3

Threatening ♘b5.

19...c6 20 ♖xh6!

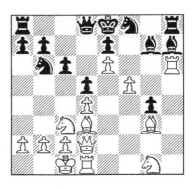

Offering the exchange to remove Black's only good piece.

20...♘c4

He must decline the gifts:

a) 20...♗xh6?? 21 ♕xh6 (threatening 22 ♕h5+) 21...♕c8 22 ♕g7 ♖g8 23 ♕f7+ ♔d8 24 ♗d6! finishes Black off.

b) 20...♗xd4?? 21 ♘b5! ends the game.

21 ♕g5!

I insist!

21...♕b6

Acceptance is disastrous once again: 21...♗xh6? 22 ♕xh6 ♕b6 23 ♗xc4 dxc4 24 ♕g7 ♖g8 25 ♕f7+ ♔d8 26 f6.

22 ♗xc4 ♗xd4

Tricky. Black threatens 23...♗e3+ winning the queen.

23 ♖xd4!

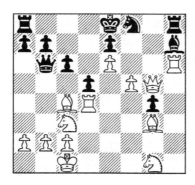

Black's game collapses after the removal of his only dangerous piece.

23...♕xd4 24 ♘ge2 ♕xc4 25 ♕h5+ ♗g6

Or instead 25...♔d8 26 ♗e5 ♖g8 27 ♕f7 and there is no good way to stop ♖xh7.

26 fxg6 ♖xh6 27 ♕xh6 1-0

Summary

Allowing e5 without first exchanging on e4 gives White a large space advantage.

Game 24
R.Vaganian-J.Adamski
Copenhagen 2006

1 d4 ♘f6 2 ♘c3 d5 3 ♗g5 ♘bd7 4 ♕d3 c5

This may be the most logical response to 4 ♕d3. White has already moved his queen once, and so Black hopes to make her move a second time by countering immediately in the centre and forcing the queen to recapture on d4.

5 0-0-0!?

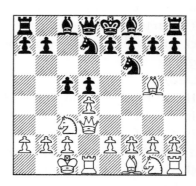

He allows ...e5 with tempo. Probably stronger is 5 ♘f3!, as played by GM Hammer in our next game.

5...cxd4 6 ♕xd4 e5

With 6...e6 7 e4 White achieves e4 in one move, without taking time for f3. This makes up for his earlier tempo loss of moving his queen twice: 7...dxe4 8 ♘xe4 ♕a5? (Black doesn't have time for such a fishing expedition and has to play 8...♗e7) 9 ♗xf6 gxf6 10 ♘xf6+ ♘xf6 11 ♕xf6 ♖g8 12 ♗b5+! 1-0 J.Hector-N.Kirkegaard, Copenhagen 2006.

7 ♕a4 d4 8 ♘d5 ♗e7 9 ♘xe7 ♕xe7 10 f4!?

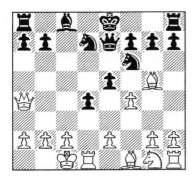

Risky, even though White has the bishop pair and the move disrupts Black's pawn centre, because it is actually Black who is ahead in development, so opening the game may blow up on White!

The more prudent alternative 10 e3! dxe3 11 ♗xe3 0-0 12 h3 gives White an edge due to his bishop pair.

10...0-0 11 fxe5 ♘xe5 12 ♘f3

Or 12 ♕xd4 ♗f5 13 ♘f3 ♖ac8 14 e4 ♕c7 15 c3 ♘xe4 16 ♕xe5 ♕xe5 17 ♘xe5 ♘xg5 with equality.

12...♘c6?!

Instead of this meek retreat, Black should focus on c2 with 12...♗f5! 13 ♘xd4 ♗g6 14 e3 ♘eg4, which gives Black full compensation for the pawn.

White must deal with problems on e3, f2 and c2.

13 ♘xd4 ♘xd4 14 ♕xd4 ♗f5 15 ♗xf6 gxf6 16 e4!

Returning the pawn to catch up in development.

16...♖fd8 17 ♕e3 ♖xd1+ 18 ♔xd1 ♕xe4 19 ♕xe4 ♗xe4 20 ♗d3! ♖d8 21 ♔e2 ♗xd3+ 22 cxd3

White stands just a shade better in the rook ending because Black has more targets to defend.

22...♔g7?!

He needed to take control over the c-file first with 22...♖c8! 23 ♔d2 ♔f8.

23 ♖c1 ♖d7 24 ♖c5!

The rook operates best on the fifth rank where it can harass both kingside and queenside.

24...♔g6 25 g4! b6 26 ♖b5 ♖d4 27 h3 ♖a4 28 a3

28...♖a5?!

A bad practical decision. King and pawn endings are nightmares over the board and almost nobody plays them correctly. Indeed, Kasparov lost a similar ending to Topalov in his final game before retirement. GM Larry Christiansen and I were doing the commentary for Chess.FM that day. Larry said something like: the king and pawn ending is probably a draw with computers playing, but here, Kasparov will mess things up and lose. And lose he did.

Adamski should have followed Christiansen's advice and kept rooks on the board. The drawing plan is then to try to force the undoubling with ...f5, beginning with 28...♖f4!. For example:

a) 29 ♔e3 ♖f1 30 d4 f5 31 ♖d5 fxg4 32 hxg4 ♖b1 33 ♖b5 ♖g1 34 ♔f3 ♖f1+ with a probable draw.

b) 29 ♖d5 f5 30 ♔e3 ♖f1 31 ♖d6+ f6 32 ♖d7 fxg4 33 hxg4 a5 34 ♖b7 ♖g1 35 ♔f3 ♖f1+ 36 ♔e2 ♖g1 37 ♔f3 and it's a draw.

29 ♖xa5 bxa5 30 ♔e3 f5 31 ♔f4 fxg4 32 hxg4 ♔f6 33 a4 h6?

This benign-looking move loses. Black must play with mathematical precision to score the half-point: 33...♔e6! draws after 34 ♔e4 f6 35 d4 ♔d6 36 ♔f5 ♔d5 37 ♔xf6 ♔xd4 38 ♔g7 ♔e3! 39 ♔xh7 ♔f4 40 ♔g6 ♔xg4 41 ♔f6 ♔f4 42 ♔e6 ♔e4 43 ♔d6 ♔d4 44 ♔c6 ♔c4 45 ♔b7 ♔b4 46 ♔xa7 ♔xa4 47 ♔b6.

34 d4 ♔e6 35 ♔e4 ♔d6 36 d5!

The winning move. Essentially White is up a pawn, since his g-pawn holds back both Black kingside pawns. Instead, 36 ♔f5? blows the win: 36...♔d5 37 ♔f6 ♔xd4 38 ♔xf7 ♔e5! 39 ♔g6 ♔f4 40 ♔h5 a6 41 b3 ♔f3 42 ♔h4 ♔f4 draws.

36...f6

36...♔d7 won't save Black either: 37 ♔e5 ♔e7 38 d6+ ♔d7 39 ♔d5 f6 40 ♔c5 f5 41 gxf5 h5 42 f6 ♔e6 43 ♔c6.

37 ♔d4 a6 38 b3!

Zugzwang!

38...♔d7 39 ♔c5 f5 40 gxf5 h5 41 ♔d4!

Refusing to make it a race.

41...h4 42 ♔e4 h3 43 ♔f3 1-0

Of course, 43...♔d6 is met by 44 f6 and Black can't touch the pawns.

Summary

5 0-0-0!? allows Black to kick the white queen around similar to a Centre-Counter with colours reversed. 5 ♘f3!,

as in the next game, may be a better try for an advantage for White against an early ...c5.

1 d4 d5 2 ♗g5 ♘d7 3 ♘c3 ♘gf6 4 ♕d3 c5 5 ♘f3!

More accurate than castling as Vaganian did in the previous game. White sensibly takes control over e5 before castling.

5...cxd4 6 ♕xd4 e6 7 e4!

White got nothing after 7 ♗xf6 ♘xf6 8 0-0-0 ♕b6 9 e4 ♕xd4 10 ♗b5+ ♘d7 11 ♘xd4 dxe4 12 ♘xe4 a6 13 ♗e2 ♘c5 14 ♗f3 ♘xe4 15 ♗xe4 ♗e7 16 f4 when White's space and Black's bishop pair balance each other out, F.Stross-J.Zawadzka, Pardubice 2006.

7...♗c5 8 ♕a4 0-0

After the passive 8...dxe4?! 9 ♘xe4 ♗e7 10 ♗xf6! gxf6 11 0-0-0 White has three advantages:

1. A lead in development;

2. A safer king; and

3. The faster attack in case Black castles kingside.

9 exd5 ♗xf2+??

I am not sure what brought this on other than a gross overestimation of his attacking potential. The sac is unsound.

Black should play 9...♕b6 10 0-0-0 ♗xf2 11 dxe6! fxe6 (Black's queen is vulnerable in the open centre and gets kicked around after 11...♕xe6) 12 ♗c4 ♘c5 13 ♕b5 (all endgames favour White due to the weakness of the e6 isolani) 13...♘fe4 14 ♕xb6 axb6 15 ♘xe4 ♘xe4 16 ♖hf1 ♗c5 17 ♔b1 h6 18 ♗c1 ♘d6 19 ♗b3 ♘f5 20 ♖de1 and e6 eventually fell in C.Lakdawala-S.Khader, Internet blitz 2010.

Instead, after 9...exd5 10 0-0-0 ♘b6 11 ♕h4 ♗e7 12 ♗d3 h6 (12...g6? 13 ♖he1 ♗e6 14 ♘d4 is even worse for Black) 13 ♗xh6 gxh6 14 ♕xh6 ♕d6. Maybe Black survives, but I wouldn't bet on it.

10 ♔xf2 ♕b6+ 11 ♕d4

Of course, not 11 ♔g3?? ♕xb2 regaining the piece.

11...♕xb2 12 ♖e1 e5 13 ♕d2

And here not 13 ♘xe5?? ♘xe5 14 ♖xe5 ♘g4+.

13...♘g4+ 14 ♔g1 f5 15 h3 ♕b6+ 16 ♗e3 ♘xe3 17 ♕xe3 ♕c7

Black imagines he has some compensation for his piece.

18 ♘xe5!

Dispelling the delusion. White has

tactics to circumvent the coming pin.

18...♖e8 19 d6! ♕xd6 20 ♗c4+ ♔f8 21

♘b5!

Offering Black a choice of how he wants to lose.

21...♕b4

21...♕xe5 22 ♕a3+ ♕c5+ 23 ♕xc5+ ♘xc5 24 ♖xe8+ ♔xe8 25 ♘c7+ wins a rook.

22 ♘g6+! 1-0

Summary

5 ♘f3! takes control over the e5-square and gives White a better version than Vaganian got last game.

Chapter Three
The Veresov: Other Defences

1 d4 ♘f6 2 ♘c3 d5 3 ♗g5

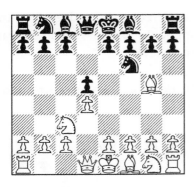

In this chapter we deal with third-move alternatives to 3...♘bd7, covered in the first two chapters:

a) 3...♗f5 is Black's most common response in this chapter. Here we have a choice of starting an argument in the centre with the sham sac 4 f3 ♘bd7 5 ♘xd5!?, which leads to complications favouring the more booked-up player (you!), or you can try the 5 ♕d2 lines, planning on castling queenside and blasting open the centre with e4.

b) With 3...c5 Black allows a Queen's Gambit Chigorin a move down. Your extra move may radically alter the assessment in such a sharp line. You have the choice between a shady gambit 4 ♗xf6 gxf6 5 e4!?, as played in Veresov-Smolianow, or the sounder 5 e3 lines, where you play in typical Chigorin fashion, often giving up both your bishops for your opponents' knights. The resulting positions are strangely favourable for your knights, although this probably won't be apparent to your opponents.

c) After 3...c6 the simplest is to play 4 ♕d3 and give Black a chance to transpose to Chapter Two. Our coverage also features a couple of independent lines.

d) 3...g6?! sees Black go Grünfeld style, and you get a revved-up Barry Attack with the simple plan: f3, ♕d2,

0-0-0, ♗h6 and mate! In the normal Barry Attack, White's knight sits on f3, which he must then move to e5, and only then play f3. Here you get a faster version.

e) 3...h6?! sees Black giving you a free move to have you take on f6 which is pure charity on his part!

Game 26
C.Lakdawala-M.Lozano
San Diego (rapid) 2010

1 d4 ♘f6 2 ♘c3 d5 3 ♗g5 ♗f5 4 f3

Playing it in pure Veresov style.

The prescribed Veresov game plan: force e4! or die trying. I prefer this plan to the Trompowsky idea of chopping on f6. That knight on c3 just looks slightly misplaced in these lines, but 4 ♗xf6 is still fully playable:

a) 4...gxf6 5 e3 e6 6 ♗d3 ♗g6 7 f4! (Nice; White gets a Stonewall Dutch set-up, minus his bad bishop) 7...c5? (like it or not he should play 7...f5!) 8 f5! exf5 9 ♕f3 and Black's game was a

mess in K.Chernyshov-R.Ovetchkin, Smolensk 2000. Indeed, his tripled f-pawns are an eyesore and White is miles ahead in development. Moreover, White has an open f-file for his rooks and his e3-pawn is not as weak as it looks, being protected easily.

b) 4...exf6 5 e3 c6 6 ♗d3 ♗xd3 (6...♗g6 7 h4! eventually forces Black to swap on d3) 7 ♕xd3 ♘a6 8 a3 ♗d6 9 e4! dxe4 10 ♘xe4 ♕a5+ 11 c3 ♗e7 12 ♘f3 0-0 13 0-0 and White's healthy queenside pawn majority gives him an edge, A.Suetin-B.Toth, Kecskemet 1972. From this point on, every trade favours White since he wins all king and pawn endings.

We'll return to and explore these Trompowsky-like lines in more detail in Chapter Seven.

4...♘bd7

Black has a very aggressive option in 4...c5:

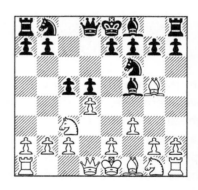

a) After 5 dxc5! d4 6 e4 dxc3 7 ♕xd8+ ♔xd8 8 exf5 cxb2 9 ♖b1 ♘bd7 10 ♗c4 g6 11 fxg6 fxg6 White stood better in T.Bromann-P.Bombek, Frydek

Mistek 2006, due to the bishop pair, his superior development and because he has chances to make something of Black's insecure king position.

b) However, after 5 e4?! cxd4! (5...dxe4 6 d5 is a reversed Albin Counter-Gambit) 6 ♕xd4 ♘c6 7 ♗b5 dxe4 8 ♗xf6 exf6 9 ♕xd8+ ♖xd8 10 fxe4 ♗g6 11 ♘ge2 ♗d6 Black stood better in E.Mozes-I.Lorincz, Hungarian League 2002, with the bishop pair and control over e5, and because White's pawn on e4 may later turn into a target.

Tossing in 4...h6 may again do more harm than good: 5 ♗h4 c5 6 dxc5! d4 7 e4 dxc3 8 ♕xd8+ ♔xd8 9 exf5 cxb2 10 ♖b1 ♘bd7 11 c6 bxc6 12 ♖xb2 and in C.Lakdawala-I.Goncalves, Internet blitz 2010, Black had to deal with the following problems: White's bishop pair, his tangled development and his insecure king.

5 ♘xd5!?

This is mainly played for shock value.

5...♘xd5 6 e4 f6!?

This move threw me! The idea is to unpin his e-pawn and bolster ...e5, which frees his position.

Instead, 6...♗xe4? is not a good decision to hand over the centre and bishop pair. Indeed, after 7 fxe4 ♘5b6 8 ♘f3, as in D.MacDonald-S.Rix, Hastings 1991/92, the opening has been a disaster for Black:

1. White owns the bishop pair;
2. White controls the centre; and

3. He has the f-file for a ready-to-order attack.

Next game we examine 6...h6! which may be Black's best prescription in the position.

7 ♗h4

7 ♗c1 ♗e6 8 exd5 ♗xd5 9 ♗d3 e5 10 c4 ♗f7 11 d5 ♗d6 12 ♗e3 ♘c5 13 ♗c2 a5 14 ♘e2 c6 15 h4 b5 16 b3 a4!? 17 b4! ♘a6 18 c5 ♗b8 19 d6 ♘xb4 20 ♗e4 gives White full compensation for the pawn, E.Hrosevitha-Xiao Cheng, Internet blitz 2005.

7...♗e6

Also playable is 7...♘e3 8 ♕e2 ♘xf1 9 exf5 ♘xh2 10 ♖xh2 ♘b6 11 c3 ♕d5 12 ♕e4 g6 13 g4! h5 14 ♗g3 ♖g8 15 fxg6 ♕xe4+ 16 fxe4 ♖xg6 17 ♖xh5 ♖xg4 18 ♔f2! when White is ready to play ♔f3 with advantage, as 18...♖xe4?? fails to 19 ♔f3 ♖e6 20 d5.

8 exd5 ♗xd5 9 ♗g3

Discouraging ...e5. I didn't like White's position in the lines 9 ♘e2 e5 10 ♘c3 ♗b4 11 a3 ♗xc3+ 12 bxc3 ♕e7 13 ♗e2, and 9 c4 ♗f7 10 f4?! e5! 11 fxe5 ♗b4+ 12 ♔f2 g5! when, suddenly,

White's king is in danger and he looks overextended.

9...e5!

Alas! He doesn't get bluffed out of playing ...e5.

10 ♘e2 c6 11 dxe5 ♘xe5 12 ♘c3 ♗b4 13 ♕d4!

Hitting e5 and b4, while preventing ...♗xc3+.

13...♕e7 14 0-0-0

14...♗xc3

Handing over the bishop pair. Black falls short of equality in other lines:

a) 14...♗f7 15 ♘e4 0-0 16 a3 ♗a5 17 ♗xe5 fxe5 18 ♕c5 ♕xc5 19 ♘xc5 b5 20 ♗d3 when White has several pluses:

1. He will occupy the hole on e4 with either bishop or knight;

2. Both the c6- and e5-pawns are targets; and

3. Black must try and exchange his light-squared bishop for White's knight to try and draw an opposite-coloured bishop ending.

b) I wasn't so sure about the line 14...0-0-0!? 15 ♕xa7 ♗xc3 16 bxc3 ♖he8 17 c4! ♗f7 18 ♖xd8+ ♖xd8 19

♗e2, but at least White has a shaky extra pawn and the bishop pair to comfort him.

15 ♕xc3 0-0-0

15...♗xa2?? loses on the spot to 16 f4 ♘g4 17 ♖e1 ♗e6 18 f5.

16 ♗xe5 fxe5 17 ♗d3 e4!

Aggressive defence. In late middlegames and endings it is critical for the defending side to stay active, even at the cost of material. Black liquidates his sickly e5-pawn away with a sacrifice. He should generate enough activity in the major piece ending to hold the game.

My opponent also considered and then correctly rejected the line 17...♗xa2? 18 b3 ♕a3+ 19 ♕b2 ♕a5 20 ♖he1 ♖he8 21 ♖e4 b5 22 ♖xe5.

The critical alternative is 17...♖he8 18 ♖he1 (18 ♗xh7?? g6! traps the bishop) 18...♔b8 19 ♖e2 and White begins to pile up on the e-pawn. However, Black has only one weakness to nurse and has chances to hold the draw. Winning isn't mission impossible, but it may be mission really, really hard!

18 fxe4 ♗xe4 19 ♗xe4 ♛xe4 20 ♛xg7 ♛e3+

Or 20...♖hg8 21 ♖xd8+ ♖xd8 22 b3 and it isn't easy to convert.

21 ♔b1 ♛e2 22 ♖de1 ♛h5 23 ♛g3 ♖hg8?!

After 23...♖d2! 24 b3 ♛g6 25 ♛c3 ♖hd8 26 g3 Black's rooks maximize their activity and it may be difficult for White to win.

24 ♛f2 ♛g5?

This trade is a bad deal for Black, who weakens his king position. Better to play 24...a6.

25 ♛xa7 ♛xg2 26 b3

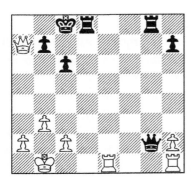

White is up a pawn and has the safer king.

26...♛g7

26...♖d2?? 27 ♖hg1 drops a rook and would be a dumb way to lose.

27 ♖hg1 ♛f7 28 ♖gf1 ♛c7 29 ♛a8+ ♛b8 30 ♛xb8+ ♔xb8 31 ♖f7!

This move looks like a no-brainer, but I used up most of my time calculating what happens when he takes my seventh rank.

31...♖g2 32 ♖ee7

White doubles first on the seventh rank.

32...♖dd2?

My opponent was down to about 12 seconds with a 5-second time-delay. The variation I calculated on my 32nd move was 32...♖d1+ 33 ♔b2 ♖dd2 34 ♖xb7+ ♔a8 35 ♖be7 ♖xc2+ 36 ♔b1! ♖b2+ 37 ♔c1 ♖gc2+ 38 ♔d1 ♖d2+ 39 ♔e1 (the point; he has exhausted his bullying checks) 39...♖d8 40 ♖a7+ ♔b8 41 ♖fb7+ ♔c8 42 ♖xh7 winning.

33 ♖xb7+ ♔a8 34 ♖a7+ ♔b8 35 ♖fb7+ ♔c8 36 ♖xh7 1-0

Summary

Black's odd but fully playable 6th move is an example of the rich possibilities for both sides in the 5 ♘xd5 line.

Game 27
C.Lakdawala-B.Baker
San Diego (rapid) 2010

1 d4 ♘f6 2 ♘c3 d5 3 ♗g5 ♗f5 4 f3 ♘bd7 5 ♘xd5 ♘xd5 6 e4 h6 7 ♗h4! g5!?

7...♘e3 also leads to tricky play after 8 ♕d3 ♘xf1 9 exf5 ♘c5 10 ♕c3 ♘a4 11 ♕b3 ♘b6 (after 11...♕xd4 12 ♗f2 ♕e5+ 13 ♘e2 ♘b6 14 ♖xf1 ♕xf5 15 0-0-0 White's development lead compensates for the missing pawn) 12 ♘e2, as in T.Bromann-R.Pruijssers, Kemer 2007.

7...g5!? 8 ♗f2 e6!

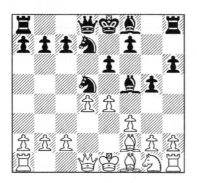

A hidden and cunning idea. White must watch out for ...♗b4+.

Instead, after 8...♗e6 9 exd5 ♗xd5 10 c4 ♗e6 11 d5 ♗f5 12 ♗d3 (12 ♗d4 to disrupt Black's castling may be a superior option) 12...♗xd3 13 ♕xd3 ♗g7 14 ♗d4 ♘f6 15 ♘e2 ♕d6 16 0-0 0-0 17 ♘g3 an attack is in the works for White, H.Heimsoth-M.Ell, Internet blitz 2004.

9 exf5!?

The only real try for an advantage. If you play 9 exf5!? be sure your life insurance policy is up to date! White's king gets bounced around in the centre and the positions are certainly not to everyone's taste.

If you don't like what is coming you can play the far safer (and more drawish) line 9 exd5 exd5 10 ♗d3 when White's only prayer for an advantage is the possible exploitation of the weakened f5-square: 10...♕e7+?! (handing White a tempo; honestly, after 10...♕f6! I don't think White has anything, as Black will castle queenside with complete equality) 11 ♘e2 ♗xd3 12 ♕xd3 ♕b4+? (an absolute waste of time; better to castle, after which White has a small edge, since he later plays ♘g3, taking control over f5) 13 ♘c3 ♘b6?! 14 0-0 0-0-0 15 a4! and White is the only one doing the attacking, M.Keller-T.Martin, German League 1996.

9...♗b4+!

Oops, I forgot about this trick. Bruce had prepared this huge improvement over a game he had against my student, John Funderberg, the previous week. Unfortunately, he craved revenge on Funderberg's teacher! There Baker played the inferior 9...exf5? when it was advantage White with the bishop pair and a healthy versus crippled majority.

10 c3

There is no turning back. It would be completely moronic to play 10 ♔e2?? ♘f4+ 11 ♔e3 c5! and White's chances of survival are slim to none.

10...♘xc3!

The point of 8...e6!.

11 bxc3 ♗xc3+ 12 ♔e2

To a lifelong London and Colle System player, such positions are rough on the nervous system! To say I was alarmed would be understating the facts. I was fully aware that my opponent was comforted by the knowledge that he had looked at this position at home with the help of computers. I, on the other hand, was left groping in the dark in this totally irrational position.

12...⏤xa1

Logical to equalize the material deficit. As in J.Smid-L.Smejkal, Svetla nad Sazavou 1998, Black can also try the riskier 12...exf5!? 13 ♖c1 ♗a5 14 ♗e1 ♗b6 15 ♔f2 ♕f6 16 ♘e2 0-0-0 when he has full compensation for the piece:

1. An attack, with the possibility of opening the centre even more with a future ...c5;

2. White's d-pawn is in danger; and

3. White's pieces are jammed on the kingside.

13 ♕xa1

Correctly rejecting avarice with 13 fxe6? which picks up an extra pawn, but also hands over another tempo to Black: 13...♕e7 14 ♕xa1 0-0-0 15 ♔d2 ♕xe6 16 ♗d3 ♘e5! and the knight

can't be touched since after 17 dxe5 ♕c4! 18 ♕c3 ♖xd3+ 19 ♕xd3 ♖d8 20 ♕xd8+ ♔xd8 21 ♘e2 ♕xa2+ Black's three connected passed pawns on the queenside are too much for White's scattered forces, who are without obvious targets.

13...exf5

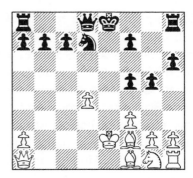

A critical point in the game. The big decision: where to put my king? The choices are f2 or out in the wide open prairie on d2. Intuitively, f2 looks like the only choice, but having put the position on computers, it seems d2 was the better bet! The longer I play chess, the less I seem to understand its depths!

14 ♗e3?

Natural and weak. White loses a lot of time with this bishop to stow his king away to f2. I should play 14 ♔d2! when the king seeks shelter in no-man's land! Now Black has a critical choice:

a) 14...♕f6?! (a superficial move which plans queenside castling) 15 ♕e1+! ♔f8 16 ♗d3 ♔g7 17 ♘e2 and

Black's king march has lost time, meaning White stands better. Indeed, Black will have to think twice before opening the game with ...c5 since his queen and king are caught on the a1-h8 diagonal. If White's bishop is given access to this diagonal Black will be in big trouble. Moreover, f5 is weak and White may hit with ♘g3 or ♕b1, while his king is annoyingly safe in the middle of the board.

b) 14...0-0! 15 ♗d3 c5 16 ♘e2 ♕a5+ 17 ♕c3! ♕xa2+ 18 ♗c2 cxd4 19 ♘xd4 ♖ac8 20 ♖a1! ♕d5 21 ♕d3 and although Black has a rook and three pawns for two bishops, I still prefer White, as Black's pawns hang on f5 and a7, while Black's king is actually in greater danger than White's, which once again feels comfortable in the middle of an open board. Moreover, if the queens come off, White will be all right. Black can't hang on to all his pawns and White's pieces are remarkably active.

14...♕e7 15 ♔f2 0-0-0 16 ♗d3 ♖he8 17 ♕c1

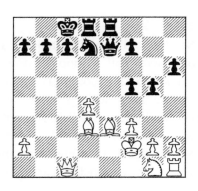

Played for three reasons:

1. It covers e3;

2. On c1, the queen fights for control of the c5-square which is important since Black's main game-opening break is ...c5; and

3. If Black manages to engineer ...c5 then White has ♕a3! tricks pinning the c5-pawn and also targeting a7.

17...f4 18 ♗d2 ♔b8?!

My opponent once again refuses to trade the knight for my d3-bishop with 18...♘e5! 19 ♕c3 ♘xd3+ 20 ♕xd3 ♕e6! 21 a3 c5 22 ♘e2 ♔b8 23 ♖c1 cxd4 24 ♘xd4 ♕d5 25 ♖c4!. White hangs on for the moment, but still Black is for choice as White must untangle from the central pin and also watch out for a slow advance on the kingside.

19 ♘e2 ♕d6?!

Black experiences difficulties coming up with an attacking plan and begins to drift. After 19...♘e5! 20 ♕b1 ♘xd3+ 21 ♕xd3 c5 22 ♖c1 cxd4 23 ♘xd4 ♕e5 24 ♗c3 ♕d5 25 ♕d2 I would rather have Black.

20 ♖d1 c5?!

Mistimed. I sensed that Baker underestimated the danger to his own king:

a) 20...♘e5?! 21 ♗b5 a6 22 ♗b4 ♕xb4 23 ♗xe8 ♘xf3 24 ♗xf7 ♘xd4 25 ♕c4 ♕xc4 26 ♗xc4 wasn't ideal either.

b) However, the game remains unclear after 20...♘b6!.

21 ♕a3!

White's pieces come to life and the open b-file becomes a big concern for Black.

21...♕e6 22 ♖b1

White must be careful: 22 dxc5?? ♘xc5 leaves his central pieces tripping over themselves.

22...♘b6?

I'm not sure what my opponent had in mind with this blunder/miscalculation, but the initiative has swung to White after the superior 22...♕d5 23 ♔f1 cxd4 24 ♖b5 ♕c6 25 ♘xd4 or 22...cxd4 23 ♘xd4 ♕d5 24 ♗c3.

23 dxc5 ♘d7??

A time-pressure blunder. I have the feeling my opponent originally planned 23...♘c4?? and then saw 24 ♕b3 with the double attack on b7 and the knight winning on the spot.

He had to try 23...♕e7 24 ♔f1.

24 ♗e4

Ganging up on b7.

24...b6

This allows deadly infiltration on c6.

25 ♘d4 1-0

Summary

6...e6! is a hidden but powerful idea for Black against the 5 ♘xd5 line. White

can chicken out and take the knight on d5 with an equal position. If you take his bishop on f5 all hell breaks loose after 7...♗b4+! Readers with heart conditions are advised against playing this way without first consulting their cardiologists!

1 ♘c3 d5 2 d4 ♘f6 3 ♗g5 ♗f5 4 f3 ♘bd7 5 ♕d2 h6 6 ♗h4 e6 7 e3!

Wisely showing restraint. One of the key skills a Veresover must develop is to know when to play e4 and when to hold back.

Here 7 e4?! is a bad idea: 7...dxe4 8 ♗c4 ♗e7 (8...♗b4! leaves White with a rotten version of the Blackmar-Diemer Gambit) 9 0-0-0 ♘b6 10 ♗b3 exf3 11 ♘xf3 ♘e4 and White had little to show for the pawn, M.Skliba-P.Herejk, Nachod 1999.

7...c6 8 ②ge2 ♗e7 9 ♗f2!

Cagey play. The bishop lurks in dark corners behind the central pawns and fulfils two purposes:

1. It avoids simplification tricks based on Black playing ...②e4 in the future.

2. It stalls castling and so doesn't reveal to Black the king's address too soon, whereas 9 0-0-0?! b5 would allow Black to begin an attack immediately.

9...b5 10 g4 ♗h7 11 ②g3 ②b6 12 h4?

White's game sours after this move. He should keep the knight out with 12 b3! with the plan of walking his king to g2 and then attacking with h4.

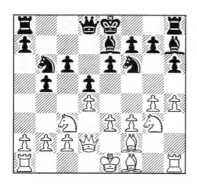

12...b4?

It was time to jump in with 12...②c4! 13 ♗xc4 bxc4 14 g5 hxg5 15 hxg5 ②d7 when Black has several advantages:

1. He exerts pressure down the open b-file;

2. He has the bishop pair and control of the light squares;

3. White's pawns are shaky and he has targets on g5 and b2;

4. White's king is a source for concern: it will not be safe to castle queenside with Black owning the b-file, but keeping the king in the centre won't be comfortable either; and

5. White won't be able to make anything of the pinned bishop on h7.

13 ②d1 ②fd7 14 ②h5 g6

There is no reason to block the bishop. I don't believe White is in a position to mount a serious offensive if Black plunges in with 14...0-0! when he is ready to blast open the centre with ...e5 and/or ...c5. If White castles queenside then Black looks faster.

15 ②f4 e5! 16 ②g2 ♕c7 17 b3 a5

He should take advantage of White's clumsy and undeveloped situation by picking a fight in the centre with 17...c5!.

18 ♗g3 ♗d6 19 ②f2 0-0-0?

There was no reason to give White a clear target. Once again the confrontational 19...c5! leaves White struggling.

20 a3!

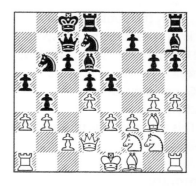

Wasting no time prising open lines.

20...exd4

After 20...bxa3 21 ♕xa5 ♖he8 22 ♗a6+ ♔b8 23 0-0 g5 24 ♗d3 White is back in business.

21 ♗xd6 ♕xd6

Avoiding 21...dxe3?? 22 ♗a6+.

22 exd4 ♕g3?

Big deal. The queen gets the boot immediately.

23 ♖h3 ♕d6 24 axb4 axb4 25 ♘d3

White's position has improved dramatically:

1. He has the safer king;

2. Black's pawn on b4 is weak and hanging;

3. The c5-square is tender; and

4. Black's bishop is buried on h7.

25...c5?!

Understandable, but this just makes matters worse.

26 ♔d1?!

Missing 26 ♖a5! cxd4 27 ♘xb4 and Black won't survive much longer.

26...♕f6 27 ♕f4!

The endgame is clearly in White's favour.

27...♕xf4 28 ♘gxf4 g5 29 dxc5! ♘xc5

If 29...gxf4 30 cxb6 ♗xd3 31 ♗xd3

♘xb6 32 ♖a7 and 32...♖d7?? walks into 33 ♗f5.

30 ♘xc5 gxf4 31 ♖a7 ♖d6 32 ♗a6+ ♔b8 33 ♖b7+ ♔a8 34 ♖xf7 ♗g6 35 ♖xf4 d4 36 ♔d2 ♖hd8 37 ♖h1 ♔a7 38 ♖a1

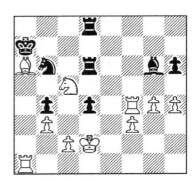

Black can resign. He is down two pawns with his king still under fire.

38...♘d5 39 ♗d3+ ♔b6 40 ♘a4+ ♔c7 41 ♖xd4

Make that three pawns.

41...♗xd3 42 cxd3 ♖f6 43 ♖c1+ ♔d6 44 ♘b6 ♔e5 45 ♖e4+ ♔d6 46 ♘xd5 ♔xd5 47 ♖cc4 ♖a8 48 ♖ed4+ ♔e6 49 ♖c6+ 1-0

Summary

Remember, you can't always force e4 in every single Veresov. It's like that song: You got to know when to hold 'em, know when to fold 'em!

Game 29
M.Khachian-A.Strikovic
Cannes 1996

1 d4 ♘f6 2 ♘c3 d5 3 ♗g5 ♗f5 4 f3 ♗g6!?

Keeping clear of all ♘xd5 tricks.

Instead, 4...♘c6!? shows that people make up all kinds of strange things when facing the Veresov. Black's idea may be ...♘b4, but it's too crude and shouldn't bother White at all: 5 e3?! (better is 5 ♕d2! intending to meet 5...♘b4? with 6 e4!) 5...♘b4 6 ♖c1 e6?! (he should play 6...c5!) 7 a3 ♘c6 8 e4 dxe4 9 fxe4 and Black must give up a piece since after 9...♗g4? (9...♗g6 10 e5 ♘xd4 11 exf6 gxf6 12 ♗e3 is also insufficient, but at least he gets two pawns for the piece in this one) 10 ♗xf6 ♕xf6 11 ♕xg4 ♘xd4 12 ♘ge2 he could resign, V.Pokhlebkin-M.Bespalov, Nizhnij Novgorod 2008.

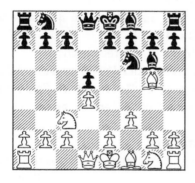

5 ♕d2 ♘bd7 6 0-0-0 e6 7 ♘h3!

This move highlights a possible defect of 4...♗g6. 7 ♘h3! is a dual purpose move which gets ready to harass the bishop with ♘f4. Also, the knight may go to f2 to prepare e4.

7...♗e7

Black's options:

a) 7...♗b4!? 8 a3 ♗a5 9 ♘f4 0-0 10 h4 h6 11 ♘xg6 fxg6 12 ♗e3 ♘b6 13 ♕d3 ♘c4 14 g4 ♕d6 15 ♗h3 ♘d7 16 g5 with a very sharp position.

b) 7...h6! 8 ♗h4 ♗b4 9 a3 ♗a5 10 ♘f4 ♗h7 11 ♘h5 0-0 12 e3 ♘e4 13 ♗xd8 ♘xd2 14 ♔xd2 ♖axd8 15 b4 ♗b6 16 ♗d3 is equal. Black's bishop pair doesn't mean much in this blocked position.

8 ♘f4 ♘g8?

After 8...♘h5! 9 ♗xe7 ♕xe7 10 ♘xh5 ♗xh5 11 h4 h6 12 e4 dxe4 13 g4 ♗g6 14 fxe4 0-0-0 White owns extra territory but Black has managed to complete development, with a solid position.

9 ♗xe7 ♘xe7 10 e4 c6 11 h4 h6 12 ♗d3 dxe4

Not a desirable move, but stalling with 12...♕c7? leads to trouble after 13 exd5 cxd5 14 ♘xg6 ♘xg6 15 ♗xg6 fxg6 16 ♖he1.

Likewise, after 12...♗h7?! 13 exd5 cxd5 14 ♗xh7 ♖xh7 15 ♖he1 ♘f6 16 g4 Black has problems, as his pieces are awkwardly posted, his king may soon come under attack and he must watch out for the undermining idea g5-g6!.

13 ♘xg6 ♘xg6 14 ♘xe4 ♕c7?!

14...♕e7! stops White's next move but Black must still be very careful after 15 h5 ♘h4 16 g4 and then:

a) 16...f5! 17 gxf5 ♘xf5 18 ♕f4 0-0 19 ♕c7 ♘b6 20 ♕xe7 ♘xe7 21 ♘c5 ♖xf3 22 ♘xe6 and White stands better, as his bishop is the superior minor piece, he may generate pressure down the g-file and his h-pawn holds back both Black's kingside pawns.

b) 16...♘xf3? 17 ♕f4 ♘g5 18 ♘d6+ ♔f8 19 ♘xb7 and Black is in bad shape.

15 ♕b4!

White has achieved a favourable Caro-Kann structure.

15...0-0-0! 16 ♘d6+ ♔b8 17 ♗xg6

The naive 17 ♘xf7?? drops a piece to 17...♕f4+!.

17...fxg6 18 ♖he1

Black experiences difficulties defending his fragile and damaged pawns.

18...♘b6 19 ♘e4 ♕f4+ 20 ♔b1 ♘d5 21 ♕b3 ♕xh4!?

He may as well gamble since playing it safe leads to unending pressure on his e-pawn with 21...♖he8 22 ♘c5 ♕f7 23 ♖e4.

22 ♘c5 b6 23 a4 a5?

Black's position can't tolerate another weakness. 23...♖he8 24 a5 ♔c8 looks bad, but had to be played.

24 ♖xe6 ♔a7

24...♔c7 25 ♕c4! bxc5 26 ♕xc5 ♔b8 27 ♖xc6 ♖d7 28 ♕b5+ ♖b7 29 ♕xd5 wins.

25 ♖xc6!

The life-span of Black's king is coming to an end.

25...♕e7

Or 25...bxc5?? 26 ♕b5!.

26 ♕b5! ♔a8 27 c4! 1-0

Summary

3...♗f5 is played to prevent White from playing e4, yet in most of the games I have looked at, White still manages to force the move later in the game.

Game 30
S.Mamedyarov-P.Dukaczewski
Bled Olympiad 2002

1 d4 ♘f6 2 ♘c3 d5 3 ♗g5 ♗f5 4 f3 c6 5 ♕d2 ♘bd7 6 0-0-0!?

Mamedyarov is not shy and castles into a possible storm. He banks on his superior development to keep his king safe. Even more radical would be to go Blackmar-Diemer style with 6 e4!?. One old game saw 6...dxe4 7 ♕f4! ♕a5 8 0-0-0 exf3 9 d5! and White's rapid development gave him full compensation for the pawn in S.Levitsky-A.Rubinstein, Vilnius 1912.

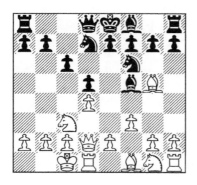

6...h6 7 ♗h4 ♕a5

If Black launches first with 7...b5?! he gets hit hard in the centre with 8 e4! dxe4 9 d5! b4 10 dxc6 bxc3 11 ♕xc3 and Black is in deep trouble, his position resembling one of those Morphy versus NN blowouts, C.Brauer-A.Glaser, German League 2006.

Otherwise, after 7...e6 8 ♖e1 (8 e4? drops a pawn to 8...dxe4 9 fxe4 ♘xe4!) 8...♗h7 9 e4 ♘xe4 10 fxe4 ♕xh4 11 ♘f3 ♕d8 12 exd5 cxd5 13 ♘xd5 ♗d6 14 ♗d3 ♗xd3 15 ♕xd3 0-0 the position looks quite equal, but Black got crushed in just a few moves: 16 ♘e3 ♖c8 17 ♔b1 ♗f4 18 g4 ♘b6 19 ♘g2! ♗d6 20 g5 h5 21 g6 and White broke through first, A.Kosteniuk-E.Korbut, Samara 2005.

8 e4!

Exploiting the queen's position on a5 to force e4.

8...dxe4 9 fxe4 ♗h7 10 d5!

The correct method of churning up trouble in the centre. Much weaker

would be 10 e5?! ♘d5 11 ♘xd5 ♕xd2+ 12 ♖xd2 cxd5 giving Black a slightly favourable ending.

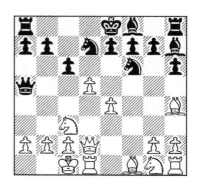

10...g5

He must play this move sooner or later to complete his kingside development.

11 ♗g3

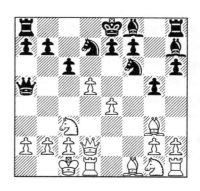

11...♗g7

Maybe Black should exchange, hoping to generate play down the c-file: 11...cxd5 12 exd5 ♗g7 13 ♗d3 ♗xd3 14 ♕xd3 ♖c8 15 ♘ge2, but I still prefer White here. Black must eventually castle kingside and when he does, White prises him open fast with h4. Also, f5 would be a nasty perch for White's knight.

12 dxc6 bxc6 13 ♘f3 0-0

He loses material if he castles the other way with 13...0-0-0 14 ♗c4 ♘c5 15 ♕e3 and then:

a) 15...♔b7 16 e5 ♘fe4 17 ♘xe4 ♘xe4 18 ♗xf7.

b) 15...♘cxe4? (free pawn, right?) 16 ♘xe4 ♘xe4 17 b4! (wrong!) 17...♕a4 18 ♕b3! ♕xb3 19 ♗a6 mate.

14 e5 ♘e4!?

Black insists on going down in a blaze of glory, but the sac is unsound. The miserable alternative is play a pawn down in the ending with 14...♘d5 15 ♘xd5 ♕xd2+ 16 ♖xd2 cxd5 17 ♖xd5 ♘b6 18 ♖d4 ♖fd8.

15 ♘xe4 ♕xa2 16 ♘c3 ♕a1+ 17 ♘b1 ♖ab8 18 ♕c3 ♘c5!

It looks like threats are mounting to White's king.

19 b4!

Ending that dream. Queens come off, and also Black's hopes of an attack.

19...♕xc3 20 ♘xc3 ♖xb4 21 ♘d4 ♖c8 22 ♗e2 a5 23 ♖hf1 e6 24 ♗h5 ♖c7 25 ♘xc6!?

Getting fancy. The simple 25 ♘de2! consolidates.

25...♖c4!

Mamedyarov probably counted on 25...♖xc6?? 26 ♖d8+ ♗f8 27 ♖xf7 ♘b3+ 28 cxb3 ♖xc3+ 29 ♔d2 ♖c2+ 30 ♔d1 and wins.

26 ♗e1 ♘d3+!

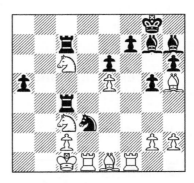

An interference shot, which somewhat resuscitates Black's game.

27 cxd3 ♖4xc6 28 d4 ♖xc3+ 29 ♗xc3 ♖xc3+ 30 ♔b2 ♖c2+ 31 ♔a1 ♗g6?!

Making it easy for White. He had to try 31...♗f5! 32 g4 ♖xh2 33 ♖c1 ♗d3 34 ♗xf7+ ♔h7 35 ♖g1, although White should still take home the full point.

32 ♗xg6 fxg6 33 ♖c1 ♖xc1+

Now White wins easily. A better try would be to make it a race with 33...♖xg2 34 ♖c8+ ♔h7 35 ♖f7 g4, although after 36 ♖cc7 h5 37 ♖xg7+ ♔h6 38 ♖ge7 ♖xh2 39 ♖xe6 g3 40 ♖cc6 h4 41 ♖xg6+ ♔h5 42 ♖g8 g2 43 ♖cg6 h3 Black's pawns are stymied and *Rybka* announces mate in 11 moves.

34 ♖xc1 ♗f8 35 ♖c6 ♔f7 36 ♖a6 ♗b4

37 ♔b2 g4 38 ♔b3 g5 39 ♔c4 h5 40 d5 exd5+ 41 ♔xd5 h4 42 ♖a7+ ♔g6 43 ♔e6 ♗d2 44 ♔d7 h3 45 g3 ♗b4 46 e6 ♔f6 47 ♖xa5! ♗f8 48 ♖a1 1-0

Summary

You are rolling the dice if you play 5 ♕d2 and 6 0-0-0!?. If you are a good attacker (and defender!) you may want to give this one a try.

Game 31
G.Veresov-Smolianow
Minsk 1963

1 d4 ♘f6 2 ♘c3 d5 3 ♗g5 c5

Allowing any opening a move down is a dangerous path, and here Black agrees to a reversed Queen's Gambit Chigorin. You may argue the Chigorin doesn't have such a great reputation. True, but any sharp opening a full move up could change the assessment dramatically.

4 ♗xf6 gxf6 5 e4?!

The nuclear option! White reasons that his development lead means more than Black's bishop pair and blasts the game wide open. However, the objective assessment of the move is '?!' if Black manages to avoid the many land mines along the way. If you have a gambler's instinct and you are pretty sure your opponent won't know the theory then let's change the assessment of 5 e4 to '!?'.

We will examine the more sober 5 e3 in the next few games.

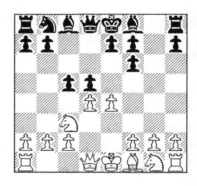

5...dxe4

Black fell dangerously behind in development after 5...cxd4!? 6 ♕xd4 dxe4 7 ♕xd8+ ♔xd8 8 0-0-0+ ♘d7 9 ♘xe4 ♔c7 10 ♘f3 e6 11 ♘d4 a6 12 ♗e2! (target: f7) 12...b6 13 ♗h5 and he never managed to shake the pressure, despite his bishop pair in an open position, I.Ibragimov-N.Sirigos, Peristeri 1993.

6 dxc5!

White should avoid playing in Albin Counter-Gambit style with 6 d5? f5 (6...♕b6! also looks good for Black) 7 ♕h5 ♗g7 8 ♘ge2 ♕b6 9 0-0-0 ♕h6+! when the queens come off and White is simply down a pawn for nothing, M.Hebden-V.Milov, Isle of Man 1995.

6...♕a5?!

Alternatively:

a) 6...♘d7?! 7 ♗c4 e6 8 ♘xe4 ♗xc5 9 ♕e2 f5?! (he probably should hang on to his bishop pair with 9...♕a5+ 10 c3 ♗e7) 10 ♘xc5 ♕a5+ 11 c3 ♕xc5 12 ♘f3 ♖g8 13 0-0 and in M.Nikolov-V.Petkov, Kavala 2007, White stood better for several reasons: he leads in development, the insecure black king is a cause for worry and White has inflicted some damage to Black's pawn structure without compensation.

b) It's tempting to take queens off the board, but Black can't afford this luxury: 6...♕xd1+? 7 ♖xd1 ♗g7?? (a colossal error for a correspondence game; Black still has a difficult game after the correct 7...♘d7 8 ♘xe4 f5 9 ♘c3 e6 10 ♘b5) 8 ♘d5 1-0 F.Schmitz-N.Berthelsen, correspondence 1990.

c) If there is a refutation to 5 e4 it lies in 6...f5! 7 ♗b5+ (I don't believe White has full compensation after 7 ♕xd8+ ♔xd8 8 0-0-0+ ♘d7) 7...♗d7 8 ♘ge2 ♘c6 9 ♕d2 e6 10 0-0 ♖g8 11 ♖ad1 (perhaps White should resign himself to a materially equal but inferior ending with 11 ♕e3 ♕g5 12 ♕xg5 ♖xg5 13 ♘a4) 11...♗xc5 12 ♘a4 ♗b4 13 c3 ♗f8 and it just doesn't feel like enough compensation for the missing pawn. Perhaps, though, White has practical chances since he still leads in development and has the safer king, I.Miladinovic-S.Smagin, Montreal 2000.

7 ♕h5 e6 8 0-0-0

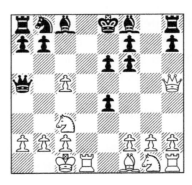

8...f5

8...♕xc5? drops a pawn to 9 ♘xe4! ♕xh5 10 ♘xf6+ ♔e7 11 ♘xh5, I.Ibragimov-H.Schut, Rochester 2001.

9 ♗b5+ ♘c6

Other moves lose:

a) 9...♘d7? 10 ♘h3! ♗e7 11 ♘g5 ♗xg5+ 12 ♕xg5 a6? 13 ♗xd7+ ♗xd7 14 ♘xe4!! fxe4 15 ♖xd7 ♔xd7 16 c6+ and the discovered attack wins the queen.

b) 9...♗d7? 10 ♘h3! ♗e7 (10...♗xb5?? 11.♘g5 wins) 11 ♘g5 ♗xg5+ 12 ♕xg5 ♗c6 13 g4! yields a winning attack.

10 g4!

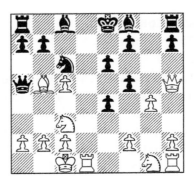

Spearing Black's snake-like central formation. An assessment:

1. White is down a pawn;

2. Black owns the centre;

3. Black has the bishop pair;

4. White is miles ahead in development; and

5. Black's king safety is a big worry for him.

Conclusion: Black controls all the static advantages while White has development and the initiative. White must strike soon before Black catches up in development and consolidates.

10...a6!

The only move. Black must tread carefully. For example:

a) 10...♗d7? 11 ♖xd7! ♔xd7 12 ♕xf7+ ♗e7 13 ♘ge2 and Black will not survive the assault.

b) 10...♗xc5? 11 gxf5 exf5 12 ♘h3 intending ♘g5 and Black's king is caught in the centre once again.

11 ♗xc6+ bxc6 12 gxf5 exf5 13 ♘ge2 ♕xc5!

13...♗xc5?? loses to 14 ♘xe4! and Black can't recapture due to the queen check on e5.

14 ♘d4 ♖b8 15 ♖he1

Taking aim at e4.

15...♗d7?

Failing to take evasive measures to avoid the sac leads to a disaster for Black. He had to counterattack vigorously with 15...♕b4! 16 ♘b3 ♗e6 17 f3 e3 18 ♕g5! ♗e7 19 ♕g7 ♖f8 20 ♖xe3 ♕f4 21 ♖dd3 c5 22 ♘e2 ♕c7 23 ♖d2 when White stands better but Black is still in the game.

16 ♘xe4!

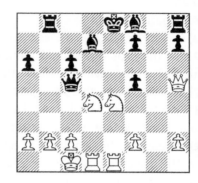

White strikes first. The position looks like it came out of a Najdorf Poisoned Pawn variation.

16...fxe4 17 ♖xe4+ ♔d8 18 ♕xf7 ♔c8 19 ♘b5!

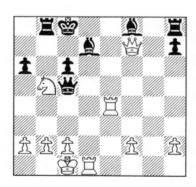

Not very hard to see. The discovered attack ends resistance.

19...♗h6+ 20 ♔b1 ♖xb5 21 ♖xd7 ♕h5

21...♕f8 fails to 22 ♕e6! ♔b8 23 ♕xc6 ♕c8 24 ♕d6+ ♔a8 25 ♖c7 winning.

22 ♖c7+ ♔b8 23 ♖b7+! 1-0

Black has a choice between getting mated or dropping his queen.

Summary

Black must cross a mine field to survive after 5 e4?!, but the line 5...dxe4 6 dxc5 f5! is critical to its soundness.

Game 32
J.Hector-A.Evdokimov
Helsingor 2008

1 d4 ♘f6 2 ♘c3 d5 3 ♗g5 c5 4 ♗xf6 gxf6

4...exf6?! doesn't have a good reputation because it hands White an easy target of the d5-pawn: 5 e3 ♘c6 6 ♘ge2! (plan: g3, ♗g2 and later ♘f4, hammering away at d5) 6...c4 7 a3 ♕a5 8 g3 ♗d6 9 ♗g2 ♘e7 10 b4! cxb3 11 cxb3 ♗g4!? 12 b4 ♕a6 13 ♘xd5 ♘xd5 14 ♗xd5 0-0 15 f3 ♗d7 16 ♔f2 didn't leave Black enough compensation for the pawn, A.Stefanova-I.Chelushkina, Turin Women's Olympiad 2006.

5 e3

A safer and sounder alternative to its psychotic cousin 5 e4?!.

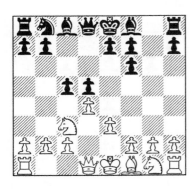

5...♘c6

Black can also clarify the central tension immediately. For example, 5...cxd4 6 exd4 h5 (to prevent ♕h5) 7 ♕f3 e6 8 0-0-0 ♘c6 9 ♘ge2 f5 10 ♔b1 ♗g7 11 h4 ♕b6 12 ♕e3 ♔f8, as played in G.West-M.Ahn, Elista Olympiad 1998. Now White should reroute his knight to d3, heading for greener pastures. After 13 ♘a4! ♕c7 14 ♘c5 White's has several trumps:

1. His knights, headed for e5 and possibly f4, look at least as good as Black's bishops;

2. Black's h-pawn is a source of concern;

3. Black's king looks more vulnerable than White's; and

4. If Black tries the cheapo 14...♘xd4??, he is the one cheapoed after 15 ♘xd4 ♕xc5?? 16 ♘xe6+.

6 ♕h5 cxd4

Black can also hold back on this exchange: 6...e6 7 0-0-0!? ♕a5 8 ♘ge2 ♗d7 9 ♔b1 b5 10 ♘f4! (target: d5) 10...b4 11 ♘cxd5 exd5 12 ♘xd5 ♗g7 13 ♗c4 0-0?! (he should have castled in the opposite direction, where White has compensation for the piece) 14 ♗d3 h6?? (he had to make a space for his king with 14...♖fd8) 15 ♘xf6+! 1-0 Bui Vinh-Dao Thien Hai, Hanoi 2009.

7 exd4 e6

Foolish is 7...♘xd4? 8 0-0-0 e5 9 ♘f3! ♗c5 (9...♘xf3?? 10 ♗b5+ ♗d7 11 ♖xd5 is crushing) 10 ♘xe5! and Black has a miserable position, V.Baci-A.Lo, correspondence 1999.

8 ♘f3!

A rare move, but a good one. Normally White castles, which I consider inferior to the text: 8 0-0-0 &b4 9 &ge2 &d7 10 g4 ₩e7 11 &g2 0-0-0 12 f4 &a5 13 &d3 &b8 14 f5 &c8 15 &f1 &c4 16 ₩h6 &hf8! 17 h4 &a8 18 fxe6 fxe6 19 &df3 &c7! 20 &b1 &b5 21 &xf6 &fc8 (there are too many black attackers around the white king) 22 c3 (22 &xe6 &xb2!) 22...&xb2 23 &xe6 ₩d7 24 &xb2 &xe2 25 &xe2 ₩b5! 26 &c2 &f8+ 0-1 O.Sagalchik-I.Krush, Seattle 2003.

8...&b4?!

Better to refrain from this pin. It turns out that exchanging on c3 isn't much of a threat.

9 &d3 &d7?!

Others:

a) 9...₩a5?! 10 0-0 &xc3 11 bxc3 ₩xc3 12 ₩h4 f5 13 &fe1 gives White more than enough compensation for the pawn.

b) 9...f5! 10 0-0 ₩f6 11 &e2 &d7 and White gains time with c3, but at least Black gets to castle queenside.

10 0-0 &xc3 11 bxc3 &a5?

I would have been a much stronger

player if I had not squandered a misspent youth reading Nimzowitsch! Black simply doesn't have the leisure of blockading c4. The kinetics of warfare require that he motorcade his king out of the centre as quickly as possible with 11...₩e7 12 c4 dxc4 13 &xc4 0-0-0 14 &ab1, but even here White's attacking chances look quite promising.

12 &fe1 ₩e7

Black must be very careful to avoid immediate punishment:

a) 12...&c6?? 13 &xe6+.

b) 12...&f8? 13 ₩h6+ &e7 14 &h4 &c6 15 ₩g7! and the threat of &f5+ wins a pawn since 15...&f8?? is met by 16 &xe6+! &xe6 17 &f5+ &d6 18 ₩g3+ &e7 19 &e1 mate.

13 &h4! &g8?

He is really asking for it, hanging around in the centre. It was high time for 13...0-0-0! 14 ₩xd5 ₩a3 15 ₩h5 ₩xc3 16 ₩xf7 ₩xd4 17 &f3 ₩c3 18 &ab1. Still, White has the better pawn structure and possibly the superior attacking chances.

14 ₩xh7!

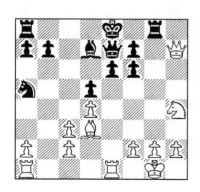

Black is in no position to launch an attack on the newly opened h-file.

14...♕f8

Forced, as 14...0-0-0? 15 ♘g6! ♕e8 (or 15...♕a3 16 ♕xf7 when White is two pawns up and menaces both ♕xf6 and also ♘e7+) 16 ♕xg8! wins the exchange.

15 ♕f5 ♕h6

After 15...♕e7? 16 ♕f4 0-0-0 17 ♘f5 ♕f8 18 ♘d6+ ♚b8 19 ♘b5+! e5 20 ♖xe5! ♖g4 21 ♕xf6 all the tactics work for White.

16 ♕xd5 ♕xh4 17 ♕xa5 ♗c6 18 d5!

Well calculated. White avoids the trap 18 g3?? ♕xh2+!.

18...b6

Cutting off the queen's connection to d5. It appears that Black's attack is beginning to take shape, but it turns out that appearance is all there is.

19 ♕a3!

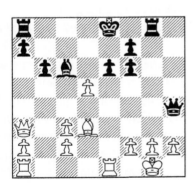

Black's attack is, indeed, a mirage.

19...♖xg2+?

The main point of 18 d5! is the line 19...♗xd5?? 20 ♗b5+ ♚d8 21 ♕d6+ ♚c8 22 ♗a6+ ♚b7 23 ♕c6+.

Instead, 19...♕g5! puts up the most resistance after 20 ♗e4 ♗xd5 21 ♕a4+ ♚f8 22 ♕b4+ ♚g7 (22...♚e8 23 f4! ♕h5 24 f5! and Black's king is in great danger) 23 ♖e3! ♗xe4 24 ♖g3 when the shattered queenside pawns could give White some technical difficulties in converting.

20 ♚xg2 ♗xd5+ 21 ♚f1 ♕h3+ 22 ♚e2 ♕f3+ 23 ♚d2 ♕f4+ 24 ♖e3 ♕xf2+ 25 ♖e2 ♕f4+ 26 ♚e1 0-0-0

Or 26...♕h4+ 27 ♖f2 and the checks are at an end.

27 ♕xa7!

He is unafraid of ghosts.

27...♖g8 28 ♗a6+ ♚d8 29 ♕xb6+

Very convenient. The queen covers g1.

29...♚d7

30 ♕e3! ♕d6

30...♕xe3 fails miserably to 31 ♖xe3 ♖g1+ 32 ♗f1 ♗g2 33 ♚f2.

31 ♕a7+ ♚d8 32 ♖b1 1-0

Summary

8 ♘f3! planning to castle kingside is White's best option in this line.

Game 33
J.Bosch-L.Ftacnik
Hamburg 2009

1 d4 ♞f6 2 ♞c3 d5 3 ♗g5 c5 4 ♗xf6 gxf6 5 e3 ♞c6 6 ♕h5 cxd4 7 exd4 e6 8 ♞f3 ♗d7!

On any other move, White plays ♗b5! and exchanges bishop for knight.

9 ♗d3

White is willing to allow Black both bishops and play in pure Chigorin style with a knight pair.

9...f5!

This miracle of self-restraint shows a deep understanding of the position. Most players would plunge forward to get the bishop pair with 9...♞b4?!, but this is exactly what White desires. Then 10 0-0-0 ♖c8 11 a3 and:

a) 11...♞xd3+ 12 ♖xd3 ♗g7 13 ♞d2! and the rook on d3 serves two functions: it protects the king, by covering sacs and tactics on c3, and is ready to swing into action on the kingside or centre to go after Black's king.

b) 11...♖xc3?! 12 bxc3 ♞xd3+ 13 cxd3 ♗a4 14 ♖de1 ♗xa3+ 15 ♔d2 0-0 16 ♖a1 ♕e7 17 h4! and White has by far the more dangerous attack, with 18 ♞g5! a serious threat and ♖h3 is in the air.

10 0-0!

Bosch is a Veresov specialist and understands it deeply. His philosophy is castle kingside if you can. The queenside can be a death trap on the open c-file. Surprisingly, it is difficult for Black to get anything going on the open g-file.

10...♕f6 11 ♖fe1 0-0-0 12 ♗b5!

Nicely timed.

12...♕g6

And not 12...♞e7?? 13 ♗xd7+ ♖xd7 14 ♞e5.

13 ♕h3 f6

Again, 13...♞e7?? 14 ♞e5! wins the exchange.

14 ♗xc6 bxc6 15 g3 ♕g4?!

Or 15...f4 16 ♕f1! ♔b7 17 ♖ad1! and then:

a) 17...♕xc2? 18 ♖d3! ♔a8 19 ♖b1! ♖b8 20 ♞e1! traps the queen.

b) 17...h5 18 ♞h4 ♕g4 19 ♞a4 ♖g8 20 ♔h1 when I actually prefer White, although this may be no more than the prejudice of a former QGD Chigorin player. Unclear would be a safe (non) assessment here.

16 ♕f1!!

A shocker! He reroutes the queen, which is the puppeteer behind the curtain, toward a6 and proves that the knight is perfectly safe on f3.

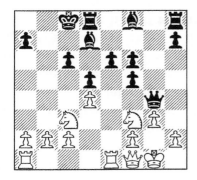

16...♔b7

After 16...♕xf3? 17 ♖e3 ♕g4 18 ♕a6+ ♔b8 19 ♘xd5! exd5 20 ♖b3+ ♔c7 21 ♕a5+ ♔d6 (forced) 22 ♕xd8 ♗g7 23 ♕a5 ♕xd4 24 ♖b7 the beleaguered black king gets no rest.

17 ♘a4! f4!

It is understandable that Ftacnik hurries to begin his own attack rather than deal with the terrors involved in 17...♕xf3?! 18 ♖e3 ♕g4 19 ♖b3+ ♔c7 20 ♕a6 ♔d6 21 ♕xa7 ♔e7 22 ♖b7 ♔e8 23 ♘b6 ♕g7 24 ♕a4! ♕e7 25 ♘xd7 ♖xd7 26 ♖xc6 ♕d6 27 ♕b5 ♖g8 28 ♖e1 and 29 ♖b6! comes next.

18 ♖ad1!

What nonchalance. White continues to find ways to leave his knight hanging on f3!

18...♖b8

Okay, let's have a look! 18...♕xf3?! 19 ♖d3 ♕g4 20 ♖b3+ ♔c7 21 ♕a6 ♔d6 22 ♕xa7 ♔e7 23 ♖b7 fxg3 24 hxg3 ♗g7 25 ♕c5+ ♔e8 26 ♘b6 h5 27 ♕d6! ♗f8 28 ♘xd7! ♗xd6 29 ♘xf6+ ♔f8 30 ♘xg4 hxg4 31 ♖xe6 leaves Black fighting for the draw.

19 ♖d3

Finally condescending to defend the knight, which has been hanging for three straight moves.

19...♗d6 20 ♖b3+ ♔a8 21 ♕d3 fxg3 22 hxg3 ♖hg8 23 ♖e3

23...♖xb3

Alternatively:

a) 23...♗xg3!? isn't a knockout: 24 fxg3 ♕xg3+ 25 ♔f1 e5 26 ♖xb8+ ♖xb8 (Black gets nowhere if he recaptures with his king: 26...♔xb8?? 27 ♘c5 ♗h3+ 28 ♔e2 and Black's attack is at a dead end) 27 ♘xe5 ♗h3+ 28 ♔e2 ♕g2+ 29 ♔e1 ♕g1+ 30 ♔d2 fxe5 31 ♖xe5 and I like White's structural advantages.

b) 23...♗f4 24 ♘h2! ♕g7 25 ♖e2 may be Black's most promising path. He can try prising open White's king position with ...h5 and ...h4 later, but White has adequate counterplay on the other side of the board. Also, White has the plan of simply walking his king over to the safety of the queenside.

24 axb3 h5 25 ♔f1!

The king simply strolls over to the other wing, where he will be secure.

25...♔b8 26 ♔e1 ♖e8 27 ♕c3

He hopes to prevent ...e5 and locks down c5.

27...e5!

Hey! Didn't you hear me? I said "prevent ...e5".

28 ♘c5

Black's trick is revealed if White takes with 28 dxe5?? ♗b4.

28...♗xc5 29 ♕xc5 e4 30 ♘h4

Black has gained central space, but suffers from dark-square weakness. One gets the sense that Black's king is in greater danger than White's.

30...♕h3 31 b4!

Threatening to undermine with b5.

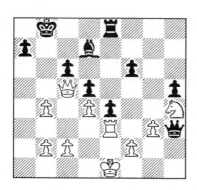

31...♕h1+ 32 ♔d2 ♕f1 33 ♕d6+ ♔c8 34 ♕xf6 ♕c4 35 ♖c3!

35 c3 ♕a2 36 ♔c1 (36 ♔c2?? c5! unleashes the bishop and wins) 36...♕a1+ 37 ♔c2 ♕a4+ is drawn.

35...♕xb4 36 ♘g6! ♖e6

36...♕xb2?? allows a dark-squared attack with 37 ♖b3 ♕a1 38 ♕d6! and then:

a) 38...♕a5+ 39 ♔c1 ♕c7 40 ♘e7+ ♖xe7 41 ♕xe7.

b) 38...♕xd4+ 39 ♔c1 ♕a1+ 40 ♖b1 wins the queen.

37 ♕h8+ ♖e8 38 ♕f6 ♖e6 39 ♕g7!

Rightly playing for the win.

39...♖xg6?!

Losing his cool. He may yet save the game in the long line 39...a5 40 ♘f4 ♖e7 41 ♕f6 ♔b7 42 ♔c1 a4 43 ♕f8! a3! 44 ♖b3 ♕xb3! 45 cxb3 a2 46 ♕xe7 a1♕+ 47 ♔c2 ♔c8 48 ♕f8+ ♔c7 49 ♘xh5 ♕f1! 50 ♕f4+ ♔b7 51 ♕e3 ♗g4 52 ♘f4 when progress will be next to impossible, despite White's two extra pawns.

40 ♕xg6 ♕xd4+ 41 ♔e1 ♕b4 42 ♔f1?!

He can take on h5 since 42 ♕xh5! d4? is met by 43 ♕c5!.

42...♕xb2 43 ♕g8+ ♔c7 44 ♖b3 ♕c1+ 45 ♔g2

Threatening mate on b8.

45...♔d6 46 ♕b8+ ♔e6 47 ♖b7 ♕g5

If 47...♕xc2?? then 48 ♕d8!.

48 ♕c7 ♕e7 49 ♖xa7 ♕d6 50 ♕d8 ♕e7 51 ♕h8 ♔d6 52 ♕b8+ ♔e6 53 ♕f4 ♕g7 54 c4!

Breaking down the protective barrier around the black king.

54...dxc4

He must, since 54...♕e7? 55 c5! ♕xc5 56 ♕h6+ wins.

55 ♕xe4+ ♔d6 56 ♕f4+

Certainly not 56 ♕xc4?? ♗h3+ 57 ♔xh3 ♕xa7.

56...♔c5 57 ♕e3+ ♔d6 58 ♕d2+ ♔e6 59 ♕e2+ ♔d6 60 ♕d1+ ♔e6 61 ♕xh5 ♕d4 62 ♕h6+ ♔e7 63 ♕g5+ ♔d6 64 ♕h6+?!

It was time to simplify with 64 ♕e3! ♕xe3 65 fxe3 c3 66 ♔f3 c2 67 ♖a1 ♔e5 68 ♔e2 c5 69 ♔d2 ♗f5 70 ♖a4 ♗d3 71 ♖f4 c4 72 g4 ♔e6 73 g5 ♔e5 74 ♖f6 ♗h7 75 ♖h6 ♗d3 76 ♖b6 and g6 cannot be stopped.

64...♗e6 65 ♕f8+ ♔d5 66 ♖a5+ c5 67 ♕d8+ ♔e4 68 ♕g5?

Missing another win with 68 f3+! ♔d3 69 ♕b6 ♗d5 70 ♕b1+ ♔e3 71 ♕e1+ ♔d3 72 ♕f1+ ♔c3 73 ♖a2!, which leaves Black helpless against White's multiple threats.

68...♗d5 69 f3+! ♔d3 70 ♖a3+?

Essentially handing Black a tempo. 70 ♖a2! forces the win: 70...c3 71 ♕g6+ ♔e3 72 ♕e8+! ♔d3 73 ♕e2 mate!

70...c3 71 ♕c1 ♕e5 72 ♕f1+ ♔d2 73

♕f2+ ♔d3 74 ♕f1+ ♔d2 75 ♕f2+ ♔d3

Unfortunately, White missed his opportunities to win and now tries his best to lose! It's like a guy who pulls off a string of robberies, feels bad about it, and immediately sets up a fund to compensate his victims!

76 ♖a1??

He should take the draw.

76...♕e2!

Gulp! Now White is totally busted. He allowed the c-pawn to travel too far down the board.

77 ♔g1 ♕xf2+! 78 ♔xf2 ♔d2??

Suddenly it's a draw, but the simple 78...c2! wins easily after 79 ♔e1 ♔c3 80 f4 c4 81 g4 ♔b2 82 ♖d1 cxd1♕+ 83 ♔xd1 c3.

79 ♖a5 c2 80 ♖xc5 ♗e6 1-0

Now in this drawn position Black lost on time. The entire game was like a balance scale, with one side going up and the other going down.

Summary

The important thing to remember from this game is that the fixed pawn struc-

structure arising out of the opening favours knights over bishops. Very few players know or understand this and your opponents will play the game as if they are winning or better, when they may be slightly worse!

Game 34
D.Arutinian-A.Kashlinskaya
Olomouc 2009

1 d4 ♘f6 2 ♘c3 d5 3 ♗g5 c5 4 ♗xf6 gxf6 5 e3 ♘c6 6 ♕h5 cxd4 7 exd4 e6 8 ♘f3 f5

8...♘e7!? was an attempt to side-step ♗b5, but 9 0-0-0 ♗d7 10 ♖e1 ♕b6 11 ♗d3 ♖c8 12 ♖e3 a5 13 ♖he1 a4 14 ♗b5!! ♗xb5 15 ♖xe6 ♕c7 16 ♖xf6 ♔d8 17 ♘e5 gave White a crushing attack in M.Rosenboom-D.Houpt, correspondence 2008.

9 ♗b5!

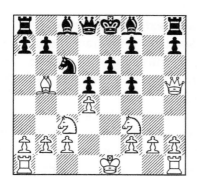

As we have seen, White fights hard to give away the bishops in this variation! He banks on the rigidity of the pawn structure to favour his knights.

9...♗g7 10 0-0!

The golden rule: castle kingside if possible.

♗d7 11 ♗xc6 ♗xc6 12 ♖fe1 0-0 13 ♘e2

White stands better. You don't believe me? Just watch. The bishops are clumsy in such structures.

13...♕d6 14 ♕h4 f6 15 ♘g3!

Eyeing h5 and ensuring that Black will not be playing ...e5 anytime soon.

15...♗e8 16 ♖e2 ♗b5 17 ♖ee1 ♗e8 18 ♘h5

No draw.

18...♗xh5 19 ♕xh5 ♖ae8 20 g3 ♕c7

If he undoubles with 20...f4 21 ♖e2 fxg3 22 hxg3 then Black must worry about a build-up on the h-file.

21 ♖e2 ♕f7 22 ♕h3! ♖c8 23 ♖ae1 ♖c6 24 c4!

Punching a hole through the wall and demonstrating that Black's control over c4 is not real.

24...♕d7

After 24...dxc4? 25 d5 exd5 26 ♖e7 ♕g6 27 ♘d4 White hits c6, e6 and f5 and Black soon collapses.

25 b3 b6

If 25...dxc4?! 26 bxc4 and d5 is coming.

26 ♘h4! ♖d8 27 ♕g2

27 ♘xf5!? is a speculative sac: 27...exf5 28 ♖e7 ♕d6 29 ♕h5 ♖f8 30 ♕xf5 ♖c7 (30...dxc4?? loses instantly to 31 ♕g4 ♖f7 32 ♖e8+ ♖f8 33 ♖1e7) 31 ♖xc7 ♕xc7 32 ♕xd5+ ♕f7 with three pawns for the piece.

27...♔f7?!

Missing his moment. Timing is critical in a chess game. Black misses his narrow window of opportunity to capture on c4, trading away his worries: 27...dxc4! 28 bxc4 ♖xc4! 29 ♖xe6 ♕xe6! 30 ♖xe6 ♖c1+ 31 ♕f1 ♖xf1+ 32 ♔xf1 ♖xd4 33 ♘xf5 ♖a4 34 ♖e2 with a balanced ending.

28 ♕f3 ♗f8 29 ♖e3 ♗b4 30 ♖1e2 ♗f8 31 ♔g2

White incrementally improves his position as long as Black must wait.

31...a5 32 h3 ♗g7?

Black finally cracks, allowing a breakthrough combination. Instead, 32...a4 holds things together.

33 ♕h5+ ♔g8 34 ♘xf5!

Breaking down the door.

34...dxc4

34...exf5?? 35 ♖e7 threatens the queen and also ♕f7+.

35 bxc4 ♕b7 36 ♔h2

Arutinian is a cool customer. His c-pawn has been hanging for 12 moves, and his knight for two!

36...♕f7 37 ♕xf7+ ♔xf7 38 d5!

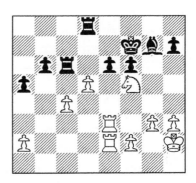

The long-awaited break arrives.

38...exd5

38...♖cc8 39 dxe6+ loses at least an exchange, no matter where Black moves his king.

39 ♖e7+ ♔g6 40 ♘xg7 dxc4 41 ♘e6 ♖d1 42 ♘f8+ ♔f5 43 ♖xh7 1-0

It is mate in three moves.

Summary

Remember: in this line, knights rule!

> ### Game 35
> ### C.McKenzie-S.Rey
> ### correspondence 1995

1 d4 ♘f6 2 ♗g5

Yes, many Veresov positions arise from a Trompowsky move order.

2...d5 3 ♘c3 c6 4 ♕d3

Perhaps for us, this is the simplest move, since Black can transpose directly to Chapter Two with 4...♘bd7, but even if Black plays other moves we are still in familiar territory and in our comfort zone.

4...b6!?

This is an idea used in the Fantasy Variation of the Caro-Kann. Black prepares to irritate the queen on d3 with ...♗a6.

Instead, 4...g6 5 f3 ♕a5 6 h4!? (as usual, Moro is the first to do something odd; his idea is to play e4, and then after ...dxe4 his bishop doesn't hang on g5, but one obvious defect with the plan is that he gives up control over g4) 6...b5 7 e4 b4 8 ♘ce2 ♗a6 9 ♕e3 dxe4 10 fxe4 ♘bd7 11 ♘f3 ♗g7 was A.Morozevich-V.Malaniuk, Alushta 1994, and now White should play 12 ♘c1 with reasonable prospects.

5 ♘f3

Being a Tromp player, I am accus-

tomed to chopping knights on f6 and would probably go for 5 ♗xf6!? when 5...gxf6 (or 5...exf6 6 e4 ♗a6 7 ♕e3 ♗e7 8 0-0-0) 6 e4 looks pleasant for White.

5...♗a6 6 ♕e3!

This odd move is an improvement over the 6 ♕d2 ♘e4 7 ♕e3 (he had to move the queen to e3 anyway, since Black has a nice position after 7 ♘xe4 dxe4 8 ♘g1 ♕d5 9 ♗f4 ♘d7) 7...♘xg5 8 ♕xg5 ♘d7 9 e4 ♗xf1 10 ♖xf1 of H.Arnold-R.Halle Allende, correspondence 1994, and here 10...e6 gives Black at least equality.

6...e6 7 0-0-0 ♗e7 8 h3 ♘bd7 9 g4 c5 10 ♗xf6 ♘xf6 11 ♘e5 ♕c7 12 f4 b5 13 g5 cxd4

Or 13...b4 14 gxf6 gxf6 5 ♘xd5 exd5 16 ♘g4 0-0-0 with complex play.

14 ♕xd4 ♗c5 15 ♕d3 ♘e4

15...♘d7? 16 ♘xd7 ♕xf4+? (Black also struggles after 16...♕xd7 17 e4) 17 ♔b1 ♔xd7 18 ♘xd5! ♕d6 19 ♗g2! exd5 20 ♕f5+ ♕e6 21 ♖xd5+ ♗d6 22 ♖xd6+! ♔xd6 23 ♖d1+ ♔c7 24 ♕f4+ regains the material with a winning position.

16 ♘xe4 dxe4 17 ♕xe4?

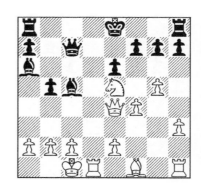

Very brave but also unsound. White should play the safer 17 ♕b3 ♗d6 18 e3 0-0 19 ♘g4.

17...♗b7 18 ♕d3 ♗xh1?

The initiative is more important than material in this position. Black takes over with 18...0-0! 19 e4 ♖fd8 20 ♕f3 ♖xd1+ 21 ♔xd1 ♗d4! 22 ♘d3 ♕c4 23 ♘c1 ♕c6 and White is on the verge of collapse.

19 ♕xb5+ ♔f8 20 ♖d7?

Unsound. Instead of unleashing the Manchurian candidate on d7, why not simply regain the material? 20 ♕xc5+! ♕xc5 21 ♘d7+ ♔e7 22 ♘xc5 and White gets two pawns for the exchange with reasonable chances.

20...♕c8 21 ♕d3

Or 21 ♖xf7+ ♔g8 and White doesn't have enough for the rook.

21...f6??

The simple block 21...♗e7 wins.

22 gxf6 gxf6 23 ♖f7+ 1-0

Black collapses after 23...♔e8 24 ♕b5+ ♗c6 25 ♕xc5. I have observed that fortune often smiles on the unsound!

Summary

4...b6 attempts to take advantage of the white queen's position by harassing her with ...♗a6.

Game 36
A.Fier-D.Lima
Vitoria 2006

1 d4 ♘f6 2 ♗g5 c6 3 ♘c3 d5 4 ♕d3 b5

This is similar to Kozul-Brkic, from Chapter Two, except that White's g1-knight and Black's b8-knight are on their original squares.

5 a3 e6

Alternatively:

a) 5...a5 6 e4 ♗a6 7 b4! ♗b7 was H.Schumacher-N.Miezis, Seefeld 2004, and now 8 ♖b1! gives an edge.

b) 5...g6 6 ♗xf6 (6 f3 is also possible) 6...exf6 7 e4 b4! 8 axb4 ♗xb4 9 exd5 0-0 10 ♗e2 ♖e8 11 ♘f3 a5 12 0-0 ♗a6 13 ♕d1 ♗xc3 14 ♗xa6 ♗xb2 15 ♗b7 ♖a7 16 dxc6 ♗xa1 17 ♕xa1 with compensation for the exchange, D.Sengupta-A.Jakubiec, Thessaloniki 2007.

6 e4 dxe4?

Black ends up with a bad Caro position because his ...b5 doesn't fit with the structure. After 6...♗e7 Black stands only a shade worse.

7 ♘xe4 ♗e7 8 ♗xf6 gxf6

He really must play this since he has nothing to show for his queenside pawn weaknesses if he plays it safe with 8...♗xf6?! 9 ♘xf6+ ♕xf6 10 ♘f3.

9 ♘f3

An assessment:

1. Black owns the bishop pair;

2. Black's pawns are slightly damaged on both wings; and

3. Black must solve the question of where to place his king. There is no obvious safe haven for it anywhere on the board.

Conclusion: White stands better.

9...♕a5+?!

Black's biggest problem is that he doesn't realize he stands worse. He should play more carefully with 9...♘d7 10 g3 ♗b7 11 ♗g2 ♕c7 12 0-0 and then pick a wing for his king.

10 ♘ed2 b4?!

Weakening his pawns for no good reason.

11 ♘c4 ♕c7 12 axb4 ♗xb4+ 13 c3 ♗e7 14 ♗e2 ♘d7 15 0-0 ♖b8 16 ♖a2

A strategic disaster is in the making for Black, as his a-pawn is a sitting duck on an open file and if he tries to dissolve with ...c5, then White simply bypasses with d5!, leaving Black's king a cause for concern down the road.

16...♖b5!? 17 ♖fa1 a6 18 ♘e3 ♖h5?!

Good luck with this 'attack'! This is like trying to break into a heavily-armed, military compound. There are defenders everywhere and Black attacks without space.

19 ♕d1!

Hitting a6.

19...♘b8

If one feels the need to make a defensive retreat like this in the middle of an assault, you know something has gone badly awry.

20 g3 ♖h6 21 b4!

Locking down targets on a6 and c6.

21...♖g6 22 ♗d3 ♖g7 23 ♕e1 0-0

Giving up on his dreams. If he con-

continues to attack with 23...f5 then 24 ♘g2 h5 25 ♔f1 ♗b7 26 ♕e3 shuts Black down.

24 ♘c4 f5 25 ♕e5!

Following three principles. When under attack:

1. Counter in the centre;
2. Centralize; and
3. Swap pieces.

25...♕xe5 26 ♘fxe5 f6

He will have to play this sooner or later, but now e6 is a new concern for Black.

27 ♘f3 ♖ff7 28 ♘fd2

Black's structure is riddled with pawn weaknesses. Now it is just a matter of which target is next.

28...♗f8 29 ♘b6! ♗b7 30 ♗c4! ♖e7 31 ♖e1 ♔f7 32 ♘b3 1-0

33 ♘c5 followed by ♖ae2 is strategic Armageddon.

Summary

One of the patterns Black inadvertently steps into is bad French or Caro-Kann structures, often with one strange move tossed in. In this case his ...b5 did not fit with the Caro pawn structure.

1 d4 ♘f6 2 ♘c3 d5 3 ♗g5 g6?!

The Grünfeld against the Veresov. White should get a dangerous attack going if he plays the normal Barry Attack plan of ♕d2, f3, 0-0-0 and ♗h6. The difference between this position and the Barry is the absence of ♘f3, which is replaced with the more aggressive f3, allowing White to speed up his attack.

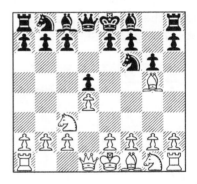

4 ♕d2

If you prefer, you can go Trompowsky style and take on f6: 4 ♗xf6 exf6 5 e3 ♗g7 6 ♗d3 0-0 7 ♕f3 c6 8 g4!, which looked like fun in A.Miles-L.Spassov, Surakarta 1982.

4...♗g7 5 ♗h6?!

Premature. 5 f3! played by Hector in our next game is the correct sequence.

5...0-0?!

5...♗xh6! intending to castle the other wing is duller and wiser: **6 ♕xh6 c5! 7 e3 ♘c6 8 0-0-0 ♕a5 9 ♘f3 ♗g4 10 dxc5** and ½-½ was R.Mateo-F.De la Paz Perdomo, Havana 2007. Of course, either side may play on.

6 0-0-0 c6 7 f3 b5 8 h4 ♘h5?

Daydreaming while his house is on fire. Black should take swift action on the queenside instead of playing on his opponent's strong wing. Better was **8...♕a5 9 h5 b4 10 ♗xg7 ♔xg7 11 hxg6 fxg6 12 ♘b1.**

9 g4 ♘g3 10 ♖h3 ♘xf1

Black invested four tempi to exchange a piece which never moved!

11 ♖xf1 f5!

He must counter vigorously in the centre, otherwise he gets crushed.

12 ♗xg7 ♔xg7 13 h5!

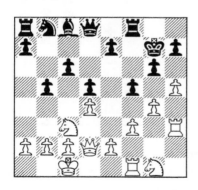

The rule of thumb in such positions is to be generous with your pawns to open lines. Take a look at Black's army. His only developed piece is his king!

13...fxg4 14 ♖h1 ♕d6 15 hxg6 ♕xg6 16 ♘h3! gxh3!?

A desperado, but the alternatives don't look so great either:

a) **16...b4 17 ♘d1 ♘d7 18 ♘f4 ♕d6 19 fxg4.**

b) **16...g3 17 ♖fg1 g2 18 ♖h2 ♗xh3 19 ♖xh3 ♔h8 20 ♖h2 ♘d7 21 ♖hxg2 ♕f6 22 ♖h2.**

17 ♖fg1 ♗e6 18 ♘d1 ♘d7 19 ♘f2 ♖f6 20 ♕c3 ♕g2?

A better attempt would be to try and make something of his passed h-pawn in the line **20...♕xg1+! 21 ♖xg1 ♔f7 22 ♕xc6 ♖g8.**

21 ♖xg2+ hxg2 22 ♖g1 ♖g6 23 ♕xc6 ♖g8 24 e4

24 ♘d3! is stronger.

24...♔f7

24...♖f8 25 exd5 ♖xf3 26 dxe6 ♖xf2 27 ♖xg2 ♖gxg2 28 ♕xg2+! ♖xg2 29 exd7 would have been a cute finish.

25 ♕xb5 ♖g5 26 f4! 1-0

Another one bites the dust after White plays f5 next move.

Summary

The Grünfeld against the Veresov is more dangerous for Black than it first appears. White gets a superior version of the Barry Attack.

Game 38
J.Hector-D.Howell
St Helier 2005

GMs Hector and Khachian are neck-and-neck in a race to see which of them gets more of their games in this book.

1 d4 ♘f6 2 ♘c3 d5 3 ♗g5 g6?! 4 ♕d2

♗g7 5 f3!

A more accurate move order than last game. White waits until Black commits to castling kingside before playing ♗h6.

5...0-0

5...h6 can be tossed in to prevent ♗h6: 6 ♗h4 0-0 7 0-0-0 c6 8 e4 b5!? (this loses a pawn, but what else?) 9 ♗xf6! ♗xf6 10 exd5! (10 ♕xh6!? e5 11 h4 exd4 12 ♘ce2 dxe4 13 fxe4 c5 14 ♘f3 leads to a mess; I'm not sure if Black survives the coming attack, but if he does his static advantages will be decisive) 10...cxd5 11 ♗xb5 e6 12 f4! and the open b-file didn't fully compensate Black for the pawn, G.Meszaros-B.Tomic, Zenica 2002.

6 0-0-0 c5 7 dxc5 ♕a5 8 ♔b1 ♘c6 9 e4 d4

Black doesn't get enough in the line 9...dxe4?! 10 ♘xe4 ♖d8 11 ♗d3 ♕xd2 12 ♖xd2 ♗e6 13 ♘e2.

10 ♘b5!

Seeing that the ending is in White's favour, whereas after 10 ♗xf6 ♗xf6 11 ♘d5 ♕xc5 12 ♘xf6+ exf6 13 ♘e2 ♖d8

14 h4 both sides are attacking.

10...♕xd2 11 ♖xd2 ♘d7 12 ♘e2 e5 13 c3!

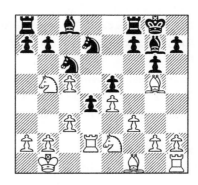

Black is slightly behind in development and isn't ready for the confrontation as White cuts open a central artery.

13...♘xc5!

Black has a difficult ending to defend in the line 13...dxc3: for example, 14 ♘exc3 ♘xc5 15 ♘d5 ♘e6 16 ♗e7! ♘xe7 17 ♘xe7+ ♔h8 18 ♘d6 wins material.

14 cxd4 exd4 15 ♘exd4 ♘xd4 16 ♘xd4 ♗xd4 17 ♖xd4 ♘e6 18 ♖d5 ♘xg5 19 ♖xg5 f5

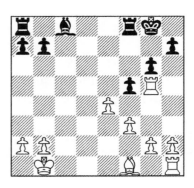

Black hopes the off-kilter position of White's rook, which for now looks like a child lost at the mall, gives him enough compensation for the pawn.

20 ♗d3 ♖d8 21 ♗c2 ♔f7 22 exf5 ♔f6 23 h4 ♗xf5 24 ♗xf5 gxf5 25 ♖h5 ♔g6 26 g4! fxg4?!

Black's best drawing chance lies in 26...♖d5! 27 ♖e1 ♖ad8 28 ♖xf5 ♖xf5 29 gxf5+ ♔f7! and conversion will not be easy.

27 fxg4 ♖ac8?

He had to try 27...h6!.

28 ♖g5+ ♔h6 29 ♖e1 ♖c6 30 a3 ♖d2 31 ♖b5 b6 32 ♖e7

Threatening a7 and also 33 ♖h5+. Black is busted.

32...♖d4

Dropping a rook, but 32...♖c5 33 ♖xc5 bxc5 34 ♖xa7 ♖d4 35 g5+ ♔g6 36 ♖a6+ ♔g7 37 ♖h6 was hopeless.

33 ♖h5+ ♔g6 34 ♖exh7 1-0

Summary

5 f3! waiting for Black to castle is White's best move order. After all, we don't want to spook Black into castling queenside.

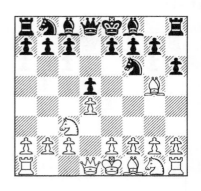

Game 39
C.Lakdawala-Barquin
San Diego (rapid) 2010

1 d4 d5 2 ♘c3 ♘f6 3 ♗g5 h6?!

Black wants the bishop pair so badly that he is willing to invest a tempo to achieve it.

4 ♗xf6

Of course. When you make this move be sure to thank your opponent for the free tempo!

4...exf6 5 e3 c6

After 5...♗f5?! 6 ♕f3! ♗xc2 7 ♖c1 ♗g6 8 ♕xd5 8...♘c6 9 ♗b5 ♕xd5 10 ♘xd5 0-0-0 11 ♗xc6 bxc6 12 ♘f4 I doubt that Black's bishops make up for the damage to his pawn structure.

6 ♗d3 ♗d6 7 ♕f3

Seizing control over f5.

7...0-0

Or 7...♘a6 8 a3 ♘c7 9 ♘ge2 ♘e6 10 h4 h5 11 e4! (playing his trump card and achieving the healthy majority on the queenside) 11...dxe4 12 ♗xe4 ♕b6 13 0-0-0 with a clear advantage to White in R.Bellin-J.Prins, Guernsey 2008. White has the better development, the stronger pawn centre, more space and a strong queenside pawn majority versus Black's crippled majority on the kingside, while the only factor Black can take consolation in is his bishop pair.

An IM once told me in an accusing

tone that I am afflicted with the Chigorin disease, where I secretly love knights and despise bishops. I cannot tell a lie and confess this to be true. Believe it or not, here I would have taken the other knight without hesitation: 8 ♗xa6!? bxa6 9 ♘ge2 ♖b8 10 ♖b1 0-0 11 0-0 when I prefer the knights and the better structure over Black's bishop pair.

8 ♘ge2 ♖e8 9 h4

With two possible ideas:

1. Play for g4-g5 to open lines; and

2. Play for h5 and g4 to take control over the light squares and f5.

9...b5

10 ♘g3

Alternatively:

a) 10 ♗xb5?? is an incorrect combination: 10...cxb5 11 ♕xd5 ♖e7 12 ♕xa8 ♗b7 13 ♕xa7 ♗xg2 and Black wins.

b) I felt 10 e4!? opened the game prematurely and didn't care for White's game after 10...b4 11 ♘d1 dxe4 12 ♗xe4 ♕e7 13 ♗d3 ♗b7, but if I had looked deeper, I may have changed my mind after 14 ♘e3 c5 15 d5 ♘d7 16

♘f5 ♕f8 17 ♘xh6+! gxh6 18 ♕g4+ ♔h8 19 ♕xd7 ♖e7 20 ♕g4. By now I like White, but *Rybka* claims it's even!

10...a5

He would rather let me expend the energy to play the knight to f5, and then take it with his inferior bishop.

11 ♘ce2 ♖a7 12 ♘f5

I didn't want to commit to 12 h5?! just yet, because I still wanted to leave the option open for g4-g5. I saw 12...♘d7 13 ♘f5 ♗f8 14 ♖h4 ♘b6 15 ♘eg3 ♘c4 16 ♖g4 ♔h8 17 0-0-0?! a4 and was concerned that his attack was gaining momentum while mine had stalled.

12...♗xf5 13 ♕xf5 g6 14 ♕f3 ♔g7

14...h5? walks into 15 g4 hxg4 16 ♕xg4 ♕c8 17 ♕f3 ♘d7 18 h5 g5 19 h6, favouring White.

15 g4 ♖ae7 16 h5

16...♘a6?

He seriously underestimates the attacking potential and allows the opening of the h-file. 16...g5 creates an eyesore on f5 and weakens the light squares, but at least his king is a lot safer than in the game continuation.

17 hxg6 fxg6 18 0-0-0

In the game, I considered the Kamikaze sac 18 &xg6?? &xg6 19 &xh6+?? &xh6 20 Wxf6+ &h7 21 0-0-0 and for a moment I thought maybe it was a forced mate, until I saw 21...&g7! and White's attack is at a dead end, leaving him a rook and a piece in the hole.

18...&b4?

Begging White to sac! My opponent again underestimates the force of White's attack. Instead:

a) 18...&h8?! 19 a4! &b4 20 axb5 cxb5 21 &xb5 when White's king is safer than it looks and Black doesn't have full compensation for the pawn.

b) Best was 18...&b7! 19 c3. White stands better, but Black is in the game.

19 &xg6!

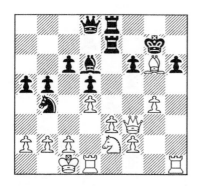

19...&h8!

Only move. Taking leads to mate: 19...&xg6?? 20 &xh6+ &xh6 21 Wxf6+ &h7 22 &h1+ &g8 23 &h8 mate.

20 &f5 &xa2+ 21 &d2

Heading to the safety of the other shore on the kingside. There is no reason to run to the danger zone on the

queenside.

21...a4 22 &a1

22 c3 b4 23 &a1 b3 24 &b1 wins a pawn, but I was after his king.

22...&b4 23 c3 &a6 24 &d3 Wc8

To cover f5.

25 &h5

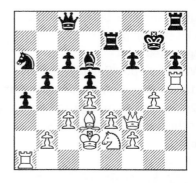

With the simple plan of tripling on the h-file and crashing through on h6.

25...&c7 26 &ah1 &e6

26...&e8 would make White work a bit harder for the win after 27 g5! fxg5 28 &xg5+! hxg5 29 &xh8 &c7 (or 29...&xh8 30 Wf8 mate) 30 Wh5.

27 &xh6!

27...&xh6 28 &xh6 1-0

Summary

As a sometime Trompowsky player, I jump for joy when Black sacrifices a tempo with 3...h6. In many lines White takes on f6 unprovoked, so 3...h6 is a pleasant surprise for White.

Game 40
S.Chekhov-V.Sokolovsky
Voronezh 2009

---

1 d4 ♘f6 2 ♘c3 d5 3 ♗g5 h6?! 4 ♗xf6 exf6 5 e3 ♗b4

Logical. Black wants to inflict damage of his own to White's pawn structure.

6 ♘ge2!

This plan also appears in some lines of the Trompowsky. White denies Black any structural damage on c3 and also prepares to fianchetto his bishop for maximum control over e4. The alternative is to allow Black to trade on c3: 6 ♗d3 ♗xc3+ 7 bxc3 c5 8 ♘f3?! (8 dxc5!, to clear d4 and create a target on d5, is worth the tripled pawns) 8...c4! 9 ♗e2

0-0 10 0-0?! (last chance for 10 e4!) 10...♖e8 and in N.Kuijf-*Comp Zarkov II*, The Hague 1993, White was in the embarrassing situation of having been strategically outplayed by a computer! Black stood better for four reasons:

1. c3 is a fixed target;

2. It will be next to impossible for White to achieve the freeing e4 pawn break, especially if Black follows with ...f5;

3. Black has a clamping space advantage; and

4. White's 'good' bishop performs no better than Black's bad bishop. However, just like in *Terminator*, the human managed to overcome the machine in the end.

6...0-0 7 a3 ♗a5 8 b4 ♗b6 9 g3 ♗g4?!

9...f5! denies e4 ideas from White.

10 ♗g2 c6 11 h3 ♗h5?!

Instead, 11...♗xe2?! 12 ♘xe2 f5 13 ♕d3 g6 14 c4 dxc4 15 ♕xc4 gives White queenside pressure, but 11...♗f5! keeps the bishop active and fights for the critical e4-square.

12 ♕d2!

Planning ♘f4, followed by e4!

♘d7 13 ♘f4 ♗g6 14 0-0 ♗c7

Intending 15...♘b6 and ...♘c4.

15 e4!

Achieving the thematic pawn break, which gives White the better pawn majority.

15...dxe4 16 ♘xe4 f5?!

There is no reason to demote the bishop to a menial role on g6. Instead better to just fire the bishop with

16...♗xe4! 17 ♗xe4 ♘b6 18 c3 ♘c4 19 ♕d3 ♗xf4 20 ♕xc4 ♗c7. Here White can eventually transform his majority into a passed pawn, while Black cannot on the other wing, but the presence of opposite-coloured bishops gives Black hopes of a draw.

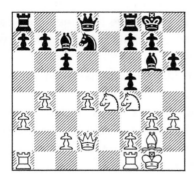

17 ♘c5 ♘xc5 18 bxc5 ♕f6 19 c4 b6 20 d5!

Wasting no time in creating a passed pawn.

20...bxc5

Black is unlikely to save himself in the line 20...♗xf4 21 ♕xf4 cxd5 22 ♗xd5 ♖ae8 23 c6.

21 dxc6 ♖ad8

21...♕g5 22 ♖ab1 ♖fd8 23 ♗d5 keeps a grip on the position.

22 ♘d5 ♕d6 23 ♕f4!

Breaking down the blockade and threatening ♘xc7.

23...♖c8

23...♗xf4 24 gxf4 ♗d6 25 ♖ab1 ♗h5 26 ♖b7 ♗e2 27 ♖c1 is lost for Black.

24 ♖ab1 ♖fe8 25 ♘xc7! ♕xf4 26 gxf4 ♖xc7 27 ♖b7 ♖ec8 28 ♖xc7 ♖xc7 29 ♖b1

There is no defence to ♖b7 and the destruction of the blockade on c7. Black's king is too far away to help, while the bishop avoids participation and continues to sulk on g6.

29...♔f8 30 ♖b7 ♖c8 31 ♖xa7 ♔e8 32 a4 ♗h5 33 a5 ♗d1 34 a6 ♗a4 35 ♖b7 ♗xc6 36 ♗xc6+ ♖xc6 37 a7 ♖g6+ 38 ♔f1 1-0

Summary

Some of my older Veresov books claim equality for Black in the 3...h6 line, but I don't believe them. My Trompowsky instincts tell me that Black will later be made to pay for wasting a tempo.

Chapter Four
Veresov versus French: Lines with ...♘f6

1 d4 ♘f6 2 ♘c3 d5 3 ♗g5 e6 4 e4

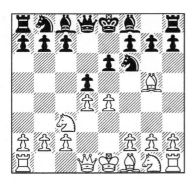

Many of your opponents just don't want to deal with the main lines of the Veresov and will sidestep them, choosing to transpose into other openings. The most common switch is to French lines with ...♘f6. In 2010, so far I have played nine Veresovs over the board and six of them turned into French ...♘f6 lines! That's a pretty high percentage, so this is quite an important chapter for those of you keen to take up the Veresov.

We reach the French via 1 d4 ♘f6 2 ♘c3 d5 3 ♗g5 and at this point, your opponent begins to get cold feet, realizing he doesn't know a thing about the Veresov and impulsively he responds with 3...e6 4 e4, and lo and behold, we have the French. The really wonderful benefit for you is that about 80% of your opposition will be unfamiliar with the black side of the French! This is not an opening conducive to groping in the dark and winging it!

After 4 e4 Black chooses among the following:

a) 4...dxe4 brings us to Rubinstein French lines with Black committed to ...♘f6 and White to ♗g5. Black hopes the insertion of the move pair favours him since he may get freeing trades with the bishop already posted on g5. After 5 ♘xe4 ♗e7 we chop the knight with 6 ♗xf6 to maintain our outpost on e4, leaving Black with a further choice:

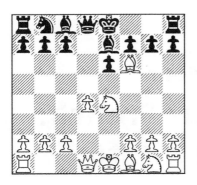

a1) 6...♗xf6 is the solid choice. Black gets the bishop pair and hopes to hit back in the centre with ...c5. Even when he does manage it, White's development tends to mean more than Black's bishop pair. Your extra space gives you attacking chances, especially if you decide to castle queenside.

a2) 6...gxf6!? is a super-aggressive option once played by Gurevich on Kasparov. Black agrees to the slight damage to his pawn structure, but in return he gets control over e5 and doesn't give White the option to take the bishop on f6. White's best line is to fianchetto and fight for control over d5.

b) Black can also head for the Classical French by playing 4...♗e7 5 e5 ♘fd7. Now I recommend the Alekhine-Chatard Gambit with 6 h4!?. It scores very well for White who gets a long-lasting initiative for only one pawn. Black can accept the pawn and try to ride out the storm, but more often than not he gets capsized by the turbulence. Black can also choose to decline the gambit, but even in the declined lines,

Black has no easy path to equality.

c) With 4...♗b4, Black enters the wild McCutcheon French. We take the air away with 5 exd5, the Lasker line. Black's choices are:

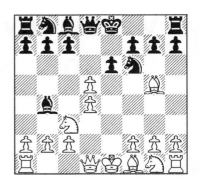

c1) 5...exd5 is the move most of your opponents will play, as in Lakdawala-Sevilliano. We go into a delayed Exchange French and deny Black his favourite set-ups. Black's bishop isn't so well placed on b4 in the Exchange lines. He will either have to take on c3, weakening his dark squares, or retreat the bishop later, losing a tempo.

b) 5...♕xd5 is usually awarded an '!' by the opening theorists. Then why does Black score so poorly with the line? We respond with 6 ♗xf6 with an unbalanced game, but I still believe slightly in White's favour.

Game 41
J.Smeets-J.De Jager
Dutch League 2010

1 e4 e6 2 d4 d5 3 ♘c3 ♘f6 4 ♗g5

Our move order would, of course, be 1 d4 ♘f6 2 ♘c3 d5 3 ♗g5 e6 4 e4.

4...dxe4

Transitioning from the Classical to the Rubinstein French. Black abdicates the centre with the intention to hit back later with ...c5, just as in a ...♘d7 Caro-Kann, but without having wasted a move on ...c7-c6. He also hopes that the inclusion of the moves ...♘f6 and ♗g5 will be in his favour and increase the likelihood of freeing trades.

5 ♘xe4

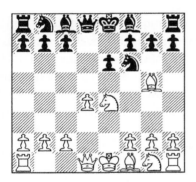

5...♗e7

Alternatively, 5...♘bd7 6 ♘f3 and then:

a) 6...♗e7 7 ♘xf6+ ♗xf6 8 h4! 0-0 9 ♗d3 (this position has similarities to our lines in Chapter Two) 9...c5 10 ♕e2! cxd4 11 ♕e4 g6 12 0-0-0 ♕a5?! 13 ♗xf6 ♘xf6 14 ♕xd4 ♘h5 15 a3 ♖d8 16 ♕e3 and in G.Kasparov-A.Shirov, Frankfurt (rapid) 2000, White had multiple dark-square invasion plans:

1. ♕h6, ♘g5 and h5, followed by ♘xh7 or simply hxg6;

2. g4, ♕f4, chase the knight away and then ♕h6; and

3. g4-g5 and possibly ♘e5 and ♘g4, followed by h5.

b) 6...h6 7 ♘xf6+ ♘xf6 8 ♗h4 c5 9 ♗b5+ ♗d7 10 ♗xd7+ ♕xd7 11 ♕e2! (a recurring theme: you temporarily sac your d-pawn, castle queenside, and then regain the pawn with a development lead) 11...cxd4 12 0-0-0 ♗c5 13 ♕e5! ♕e7 14 ♘xd4 0-0 15 ♖he1 ♖fd8 16 f4 ♖d5? (White had an edge but Black is busted after this blunder) 17 ♕xd5 exd5 18 ♖xe7 ♗xe7 19 ♘f5, winning a pawn and holding on to the initiative, V.Anand-M.Gurevich, Bastia (rapid) 2004.

6 ♗xf6

White wants to minimize the exchanges and is willing to trade bishop for knight to keep his powerful outpost on e4.

6...♗xf6

Next game, we examine the more dynamic and also more risky recapture 6...gxf6!?.

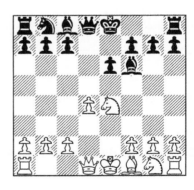

7 ♘f3 ♘d7

7...♘c6?! is a strategically dubious

move. My opponent gambles that he can force a favourable ...e5 break: 8 c3 0-0 (8...e5!? 9 d5 ♘e7 10 ♗b5+ ♗d7 11 ♕b3 isn't very tempting for Black) 9 ♗b5! ♕d5 10 ♗d3! ♖d8 (the point of White's manoeuvre is that 10...e5?! 11 dxe5 ♗xe5?? drops the queen to 12 ♘f6+! ♗xf6 13 ♗xh7+) 11 ♕c2 ♗e7 12 ♘ed2 h6 13 0-0 ♗d7 (he still can't force the break 13...e5? because 14 ♗h7+ ♔h8 15 ♗e4! wins a pawn) 14 ♖fe1 ♗e8 15 ♖e2 ♗f6 16 a3 ♔f8 17 ♖ae1 and Black can't free himself with ...c5 or ...e5 breaks, leaving his bishop pair meaning nothing in the blocked position, C.Lakdawala-J.Arnold, San Diego (rapid) 2010.

8 ♕d2 0-0 9 0-0-0

9...♗e7

Black prepares the freeing break ...c5.

10 ♕f4

Designed to discourage ...c5. Alternatives are:

a) 10 ♗d3 b6 11 h4 ♗b7 12 ♘eg5 ♘f6 13 c3 ♗xf3 14 gxf3 c5 15 dxc5 ♕c7 16 ♔b1 bxc5 17 ♖dg1 ♖fd8 18 ♕c2 h6

19 ♗h7+! ♔f8 20 ♘xf7! gave White a dangerous attack for the piece in V.Anand-E.Bareev, Wijk aan Zee 2004.

b) 10 h4 ♘f6 11 ♘xf6+ ♗xf6 12 ♗d3 c5 13 dxc5 ♕c7 14 ♘g5 h6! 15 ♘e4! (after 15 ♘h7? ♗e5! White can't take on f8 due to Black's pin trick on f4) 15...♗e5 16 ♔b1 f5 17 ♘d6 ♕xc5 18 ♘c4 ♗f6 19 f4! b5 20 ♘e5! ♗xe5 21 fxe5 ♕xe5 22 ♖he1 ♕c5 23 g4! and White had sufficient compensation for the pawn, V.Anand-T.Radjabov, Dubai (rapid) 2002.

10...c5?

Opening the centre too soon. He should patiently develop with 10...b6! 11 ♗c4 ♘f6! 12 ♘xf6+ ♗xf6 13 d5?! (13 ♗d3!) 13...e5! and Black stood better in A.Chudinovskih-D.Kovalev, Yuzhny 2008, since 14 ♘xe5?? hangs the queen to 14...♗g5.

11 d5!

Correctly assessing that the game opening up favours his development lead over Black's bishop pair. After the opening of the d-file:

1. White's activity grows sub-

stantially due to his powerful central-ized pieces;

2. White's rook on d5 has possibili-ties of swings over to g5 or h5; and

3. The presence of Black's c-pawn impinges upon Black's counterplay down the c-file and also plugs up the c5-square, making it unavailable for his pieces.

11...exd5 12 ♖xd5 ♕b6

If 12...♕a5? 13 a3 and then:

a) 13...♘b6 14 ♖h5 and White's pieces loom ominously over the king-side, but perhaps this is Black's best shot here.

b) 13...♘f6? 14 ♘xf6+ ♗xf6 15 ♗d3 ♗e6 16 ♖h5 h6 17 ♖xh6! yields a crush-ing attack.

13 ♗c4 ♕b4?!

After 13...♘f6 14 ♘xf6+ ♗xf6 15 c3 ♗e6 16 ♖d6 ♕c7 17 ♗xe6 fxe6 18 ♕d2 Black has no compensation for his weak e-pawn. Still, this may be Black's best line.

14 ♗b3 ♘f6

The rook floats in the centre like a drifting cloud. Normally in the early middlegame, we post our rooks on the first rank, keeping them a safe distance from the enemy pieces. Here Smeets accurately determines that Black can't capitalize on the rook's position.

15 ♖e5! ♗d6?!

15...♗d8 16 ♘fg5! puts tremendous pressure on Black.

16 ♘xf6+ gxf6 17 ♕xf6!

Far more energetic than trying to milk the superior ending after 17 ♕xb4 cxb4 18 ♖d5.

17...♗xe5 18 ♘xe5 ♗e6 19 c3!

Transferring the bishop to c2, to take aim at the black monarch.

19...♕e4?!

Slightly superior, but still insuffi-cient was 19...♕b6 20 ♗c2 ♖fd8 21 ♕g5+ ♔f8 22 ♕h6+ ♔e7 23 ♖e1! when Black can't escape the crossfire.

20 ♕g5+ ♔h8 21 ♗c2 ♕e2 22 ♕f6+ ♔g8 23 ♗d3! ♕h5 24 g4! 1-0

Now 24...♕h3 25 ♗f1! traps the queen.

Summary

Try to capitalize on your space advantage to whip up an attack through queenside castling versus the Rubinstein French. If Black achieves his freeing ...c5 break, this doesn't automatically alleviate his worries since he falls behind in development in a wide-open position.

Game 42
G.Kasparov-M.Gurevich
Sarajevo 2000

---

1 e4 e6 2 d4 d5 3 ♘c3 ♘f6 4 ♗g5 dxe4 5 ♘xe4 ♗e7 6 ♗xf6 gxf6!?

An aggressive option which I sometimes play when on the other side of the board. Black allows damage to his structure, but takes control over e5 and retains the bishop pair.

7 ♘f3 a6

Planning a Meran Slav strategy with ...b5, ...♗b7, ...♘bd7 and ...c5 to challenge the centre and open the game for his bishops. Alternatively:

a) 7...f5 8 ♘c3 a6 9 g3! b5 10 ♗g2 ♗b7 11 0-0 c5 12 d5!! (a sparkling strategic piece sac) 12...b4 13 dxe6! (otherwise, Black wins a pawn for nothing) 13...bxc3 14 exf7+ ♔f8 15 ♕e2 cxb2 16 ♖ad1 ♕b6 17 ♖fe1 ♕f6 18 c3! ♗e4 19 ♘h4! ♘c6 20 ♗xe4 fxe4 21 ♕xe4 ♖d8 22 ♖b1 ♖d2 23 ♘f3 ♖d6 24 ♖xb2 ♔xf7 25 ♖b6 and Black never managed to shake off the pressure, which was worth more than the piece, V.Ivanchuk-S.Volkov, Saint Vincent 2005.

b) 7...b6!? is designed to deter White from a fianchetto: 8 ♗c4! (remaining flexible; 8 g3?! ♗b7 is not as effective: 9 ♕e2 ♕d5! 10 ♘ed2 ♘c6 11 c3 0-0-0 12 ♗g2 ♕h5 and at the minimum, Black had equality in F.Hellers-U.Andersson, Haninge 1989) 8...♗b7 9 ♕e2 c6 10 0-0 ♘d7 11 ♗a6! (principle: when your opponent has the bishop pair, swap one of them off if possible) 11...♗xa6 12 ♕xa6 ♕c7 13 c4 and in A.Shirov-J.Timman, Wijk aan Zee 2004, White had managed to remove one of Black's bishops, seize a space advantage and have the safer king.

8 g3!

Kingside fianchettoes are peculiar in king pawn openings, yet this is probably White's best plan. The idea is to challenge the h1-a8 diagonal and fight for control over d5. A couple of other options:

a) 8 ♗d3 f5 9 ♘c5 b6 10 ♘b3 ♗b7 11 ♕e2 ♕d6! (fighting for e5) 12 0-0-0 ♘d7 13 ♖he1 b5 with dynamically equal chances, Z.Hracek-A.Morozevich, German League 1999.

b) 8 ♗c4 b5 9 ♗b3 ♗b7 10 ♕e2 ♗d5

(even better is 10...f5 11 ♞c3 c5! – correctly timed where White can't take advantage of his development lead – 12 dxc5 13 0-0-0 ♞d7 when Black has at least equality if not better) 11 0-0 c6 12 ♞ed2 ♞d7 13 a4 and White doesn't have anything, J.Becerra Rivero-C.Lakdawala, Internet blitz 2010.

8...b5 9 ♗g2 ♗b7 10 ♕e2 ♞d7

He can also push forward with 10...f5 11 ♞ed2?! (too meek; White should try 11 ♞c3!) 11...♞d7 12 0-0 0-0 13 ♖ad1 ♗d5! 14 ♖fe1 c6 15 ♞f1 ♞f6 16 ♞e3 and Black's grip on the light squares assures him equality, C.Lakdawala-'Cyclones', Internet blitz 2010.

11 0-0!

Superior to 11 0-0-0 0-0 12 h4 ♗d5! 13 ♕e3 ♔h8 14 ♔b1 ♖g8 15 ♞c3 c6 16 ♞xd5 cxd5 17 ♗f1 f5 18 ♗d3 ♗f6 19 ♖dg1 when Black has a structural plus and her king is relatively safe, A.Kosteniuk-Huang Qian, Beijing 2008.

11...0-0

11...c5!? is risky but playable: 12 ♖ad1 ♕c7 13 ♖fe1 0-0? (after 13...cxd4

14 ♞xd4 0-0 15 ♕d2 ♞e5 16 ♕f4 ♔g7 Black is on the edge, but still may be okay here) 14 d5! ♗xd5 15 ♖xd5 exd5 16 ♞c3 ♗d6 17 ♞h4! gave White a murderous attack with very little investment in A.Zhigalko-D.Novitzkij, Minsk 2006.

12 ♖fd1!

Subtle. Most players would mechanically post the rooks on d1 and e1, but Kasparov leaves a rook on a1 to reserve the right to play a4 at some point.

12...♗d5!

Black essentially has two plans in this line:

1. Play for ...c5 if he can get away with it without punishment; or

2. Post the bishop on d5 and then back it up with ...c6.

13 c3 f5

Black usually plays this move sooner or later, grabbing more central territory but weakening e5.

14 ♞ed2 c5?!

As I researched this line, I was struck at just how often Black played this move prematurely. The need to fight back against White's central space advantage is understandable, but by opening too early Black is unprepared for the ensuing conflict in the middle. Better is 14...♗f6 15 ♘e5 ♘b6 16 ♕h5 with only a micro-edge to White.

15 dxc5 ♘xc5 16 ♘f1! ♕c7!?

Allowing the exchange sac. The alternative is to suffer quietly with 16...♗d6 17 ♘e3 ♗c6 18 ♘g5 ♕xg5 19 ♖xd6 ♗xg2 20 ♔xg2.

17 ♖xd5!

This strategic exchange sac keeps cropping up in this line. White destroys the integrity of Black's central structure and removes Black's best piece.

17...exd5 18 ♘e3 ♗f6 19 ♘d4

More accurate was 19 ♘xd5! ♕d6 20 ♘d4 ♖ae8 21 ♕h5 ♗xd4 22 cxd4 ♘d7 23 ♕xf5 ♔h8 24 ♗f3 ♕e6 25 ♕f4 when White's two pawns for the exchange and powerhouse pieces give him a clear advantage.

19...♗xd4 20 cxd4 ♘e4 21 ♘xd5?!

This may be the wrong pawn to capture. Better was 21 ♘xf5! ♔h8 22 ♗xe4 dxe4 23 ♕xe4 ♖ae8 24 ♕f3 ♕c2 25

♘e3! ♕g6 (25...♕xb2?? 26 ♕f6+ ♔g8 27 ♘f5 ♕xa1+ 28 ♔g2 mates) 26 ♘f5 with both material and strategic advantages.

21...♕d6 22 ♘e3 ♕f6 23 ♕h5 ♖ad8 24 ♘xf5 ♘d6 25 ♘e3 ♕xd4 26 ♖d1 ♕g7?!

Black can take the b2-pawn: 26...♕xb2! 27 ♕g5+ ♕g7!! 28 ♕xg7+?! (perhaps White should refrain from the following combination and keep the pieces on the board with 28 ♕h4) 28...♔xg7 29 ♖xd6 ♖xd6 30 ♘f5+ ♔f6 31 ♘xd6 ♔e5 32 ♘e4 ♖c8. Now it is White who struggles for the draw: 33 f4+ ♔d4! 34 ♘d6 ♖c2 35 ♘xf7 ♖xa2 36 f5 b4 37 f6 b3 38 ♘g5 ♔e3 39 ♘e4! b2 40 ♘c3 ♖a1+ 41 ♗f1 ♔d4! 42 f7 ♔xc3 43 f8♕ b1♕ 44 ♕f6+ with a draw by perpetual check since Black's king has no hiding spot.

27 ♖d5 ♔h8 28 ♕d1 ♘b7 29 b4 ♖xd5 30 ♕xd5 ♘d8 31 ♕d6 ♘e6 32 ♕xa6

Since the direct attack on Black's king didn't come to fruition, Kasparov now switches to plan B: win the ending.

32...♘d4 33 h4 f5! 34 ♘d5 ♘e2+!

The beginning of a vicious counterattack. Black fights to get in ...f4! prising open White's defences.

35 ♔f1!?

Kasparov puts his head into the lion's mouth. Only his legendary fighting spirit and calculation power allow him to enter such danger zones with confidence. He refuses to move the king in the other direction, with a draw.

I had the opportunity to play Kasparov three 5-0 games over the ICC in 1998, and in the greatest fluke in all of sports history managed to break even. Kasparov played anonymously on his coach's account in preparation for an ICC blitz match versus GM Peter Svidler. He used the account 'Dahlia', while I was on an account called 'Bodhiboy'. After he smoothly won the first game, the second petered out to a draw. Kasparov flagged in our final game in a totally winning rook and pawn ending after declining a draw offer. My friend, the late GM Tony Miles, was the only other ICC player to break even with the World Champion that day and I believe Tony's sole win came when he flagged Kasparov in a drawn position! David Bowie described it best when he sang: "We can be heroes, just for one day!" Had I known my opponent's identity, it would be a pretty safe bet that I would have quivered like large bowl of jelly and gotten slaughtered every game. Ignorance truly is bliss!

Here if Kasparov wanted a draw, he had it with 35 ♔h2! f4 36 ♕d6 fxg3+ 37 fxg3 ♖g8 38 g4! ♕xg4 39 ♕e5+ ♖g7 40 ♕e8+ ♖g8 41 ♕e5+.

35...f4!

Gurevich discards the knight to launch his own attack.

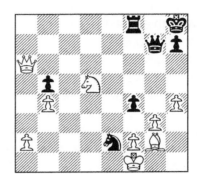

36 ♔xe2!?

Once again, refusing to take the draw after 36 ♕d6 ♘xg3+! 37 fxg3 fxg3+ 38 ♔e2 ♖f2+ 39 ♔e3 ♖xg2 40 ♕b8+ ♕g8 41 ♕e5+.

36...fxg3

Or he can push back with 36...♕e5+ 37 ♔d3 f3 38 ♗xf3 ♖xf3+ 39 ♘e3 ♖xf2 40 ♕c8+ ♔g7 41 ♕d7+ ♖f7 42 ♕g4+! (trading queens is a bad decision: 42 ♕d4? ♕xd4+ 43 ♔xd4 ♖f3 44 g4 ♖h3 45 h5 ♔f6 46 ♘d5+ ♔g5 47 ♘c7 ♔xg4 48 ♘xb5 ♖xh5 49 ♘d6 ♖h2 and Black's h-pawn sails smoothly towards promotion, while for White's pawns it's a long, long way to Tipperary!) 42...♔h6 43 a3 with a draw being the most likely result.

37 ♕d6!

Kasparov is finally willing to split the point. IM Tony Saidy once told me that Kasparov's hidden talent is his ability to push the aggression to the edge without actually plunging off the cliff with a loss.

37...♕b2+?

Gurevich overestimates his attack and goes for the full point. He had the draw with 37...♖xf2+ 38 ♔e3 ♖xg2 39 ♕b8+ ♕g8 40 ♕e5+.

38 ♔d3 ♖xf2?

It looks like he is closing in for the kill, but Kasparov had seen deeper. It was time to grovel with 38...♕b1+ 39 ♔d4 ♕b2+ 40 ♔c5 ♕xf2+ 41 ♔xb5 ♕e2+ 42 ♔b6 ♕f2+ 43 ♕c5! ♔g7 44 ♗h3 g2 45 ♗xg2 ♕xg2 46 ♕e7+ ♖f7 47 ♕e5+ ♔g8 when the exposed position of White's king could make victory difficult.

39 ♕b8+ ♔g7 40 ♕xg3+ ♔h8 41 ♕b8+ ♔g7 42 ♕c7+ ♔f8 43 ♕e7+ ♔g8 44 ♕g5+ ♔h8

A draw?

45 ♗e4!

No! Centralization with a vengeance. White's king is strangely secure out in the open.

45...♕c2+ 46 ♔d4 ♕d2+ 47 ♔c5 ♕xg5

Black has nothing better.

48 hxg5 ♖xa2 49 ♔xb5 ♖e2 50 ♘c3 ♖e3 51 ♔c4 ♖g3 52 b5 ♖xg5 53 b6 1-0

The b-pawn costs Black a rook, and Gurevich is pretty sure that Kasparov knows how to checkmate with knight and bishop!

Summary

In the feisty 6...gxf6 line of the Rubinstein French, Black allows his pawns to be compromised, hoping he is compensated by the extra central control and the bishop pair. White's best line is to fianchetto and take aim at the d5 pawn break. Remember to fight for d5 and also look for exchange sacs on that square.

> *Game 43*
> **A.Grischuk-S.Brynell**
> German League 2002

1 e4 e6 2 d4 d5 3 ♘c3 ♘f6 4 ♗g5 ♗e7 5 e5

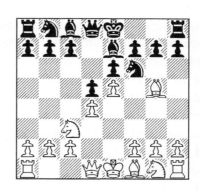

5...♞fd7

There are also two sidelines you should be aware of:

a) 5...♞e4?! 6 ♗xe7 ♛xe7 7 ♞xe4 dxe4 8 ♛e2! (a key move which comes close to a refutation of this line; White covers against ...♛b4+ and also hits Black's loose e4-pawn) 8...♗d7 9 0-0-0 ♗c6 10 g3! ♞d7 11 ♗g2 f5 12 exf6 ♞xf6 13 ♞h3 (13 f3! also looks good after 13...exf3 14 ♗xf3 ♗xf3 15 ♞xf3 0-0-0 when Black will suffer due to his isolani on the e-file) 13...h6? 14 ♞f4 ♛f7 15 ♗h3 ♗d7 16 d5! exd5 17 ♗xd7+ and 17...♛xd7? is met with 18 ♞xd5!.

b) 5...♞g8 and now:

b1) 6 ♗e3! is very logical: White keeps pieces on the board to maximize his space advantage and attempts to punish Black for ...♞g8. Thus he doesn't give the knight an easy out by exchanging on e7, and after 6...b6 7 ♞h3 ♗a6 8 ♗xa6 ♞xa6 9 ♛g4 g6 10 0-0-0 c6 11 ♞f4 ♛d7 12 ♛e2 ♞c7 13 g4! in P.Ricardi-M.Frank, Villa Ballester 1997, Black was more congested than if he had a bad cold!

b2) You can also continue in Alekhine-Chatard style with 6 h4; the only difference being Black's knight on g8 rather than on d7.

6 h4!?

The Alekhine-Chatard Gambit is for those thrill-seekers who don't want to grind their opponents and win by one tempo in 80 moves. In case you are under the impression that this is an unsound gambit, it scores a hefty 59% for

White according to my database.

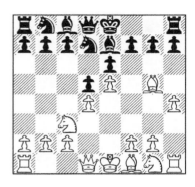

6...♗xg5

Declining the gambit doesn't absolve Black of his problems either. We examine those lines next game.

7 hxg5 ♛xg5 8 ♛d3!

White played 8 ♞h3 and ♛g4 in the old days. 8 ♛d3! is an improved version.

8...g6

8...h6 avoids weakening the dark squares, but doesn't slow down White's kingside and central initiative: 9 ♞h3! ♛h4!? (with the idea of keeping White's queen away from g3) 10 0-0-0 a6 11 g3 ♛e7 12 ♞f4 c5 13 ♗h3! ♞c6? 14 ♗xe6! ♞xd4 15 ♞cxd5 ♞xe5 16 ♛e4 ♛d6 17 ♗xc8 ♖xc8 18 ♖he1 f6 19 c3 ♞b5 20 ♞g6 and 1-0 in E.Vovsha-M.Cherkasova, Biel 2003, is a brutal example of the terrible fate which may befall Black if the game opens up.

9 ♞f3

A decision you will have to make is whether you want this knight on f3, or on h3, where it can go to f4, followed by sac ideas on d5.

9...♕e7 10 0-0-0 a6 11 ♕e3!

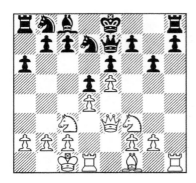

Those kingside dark squares leak like an old roof. One must be part adventurous and part crazy to take on Black's position!

11...c5

He wants freedom, but at the high cost of opening the centre for White. The passive alternative 11...♘b6 doesn't look like a relaxing holiday for Black either: 12 ♗d3 ♗d7 13 ♔b1 ♘c6 14 ♖h6! (ensuring that he regains his pawn while retaining a strategic edge) 14...♘a5 15 ♕g5! (the ending is clearly in White's favour) 15...♘a4 16 ♘xa4 ♗xa4 17 ♕f6 ♔d7 18 ♖dh1 ♗b5 19 ♖xh7 ♖xh7 20 ♖xh7 ♕xf6 21 exf6 and pawns begin to fall, F.Stross-M.Srba, Prague 2004.

12 dxc5 ♕xc5 13 ♕f4 ♘c6 14 ♗d3 ♕b4 15 ♗e4!!

The extra exclam is for pure courage. This remarkably nonchalant move threatens to chase off the queen with a3 and then sac on d5 if Black declines the piece.

15...dxe4!?

One must have great confidence in his defensive abilities to play such a move. He could also take the safer path with 15...♘b6 16 a3 ♕e7 17 ♗d3 ♗d7 18 ♘g5 h5 19 ♖h3 0-0-0 20 ♘e2 ♖df8 21 ♕e3 which gives White full strategic play for his material, but Black continues to cling tightly to his extra pawn.

16 ♘xe4

17...♖f8?!

Better was 16...♔d8!:

a) 17 ♘fg5 ♔c7 18 ♘xf7 ♖f8 19 ♖xh7 ♘d8 20 a3 ♕a4 21 ♕d2! ♘xf7 22 ♘g5! ♔b8 23 ♘xf7 ♕c6 24 ♕h6 ♖g8 25 ♕g5 when White has two pawns for the piece and an enduring attack.

b) 17 ♕xf7 threatens to pick off the rook next move with a queen check on f6: 17...♕e7 18 ♕f6! ♕xf6 19 exf6 ♔c7 20 ♘fg5 ♘f8 21 ♘f7 ♖g8 and now White can take the immediate draw with 22 ♘h6 ♖h8 23 ♘f7.

17 a3 ♕e7 18 ♕e3?!

Black can't hold things together in the line 18 ♖xh7! ♔d8 19 ♘h4! ♔c7 20 ♕g3 ♖g8 21 ♘d6 ♘d8 22 ♕c3+ ♘c6 23 f4.

18...♖h8 19 ♘fg5 ♘dxe5??

Cracking under the strain. His only hope was 19...f5! 20 ♘d6+ ♔f8 21 ♘gf7 ♔g7! 22 ♘xh8 ♔xh8 23 f4 and then pray he can hang on.

20 ♘xh7

Threatening a devastating check on f6.

20...♖xh7 21 ♖xh7 ♕f8

21...♘d7 22 ♖h8+ ♘f8 23 ♕h6 ♗d7 24 ♘f6+ mates.

22 ♘f6+ 1-0

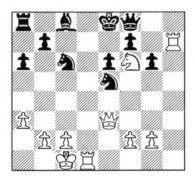

After 22...♔e7, 23 ♕c5+ wins the queen or 23 ♕g5! forces mate in 9.

Summary

The Alekhine-Chatard Gambit offers enduring pressure for the bargain price of just one pawn.

Game 44
E.Vorobiov-A.Rychagov
Aghios Kirykos 2009

---

1 e4 e6 2 d4 d5 3 ♘c3 ♘f6 4 ♗g5 ♗e7 5 e5 ♘fd7 6 h4 0-0

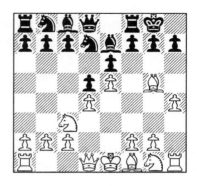

Black isn't interested in taking the offered pawn and suffering for the next 30 moves. Other decline lines are:

a) 6...a6 7 ♕g4 ♗xg5 8 hxg5 c5 (ensuring the destruction of White's pawn centre, but also ensuring White open lines!) 9 ♘f3 ♘c6 10 dxc5 ♘dxe5 11 ♘xe5 ♘xe5 12 ♕g3 ♘g6 13 0-0-0 ♗d7 14 ♗d3 ♕b8 15 ♕e3 ♘e7 16 ♗xh7! g6 17 ♗xg6! ♖xh1 18 ♖xh1 ♘xg6 19 ♘xd5 with three pawns and an attack for the piece, J.Degraeve-M.Gurevich, Belfort 1997.

b) 6...c5 7 ♗xe7 ♔xe7 8 dxc5 ♕c7 9 f4 ♕xc5 10 ♕d2 ♘c6 11 ♘f3 ♘b6 12 a3 a5 13 h5 h6 14 0-0-0 ♗d7 15 ♔b1 a4 16 ♖h3 ♖ac8 17 ♘b5 ♖hd8 18 ♘d6 ♖b8 19 ♖g3 ♔f8 20 ♕d3! and 1-0 was the brutal A.Morozevich-V.Korchnoi, Biel 2003; 20...♔g8 21 ♘xf7! destroys Black.

c) 6...h6 7 ♗xe7 ♕xe7 8 f4 a6 9 ♕g4 f5 (9...0-0 looks better, but White will still play 0-0-0 and go after Black's king) 10 exf6 ♘xf6 11 ♕g6+ ♕f7 12 ♗d3 ♕xg6 13 ♗xg6+ ♔e7 14 ♘f3 gave White a bind in the endgame, D.Velimirovic-R.Lontoc, Nice Olympiad 1974.

7 &d3 c5 8 ♕h5!

The queen enters like a shooting star and threatens the beginner's checkmate on h7. There is no turning back, White's centre is on the verge of collapse and he must play for mate.

8...g6 9 ♕h6 cxd4

9...♘c6 10 ♘h3 ♖e8! (clearing the way for ...&f8) 11 h5 &f8 12 ♕xf8+ ♘xf8 13 &xd8 ♖xd8 14 hxg6 fxg6 (after 14...hxg6 15 dxc5 ♘xe5 16 f4! ♘ed7 17 ♘a4 Black is still a bit cramped) 15 ♘b5 c4 16 &f1 a6 17 ♘d6 ♘xd4 18 0-0-0 ♘c6 19 f4 b5 and in Y.Pelletier-B.Zueger, Lenzerheide 2006, even with the reduced material White had full compensation for the pawn, and Black is having trouble dealing with the plan g4, &g2 and f5.

10 ♘f3!

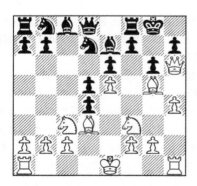

Unruffled, White makes a low-key developing move with a knight hanging on c3. He relies on the power of his ominous build-up in the vicinity of Black's king. 11 h5 is now a game-ending threat. It is Black's turn to find a good move.

10...♘xe5!

Black finds the only way to continue playing. White's knight must be deflected from g5, otherwise 11 h5 creates havoc. Black can't survive the assault after 10...dxc3? 11 h5 cxb2 12 ♖b1, while after 10...♖e8? 11 ♘b5 ♘c6 12 h5 &f8 13 hxg6 &xh6 14 gxf7+ ♔xf7 15 &xd8 ♖xd8 16 ♖xh6 ♘dxe5 17 ♘xe5+ ♘xe5 18 ♖xh7+ ♔f6 19 ♘xd4 White wins a pawn.

11 ♘xe5 ♘c6?

11...dxc3! saves Black: 12 ♘xg6 fxg6 13 &xg6 hxg6 14 ♕xg6+ ♔h8 15 ♕h6+ ♔g8 (White should take a draw since going all out puts him at risk) 16 ♖h3 cxb2 17 ♖b1 ♖f7 18 ♖g3 &xg5 (18...♖g7?? 19 ♕xg7+! ♔xg7 20 &xe7+ wins) 19 ♖xg5+ ♕xg5 and now White should take the perpetual check with 20 ♕xg5+.

12 ♘f3!!

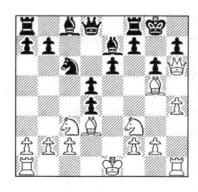

What goes up must come down! Moves like this are why we play chess. White pursues his plan with the tunnel-vision of an angry pitbull. His goal: protect g5 in order to play h5!.

Instead, Black's massive pawn cen-. tre offers him compensation in the line 12 ♘xc6? bxc6 13 ♘e2 e5.

12...dxc3 13 h5 cxb2 14 ♖b1 ♗b4+ 15 ♔e2!

Connecting his rooks just in case he needs the b1-rook in the assault. It looks like it's time for Black to resign. His queen is under attack and his king in mortal danger, but Rychagov continues to put up fierce resistance under extreme pressure.

15...f6! 16 hxg6 ♕e7 17 gxh7+ ♔h8

Black manages to seal the h-file with a human shield on h7.

18 ♘h4!

The second wave of the assault begins. Target: g6.

18...♘e5 19 ♗f4 ♕g7 20 ♖xb2 a5

20...♕xh6 21 ♗xh6 ♗e7 22 f4 eliminates the protector of g6.

21 ♕h5 ♗d7!

Black clings to life, continually finding the only move in the most dire situations.

22 ♗xe5

Destroying the key defender of g6.

Of course, he isn't interested in a petty gain of material after 22 ♗h6?!.

22...♗e8!

Just in time.

23 ♗g6! ♗b5+

23...fxe5 24 ♗xe8 ♖f6 25 ♘g6+ ♖xg6 26 ♕xg6 leaves Black down a rook.

24 ♔d1 fxe5 25 ♗f7!

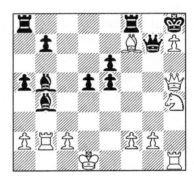

White will have his way! Vorobiov adds the cherry on top of a breathtaking attacking game with a clearance shot. The long awaited ♘g6+ can no longer be prevented.

25...♕xf7 26 ♘g6+

The Cinderella knight has all its wishes fulfilled in this game.

26...♔g7 27 ♕h6+! 1-0

White mates first after 27...♔f6 28 ♘xf8+ ♔e7 29 ♕g5+ ♔d6 30 h8♕ ♕xf2 31 ♕hxe5+.

Summary

Contrary to what might be expected, declining the Alekhine-Chatard Gambit doesn't automatically protect Black from a ferocious attack.

Game 45
C.Lakdawala-E.Sevilliano
San Diego (rapid) 2010

Do you have a boogieman in chess? Mine is one of the strongest IMs in the world, the 2008 US Open Champion Enrico Sevilliano. My dismal lifetime score before this game was four losses and about 12 draws, despite four or five winning positions. Even more disconcerting is the fact that Sevilliano's amiable personality and thug-like chess style don't match at all. Playing Enrico is exactly like having your mild-mannered and soft-spoken neighbour drop in for a cup of tea, and then immediately after the tea, put a knife to your throat and issue demands for your wallet!

1 d4 ♘f6 2 ♘c3 d5 3 ♗g5 e6 4 e4 ♗b4 5 exd5

The day before this game was played, John Emms emailed me and suggested the Lasker Variation against the McCutcheon French for this book. He reasoned that it bypasses the heavily-analysed lines and contains a drop of poison. I spent the entire morning of the previous day studying the Lasker line, which certainly threw my opponent, who seemed to only be familiar with mainlines like 5 e5 h6 and then 6 ♗d2 or 6 ♗e3!?. If you decide to play the mainline, make sure you investigate it deeply before testing it out over the board.

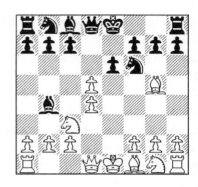

5...exd5

It's an Exchange French, but on *our* terms. French players always have a favourite aggressive arrangement against the Exchange lines. For instance, they often favour ...♘c6, ...♗d6, ...♘ge7, ...♗g4, ...♕d7 and castle queenside. By playing a late exchange line, we deny French players their cherished set-ups.

Next game we look at 5...♕xd5.

6 ♗d3

In this position, I also like the line 6 ♕f3 c6 7 ♗d3 ♘bd7 (7...h6?! looks untrustworthy after 8 ♗xf6 ♕xf6 9 ♕xf6 gxf6 when Black's bishop pair doesn't fully compensate for the damaged structure, K.Spraggett-A.David, Metz 2009) 8 ♘ge2 0-0 9 0-0-0 ♗e7, as in L.Fressinet-Y.Pelletier, Istanbul Olympiad 2000. Let's assess: it's an opposite wings attack position, but Black felt the need to waste a precious tempo with his last move because the bishop on b4 gets in the way of his pawn storm. He can also save the tempo by exchanging for the knight on c3, 9...♗xc3 10 ♘xc3 b5, but I don't like Black here either. White has the bishop pair and controls the dark squares. It's doubtful Black will make something tangible happen from his queenside attack.

6...c5?!

Sevilliano excels in open games, but this move is over-enthusiastic and he simply falls behind in development. He should behave himself and castle: 6...0-0 7 ♘ge2 ♗g4?! (better is 7...c6) 8 0-0 c6 9 f3 ♗h5 10 ♘f4! ♗g6 11 ♘xg6 hxg6 12 f4! ♗e7 13 f5 with the bishop pair and attacking chances, T.Bromann-J.Sorensen, Danish League 2009.

7 dxc5 d4 8 a3 ♗xc5?

Only making matters worse. He should go for 8...♗xc3+ 9 bxc3 dxc3 10 ♘e2 0-0 11 0-0 ♘bd7 12 c6 bxc6 13 ♘xc3 when White's bishops are meaningful in the open position, but it isn't the end of the world for Black.

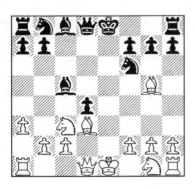

9 ♘e4 ♗e7 10 ♗xf6 ♗xf6 11 ♘xf6+?!

Unlike my opponent, I just don't have the open-game gene. I tend to over-finesse and try to control some weak square when I should be going after the opponent with a meat axe! I remember one exasperated ICC kibitzer offering me this piece of constructive criticism after I had botched a similar game: "It's called the initiative. You ought to try it sometime! Idiot!!"

Here I should play 11 ♕h5! g6 12 ♕h6, but I had a blind spot and missed this obvious move. After 12...♗f5 13 ♘f3 Black is in big trouble.

11...♕xf6 12 ♕f3 ♕b6

The ending would be clearly in White's favour. I would simply pile on the weak d4-pawn.

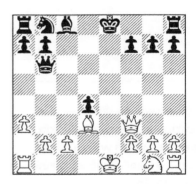

13 0-0-0 0-0 14 ♘e2 ♘c6 15 ♔b1?!

I considered and then rejected the stronger 15 ♗e4!:

a) I was unjustifiably afraid of 15...♘e5, but then 16 ♕h5 (16 ♗xh7+?? fails miserably to 16...♔xh7 17 ♕h5+ ♕h6+ and oops, it's a check and I don't get my piece back!) 16...f5 17 ♘xd4! fxe4 18 ♕xe5 ♖xf2 19 ♕e8+ ♖f8 20 ♕xe4 with an extra pawn.

b) 15...♗d7 16 ♕d3! (sigh... I missed this one too) 16...g6 17 ♘xd4 and Black doesn't have sufficient compensation for the pawn.

15...♗e6 16 ♘f4 ♖ae8 17 ♖he1 ♕c5?

I couldn't believe my eyes! My opponent misses a simple double-attack. At this point, I felt like a homeless and destitute man, who, rummaging through the trash, finds a 7-carat diamond! I had a feeling my Sevilliano curse was about to end.

18 ♘xe6 fxe6 19 ♕h3!

Enrico said he totally forgot about this move, which wins a pawn.

19...g6 20 ♖xe6 ♖xe6 21 ♕xe6+ ♔g7 22 f3 ♘e5 23 ♖e1

I just wanted to simplify. *Rybka* says 23 ♗e4! is very strong. By now the old paranoia had kicked in and I was wondering just how I would bungle this one.

23...♘xd3 24 cxd3 ♖f7 25 ♕e5+

A critical point. I was certain the rook ending was a win for White. If I were braver I could also play for an attack with 25 ♖e5 ♕c7 26 h4.

25...♕xe5 26 ♖xe5

Black is busted in the rook ending.

My plan:

1. Tie him down to his weak d4-pawn;

2. Centralize my king;

3. Play ♖b5 and force ...b6;

4. Push my queenside pawns to a4 and b5 to fix another potential target on a7; and

5. Slowly create a passed pawn on the kingside with my majority.

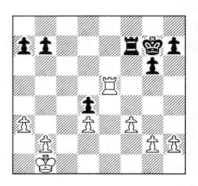

26...♖d7 27 ♔c2 ♔f6 28 f4 h5

The subtle 28...h6! intending ...g5 pretty much forces White to create a weakness with the concession 29 h4 h5. Now Black has ...♔f5 and ...♔g4 in case White's rook wanders off the fifth rank. Here, though, is White's winning technique: 30 ♔d2 ♖d6 31 ♖b5! ♖d7 32 a4 ♔e6 33 a5 ♔f6 34 b4 ♔e6 35 ♔e2 ♔f6 36 ♔f3 ♖e7 37 ♔f2 ♖d7 38 ♖c5 ♔f7 39 ♔f3 ♔f6 40 ♔e4 ♖e7+ 41 ♔xd4 ♖e2 42 ♖c7 ♖xg2 43 ♖xb7 and the race will not even be close.

29 g3

White shouldn't lock with 29 h4 if he has a choice.

29...♖d6 30 ♖b5!

As in the Vaganian-Adamski game from Chapter Two, White uses the fifth rank effectively here to create weaknesses and box in Black's king.

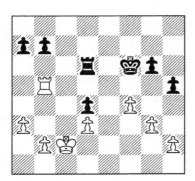

30...b6

The alternative is to defend passively with 30...♖d7.

31 ♔d2 ♖d7 32 a4 ♖d6 33 b4 ♖d7 34 ♖e5 h4?!

This aggression makes White's task easier. Now his h-pawn is separated and weak.

35 g4 h3 36 g5+

Bottling up his king.

36...♔f7 37 b5

To fix an additional target on a7.

37...♔f8 38 ♖e4!

There is no good defence to ♔e2, ♔f3, ♔g4 and ♔xh4.

38...♔f7 39 ♔e2 ♖c7 40 ♔f3 ♖c2 41 ♔g3 ♖g2+ 42 ♔xh3 ♖g1 43 ♔h4 ♖g2 44 ♖xd4

I confess to a bit of bravado on my part since I knew I was winning anyway and was happy to offer the h2-pawn to free my king. Shantideva, a 7th Century Buddhist monk, correctly observed: "When they find a dying serpent, even crows behave like soaring eagles!"

44...♔e6 45 ♖d8!

Intending 46 ♖f8 and ♖f6+. The game is over. Only the hope based on the happy memories of my previous incompetence in past games kept my opponent playing on!

45...♖xh2+

The main idea behind 45 ♖d8 is 45...♔f5? 46 ♖f8+ ♔e6 47 ♖f6+.

46 ♔g4 ♖g2+ 47 ♔f3 ♖a2 48 ♖f8

The g-pawn falls, and with it all of Black's hopes. White is too far ahead in the race.

48...♖xa4 49 ♖f6+ ♔e7 50 ♖xg6 ♖a5 51 ♖g7+ ♔e6 52 ♔e4 ♖xb5 53 f5+ ♔d6

53...♖xf5?? drops the rook to 54 ♖g6+.

54 ♖xa7

It's a good thing chess pieces can't become overweight! The perpetually-hungry pig eats his fill at the trough.

54...♖b1 55 g6 ♖g1 56 g7 1-0

57 f6 followed by ♖a8 wins. Free at last, free at last! The curse ends.

Summary

If Black responds to the Lasker line of the McCutcheon with 5...exd5, he ends up in an Exchange French, unable to enter his favourite set-up, and with his bishop possibly misplaced on b4.

Game 46
J.Hector-T.Bromann
Stockholm 2002

1 e4 e6 2 d4 d5 3 ♘c3 ♘f6 4 ♗g5 ♗b4 5 exd5 ♕xd5

The books say this move may be superior to recapturing with the pawn.

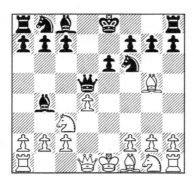

6 ♗xf6 ♗xc3+

Or 6...gxf6 7 ♘ge2 ♘c6 and then:

a) 8 a3 ♗xc3+ 9 ♘xc3 ♕xd4 10 ♕xd4 ♘xd4 11 0-0-0 c5 12 ♘e4 b6 13 c3 ♘b3+ 14 ♔c2 ♘a5 15 b4 ♘b7 16 ♘xf6+ ♔e7 17 ♘e4 with equal chances, A.Morozevich-A.Kovalev, Moscow 1994.

b) 8 ♕d2! ♕g5 9 f4! (superior to 9 ♕xg5?!; it probably wasn't so bright of me to straighten out his pawns with 9...fxg5 10 0-0-0 ♗d7 11 ♘e4 ♗e7 12 g3 0-0-0 13 ♗g2 h6 14 ♖he1, which left Black a touch better in C.Lakdawala-J.Becerra Rivero, Internet blitz 2010) 9...♕a5 10 0-0-0 ♗d7 11 a3 ♗d6 12 ♘e4 ♕xd2+ 13 ♖xd2 ♗e7 14 g3 ♘a5 15 ♘2c3 0-0-0 16 d5 and White's space and superior piece placement outweigh Black's bishop pair. Also, b4 is in the air, F.Bellin-F.Ranieri, Palermo 2007.

7 bxc3 gxf6 8 ♕d2 ♕a5

Given by some authors as Black's optimal line. Black discourages c4 because the ending is equal. Okay, fine, so we go for another plan!

Your opponents may not know the theory and prefer the natural 8...c5. An example: 9 ♘f3 ♘c6 10 ♕e3!? cxd4 11 cxd4 ♗d7 12 ♗d3 ♕a5+ 13 ♔e2! (Black's big decision is where to put his king) 13...0-0-0 14 ♖hb1 e5 15 dxe5 ♘xe5 16 ♘xe5 ♕xe5 17 ♕xe5 fxe5 18 ♗e4 ♗c6? (he should play 18...b6 19 a4 ♗e6 20 a5) 19 ♗xc6 bxc6 20 ♖b3 ♔c7 21 ♖ab1 ♖b8? (he was in trouble anyway, but this loses the pawn ending) 22 ♖xb8 ♖xb8 23 ♖xb8 ♔xb8 24 ♔d3 ♔c7 (or 24...f5 25 g4! fxg4 26 ♔e4 and wins) 25 ♔e4 ♔d6 26 g4! ♔e6 27 h4 f6 28 f4 exf4 29 ♔xf4 h6 30 c3! a6 31 a3! a5 32 a4 ♔e7 (32...c5 33 c4 zugzwang!) 33 ♔f5 c5 34 c4 1-0 J.Capablanca-W.Shipley, Philadelphia (simul) 1924.

9 ♘e2!

I like this move. White plans to transfer the knight to b3, where it harasses Black's queen and controls c5.

9...b6 10 ♘c1 ♗a6 11 ♘b3 ♕a4 12 ♕f4! ♕c6?

After 12...♘d7! 13 ♕e4 ♖b8 14 ♗xa6 ♕xa6 15 f3 ♕c4 16 ♕e3 ♖g8 17 ♔f2 *Rybka* says equal, but I prefer White:

1. Who is about to break the c4 blockade with ♘d2;

2. Who has the more secure king;

3. Who will play for the c4 and d5 (or c5) pawn breaks, maybe even tossing in a4-a5, depending on how Black responds.

13 0-0-0! ♗xf1 14 ♖hxf1 ♘d7 15 d5!

Principle: open the game when ahead in development.

15...♕xc3?

Alternatively:

a) 15...exd5 16 ♖fe1+ ♔d8 17 ♕f5 ♖e8 18 ♘d4! ♕d6 (forced) 19 ♖xe8+ ♔xe8 20 ♕xh7 and Black is busted.

b) 15...♕b7! (best) 16 dxe6 fxe6 17 ♖fe1 0-0-0! 18 ♖xe6 ♕xg2 19 ♘d4 when White continues to apply pressure on the light squares around Black's king.

16 ♖fe1

White threatens both the e6-pawn and also ♖e3, leaving Black's queen without an exit.

16...e5??

Missing the threat. Black must place his hopes on 16...♘c5! 17 ♘xc5 bxc5! 18 ♕xc7 ♕a3+ 19 ♔d2 ♕b4+ 20 ♔e2 ♕c4+ 21 ♔f3! ♕c3+ 22 ♖e3 ♕xc2 23 ♖dd3 0-0 24 ♕g3+ ♔h8 25 ♕f4 ♔g7 26 dxe6 fxe6 27 ♕g4+ ♔h8 28 ♕xe6 and Black fights for his life because his king is far less secure than White's, but this was his only recourse.

17 ♖e3!

Trapping Black's queen, but with a catch: White can't take it because if he does, his own queen hangs.

17...c5 18 a3!

Ensuring that there will be no squirming out via b4.

18...c4 19 ♕h6 ♕xe3+ 20 fxe3 cxb3 21 cxb3 0-0-0 22 ♖d2 ♔b8 23 b4 b5 24 e4 ♖dg8 25 ♕h5 ♖g6 26 ♕e2 a6 27 a4 1-0

Summary

5...♕xd5 is usually awarded an '!' by the opening theorists, but White still scores a whopping 61% against this line, so I'm not buying that Black gets the promised easy equality.

Chapter Five
Veresov versus French: Lines without ...♞f6

1 d4 d5 2 ♞c3 e6 3 e4

We cover four critical French lines in this chapter arising from the move order 1 d4 d5 2 ♞c3 e6 3 e4. The only difference from Chapter Four is that Black hasn't committed to an early ...♞f6:

a) After 3...♝b4 we have the Winawer Variation. Now, if you already know and enjoy the main lines of the Winawer, then by all means go into these. However, for the rest of us it may be easier not to commit to such a huge effort in learning so much theory. Let's circumvent the main lines against the Winawer, which your opponents undoubtedly want you to play, and instead begin 'Operation Annoy The French Player' by playing the delayed Exchange French. The positions will be similar to the Lasker line we play versus McCutcheon, but possibly even better for White. My feeling is that Black's bishop is misplaced at b4 and he really wants it posted on d6 or e7. On b4 Black will either exchange for your knight on c3, giving you the dark squares in exchange for a slight weakening of your pawn structure, or lose a tempo and retreat the bishop later. If Black retreats, remember the manoeuvre ♞ce2! and transfer the knight over to the king's wing for a build up to your attack.

b) In the version of the Rubinstein after 3...dxe4 4 ♞xe4 ♞d7, we haven't committed our bishop to g5, as in Chapter Four which usually leads to freeing trades for Black. Black's king is in more peril in this version than in the last chapter. Nakamura-Akobian may be Black's optimal line, but even here we tend to keep a slight edge with accurate play.

c) Black goes into a crouch and constructs a Caro-Kann-like fortress in the Fort Knox line, with the manoeuvre 4...♞d7, 5...♝c6 and often ....♝xf3 followed by ...c6. We can be content with our extra central space and the bishop pair.

d) Last we have the 'Swearing in Church' line where Black blocks his c-pawn, mimicking us, and playing his own knight to c6. Let's be consistent and deal with it by playing a delayed Exchange. I used to play this line as Black, but pretty much gave it up because I hated the lifeless positions I got after the exchange on d5. White is up a move in a symmetrical position and that has to be worth something. If anything, you make Black sweat to equalize.

Game 47
W.Steinitz-S.Winawer
Paris 1867

1 e4 e6 2 d4 d5 3 ♞c3 ♝b4 4 exd5

Singing from the same book of hymns! Once again we avoid main lines and go with another annoying delayed Exchange against the Winawer.

4...exd5

Although in the Lasker McCutcheon it is considered best, 4...♛xd5?! is inferior here. White either gains time on the queen or picks up the bishop pair and strengthens his centre: for example, 5 ♞f3 ♞f6 6 ♝d3 b6 7 0-0 ♝xc3 8 bxc3 ♝b7 (8...♝a6 to remove White's bishop pair is a consideration; however, exchanging on d3 strengthens White's centre) 9 c4 ♛h5 10 ♝e2 h6 11 ♜e1 ♛a5 12 a4! deprives the queen of a safe haven at a4, E.Rozentalis-H.Westerinen, Gausdal 2006. Thus:

1. Black's queen gets bounced around;

2. White's bishop pair is meaningful in the open position;

3. White controls the centre; and

4. White leads in development.

5 ♝d3

Noted chessologist IM John Watson explores the interesting 5 ♛f3!? in his

Dangerous Weapons book on the French. He used to live in San Diego and it was a learning experience to analyse with him. He is one of the most creative analysts I have ever worked with. When we covered an opening position I would point out two or three ideas, while John banged out 10 or 15 ideas! Not all were sound, and many were a bit out there, but he never ran dry!

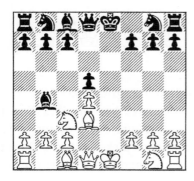

5...♗e6?!

This is awfully passive, but hey, it's 1867, and Winawer didn't have access to any of Watson's books (or ebooks for that matter) at the time!

6 ♘f3

Or 6 a3 ♗xc3+ 7 bxc3 ♘c6 8 ♕f3 ♕d7 9 ♘e2 0-0-0 10 0-0 ♘ge7 11 ♘g3 h5 12 h3 h4 13 ♘h5 ♖dg8 14 ♘f4 g5 15 ♘xe6 ♕xe6 and I trust White's pair of bishops over Black's attacking chances, N.Pedersen-I.Rajlich, Budapest 2006.

6...h6?!

I believe in the infallibility and interconnectedness of chess karmic law: one lousy move leads to another. Hav-ing posted his bishop on e6 prematurely, Black fears ♘g5 and wastes another tempo, as well as weakening his kingside.

7 0-0 ♗xc3?

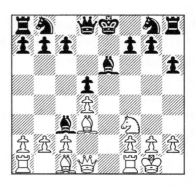

I love annotating these old games, rejoicing in the malicious pleasure of awarding question marks to great players simply because they didn't have the strategic knowledge base of the modern player. The founding father of the Winawer mistakenly captures on c3 without waiting for White to expend a tempo with a3. On top of it, a3 is now available for White's bishop.

8 bxc3 ♘d7 9 ♖b1 ♘b6

Now White conveniently gets to play ♘e5, unchallenged by a knight on d7. The alternatives are worse, though:

a) 9...♖b8?! deprives Black of queenside castling.

b) 9...b6?! turns the queenside light squares into Swiss cheese.

10 ♘e5 ♘e7 11 f4!

Luckily for Steinitz, this game was played before Nimzowitsch's time.

Players damaged by too much Nimzowitsch in their youth (I include myself in this unfortunate group) would automatically refrain from this move, fearing some kind of light-square blockade. In this position, how-ever, the dynamic factors overwhelm static subtleties.

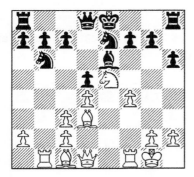

11...♗f5

11...g6 is too slow since after 12 ♕e2 ♕d6 13 ♖b3! Black doesn't have time to castle queenside with ♗a3 is coming.

12 ♗xf5?!

There is no reason to allow Black's knight to reach d6. Black is completely busted after 12 ♗a3! ♗xd3 13 ♕xd3! 0-0 14 f5 since 14...f6 drops an ex-change to 15 ♗xe7 ♕xe7 16 ♘g6.

12...♘xf5 13 ♗a3 ♘d6 14 f5

No more f5 blockade.

14...♘e4?

It's a good thing Winawer special-ized in closed games! He doesn't have the time for such adventures but to be fair, he is still quite lost after the supe-rior 14...♕g5 15 ♕e1 ♘e4 16 c4!.

15 f6!

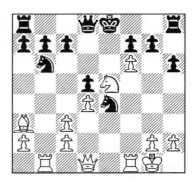

15...g6

The only move, as shown by:

a) 15...gxf6? 16 ♕h5! ♘g5 17 ♘xf7! ♘xf7 18 ♖be1+ which regains the piece with a deadly attack.

b) 15...♘xc3?? 16 fxg7 ♖g8 17 ♖xf7! ♘xd1 18 ♖f8+ ♖xf8 19 gxf8R mate. The sweet dream of all chess players comes true. Mate with underpromotion!

c) 15...♘xf6?? 16 ♕e1 (threatening a horrific discovery) 16...♘e4 17 ♘xf7.

16 ♕g4 ♕c8 17 ♕xg6!!

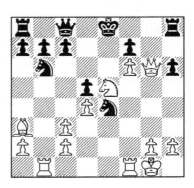

Have you noticed that some people just lead charmed chess lives, while others win their games by one tempo in opposite-coloured bishop endings?

17...♕e6

Or 17...fxg6 18 f7+ ♔d8 19 f8R+ (there it is again, the treasured under-promotion!) 19...♖xf8 20 ♖xf8 mate.

18 ♕g7 0-0-0 19 ♘xf7!

Allowing his queen to be trapped – at a very high price.

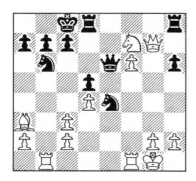

19...♘xc3

If 19...♖dg8 20 ♘xh8! ♖xg7 21 fxg7 and the g7-pawn turns into a queen.

20 ♘xd8 ♖xd8 21 f7 ♘d7 22 ♖be1 ♘e2+ 23 ♔h1 c5 24 ♗xc5 ♕e4 25 f8♕ ♘xf8 26 ♖xf8 ♘g3+

I question the validity of Black's 'combination' at this point; however, criticism would be the equivalent of throwing a bucket of water on a man already drowning in the middle of the ocean.

27 ♕xg3

Was Winawer hoping for 27 ♔g1 ♕xe1+ 28 ♖f1 ♕xf1 mate?

27...♖xf8 28 ♗xf8 1-0

Sorry, no back-rank mate.

Summary

Once again we invoke our strategy, Operation Annoy The French Player, through a delayed Exchange French with 4 exd5 in response to the Winawer.

Game 48
V.Korchnoi-R.Vaganian
Skelleftea 1989

1 e4 e6 2 d4 d5 3 ♘c3 ♗b4 4 exd5 exd5 5 ♗d3 c6

6 ♗f4!?

Korchnoi doesn't want to block his queen's access to f3 or h5. Others:

a) 6 ♘ge2 ♘e7 7 0-0 0-0-0 8 ♘g3 ♘d7 9 ♗g5 ♕c7 10 a3 (I prefer 10 ♘ce2!) 10...♗d6 11 ♕h5 ♘g6 12 ♘f5 saw White build up his forces around Black's king, V.Kramnik-M.Castells Briones, Barcelona (simul) 2002.

b) Korchnoi, in his notes to this game, gave 6 ♕f3 as his preference: 6...♘f6 (after 6...♕f6 allowing a queen swap is dead equal, so White boldly offered a pawn for development with 7 ♗f4!? which Black declined in

R.Rabiega-S.Giemsa, Berlin 2009) 7 ♗g5 ♘bd7 8 ♘ge2 0-0 9 0-0-0 ♗e7!? (here it is, the tempo loss; Black's bishop is in the way of his pawn storm, and he doesn't want to exchange it for the knight and lose control over the dark squares) and we've again reached L.Fressinet-Y.Pelletier, Istanbul Olympiad 2000. As mentioned on page 124, White's extra tempo matters in a big way in opposite-wing attacks.

6...♘e7

Or 6...♘f6 7 ♕f3 0-0 8 h3 (more dynamic is 8 ♘ge2 ♗g4 9 ♕g3 ♗xe2! 10 ♗xe2 ♖e8 11 ♗h6 g6) 8...b6!, as in P.Nikac-M.Drasko, Ulcinj 1997, intending to remove the attacking light-squared bishop on d3, equalizing the game.

7 ♕h5?!

The rule of thumb: swing the queen into h5 any time your opponent plays ...♘e7. However, this is the exception. If Black has access to...♘d7 and ...♘f6 it is better to forgo ♕h5. Indeed, ♕h5! is only best when Black has already committed his b8-knight to c6.

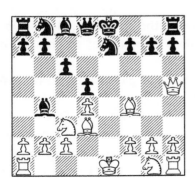

7...♘d7 8 ♗g5!? h6 9 ♘f3 ♖g8

Black gives up his right to castle kingside in order to threaten the bishop. Instead after 9...0-0 10 0-0 f5 Korchnoi in his notes claims Black stands slightly better at this point. However, *Rybka* vehemently disagrees giving the line 11 ♗xf5! ♖xf5 12 ♗xe7 ♖xh5 13 ♗xd8 ♘b6 14 ♗xb6 axb6 15 ♘e5 ♗xc3 16 bxc3 and Black struggles without full compensation for the pawn.

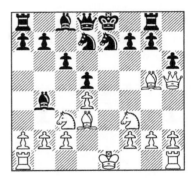

10 0-0!?

I said "threaten the bishop!" Korchnoi unleashes a spectacular piece sac to complicate. The funny thing is, Korchnoi criticized his own sac in his notes to the game in *Informant 48*! I believe he is being a bit hard on himself and certainly the confusion he creates gives him full practical chances for his sac. As Alekhine once said: "Chess is not all logic!"

I witnessed Korchnoi's staggering analytical powers at the 1983 US Open in Pasadena. Korchnoi played to warm up before his Candidates Finals match against a kid named Kasparov. At the US Open, I saw Korchnoi analyse his win against GM Dmitry Gurevich. Gurevich would suggest a line and Korchnoi would wave it off with a gesture of his hand, and demonstrate he had seen about 10 ply deeper! And this was when Korchnoi was past his prime. It was like watching a cyborg play a human. What freaked me out even more was the fact that I had played and lost to Gurevich the round before, and next to Korchnoi one could really see the difference between a Grandmaster and a contender for the World Championship.

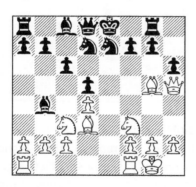

10...hxg5 11 ♘xg5 g6?

Vaganian gets boggled by his defensive choices in the fog of war and misses the tricky 11...♖f8! 12 ♘e6! (threatening Black's queen and also mate on g7) 12...♘f6! 13 ♘xg7+ ♔d7. Here the computers like Black, but White still should have his chances in the coming complications.

12 ♕h7 ♘f8?

It was imperative to play 12...♖f8!

13 ♖ae1 ♘f6 14 ♕g7 ♕d6 (not 14...♘h5? 15 ♘h7!!) 15 ♘xf7! ♖xf7 16 ♗xg6 ♔d8 17 ♕xf7 ♘xg6 18 ♕xg6 with a rook and three pawns for two bishops.

13 ♕xf7+ ♔d7 14 ♖ae1 ♔c7 15 ♖e2?

Allowing Black to slip out of the net. Black can't survive after 15 ♖e5! ♗d7 (15...♗d6 16 ♖fe1! ♗xe5 17 ♖xe5 also looks grim for Black) 16 ♖fe1 ♖c8 17 ♕f4! and if 17...♗d6 18 ♘f7! wins.

15...♗d7 16 f4

After 16 ♖fe1 ♘f5! 17 ♕xg8 ♕xg5 Black is back in the game.

16...♖h8 17 ♖fe1 ♘f5 18 ♗xf5 gxf5 19 ♕g7 ♖h5 20 ♘f7!

Hitting the queen and taking control over the d6-square. Black is unable to block a check on e5 and his king goes for a ride.

20...♕h4 21 g3 ♕g4 22 ♕e5+ ♔b6 23 a3?!

23 ♘a4+! ♔b5 24 ♘c5! ♗xe1 25 ♖xe1 ♔b6 26 ♘a4+ ♔a5 27 ♕c7+! b6 (27...♔xa4 28 ♕xb7 forces mate) 28 ♘xb6!! axb6 29 ♕b7 mates in nine moves.

23...♖e8?!

The complexity of the position is too much, even for these two great players. Vaganian misses 23...♗xc3! 24 bxc3 ♚a6! with a totally unclear position.

24 ♘xd5+!

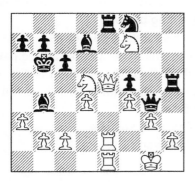

Beginning the second wave of the attack.

24...cxd5 25 ♕f6+ ♗c6 26 ♖xe8 ♗xe1 27 ♖xe1 ♘d7 28 ♕d8+ ♚a6

29 b4!

Just as Black's king felt he made a clean getaway, the b-pawn enters the attack, and one look in his rear-view mirror shows the queen ready to deliver checkmate on a5.

29...♘b6 30 ♘g5 ♖h6 31 ♕f8 ♖g6

31...♕h5 32 h3 ♘a4 33 ♕xf5 is a slow death.

32 ♕c5 ♘c4 33 ♘e6?!

For the second time in the game, Korchnoi misses a knockout punch: 33 a4! ♗xa4 34 b5+! ♗xb5 35 ♖a1+ ♘a5 36 ♕c3! and 36...b6 is met by 37 ♕c8 mate.

33...♖xe6 34 ♖xe6 ♕d1+ 35 ♚g2

35...♕xc2+?

Are you ready for a mind-blower? Black to play and force stalemate! Problemists out there, are you watching? 35...b6!! (two exclams are not enough!) 36 ♕xc6 ♘e3+!! 37 ♖xe3 (forced, since White walks into a mate after 37 ♚f2?? ♘g4+ 38 ♚g2 ♕d2+ or 37 ♚h3?? ♕h5 mate) 37...♕f1+! 38 ♚xf1 and it's stalemate!

36 ♚h3

Black runs out of checks and White threatens b5+!.

36...♕a4 37 ♚h4!

White's plan:

1 Black is in zugzwang and must move his knight;

2. Play ♕a5+! swapping queens;

3. Play ♔g5 to make way for his h-pawn; and

4. Play h4 and promote.

37...♘d2!

Better than both:

a) 37...♘b6? 38 ♕a5+! ♕xa5 39 bxa5 ♔xa5 40 ♔g5 and the h-pawn has given its marching orders to the queening square.

b) 37...♘xa3? 38 g4! fxg4 39 f5 and Black is curiously helpless to stop the passed f-pawn or exploit White's exposed king position.

38 ♕xd5

It's important to remove this pawn in case Black wins White's d-pawn and makes it a race.

38...♕b5

Black tires of the paralysis and agrees to the queen swap.

39 ♕xb5+ ♔xb5 40 ♖e5+ ♔c4 41 ♖xf5

The kingside passers are too much for Black's minor pieces.

41...♘f3+ 42 ♔h5 ♘xh2 43 g4 ♗f3 44 ♖g5 ♔xd4 45 ♔h4! ♔e4 46 f5 ♗d1 47 ♖g7 ♔e5 48 ♔h3 ♘xg4 49 ♖xg4 ♗c2 50

♖g5 ♗xf5+ 51 ♔g3 ♔f6 52 ♔f4 ♗d7 53 ♖e5!

Sealing off Black's entry to the queenside.

53...♗c6 54 ♖a5

In general, try to force your opponent's pawns on the same colour as his remaining bishop.

54...a6 55 ♖e5 b6 56 ♖e2 a5

Vaganian tries to take all the pawns off the board. The problem is Korchnoi has one remaining, which is all he needs.

57 ♖e5 axb4 58 axb4

Zugzwang!

58...♗g2

Alternatively:

a) 58...♗d7 59 ♔e4 ♗c6+ 60 ♔d4 ♔f7 61 ♔c4 ♔f6 62 ♖b5! wins the king and pawn ending.

b) 58...b5 59 ♖c5 ♗d7 60 ♔e4 ♔e6 61 ♔d4 ♔d6 62 ♖h5 ♗c6 63 ♖h6+ ♔c7 64 ♔c5 ♗d7 65 ♖h7 ♔c8 66 ♖xd7! and once again the king and pawn ending wins for White.

59 ♖b5 ♔e6 60 ♔e3 ♗f1 61 ♖xb6+ ♔e5 62 ♖c6 1-0

Summary

Remember the manoeuvre ♕h5! if Black posts his knight on e7 early *and* plays ...♘bc6. Then Black doesn't have the resource ...♘d7-f6, and experiences difficulties ejecting the queen without the help of the knight. People who say the Exchange French lines are boring should take a closer look at this game!

Game 49
N.Short-A.Beliavsky
Dortmund 1995

1 e4 e6 2 d4 d5 3 ♘c3 ♗b4 4 exd5 exd5 5 ♗d3 ♘c6

Black immediately hits d4. If White blocks with a knight, this deprives him of ♕f3 and ♕h5 possibilities.

6 a3! ♗xc3+

After 6...♗e7 7 ♘ce2! (both knights head for the kingside) 7...♘f6 8 c3 h5 9 ♘g3! g6 (White's idea is 9...h4 10 ♘h5, picking off the defender of the dark squares) 10 h3 ♗e6 11 ♘f3 h4 12 ♘f1 ♕d7 13 ♗f4 a6 14 ♘e3 ♕e7 15 0-0

(somehow White's pieces are in perfect harmony, whereas Black's are out of alignment) 15...g5?! (making matters worse; it is rarely a good idea to begin attacking as a solution to your inferior position) 16 ♗h2 ♕d7 17 b4 ♗d8 18 ♖e1 ♔f8 19 c4! and Black wasn't ready for the central confrontation in J.Hickl-L.Johannessen, Bled Olympiad 2002.

7 bxc3 ♕f6 8 ♖b1 ♘ge7 9 ♘e2 ♘g6?

I know what you're thinking. Dynamically equal, right? White's bishops and Black's better pawn structure balance each other out? Well, according to the database, Black scores 0% from this position with eight unanswered losses.

Better is 9...0-0 which brings up Black's score to 25%! Then after 10 0-0 b6 (sac'ing the c-pawn; he didn't want to get kicked around with 10...♕d6 11 ♗f4 ♕d8 12 ♖e1) 11 ♗f4 ♘g6 12 ♗xc7 ♘a5 13 ♖e1 ♗d7 14 ♗g3 ♖ac8 15 h4! h5 (15...♘xh4 16 ♘f4 ♗e6 17 ♕h5 ♘f5 18 ♗xf5 ♕xf5 19 ♕xf5 ♗xf5 20 ♘xd5 ♘c6 21 ♘e3 leaves White a pawn to the good) 16 ♗xg6 fxg6 17 ♘f4 and Black is a whisker away from being busted, J.Magem Badals-M.Apicella, Andorra 1996.

10 0-0 0-0 11 f4!

Here it is again, the battering ram along the f-file. Black can't hold the blockade on f5 and White's f-pawn ploughs its way through the defensive barrier with ease. Every black piece is on the wrong square. For instance, his queen on f6 is a horrible blockader and can easily be driven away.

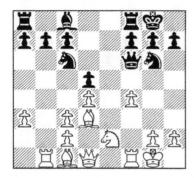

11...♗f5

Already Black may not have a way to save the game. Indeed, after 11...♘ge7 12 f5 White's threats include ♘g3, ♘h5 and f6, obliterating Black's defences, as well as ♗f4, picking off c7.

12 ♗xf5 ♕xf5 13 ♘g3 ♕d7 14 f5 ♘ge7

He didn't have the stomach for 14...♘h8. All very Kafkaesque. The knight is sent to the back of the line on h8, where it is a laughing stock and the butt of the other pieces' jokes! Then 15 f6 g6 16 ♕d2 ♘d8 17 ♕h6 ♘e6 18 ♘f5! gxf5 (18...♖fe8 19 ♖f3! leads to the same end) 19 ♖f3 ♘g6 20 ♖h3 mates.

15 f6

Something wicked this way comes!

15...♘c8

If 15...gxf6?? 16 ♘h5 ♔h8 17 ♘xf6 ♕e6 18 ♕h5.

16 fxg7 ♖e8 17 ♘h5 ♖e6 18 ♕g4 1-0

Summary

These lines are deceptive. The delayed Exchange lines are not the same as exchanging on the third move. Here we see a high-level player get blown away without any obvious error on his part. All it takes is to put one or two pieces on the wrong squares and White's attack can run amok. Also, keep a sharp eye out for f4! Play it when you feel that Black can't hold the blockade on the f5-square.

Game 50
J.Polgar-M.Rivas Pastor
Salamanca 1989

1 e4 e6 2 d4 d5 3 ♘c3 ♗b4 4 exd5 exd5 5 ♗d3 ♘f6 6 ♘ge2

Logical. We don't mind blocking our

queen since we don't have access to h5 and we would lose time with our queen on f3.

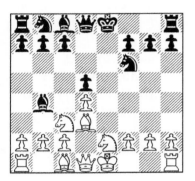

6...h6?!

Stops the pin, but creates a big sac target on h6. White also has access to simple plans like a future f3, g4, h4 and g5. Preferable was 6...0-0, although even here 7 0-0 c6 8 ♗g5 left Black wishing his bishop was on e7 rather than on b4, I.Nataf-V.Rosinovsky, Aubervilliers 2001.

7 ♗e3 c6 8 ♕d2 a5?

Black is nervous about sacs on h6 and so refrains from castling kingside. His last move compounds his troubles by making queenside castling next to impossible. Rivas Pastor is under the mistaken impression that queenside castling by White is imminent and begins attacking the non-existent king on that side of the board. He should play something like 8...♗e6 9 0-0 ♘bd7 10 ♘f4 0-0! with a slightly worse but playable position.

9 a3 ♗e7 10 f3!

Black's problem: where to put his

king? Either wing is unsafe. Meanwhile Polgar keeps Black guessing about the status of her own king and keeps it in the centre for now, while also annexing large amounts of territory on the kingside.

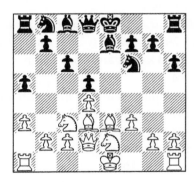

10...♘a6 11 g4 ♘h7 12 ♘g3 ♘g5 13 ♕e2 b5 14 f4! ♘h7 15 g5! hxg5 16 fxg5 g6 17 h4 b4 18 ♘a4!

It would be unwise to allow Black's knight to trade itself off for White's bishop on d3 with 18 axb4? ♘xb4.

18...bxa3 19 bxa3 ♘f8 20 ♗f4! ♘e6 21 ♗e5 ♖g8 22 0-0!

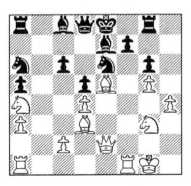

Hiding in plain sight. Black's passivity ensures that White's king remains safe out in the open.

22...♖a7 23 c4! ♗d6 24 cxd5 ♗xe5 25 ♕xe5 ♕xd5

Trading queens at the high cost of granting White's knight access to e4. However, after 25...cxd5 it's just a matter of time before d5 falls: for example, 26 ♖ac1 ♘ac7 27 ♘b6 ♗a6 28 ♗xa6 ♖xa6 29 ♖c6! ♖f8 30 ♘e2! and Black is tied up in a knot and d5 is doomed.

26 ♘e4

The knight is an octopus, spreading its power over f6, d6 and c5.

26...♕xe5 27 dxe5 ♔d8

Hopeless, as is 27...♔f8 28 ♘d6 ♔g7 29 ♘b6! ♖c7 30 ♘bxc8.

28 ♖ad1 ♘b8 29 ♗c4+ ♗d7

Black is helpless. For example:

a) 29...♖d7 30 ♘f6.

b) 29...♔e7 30 ♘d6 ♖f8 31 ♖xf7+! ♖xf7 32 ♘xc8+.

30 ♖xf7 ♖e8 31 ♘b6

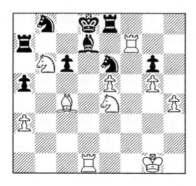

Attackers all across the board are drawn to the d7-square like flies to a garbage can!

31...♖b7 32 ♘xd7 ♖xd7 33 ♖fxd7+ 1-0

34 ♘f6 follows.

Summary

The tip from this game is to stall castling if you can and keep Black guessing about the address of your king.

Game 51
**J.Magem Badals-
C.Matamoros Franco**
Ubeda 1996

1 e4 e6 2 d4 d5 3 ♘c3 ♗b4 4 exd5 exd5 5 ♗d3 ♘e7

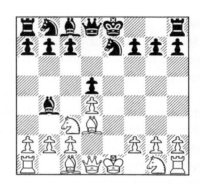

6 ♕h5 ♘bc6

Others:

a) 6...♗e6 7 ♘ge2 ♕d7 (worrying White about ...♗g4) 8 0-0 ♘bc6 9 ♕g5 ♘g6 10 f4!? ♗e7 11 ♕h5 f5 (now all hell breaks loose!) 12 g4!? 0-0 13 g5 (targeting h7) 13...♘b4 14 ♖f3 c5 15 ♗b5 ♕c8 16 ♖h3 ♔f7! 17 ♗a4 ♗d7 18 a3! ♗xa4 19 axb4 ♗xc2 20 ♘xd5 with total chaos all across the board, E.Paehtz-T.Fomina, Warsaw 2001.

b) 6...c5?! looks overly ambitious. True, Black wins an exchange, but at too high a cost: 7 dxc5 d4 8 a3 ♕a5 9 axb4 ♕xa1 10 ♘ce2. For the exchange White gets two pawns, while Black's queen is badly out of touch on a1 and his king is in serious danger. Moreover, both f7 and h7 are sore spots which White may exploit after 10...♘bc6 11 ♘f3 ♘xb4 12 ♗b5+:

b1) 12...♘bc6 13 0-0 ♕a2 14 ♘exd4 0-0 15 ♗d3 ♘g6 16 ♘b3 ♖d8 17 ♖e1 ♘ce7 18 ♘g5 h6 19 ♖xe7! and Black found himself swamped by attackers in R.Rabiega-D.Krumpacnik, Graz 2008.

b2) 12...♘ec6 13 0-0 0-0 14 ♗c4! and White threatens ♘g5! hitting f7 and h7. Black's king finds itself all alone after being abandoned by the queen over on a1.

7 a3 ♗a5!?

After 7...♗xc3+ 8 bxc3 g6 9 ♕f3 0-0 10 ♘e2 ♗f5 11 h4! White looks good, with dark-square control and an attack brewing, S.Dvoirys-C.Bauer, New York 2000.

8 ♘f3 ♗e6 9 b4 ♗b6 10 ♘e2!

A recurring theme: ♘c3-e2! heading for g3 or f4.

10...♕d7 11 b5! ♘d8!?

After this move Black gets congested in a big way. All chess players are terrified by the rhyme: "A knight on the rim is grim!" Nevertheless, I would head for the rim with 11...♘a5 12 ♘e5 ♕c8 13 0-0 and then try and swap off an attacker with 13...♘c4.

12 ♘e5 ♕c8 13 ♗g5 ♘f5 14 c3 0-0 15 g4?!

White misses a powerful shot with 15 ♗f6!!.

Then:

a) 15...gxf6 16 g4! fxe5 17 gxf5 f6 18 fxe6 e4 19 ♖g1+ ♔h8 20 ♘f4 ♖g8 21 ♖xg8+ ♔xg8 22 ♕e8+ ♔g7 23 ♕e7+ ♔g8 24 ♘h5 wins.

b) 15...h6 16 ♘g4! ♗d7 17 ♗xf5 ♗xf5 18 ♘xh6+ gxh6 19 ♕xh6 mates.

c) 15...g6! (best) 16 ♕g5 h6 17 ♕d2 ♔h7 18 0-0 and White has a winning attack, but for now at least Black is still breathing.

15...g6?!

15...f6! 16 ♘g3! fxe5 17 ♘xf5 ♗xf5 18 ♗xf5 g6 19 ♗xg6 hxg6 20 ♕xg6+ ♔h8 21 ♗f6+ ♖xf6 22 ♕xf6+ ♔h7 23 0-0-0! had to be tried.

16 ♕h3 ♘g7 17 ♗f6 ♘e8

Alternatively:

a) 17...♘h5? 18 ♕xh5!! gxh5 19 gxh5 ♗f5 20 ♗xf5 ♕xf5 21 ♖g1+ ♕g6 22 hxg6 leaves White up a piece.

b) 17...♗d7 18 ♕h6 ♘de6 19 h4 ♘e8 20 ♗e7 is similar to the game.

18 ♗e7

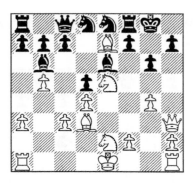

Winning a full exchange and keeping the attack.

18...f6 19 ♕h6?!

19 ♗xg6! hxg6 20 ♘xg6 forces resignation.

19...♘g7 20 ♗xf8 ♔xf8 21 ♕f4 ♔e7 22 g5!

White is unrelenting in his pursuit of Black's king.

22...fxe5 23 ♕f6+ ♔e8 24 ♕xg7 e4 25 ♗c2 ♕d7 26 ♕h8+ ♔e7 27 a4 ♗a5 28 ♕xh7+ ♗f7 29 ♕h8 ♕f5 30 h4 a6 31 ♕f6+!?

A practical decision. He can also keep queens on and continue attacking after 31 ♖a3 ♕f3 32 ♖g1.

31...♕xf6 32 gxf6+ ♔xf6 33 ♔d2 ♘e6 34 f3! exf3 35 ♖af1 axb5 36 axb5 ♗b6 37 ♖xf3+ ♔e7 38 ♖hf1 ♗e8 39 ♖e1

♔d6 40 ♖f6 ♗d7??

40...♔e7 was forced.

41 ♘f4 1-0

Summary

Note the similarities of this game to Korchnoi-Vaganian earlier in the chapter. Once again ♕h5! created trouble for Black.

Game 52
G.Kamsky-V.Akobian
US Championship,
Saint Louis 2009

---

1 e4 e6 2 d4 d5 3 ♘c3 dxe4 4 ♘xe4 ♘d7 5 ♘f3 ♘gf6 6 ♗d3

A safe alternative for White is the line 6 ♘xf6+ ♘xf6 7 c3 c5 8 ♘e5! and:

a) 8...a6 9 ♗e3 ♕c7 10 ♕a4+ ♘d7 11 ♗b5 cxd4 12 ♗xd7+ ♗xd7 13 ♕xd4 f6 14 ♘xd7 ♕xd7 15 ♕xd7+ ♔xd7 16 0-0-0+ ♔c6 17 ♖d4 b5 18 ♖hd1 ♗e7 19 ♖d7 ♖he8 was L.Dominguez Perez-J.Nogueiras, Havana 2008. Depressingly enough, this is all theory. GMs like Bareev, Akobian and Meier are geniuses at holding draws with this line against top opposition but the rest of us prefer White!

b) 8...cxd4?! gives White what he wants after 9 ♗b5+ ♗d7 10 ♘xd7 ♘xd7 11 ♕xd4 a6 12 ♗e2, which looks like a bad c3 Sicilian position for Black. White's bishop pair in the open position makes life tough for Black, R.Loos-P.Rodriguez Ferrer, Cullera 2005.

6...c5 7 ♘xf6+

I think this is the best way for White to proceed. Alternatives:

a) 7 0-0 cxd4 8 ♘xd4 ♗e7 9 c3 0-0 10 ♖e1 ♘xe4 11 ♗xe4 ♘f6 12 ♗f3! (going for Catalan-like play rather than aiming at Black's well-protected king) 12...♕c7 13 ♘b5 ♕b6 14 a4 a6 15 ♗e3 ♗c5 16 ♗xc5 ♕xc5 17 ♕d6! ♕xd6 18 ♘xd6 ♖b8 19 a5 with a bit of a queenside bind, R.Ponomariov-V.Akobian, Khanty Mansiysk 2009.

b) I'm not crazy about 7 ♕e2, though, where White often gives up the light-squared bishop for a knight, in exchange for a development lead: 7...cxd4 8 0-0 ♘xe4 9 ♗xe4 ♘c5! 10 ♖d1 ♗e7 11 ♘xd4 ♘xe4 12 ♕xe4 0-0 13 ♗f4 ♕b6 14 a4 ♗d7 15 a5 ♕a6! and Black's control over the light squares keeps him equal, despite White's piece activity in the centre, V.Anand-V.Milov, Bastia (rapid) 2005.

7...♘xf6 8 ♗e3

A critical position for our line.

8...♘d5?!

The ambition of youth! Black, al-ready lagging in development, allows himself to fall behind further to pick up the bishop pair.

Instead, after 8...cxd4 9 ♗xd4 ♕a5+! (the idea is to make it difficult, if not impossible, for White to castle queenside) 10 c3 ♗e7 11 ♕c2 ♗d7 12 0-0 ♗a4 13 b3 ♗c6 14 ♘e5 ♕d5 15 ♘xc6 ♕xc6 16 a4 the bishops give White the edge, but Black is solid and has reasonable chances to hold the draw, R.Ponomariov-A.Anastasian, Moscow 2005.

Next game we examine 8...♕c7!.

9 ♘e5! ♗d6

If 9...♘xe3?! 10 fxe3 ♗d6 11 0-0 ♗xe5 (or 11...0-0? 12 ♗xh7+ ♔xh7 13 ♕h5+ ♔g8 14 ♘xf7 ♖xf7 15 ♕xf7+ with a horrific attack without any material investment) 12 dxe5 looks rough for Black who:

1. Faces an attack on the f-file and kingside;

2. Falls seriously behind in development; and

3. Suffers from the cramping effect of the e5-pawn.

10 ♕h5 ♕c7

Or 10...g6?! 11 ♕h6 ♘xe3 12 fxe3 cxd4? (Black's position is riddled with dark-square holes after 12...♗xe5 13 dxe5, but this is how he must proceed) 13 ♘xf7! ♚xf7 14 ♗xg6+! ♚g8 (forced) 15 0-0 ♕c7 16 ♖f3! ♕g7 17 ♗f7+ ♕xf7 18 ♕g5+! ♕g6 19 ♕d8+ ♚g7 20 ♕xd6 and Black has no way to deal with threats like ♖g3, doubling rooks on the f-file and ♕e7+.

11 ♗b5+ ♚f8 12 0-0-0 a6

At this stage, allowing White to open the f-file with 12...♘xe3? 13 fxe3 would be insane.

13 ♗c4 ♘f6 14 ♕f3 ♖b8

Everything is under control. Black can't win a piece with 14...cxd4 15 ♗xd4 ♗xe5?? 16 ♗xe5 ♕xe5 because of 17 ♖d8+ ♚e7 18 ♖xh8 and White is up an exchange with a powerful attack to boot.

15 ♗f4 b5 16 ♖he1!!

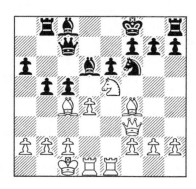

The irksome bishop refuses to budge.

16...cxd4!

Good defence by Akobian who finds the only path through the jungle in an attempt to survive. A less-skilled defender would have walked into either:

a) 16...bxc4? 17 dxc5 ♕xc5 18 ♘d7+!.

b) 16...♗b7? (hits both queen and bishop) 17 ♕g3! (threatens ♘g6+!) 17...♚g8 18 dxc5 ♕xc5 19 ♖xd6! ♕xd6 20 ♘xf7 with threats everywhere.

17 ♖xd4! ♖b6!

17...bxc4?? 18 ♘g6+ wins.

18 ♗b3 ♗b7 19 ♕h3!

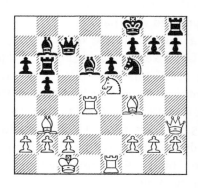

The pressure reaches a boiling point. Black must be vigilant for sacs on f7 and e6.

19...a5?

He had to try 19...♕e7 20 ♖ed1 ♚g8!, although even here Black's survival is doubtful.

20 ♖xd6!

The storm begins.

20...♖xd6

20...♕xd6?? 21 ♘g6+ picks off the queen.

21 ♘xf7!

Just look at the perfect harmony on White's side, whereas Black is in total disarray. White's pieces provide the chorus to the knight's solo.

21...♔xf7 22 ♕xe6+?

Still winning of course, but 22 ♖xe6! forces immediate resignation.

22...♖xe6 23 ♗xe6+ ♔g6 24 ♗xc7 ♖e8

24...a4 25 f4 ♗d5 26 f5+ ♔h5 27 ♖e5 ♗xg2 28 ♖xb5 wins without much trouble.

25 ♗xa5

How convenient. White picks off a pawn and at the same time covers his rook on e1, eliminating any ideas Black may have had of exploiting the pin on the e-file.

25...♗xg2 26 f4 h5 27 ♖e5 ♔h6 28 ♗d2 ♗c6 29 ♖c5

Of course, the bishop on e6 can't be touched due to the discovered check.

29...♗d7 30 ♗xd7 ♘xd7 31 ♖xb5 ♖e2

Akobian still hopes to make it a race by picking off h2 and then racing his h-pawn down the board. Kamsky, one of the most accurate technical players in the world, denies his opponent even a trace of counterplay.

32 h4 ♘f6 33 f5+ ♔h7 34 ♔d1 ♖h2 35

♗e1! ♘g4 36 ♖b3!

Covering the entry points for the knight. The a-pawn is ready for launch.

36...♖h1 37 a4

Lift-off.

37...♖f1 38 a5 ♖xf5 39 a6 ♖f7 40 ♖a3 ♖d7+ 41 ♔c1 1-0

Summary

Black's position after 8 ♗e3 is rather fragile, being behind in development and space. He can easily wind up in a position similar to an Open Sicilian gone wrong for Black.

Game 53
H.Nakamura-V.Akobian
Montreal 2008

---

1 e4 e6 2 d4 d5 3 ♘c3 dxe4 4 ♘xe4 ♘d7 5 ♘f3 ♘gf6 6 ♗d3 c5 7 ♘xf6+ ♘xf6 8 ♗e3 ♕c7!

Black's best choice in the position.

9 ♕e2 a6!

Avoiding the common error 9...♗e7? 10 0-0-0 a6 11 dxc5 ♗xc5 12 ♗xc5

147

♕xc5 13 ♘e5 with a similar position as in our game, except White is up a full tempo since Black has moved his bishop twice, R.Antonio-J.Al Huwar, Subic Bay 2009.

10 0-0-0 b5

The threat of 11...c4 forces White to break the central tension.

Instead, 10...♘d5 11 dxc5 ♘xe3 12 ♕xe3 ♗xc5 13 ♕g5 g6 (perhaps Black should risk 13...0-0 14 ♕h4 h6 15 ♖he1) 14 h4 ♗e7 15 ♕e3 ♗d7 16 ♔b1 0-0-0 17 ♘e5 ♗c5 18 ♕e2 ♗e8 19 h5 left White with a pull, despite Black's bishop pair in C.Peptan-A.Maric, Budva 2003.

11 dxc5 ♗xc5 12 ♗xc5

After 12 ♗g5 ♗b7 13 ♘e5 (13 ♗xf6!) 13...♗d6 14 f4? (14 ♗xf6 gxf6 15 ♘g4) 14...♘d5! White found it awkward to deal with the undermining threat of ...h6 in A.Shirov-Y.Drozdovskij, Mainz (rapid) 2007.

12...♕xc5 13 ♘e5 ♗b7 14 ♖he1 0-0

An instructive moment. I showed this position to several students and asked for an assessment. Nearly every one of them gave Black the thumbs up with statements like: "Black's attack is well underway, while White's hasn't started." Or, "Black is clearly faster with the open c-file."

The truth is, White's attack is more potent. First of all, because Black's knight will be ejected with tempo. Second, ♕e4! creates serious weakness in Black's kingside structure. Black's only plan of attack lies in a pawn storm with

...b4, ...a5, ...a4 and probably ...a3, but this simply takes too long.

15 g4!

Impulsive, committal, and very powerful!

White does weaken the f4-square, but more importantly he doesn't lose a tempo wasting a move with f2-f4. He threatens 16 g5, followed by (after 16...♘d5) ♕e4, ♘g4, ♘f6+ and ♕h4 with a winning attack.

15...♕b4!

Fighting for the f4-square and sidestepping White's attacking ideas based on ♕e4. If Black doesn't take swift measures and develops calmly with 15...♖ad8?, he gets swept away by the tide of the attack: 16 g5 ♘d5 17 ♕e4 g6 18 ♘g4! (exploiting the punctured dark squares; one threat is ♕e5 and ♘h6 mate) 18...♘b4 19 ♘f6+ ♔g7 20 ♕h4 h5 21 gxh6+ ♔h8 22 ♘d7! with a crushing double threat.

16 h4 ♘d5 17 ♕e4!

Great judgement, and also the sign of flexibility. White hasn't signed a legally-binding contract which stipulates he must checkmate at any cost. He can also play for the superior ending, as he has three factors in his favour: a pin on the d5-knight, a space advantage and the superior pawn majority.

17...♛xe4

I would have tried my luck in the line 17...f5!? 18 ♛xb4 ♞xb4 19 gxf5 ♞xd3+ 20 ♞xd3 ♝f3 21 ♖d2 exf5 22 ♖e3 ♝g4 23 ♞f4, even though the knight is superior to the bishop.

18 ♝xe4

18...♖fd8?

The wrong plan. Doubling rooks on the d-file allows White to mirror this plan. Black begins to get tangled on

two pins, lateral and horizontal, on the d5-knight. Alternatively:

a) 18...f6? 19 ♞d7 ♖fe8 20 ♝xd5! ♝xd5 21 ♞b6 ♖ad8 22 ♞xd5 exd5 23 ♖xe8+ ♖xe8 24 ♖xd5 with good chances of conversion due to the extra pawn and the vulnerability of Black's queenside.

b) 18...♖fc8! 19 g5 ♖c7 20 ♖d4 f6!? 21 gxf6 gxf6 22 ♞d3 with only a slight edge for White, who can still go after targets like e6.

19 f4! ♖d6 20 ♖d4 ♖c8 21 ♖ed1

That poor knight is pinned on both the diagonal and the d-file.

21...f6 22 ♞f3 h5?

A critical moment. This move isn't as strong as it looks and makes matters worse. Black gives up a pawn to wreck White's kingside pawn structure, but the trouble is he never gets the pawn back. However, if he plays passively and tries to hang tough, White continues to make progress with the plan of b3 and c4, exploiting the pins. Even then, Black may still save himself: 22...♖cd8! 23 h5 h6 24 a3! (threat: b3! followed by c4)

24...a5 25 ♘d2! a4 26 ♗f3! (clearing e4 for the knight) 26...f5 27 gxf5 exf5 28 c4! bxc4 29 ♘xc4 ♖c8 30 ♔d2 ♖xc4 31 ♖xc4 ♘b6+ 32 ♔c3 ♘xc4 33 ♔xc4! ♖b6 34 ♖d8+! ♔h7 35 ♗d1 ♖xb2 36 ♗xa4 (threatens 37 ♗e8! and ♗g6 mate) 36...g5!, which may still save Black.

23 gxh5! ♖cd8 24 f5 e5 25 ♖4d2 ♔f7

Black's only chance is to liberate himself from both pins. He plans ...♔e7, ...♗c6 and then to move his knight. Nakamura, with only a small window for action, must act quickly while Black is still hampered by the pins.

26 ♘h2!

With two ideas:

1. ♘g4 and a possible ♘e3, working the pin; and

2. ♘g4 and h6, exchanging and un-doubling the h-pawns.

26...♔e7 27 ♘g4 ♗c6

Covering himself against ♘e3 ideas.

28 a3!

Now the b3, c4 plan is in the air.

28...♘e3

I have learned to my sorrow, time after time on ICC, that whenever Nakamura 'falls' for a combination, bets are he has already seen it and found a hole! Such is the case here.

28...♗a8 is superior, but still fails to save the game: 29 b3 ♗c6 30 c4 bxc4 31 bxc4 ♘c3 32 ♖xd6 ♖xd6 33 ♖xd6 ♔xd6 34 ♗xc6 ♔xc6 35 ♘xe5+! ♔d6 (35...fxe5?? 36 f6 gxf6 37 h6 and the pawn promotes) 36 ♘f7+! ♔e7 37 h6! gxh6 38 ♘xh6 and White's passed c- and h-pawns win the game.

29 ♖xd6 ♖xd6 30 ♖xd6 ♔xd6 31 ♘xf6!

Picking up a second pawn. Akobian must surely have regretted sac'ing his h-pawn now. Black's hopes grow dim like the setting sun. Nakamura is one of the most tactically alert players in the world and rarely misses such shots, even in one-minute games. In effect, he is the World Cheapo Champion!

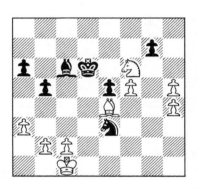

31...♗xe4

White's point is 31...gxf6 32 h6! and Black's pieces are curiously helpless to prevent the coronation of the h-pawn. Or 31...♔e7 32 ♘g8+! ♔f7 33 ♗xc6 ♔xg8 34 ♗b7 a5 35 ♗e4 and Black is helpless to prevent the birth of a queenside passed pawn.

32 ♘xe4+ ♔e7 33 f6+!

An instructive variation on a theme. White temporarily gives up a pawn in order to turn his h-pawns into passers.

33...gxf6 34 h6 ♔f7 35 h7 ♔g7 36 ♘xf6

This must have been annoying for Akobian. White's knight is a multi-tasker who has regained the sac'ed pawn, is untouchable on f6 and secures the h-pawn.

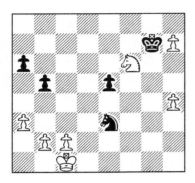

36...♘f5!

Akobian puts up maximum resistance. His plan: ...♘h6 and ...♘f7, which covers the queening square and wins the lead h-pawn. Despite his tenacity, however, Black's position is beyond repair.

37 h5 ♘h6 38 ♔d2 ♘f7 39 ♘g4 ♔xh7

Knight endings are the closest thing to a king and pawn ending. Black is doomed because White stays up a pawn and his h-pawn is dangerous. Moreover, White's powerful, centralized king threatens to raid the queenside, whereas Black's king is assigned the menial task of watching over the passed h-pawn, and so White can create a passed pawn on the queenside.

40 ♔d3 ♘d6

He can't allow the king to e4.

41 ♘xe5 ♔h6 42 ♔d4 ♔xh5 43 ♔c5 1-0

Black's king is a million miles away from the action.

Summary

You don't have to force checkmate in every Rubinstein French. Sometimes you win just by squeezing the opponent with your extra space.

Game 54
E.L'Ami-M.Luch
Maastricht 2007

1 d4 e6 2 e4 d5 3 ♘c3 dxe4 4 ♘xe4 ♗d7

The Fort Knox Variation, as the name implies, is a line where Black gives up the centre, space and often a bishop for a knight, all in the name of solidity. You can expect an easy edge out of the opening, but winning, well, that is another matter! But take heart, the Maginot Line didn't work out so well for the French in World War II. The secret: be patient, and chip away at Black slowly, and you may deny your opponent his half point.

5 ♘f3 ♗c6 6 ♗d3 ♘d7 7 0-0 ♘gf6 8 ♘ed2!

This is now considered to be the main line against the Fort Knox French. White avoids trades which give Black relief in his cramped situation, and

White fights for a grip on the e5-square with ♘c4.

8 ♘g3, the old mainline, doesn't make as much sense, as the knight has no great prospects on g3.

8...♗e7 9 ♘c4 ♗d5

A crossroads. Black has several plans:

1. Play ...♗xf3 and ...c6, turning it into a Caro-Kann position where Black cedes the bishop pair in exchange for a super-solid game.

2. Play ...♗e4 and swap bishop for bishop, simply reducing the number of white pieces on the board and removing a dangerous attacker.

3. Play ...0-0 followed by ...b6, retaining the bishop, and shoot for the ...c5 pawn break.

Let's examine the specifics:

a) After 9...♗xf3 10 ♕xf3 c6 11 c3 0-0 12 ♗f4 ♘b6 13 ♘e5 ♘fd5 14 ♗g3 Black's position is solid, but also rather lifeless, as he is short on space and White owns the pair of bishops. Moreover, White is ahead in development and the freeing ...c5 is not very tempt-

ing since White's development lead and bishop pair would come alive.

b) 9...♗e4 sees Black enter super-grovel mode and want to swap without giving up the bishop pair: 10 ♗xe4 ♘xe4 11 ♕e2 ♘ef6 and now 12 ♖d1! puts the clamp on both the ...c5 and ...e5 breaks, leaving Black with a lifeless but still solid position, F.Vallejo Pons-M.Suba, Dos Hermanas 2002.

c) 9...b6 10 ♘ce5 ♗b7 (now White has a promising sac...) 11 ♘xf7! ♔xf7 12 ♘g5+ ♔g8 13 ♘xe6 ♕c8 14 ♖e1 with two pawns for the piece, Black's h-rook sitting it out on the sidelines where it will be out of the action for a long time, and a shaky black king, especially on the light squares and the a2-g8 diagonal.

10 ♘ce5 ♘xe5 11 ♘xe5 0-0 12 ♕e2 c5 13 dxc5 ♗xc5 14 ♗g5 ♗e7 15 ♖ad1 ♕c7 16 c4 ♗c6 17 b4!

The beginning of an insurrection on the other wing. White finds a clever method of activating his queenside majority, as the pawn can't be touched. Instead, going for the bishop pair is a false path: 17 ♘xc6?! bxc6! followed by ...c5 equalizes, due to Black's dark-square power and also his grip on the d4-square.

17...♖ad8

Taking on b4 is suicide: 17...♗xb4?? 18 ♗xf6 gxf6 19 ♗xh7+ ♔xh7 20 ♕h5+ ♔g7 21 ♕g4+ ♔h7 22 ♖d3 mates.

18 b5!

A good decision. White gives up control over c5, but in return he shackles Black's bishop to e8.

18...♗e8

In case Black thinks about rerouting the bishop to c8 with 18...♗d7? then comes 19 ♗xf6! ♗xf6 20 ♗xh7+! ♔xh7 21 ♕d3+! ♔g8 22 ♘xd7 (strangely enough, Black can't do a thing about the pinned knight) 22...♗e7 23 ♕d4 ♖fe8 24 ♖d3 ♗f8 25 ♖fd1 and the knight continues to lounge serenely within Black's borders.

19 f4 ♕c5+?

The start of a bad plan. He should try to untangle with 19...h6 20 ♗h4 a6 21 a4 ♗d7! 22 ♖f3! when clearly an attack is brewing, but Black has

counter chances due to the open centre in case White goes crazy on the attack.

20 ♔h1 ♘d7? 21 ♕e4!

Threatens mate and b7.

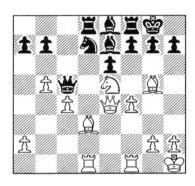

21...f5!

21...g6 22 ♗xe7 ♕xe7 23 ♕xb7 is hopeless for Black.

22 ♘xd7 ♖xd7!

The best choice in a difficult situation:

a) If 22...♗xd7? 23 ♗xe7 ♕xe7 24 ♕xb7 and Black can resign.

b) 22...fxe4? 23 ♘xc5 ♗xg5 24 ♗xe4 ♖xd1 25 ♖xd1 ♖xf4 26 g3! ♖f2 27 ♘xe6 ♗e7 28 ♗xb7 ♗f7 29 ♗d5 ♗xe6 30 ♗xe6+ ♔f8 31 a4 and the opposite-coloured bishops won't save Black.

23 ♕xe6+ ♔h8 24 ♖fe1 ♗xg5 25 fxg5 ♖d8

After 25...g6 26 ♗f1 ♖xd1 27 ♖xd1 ♗f7 28 ♕d6 White wins easily.

26 ♗f1

Rybka found the amazing line 26 ♖e5!! ♕a3 27 ♖xf5! ♖xf5 28 ♕xf5 ♗g6 (this looks crushing, but...) 29 ♗f1!!. This trick allows White to exploit the back rank and take the point. It is lines like this which tend to incite in humans a Frankenstein complex, believing computers, our creation, have taken over chess. The way I look at it is: computers are just a tool we humans invented, therefore we take full credit for all their great moves! After all, an Olympic weight lifter doesn't fear competition from a forklift, who can certainly out-lift the human!

26...♗f7 27 ♕e2 ♖de8 28 ♕f3 ♖xe1 29 ♖xe1 b6 30 ♕e3 ♖c8?!

The ending is easy for White. Black had to try 30...♕c8 31 ♕f4 ♗e6.

31 ♕xc5 ♖xc5 32 ♖e7 ♔g8 33 ♖xa7 ♗xc4 34 ♗xc4+ ♖xc4 35 ♔g1 ♖c2 36 a4 ♖b2 37 h4 g6 38 g3 ♖b4

Or 38...♔h8 39 ♖a6 ♖b4 40 ♔f2 (goal: c3) 40...♔g7 41 ♔e3 ♔f7 42 ♔d3 ♔g7 43 ♔c3 ♖g4 44 a5! ♖xg3+ 45 ♔c4 bxa5 46 b6 ♖g4+ 47 ♔c5 ♖b4 48 ♖xa5 ♖b1 49 ♖b5 and wins.

39 ♔f2

White's king strolls to the queenside to assist the pawn promotion.

39...f4 40 gxf4 ♖xf4+ 41 ♔e3 ♖xh4 42 a5! 1-0

The b-pawn costs Black his rook.

Summary

The Fort Knox lives up to its name. Black gives up space and usually the bishop pair to boot, and dares White to come after him in the bunker!

Game 55
J.Peters-C.Lakdawala
Southern California State
Championship 2008

IM and *Los Angeles Times* chess columnist Jack Peters and I have been friends for over 30 years. He was the undisputed king of Southern California chess in the 70's and 80's. As his crown prince, I ruled in the 90's, only to be unceremoniously ousted myself by a pair of tyrants, GMs and co-rulers, Khachian and Akobian, around 2002.

1 e4 e6 2 d4 d5 3 ♘d2 dxe4

One of the benefits Black gets from the Rubinstein lines is that he gets the same positions from 3 ♘c3 and also from the Tarrasch 3 ♘d2, so it saves a lot of study time.

4 ♘xe4 ♗d7

The Fort Knox Variation, the dullard's paradise, was a moronic choice on my part because after the 5th round, I was in 2nd place and desperate to beat Jack with the black pieces. As I explained to him later, I was "grovelling for the win!"

5 ♘f3 ♗c6 6 ♗d3 ♘d7 7 0-0 ♘gf6 8

♘ed2 ♝e7

9 ♘c4

I had this position against GM Tigran Petrosian (no, not the World Champion, the other one!) at the 2008 National Open G/10 Championship. The game went 9 ♖e1 (securing e4 first) 9...0-0 10 b3 ♝xf3 11 ♕xf3 c6 12 ♝b2 ♖e8 13 ♘c4 ♕c7 14 ♘e5 ♖ad8 15 ♖ad1 (I expected Tigarano to go ballistic and sac on h7) 15...♝f8 16 c4 ♘xe5!? 17 dxe5 ♘d7 18 ♝xh7+!? (there we go!) 18...♚xh7 19 ♕xf7 ♖e7 20 ♕h5+ ♚g8 21 ♖d3 g6! (throughout my life, I have always been an incompetent attacker and an excellent defender; here my defensive instincts were correct as Black avoids the false path 21...♖f7? 22 ♖h3 ♖f4 23 g3 ♕a5 24 ♚f1 ♖f5 25 ♕h7+ ♚f7 26 g4! ♖f4 27 ♝c1! which evicts the rook from the f-file, giving White a deadly attack) 22 ♕xg6+ ♝g7 23 ♖ed1 ♖c8 24 h4 ♘f8 with a complex position, probably in White's favour. After securing an advantage, later I botched the game with both our clocks hanging. Sadly, most IMs just don't

have the quick sight of the board that the majority of GMs possess. As a result we tend to get burned in the time scrambles.

9...0-0!?

I decided to allow him his 'threat' ♘a5. Instead, 9...0-0 10 ♖e1 b6 11 ♘ce5 ♘xe5 12 dxe5 ♘d7 (12...♘e4!? is a possibility) 13 ♘d4 ♝b7 14 ♕g4 ♖e8 15 ♝h6 ♝f8 16 ♝g5 ♝e7 17 h4 and the cramping e5-pawn gives White attacking chances, with the weak c6-square also a concern for Black, I.Smirin-A.Chernin, Moscow 1994.

10 ♘a5

Jack was under the impression that my last move was a blunder.

10...♝d5!

An important move: c4 must be provoked, which weakens his d4-square and his dark squares later.

11 c4 ♝xf3 12 ♕xf3 c6!

My opponent missed this idea, which regains the pawn. Of course, Black is strategically busted after the lame 12...b6?? 13 ♘c6 ♕e8 14 ♝d2 and Black will never unravel.

13 ♘xb7 ♕b6 14 ♘c5 ♘xc5 15 dxc5 ♗xc5

Assessment:

1. Black controls d4;

2. Black has dark-square control;

3. White has the bishop pair, which glares in the direction of Black's king; and

4. Critical to the coming moves is White's b4-pawn break, which would open the game and get his queenside pawn majority in motion.

Perhaps the position is dynamically balanced.

16 ♖b1!

A new move and an improvement over 16 ♗g5?! ♗d4! 17 ♖ab1 a5 18 ♖fd1 ♖fd8 19 ♗h4 c5 when Black already stands better due to his iron grip on the dark squares, R.Castineira-A.Anastasian, Ubeda 2001.

16...a5 17 a3!

White must react vigorously before Black establishes a central bind on the dark squares. After 17 b3?! ♗d4! 18 a3 c5 Black is better.

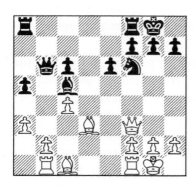

17...♗d4?!

Chickening out. Fear leads to hesitation; hesitation leads to defeat. I should have gone forward with 17...a4! 18 b4! axb3 19 ♖xb3 ♕c7 20 ♗b2 e5! (after 20...♗e7?? 21 ♗xf6! ♗xf6 22 ♗xh7+! ♔xh7 23 ♕h5+ ♔g8 24 ♖h3 ♗h4 25 ♖xh4 f6 White should win, not due to his extra pawn, but to the insecure situation of Black's king) 21 ♕g3 ♖fe8 22 ♖e1 ♗d6. I had analysed the position up to this point and reasoned that White stood clearly better after 23 c5 ♗xc5 24 ♗xe5, but I had missed: 24...♗xf2+!! 25 ♔xf2 ♖xe5! 26 ♖xe5 ♕xe5! 27 ♕xe5 ♘g4+ 28 ♔e2 ♘xe5 with an extra pawn and good chances to convert.

18 b4 axb4 19 axb4

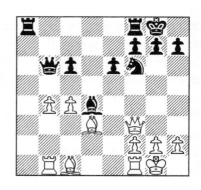

18...♖fd8?

Black weathers the attack after 19...c5! 20 bxc5 ♕xc5 21 ♖b5 ♕c7 22 ♖g5 ♖fd8 23 ♗f4 ♕e7. Perhaps the pharmaceutical industry may some day invent a drug designed to prevent paranoia in chess players! I analysed to this point and once again misassessed it as being in White's favour, seeing ghosts everywhere and believing he had an attack. Black's grip on the dark squares keeps his king a lot safer than it looks and chances are balanced.

20 c5! ♕c7 21 ♗f4

Now White enjoys a slight but nagging advantage.

21...♕d7

Allowing the bishop to entrench itself on d6. I had planned 21...♗e5?, but realized it loses after 22 ♗xe5 ♕xe5 23 ♕xc6 ♘g4 24 g3 ♕h5 25 ♕g2! when Black has nothing and White's passers carry the day. Likewise, after 21...e5?? 22 ♗g5 Black doesn't have a good response.

22 ♗d6 e5!

Avoiding multiple losing lines:

a) 22...♘e8? 23 ♖fd1! ♗f6 (or 23...♘xd6 24 ♗xh7+! ♔xh7 25 ♖xd4 ♕e7 26 cxd6! and 26...♖xd6?? isn't possible due to 27 ♕d3+) 24 ♗e4 ♖ac8 25 ♗f4! and c6 falls.

b) 22...♘d5?? 23 ♕e4.

23 ♗f5 ♕e8

Certainly not 23...♕b7?? 24 b5.

24 ♕b3 g6 25 ♗d3 ♕d7

Threatening ...♘e8.

26 b5

26...♗xc5??

Finally succumbing to White's pressure with a hallucination.

26...cxb5! saves Black: 27 ♗xb5 ♕f5! (the counterattack on f2 ties White down, at least enough for Black to save himself) 28 ♗c6 ♖a6! 29 ♗b7 (29 ♕b7?? allows Black a huge attack after 29...♖a2 30 ♔h1 ♘g4) 29...♖axd6! 30 cxd6 ♖xd6 and the knight and pawn offer full compensation for the exchange. In fact, I even prefer Black here.

27 ♗xc5 ♕xd3 28 ♗e7!

Bleep! (Please insert favourite expletive). Uhm... yes, there is that! For some reason, I had only analysed a queen trade. If an undertaker had been observing the game at this point, just one look at me would have brought a smile to his face at the possibility of a bit of business coming his way! I should have resigned, but played on only because Jack was in his customary time trouble.

28...♕f5 29 ♗xd8 ♖xd8 30 bxc6 ♖c8 31

♖fc1 ♔g7 32 h3 ♖c7 33 ♕c4 ♘e4 34 ♕c2 ♔f6 35 ♖b7 ♖c8 36 c7 ♔e7 37 ♖d1 ♘d6 38 ♕c5 1-0

After the game, Jack poured alcohol on the wound by informing me that the last time he beat me was 1994!

Summary

The Fort Knox appeals to players who like trench warfare (i.e., me!). Black forces the position he wants at the high price of the bishop pair and space.

Game 56
R.Fischer-T.V.Petrosian
9th matchgame,
Buenos Aires 1971

1 e4 e6 2 d4 d5 3 ♘c3 ♘c6

IM John Watson calls his *Dangerous Weapons* chapter on this line 'Swearing in church'. Like the Guimard French where Black plays ...♘c6 before playing ...c5, this line tends to raise eyebrows. Of course, we Veresovers thrive on blocking our c-pawns with our knights!

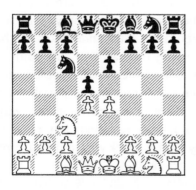

4 ♘f3 ♘f6 5 exd5

Let me tell you a little secret. French players are involved in a world-wide conspiracy. They all claim to cherish playing the black side of Exchange French, but this is misinformation designed to throw off White. The truth is they actually hate *all* irritating exchange lines! I am a French player and one time my opponents, all of them lower rated, hit me with 8 (!) Exchange Frenches in a row. Each time they exchanged my d5-pawn I remember grating my teeth and fighting the urge to strangle them!

5...exd5

5...♘xd5 is also possible, but doesn't equalize if White reacts correctly: 6 ♘e4! ♗e7 7 ♗d3?! (7 c3! 0-0 8 ♗d3 gives White the normal Rubinstein edge) 7...♘db4! and Black got rid of the powerful attacker, B.Abramovic-Z.Nikolic, Novi Sad 1985. Here 8 ♗c4 wasn't possible since Black has the tactic 8...♘xd4!.

6 ♗b5 ♗g4

Black has many choices from this position:

a) 6...♗b4 sees Black agree to continue the symmetry a while longer: 7 ♘e5 0-0 8 ♗xc6 bxc6 9 0-0 ♗xc3 10 bxc3 ♘e4 11 ♗a3 ♖e8 12 f3!? ♘xc3 13 ♕d3 ♘a4 14 ♖ae1 ♖e6?! (14...♗d7) 15 f4 and White had an attack brewing, N.De Firmian-M.Cordara, Ticino 1993.

b) 6...♗d7 7 0-0 ♗d6?! 8 ♖e1+ ♘e7 9 ♗g5 c6 10 ♗xf6 gxf6 11 ♗d3 and Black must take care to avoid trades from this point on due to his broken pawn structure, M.Ebeling-J.Kekki, Helsinki 1993.

c) The problem with 6...♗d6?! is that it doesn't address the problem of how to deal with the pin if White plays ♗g5: 7 0-0 0-0 8 ♗xc6 bxc6 9 ♘e5 ♗b7 10 ♗g5 and Black decided to backtrack, ceding a tempo with 10...♗e7 in A.Rodriguez-C.Florez Fernandez, Merida 1992.

d) Players as strong as GM Rozentalis have tried the turkey 6...a6?!. I love it when they give up a move to force the move I wanted to play in the first place! I remember reading an online article once which had the nerve to claim Black stood better after the dubious 6...a6. As the old saying goes: "Don't believe everything you read!" Here 7 ♗xc6+ bxc6 8 0-0 ♗e7 9 ♘e5 ♗b7 10 ♘a4! is all very Nimzowitschian: c5 is firmly blockaded and can even be backed up with ♘d3. Black is essentially stuck with his pawn weaknesses.

e) Next game we examine 6...♗e7.

7 h3 ♗xf3 8 ♕xf3 ♗e7 9 ♗g5 a6

White had a nagging pull after 9...0-0 10 0-0-0! ♘e4 11 ♗xe7 ♕xe7 12 ♖he1 ♕g5+ 13 ♕e3 ♕xe3+ 14 ♖xe3! ♘d6 in L.Fressinet-O.Foisor, Saint Affrique 2000. Here White should play the simple 15 ♗xc6 bxc6 16 ♘a4 and pick on the sickly black pawns on the queenside.

10 ♗xc6+ bxc6 11 0-0 0-0 12 ♖fe1 h6 13 ♗h4 ♕d7 14 ♖e2 a5 15 ♖ae1 ♗d8

After 15...♖fe8 16 b3 ♗d8 17 ♖xe8+ ♘xe8 18 ♗xd8 ♕xd8 19 ♘a4 White's advantages are a blockade on c5, ownership of the e-file, and targets on c6 and a5.

16 b3 ♖b8 17 ♘a4!!

Although Fischer certainly dealt with multiple negative personality issues during his lifetime, most players consider his chess moves sacrosanct. My big brother *Rybka* and I would both be racked with remorse if we dared criticize his move. So we won't!

Black gets tied up like a pretzel after the simple 17 ♗g3! ♖e8 18 ♗e5! ♖e6 19 ♕d3! when he must also deal with ♕a6 ideas. All this being said, Fischer's 17 ♘a4!! is the birth of a profound series of wobbly-looking ideas which conspire to create a perfectly-shaped whole.

17...♘e4 18 ♗xd8 ♖bxd8 19 ♕f4!

This looks like a silly strategic error since it allows Black ...♕d6 with tempo. Keep watching.

19...♕d6 20 ♕xd6!

Amazing! Now he voluntarily corrects Black's misaligned pawns.

20...cxd6 21 c4! ♘f6

22 ♖c1!

Black is also hard pressed to hold the game after 22 c5!.

22...♖b8

22...♖fe8 23 ♖xe8+ ♖xe8 24 cxd5 cxd5 25 ♘c3 ♖c8 26 ♘e2 ♖xc1+ 27 ♘xc1 in essence leaves White a clear pawn up, since Black's doubled d-pawns are useless for the purposes of the establishment of a passed pawn.

23 cxd5 cxd5

Fischer's sequence produced:

1. A queenside majority;

2. Black is saddled with sickly doubled isolanis on the d-file; and

3. White controls the c-file, giving him opportunities for rook raids to c6, menacing d6 and perhaps later the a5-pawn.

24 f3 ♘h5 25 ♖c6 ♘f4 26 ♖d2 ♖fe8!?

Refusing to get tied down to passive defence with 26...♖fd8.

27 ♖xd6 ♖e1+ 28 ♔f2 ♖h1 29 ♔g3 ♘h5+ 30 ♔h4!

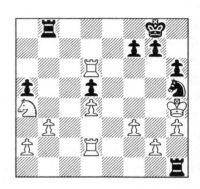

Fischer is willing to endure inconvenience in exchange for material and jams his king in the corner the way a traveller would with an oversized bag on a plane. For the next ten moves, Petrosian sacs pawns left and right, making a mighty effort to weave mating nets or, failing that, bag a perpetual check.

30...g6 31 ♖xd5 ♖e8 32 ♖xa5 ♖ee1 33 ♘c3 ♘f4 34 ♔g4 ♘e6 35 ♖e5 f5+ 36 ♔g3 f4+ 37 ♔h4

And not 37 ♔f2??, met by 37...♖hf1 mate.

37...♔h7 38 ♘e4 g5+ 39 ♔g4 ♘g7!

Black threatens ...♔g6 and ...h5 mate.

40 ♘xg5+!

40...hxg5 41 ♖xe1 ♖xe1 42 ♔xg5 ♘e6+ 43 ♔f5 ♖e2!

Clever, but by this point White has collected too many pawns for his piece.

44 ♖xe2 ♘xd4+ 45 ♔e5 ♘xe2 46 a4 1-0

The knight is overwhelmed by the army of white pawns. Sorry Morphy, Capa and Kasparov. The three of you must fight it out to see who gets the title of second-best player of all time. Fischer, like Ali, was the greatest.

Summary

I used to play the 3...♘c6 line as Black, but abandoned it due to the annoying 4 exd5! Exchange line. Symmetry is no fun when you are the guy down the move.

Game 57
**M.Kobalia-
Nguyen Ngoc Truong**
Al Ain 2008

---

1 e4 e6 2 d4 d5 3 ♘c3 ♘c6 4 ♘f3 ♘f6 5 exd5 exd5 6 ♗b5 ♗e7

Black sensibly inoculates himself from the pin on g5.

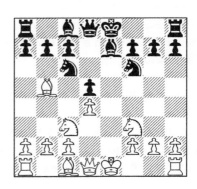

7 ♘e5 ♗d7 8 0-0!

There is no rush to exchange since 8...♘xe5? drops a pawn.

8...0-0 9 ♖e1 a6?!

How quick they are to make this concession. I would hold off for a while at least, and play 9...♖e8 10 ♗f4 h6. Perhaps then White has nothing better than to take on c6, although after 11 ♗xc6 ♗xc6 12 ♕f3 ♗b4 13 a3 ♗xc3 14 ♘xc6! bxc6 15 ♕xc3 ♕d7 16 f3! Black still has troubles: his c6-pawn, the a-pawn, the dark squares and with his knight, which for now has no scope. Perhaps he should manoeuvre it to e6.

10 ♗xc6 ♗xc6 11 ♗g5

Playing for central pressure over the structural damage which he can inflict with 11 ♘xc6 bxc6 12 ♘a4.

11...♘e4?

Drifting into a wretched ending. His best shot was to curl up into a ball and hope to unravel later with 11...♗e8! 12 ♕d3 c6 13 ♖e3 h6 14 ♗h4 ♘d7 15 ♖ae1 ♖e8. Admittedly, matters are not pleas-

pleasant for Black, but this is far better than what happens in the game.

12 ♗xe7 ♕xe7 13 ♘xc6 bxc6 14 f3!

This deceptively strong move is even better than winning a clear pawn with 14 ♕e2 ♕h4 15 ♘xe4 ♖fe8 16 f3 dxe4 17 fxe4.

14...♘xc3 15 ♖xe7 ♘xd1 16 ♖xd1 ♖ab8 17 b3 ♖bc8

17...♖fc8? 18 ♖de1 ♔f8 19 ♖d7 and White's threat to double on the seventh forces 19...♖e8 20 ♖xe8+ ♖xe8 21 ♖xc7 which is hopelessly lost for Black.

18 ♖d3 ♖fe8 19 ♖xe8+ ♖xe8 20 ♔f2 f5 21 ♖c3 ♖e6 22 b4!

Bye, bye a6-pawn!

22...f4 23 ♖a3 ♔f7 24 ♖xa6 ♔e7 25 ♖a3!

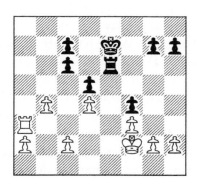

The correct plan:

1 Manoeuvre the rook back to c3;

2. Play a4;

3. Post the rook at c5; and

4. b5! either wins another pawn or swaps rooks, which forces Black into a pawn-down king and pawn ending.

25...♔d7 26 ♖c3!

Like an echo, the rook returns to c3.

26...♖h6 27 h3 ♖e6 28 a4 ♔c8 29 ♖c5! ♔d7 30 b5!

His long-term plan comes to fruition.

30...♖e3

Or 30...g6 31 a5! cxb5 32 ♖xd5+ ♖d6 (any other move drops a second pawn, but now White wins the king and pawn ending) 33 ♖xd6+ cxd6 34 ♔e2 d5 35 ♔d3 b4 36 c4! and wins.

31 ♖xc6 ♖a3 32 ♖c5 ♔d6 33 c4! dxc4 34 ♖xc4 g5 35 ♔g1 ♔d7 36 h4!

Giving his king access to Black's pawns on that side of the board through the winding road of h3 and g4.

36...♖a1+ 37 ♔h2 gxh4

Or 37...h6 38 hxg5 hxg5 39 ♔h3 ♖a2 40 g3 ♖f2 41 ♖c3 ♖d2 42 gxf4 gxf4 43 ♖c4 and f4 falls to ♔g4 and ♔xf4.

38 d5 h3 39 ♔xh3 ♖h1+ 40 ♔g4 ♖g1 41 ♖c2 ♖a1 42 ♔xf4 ♖xa4+ 43 ♔e5 ♖b4 44 g4 ♖b3

If 44...♖xb5 45 ♖h2 c6 46 ♖xh7+ ♔d8 47 ♔e6 ♖xd5 48 f4 ♖d4 49 g5 ♖xf4 50 g6 and the g-pawn wins a whole rook.

45 ♖h2 ♖e3+ 46 ♔f4 ♖e7 47 ♖h6 ♖f7+ 48 ♔g3 ♔e8 49 f4 ♖d7 50 ♔h3

I don't really get this move, which doesn't hurt White. Surely 50 f5 is more useful?

50...♖xd5 51 ♖xh7 ♖c5 52 g5 ♔f8 53 ♔g4 ♔e8 54 f5 1-0

Summary

So far, I haven't found a clear way for Black to equalize in the Exchange variation of the 3...♘c6 French.

Chapter Six
1 d4 d5 2 ♘c3:
Second Move Alternatives

1 d4 d5 2 ♘c3

In this chapter, we mainly concentrate on Black's second-move options after: 1 d4 d5 2 ♘c3, which include:

a) After 2...♗f5 Black may refrain from playing an early ...♘f6.

b) 2...♘c6 sees Black mirror the Veresov.

c) With 2...c5 Black scoffs at the Veresov and attempts to take over the initiative immediately!

d) With 2...g6 Black plays it Grünfeld style.

e) We also cover some of Black's more ridiculous attempts like 2...e5?!. If this alternate-universe reversed Albin Counter-Gambit works, then I am willing to concede that Black stands better from move one!

Game 58
Z.Varga-B.Lengyel
Budapest 1994

1 d4 d5 2 ♘c3 ♗f5

In a little tweak, Black plays his bishop out before moving his knight to f6, possibly to avoid pins based on ♗g5.
3 f3

You can also hold back on f3 and play 3 ♗g5 h6 4 ♗h4 c6 5 ♕d2 ♘d7 when 6 f3 ♘gf6 7 0-0-0 transposes to a mainline Veresov from Chapter Three.

3...e6

The independent route. Instead, 3...♘f6 4 ♗g5 ♘bd7 5 ♘xd5 or 5 ♕d2 transposes to Chapter Three.

4 e4 ♗g6 5 ♗d3

Guarding the knight with 5 a3!?, which protects e4, looks a tad slow: 5...dxe4 6 fxe4 e5! (a vigorous reaction; Black sacs a pawn in an ending with little hope of regaining it, but his development lead compensates) 7 dxe5! ♕xd1+ 8 ♔xd1 ♘c6 9 ♗f4 0-0-0+ 10 ♔c1 f6! 11 ♘f3 fxe5 12 ♘xe5 ♘xe5 13 ♗xe5 offered full compensation for the pawn in J.Hector-J.Smeets, Fuerth 2002.

Next game we look at 5 ♘ge2.

5...♘f6

After 5...♘c6 6 ♘ge2 ♗b4 7 a3 ♗a5 White overpressed with 8 h4?! in J.Hector-E.Berg, Swedish Team Championship 2003, but the simple 8 0-0! is an easy improvement.

6 ♘ge2 ♗e7

Nobody has yet tried the logical 6...c5! 7 exd5 ♘xd5 8 ♘xd5 ♕xd5 9 c4 ♕d7 10 ♗xg6 hxg6 11 ♗e3 cxd4 12 ♕xd4 ♕xd4 13 ♘xd4 a6, which looks

like an ending arisen from a c3 Sicilian. White has a tiny spatial edge and his queenside pawn majority looks slightly better than Black's kingside majority. If I had to bet though, I would put my money on a draw.

7 ♗e3 ♘c6?!

This bogs him down. He needs ...c5 for future counterplay. Perhaps Black should cede some territory whilst freeing himself a bit with 7...dxe4 8 ♘xe4 ♘bd7 and only then play for ...c5.

8 e5 ♘d7 9 ♗f2 ♗xd3 10 cxd3!

This unstereotyped recapture is effective because:

1. It opens the c-file for a rook;

2. White understands that Black needs ...c5 eventually, but when he does play it, White will respond with dxc4 and then has a back-up d-pawn and can push d4 again; and

3. ♕b3 becomes a possibility.

On the flipside, Black eliminates White's good bishop and best attacker.

10...♘cb8

Black experiences respiratory problems and craves air with a ...c5 break.

11 ♕b3 b6 12 f4 f6?

Breaking the principle: don't allow the game to open when behind in development.

13 ♖c1

Missing an opportunity to punish Black's last move: 13 f5! fxe5 14 fxe6 ♘f8 15 ♘xd5 ♘xe6 16 0-0 and Black finds himself dangerously lagging behind with a king stuck in the centre.

13...c6!

Correcting his error.

14 0-0 h5?

A continuation of his flawed policy of allowing the centre to remain fluid while behind in development. Black equalizes after 14...f5! (closing the position) 15 ♘d1 0-0 16 ♘e3 a5.

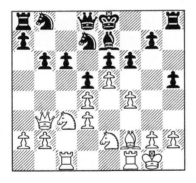

15 ♘d1

Both players remain oblivious to the f5! break, but White's move is not bad. He clears the d-file to put pressure on c6 and prepares to transfer the knight to the superior e3-square. Again, though, 15 f5! makes Black sweat: 15...fxe5 16 fxe6 ♘f8 17 dxe5 ♘xe6 18 ♗e3 ♕d7 19 d4 ♘a6 20 ♘g3. This looks like a French gone wrong for Black.

15...c5? 16 dxc5?!

16 f5! ♘f8 17 exf6 ♗xf6 18 dxc5 is simply dreadful for Black.

16...♘xc5 17 ♕c2 a5 18 ♘ec3

White prefers to go for a strategic squeeze, but why not open the game? 18 exf6! gxf6 19 f5 e5 20 d4 ♘e4 21 ♗e3 leaves Black's king in a precarious position.

18...♘c6 19 a3?!

Better was 19 d4.

19...♖c8?!

19...fxe5! 20 fxe5 d4! and Black is back in business.

20 d4 ♘d7 21 ♕d3

Sigh... Get on with it, man! 21 f5! and he should play it the following move also.

21...♕c7 22 ♘e3 ♕b7

Alternatively:

a) 22...♘xd4? 23 ♕xd4 ♗c5?? 24 ♕d3 d4 25 ♘b5 retains the extra piece.

b) 22...0-0 23 f5! ♘dxe5 24 dxe5 ♘xe5 25 ♕d1 and Black doesn't have enough for the piece.

23 ♘cxd5!

At last, White wakes up and forcefully destabilizes Black's position with a promising piece sac, getting two good central pawns for the piece.

23...exd5 24 ♘xd5 ♘d8

Really not a blunder since Black's position was on the verge of collapse anyway, as shown by:

a) 24...♔f8 25 e6 ♘db8 26 ♘xb6! ♕xb6 27 ♕g6 ♘d8 28 ♖xc8.

b) 24...♗d8 25 e6 ♘f8 26 ♖fe1 g6 27 f5 g5 28 ♗g3 b5 29 e7 ♗xe7 30 ♖xc6!.

25 ♕b5?

Robert Plant of Led Zeppelin described it in a song: "Been dazed and confused for so long, it's not true." Varga misses 25 ♕g6+! ♔f8 26 ♘xe7 ♖h6 27 ♕g3!.

25...h4? 26 h3?

26 ♖xc8! ♕xc8 27 e6! ♘xe6 28 ♖e1 ♔f7 29 f5 wins.

26...♔f8 27 ♗e3 ♖h5?? 28 ♖xc8! 1-0

28...♕xc8 29 ♖c1 followed by ♖c7 regains the material with interest.

Summary

Yes, I know. This game was teeming with blunders. One of the charms of the Veresov I have grown to love is its disorienting nature (hopefully just for your opponent!). In this game both players drifted and missed thematic ideas. This will occasionally happen to you too (Lord knows it happens to me all the time!). When it does, just embrace the chaos and stay aggressive. The longer you play the Veresov, the less crazy it gets.

Game 59
M.Khachiyan-B.Dolinskij
Moscow 1996

1 d4 d5 2 ♘c3 ♗f5 3 f3 e6 4 e4 ♗g6 5 ♘ge2

White avoids posting a bishop on d3, with the inevitable trade for the g6-bishop. Since he controls more space, he avoids exchanges.

5...♘f6

If Black wants to avoid a closed French/Advance Caro structure, he should open the game a bit with 5...dxe4!? 6 fxe4 ♘f6 and now 7 ♗g5?! was a bit superficial, leading to swaps in B.Maksimovic-J.Nikolac, Bjelovar 1979. Better to kick immediately with 7 e5! ♘d5 8 ♘xd5 exd5 9 ♘f4 ♗e4 10 ♗d3 when White's extra space and development give him the advantage.

6 e5 ♘fd7 7 h4!

7 ♘f4?! doesn't take into account the health of his centre: 7...c5 8 ♘xg6 hxg6 9 f4 cxd4 10 ♕xd4 ♘c6 saw White getting kicked around, J.Mense-

T.Visschedijk, German League 2004.
7...h6 8 ♘f4 ♗h7 9 ♗d3!

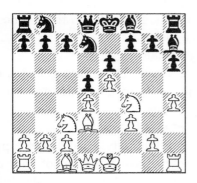

Generally this should help Black, who benefits from trades, especially of White's good bishop. But here Khachian understands that the swap subtlety weakens the light squares around Black's king, with the help of a sac on e6.
9...♗xd3 10 ♕xd3

Khachian has his eyes on an e6 sac followed by ♕g6+. He wants more than just space after 10 cxd3 c5 11 dxc5 ♗xc5 12 d4 ♗b4.
10...♗e7

Instead, 10...c5 11 ♘cxd5! exd5 (Black gets smacked down after the careless 11...cxd4?? 12 ♘xe6!) 12 e6 ♘f6 13 ♕b5+ ♗d7 (13...♘c6?? 14 ♕xb7 ♘e7 15 ♕b5+ wins) 14 ♕xb7!? fxe6 15 ♘xe6 ♕c8 16 ♕xa8! ♕xa8 17 ♘c7+ ♔f7 18 ♘xa8 ♗d6 finds us in an interesting and difficult-to-assess ending.
11 ♘xe6!?

The e6- and g6-squares become ground zero for a nuclear test explosion. Having played Melik Khachian many times, I can tell you the man is not shy when it comes to eyebrow-raising sacs! In this case, the sac looks sound enough for at least a draw.

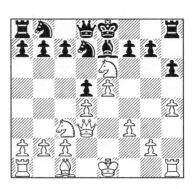

11...fxe6 12 ♕g6+ ♔f8 13 ♕xe6 c6?!

Black needs to shake things up in the centre to challenge White's wing attack. I would play the disruptive 13...c5! 14 ♘xd5 ♘c6 which either forces White to give the perpetual check or take great risks going for the full point.
14 ♘e2!

Heading for g6 or e6.
14...♕e8?

I wonder what Khachian would have played after the correct 14...♗xh4+! 15 g3 ♗g5 16 f4 ♗e7 17 ♕f5+ ♔g8. Now would he take the draw after 18 ♕e6+? Knowing Melik, more than likely he would have turned up the volume a notch, and avoided the perpetual with 18 ♗e3! where White's attack is a well-oiled machine. His plan:

1. Castle queenside;
2. Play g4 with the possibilities of g5, ripping open lines; but

3. His obvious difficulty: he remains down a piece for only one pawn!

15 ♘f4

Threatening devastation on g6 and forcing Black's next move.

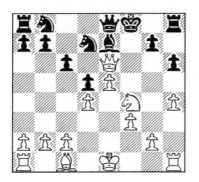

15...♗b4+ 16 c3 ♕xe6 17 ♘xe6+ ♔f7 18 ♘c7 ♗a5 19 ♘xa8 ♖c8

19...♘a6? 20 b4 ♗d8 21 a4 makes the situation even worse for Black, who has trouble winning the a8-knight.

20 b4 ♗d8 21 f4 ♔e6?

Black may be shell-shocked and loses a couple of tempi. His position remains dismal even after the correct 21...♘a6 22 f5 ♔f8 23 g4 ♖xa8 24 g5!.

22 g4 ♘a6 23 f5+ ♔e7 24 g5!

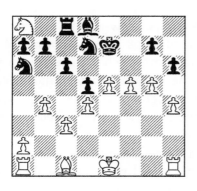

The armada surges forward.

24...h5

24...hxg5? 25 hxg5 ♖xa8 26 ♖h7 ♔f8 27 ♖h8+ ♔e7 28 g6 and there is no defence to ♖g8.

25 g6! ♖xa8

He finally eliminates the doomed knight, only to be obliterated on the other wing.

26 ♗g5+ ♔f8 27 0-0!

Chess pundits advise: don't push too many pawns in front of your castled king. Khachian obviously differs with this theory!

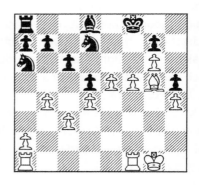

27...♘c7 28 ♖ae1

Or 28 f6! ♘e6 29 fxg7+ ♔g8 30 ♗h6! ♗e7 31 ♖f7 ♖e8 32 ♖af1, which leaves Black helpless against the idea ♖1f5!, ♖xh5, move the bishop and ♖5h7.

28...♘e8

The stampede can't be held back after 28...♗xg5 29 hxg5 a5 30 e6 ♘b6 31 e7+ ♔g8 32 f6.

29 ♗xd8! 1-0

29...♖xd6 30 e6 wins a knight since White also threatens 31 e7+.

Summary

It isn't easy to take advantage of 2...♗f5, but Khachian's 5 ♘ge2 avoids swaps and plays to his space advantage.

> ### Game 60
> ### B.Spassky-G.Gilquin
> Corsica (rapid) 1997

1 e4 ♘c6 2 d4 d5 3 ♘c3

Our move order would be 1 d4 d5 2 ♘c3 ♘c6 3 e4.

3...dxe4!?

I don't claim to understand the motivation behind this line where Black allows White to push his knight around with gain of development. 3...e6 transposes to the 'Swearing in Church' line of the French, covered in Chapter Five.

4 d5 ♘e5 5 ♗f4!

Turning it into a real gambit. White can also play the meeker and safer 5 ♕d4 ♘g6 6 ♕xe4 ♘f6 7 ♕a4+ ♗d7 8 ♗b5 a6 9 ♗xd7+ ♕xd7 10 ♕xd7+ ♘xd7 11 ♘f3 h6 12 ♗e3 0-0-0 13 0-0-0 ♘de5

14 ♘xe5 ♘xe5 when White's advanced d-pawn gave him a safe edge in S.Tiviakov-J.Becker, Eupen 2000, but enough to win? I have my doubts.

5...♘g6 6 ♗g3 a6

Black declines the gambit. Next game we examine the gluttonous 6...f5!?.

7 ♗c4 ♘f6 8 ♕e2!

Threatening e4 and intending to castle queenside.

8...♗g4 9 ♕e3!?

Breaking News: Hell Freezes Over!

We all tend to mellow with age. I can't imagine the 19-year-old Spassky, who worshipped at the altar of sacrifice, playing this move. Even a registered chickenheart like me would sac with 9 f3!? exf3 10 ♘xf3. Does this mean I am braver than Spassky? For the pawn White gets ample compensation:

1. A lead in development which is bound to increase – just look at the constipated bishop on f8!

2. Open f- and e-files for his major pieces;

3. A cramping d5-pawn, which, if challenged with ...e6 or ...c6 at some later point, opens even more lines for White; and

4. Black's king stranded in the centre. If he goes queenside it looks easy to rip Black open with ♗xa6!.

9...♕d7 10 h3 ♗f5

Or 10...♗h5 11 ♘ge2 ♗xe2 (to reduce White's attackers) 12 ♕xe2 0-0-0 (he either plays this or sits around and awaits execution with his king in the middle) 13 0-0-0 ♔b8 14 ♗xa6! bxa6 15 ♕xa6 ♕c8 16 ♕b6+ ♕b7 (16...♖a8 17 ♗xc7 ♖d7 18 ♕a5+ ♔b7 19 ♖d4! forces mate) 17 ♗xc7+.

11 0-0-0 b5

11...0-0-0?? 12 ♕a7 shows one great benefit of stationing the queen on e3.

12 ♗b3 ♕c8

Black's dilemma is that if he tries to free his kingside pieces at the cost of opening the game, he faces 12...c5!? 13 dxc6 ♕xc6 14 ♘ge2 and then:

a) 14...e5! 15 ♗g5! ♕c8 16 ♗xe5! ♘xe5 17 ♘g3 ♘d3+! 18 cxd3 ♗e6 19 ♗xe6 fxe6 20 ♔b1 ♕c5 21 ♘gxe4 ♘xe4 22 ♘xe4 ♕xg5 23 ♘xg5 ♔d7 24 ♖he1 ♖e8 and White has an extra pawn, with conversion to the full point requiring some technique.

b) 14...e6?! 15 ♘d4 ♕b7 16 ♘xf5 exf5 17 ♘d5! (hits the f6- and c7-squares) 17...♖c8 18 ♗g5! ♗e7 19 ♕xf5 0-0 20 h4! ♖fd8 21 h5 ♘f8 22 h6 with a crushing attack.

13 ♘ge2 e5!

Of course this move, the point of 12...♕c8, blasts the game open and

plays into White's hands. The alternative is even worse, which is to do nothing and continue to stare at the f8-bishop and h8-rook, who remain cryogenically frozen to their squares.

14 dxe6 fxe6

Even worse is 14...♗xe6?! 15 ♘xe4 ♗e7 16 ♘xf6+ ♗xf6 17 ♕c5!, which prevents castling, threatens 18 ♖he1 followed by ♕c6+, and hits c7.

15 f3!

The Spassky of old returns with a vengeance. The secret in such positions is never count pawns. Just repeat the mantra: open lines, open lines!

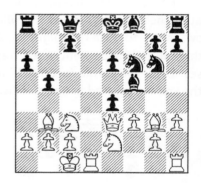

15...exf3 16 ♘d4!?

Rybka gives 16 ♕xf3 c5 17 ♗c7! (threatening both 18 ♕c6+ and also 18 ♖d8+) 17...c4 18 ♗xc4! bxc4 19 g4 with complications that appear favourable to White.

16...♘e7?

After this, Black looks like a goldfish that accidentally flops out of his bowl. He struggles for a while, but death is certain.

It was time to bail out with

16...♗c5! 17 ♕xf3 ♗xd4 18 ♕c6+! ♔f7 19 ♖xd4 ♘e7 20 ♕xc7 ♕xc7 21 ♗xc7 ♖hc8. This only gives White the superior ending, which looks pretty good from Black's perspective if you consider what happened in the remainder of the game.

However, 16...fxg2?? 17 ♘xe6! threatens two (!) double checkmates on the next move: 17...♗xe6 18 ♗xe6 gxh1♕ 19 ♗xc8+ ♗e7 20 ♖xh1 ♖xc8 21 ♕e6 and Black is crushed.

17 ♘xe6 ♗xe6 18 ♗xe6 ♕b7 19 gxf3 c6 20 ♖he1 ♕a7 21 ♕e5 ♘g6

Not that other moves were so wonderful for him.

22 ♗f7+!

Double check. No need to move the queen.

22...♔xf7 23 ♕e6 mate (1-0)

Summary

The position after 3...dxe4 4 d5 ♘e5 looks to me like a poor man's version of the Alekhine's Defence on the queenside. White's 5 ♗f4 turns it into a promising gambit.

Game 61
M.Apicella-V.Vaisman
French Championship,
Angers 1990

1 e4 ♘c6 2 d4 d5 3 ♘c3 dxe4!? 4 d5 ♘e5 5 ♗f4 ♘g6 6 ♗g3 f5!?

Black hangs on to his extra pawn for dear life and dares White to do something about it.

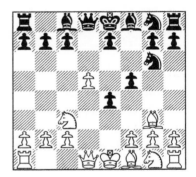

7 ♘h3!

Controlling f4 and keeping options open for a future ♘g5.

7...e5 8 dxe6 c6!

Probably superior to the alternatives:

a) 8...♕xd1+ 9 ♖xd1 c6 10 ♗c4 h6 11 0-0 ♘f6 12 f3! ♗c5+ 13 ♔h1 b5 14 ♗b3 e3!? (virtually a pawn sac; the alternative 14...exf3 15 ♖xf3 ♘e7 16 ♗e5 looks tough for Black) 15 ♖fe1 ♔e7 16 ♘f4 ♘xf4 17 ♗xf4 and e3 is doomed, M.Apicella-S.Soetewey, Brussels 1993.

b) 8...♗xe6?! 9 ♘b5! ♗d6 10 ♗xd6 cxd6 11 ♕d4 ♘h6 12 ♘xd6+ ♔f8 13 0-0-0 ♘f7? (13...♕f6 is better) 14 ♘xf5!

saw White steal a pawn in broad daylight in I.Rogers-C.Laird, Noosa 1998.
9 ♕xd8+ ♚xd8 10 ♘g5 ♘h6 11 0-0-0+ ♚e8

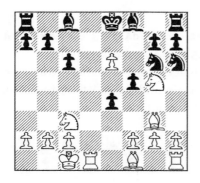

12 ♗c4!?

You don't see this too often. White goes all in and sacs a piece with queens off the board! However:

1. He gets at least two pawns for the piece;

2. Black's king has already moved and remains drifting in the centre;

3. The e6-pawn chokes the development of Black's queenside; and

4. White has a huge development lead and powerfully centralized pieces.

If White gets all of this then why don't I award his last move an exclam? My reasoning is: bravest doesn't always equal best when it comes to how we pick our lines. I see this tendency with some of my students. They go for some spectacular and speculative sac when a simple quiet move secures a clear and safe advantage. When I point out the advantages of the quiet line, they invariably argue against the tyranny of

suppressing art! Sometimes it is trying to be the chess parent to stubborn offspring!

I would go for the low-risk and promising **12 h4!**. For example:

a) 12...f4 13 ♗h2 ♘g4 14 ♘cxe4 ♘xh2 15 ♖xh2 ♘e5 16 ♖h3 h6 17 ♘f3 ♘g4 18 ♘d4 when I don't see Black's compensation for the pawn.

b) 12...♗c5 13 h5 ♘e7 14 ♗c4 and Black's game is a tangled mess.

12...f4 13 ♘cxe4!?

White can also regain some of his material with 13 ♘f7 fxg3 14 ♘xh8 ♘xh8 15 hxg3.

13...♗e7 14 ♖he1 fxg3 15 hxg3

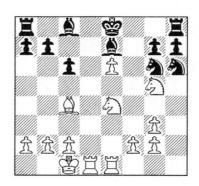

15...♗xg5+!

Reducing the attackers and making room for the king on e7. An example of some of the dangers Black faces is the line: 15...♘e5 16 ♗b3 a5 17 a4 ♘hg4? 18 f3 ♘f6 19 ♘d6+ ♗xd6 20 ♖xd6 ♚e7 (not 20...♘g6?? 21 e7! ♘xe7 22 ♗f7+ ♚f8 23 ♖d8+ ♘e8 24 ♖xe8 mate) 21 ♖xe5!.

16 ♘xg5 ♚e7 17 f4 b5?!

Understandably Black is weary of

being pushed around and desires to push back, but this move creates a fresh weakness on c6.

18 ♗d3!

This controls f5, threatens tricks like ♘xh7 and the bishop may redeploy to e4, where it looks at both wings.

18...♘f8 19 ♗e4! ♖b8

Black must let another pawn fall, as 19...♗b7? fails to 20 ♘xh7! overloading the f8-knight.

20 ♗xc6 ♗b7 21 ♗xb5 ♗xg2 22 ♗c4 ♖c8 23 ♗b3 ♗c6 24 ♘f7!

24...♘xf7

I don't see a way for Black to save himself. For instance: 24...♖g8 25 g4! ♘xg4 (25...a5 26 f5 ♘xg4 27 f6+! ♘xf6 28 ♘d6 wins) 26 ♘d6 wins material, since 26...♖c7?? 27 ♘f5+ ♔f6 28 e7 is hopeless for Black.

25 exf7+ ♔f6 26 ♖d6+ ♔f5 27 ♖e5+ ♔g4 28 ♖g5+ ♔h3 29 ♖xg7 1-0

There is no defence to 30 ♖g8.

Summary

6...f5!? is incredibly risky. In fact, I believe this entire line stinks for Black!

Game 62
L.Aronian-B.Annakov
Moscow 1995

I used to play Levon Aronian when he was a teenage IM on the ICC around the time this game was played. He had such an unassuming, stodgy style (like Reshevsky), that it never occurred to me that just a few years later he would be a contender ranked in the top five players in the world.

1 d4 d5 2 ♘c3 c5 3 e4!

The Albin Counter-Gambit, but a full move up since it's White who plays it.

3...cxd4?!

Black declines the gambit and fires back with the offer of a dubious one himself. I think the best route for Black in this position is to decline the gambit with 3...♘f6! 4 e5 and then:

a) 4...♘e4 5 ♘xe4 dxe4 6 d5 ♕c7 7 ♗f4 g5! 8 ♗g3 ♗g7 9 ♕h5 ♗xe5 10 0-0-0! (sidestepping 10 ♕xg5 ♕a5+!) 10...♗f4+ 11 ♔b1 ♘d7 and now, instead of the 12 ♕h6? of G.Portisch-C.Csiszar, Zalaegerszeg 1992, 12 ♕xg5! leaves White slightly better.

b) 4...♘fd7 transposes to a line in the Alekhine, which comes from the order 1 e4 ♘f6 2 ♘c3 d5 3 e5 ♘fd7 4 d4 c5. Now 5 e6!? fxe6 6 ♘f3 was seen in J.Hector-M.Konopka, German League 1997, and gives White reasonable compensation for the pawn, with his control over e5 and Black's clogged situation with both bishops.

Next game we'll look at Black's third option, 3...dxe4.

4 ♕xd4 ♘c6!

Obligatory, since 4...dxe4? 5 ♕xd8+ ♔xd8 6 ♗f4 led to an ending where Black's king was in real peril in the game H.Mayerhofer-I.Somerlik, Hrabyne 1995.

5 ♕xd5 ♗d7

This is the kind of shaky gambit you encounter at chess clubs all over the world. You know in your heart that your opponent's sac shouldn't work, but the reality is that you must endure his initiative for the next 20 moves or so. Watch how Aronian patiently rebuffs his opponent's attempts to make something concrete with his initiative.

6 ♘f3 ♘f6 7 ♕d1!

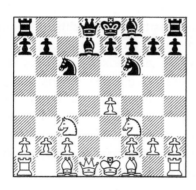

A psychologically difficult move to make, but a good one. Most players regard the retreat of an already developed piece back to its original square as a kind of defeat. However, keeping the queen 'developed' elsewhere simply hands Black a convenient target for

his pieces. A parallel can be made between Aronian's move and a line of the French: 1 e4 e6 2 d4 d5 3 ♘c3 ♗b4 4 e5 b6 5 ♕g4 ♗f8!. There the bishop returns to its place of birth to avoid weakening or moving the king.

7...e5 8 ♗d3!

Aronian consolidates, avoiding the sharper 8 ♗c4.

8...♗b4 9 ♗d2 0-0 10 h3!

Aronian's careful play demonstrates that Black has only fishing chances for the pawn.

10...♖e8 11 ♘e2!

Principle: trade down when ahead in material.

11...♗xd2+ 12 ♕xd2 ♕b6 13 c3 ♖ad8 14 ♕c2 ♖c8 15 ♕b3 ♕a5 16 0-0 ♗e6

It looks like Black is getting somewhere kicking White around, but in reality he is building a castle in the sky since White's position doesn't deteriorate in any way. It goes against our human nature to allow the opponent to bully us for this long. See, though how Aronian humbly forebears the insults and turns the other cheek in response to his opponent's shoving, patiently waiting for his turn to be in control. This patience is often misinterpreted as lethargy or cowardice by players on the club level. It's not, and I remind them to re-read the story of the tortoise and the hare we read as children!

17 ♕c2!

He isn't afraid of ghosts on the c-file.

17...b5

Naturally, 17...♘b4?? fails to the simple 18 cxb4! ♖xc2 19 bxa5, winning a piece.

18 ♘g5 ♗c4 19 ♘f3!

I discovered long ago that it annoys opponents if I repeat a position twice, and then pull the rug out from under them, refusing to repeat a third time. Perhaps Aronian's motives for repetition were not as Machiavellian as mine, and he simply repeated to get closer to the move 40 mark and avoid time trouble.

19...♖cd8

Realizing that White may just be toying with him and would most certainly have avoided the draw after 19...♗e6 20 b4! ♕b6 21 ♖fb1 with a4 to follow.

20 ♗xc4 bxc4 21 b4 cxb3

After 21...♕c7 22 ♖fd1 Black has zip for the pawn.

22 axb3

White removed the air out of Black's initiative with carefully sustained defence. Watch how he keeps improving his game, little by little.

22...♕b6 23 ♖a4 a6 24 ♘d2!

Protecting b3 and keeping the possibility of c4 as a nice perch for the knight.

24...♕c5 25 ♘c4

Avoiding the silly trap 25 ♖xa6?? ♘b4.

25...a5 26 ♖fa1

The initiative swings over to White, who retains his extra pawn and now eyes a new target on a5.

26...♖a8 27 ♘c1!

Incremental adjustments. See how he slowly brings all his pieces into play? The knight wasn't doing much on e2, but on c1 it covers b3 and prepares to enter the fight from d3.

27...♖ed8 28 ♘e3 ♕d6?

Black is under the impression that he still has the initiative and misses White's threat. However, if 28...♖ab8 29 ♖c4 ♕b5 30 ♘d3! ♘xe4 31 ♘xe5! ♘xe5 32 ♖xe4 White stays up a pawn.

29 b4!

Another one bites the dust!

29...♖ac8

Realizing the futility of 29...♕c7 30 ♘b3.

30 bxa5 ♘d4 31 ♕b2

Even two pawns up, Aronian doesn't mind dancing to his opponent's tune for a while longer.

31...♖b8 32 ♕a2 ♘e6 33 ♘b3 ♕d3?!

His position is still busted after the superior 33...♕a6.

34 a6!

The c3-pawn doesn't matter. The advancing a-pawn paralyses Black.

34...♕xc3 35 a7 ♖xb3

35...♖a8 36 ♖c4! ♕d3 37 ♖d1 traps the queen in mid-board.

36 ♖c4 1-0

I realize this low-key game isn't the most exciting in the book, but it's instructive. In books and magazines it's always the attackers who get all the attention and glory. In real life patient defenders win just as often.

Summary

Declining the Reversed Albin with 3...♘f6! looks like Black's best route to equality.

1 d4 d5 2 ♗f4

For more information on the London System please order several copies of my excellent book *Play the London System*!

2...c5 3 e4!

Darwinian law states that the powerful always oppress and prey on the weak. GM Grachev, who probably views an old IM like me the same way a hungry young cheetah looks upon an elderly and well-fed gazelle, signals his refusal to play strategic chess and attempts to take my head off with a Reversed Albin Counter-Gambit. The extra move means a lot in the open position and Black must continue with great care.

3...dxe4!?

In this case common sense bows to pure greed! As I mentioned last game, the more prudent decision would be to decline the gambit.

4 d5 ♘f6 5 ♘c3

You get this position from the Veresov via: 1 d4 d5 2 ♘c3 c5 3 e4 dxe4 and then 4 d5 ♘f6 5 ♗f4.

5...a6

A strategic trap to watch for is 5...e6? 6 ♗b5+ ♗d7 7 dxe6! fxe6 and White picked off both e-pawns, C.Lakdawala-B.Baker, San Diego 2007.

6 ♕e2!

This is also my favourite plan when I'm White in this position. The idea is to castle queenside and then go after Black's king.

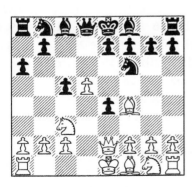

6...♗f5

Hanging on to the extra pawn. Other moves:

a) 6...♘xd5? 7 0-0-0 e6 8 ♕xe4 (White regains his pawn while retaining his massive development lead) 8...♗e7 9 ♖xd5!? (uncharacteristically reckless! Black gets clobbered after the more patient 9 ♗c4!) 9...exd5 10 ♘xd5 ♗e6?? (panic; Black should play 10...f5! 11 ♕a4+ ♔f8 12 ♘xe7 ♕xe7 13 ♘f3, but White still has huge compensation for the exchange as Black's entire army is snoozing on the last rank) 11 ♘c7+ ♔f8 12 ♕xb7 ♗g5 13 ♘e2 ♗xf4+ 14 ♘xf4 ♗c8 15 ♕b6! 1-0 C.Lakdawala-B.Bereick, Internet blitz 2009.

b) 6...♗g4!? 7 f3 exf3 8 ♘xf3 g6 9 0-0-0 with big compensation for the pawn thanks to White's development lead, the pressure down the e-file, and because the d5-pawn hampers Black's harmony and cramps him.

7 0-0-0 ♘bd7

Black doesn't have the luxury for such aggression as 7...b5?!. Indeed, after 8 f3 exf3 9 gxf3! b4? 10 ♘e4 ♗xe4 11 fxe4 in C.Lakdawala-V.Krishnan, San Diego (rapid) 2009, for only one pawn White had:

1. A large development lead;

2. A space advantage with cramping central pawns;

3. The bishop pair; and

4. An attack.

8 h3!

This is played to induce the weakening ...h5.

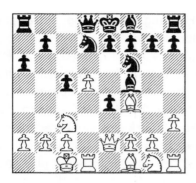

8...h5

Or 8...♕b6 9 g4 ♗g6 10 f3 e5 11 dxe6 fxe6!? 12 fxe4 e5 13 ♗h2 0-0-0 14 ♘f3 ♕e6 15 ♘h4 ♗f7 16 ♗g2 c4 17 ♔b1 ♗c5 18 ♘f5 with an edge for White, L.Winants-O.Korneev, Warsaw 2005.

9 f3 e3!?

Trying to cool off his initiative. Accepting the pawn is very dangerous: 9...exf3 10 ♘xf3 ♕a5 11 ♔b1 0-0-0? (Grandmaster Magerramov misses the next move) 12 ♘e5! threatened 13 ♘xf7 as well as 13 ♘c4 in C.Lakdawala-E.Magerramov, Internet blitz 2007.

10 ♕xe3 ♕a5 11 ♘ge2 0-0-0 12 ♘g3 ♗g6 13 ♘ge4 ♘xe4

An example of the perils for Black is the line 13...h4? 14 ♘g5 (threatening ♗d3, which undermines f7) 14...♘h7 15 ♘e6! fxe6 16 dxe6 ♘b6 17 ♖xd8+ ♔xd8 18 ♕e5 ♘c8 19 ♕b8 ♕b6 20 ♗b5! clearing the d-file for the rook mates.

14 fxe4 e5?

As rancid as it looks, 14...f6 had to be played.

15 dxe6 fxe6 16 ♗c4 ♕b6 17 ♗g5! ♖e8

18 ♕g3!

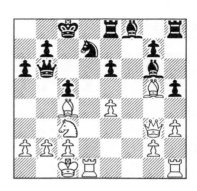

Black's pieces are totally out of sync.

18...h4

Black is quickly reduced to helplessness if he goes passive with 18...♗f7 19 ♖hf1 ♗g8 20 ♖f3, and he gets crushed after 18...♕b4?? 19 ♖xd7! ♔xd7 20 ♖d1+ ♔c6 (or 20...♔c8?? 21 ♗xe6+ ♖xe6 22 ♖d8 mate) 21 ♕d3 ♔b6 22 a3! ♕a5 23 ♗d8+, which picks off the queen.

19 ♗xh4 ♗h5 20 ♖d2 ♕c7 21 ♕xc7+

Why not? He is up a pawn now.

21...♔xc7 22 g4 ♗g6 23 ♗g3+ ♔c8 24 h4! ♘b6

Avoiding the trap 24...♘f6? 25 ♖hd1! (threat: mating with ♗xe6+!) 25...b5 26 ♘xb5! axb5 27 ♗xb5 and Black collapses since 27...♖e7 runs into 28 ♗a6+ ♖b7 29 ♖d8 mate.

25 ♗e2 ♗e7 26 ♔b1

But not 26 g5?? ♗xg5.

26...♗f6 27 e5 ♗e7 28 h5 ♗h7 29 ♗f3 ♘c4 30 ♖e2 ♗g5!

Threatening to fork on d2.

31 ♗e1!

After 31 ♘e4?! ♗xe4 32 ♗xe4 ♘d2+

33 ♔a1 ♘xe4 34 ♖xe4 ♖hf8 Black remains active and conversion won't be easy for White.

31...♗f4?

I felt pretty good around here. Maybe I was clawing my way back into the game? There I was, thinking these beautiful thoughts, when Grachev's next move rudely dispelled this daydream. The experience of facing down a top-tier GM is really just enduring a series of surprising jolts. Go back to the time when you discovered that Darth Vader was actually Luke Skywalker's father. Yes, the shocks are just like that!

Better was 31...♖d8.

32 ♗e4!

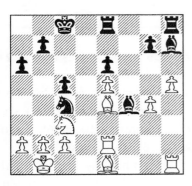

Taking Black's best piece out of the equation.

32...♗xe5 33 ♗xh7?!

Good enough, but he had better. Both sides miss the trick 33 ♗d3! ♗xc3 34 ♗xc3 ♗xd3 35 cxd3 ♘d6 36 ♗xg7 and I would resign here.

33...♖xh7 34 b3! ♘a3+

34...♗xc3 35 ♗xc3 ♘d6 36 ♖f1 ♖e7 37 ♖f8+ ♔d7 38 ♗e5 is busted for Black

who is hopelessly passive, with a silly-looking rook on h7. Moreover, his knight is dominated by White's monster bishop, while White's rooks rule.

35 ♔b2 ♗xc3+ 36 ♗xc3 ♘b5 37 ♗e5 ♔d7

There is no saving the game. For example:

a) 37...♘d4 38 ♖f2 ♘c6 39 ♗d6 sees White menace both ♗xc5 and ♖f7.

b) 37...♖f8 38 ♖hh2! ♘d4 39 ♖hf2 ♖xf2 40 ♖xf2 and there is nothing to be done about ♖f7.

38 ♖d1+ 1-0

38...♔c8 39 ♖f2 is hopeless.

Summary

Accepting the Albin Counter-Gambit a full move up is a pretty scary prospect for Black. That extra move gives White a long-lasting initiative plus attacking chances for the pawn.

Game 64
Buyakhin-M.Botvinnik
USSR 1968

I had the honour of playing the great Mikhail Botvinnik in a simul in Montreal when I was 15-years old. I plotted with my friend, Andy, another junior who also played the legend. We grudgingly conceded Botvinnik had an edge over us strategically, but he was weak (for a World Champion!) tactically, and that we both had excellent chances to whip him should complications arise! We had unearthed his Achilles heel and were ready to strike! Oh, the innocence of youth.

In the game, by some miracle I managed to outplay Botvinnik strategically on the black side of a King's Indian and reduce him to moving back and forth. I was so close to the win that I visualized the headlines in the following day's newspaper: 'Boy Genius Defeats 3-Time World Champ!!!' Tragically my fantasy world disintegrated quickly when Botvinnik unexpectedly sac'ed a piece (rather unsoundly), confusing the living daylights out of me, and swindled me of the point. Could it be that Andy and I maybe needed to reassess our theory about Botvinnik the tactical weakling?

1 d4 g6 2 ♘c3 d5

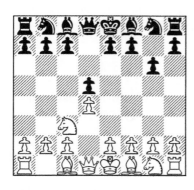

3 e4 dxe4 4 ♘xe4 ♗g7 5 ♘f3 ♘d7

Black gets into trouble quickly after the logical-looking but weak 5...♗g4? 6 ♗c4! with the threat of 7 ♗xf7+!. Then:

a) 6...e6 7 ♗g5 ♗xf3 8 ♕xf3 f6 9 ♗e3 ♕e7 10 ♘c5 ♘c6 11 0-0-0 0-0-0 12 ♗a6! and already 1-0 in R.Gukasian-

P.Natacheev, Anapa 2008.

b) 6...♘f6 7 ♘eg5! ♖f8 (Black is busted after 7...e6 8 ♘xf7!) 8 ♘xf7! ♗xf3 9 ♘xd8 ♗xd1 10 ♘e6 ♗xc2 11 ♘xg7+! ♔d7 12 ♘e6 when Black had managed to keep the material even, but White still had a strong initiative in P.Rosen-F.Lindgren, Stockholm 1996.

Next game we look at 5...♘h6.

6 ♗c4 ♘b6 7 ♗b3 a5 8 c3 a4 9 ♗c2 ♘f6 10 ♘xf6+ ♗xf6?

A rare strategic error by the Mr. Spock of the chess world. Black should play the unnatural 10...exf6! 11 0-0 0-0 12 ♖e1 ♗e6!. Let's assess:

1. White's healthy four versus three pawn majority on the queenside means a win should the game reach a king and pawn ending;

2. White controls extra central space;

3. The extra pawn surrounding Black's king keeps it safe; and

4. Black keeps a grip on the central light squares for now. The fight will revolve around how well Black holds on to his control. White may try to expand

with b3 and c4, but this could weaken his d-pawn.

Conclusion: chances may be dynamically balanced.

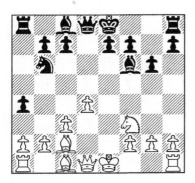

11 ♗h6!

Pinpointing the flaw with Black's last move. Black's king is stranded in the centre and experiences difficulties castling.

11...♖a5!?

The rook volunteers for a risky mission to eject the intruder on h6.

12 0-0 ♖h5 13 ♕c1 ♖g8

Threatening 14...g5.

14 ♗f4 ♖a5 15 ♖e1 g5?!

Even Botvinnik had his off days. Attempting to wrest the initiative from a position of weakness rarely works. He should just defend with 15...♗e6 16 ♘d2! ♔f8 17 ♗h6+ ♗g7 18 ♘e4 ♗d5.

16 ♗e5 ♗xe5 17 ♖xe5 ♖xe5 18 ♘xe5 ♕d6

Unappealing are:

a) 18...h6?! 19 ♕d1! which threatens both the a-pawn and ♕h5.

b) 18...♗g7 19 ♕d1 a3 20 bxa3 f6 21 ♘d3.

19 ♗xh7 ♖g7 20 ♕c2 f6 21 ♘f3 ♗d7 22 c4 c5 23 ♗e4 g4 24 dxc5 ♕xc5 25 ♘d2 ♗c8 26 ♖e1 ♔f7 27 ♕c3 ♖g5 28 g3 ♕c7 29 ♗g2 ♖c5 30 b3 axb3 31 axb3

White has his extra pawn on the queen's wing. Time to slowly nurture it forward.

31...♖h5 32 ♘f1!

Little moves like this are deceptively hard to find in our own games. White patiently improves the position of his knight to e3.

32...♘d7 33 ♕d4 ♘e5 34 ♕e4 ♕b6 35 ♕e3 ♕xe3!?

Trying his luck in a pawn-down endgame. He probably feared for the safety of his king had he kept queens on the board after 35...♕b4 36 ♖a1.

36 ♘xe3 ♖h8 37 ♖a1!

Both ♖a8 and ♖a7 are in the air.

37...♗d7?!

Giving up a second pawn in the hope of getting somewhere with his bishop over White's knight. He probably should have stayed passive with 37...♖d8 38 ♖a8 ♔e8 39 ♔f1, although then Black has no useful plan.

38 ♗xb7 ♖b8 39 ♖a7 ♘c6 40 ♗xc6 ♗xc6 41 ♖a3

He wants two connected passed pawns over the line 41 ♘xg4 ♖xb3 42 ♖a1.

41...♗f3 42 ♔f1 e5 43 ♔e1 ♔g6

43...♖h8 44 ♘f1 ♖d8 45 ♘d2 doesn't get Black anywhere.

44 ♔d2 f5 45 ♔c3 f4 1-0

Resignation looks a bit premature, but it isn't: 46 ♖a6+ ♔g5 47 gxf4+ exf4 48 ♖a5+ ♔g6 49 ♘d5 ♗xd5 50 ♖xd5 ♖h8 51 c5 ♖xh2 52 c6 ♖h7 53 b4 easily wins the queening race.

Summary

The ...d5 and ...g6 set-up looks playable if Black sidesteps several opening traps and doesn't mind a slightly more cramped game.

> ### Game 65
> **K.Chernyshov-A.Panchenko**
> Zalakaros 2003

1 ♘c3 d5 2 d4!

Brilliantly recovering from his shaky first move by steering the game into a Veresov! Just kidding, 1 ♘c3 is a perfectly good move.

2...g6 3 e4 dxe4 4 ♘xe4 ♗g7 5 ♘f3 ♘h6

6 ♗f4

Others:

a) 6 c3 0-0 7 ♗c4 b6 8 0-0 ♗b7 9 ♕e2 ♘d7 10 ♖e1 ♘f5 11 ♗f4 ♘f6 12 ♘g3 ♘d6 13 ♗b3 e6 14 ♖ad1 and Black experiences difficulties engineering either ...e5 or ...c5, H.Vatter-J.Hofrichter, Leimen 2001.

b) 6 ♗c4 isn't as logical since Black has the manoeuvre ...♘f5 and ...♘d6! which may lead to exchanges: 6...♘f5 7 c3 0-0 8 0-0 ♘d7 9 ♗f4 ♘d6! and now White agreed to the loss of time with 10 ♗d3, but even then Black was yet to fully equalize in M.Kaminski-J.Kiedrowicz, Bielsko Biala 1991.

6...♘f5 7 c3 ♘d6 8 ♘g3

In general, the side with more space should dodge exchanges.

8...♗g4

A common strategy for Black: elimi-

eliminate the knight, which controls the important e5-square, and then change the pawn structure to suit his remaining bishop with ...c6.

9 h3 ♗xf3 10 ♕xf3 c6

Assessment:

1. Black developed harmoniously at the cost of the bishop pair;

2. Besides the bishop pair, White also controls more central space due to his d4-pawn; and

3. Black must make a crucial decision: should he free himself by fighting to play ...e5!? at some point. Doing so opens the game for White's bishops, but also frees Black. The alternative is to go the passive route, and remain solid but cramped and forgo ...e5.

Conclusion: White has a slight but enduring advantage.

11 h4!

White uses his h-pawn as a battering ram and gets Black skittish about castling kingside.

11...h5

Perhaps an overreaction. Better was 11...♘d7 12 0-0-0 0-0 13 h5 ♕a5 14

♔b1 ♕d5!, taking the sting out of the attack by exchanging queens. However, after 15 ♗e2 ♕xf3 16 ♗xf3 White still controls the game with his bishop pair, central space and kingside space. Moreover, Black hasn't achieved either the ...c5 or ...e5 pawn breaks, but still Black remains super-solid and such positions are not so easy to win with the white pieces.

12 ♗e5!

Well timed, just before Black plays ...♘d7, controlling e5.

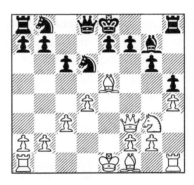

12...♔f8?!

As a consequence of this move, the h8-rook won't see daylight for a long time, but after 12...0-0 13 ♖h3! suddenly the sac on h5 becomes a very real threat and puts pressure on Black to come up with a good defence:

a) 13...♕a5?! 14 ♘xh5! ♗xe5 15 b4! ♕c7 16 dxe5 ♘f5 17 ♕e4 ♘d7 18 f4 with an extra pawn and attacking chances.

b) 13...f6?! 14 ♗f4 e5 15 dxe5 fxe5 16 ♗g5 ♖xf3 17 ♗xd8 ♖f7 18 ♗d3 when the g6-pawn is a clear target, and

White also has potentials of occupying holes on e4 and g5.

c) In this case the passive choice is best: 13...♘e8! 14 ♗c4 ♘d7 15 ♗xg7 ♘xg7 16 0-0-0 ♕c7 17 ♘e4 and g4 follows, but Black may get central counterplay with a well-timed ...e5.

13 ♗d3

Threatening to clip g6.

13...♔g8 14 0-0-0 ♘d7 15 ♖he1!

The bishop refuses to budge from its advanced outpost on e5. Black can't afford to take it.

15...♘f6!

Black realizes the futility of trying for the ...e5 break and shores up the defensive barrier around his king. This strategy leaves him totally passive. Essentially Black is saying: "Here I am, come and get me if you can!"

16 ♕e2 ♕d7 17 ♗f4 ♖e8 18 f3 e6

19 c4?

Violating the physician's oath: "First, do no harm." I would wait before agreeing to this impatient and committal move, which grabs more territory and also weakens his d-pawn.

White reasons that in such situations one must take strategic risks in order to make progress. True, but what is the rush? White's pieces are not in their optimal spots yet.

White should play 19 ♔b1 ♘d5 20 ♗e5 ♕e7 21 c4! (the right moment for this move) 21...♘b4 22 c5! ♗xe5 (if 22...♘f5? 23 ♗xf5 exf5 24 ♕d2! – threatening both g7 and b4 – 24...♕xh4 25 ♗f6!! wins material) 23 dxe5 ♕xh4 24 ♘xh5 ♖xh5 25 g4 ♘e4! (threatening a strange fork on f2) 26 ♕xe4 ♘xd3 27 ♖xd3 ♖h8 28 ♖d7 when White's space and absolute control over the d-file leave Black with serious problems to solve.

19...♕d8?

There is a fine art to grovelling. The formula: lie low and patiently wait until your opponent overpresses. Then strike hard! Now is the moment to fight back with 19...b5! which generates counterplay:

a) 20 c5?! ♘f5 and all of a sudden I like Black, who controls d5 and may add pressure to the weak d4-pawn.

b) 20 ♗e5 bxc4 21 ♗xc4 ♘xc4 22 ♕xc4 ♔h7 23 ♘e4 ♘xe4! 24 fxe4 ♖d8 25 ♕c5 ♖he8 and I'm not so sure White stands better. His own weaknesses balance out with Black's weak c6-pawn.

c) 20 b3!? bxc4 21 bxc4 ♖d8 when White's king has been weakened and his d-pawn a cause for concern.

20 ♔b1 ♕d7 21 ♗e5 ♕d8?!

It was time to get active with 21...b5!. Should White accept, then

Black gets compensation through the open b-file and ownership of d5.

22 ♕f2 a6 23 ⧄f1!

The knight wasn't doing much on g3. He manoeuvres it to e3 where it watches c4 and helps force an eventual d5 break.

23...b5!?

At last he fights back, but he was slow to pull the trigger and allowed White to reposition and absorb the break.

24 cxb5! cxb5 25 ⧄e3 ♕b6 26 ♕g3 ♖d8 27 d5!

Black is not ready for a game opening with his rook oversleeping on h8.

27...⧄de8

27...⧄xd5? 28 ⧄xd5 exd5 29 ♗xg6! fxg6 30 ♕xg6 ♕c7 31 ♕g5! ♖h7 32 ♖xd5 leaves Black totally tangled up and busted.

28 dxe6 ♕xe6 29 f4!

Now f5 cannot be held back.

29...⧄g4 30 ♗xg7 ⧄xg7 31 f5 ♕e5 32 ♕f3 ⧄xe3 33 ♖xe3 ♕f6 34 fxg6 ♕xf3 35 ♖xf3 fxg6 36 ♖f6!

Pawns begin to fall.

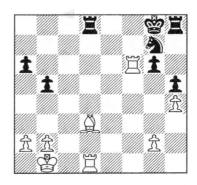

36...⧄f5 37 ♖xg6+ ♔f7 38 ♖xa6 ⧄e3

38...⧄xh4 39 ♖f1+ ♔g7 40 ♗xb5 and the two connected passed pawns on the queenside win easily.

39 ♗g6+ ♔g7 40 ♖xd8 ♖xd8 41 ♗xh5

Efficient. He picks up another pawn and also covers Black's sneaky mating threat on d1.

41...♖d2 42 ♖g6+ ♔h8 43 ♖e6! ♖xg2 44 ♖e2 ♖d1+ 45 ♔c2 ♖g1 46 ♖e4 ♖h1 47 ♗e2 1-0

Summary

The position after 5...⧄h6 looks a bit like a line of the Alekhine: 1 e4 ⧄f6 2 e5 ⧄d5 3 d4 d6 4 ⧄f3 dxe5 5 ⧄xe5 c6, where Black's game is dependable but lacks space.

Game 66
J.Mrkvicka-R.Sicker
correspondence 1998

1 d4 d5 2 ⧄c3 e5?!

The Yiddish word Chutzpah best describes this audacious attempt to seize the initiative on the second move!

3 dxe5 d4 4 ♘b5!

The only path to advantage. 4 ♘e4?! allows Black dynamic equality after 4...♕d5! 5 ♘g3 ♘c6 6 e4 ♕xe5 7 ♘f3 ♕a5+ 8 ♗d2 ♗b4, as in S.Marder-J.Hector, Copenhagen 2001.

4...♗c5

Black also struggles to regain his material in the line 4...c5 5 a4! a6 6 ♘a3 ♘c6 7 ♘f3 ♗e6 8 e3, but I think this is better for him than the game continuation.

5 ♘f3 ♘c6 6 c3!

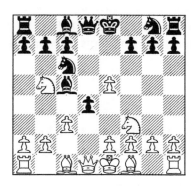

The Smith-Morra Gambit (sort of!). White takes over the initiative while

retaining his extra pawn.

6...dxc3 7 ♕xd8+ ♔xd8 8 ♘xc3 ♘b4 9 ♗g5+ ♘e7

9...f6? 10 0-0-0+ ♔e8 11 exf6 ♘xf6 12 ♗xf6 gxf6 13 a3 ♘c6 14 ♘d5 picks off another pawn.

10 ♖c1

How Petrosianic. Safety first. White reasons that Black may get counterplay if White castles queenside. Nevertheless, I would play it anyway: 10 0-0-0+ ♔e8 11 a3 ♘bc6 12 e3 ♗g4 13 ♗b5 ♘g6 14 ♖d5! ♗e7 15 ♗xe7 ♘gxe7 16 ♖c5! a6 17 ♗xc6+ ♘xc6 18 ♘d4 ♘xd4 19 exd4 c6 20 ♘e4 and White's extra pawn, space and powerhouse knight should win without trouble.

10...h6 11 ♗d2 ♗b6 12 a3 ♘bc6 13 ♘a4 ♘g6 14 ♗c3 ♗g4 15 ♖d1+ ♔e7 16 ♘xb6 axb6 17 e6!

Trading in the vulnerable clunker on e5 for a new model on g7.

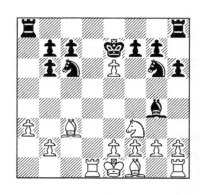

17...♗xe6 18 ♗xg7 ♖hd8!

Agreeing to give up a second pawn with the prayer that his development/endgame attack may materialize into something tangible. 18...♖h7?

would hang on to the h-pawn at a high cost of the rook's fall from grace on the terrible h7-square.

19 ♖xd8 ♖xd8 20 ♗xh6 ♗b3 21 ♘d2?!

21 ♗d2! consolidates easier after 21...♘ge5 22 ♘xe5 ♘xe5 23 e4 ♘c4 24 ♗xc4 ♗xc4 25 h4! and the opposite-coloured bishops won't save Black; the h-pawn is too strong.

21...♘d4 22 e3 ♘c2+ 23 ♔d1?!

Normally, after a move like this, I would say that this looks like panic, except for the fact that this is a correspondence game! How do you panic when you and your army of computers have 48 hours to find a defence?

After 23 ♔e2! ♗a4 24 f3 I don't see a way for Black to continue the attack.

23...♘xe3+ 24 ♔e2?!

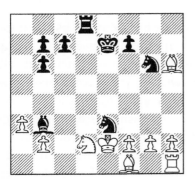

Could it be that we are witnessing a game played by the only honest correspondence player in the known universe, who actually makes the moves on his own without the help of ten computers? If he had turned on *Rybka*,

it would have told him to unravel with 24 ♔c1! ♘g4 25 ♘xb3 ♘xh6 26 ♗e2.

24...♘f5 25 ♗g5+?

This pawn is meaningless. He needs to develop and also eliminate an attacker with 25 ♘xb3! ♘xh6 26 g3!.

25...f6 26 ♗xf6+ ♔xf6 27 ♘xb3 c5?

27...♘f4+! 28 ♔f3 ♘d3 29 g3 c5 and Black achieves queenside counterplay.

28 ♔e1 ♘f4 29 g3 ♘d3+ 30 ♗xd3 ♖xd3 31 ♘c1!

Repelling the invader. At last, White begins to take control.

31...♖d6 32 h4 c4 33 g4 ♘d4 34 f4

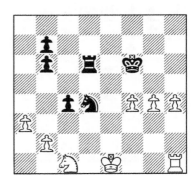

It's easy now. Connected passers like this always remind me of the movie *Night of the Living Dead*. The trio of flesh-loving zombies simply move forward with no barricade to halt them.

34...b5 35 h5 b4 36 axb4 ♘c2+ 37 ♔e2 ♘xb4 38 h6 1-0

Summary

4 ♘b5! refutes Black's cheeky 2...e5?!.

Chapter Seven
Veresov versus Caro-Kann

1 d4 d5 2 ♘c3 c6 3 ♗g5

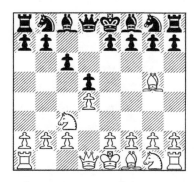

You have a choice against Black's offer of a Caro-Kann, which normally arises after the move order 1 d4 d5 2 ♘c3 c6:

a) Simply play 3 e4 and go into a mainline Caro. The potential for trouble with this approach may be that your opponent probably knows Caro lines better than you do since it is his bread and butter opening. Now if you play Caro as Black, or just tend to do well when you are White against Caro and know it well, then take this route.

b) You obstinately force the game into Veresov paths with 3 ♗g5!?. I remember when FM Duckworth played this on me, the move came as a real shock. I realized that I had not avoided the Veresov after all, and as a Caro player would definitely have preferred him to enter mainlines of the Caro-Kann.

In this line with 3 ♗g5!? you follow up with e3 and f4 leading to a strange Reversed Stonewall Dutch, but with a few twists in your favour. Here is what you get in your Stonewall:

1. Your bishop is on the outside of the chain on g5 instead of on c1.

2. Black doesn't know you are about to play a Stonewall and often replies with the passive ...♘d7. It would be better for your opponent to later post his knight on c6 (after playing ...c5 of course; as far as I know, two pieces can't share the same square!) where it would put more pressure on your centre.

3. ...c6 probably costs him a tempo since at some later stage Black needs to play ...c5.

4. Your knight is on c3, which is a bit odd. The typical placement would be d2. In the games I researched, I didn't see any big problem for White with the c3 placement other than the danger of pins with ...♗b4, but these seem to be easily avoided. The other problem could be that you don't have a c-pawn backing up d4 and Black uses this to add pressure on d4.

Conclusion: I think you get more benefits than problems as White in this line when we compare it to the normal Stonewall set-up.

Game 67
E.Bricard-O.Todorov
St Affrique 2000

1 d4 d5 2 ♗g5

Our Veresov move order is 2 ♘c3 c6 3 ♗g5.

2...c6 3 ♘c3 ♘f6

Black dares White to take on f6.

4 e3!?

Against the Caro, I'm recommend-ing a departure to our normal plan of forcing e4 at all costs. Let's go for a funky reversed Stonewall Dutch set-up with White's knight on c3. If anything, it is certain to confuse your opponents. If the positions in this chapter don't appeal to you, don't worry, you can steer the game back to familiar waters with the alternatives:

a) 4 ♕d3 ♘bd7 and now 5 e4 or 5 ♘f3 transposes to Chapter Two.

b) 4 ♕d2 ♗f5 5 f3 transposes to Chapter Three.

4...♘bd7 5 f4!

I like this rarely played move, which turns the game into a confusing ver-sion of a Stonewall Dutch, for the rea-sons given above.

The main move is 5 ♘f3 which to my mind, leads to paralysing boredom after 5...g6! 6 ♗d3 ♗g7 7 0-0 0-0 and White had nothing in I.Miladinovic-D.Vocaturo, Rome 2005. For instance, if he plays his thematic break with 8 e4 dxe4 9 ♘xe4 ♘xe4 10 ♗xe4 ♘f6 11 ♗d3 ♕b6 12 b3 ♗g4, Black should be very happy with the outcome:

1. White's d-pawn is under some pressure and he must weaken with c3;

2. Black gets rid of his bad bishop by swapping for the knight on f3;

3. Black has plans like ...♗xf3, ...♖ad8, ...♖ac8 and ...c5, with lots of play against the central pawns; and

4. True, White gets the bishop pair in the open position, but it's hard to see White turning his one trump into a win.

5...g6

Black's most harmonious response. Alternatives:

a) 5...♕b6 doesn't bother White since he didn't plan on queenside castling anyway: 6 ♖b1 e6 7 ♘f3 ♕a5 8 ♗d3 ♗b4 9 0-0! c5 10 ♗xf6 ♘xf6 11 ♗b5+ ♔e7!? was N.Napoli-M.Mrsevic, Nis 2008, which White went on to win. Here 9....♗xc3 10 bxc3 ♕xc3 would give White decent compensation for the pawn in the form of his dark-square control, his development lead, possibly leading to an attack, his central clamp on e5, the bishop pair and the open b-file.

b) 5...♕a5 6 ♗d3 ♘e4 7 ♗xe4 dxe4 8 ♕d2 f6 9 ♗h4 e5?! saw Black getting a little excited. He didn't get full compensation for the pawn after 10 fxe5 ♗b4 11 exf6 0-0 12 ♘ge2 ♘xf6 13 0-0 in P.De Souza Haro-F.Moura, Vitoria 2006.

6 ♗d3 ♗g7 7 ♘f3 0-0 8 0-0 c5

Black finally hits back to challenge White's central control, but he still must live with his passive d7-knight and the fact that he expended two

tempi to play ...c5. Other plans for Black are:

a) 8...♕b6 9 ♘a4?! (I would sit tight with 9 ♖b1 c5 10 b3) 9...♕a5 10 c3 c5 (Black gets good play after 10...b5!) 11 ♘e5 c4 12 b4 ♕c7 13 ♗c2 with an equal position in G.Haubt-D.Troyke, German League 2009.

b) 8...♘g4!? 9 ♕d2 f6 10 ♗h4 ♘h6 11 e4 dxe4 12 ♗c4+ ♔h8 13 ♘xe4 ♘f5 14 ♗f2 ♘b6 15 ♗b3 with an edge to White due to his central space, C.Hardt-K.Neumeier, Austrian League 1997.

9 ♕e1!

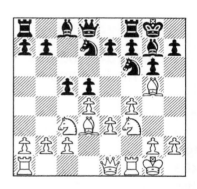

With the centre stable, White's plan is simple. Transfer everyone to the kingside and play for mate.

9...h6!?

He wants to avoid ♕h4 and ♗h6. The trouble is, ...h6 weakens g6 and now f5 creates problems for Black.

10 ♗h4 b6 11 ♘e5 ♗b7 12 ♖d1 ♕c7 13 f5!

It takes good judgement to make a move like this. White allows the destabilization of his centre to strike at Black's weakest point, g6.

13...g5

Black has good reason to fear 13...♘xe5?! 14 dxe5 ♘g4 15 ♕g3 h5 16 fxg6 ♗xe5 17 gxf7+ ♖xf7 18 ♕h3 ♗xh2+ 19 ♔h1 ♖g7 20 ♖f5.

14 ♗g3 ♘h5

15 ♘xd7

15 ♘g6!? leads to strange complications after 15...♘xg3 16 ♘xe7+ ♔h8 17 ♕xg3 ♕xg3 18 hxg3 ♘f6. The question now is: can White's knight get out alive? Yes it can, with 19 dxc5 bxc5 20 ♗b5!, but Black gets some counterplay after 20...♖ab8 21 b3 ♘g4 with a crazy position which *Rybka* helpfully claims is equal!

15...♘xg3

White stands better after 15...♕xd7?! 16 ♗e5 f6 17 ♗g3 ♘xg3 18 ♕xg3 when Black experiences difficulties activating his entombed bishop on g7. The trouble is he needs to play ...e6 to free the piece, but this punctures the light squares around his king.

16 ♕xg3

I would go for the ending after 16 f6!? ♘xf1 17 fxg7 ♕xh2+ 18 ♔xf1 ♕h1+ 19 ♔f2 ♕xe1+ 20 ♖xe1 ♖fd8 21 ♘e5 ♔xg7 22 g4 when White gets two knights and kingside pressure for a rook and two pawns.

16...♕xd7 17 dxc5!

Now the health of Black's d5-pawn becomes an issue.

17...bxc5 18 h4

As well as Black's king!

18...♗f6 19 ♗b5 ♕c8?

After 19...♕d8! 20 ♘xd5 ♗xd5 21 c4 ♕b8! 22 ♕xb8 ♖axb8 23 ♖xd5 Black struggles to draw, but the opposite-coloured bishops should give him good chances to achieve this.

20 ♘xd5 ♗xd5 21 ♖xd5 ♖b8 22 hxg5

hxg5

Black gets wiped out after 22...♗xg5?? 23 f6 exf6 24 ♖xf6 ♔g7 25 ♖xg5+.

23 ♗d7!

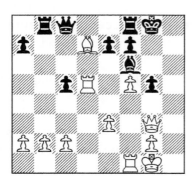

White finds a clever manoeuvre to hang on to his extra material.

23...♕a6 24 b3 ♔g7

White remains up a pawn after 24...♕xa2 25 ♖xc5.

25 a4 ♕e2?

Incorrectly banking on a non-existent attack, which in reality is all appearance and no power – a bit like the Wizard of Oz! He should protect c5.

26 ♖xc5 ♖h8 27 ♗b5 ♕h5 28 ♗d3 g4?

Dropping another pawn. White defends comfortably after 28...♖b4 29 ♔f2!.

29 ♖c4 1-0

Summary

What I like about this line is that you first induce Black to play the passive ...c6 and ...♘bd7, which work fine for Black if White plays the lame 5 ♘f3 system. Only then do you pull the old switcheroo and trick Black into a passive version of a Reversed Stonewall Dutch with 5 f4!

1 d4 ♘f6 2 ♘c3 d5 3 ♗g5 c6 4 e3 ♘bd7 5 f4! g6 6 ♘f3 ♗g7 7 ♗e2

A positional idea over the more hostile 7 ♗d3, which aims the bishop directly at Black's king. With 7 ♗e2, White plans ♘e5 and ♗f3. GM Blatny once tried this plan on me at an American Open in a similar position and confused the daylights out of me. Then with true generosity of spirit, flagged in a winning position! Possibly he had so many wonderful lines available that it may have confused him! White's plans include:

1. g4, g5, h4 and attack;

2. Play for e4; and

3. The bishop on f3 in conjunction with his knight on c3 makes ...c5 difficult for Black to achieve because his d5-pawn could get tender.

7...0-0 8 0-0 b6

8...♘e8 intends to break at some point with ...f6 and ...e5, but now, instead of 9 e4!?, as in G.Trikaliotis-E.Palamidas, Ikaros 1997, 9 f5! messes up Black's plan.

9 ♘e5 ♗b7 10 ♗f3 ♖c8 11 ♕e1 ♗a6 12 ♖f2 ♖c7 13 ♖d2

Clearing the way for the queen to

h4, and also making Black nervous about ever playing ...c5.

13...♘e8 14 e4!

White enters complications rather than building up on the kingside.

14...f6 15 ♘xd7 ♖xd7 16 ♗h4 ♗b7

Black refuses to cede central space with 16...dxe4 17 ♕xe4 ♖d6 18 ♖e1.

17 ♖ad1 ♔h8 18 f5!?

White goes directly after Black's king rather than take a territorial advantage with 18 e5.

18...gxf5 19 exf5 ♘d6 20 ♖e2 ♖g8?

Black decides to defend passively and begins to run out of counterplay. He should fight back by sac'ing an ex-

change for a pawn to roll his central pawns in the line 20...♘xf5! 21 ♗g4 ♘xh4 22 ♗xd7 ♕xd7 23 ♕xh4 e5 when the battle revolves around White's ability to blockade Black's centre.

21 g4 ♗h6 22 ♗g3 ♘f7 23 h4 ♗f8 24 ♖g2 ♘d6 25 ♘e2!

This is a move I would never play in a million years. This is where a positional player would be tempted to play it safe and throw in the knee-jerk 25 b3? first, keeping the knight out of c4 and only playing ♘e2-f4 on the next move. However, this is too slow if Black reacts vigorously with 25...h5! 26 ♗f4 hxg4 27 ♗xg4 ♗c8 28 ♕e2 ♖b7 29 ♗h3! (threat: ♕h5) 29...♖g7! 30 ♖xg7 ♗xg7 31 ♖e1 and although Black's position remains dismal, at least he has avoided the direct mating attack.

25...♘c4?

Looks nice but he doesn't have the time, despite simultaneously attacking b2 and the fork on e3.

After 25...h5! 26 gxh5 ♘xf5 27 ♘f4 ♗h6 28 ♘g6+ ♔h7 29 ♗f2 ♗c8 30 ♕e2 e6! 31 ♕d3! (31 ♕xe6? ♘e3!) 31...♖dg7 for the moment the defence holds.

26 ♘f4!

Who cares about b2?

26...♘xb2 27 ♘e6 ♕e8 28 g5! ♘xd1 29 ♕xd1

White invested a full exchange and a pawn. His compensation?

1. A slow but unstoppable attack;

2. Black's rooks and bishop sit by idly as their monarch gets mugged by the powerful knight on e6 and the surging pawns; and

3. White threatens 30 ♗h5! followed by ♗f7. If he regains his material Black's position remains horrible without the comfort of extra material.

29...♕c8 30 ♗h5! ♗g7?

The h8-square will be the final resting place for Black's king. With each move the coffin moves lower and lower into the grave. He should offer the rook for the knight with 30...♖g7!.

31 ♗f7

This is really not an error since virtually everything wins. In possible time trouble, White misses the not-so-hard-to-see shot 31 ♗g6! h6 (the bishop is untouchable) 32 gxh6 ♗f8 33 ♗f7 c5 34 ♕h5 cxd4 35 ♗xg8, which mates in six moves.

31...♖f8 32 ♕h5 fxg5

32...♖xf7 33 g6! mates quickly.

33 ♗g6

33 ♘xg5! h6 34 ♕g6 hxg5 35 ♕h5+ ♗h6 36 ♕xh6 mate.

33...h6 34 ♗e5! ♖f6 35 hxg5 1-0

Summary

Developing the bishop on e2 with the idea ♗f3 is a refinement over the normal placement on d3.

Game 69
K.Chernyshov-A.Kosteniuk
Moscow 2001

1 d4 d5 2 ♘c3 ♘f6 3 ♗g5 ♗f5 4 ♗xf6!?

Mixing Trompowsky ideas with a Veresov flair. We looked at this move briefly in the notes to Lakdawala-Lozano in Chapter Three. Now we examine it more closely.

4 f3 was covered in Chapter Three.

4...exf6

Next game we examine the more risky g-pawn recapture.

5 e3 c6

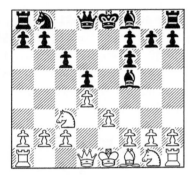

You may also reach this position through the move order: 1 d4 d5 2 ♘c3 c6 3 ♗g5 ♗f5 4 e3 ♘f6 5 ♗xf6 exf6.

6 ♗d3 ♕d7

It's probably more accurate to make White work to swap bishops after 6...♗g6 7 ♘ge2 ♗d6 8 h4!? (I wanted to force him to exchange on d3) 8...0-0 9 h5 ♗xd3 10 ♕xd3 ♖e8 11 ♔f1!? b5!? 12 a3 a5 13 e4 (principle: counter in the centre when attacked on the wing) 13...dxe4 14 ♘xe4 ♗f8 15 ♖h3! ♘d7 16 ♖f3 ♕e7?! 17 ♘2g3 b4 18 axb4 axb4 19 ♖e1 (threat: 20 ♘xf6+) 19...♕d8 20 ♖fe3 g6 21 ♕c4 ♖e6 22 hxg6 hxg6 23 ♘g5!? (What is happening to me? Has the Veresov turned me into a thug like my brother Jimmy?!) 23...fxg5 24 ♖xe6 fxe6 25 ♖xe6 ♔h7 26 ♕d3?! (after 26 ♘e4! ♗e7 27 ♕xc6 ♖a1+ 28 ♔e2 ♘f8 29 ♖e5 ♖a7 White has full compensation for his piece) 26...♘f6?! 27 ♘e4 ♗e7? 28 ♘xg5+ ♔g7 29 ♖xf6?? (a time-

pressure freakout! 29 ♖e1! is drawn by perpetual check) 29...♔xf6!. Aaak! I forgot about this recapture and now must consume an extra large slice of humble pie! We were both below a minute but Black had everything under control with an extra rook in C.Lakdawala-Griffith, San Diego (rapid) 2010.

7 ♗xf5 ♕xf5 8 ♘ge2 ♗d6 9 ♘g3

9 0-0 0-0 10 ♘g3 ♕g6 11 ♕d3 ♕xd3 12 cxd3 ♘a6 looks equal, but I would rather play White and try a minority attack (I'm allowed to do this since I was born in India) on the queenside.

9...♕e6 10 ♕f3 g6 11 0-0

Going the other way looks risky after 11 0-0-0?! f5 when the centre is closed and Black has an automatic attack on the queenside.

11...f5 12 ♘ce2

The knight was useless on c3. Also White needs to work in c4.

12...♘d7 13 ♘f4 ♕e7 14 b3!

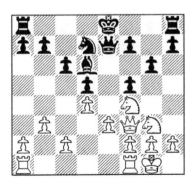

The correct plan. Force c4 and destabilize Black's centre.

14...h5 15 c4 h4 16 ♘ge2 dxc4 17 bxc4 ♘f6 18 c5 ♗c7 19 ♘c3 ♘e4 20 ♖fc1

0-0-0

The game heats up. Who gets there first? 20...0-0 21 ♘xe4 fxe4 22 ♕g4 was the more positional option.

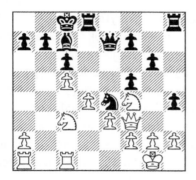

21 ♘h3?!

Avoiding the ending after 21 ♘xe4 fxe4 22 ♕g4+ ♕d7 23 ♕xd7+ ♖xd7 24 ♘e2 when chances are balanced. Black will push on the kingside, but may also overextend there, while White will double on the b-file.

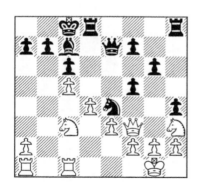

21...♘f6?!

I have heard chess teachers declare that a bad plan is better than no plan. I disagree. Nothing sours a good position quicker than engaging a bad plan. It's often better to actually just drift and do nothing, rather than move in the wrong direction. Black's knight needs to keep firm control over the d5-square and, instead, goes off on an attacking adventure. She should play 21...♕e6! (planning ...g5) 22 ♘xe4 fxe4 23 ♕d1 g5! 24 ♕b3 ♖hg8 25 ♕xe6+ fxe6 26 g4 e5, which puts pressure on d4 while White's knight languishes on h3.

22 ♖ab1 ♘g4? 23 d5!

The h-pawn is meaningless as long as lines open quickly on the queenside. Suddenly the energy latent in White's pieces bursts forth.

23...cxd5 24 ♘xd5 ♗xh2+ 25 ♔h1 ♕e4

Black's position is more precarious than it looks. For example, 25...♕e6 26 c6! ♖xd5 (26...♕xd5?? 27 cxb7+ ♔b8 28 ♖c8+ overloads the d8-rook) 27 ♘g5! ♘e5 28 cxb7+ ♔b8 29 ♘xe6 ♘xf3 30 ♘c5! (threatening mate on a6) 30...♖xc5 31 ♖xc5 ♗g1 32 gxf3 ♗xf2 33 ♖e5 wins.

26 ♘c3! ♕e7

Or 26...♕xf3 27 gxf3 ♘xf2+ 28 ♔xh2 ♖d2 29 ♘xf2 ♖xf2+ 30 ♔h1 ♖xf3 31 ♘b5! ♖xe3 32 ♘d6+ ♔d7 33 ♖xb7+

♗c6 34 ♖xf7 ♖b8 35 ♘c4 ♖g3 36 ♘a5+ and the c-pawn's march is decisive.

27 ♘b5 ♔b8 28 c6 ♖c8 29 c7+!

Now White finds one sparkling shot after another.

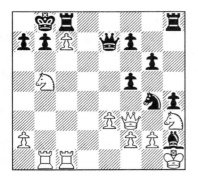

29...♔a8

White's brilliant point is seen in the line 29...♗xc7?? 30 ♕xb7+! ♔xb7 31 ♘xc7+ ♕b4 32 ♖xb4 mate.

30 ♖c4!

A terrific dual-purpose attacking move.

1. White threatens ♖a4 with devastating effect.

2. White prevents the defensive idea ...♕e4.

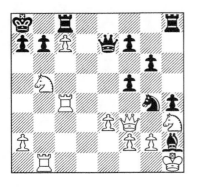

30...a6 31 ♖a4

Threatening mate on a6.

31...♗xc7 32 ♖xa6+ ♔b8 33 ♘d4?

Right piece, wrong square. He misses the immediate put away with 33 ♘a7! ♗e5 34 ♖ab6 ♖c7 35 ♘c6+ ♖xc6 36 ♕xc6.

33...♗d8!

Keeping control over b6 is crucial for her survival. Possibly White expected 33...♗e5? 34 ♘c6+ ♖xc6 35 ♕xc6 ♖c8 36 ♕b6.

34 ♕d5?

He had to settle for the prosaic grind-out win after 34 ♘c6+ ♖xc6 35 ♖xc6 ♕e4 36 ♕xe4 fxe4 37 ♖d6 ♘e5 38 ♖d4 f5 39 ♘f4.

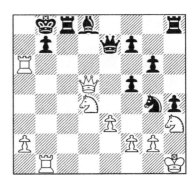

34...♖c5?

The startling 34...♕b4!! draws by force after 35 ♖xb4 ♖c1+ 36 ♘g1 ♘xf2+ 37 ♔h2 ♘g4+.

35 ♘c6+ ♖xc6 36 ♖xc6 ♔a7??

Hanging a rook, but White wins anyway after 36...♖e8 37 ♔g1 ♘e5 38 ♖a6.

37 ♕d4+ ♔b8 38 ♕xh8 1-0

Summary

Capturing on f6 unbalances the game and turns it into a kind of pseudo-Trompowsky, with that strange knight sitting on c3. The e-pawn recapture is Black's most solid choice.

> ## Game 70
> ## R.Bellin-K.Lie
> Gausdal 1996

1 d4 ♘f6 2 ♘c3 d5 3 ♗g5 ♗f5 4 ♗xf6 gxf6

Black seeks a fight and recaptures with his g-pawn. This weakens his structure somewhat, but also opens the g-file for his rook and strengthens his pawn centre.

5 e3

Once again we avoid f3 lines in this chapter. We don't want to open the game immediately after giving up the bishop pair. Nor do we wish to weaken our dark squares with 5 f3?!.

5...c6

The move order 1 d4 d5 2 ♘c3 c6 3

♗g5 ♗f5 4 e3 ♘f6 5 ♗xf6 gxf6 would also bring about this position.

6 ♗d3 ♗g6 7 f4!

There is our Stonewall structure again. We threaten f5.

7...♗xd3

Others:

a) 7...e6?! allows a promising pawn sac: 8 f5! exf5 9 ♕f3 looked rosy for White in M.Spal-J.Hostinsky, Czech League 1995. Those tripled f-pawns are an eyesore and e3 is not as weak as it looks.

b) 7...f5!? 8 ♘f3 ♘d7 9 0-0 e6 10 ♘e2 ♗g7 11 c4 dxc4 12 ♗xc4 ♘b6 13 ♗b3 ♘d5 14 ♕d2 0-0 15 ♘e5 ♖c8 16 ♖ac1 ♖c7 17 ♗xd5 ♕xd5 18 ♖c5 ♕d6 19 ♖fc1 ♖d8 20 b4 ♗f8 21 ♕c2 f6 22 ♘d3 was G.Veresov-J.Abakarov, USSR 1974, where the knights didn't suffer from inferiority complexes against their bishop counterparts. Black's breaks have been shut down and the grand old man of the opening was able to convert his edge from this position.

8 ♕xd3 ♕c7 9 ♘ge2 ♘d7 10 e4!

The end of an era. The Stonewall

fades away and the game begins to look like a real Bronstein-Larsen Caro-Kann position.

10...dxe4

Black was probably better off entering 10...e6 11 f5! 0-0-0 12 0-0-0 ♗d6 13 fxe6 fxe6 14 exd5 exd5 with the superior pawn structure for White.

11 ♕xe4 0-0-0 12 0-0-0 e6 13 f5!

This move messes up the opponent's plans. If Black had time to play ...f5 his position would look nice.

13...♖e8 14 ♔b1 ♗d6 15 g3 ♔b8 16 ♖hf1 ♘b6 17 ♕d3!

If he tries to wreck the structure immediately with 17 fxe6 ♖xe6 18 ♕h4 ♘c4! 19 d5 cxd5 20 ♘xd5 ♕c5 then Black gets compensating piece activity.

17...e5?

Dreadfully weakening his light squares, but Lie did become a GM a few years after this game was played. In my experience, I have encountered a number of GMs whom I consider strategically suspect and in desperate need of coaching in planning and judgement! But never ever have I met one who isn't a tremendously-gifted tactician. My sad conclusion: tactics and calculation are far more important skills than positional understanding in chess. This is why I always wince when I see a seasoned 30-year veteran of the game with excellent understanding, losing to some snot-nosed 12-year-old who calculates like a machine and possesses the strategic insights of a slightly below-average chimp!

Black should hang in there with the patient 17...♕e7 18 ♘e4 ♖hf8 19 ♘xd6 ♕xd6 20 ♘c3.

18 d5!

Firmly seizing control over e4 and d5.

18...♖d8 19 ♕e4 cxd5 20 ♘xd5 ♘xd5 21 ♖xd5 ♗c5 22 ♖fd1 ♖xd5 23 ♖xd5 ♖c8 24 ♘c1!

Total domination of the light squares. A classic good knight versus bad bishop position arises. Possible flight plans for the knight include ♘b3-d2-e4 or, if Black moves his bishop off the g1-a7 diagonal, then ♘d3-b4-d5, although this one is less likely to occur.

24...♕c6 25 a3 a6 26 ♕c4 ♗g1 27 ♕xc6 bxc6 28 ♖d1!

Daring Black to capture on h2.

28...♗c5!

It's important to know when to go forward and when to back down. If Black stubbornly proceeds with 28...♗xh2? 29 ♘e2 ♖g8 30 ♖h1 ♗xg3 31 ♖g1 ♖g5 32 ♖xg3 ♖xf5 33 ♖g8+ ♔c7 34 ♖g7 h5 35 ♘g3 then his pawns begin to fall.

29 ♘b3 ♗b6 30 c4 ♖d8 31 ♖xd8+ ♗xd8 32 ♘c5 a5 33 ♔c2 ♔c7 34 ♔d3 ♗e7 35 ♘e4

The knight rules over the sickly bishop, who must forever cover f6.

35...♔d7

Or 35...c5 36 ♔e3 ♔d7 37 ♔f3 ♔e8 38 ♘d2 (threatening to enter via d5 with ♔e4 and ♔d5) 38...♔d7 39 ♔g4! (a nice fakeout; the king heads for the kingside pawns) 39...h6 40 ♘e4 ♔e8 41 ♔h5 ♗f8 42 ♘xf6+ ♔e7 43 ♘e4 ♔e8 and White simply creates a passer with g4, h4 and g5, winning easily.

36 c5!

Ensuring queenside king entry.

36...♔c7 37 a4 ♔d7 38 ♔c4 ♔c7 39 g4 h6 40 h4 ♔b7 41 b4 axb4 42 ♔xb4 ♔a6 43 ♘d6! ♗f8

If 43...♗xd6 44 cxd6 ♔b7 45 ♔c5 e4 46 a5! e3 47 a6+ ♔xa6 48 d7 e2 49 d8♕ e1♕ 50 ♕a8 mate.

44 h5 ♗g7 45 ♘xf7 e4 46 ♘d8 e3 47 ♔c3 ♗f8 48 ♘xc6 ♗xc5 49 ♔d3 e2

49...♔b6 50 ♘d8! leaves Black in zugzwang: 50...♔a6 (50...♔a5?? 51 ♘b7+) 51 ♘f7 ♗f8 52 ♔xe3 ♔a5 is similar to the game.

50 ♔xe2 ♔b6 51 ♘d8 ♔a5

A blunder but it didn't matter, as 51...♗e7 52 ♘f7 ♗f8 53 ♔e3 ♔a5 54 ♔e4 ♔xa4 55 ♔d5 ♔b4 56 ♔e6 ♗g7 57 ♘xh6! ♗xh6 58 ♔xf6 finishes Black off.

52 ♘b7+ 1-0

Summary

4...gxf6 lines tend to lead to sharper games than the e-pawn recapture. Begin with a Stonewall, but be mindful of the fact that you may want to later play e4 and turn the game into a type of Bronstein-Larsen Caro-Kann.

Game 71
R.Hasangatin-D.Tishin
Alushta 2005

---

1 d4 d5 2 ♗g5 c6 3 ♘c3 ♗f5 4 e3 ♕b6

Black tosses in ...♕b6 in conjunction with ...♗f5. Instead, 4...♘d7 (intending ...♘f6 without allowing doubled pawns) 5 ♗d3 ♗xd3 6 ♕xd3 ♘gf6 7 e4 dxe4 8 ♘xe4 ♘xe4 9 ♕xe4 ♕a5+ 10

♗d2 ♕b6 was B.Rozow-M.Heinrich, German League 2001, and now 11 0-0-0 looks similar to positions we examined in Chapter Three.

5 ♖b1

Defence of the b-pawn isn't strictly necessary. He can just ignore it and continue to develop with 5 ♗d3:

a) 5...♕xb2?! sees Black quench his thirst by taking a sip of poisoned Kool-aid! This is an unbelievably risky pawn grab in view of 6 ♘ge2 ♗xd3 7 cxd3 ♕b6 8 ♖b1 ♕c7 9 ♕b3 b6 10 0-0, as occurred in O.Castro Rojas-J.Cuartas, Fusagasuga 1999. For the pawn White has:

1. A massive development lead; in fact, he leads by five to six tempi!

2. The open c-file is a cause for concern for Black, and White can set up sacs on d5 or also try ♘b5 ideas;

3. e4 is coming with e5 or f4-f5 ideas; and

4. Black must pin his survival hopes on the relatively closed nature of the game (for the moment!).

b) Black should decline with

5...♗xd3 6 ♕xd3 ♘d7 7 ♗f4 ♘gf6 8 0-0-0 e6 9 ♘ge2 ♗e7 when he looks fine, P.Mozelius-G.Sigvardsson, correspondence 2002.

5...e6 6 ♗d3 ♗xd3

Next game I play the more accurate 6...♗g6.

7 cxd3 ♗e7 8 ♘f3

I would invest a tempo to keep the bishop on the board and control e5 with 8 ♗f4.

8...♘f6

He probably didn't like 8...♗xg5 9 ♘xg5 ♘f6 10 f4.

9 0-0 ♘bd7

Perhaps he should prevent White's next move with 9...a5.

10 b4!

Picking up some useful queenside space.

10...0-0 11 ♘e5 ♕d8 12 f4

A Stonewall, but with our bad bishop on the outside of the pawn chain.

12...♘e8 13 ♗xe7 ♕xe7 14 ♘f3 f5 15 ♕e2 ♘d6 16 ♖fc1

Black has probably equalized

through careful play. White hopes to get something going on the queenside.

16...a5!?

And so does Black!

17 ♕b2 b5?!

Pushing it too far, he weakens c6. Black should be content with 17...axb4 18 ♕xb4 ♖a7 19 a4.

18 ♘e2 ♖fc8 19 a3 axb4 20 axb4 ♖a6 21 ♘e5 ♘b7 22 ♖a1 ♖xa1 23 ♖xa1 ♘xe5 24 fxe5

He doesn't like the idea of giving Black an opportunity to dissolve the backward c-pawn. A better option: 24 dxe5 which opens d4 for his knight. I prefer White after 24...c5 25 bxc5 ♕xc5 26 ♘d4 b4 27 ♖b1 ♕b6 28 h3 ♘d8 29 ♔h2 ♖b8 30 ♕a2 ♕b7 31 ♕a4 ♔f7 because Black's passer is firmly blockaded and his pieces have been forced into a defensive posture. Moreover, Black's king may not be as safe as it looks and White may try shenanigans on the other side with a well-timed g4.

24...♘d8 25 ♕c3 ♖c7 26 ♖a5 ♔f8 27 g3 ♔e8 28 h4 g5!?

Black just has an itchy trigger finger and refuses to defend passively. The problem with this move is that it gives f4 to White's knight, but on the plus side he exposes White's king.

29 hxg5 ♕xg5 30 ♔f2 h5 31 ♔e1!!

This deceptively deep pawn sac displays remarkable judgement. White forces a pawn-down ending, realizing that it is Black who is in danger of losing. If Black refuses the pawn, White's king marches to safety to d2.

31...♕xe3 32 ♖a8! h4!

Black hurries to eliminate his h-pawn before he loses it. Black fights for his life in the ending after 32...♕g5? 33 ♕c5 ♕e7 34 ♘f4 ♕xc5 35 dxc5 ♔e7 36 d4 when White gets the same ending as in the game, but with an extra pawn.

33 ♕c5! ♕h6!

33...hxg3?? 34 ♕d6 ♖d7 35 ♕xe6+ ♖e7 36 ♕g8+ mates.

34 gxh4 ♕xh4+ 35 ♔d1 ♕e7 36 ♘f4 ♕xc5 37 dxc5

One of my greatest joys in life is conning students. I asked some of them to assess the position. Every one of them said something like: "Black is up a pawn, but it may be hard for him to win." The truth is, even a clear, connected passed pawn up, Black fights for survival! White's trumps in the position:

1. A massive space advantage;

2. A powerfully posted rook and knight, which show a clear contrast to Black's limping rook and knight;

3. White's king may even take a walk to f6!

4. The congestion is so bad that Black is in grave danger of zugzwang; and

5. Black's king is in danger of being hunted down in endgame mating attacks.

37...♔d7 38 ♘g6 ♔e8 39 ♘f4 ♔d7 40 ♘h5 ♔e7 41 ♘f6 d4?

Patience is one of the most underrated character traits necessary for a strong chess player. I just love it when my opponent is defending and keeps active at all costs, when he should be in a holding pattern. Here Black artificially isolates White's e-pawn and hopes to win it with a well timed ...♘f7. The problem: the moment for ...♘f7 never arrives and he virtually ensures that White regains his pawn.

It's tough on the ego, but Black should just grovel with 41...♖b7 and wait to see how White makes progress.

42 ♔e2 ♖b7

42...♘f7?? would not be such a 'well-timed' moment for ...♘f7 because of 43 ♖e8 mate!

43 ♔f3 ♖c7 44 ♔g3 ♖b7 45 ♔h4 ♖c7 46 ♔h5 ♖b7 47 ♘g8+ ♔e8 48 ♘f6+ ♔e7 49 ♔h4 ♖c7 50 ♔g3

White isn't sure how to proceed and marks time for the moment.

50...♖b7 51 ♔f4 ♖c7 52 ♖a1

Testing new entry routes via the g- or h-file.

52...♘f7 53 ♘g8+ ♔d8 54 ♘f6 ♖c8 55 ♘h5 ♔d7 56 ♖a7+ ♖c7 57 ♘f6+ ♔d8 58 ♖a8+ ♖c8

If 58...♔e7?? 59 ♖e8 mate. There it is again.

59 ♖a2 ♖c7 60 ♖g2 ♖e7 61 ♖g8+ ♔c7 62 ♘e8+ ♔d7 63 ♘f6+ ♔c7 64 ♘e8+ ♔d7 65 ♘d6! ♘d8 66 ♖g1?!

White can engineer zugzwang: 66 ♔g5! ♖h7 67 ♔g6 ♖e7 (67...♖h3?? 68 ♖g7+!) 68 ♖f8 ♔c7 69 ♔f6 ♖h7 70 ♖g8 ♔d7 71 ♔g5! ♖e7 72 ♔g6! ♔c7 73 ♖h8 ♖d7 (or 73...♔d7 74 ♔f6 with zugzwang!) 74 ♖e8 (zugzwang!) 74...♔b8 75 ♘xf5! and wins.

66...♔c7 67 ♖a1 ♔b8 68 ♔g5 ♖g7+ 69 ♔f6 ♖d7

Ambition is followed by immediate retribution! 69...♖g3? 70 ♔e7! ♖g8 71

♔d7 f4 72 ♖f1 ♖f8 73 ♔e7. We have seven fruit trees in our backyard and my wife, son and I are three of the laziest/incompetent gardeners in America. Our yard is always littered with unpicked fruit. Here Black's pawns fall like the rotten fruit in our yard!

70 ♖h1 ♔c7 71 ♖h4 ♔b8 72 ♔g6!

Covering h7 before picking up the d-pawn.

72...♔c7 73 ♖xd4 ♖e7 74 ♖h4 ♖d7 75 ♔f6 ♔b8 76 d4 ♔a7 77 ♖h8 ♔a6 78 ♖h1

78 ♖g8! ♔a7 79 d5! cxd5 80 ♘c8+! ♔b7 81 ♘b6 ♔c6 82 ♘xd7 ♔xd7 83 ♖g7+ ♔c6 84 ♖a7 d4 85 ♔e7 wins.

78...♔a7 79 d5!

The long-awaited breakthrough.

79...cxd5 80 ♘xb5+ ♔b7 81 ♘d6+!

Braver and more accurate than 81 ♘d4.

81...♔c6 82 ♖c1!

White's pawns are ready to roll forward.

82...d4 83 b5+ ♔d5 84 c6 ♖c7 85 ♘e8 ♖c8 86 c7 ♘b7 87 ♘d6!

In the words of Jim Morrison: break

on through to the other side! The liquidating move wins the queening race easily.

87...♘xd6 88 exd6 ♔xd6 89 b6 ♔d7 90 ♔e5 d3 91 b7 ♖xc7 92 ♖b1 ♖xb7 93 ♖xb7+ ♔c6 94 ♖b3 1-0

Summary

...♕b6 in conjunction with ...♗f5 is fully playable as long as Black refrains from taking the 'free pawn' on b2.

Game 72
M.Duckworth-C.Lakdawala
US G/60 Championship, Commerce 1998

1 d4 d5 2 ♘c3 c6

FM Mark Duckworth and I are often associated with the demeaning and derogatory term 'Quickplay Expert'. Translation: These players possess some natural tactical talent, but due to laziness and their shallow understanding of the game, they only survive in games with low clocks where they swindle their honest opponents! Hikaru Nakamura once went off on a tirade on me on ICC when he was losing a 5-0 game (normally I am his punching bag on ICC). He kibbed the following to onlookers: "I don't know any other player who plays like a strong GM on ICC, but has such weak results OTB besides 'Kawas'!" My friend, National Master David Hart, saw the kib and told me: "I guess the irony of Nakamura's own 'Quickplay Expert' status was lost on him!"

But I digress. Where was I? Oh, yes, back to Duckworth. We were tied for first place in the 1998 US G/60 Championship. All the other titled players were safely out of the way and it came down to the two of us 'Quickplay Experts'. Besides my kid brother Jimmy, nobody else had ever ventured a Veresov on me. I used my standard anti-Jimmy formula of dodging mainlines and going directly to the French or Caro-Kann, where I was sure to outbook the streetsmart Duckworth. His next move came as a total surprise.

3 ♗g5

Oh, no! I hadn't bypassed the Veresov after all!

3...♕b6

The difference between playing his move before ...♗f5 is the fact that b7 is covered and Black is happy to capture on b2.

4 ♖b1

Sac'ing the b-pawn isn't very convincing here: 4 ♕d2?! ♕xb2 5 ♖b1 ♕a3

6 e3 e6 7 ♗d3 ♗e7 8 h4 ♘f6 9 ♘ge2 ♘bd7 10 ♗f4 ♗d8! (making room for the queen on e7) 11 h5 ♗a5 12 ♖b3 ♕e7 13 h6 g6 and White doesn't have enough compensation for a pawn, C.Hauke-V.Alterman, Biel 1994.

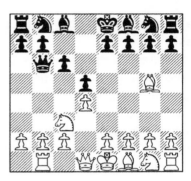

4...♗f5 5 e3 e6 6 ♗d3 ♗g6

Superior to capturing on d3. Why give White a free move or open the c-file?

7 ♘ge2 ♘d7 8 0-0 ♘gf6 9 f4?!

Here the Stonewall is mistimed. He should play 9 b4!.

9...♘g4 10 ♕d2 f5!

One Stonewall deserves another!

11 h3 ♘gf6 12 ♗xf6

He eliminates his bad bishop.

12...♘xf6

The position looks equal, but it isn't. The difference? Black's knight has immediate access to e4, while White's knights remain far away from e5. Black has the edge.

13 a3 ♗e7 14 ♔h2 0-0 15 ♘g1 ♘e4 16 ♘xe4?

A strategic error. Now his knight languishes on g1 and will never reach its goal of e5. Duckworth should settle for the line 16 ♕e1! ♗h5! 17 ♘f3 ♗xf3 18 gxf3 ♘xc3 19 ♕xc3 (19 bxc3 ♕c7 20 a4 c5 21 ♖g1 c4 22 ♗e2 and White must be ever vigilant about the health of his a4- and c3-pawns) 19...c5 20 ♖fe1 cxd4 21 ♕xd4 ♗c5! 22 ♕e5 ♖f6 with a minimal edge to Black.

16...fxe4 17 ♗e2 c5 18 c3 ♖ac8 19 ♖fc1 ♖c6 20 ♗d1 c4

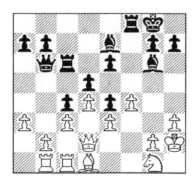

My plan:

1. Play ...b5, ...a5 and ...b4;
2. Double rooks on the b-file;
3. Exchange on c3; and
4. Enter via b2, or go after his fixed target on c3.

I didn't see much counterplay for him on the kingside. In fast games such mindless plans are of great value since you play the next ten or so moves very quickly and avoid burning up time on your clock.

21 ♕e1 ♕c7 22 ♖c2 b5 23 g4 a5 24 ♖g2 b4 25 axb4 axb4 26 ♖a1 bxc3 27 bxc3 ♖b6 28 h4 ♖fb8 29 h5 ♗e8 30 ♗e2 ♖b2 31 g5

White's dilemma: no targets for him on the kingside and he experiences great difficulties opening lines. Meanwhile Black works on his very concrete target at c3.

31...♗d7 32 ♔h1 ♕b7 33 h6!

He wants to worry me about the back rank with possibilities of check on a8 followed by ♖h8. His trouble is that there is no easy way to open the king-side.

33...g6 34 ♗f1 ♖b1!

The fewer attackers the better.

35 ♖xb1 ♕xb1 36 ♕f2 ♕a1 37 f5!

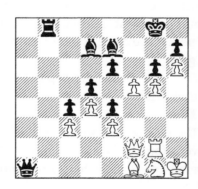

I knew he would go for this and avoid 37 ♘e2? ♖b2 38 ♔h2 ♗d8! when it's just a matter of time before c3 falls.

37...exf5 38 ♕f4

Entry, but at a very high cost.

38...♖e8!

Ha! Human intuition rules. The computers heartily recommend the false path 38...♖b6? 39 ♕e5 ♗f8 40 ♕xd5+ ♗e6 41 ♕e5 ♕xc3 42 ♖a2 ♕b4 43 ♖a8 (threatening mate on g7) 43...♕e7 44 ♘h3 c3 45 ♘f4 c2 46 ♘d5! ♕b7 (not 46...♕xg5?? 47 ♕g7 mate) 47 ♘xb6 c1♕ 48 ♖xf8+! ♔xf8 49 ♕f6+ ♗f7 50 ♕g7+ ♔e7 51 ♕f6+ ♔e8 52 ♕h8+ when it's perpetual check.

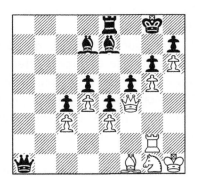

39 ♕e5 ♗f8 40 ♕xd5+ ♗e6 41 ♕b5 ♖c8 42 ♕e5 ♗f7

Black's king feels cosy and gets tucked in with a warm blanket of friendly pieces and pawns. Meanwhile, c3 falls.

43 ♕f4 ♕xc3 44 ♖a2 ♕b4 45 ♖a6 c3 46 ♘e2 c2 47 ♕e5! ♕e7

Much as I love to conjure phantoms, Black can actually grab the material and live to talk about it: 47...c1♕! 48 ♘xc1 ♖xc1 49 ♖a8 ♖xf1+ 50 ♔g2 sees White threaten ♕g7 mate. I saw to this point and didn't have the time to work out if I had a win/mate or had to settle for a perpetual. It turns out Black achieves the win after 50...♕d2+! 51 ♔xf1 ♗c4+ 52 ♔g1 ♕xe3+ 53 ♔h2 ♕f2+ 54 ♔h1 ♕h4+ 55 ♔g2 ♕xg5+ 56 ♔f2 ♕xh6, since it eliminates White's ♕g7 mate threat. Needless to say I didn't see all of this and played it safe.

48 ♘c1 ♕xg5!?

I think we were both down below the one minute mark by now. Shockingly, I didn't simplify with 48...♕xe5 49 dxe5 ♗e7 which also wins.

49 ♖a7 ♕xh6+ 50 ♔g2 ♕xe3 51 ♖xf7

He has no prayer for a perpetual check.

51...♔xf7 52 ♕d5+ ♔f6 53 ♗e2 ♕xc1 54 ♕e5+ ♔g5 55 ♕g3+ ♔h6 56 ♕h2+ ♔g7 57 ♕e5+ ♔g8 58 ♗c4+ ♖xc4 59 ♕e6+ ♔g7 0-1

Hooray! I become US (gulp!) Quick-play champ!

Summary

3...♕b6 4 ♖b1 doesn't seem to bother White much since he never planned on castling queenside anyway. Also, I sincerely apologize to the reader for this '0-1' outrage, and promise to work hard to pepper the remainder of the book with '1-0' games! As I was working on Chapter Six, my son Tim walked by and asked: "Hey dad, why does White win all the games in your book?" I calmly replied: "Death to Black!" He gave me the trying look of a dutiful son who endures the irrational meanderings of a senile parent.

Chapter Eight
Veresov versus Dutch

1 d4 f5 2 ♘c3

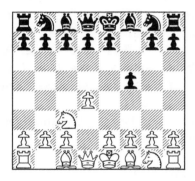

Unlike some of the earlier chapters in this book where your author suggests some of the more dubious Veresov lines with a distinctively apologetic tone, in this chapter I can confidently tell you that the Veresov is one of the best methods of meeting Dutch. With 2 ♘c3! our goal is simple: blast open with e4! When it happens, Black often finds himself unprepared and behind in development. Dutch players have three choices:

a) Black meets the Veresov approach with a Stonewall Dutch Struc-ture, 2...♘f6 3 ♗g5 d5, when our plan of ♕d2, f3 and playing for e4 looks effective.

b) Black goes 2...♘f6 3 ♗g5 e6 and allows White the e4 break. After 4 e4 fxe4 5 ♘xe4 Black falls behind in space and development. I suggest a promising pawn sac line where White stands better whether Black accepts or declines.

c) Black meets the Veresov with a Leningrad Dutch/Stonewall hybrid formation, 2...d5 3 ♗g5 g6.

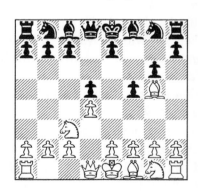

Black's problem is, he really doesn't want to play ...d5, but he must. Other-

Otherwise, White has the killer idea h4-h5!, sac the exchange on h5 and follow with e4! This gives White a murderous attack, so Black is virtually forced into the weakening ...d5 move. Our normal plan f3, ♕d2, possibly castle queenside, and force e4 also works very well here. Another wonderful benefit is that Leningrad players are prodded into a Stonewall structure, which they are not used to and usually bungle with great consistency!

Game 73
B.Gelfand-P.Nikolic
Munich 1994

1 d4 f5 2 ♘c3 d5

This move is played less than the mainline 2...♘f6. Presumably Black is afraid of 3 ♗g5 and ♗xf6, and delays the development of the g8-knight. In my opinion, Black is afraid of ghosts and the ♗g5 and ♗xf6 lines give White nothing.

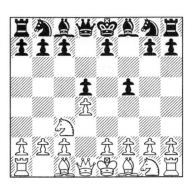

3 e4!?

What shall we call this? The Pseudo-Staunton Gambit? Honestly, I'm itching to hand out a '?!' for this move, but I realize that there is a practical side to chess and the move certainly sets difficult problems for Black. So let's settle for '!?' and get the more vulgar lines out of the way first for the hotheads among our readers, whose hearts skip a beat at such speculation.

Next game we examine 3 ♗f4!.

3...dxe4

It's not likely that a player of Nikolic's calibre would fall for the silly 3...fxe4?? 4 ♕h5+ g6 5 ♕xd5 ♘f6 6 ♕xd8+ ♔xd8 and Black had a rancid ending with no compensation for the damage he had sustained to his structure in C.Babos-F.Bohiltea, Sovata 2001.

4 ♗f4!

More accurate than immediately playing 4 f3 e5! 5 dxe5 ♕xd1+ 6 ♔xd1 ♘c6 7 ♘d5! ♔d8 8 f4 ♗e6 9 ♘e3 ♗c5 when if anyone stands better it's Black, L.Guidarelli-J.Le Roux, Besancon 2006.

4...♘f6 5 f3 exf3 6 ♘xf3 e6 7 ♗c4 ♗d6 8 ♕d2 0-0 9 0-0-0 c6

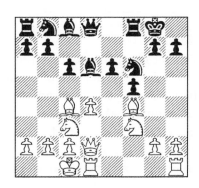

For the pawn White gets:

1. A jump in development made more important by the fact that we have opposite-wing castling;

2. A hole on e5 to occupy; and

3. A backward e6-pawn to pick on.

Conclusion: White nearly gets full compensation, but for the record I would still take Black, who looks solid and controls d5.

10 ♗g5

To prevent ...♘d5.

10...♘a6!

Multi-purpose defence. The knight heads for c7 where it protects his weak spot e6, and Black also plans to stick the knight on d5 since the other one on f6 can't move.

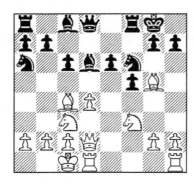

11 ♕e1!?

Technically, this move is probably incorrect for refusing the opportunity to bailout into a sharp and possibly equal ending with the line 11 ♗xa6! bxa6 12 d5! cxd5 13 ♘xd5 ♘xd5 14 ♗xd8 ♗f4 15 ♗g5 ♗xd2+ 16 ♗xd2 when Black's extra pawn doesn't mean much as long as White keeps his grip

on e5. From a psychological standpoint, Gelfand didn't sac in the opening just to get a probable drawn ending. It would be a little like ordering a steak and then asking the waiter to put a scoop of ice cream on top of it.

11...♘c7

Black won the opening battle and stands better. White just doesn't have full compensation for the pawn. Sensing this, Gelfand ups the ante with his next move.

12 g4!?

Thematic in such positions. If you are willing to sac on move three, then there is no place for half measures. White must be willing to give until it hurts to hang on to the initiative.

12...b5

He can also take the second pawn and make White prove it with 12...fxg4 13 ♘e5 ♘cd5 14 ♘e4 ♗e7.

13 ♗b3 b4

13...a5? fails to 14 gxf5.

14 ♘e2 ♘cd5 15 gxf5 exf5 16 ♘e5 ♗e6 17 ♖g1 ♕e8 18 ♗h6 ♘g4 19 ♗xg7

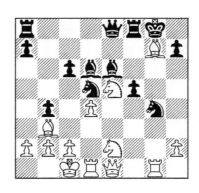

Of course the sac isn't for real and

White regains the piece. Then again, Black isn't bothered much about it either. His king remains relatively safe for the moment.

19...♔xg7 20 h3 ♔h8 21 hxg4 fxg4 22 ♖h1

The pressure is on for both sides. Black's king faces a rook down the open h-file, while White's problem is the two connected passers on the g- and h-files which spell doom if his attack fades. If given a choice, I would take Black here.

22...♗xe5!

Risky, but excellent judgement. He opens up d4 for White's knight in order to eliminate the monster on e5. White also doesn't quite have full compensation in the line 22...♗f5! 23 ♘g3 ♗g6 24 ♖h4 ♗xe5 25 dxe5 ♖f4 26 e6 ♕e7 27 ♖h2 ♖f6. If Black survives the next 15 moves or so, he takes home the point with his two connected kingside passed pawns.

23 dxe5 ♕g6 24 ♘d4 a5 25 ♕d2!

Intending to double with tempo on the h-file with ♖h6.

25...♗g8 26 ♖h6 ♕g7 27 ♘xc6 g3!

Black navigated the complications exceptionally well and now forces White on the defensive with his surging g-pawn.

28 ♖hh1

It is always a bad sign when you are forced into a retreat in the middle of an attack.

28...♖f2 29 ♕d4 ♘f4!

Threatening the cheapo on e2.

30 ♔b1 ♖f8?

Missing a forced win with 30...♘e2! 31 ♕e3 ♖af8 32 e6 (32 ♗xg8 g2!) 32...g2 33 ♖he1 g1♕ 34 ♖xg1 ♕xg1! 35 ♕xe2 ♖xe2 36 ♖xg1 ♗xe6 37 ♘xa5 h5! and the h-pawn wins the game.

31 ♗xg8 ♖xg8 32 ♘d8!

A good practical try, threatening future tricks on e6 or f7.

32...♖f8 33 ♕c5 ♖e2 34 ♖d7! g2! 35 ♖c1 ♖xe5?

A blunder in a winning position. Black wins in problem-like fashion after 35...♕g8! 36 ♕d4 ♕g6! 37 e6+ ♔g8 38 ♘f7 (threatening mate) 38...♕xc2+!! 39 ♖xc2 ♖e1+ 40 ♖c1 ♖xc1+ 41 ♔xc1 ♘e2+ 42 ♔d2 ♘xd4 43 ♘h6+ ♔h8 44

e7 ♘e6!! 45 exf8♕+ ♘xf8 and White is helpless to stop Black's promotion.

36 ♘f7+!

A cruel reversal of fortune for Black.

36...♔g8

Instead, 36...♖xf7 37 ♖d8+ wins a full queen and 36...♕xf7 37 ♖xf7 ♖xc5 38 ♖xf8+ ♔g7 39 ♖xf4 ♖g5 40 ♖g1 followed by ♖f2 picks off Black's last hope, the g-pawn.

37 ♘xe5

What a nightmare for Black, whose well-crafted fortress crumbles like a sandcastle as the tide rolls in. White halts the queening attempt on g1 and is up a rook.

37...♕f6 38 ♘g4 ♕e6 39 ♕g5+ ♘g6 40 ♖dd1 ♔g7 41 ♕h6+ ♔g8 42 ♘e3 1-0

Summary

The Pseudo-Staunton looks like a pretty risky method of meeting Black's Stonewall Dutch, but obviously we must factor in the practical chances as well in the assessment of the gambit.

> *Game 74*
> **E.Bareev-A.Onischuk**
> Elista Olympiad 1998

1 d4 f5 2 ♘c3 d5 3 ♗f4!

The Veresov and London merge. Aristotle said: "Nature abhors a vacuum and the bishop is ready to swoop in on e5!" (I'm not sure if Aristotle threw in the part about the bishop covering e5.) The London set-up is the most logical

choice against the Stonewall.

Everyone please calm down! I know what you are going to say. That this move is a clear violation of the Geneva Convention, and that the rules of engagement call for a more Veresovian approach. My response: for once in this book, let's play positional chess and forgo our normally violent instincts to annihilate Black. Black weakens e5 so we take aim at e5. And if you don't cease and desist with the anti-London talk, you leave me no choice but to ask you to buy my excellent London book once again!

3...♘f6

With 3...a6?! Black worries about ♘b5 and wastes time covering this not-so-dangerous threat: 4 f3 c5? (and now he opens the game when behind in development) 5 e4 dxe4 6 dxc5 ♕xd1+ 7 ♖xd1 and Black found himself too far behind, with the threats including ♘d5 and ♘a4, as well as fxe4 in C.Lakdawala-'QvC', Internet blitz 2010.

4 e3!

The f3 and ♕d2 set-ups work better

when White's bishop is posted on g5 rather than f4. If even after my earlier lecture on the glories of the London System, you still want to avoid it and remain incorrigibly violent, then try 4 f3 e6 5 e4 ♗b4 6 exf5 exf5 7 ♕d2 0-0 8 0-0-0 b6 9 a3 ♗d6 10 ♘h3 c6 11 ♗d3 g6 12 ♖he1 when White's king looks safer and she still controlled the key central dark squares f4 and e5 in A.Stefanova-D.Bescos Cortes, Zaragoza 1999.

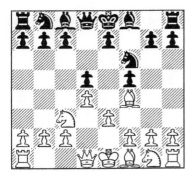

4...c6 5 ♘f3 ♗e6

On 5...g6?! I heartily recommend going psycho with 6 h4! ♗g7 (6...h6 7 ♘e5 ♖g8 ruins Black's kingside castling option, but perhaps still this is how Black should play it) 7 h5! ♘xh5 8 ♖xh5 gxh5 9 ♘g5 with a monster attack for the bargain price of only an exchange, F.Liardet-G.Gris, Geneva 2004.

6 ♗d3 g6 7 h4! h6

7...♗g7 is met by 8 h5! This offer of an exchange should be old hat by now. After 8...♘bd7 9 ♘e2 ♗f7 10 ♘g5 Black was getting pushed around in I.Soko-lov-A.Bachofner, Amsterdam 2002.

8 ♘e5 ♖g8 9 f3

A useful and flexible move which prevents ...♘e4 and prepares a future e4 or g4 break.

9...♘bd7 10 ♘e2 ♘h5 11 c3

Refusing to waste time preserving the bishop with 11 ♗h2 ♘xe5 12 ♗xe5 ♗g7.

11...♘xf4 12 exf4

The strategic threats are ♕c2 and g4 or h5.

12...h5

After 12...♘f6 13 ♕d2 White slowly prepares a g4 break.

13 ♕c2 ♗h6 14 g4!?

Undeterred, he makes the thematic break.

14...♘xe5 15 fxe5 hxg4 16 fxg4 fxg4 17 ♗xg6+ ♔d7 18 0-0!

Forget about all that stuff I said earlier about playing positional chess! Actually, believe it or not, castling kingside takes fine strategic judgement. White's king obviously enjoys the great outdoors and feels comfortable on the breezy kingside:

1. Black's g-pawn shields White's

king and keeps it a lot safer than it looks; and

2. Should more pieces come off the board, White would be happy to move his king forward and eat the g-pawn later on.

18...g3!?

The pawn goes on a suicide mission in an attempt to open lines for his comrades.

19 ♗f5!

He isn't going to allow the bishop to participate in the attack. Also, this eliminates Black's bishop pair.

19...♗xf5 20 ♕xf5+ ♔c7 21 ♔g2 ♕d7!?

A sign of White's dominance. Black tries his luck in a pawn-down ending realizing that his extended g-pawn is not long for this world.

22 ♕xd7+ ♔xd7 23 ♖f3 ♖g4 24 ♔h3

White isn't content to simply trade g-pawn for h-pawn.

24...♖ag8 25 ♖xg3 ♖xg3+ 26 ♘xg3 ♖f8

This is probably what Onischuk envisioned when he agreed to the ending. Black threatens to infiltrate on f2.

27 ♖e1!

Challenging on the second rank is the correct path since after 27 ♖f1? ♖xf1 28 ♘xf1 ♗c1 29 b3 ♗b2 30 ♘g3 ♗xc3 31 ♘e2 ♗d2 Black regains his lost pawn and may just hold the game, despite that passed h-pawn.

27...c5

If 27...♖f2 28 ♖e2 ♖xe2 29 ♘xe2 and the point is that Black is denied ...♗c1.

28 dxc5 ♔c6 29 ♔g4

Avoiding the careless 29 b4? ♗d2.

29...♖g8+ 30 ♔h5!

He sees that Black can't keep his king boxed in on the h-file forever.

30...♖xg3 31 ♔xh6 ♔xc5!

The path to the stiffest resistance. 31...♖g2?! 32 b4 ♖xa2 33 ♖g1! allows White's king access to the g-file and leaves the h-pawn unimpeded.

32 ♖e2 b5 33 h5 a5 34 ♔h7 ♔c4

Black plans ...b4 to try and get his own passed d-pawn.

35 ♖f2!

The start of a clever manoeuvre designed to back Black's king off. Also, White threatens ♖f7, creating a second passed pawn.

35...b4 36 ♖f4+! ♔c5 37 h6! bxc3 38 bxc3 ♔c6

Black loses the race after 38...♖xc3? 39 ♖g4! d4 40 ♔g7 ♖h3 41 h7 d3 42 h8♕ ♖xh8 43 ♔xh8 d2 44 ♖g1 ♔d4 45 ♖d1 ♔d3 46 ♔g7 ♔e2 47 ♖xd2+ ♔xd2 48 ♔f7.

39 ♔h8 ♔d7 40 c4 ♔e6 41 cxd5+ ♔xd5 42 ♖f8!

The rook ends its king's imprisonment from the dungeon of h8.

42...♔xe5 43 h7 ♖g2 44 ♖g8 ♖xa2 45 ♔g7 ♖h2 46 h8♕ ♖xh8 47 ♖xh8 a4 48 ♔g6 a3 49 ♖a8 1-0

Summary

Against the ...f5 and ...d5 Stonewall, you will follow Aristotle's advice and play the London. And you will like it! Just kidding. If these London positions fill you with a nameless dread, then begin with a faux London with 3 ♗f4, but take the option of returning to your Veresovian ways with 4 f3 and play for e4.

Game 75
T.Dao-N.Babu
Udaipur 2000

---

1 d4 f5 2 ♘c3 ♘f6 3 ♗g5

Back to a Veresov approach now that Black has developed his knight!

3...d5 4 ♕d2

Next game we'll consider the immediate 4 f3.

4...c6

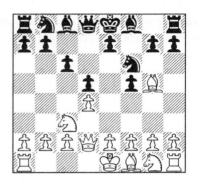

Other choices:

a) 4...e6 5 g4!? is a strange wing gambit which may well be sound: 5...fxg4 6 e4 (6 h3! looks logical when Black should probably decline with 6...g3) 6...♗e7 7 e5 ♘h5 8 ♗e3?! c5 9 ♗e2 cxd4 10 ♕xd4 ♘c6 11 ♕xg4 g6 12 ♘f3 and now it looks like a nice French for Black who owns f5, A.Stefanova-K.Spraggett, San Sebastian 1999.

b) Nobody has tried 4...♘e4?! and with good reason. It doesn't make much sense since Black falls behind in development after 5 ♘xe4 and then 5...fxe4 6 f3 ♗f5 7 g4 ♗g6 8 ♘h3, or 5...dxe4 6 f3 ♘c6 7 0-0-0 when White threatens both d5 and fxe4.

5 f3 ♗e6 6 e3!

In this case the restrained approach could be best, although after 6 ♘h3 ♘bd7 7 ♘f2 h6! (good timing, which induces White to capture since f2 is currently occupied by a knight, and White doesn't have the option of playing to h4) 8 ♗xf6 ♘xf6 9 e4 g6 10 exf5 (he wants the e5 hole for his pieces) 10...♗xf5 11 ♗d3 ♕d6 12 0-0 0-0-0 13

♗xf5+ gxf5 14 ♘d3 White may still have had a tiny edge in L.Schandorff-M.Bartel, Istanbul 2003, for these reasons:

1. White controls e5;

2. He may be able to play ♕f4 at some point with a slightly better ending;

3. Black has a perpetually backward pawn on the e-file.

6...♘bd7 7 ♗d3 ♘b6 8 ♘ge2 ♕d7 9 0-0 h6 10 ♗f4!

Provoking ...g5.

10...♗f7

10...g5 11 ♗e5 ♗g7 12 a4 ♘c4 13 ♗xc4 dxc4 14 a5! intending ♘a4 and ♘c5 gives White a strategic advantage.

11 e4 e6

11...dxe4 12 fxe4 g5 13 ♗e5 f4 14 b3 ♗g7 15 a4! looks like a position arising from a King's Gambit, except White isn't down the pawn.

12 exd5

Black isn't bothered by 12 e5?! which makes e5 inaccessible for White's pieces.

12...exd5 13 ♘g3!

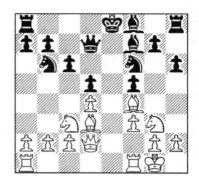

White begins a series of probing manoeuvres designed to create weaknesses in Black's overall structure.

13...g6

The passive 13...♗g6 14 b3 doesn't look like an improvement.

14 ♖fe1+ ♔d8

I don't believe in Black's compensation if he hands over the h-pawn with 14...♗e7 15 ♗xh6 0-0-0 16 b3, and 14...♗e6?? loses material on the spot to 15 ♖xe6+ ♕xe6 16 ♖e1.

15 b3!

Now Black's knight looks silly on b6.

15...♗g7 16 ♘ce2 ♘e8

Black begins to drop pawns if he gets cute with 16...♘c4?! (just because he can play it doesn't necessarily mean he should play it) 17 bxc4 dxc4 18 ♗xf5 gxf5 19 ♗e5 ♘e8 20 ♕f4.

17 h4!

Instructive. The positional threat of 18 h5 forces more concessions from Black.

17...h5

Swiss cheese! Just look at the holes on g5, f4 and e5.

18 a4 ♘c8 19 c4!

It is in White's best interest to try and break open the centre while Black's king remains homeless in the middle.

19...♗f6 20 ♗e5!

Note how often Black gets stuck with a bad light-squared bishop in these lines.

20...♘e7

After 20...♗xe5 21 dxe5 dxc4 22 bxc4 ♔c7 23 ♕c3 ♗e6 24 ♖ab1 Black's king is in huge danger of being hunted down.

21 ♖ad1 ♗xe5

21...♖g8 22 ♗xf6 ♘xf6 23 c5 is slow death.

22 dxe5 ♘c7 23 ♘f4 ♗e6

Or 23...♘e6 24 ♘ge2! with a replacement on the way.

24 ♘ge2 ♔e8 25 ♘d4 ♔f7

Black gets asphyxiated after 25...dxc4 26 ♗f1! c3 27 ♕c1! ♕c8 28 ♗c4! ♗xc4 29 bxc4 ♔f8 30 ♕xc3.

26 ♘h3!

♕g5 is in the air.

26...♔g7 27 ♕g5 c5 28 ♘xe6+ ♘xe6

28...♕xe6 29 ♘f4 ♕f7 30 cxd5

♘exd5 31 ♗c4 ♖ad8 32 ♘xd5 ♘xd5 33 ♗xd5 ♖xd5 34 ♕f6+! wins a full rook.

29 ♕f6+ ♔h6 30 ♘g5!

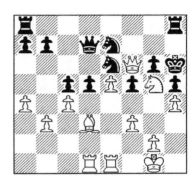

Threatening the knight on e6 and the fork on f7. Black has no defence.

30...♘g7

If 30...♘xg5?? 31 hxg5+ ♔h7 32 ♕f7 mate.

31 ♘f7+ ♔h7 32 ♘xh8 ♖xh8 33 cxd5 ♘xd5 34 ♕d6 ♘e8?

A bit of a booboo from Babu! But White was winning anyway.

35 ♕xd7+ 1-0

Summary

You don't have to enforce e4 every time against the Dutch. Sometimes you may consider the quieter e3 lines, engineering e4 only later on.

> ## Game 76
> ## I.Sokolov-B.Weick
> Mainz (rapid) 2003

1 d4 f5 2 ♘c3 ♘f6 3 ♗g5 d5 4 f3 ♘c6

The sincerest form of flattery! Black

blocks his c-pawn with his knight in the spirit of the Veresov, immediately fighting for control over e5.

Alternatives will be considered in the next game.

5 ♕d2 e6 6 ♘h3!

The most flexible of White's options:

1. The knight may play to f2 to help force the e4 break;

2. The knight may also head for open pastures on f4;

3. White doesn't castle queenside early and keeps Black guessing about his king; and

4. White keeps options open for either e3 or e4.

Others:

a) 6 0-0-0!? is very committal; I wouldn't let Black know my king's address this early. Then 6...♗b4 7 e3 0-0 8 ♘h3 ♖b8! 9 ♘f4 b5! 10 a3 ♗e7 11 ♘xb5 ♗d7 12 ♘c3 ♕c8 saw the open b-file give Black excellent compensation for the pawn in E.L'Ami-F.Nijboer, Groningen 2004.

b) 6 e4!? dxe4 7 ♗b5 ♗b4! 8 fxe4 ♘xe4 9 ♗xd8 ♘xd2 10 ♗xc7 ♘e4 11 ♘ge2 ♗d7 12 0-0 ♗xc3 13 bxc3 ♖c8 when Black's structural advantage and White's bishop pair balance the game, L.Schandorff-S.Kindermann, German League 2003.

6...♗e7 7 ♘f4 0-0 8 e3 a6

Avoiding ♗b5 and ♗xc6, which kills a defender of e5. Black decides against pushing pawns in front of his king with 8...h6 9 ♗xf6 ♗xf6 10 0-0-0 a6 11 h3 b5 12 g4, which leads to a sharp opposite-wings attack situation.

9 h4 ♕e8

Setting up for his next move.

10 h5 ♘e4?!

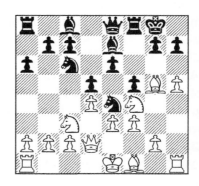

Clever but favouring White!

11 fxe4 ♗xg5 12 e5

Advantage White:

1. He owns f4, since if Black ever plays ...♗xf4 he ends up with a bad bishop;

2. White's attack looks faster since he has a clear plan of a3, ♗d3, and play for g4; and

3. Black's attack on the other wing looks harder to organize.

12...♗h6 13 a3! ♗d7 14 ♗d3 ♖c8 15 ♘ce2 ♘d8 16 c4!

Black gets counterplay after the automatic 16 0-0-0?! c5: for instance, 17 c3 c4 18 ♗c2 (or 18 ♗b1?! ♘c6 19 ♖dg1 ♘a5! and White's queen doesn't have access to c2 since it gets hit by a bishop on a4) 18...b5 19 ♖dg1 a5 20 g4 fxg4 21 ♖xg4 ♘c6 22 ♗b1 b4 23 ♕c2 ♖f5 24 ♕d1 ♖f7 25 ♕c2 leads to a draw.

16...c6

After 16...c5!? 17 cxd5 exd5 18 0-0! the powerful knight post on f4 allied to his pressure on d5 leaves White in strategic control.

17 c5! ♘f7 18 g4!

The time has arrived.

18...♘g5 19 0-0-0 fxg4?

He should try and open lines with 19...♖b8.

20 ♕c2 ♕e7 21 ♖dg1 ♖b8 22 ♖xg4 b6 23 ♖hg1

White has a buffet of wins. Another one would be 23 ♖xg5 ♕xg5 24 ♗xh7+ ♔f7 25 ♖g1 ♕h4 (25...♕d8 26 ♖xg7+!! mates) 26 ♕g6+ ♔e7 27 ♕xh6! gxh6 28 ♘g6+.

23...bxc5 24 ♖xg5!

Removing the defender of h7. Black collapses quickly.

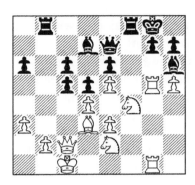

24...♖xf4

The rook can't be touched: 24...♗xg5 25 ♗xh7+ ♔h8 (25...♔f7 26 ♕g6 mate) 26 ♘g6+ forks.

25 ♗xh7+ ♔f7 26 ♕g6+ ♔f8 27 exf4

27 ♘xf4! ♗xg5 28 h6! ♗xh6 29 ♖f1 leads to mate.

27...♗xg5

The naive 27...♗e8 is dealt a harsh blow with 28 ♕xh6! gxh6 29 ♖g8+ ♔f7 30 ♖1g7 mate.

28 fxg5 ♗e8 29 ♖f1+ ♗f7 30 h6 1-0

Summary

Keep in mind the ♘h3 plan, whose hallmark is flexibility.

Game 77
C.Lakdawala-B.Baker
San Diego (rapid) 2007

1 d4 f5

If Black's name has a familiar ring it

is because National Master Bruce Baker and I have played well over 200 tournament games over the last ten years in our weekly Saturday tournaments. My books are plastered with our games like wallpaper!

2 ♘c3 ♘f6 3 ♗g5 d5 4 f3 c5?!

Overly ambitious. Instead, 4...e6 5 e4 ♗e7 6 exf5 exf5 7 ♕d2 0-0 8 0-0-0 c6 9 ♗d3 ♘h5 10 ♗xe7 ♕xe7 11 ♖e1 ♕d6 12 ♘h3 ♘d7 13 ♕g5 g6 14 ♘e2 ♕f6 was K.Sakaev-V.Malaniuk, Elista 1998, where Malaniuk had handled Black well, but I still prefer White's dark-square control and good bishop after 15 ♕h6 or 15 ♕d2.

5 e4

Logically opening the position when leading in development in an attempt to punish the premature ...c5 break. Here 5 e3 just seems too obliging and passive: 5...e6 6 ♗b5+ ♗d7 7 ♗xd7+ ♘bxd7 8 ♘ge2 ♗e7 9 0-0 0-0, as in M.Panic-P.Raab, German League 2008. On a side note, White's name is most certainly not a good one for a chess player!

5...♘c6

Black also lags dangerously behind after 5...dxe4 6 dxc5 ♕a5 7 ♕d2 ♕xc5 8 0-0-0 ♘c6 9 fxe4 fxe4 10 ♗b5.

6 ♗b5

6 ♗xf6?! helps Black develop and gives up control over the dark squares.

6...fxe4 7 fxe4

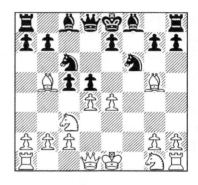

7...♗g4

Perhaps Black should remove pieces from the board with 7...♘xe4 8 ♘xe4 dxe4 9 ♗xc6+ bxc6 10 dxc5 ♕a5+ 11 ♕d2 ♕xc5 12 ♘e2 when he has an extra pawn and also owns the pair of bishops. However, Black's structure isn't pretty and he remains woefully undeveloped. Conclusion: Advantage White.

8 ♘ge2 cxd4!?

Handing White a tempo. Once again I would have taken the opportunity to remove a few attackers with 8...♘xe4!.

9 ♕xd4 dxe4?

Allowing White to keep queens on the board is fraught with peril. He should force an inferior ending with

9...♗xe2! 10 ♔xe2! dxe4 11 ♖ad1 ♕xd4
12 ♖xd4 ♖c8 when Black struggles, but
his position is off the critical list.

10 ♗xf6!

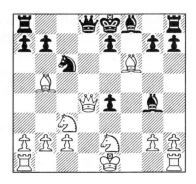

This move:

1. Regains the pawn;

2. Increases White's development
lead; and

3. Keeps queens on the board.

10...gxf6

Instead, 10...exf6?? 11 ♕xe4+ wins a
piece, and after 10...♗xe2? 11 ♗xc6+
bxc6 12 ♗xg7 ♖g8 13 ♕xd8+ ♖xd8 14
♗xf8 ♗h5 15 ♗h6 ♖xg2 16 ♖c1 White
should consolidate without trouble.

11 ♕xe4 ♗d7 12 0-0-0

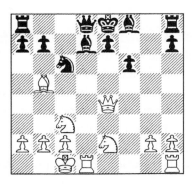

Black is in a bad way, but now finds
the only move to stay alive for the moment.

12...♕c8!

An excellent defensive move. Black's
only prayer is to get off the d-file and
fight for the light squares. Self-
destruction is very easy under such
strain: for example, 12...♗h6+?! 13 ♔b1
♔f7?? 14 ♕d5+ ♗e6 15 ♕h5+ picks off
the queen.

13 ♔b1 a6 14 ♗a4?!

Once again plagued by my weak
spot: a lack of attacking intuition. I
tend to calculate well if there is a single, long string. Problems arise when
multiple strings of analysis arise. I considered the sac 14 ♘d5! ♗f5 15 ♘xf6+
♔f7 16 ♗c4+ ♔xf6 and horribly misassessed it as unclear. In fact, White's
attack has reached overwhelming momentum: 17 ♖hf1 ♔g6 18 ♘f4+ ♔h6 19
♕e3! ♔g7 20 ♕g3+ ♔h6 21 ♕h4+ ♔g7
22 ♕g5+ ♗g6 23 ♘h5 mate. It's de-
pressing to come home from a tournament and plug your game into a
computer, which informs you just how
much you missed over the board.

14...b5 15 ♗b3 ♖b8 16 ♖xd7!

Eliminating a key defender of the
light squares. I would describe myself
as a courageous coward, in that I force
myself to make such sacs, overriding
the voice of my inner chicken! Normally
I am engaged in a constant tug-of-war
between my heart (the inner chicken)
and my mind (the one that yells: "Sac
you coward! Go for it!"). Saying this, I

rarely allow the inner chicken to win the battle! Over the years I have come to realize that courage is not the same as fearlessness. Courage is acknowledging your inner demons and then facing them down.

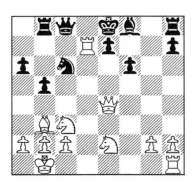

16...♕xd7 17 ♖d1 ♕c7 18 ♕e6

18 ♕f5! ♘e5 19 ♕h5+ ♘g6 20 ♘d5 ♕d6 (20...♕e5?? 21 ♕xe5 ♘xe5 22 ♘c7 mate would be a cute finish) 21 ♘ef4 f5 and now 22 ♘xg6 overloads Black's queen.

18...♘e5?

Losing immediately, but there was no saving the game at this point: for instance, 18...♘d8 19 ♕g4 with too many threats.

19 ♘d5 1-0

Summary

The Stonewall Dutch is considered a closed line. Thus Black often gets surprised by how quickly White is able to open the game with the Veresov approach. That ♘c3 and f3 pair changes the equation and Black must be ever vigilant for a quick e4! break.

Mr. Champion certainly lucked out with an excellent surname for a chess player! Other good chess names are Hammer and Powers. My unimpressive surname, Lakdawala, translates from the Gujarati (one of a million Indian languages) as: 'Guy who sells wood'. But I would be remiss if I didn't also point out that my first name, Cyrus, means 'He who radiates like the sun!' What do you think about that Messrs. Champion, Hammer and Powers?

1 d4 f5 2 ♗g5 ♘f6 3 ♘c3 e6

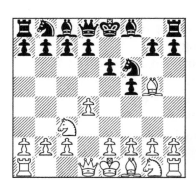

Black allows White e4 hoping for a solid game in return.

4 e4 fxe4 5 ♘xe4 ♗e7 6 ♗xf6!

Just like we do in the Rubinstein French lines. Maintaining the powerful e4-knight is our top priority.

6...♗xf6 7 ♕h5+! g6 8 ♕h6

A key position to remember. White gets terrific compensation if Black takes on d4 and he gets a strategic edge if Black declines.

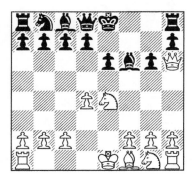

8...♗xd4?!

Gulp! Mr. Champion relies a wee bit too much on the power of his name to see him safely though this game. He goes grabbing pawns and falls way behind in development against one of the greatest pure tacticians of all time. Next game we examine the more reliable decline lines.

9 0-0-0 ♘c6?

Even after the superior 9...♗f6! 10 h4 ♛e7 11 ♘xf6+ ♛xf6 12 h5 Black found himself totally on the defensive, with every piece but his queen on the first rank in J.Krouzel-R.Fiala, Czech League 2000.

10 ♘f3?

Miraculously for Black, Tal misses a simple combination! But let's remember, it is a simul and he probably banged out the automatic 10 ♘f3 in less than a second.

Instead, 10 ♖xd4! ♘xd4 11 ♛g7 ♖f8 12 ♛xd4 ♛e7 13 ♘f3 b6 14 h4 ♗b7 15 ♛e3 0-0-0 16 ♗d3 ♔b8 17 a3 e5 18 c4

d6 19 ♖e1 was M.Kahn-F.Seifert, Leutersdorf 2000, where for some strange reason White agreed to a draw in a clearly superior position. My opponents are never this courteous!

10...♗f6 11 ♗b5

The standard plan 11 h4 intending to push again was also available.

11...♛e7 12 ♖he1

He can also play for the cheapo 12 ♛f4 ♗xb2+?? (12...0-0 is forced) 13 ♔xb2 ♛b4+ 14 ♔a1 ♛xb5 15 ♘f6+! ♔d8 (15...♔e7 16 ♘d5+! also does the job) 16 ♘xd7!.

12...♗g7 13 ♛f4 d6 14 ♖xd6!?

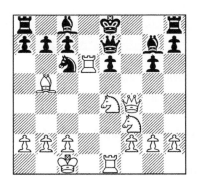

The wizard strikes. *Rybka* says it's a sound sac, but only good for a draw.

14...♖f8!?

Playing for the win? A draw is for the taking after 14...cxd6 15 ♘xd6+ ♔d8 16 ♘f7+ ♔e8 17 ♘d6+.

15 ♖xc6!

Dazzling stuff, and all the more impressive from a simul game. I had a student named Jack Miller who played Tal in a simul about 20 years ago. Tal won in mind-bending fashion similar

15...☐xf4 16 ☐xe6+ ♗d7??

It is pretty clear that Black's head reels from the complications. He had to play 16...♔f8! (box!) 17 ☐xe7 ♔xe7 18 ♘eg5+ ♔d6! with total chaos.

17 ♘d6+!

The power and the glory!

17...♔f8 18 ☐xe7

Down a full piece, Black can resign.

18...♗xb5 19 ♘xb5 ♗xb2+ 20 ♔xb2 ☐b4+ 21 ♔c1 ☐xb5 22 ☐xc7 1-0

Summary

Black is especially asking for it when he grabs the d4-pawn in this line. White gets a huge initiative and can virtually regain his pawn at will.

Game 79
V.Popov-A.Neiksans
Pardubice 2000

---

1 d4 f5 2 ♘c3 ♘f6 3 ♗g5 e6 4 e4 fxe4 5 ♘xe4 ♗e7 6 ♗xf6! ♗xf6 7 ♕h5+! g6 8 ♕h6

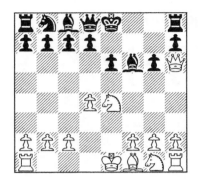

8...♘c6!

Declining is the wiser course. Another way to do so would be 8...b6!? 9 ♘f3 ♗b7 10 ♗d3 ♕e7 and then:

a) 11 c3! ♕e7 (11...d5?! 12 ♘xf6+ ♕xf6 13 ♗b5! leaves White in a classical good knight versus bad bishop scenario) 12 ♕f4! (remember this double attack) 12...0-0 13 ♕xc7 ☐ab8 14 0-0 ♗a8 15 ☐fe1 ♗g7 16 ♕g3 with advantage White in K.Gawehns-A.Dunne, correspondence 1997. Here Black's pawn structure is shaky, while White controls more central space and the central dark squares. Moreover, White has the safer king, may prepare an attack with h4 and, of course, he is a pawn up.

b) 11 0-0-0 ♘a6! (covering the sensitive c7-square) 12 c3 ♗g7 13 ♕e3 0-0-0 14 ♔b1 ♘b8 15 ☐he1 ♘c6 and Black has equalized. His bishop pair makes up for White's space, R.Ash-A.Yusupov, Winnipeg 1986.

9 c3 ♕e7!?

Everyone seems to play this, but it's a sac! Instead, after 9...d6 10 ♗d3 ♕e7

11 ♘xf6+ ♕xf6 12 ♘f3 ♗d7 13 0-0 0-0-0 14 ♖fe1 Black must suffer passively, but his extra pawn should give him some comfort.

10 ♕f4!

Old faithful! This double attack constantly crops up in these lines.

10...0-0 11 ♕xc7

Now comes a forcing line critical to the evaluation of the opening.

11...♗xd4!

Instead, 11...d5 12 ♕xe7 ♗xe7 13 ♘d2 e5!? (the cost of freedom is an isolani) 14 dxe5 ♘xe5 15 ♘gf3 ♘d7 16 ♘b3 was A.Kochemasov-K.Ter Veen, correspondence 2005. I always prefer White in such situations, as I just don't believe in Black's activity as full compensation for the missing pawn.

12 cxd4 ♕b4+ 13 ♘d2 d6!

With the unstoppable threat 14...♖f7, trapping White's queen. The question is: does White get enough for the queen?

14 ♖c1?!

A questionable decision. 14 a3! is a huge improvement: 14...♕xb2 15 ♖b1

♕xa3 16 h4! ♖f7 17 ♖h3! (the point; White doesn't lose his queen) 17...♖xc7 18 ♖xa3 ♘xd4 19 ♗d3 when Black's three pawns don't fully compensate the piece since it looks very difficult to advance them without losses.

14...♖f7 15 ♖xc6! ♖xc7 16 ♖xc7 ♕xb2 17 ♗d3 ♕xd4 18 ♗b1

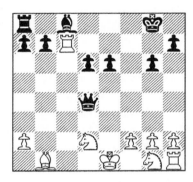

What a mess. The material count is rook and two knights versus queen and two pawns. King safety will be the deciding issue to see who stands better.

18...♕b6 19 ♖c1 ♗d7 20 ♘gf3 ♗b5!

Black gives notice that White's king must sit it out in the centre.

21 h4!

With a purpose: White lets Black know that his own king isn't so safe with h5 coming, and that he may activate his rook with ♖h3.

21...♗a6!

Idea: 22...♕b5.

22 ♔d1!

What a battle! His move is much stronger than 22 a4?! ♕a5 23 ♗a2 ♕xa4 24 ♗b3 ♕d7 25 ♔d1 d5 when Black has everything under control.

22...♕xf2 23 ♖e1 ♖f8

Or 23...♖e8 24 h5! and then:

a) 24...♗b5?! 25 hxg6 ♗a4+ 26 ♗c2 ♗xc2+ 27 ♖xc2 (threatening 28 ♘e4!) 27...♕xg2 28 gxh7+ ♔h8 29 ♖g1 ♕f2 30 ♖c7 when Black is tied up and fighting for survival.

b) 24...gxh5! 25 ♗f5! e5 26 ♘e4 ♕xa2 27 ♘f6+ ♔f7 28 ♘xe8 ♔xe8 29 ♖c2 with two rooks and a knight for a queen and five pawns.

Conclusion: I'm forced to cop out with a plea of unclear.

24 h5 g5!?

Black had a difficult choice:

a) 24...♕xg2 25 hxg6 hxg6 26 ♖xe6 ♕h1+ 27 ♖e1 ♕h3 28 ♗e4 when I don't trust Black's position.

b) 24...gxh5 25 ♖c7 ♖f7 26 ♖c8+ ♔g7 27 ♘g5 ♖e7 28 ♗xh7 ♕d4 29 ♖g8+ ♔f6 30 ♖g6+ ♔f5 31 ♖g7+ ♔f6 32 ♖g6+ with perpetual check.

25 ♖xe6!?

25 ♖c7 ♕b6 26 ♗xh7+ ♔h8 27 ♖e7 e5 28 ♘xg5 ♕b2 29 ♗c2 ♕a1+ 30 ♗b1 ♗d3! 31 ♖xb7 ♗xb1 32 ♖xb1 ♕xa2 and it remains a mess.

25...♕xg2 26 ♖c7 ♕h1+ 27 ♖e1 ♕g2??

27...♕xh5! 28 ♗xh7+ ♔h8 29 ♗e4 ♖f7 30 ♖c8+ ♔g7 31 ♗d5 g4 32 ♗xf7 ♕xf7 33 ♘d4 ♕xa2 34 ♖c7+ is also nightmarishly hard to evaluate!

28 ♗xh7+ ♔h8 29 ♗g6!

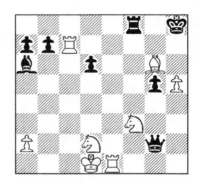

It's all over. Black's king can't be defended and there isn't a perpetual in sight.

29...♕f2

Or 29...♗b5 30 ♖ee7 ♕h1+ 31 ♘e1 ♗a4+ 32 ♔c1 ♖d8 33 h6! ♗c6 34 ♖h7+ ♔g8 35 ♖cg7+ ♔f8 36 ♖h8 mate.

30 ♘xg5 ♕f4 31 ♘gf3

The more efficient path lies in 31 ♘f7+! ♔g7 32 ♘e5+! ♔h6 33 ♘ef3! ♖h8 34 ♖ee7 ♕a4+ 35 ♔e1 when Black's king is cornered.

31...♕a4+

31...♕f6 32 ♖ee7 ♕a1+ 33 ♘b1 ♕f6 34 ♖h7+ ♔g8 35 ♗e4! menaces both ♗d5+ and also h6.

32 ♗c2 ♕g4 33 ♖h7+ ♔g8 34 ♖g1 1-0

Summary

Declining the d-pawn is the superior route for Black in this line.

Game 80
A.Krivonogov-P.Yanin
Novgorod 1998

1 d4 f5 2 ♘c3

Note too the continuation 2 ♗g5 (don't worry, we will transpose to our Veresov position soon) 2...g6 3 ♘c3 (there!) 3...♗g7 (Black gets into trouble quickly if he avoids ...d5) 4 h4! ♘f6?! (4...h6) 5 h5! ♘xh5 6 ♖xh5! gxh5 7 e4 0-0 8 ♗c4+ ♔h8 9 ♕xh5, which gave White a blistering attack for the exchange in D.Gormally-S.Barua, Manchester 1997. Trust me on this one. GM Akobian once slaughtered me with a similar sac when in a moment of temporary insanity, I abandoned my beloved Slav and essayed a Leningrad Dutch.

2...d5

This move is played slightly less often than 2...♘f6. I feel that the 2...d5 move order is a bit inaccurate since White can pull the switcheroo to a favourable London with 3 ♗f4!. Black should probably play 2...♘f6 to make White commit a bishop to g5, and only then should he play 3...d5. Of course, this is all from the heavily-biased perspective of a London System lover!

Instead, the immediate 2...g6 runs into 3 h4! ♘f6 (Black stops the h5 pawn push) 4 h5! (oh, no he doesn't!) 4...♗g7 (or 4...♘xh5 5 ♖xh5! gxh5 6 e4 with monster compensation for the exchange in S.Plischki-T.Braun, Liberec

2007; it's not a good sign when the only developed piece is the king!) 5 h6! (get back, get back, get back to where you once belonged!) 5...♗f8 6 ♗g5 d5 7 ♕d2 e6 8 0-0-0 ♗b4 9 f3 0-0 10 ♘h3 c6 11 a3 ♗a5 12 e4! ♗xc3 13 ♕xc3 fxe4 14 ♗xf6 ♖xf6 15 fxe4 dxe4 16 ♗c4 left Black undeveloped and his king in danger in G.Moehring-M.Knezevic, Hradec Kralove 1978.

3 ♗g5

White is obviously a London hater! As you know, I prefer 3 ♗f4! at this point.

3...g6

What I like about the Veresov versus the Dutch is that we force Black to stir the pot of a peculiar Stonewall/Leningrad soup, something which confuses both Stonewall and Leningrad players. If he insists on a Stonewall, Black could play:

a) 3...c6 4 ♕d3!? (the idea may be to help out enforcing f3 and e4 later on) 4...♗e6 5 h4 ♘a6 6 a3 ♕a5 7 ♘h3 0-0-0 8 ♗f4 ♗d7?! 9 ♘g5 ♘h6 10 e3 e6 11 ♖a2! (setting up a cheapo!) 11...♖e8? 12

b4! ♕b6 13 ♘a4 ♗xb4+ (Black now realized that 13...♕d8?? is met rudely with 14 ♕xa6!) 14 axb4 ♕xb4+ 15 c3 when Black was down a piece and under heavy fire in R.Knaak-P.Welz, Berlin 1990.

b) 3...h6 is a move examined by GM Neil McDonald in *Play the Dutch*. After 4 ♗f4 it's back to a Londony Stonewall – certain death for Black! For example, 4...♘f6 5 e3 e6 6 ♘f3 ♗d6 7 ♗d3 0-0 8 0-0 ♗d7 9 ♘e2 ♗e8 10 c4 ♗h5 11 ♗xd6 ♕xd6 12 ♘f4 ♗xf3 13 ♕xf3 c6 14 b4! and White's queenside play is well underway, A.Moiseenko-G.Rechlis, Israeli League 2008.

4 f3 ♘f6

Slightly more accurate may be 4...♗g7 which gives Black more options.

5 ♕d2

Cooked to order. Now our position looks very, very, Veresovy! When in doubt my brother, Jimmy, the Veresov god (so he believes himself to be), would apply his formula against virtually any Black set-up: d4, ♘c3, ♗g5, f3, ♕d2 and castle queenside.

5...♗g7 6 0-0-0

Alternatively, 6 ♘h3 ♗e6 7 0-0-0 ♘bd7 8 ♗h6 0-0 9 ♗xg7 ♔xg7 10 ♘f4 ♗f7 11 h4 c5 12 e3 ♕a5 13 h5 ♖ac8 14 hxg6 hxg6 15 a3 ♖h8 16 ♗b5 e6 17 ♗xd7 ♘xd7 18 dxc5! ♕xc5 19 e4 and Black had problems in R.Kempinski-M.Krasenkow, Warsaw 1997:

1. His king is insecure;

2. White applies pressure to Black's centre;

3. Black dark squares look shaky; and

4. For now his bishop remains bad since his pawns remain fixed on light squares.

6...♗e6 7 e4!?

He can also prepare this break with the slower 7 ♘h3 and follow with ♘f2 and e4, or even g4.

7...fxe4 8 fxe4 dxe4

8...♘xe4!? 9 ♘xe4 dxe4 is also possible.

9 ♘ge2 0-0 10 ♘g3 ♗d5?

This is an important piece. He throws away good money to a lost cause. The advanced e-pawn will fall later anyway, and Black will be made to pay dearly for giving up the defender of the light squares. Better to return the pawn with 10...c6.

11 ♗e2 ♘c6 12 h4 h5 13 ♘xd5 ♕xd5 14 ♕c3 ♔h7?!

I would not give ground. Better was 14...b5!?.

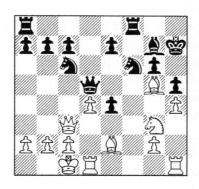

15 ♗c4 ♕d6 16 ♕e1!

This covers the knight and hits e4. If White regains the pawn he stands clearly better with his bishop pair and safer king.

16...e3 17 c3 a6 18 ♗xe3 b5 19 ♗b3 a5 20 ♖f1 a4 21 ♗f4 ♕d8

Backing off again, but this time by necessity: 21...♗h6? 22 ♗xh6 ♔xh6 23 ♗c2 and the threat of ♕e3+ followed by ♕g5 gives White a powerful attack.

22 ♗c2 a3 23 b3 b4

This leads to a terrible position, but I am at a loss for useful suggestions for Black, who may well be busted here.

24 d5! ♘a5

After 24...♘a7 25 c4 Black is in no position to attack.

25 cxb4 ♘b7 26 ♕e2

Simple chess. h5 and g6 are in White's crosshairs and there isn't a thing Black can do about it.

26...♗h6 27 ♘xh5 ♘xd5 28 ♗xh6 ♖xf1 29 ♕xf1 ♔xh6 30 ♕d3! ♕g8 31 ♕d2+!

Winning a piece. Black can resign.

31...♔h7 32 ♕xd5 ♕xd5 33 ♖xd5 ♘d6 34 ♘f4 1-0

Summary

Although I prefer the slower ♘h3 lines,

if White chooses he can play for an earlier e4 and sac a pawn temporarily. It looks to me like he gets the edge in this line also.

Game 81
S.Sergienko-A.Mukhin
Voronezh 1999

1 d4 f5 2 ♘c3 ♘f6 3 ♗g5 g6 4 f3 d5 5 ♕d2 ♘c6

Black fights for e5.

6 0-0-0 ♗e6

This move may be slightly more accurate than 6...♗g7 7 ♗h6! (logical, since Black wasted a tempo with ♗g7) 7...0-0 8 ♘h3 a6 9 ♗xg7 ♔xg7 10 ♘f4 ♕d6 11 e3 ♗e6 (a bad bishop since he can't play ...e5 any time soon) 12 h4 ♗f7 13 h5 g5 14 h6+ ♔h8 15 ♘h3 g4 16 ♘g5 ♗g6 17 ♘e2 e5 18 dxe5 ♕xe5 19 ♘f4 ♖ae8 20 ♗d3! ♕xe3 21 ♕xe3 ♖xe3 22 ♘fe6 and White's dark-square control gave him more than enough for the pawn in I.Sokolov-M.Illescas Cordoba, Wijk aan Zee 1997.

7 ♘h3 ♕d7 8 ♘f4 0-0-0?!

Black mistakenly feels safer castling on the same wing as White.

9 e3 a6 10 ♘a4!

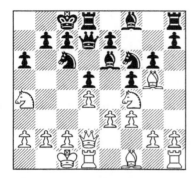

Off on an unannounced visit into Black's camp. Black's pieces are caught in a massive traffic jam and can't stop the knight from landing on c5.

10...♗f7 11 ♘c5 ♕d6 12 ♘fe6!!

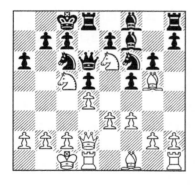

A beautiful shot which emphasizes the dishevelled nature of Black's pieces, who stumble over each other.

12...♗xe6 13 ♗f4!

The point. White demands ransom in exchange for the life of Black's queen.

13...♘e5 14 ♕b4! ♕c6

Instead, 14...♕b6 drops an exchange to 15 ♕xb6 cxb6 16 ♘xe6 ♘c6 17 ♘xd8.

15 ♗xe5

Black's pieces are in a hopeless tangle, unable to eject the growing number of intruders.

15...♖g8 16 ♖d3!

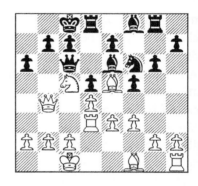

The tipping point. Black quickly buckles under the pressure.

16...♘e8

16...♘d7 17 ♘xd7 ♕xd7 18 ♖c3 c6 19 ♗xa6 ♗g7 20 ♖b3 doesn't help a bit.

17 ♖b3 ♗d7 18 ♗xa6 1-0

Summary

If Black avoids opposite-wings castling, there is no guarantee of safety for him on the queenside.

Game 82
S.Savchenko-M.Babar
Bad Wiessee 2000

1 d4 f5 2 ♘c3 ♘f6 3 ♗g5 d5 4 f3 g6 5

♕d2 ♗e6 6 ♘h3 c6

Played to avoid the tempo loss incurred after 6...♗g7 7 ♗h6.

7 ♕e3!

I like this bizarre and interesting plan. White makes an artificial move in an attempt to force Black to make an artificial move!

7 0-0-0 would be standard play: 7...♘bd7 8 ♘f4 ♗f7 9 h4 h6 10 ♗xf6 ♘xf6 11 e3 ♕c7 12 g4! fxg4 13 fxg4 ♘xg4 14 ♗h3 and White got excellent compensation for the pawn in A.Hagen-R.Tozer, Copenhagen 2001.

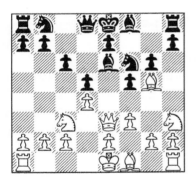

7...♕d6

The queen becomes a target, but he had no choice since 7...♗f7?? 8 ♗xf6 drops a piece, while 7...♕d7?! 8 ♘f4 ♔f7 9 ♘d3 threatens to fork and makes Black dance further to avoid it.

8 ♗f4!

Forcing the queen to d7, where it gets in the development path for his knight.

8...♕d7 9 ♘g5!?

But this seems like a waste of time. White looks faster after 9 0-0-0 ♗g7 10

♗h6 0-0 11 ♗xg7 ♔xg7 12 ♘f4 ♗g8 13 h4 b5 14 h5 when, once again, the dark squares around Black's king look ripe for exploitation.

9...♗g8 10 0-0-0?!

It seems White insists on the eccentric. I would make an effort to contain Black's expansion on the kingside with 10 h4!.

10...h6 11 ♘h3 g5 12 ♗e5 ♗g7 13 ♕d2

White, like an investor who makes a fortune and then loses it speculating on the stock market, gained time earlier, only to lose it back.

13...♗h7 14 e4

At last, White reforms from his previously Nimzovitchian ways and plays normally!

14...e6

Rejecting the sharper alternative 14...fxe4 15 fxe4 0-0 16 ♘f2 when h4 may follow. White looks very quick in the attack.

15 exf5 exf5 16 ♘f2 0-0 17 h4

White always looks faster to me in these lines. Notice how the inducement of ...♕d7 clogs Black's natural development on the queenside.

17...g4 18 h5! ♕f7 19 ♗f4 ♘xh5 20 ♗xh6 ♘g3 21 ♗xg7 ♕xg7 22 ♖h4 ♘xf1 23 ♖xf1

A picture of hopelessness. Black lies injured on the train tracks and lacks the strength to get out of the way of the oncoming train. He hasn't even finished developing while White's attack is well underway.

23...♘d7 24 ♖fh1 ♗g6 25 ♘e2!

He doesn't want the pawn. Instead he occupies f4 for his knight.

25...♘f6 26 ♘f4 g3 27 ♘2d3

Strategic disaster:

1. The f4-knight's big brother heads for e5;

2. White's rooks control the h-file;

3. Black's bishop clearly isn't the sharpest tool in the woodshed!

4. Black's loose g3-pawn can be picked up at any time; and

5. Black's king's days are numbered.

27...♖ae8?

27...♗f7 28 ♘e5 ♖ae8 29 ♕b4 was also hopeless.

28 ♖h8+ 1-0

Summary

When Black develops his bishop to e6, keep in mind White's strange ♕e3! plan. It looks to me like Black gets the worst of it after both sides lose time.

Chapter Nine
Modern, Pirc and Philidor

1 d4 d6 2 ♘c3 g6 3 e4 ♗g7 4 ♗g5

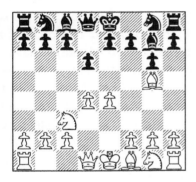

Some of your opponents may totally bypass the Veresov and meet 1 d4 with 1...g6, or 1...d6. Others will see the Veresov coming and attempt to dodge it this way into a Pirc or Philidor: 1 d4 ♘f6 2 ♘c3 d6 3 e4 and now 3...g6 transposes to a Pirc and 3...♘bd7 turns the game into the Lion Variation of the Philidor.

Against the Modern, let's go with the surrealistic Byrne System where our bishop leaps out into space on g5, pinning his e-pawn and attacking the

future knight on f6! This system has three advantages:

1. Most Modern/Pirc players won't be as familiar with this set-up.

2. White scores a very good 59% against both the Modern and Pirc with the Byrne System. There is an old saying which goes: "There are lies; there are damned lies; and then there are statistics!" which essentially says that anyone can try to prove anything that suits them by offering up the appropriate stats! However, while researching this chapter, I looked over many games in this line against both Modern and Pirc and saw that black players were genuinely confused, and that the set-up has real bite to it.

3. The GM Modern/Pirc experts all offer terrifying warnings about the Byrne System to their readers! For instance, Davies calls the Byrne: "one of the most dangerous at White's disposal, yet it tends to crop up surprisingly little in practice." Alburt and

Chernin call it the "real tiger of the Pirc." And speaking of tigers, Tiger Hillarp Persson calls it "one of the most poisonous against the Pirc", but claims Black is okay against it in the Modern. If the system makes the top GMs of the line this nervous, it is a good bet the Byrne will give you the capability of terrorizing some of your opponents with it too.

We aren't going to mess around either with the Lion, which is a Philidor coming from a Pirc move-order. 4 g4!? is the most aggressive option at our disposal and the one most likely to put a normally quiet Philidor opponent off his stride.

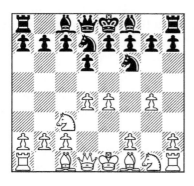

By contrast, in the Lion's Yawn, 1 d4 ♘f6 2 ♘c3 d6 3 e4 e5, Black invites a queen exchange at the cost of castling privileges. I suggest you bypass Black's specialty ending in favour of the more aggressive 4 ♘ge2 which keeps the central tension. From this point, Black has a choice of playing in normal Philidor fashion with 4...♘bd7, where we follow with the plan f3, ♗e3, ♕d2 and

0-0-0, all in Veresov style or Black can give up the centre with 4...exd4, the Antoshin Philidor. Our space advantage still should give us the edge, despite Black's super-solid set-up.

Game 83
S.Rublevsky-G.Chepukaitis
St Petersburg 2001

Not all chess geniuses are Grandmasters. Genrikh Chepukaitis, also known as 'Smartchip' on ICC, was a legendary blitz player, who, back in the 70's won the 5-minute championship of Leningrad ahead of Korchnoi and Petrosian. He could easily have annexed the GM title had he had the inclination. But Chepukaitis was a true amateur, who played only for the love of the game. I had the pleasure of many wild encounters over the ICC against the blitz giant despite my great exertions to keep things dull! So intense was his fighting spirit that he never ever took draws and to my exasperation, played until bare kings remained! I never knew who I was playing until it was announced that he had passed away. It was shocking news to me since I assumed Smartchip was some teenage hotshot GM incognito. He certainly never played chess like a senior citizen! I remember my friend, IM David Vigorito, aka 'Fluffy', bitterly complaining to me of how 'Smartchip' tormented him on a regular basis over the ICC with his neanderthal style of play!

1 e4 g6 2 d4 d6 3 ♘c3 ♗g7 4 ♗g5

"Into midair," writes GM Tiger Hillarp Persson, who continues: "this line is one of the most poisonous against the Pirc move order, but against the Modern it loses some of its venom." I believe Black must also be very careful in the Modern move order. We pin his e-pawn and deny Black ...e6.

4...h6?!

The black side of a Modern is not an easy position to navigate, and sometimes it's easy to turn into a blind loyalist to a corrupt party! Black tosses in ...h6 before deciding on his actual set-up and pays much too high a price for ejecting the irritating bishop. 4...h6?! weakens g6 and makes it a lot easier for White to sac.

5 ♗h4 a6

Smartchip's Modern! Chepukaitis specialized in Tiger's Modern even before Tiger did.

6 ♘f3

Flexibility is the key to the Byrne System. The realm of possibilities include f3, f4 and ♘f3 ideas. After 6 f4 b5 7 ♘f3 ♗b7 8 ♗d3 Black's insertion of ...h6 leaves him vulnerable to e5-e6 ideas. Still, Black should be okay here, since he may meet e6 with ...f5.

6...♘d7?!

Perhaps Black should throw in 6...b5! while he can: 7 a4 b4 8 ♘d5 a5 9 e5!? (9 ♗c4 gives White a safe edge) 9...dxe5 10 dxe5 ♗b7 11 ♗c4 g5 12 ♗g3 e6 13 ♘e3 ♕xd1+ 14 ♖xd1 ♘d7 15 ♗b5 0-0-0 with a complex struggle, P.Smirnov-V.Tseshkovsky, Krasnoyarsk 2003.

7 a4 b6

The Hippo structure doesn't work well for Black since he needs ...e6 and can't achieve it without the weakening ...g5. Instead, 7...c5 8 d5 ♕a5 9 ♖a3 ♘gf6 10 ♘d2 gives White a favourable version of the Schmid Benoni, which we examine in Chapter Ten. That early ...h6 could lead to trouble on the king-side when White achieves f4.

8 ♗c4 g5?

Smartchip, like most coffeehouse players, was tragically defence-challenged. A fire-breathing dragon if he had the initiative, but on the other end when defending, he lacked patience and would routinely lash out like this. He intends to play ...e6 after the bishop retreats. The problem: the bishop has no intention of retreating.

If Chepukaitis had foreseen the sacrificial cascade which follows he would surely have gone in for 8...♗b7! 9 ♕e2 g5 and the white sacs don't have the same force since Black's queen is no longer trapped.

9 ♗xg5!!

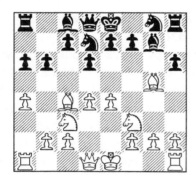

Just watch, more sacs follow.

9...hxg5 10 ♗xf7+!

Unceremoniously stripping the emperor of his bodyguard and sending him out into the street to face the angry mob.

10...♔xf7 11 ♘xg5+ ♔g6

11...♔f6?? 12 ♕g4 ♘f8 13 ♘d5+ ♔g6 14 ♘e6+ leads to total annihilation.

12 ♘e6 ♘h6

A sad necessity, since 12...♕e8?? 13 ♕g4+ ♔h6 (or 13...♔f7 14 ♕xg7+ ♔xe6 15 d5 mate) 14 ♕xg7+ ♔h5 15 ♕g5 is mate.

13 ♘d5

Of course he can also just eat the queen, but this move rubs it in a bit more.

13...♘f6

13...♕e8 14 ♕h5+!! ♔xh5 (14...♔h7 15 ♘g5+ mates in three moves) 15 ♘df4+ ♔h4 16 g3+ ♔g4 17 h3+ ♔f3 18

♘g5 mate would be a horrible way to exit the chessboard.

14 ♘xd8 ♖xd8 15 ♘xe7+ ♔f7 16 ♘xc8 ♖dxc8 17 f3

The position has settled:

1. The material balance of queen and four pawns clearly outstrips Black's three minor pieces; and

2. Black's king safety is just a temporary matter. Once White castles and starts to push his pawns, Black will feel the heat shortly.

Conclusion: Black is dead lost and simply awaits the second wave of the attack.

17...♘hg8 18 c3 c5 19 ♕b3+ ♔g6 20 0-0 ♖ab8 21 ♕e6 ♔h7 22 e5 ♘e8 23 f4 ♘c7 24 ♕f5+ ♔h8 25 ♖f3

The queen gets help from another attacker.

25...♘h6 26 ♖h3 ♔g8 27 ♕g6 ♘f7 28 e6 ♘xe6

An annoying Smartchip trademark: the bugger never resigned and always played on till kingdom come! 28...♘h8 29 ♕h7+ ♔f8 30 ♖g3 ♘xe6 31 f5 is slaughter.

**29 ♕xe6 cxd4 30 ♕g6 ♘h8 31 ♕h7+
♔f7 32 ♖g3 ♖g8 33 ♖e1 dxc3 34 ♕f5+
1-0**

The old lion finally hangs it up, not wishing to be shown 34...♗f6 35 ♕d5+ ♔f8 36 ♖xg8 mate.

Summary

An early ...h6?! without the immediate ...g5 loosens Black's kingside and opens the possibility of sacs on f7, or just a plan of f4 and later f5.

Game 84
M.Feygin-M.Roobol
Dutch League 2007

---

1 e4 g6 2 d4 ♗g7 3 ♘c3 d6 4 ♗g5 a6

Wisely avoiding 4...h6?!.

Modern specialist GM Colin McNab advocates 4...♘d7 in *Dangerous Weapons: The Pirc and Modern*. 5 ♕d2 c5 and now:

a) 6 d5 a6 7 a4 ♕a5 8 f3 b5 9 ♘h3 ♖b8 10.♘f2 ♘e5 with unclear play in this Trompowsky-like position. White's space plus and Black's queenside activity may balance each other out, J.Hodgson-C.McNab, Grangemouth 2001.

b) Black doesn't mind transposing into a Dragon after 6 ♘f3 cxd4 7 ♘xd4. Normally White doesn't mix ♕d2 with ♗g5 in Dragons but it doesn't seem so bad for him after 7...♘gf6 8 0-0-0 a6 9 f4 ♕c7 10 g4!? b5 11 ♘d5 ♘xd5 12 exd5 ♘f6 13 ♗xf6 ♗xf6 14 g5 ♗g7 15 h4, A.Motylev-P.Pogromsky, Russian

Cup (Internet) 2004. Black may be okay with his control over the dark squares, but I still prefer White, who has the more potent attack and control over c6.

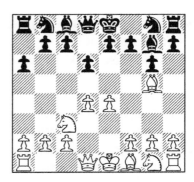

5 ♕d2 b5

5...♘d7 6 h4 h5 7 0-0-0 b5 (7...c5 may be the most accurate move, since now White found a promising sac to open lines) 8 e5! dxe5 9 dxe5 ♗xe5 10 ♖h3! with excellent compensation for the pawn in A.Caldeira-E.Capatti, Sao Paulo 2005.

6 a4

Played on the assumption that early confrontation favours the better developed side. Instead, after 6 ♘f3 ♗b7 7 a4 b4 8 ♘d5 a5 9 ♗c4! (taking advantage of the fact that Black can't toss in ...e6) 9...h6 10 ♕f4! ideas of ♘xc7+ were in the air in J.Waitzkin-Y.Lapshun, New York 1999.

6...b4 7 ♘d5 a5 8 c3 c6 9 ♘e3 bxc3 10 bxc3 ♘f6 11 ♗d3 ♗a6

Exchanges ease Black's burden.

12 f4!?

Risky. White is intent on attacking on the kingside, but pawns once pushed can't retreat, and White could be vulnerable to a ...d5 counterpunch in the centre. However, after 12 ♘e2 ♘bd7 13 0-0 0-0 14 f4 ♗xd3 15 ♕xd3 d5! 16 e5 ♘e4 17 ♘g4 f6 18 ♗h4 f5 Black's powerful knight on e4 compensated for his lack of space in B.Lindberg-M.Burwick, Swedish Team Championship 2004.

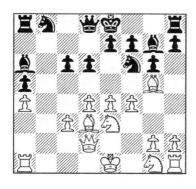

12...0-0 13 ♘f3 d5! 14 ♗xf6! exf6!

14...♗xf6?! 15 e5 just loses time and the e-file stays closed.

15 exd5!

15 e5?! fxe5 16 fxe5 f6 allows Black to chip away at his centre.

15...cxd5 16 0-0 ♕d6 17 ♖ab1 ♘d7

Swapping White's f-pawn for d5 is a bad deal: 17...♕xf4? 18 ♗xa6 ♖xa6 19 ♘xd5 ♕d6 20 ♖b5.

18 ♗xa6 ♖xa6 19 ♖b5!

Pressuring both the d5- and a5-pawns.

19...♘b6 20 ♖fb1 ♖e8 21 g3 ♕c6 22 ♕d3 ♗f8 23 ♘d2!

An assessment:

1. Black is tied down to d5 and a5;

2. He must watch for ♘b3 which hits a5 and may enter powerfully via c5;

3. His crippled pawn majority on the kingside effectively keeps him down a pawn; and

4. Black may be in a position to apply pressure on c3 or make something happen on the e-file, but at the moment his pieces stand clumsily placed.

Conclusion: White has the edge.

23...♖d8 24 ♖1b3 ♘xa4!?

He insists on staying active instead of sitting tight with 24...♗e7 and seeing how White makes progress.

25 ♖xd5!

Exploiting the overloaded black

queen to pick off d5. White's central pawns mean more than Black's passed a-pawn.

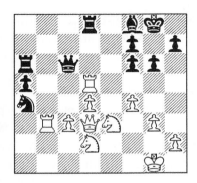

25...Ξxd5 26 ♘xd5 Ξa8?

Missing his chance to force a draw with a series of little combinations, starting with 26...♕xd5! 27 ♕xa6 ♘xc3! 28 ♕c4 ♕xd4+! 29 ♕xd4 ♘e2+ 30 ♔f2 ♘xd4 31 Ξb8 ♔g7 32 ♘c4 ♗b4 33 Ξa8 f5 34 ♘xa5 ♗xa5 35 Ξxa5 ♘e6, with a theoretical draw.

27 c4

Even stronger was 27 ♕b5! ♕xb5 28 Ξxb5, which Tetsuji's Black's knight in its prison cell on a4, and effectively halts Black's passed a-pawn.

27...Ξe8 28 ♘e4 ♗g7?

Allowing a sparkling finish. Black puts up more resistance with 28...Ξc8 29 ♘dxf6+ ♔g7 30 Ξb5 ♕xc4 31 ♕xc4 Ξxc4, but still loses after 32 Ξb7!! when he faces a mating attack. For example, 32...♘c3 33 ♘g5! forces mate, or 32...h6 33 ♘e8+ ♔h8 34 Ξxf7 ♔g8 35 Ξd7 with the terrible threat of either knight checking on f6 followed by Ξh7 mate.

29 Ξb8!

Black's rook is tied down to the fork square e7.

29...♔h8

29...♔f8 fails to 30 ♕a3+!.

30 ♘e7! ♕d7 31 ♘d6! 1-0

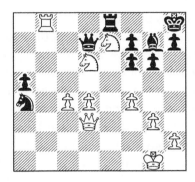

Ground Control to Major Tom! What a pretty picture: three White pieces all floating serenely in space, and all untouchable.

Summary

Generally, it's a good idea to meet an early ...b5 with a4. Picking a fight favours the player with the superior development.

Game 85
A.Shabalov-M.Zlotnikov
Mashantucket 1999

1 e4 g6 2 d4 ♗g7 3 ♘c3 d6

Be careful of the move order 3...c6. It is specifically designed against the Byrne system:

a) 4 ♗c4! d6 5 ♕f3!? (a move to warm the heart of any chess barbarian;

someone named this line the Monkey's Bum, a name which doesn't inspire confidence!) 5...e6 6 ♘ge2 b5 7 ♗b3 a5 8 a3 ♗a6 9 d5 cxd5 10 exd5 e5 11 ♘e4 h6 12 g4 ♘f6 13 ♘2g3 ♘xe4 14 ♘xe4 0-0 15 ♕h3 f5 16 gxf5 ♗c8 (I hate to bring this up, but we are still in book!) 17 ♘g3 ♖xf5!? with a chaotic position which looks like fun for both sides, V.Anand-A.Shirov, Dos Hermanas 1996.

b) If you are the type who loves to play in Vegas and are willing to gamble, then play 4 ♗g5!? regardless! Now this is a pawn sac: 4...♕b6! 5 ♘f3 ♕xb2 6 ♗d2 ♕b6. You may well have full compensation for the pawn, with a big development lead but what worries me is that the game is relatively closed for now, and it will be up to White to force it open later to get some traction with the development lead.

4 ♗g5 ♘c6

Advocated by Modern expert GM Davies. Black logically strikes at d4, which has been weakened slightly by White's refusal to play his bishop to the traditional e3-square.

5 ♘ge2

5 d5?! enhancing the g7-bishop's diagonal is just what Black wants: 5...♘e5 6 f4 ♘d7 7 ♘f3 c6 gave Black excellent counter-chances on the dark squares in A.Minasian-N.Davies, Lyons 1990.

5...a6

Alternatively:

a) 5...f6!? (so he can play e5, despite the annoying pin) 6 ♗e3 e5 7 ♕d2 ♘ge7 8 d5 ♘b8 9 0-0-0 0-0!? and White looks faster due to the loss of time incurred by ...♘c6 and ...♘b8, A.Yermolinsky-Z.Azmaiparashvili, Groningen 1993.

b) 5...h6 6 ♗e3! (giving Black ...h6 for free, but clearly it's a liability, not a strength) 6...e5 7 ♕d2 and Black will be forced to play the weakening ...h5 if he ever wants to castle kingside, T.Horvath-S.Kosanski, Celje 2007.

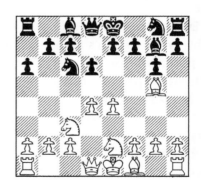

6 ♕d2 b5 7 f3

Remember, in this line you have a structural decision: f3, f4 or ♘f3, depending on the circumstance.

7...♗d7 8 g4!? h5 9 gxh5 ♖xh5 10 h4

♕c8 11 0-0-0

Trusting that his extra space will keep his king safe from Black's queenside onslaught.

11...♖h8 12 ♔b1 ♕b7 13 ♗e3

He drops back with the bishop to cover d4 and cut the e2-knight loose from its defensive duties.

13...0-0-0 14 ♖c1!

Multipurpose:

1. White opens d1 for his knight to manoeuvre to the more useful f2-square; and

2. He thinks about playing c4 and going after Black's king down the c-file.

14...♔b8 15 ♗g2 ♘f6 16 ♘d1 d5?

Creating an ugly weakness on c5. He should play it King's Indian style with 16...e5 17 d5 ♘e7 18 c4 c5!, with a decent position.

17 ♘f2

Better than 17 e5 ♘h5 18 ♘f2 ♗f5 19 ♘d3 ♗xd3 20 cxd3! e6 which also looks tough on Black.

17...e6?!

This leads to a lingering squeeze. 17...e5! 18 c3 intending ♘d3, although

still in White's favour, at least complicates the game.

18 ♘d3 ♕b6 19 c3 ♗c8 20 ♗g5!

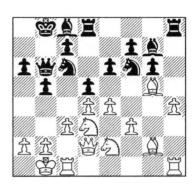

Threatening 21 e5.

20...♖df8 21 ♘ef4! dxe4?!

Allowing the f-file to open spells doom for Black. He had to hang tough with 21...♖e8.

22 fxe4 ♘h7 23 e5! ♘xg5 24 hxg5

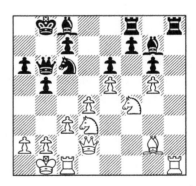

Total strategic domination by White:

1. A clamp on c5;

2. Massive space with the e5- and g5-pawn duo fixing f7 as a target.

3. Ideas of manoeuvring a knight to e4 and then landing on f6, or ma-

noeuvring a knight to g4 and going to h6; and

3. Black's king is seriously weakened.

24...♖d8

Let's say Black tries to block the f-file pressure with 24...♘e7 then 25 ♕f2 ♖d8 (25...♗b7? 26 ♘c5 threatens the bishop and also the fork on d7) 26 ♘c5 a5 27 ♘fd3 ♘f5 28 b4 a4 29 ♕f3 ♕a7 30 ♖xh8 ♖xh8 31 ♖h1 ♖xh1+ 32 ♗xh1 ♗f8 33 ♕c6 threatens b7 and infiltration to e8.

25 ♖xh8 ♖xh8 26 ♕e3 ♘a5 27 ♘c5 ♘c4 28 ♕f2

Avoiding the silly trap 28 ♕f3?? ♘d2+.

28...c6 29 ♘fd3 ♖f8 1-0

Black's game is in freefall and he resigns rather than be reduced to helplessness after 29...♖f8 30 ♘b4 ♘a5 31 ♖h1.

Summary

4...♘c6 looks to me like Black's best in the Modern versus our Byrne line. The key for White is to avoid the temptation to gain tempi with 5 d5. Just maintain the tension for as long as possible with ♘ge2, ♕d2, f3 and possibly 0-0-0 in Veresov fashion.

> ### Game 86
> **H.Nakamura-L.Kis**
> Philadelphia 2006

1 d4 g6 2 e4 ♗g7 3 ♘c3 d6 4 ♗g5 c6 5

♕d2 ♕a5

White was better too after 5...b5 6 f4 ♘d7 7 ♘f3 ♕a5 8 ♗d3 b4 9 ♘e2 c5 10 a3! (the game opens to White's favour) 10...♕b6 11 axb4 cxd4 12 ♖a5 e5 13 c3 f6 14 ♗h4 dxc3 15 ♘xc3 in B.Amin-A.Adly, Tripoli 2009.

6 f4

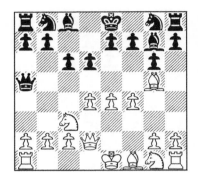

Going Austrian Attack style, the most aggressive of White's options. White must be careful when he plays this way because moving his f-pawn two squares undermines support for his e-pawn.

6...b5

Black may transpose to the Pirc at any time with 6...♘f6, after which you have choices like 7 e5 and 7 ♘f3.

7 ♘f3 ♗g4

As a Modern player myself, I have never liked mixing this move with ...b5 and generally develop the bishop to b7 after playing ...b5.

8 ♗e2 b4?

Leaving himself vulnerable to a3 tricks. ...b4 is a move Black should avoid, unless:

1. White commits to castling queenside; or

2. Black is forced to do so by White playing a4.

9 ♘d1 d5!?

Black's position has already become difficult, as shown too by:

a) 9...c5 10 ♘e3 ♗xf3 11 ♘c4! ♕a6 12 gxf3 cxd4 13 ♕xb4 ♘c6 14 ♕b3! ♕c8 15 ♕a4 and Black must move his king to deal with the threat ♘a5.

b) 9...♘f6 10 ♘f2 ♗xf3 11 ♗xf3 with a clear advantage due to the bishop pair and central space.

10 e5 e6 11 a3!

Black had better pray the position remains closed. All his pieces are fast asleep on the first rank.

11...♗f8 12 0-0 h6 13 ♗h4 c5?

He feels he must fight back in the centre, but he just isn't prepared for a central clash.

14 ♘e3 ♗xf3 15 axb4 ♕xb4 16 ♕xb4!

Not getting tempted by romantic notions of keeping queens on and trying for mate with 16 c3. A winning ending will do just fine for White.

16...cxb4 17 ♗b5+ ♘d7 18 ♖xf3 a5 19 ♗e1!

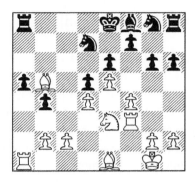

Black is virtually paralysed. White prepares to open quickly with c4!.

19...♖d8

Alternatively:

a) 19...♘e7?? is met by 20 ♗xb4.

b) 19...h5 20 c4! bxc3 21 ♗xc3 ♘e7 22 ♖xa5 ♖xa5 23 ♗xa5 is also totally hopeless. Black is down a pawn, horribly undeveloped and caught in a perpetual pin on the d7-knight.

20 c4! 1-0

Nakamura makes it look easy. Black can only await his own execution if he plays on with 20...bxc3 21 bxc3 ♘e7 22 ♖xa5 ♗g7 23 ♖a7 ♘c8 24 ♖b7.

Summary

Most Veresov players tend to favour f3 lines since this is closest to the structure they are used to. Just keep an open mind about playing Austrian Attack style with f4. It wouldn't be a bad idea to go over some Austrian Attack games, just so you know when it would be a favourable set-up.

Game 87
P.Leko-V.Topalov
Frankfurt (rapid) 1999

As I write this, India's beloved son, Anand, faces the much-despised Topalov for the World Championship title. IM Jack Peters recently sent all the titled players in Southern California a poll asking who would win the match. Logically, I felt Topalov must have the edge due to his youth. As I typed my e-mail response to Jack, I found my fingers typing the following on their on volition: "Hi Jack, Anand by a point! Best wishes, Cy." As a card-carrying member of the COA (Church of Anand) there is no way I am going to vote against our messiah! (Postscript: Prepare the elephants for the parade. Anand wins!)

1 e4 d6 2 d4 ♘f6 3 ♘c3 g6 4 ♗g5

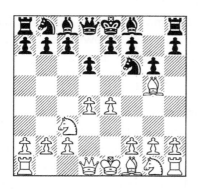

Neither Pirc nor Modern discourages us from our favourite set-up. It's worth quoting again Modern specialist GM Nigel Davies' view of this line in his *Starting Out: The Modern*: "In my opinion the Byrne System with 3 ♘c3 and 4 ♗g5 is one of the most dangerous at White's disposal, yet it tends to crop up surprisingly little in practice."

4...♗g7 5 ♕d2 h6

Black may opt to avoid chasing down the bishop with 5...c6 6 f4 b5 7 ♗d3 0-0 8 ♘f3 ♗g4 9 0-0, as in M.Kobalia-B.Rimawi, Amman 2006, but White's position looks rather easy to play: build up on the kingside and play for mate. His centre remains quite stable for an Austrian-style position of the Pirc, and this factor favours him.

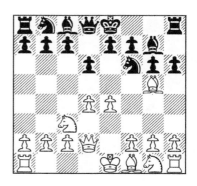

6 ♗h4 g5

Black insists on chasing down the bishop and punishing White by depriving him of the bishop pair. However, nothing in life is free. White's compensation:

1. hxg3 opens the h-file for his attack;

2. If Black doesn't take the bishop right away, then he may be vulnerable to h4 ideas;

3. White plays a knight to e2 and

then prises open with f4; and

4. White plays a knight to e2 and may recapture on g3 with a knight, which then has access to h5. This in turn may drive Black's fianchettoed bishop off the a1-h8 diagonal.

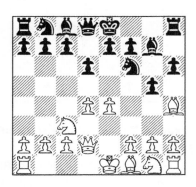

7 ♗g3 ♘h5 8 0-0-0 ♘c6

Others:

a) 8...♘d7 9 e5! (a promising pawn sac; always be on the lookout for this move) 9...♘xg3 10 hxg3 dxe5?! (Black should decline with 10...♘b6) 11 dxe5 ♗xe5 12 f4! gxf4 13 gxf4 ♗g7 14 ♖h3! c6 15 ♖g3 ♗f6 16 ♘e4 ♕b6 17 ♖b3 ♕c7 18 ♘h3 ♗g7 19 ♖g3 ♔f8 20 ♘c5! ♕d6 was S.Tiviakov-M.Mohammed Abdul, Bhubaneswar 2009, and now 21 ♕a5! ends the game.

b) 8...♘xg3 9 hxg3 ♘c6 10 ♗b5! a6 11 ♗xc6+ bxc6 12 f4 gxf4 13 gxf4 ♗g4 14 ♘f3 ♕b8 15 e5 was C.Balogh-T.Nyback, Budapest 2002. You already know how I feel about knights, so you won't be surprised when I tell you I prefer White's space over Black's bishop pair.

9 ♕e3!?

Moving the queen off the d-file gets Black nervous about e5 ideas. Instead, 9 ♗b5 ♗d7 10 ♘ge2 e6 11 ♔b1 ♕e7 12 d5 ♘e5 13 ♗xe5 ♗xe5 14 ♗xd7+ ♕xd7 15 h4 g4 16 ♕e3! left Black in a quandary about where to place his king, J.Van der Wiel-T.Chapman, Hoogeveen 2008.

9...♗d7 10 ♘ge2

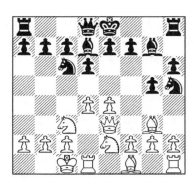

10...e6

This flexible move is played the most. Black may consider the more forcing 10...e5 11 dxe5 ♘xg3 12 hxg3 ♘xe5 13 ♘d4 ♘g4 14 ♕d2?! (14 ♕e2! intending f3 is an improvement and secures the advantage) 14...♕f6! 15 f3 ♕xd4! 16 ♕xd4 ♗xd4 17 ♖xd4 ♘e5 and Black equalized in M.Ruimy-G.Wicklund Hansen, correspondence 2002.

11 h4 ♕e7

Alternatively:

a) 11...♕f6 12 e5! dxe5 13 dxe5 ♕e7 (13...♘xe5 14 hxg5 hxg5 15 ♘e4 ♕f5 16 ♖xd7! ♘xd7 17 ♗xc7 offers terrific compensation for the exchange) 14 ♗h2 ♕b4 and now instead of the 15 g4!? of A.Shabalov-E.Vovsha, Connecticut 2002, 15 a3! ♕b6 16 ♕f3 looks promising for White.

b) 11...♘xg3 12 ♘xg3 ♖g8 (after 12...gxh4!? 13 ♘h5 ♗xd4 14 ♖xd4 ♕g5 15 ♖d2 ♕xh5 16 ♘b5 ♔d8 17 f4 a6 18 ♘c3 ♔e7 White's attacking chances compensate for the material) 13 ♘h5 ♗h8 14 g3 ♕e7 15 f4 gxf4 16 gxf4 0-0-0 17 e5 with a complex struggle ahead, J.Fluvia Poyatos-L.Marin, Banyoles 2007.

12 ♗h2 gxh4 13 ♗g1!

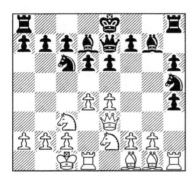

I like this subtle Bronsteinian redeployment, and am reminded of that Caro-Kann where Bronstein famously covered his sensitive f7-square with ...♗g8!! Here White's bishop wasn't doing much on h2 and so he transfers it to cover d4 and aims at a7, in the vicinity of Black's king should he castle queenside.

13...0-0-0

Topalov has no choice. The kingside is much too exposed.

14 g4! ♘f6 15 f3 ♘h7 16 ♗f2 e5 17 d5 ♘d4 18 ♘xd4!

This exchange sac drains the life out of Black's piece activity.

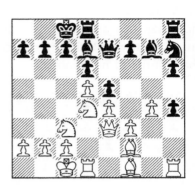

18...exd4 19 ♖xd4 ♗xd4 20 ♕xd4 b6 21 ♘b5 ♔b7

21...♗xb5? 22 ♗xb5 leaves Black with a very low white blood cell count around his king.

22 ♕c3 ♖c8 23 ♘d4!

Black must worry about how to cover c6, a6 and b7 from the occupying army.

23...♕f6 24 ♕d3! ♔a8 25 ♗xh4 ♕f4+ 26 ♔b1 ♘f8?

Black gets some counterplay after 26...♘g5! 27 ♗e2 (the immediate lunge doesn't quite do it after 27 ♕a6? ♘xf3 28 ♗b5 ♘xd4 29 ♗xd7 ♕xe4 30 ♖c1 ♖cd8) 27...h5!.

27 ♕c3

Not the strongest continuation. Black can't defend after 27 ♕a6!: for example, 27...♖b8 28 ♗b5 ♖b7 29 ♗c6 ♗c8 30 ♗d8! ♔b8 31 ♗xb7 ♗xb7 32 ♘c6+ ♔c8 33 ♘xa7+ ♔b8 34 ♗xc7+ ♔xc7 35 ♘b5+ wins.

27...♘g6 28 ♗a6 ♘xh4 29 ♗xc8 ♖xc8 30 ♖xh4

The complications have ended and White has a technical win. Nobody mops up better than Leko in such positions:

1. White is a clean pawn up;

2. His knight is superior to Black's bishop;

3. Black must cover light-squared weaknesses on the queenside; and

4. Black must nurse a weak h-pawn.

30...♔b7 31 a3 ♖g8 32 ♘e2! ♕g5 33 ♖h5! ♕e7

No choice but to hand over h6 since 33...♕g6? 34 ♘f4 ♕h7 35 ♕f6 loses it under even worse circumstances.

34 ♖xh6 f5!

Black eliminates his last weakness, but he can't overcome the two-pawn deficit.

35 gxf5 ♗xf5 36 ♘d4 ♗d7 37 ♘e6 ♗c8 38 f4 ♖g4 39 ♕c6+ ♔b8 40 ♖h8 1-0

Black hangs it up since 40...♖h4 is met with 41 ♖xc8+! ♔xc8 42 ♕a8+ ♔d7 43 ♘f8+ winning the queen.

Summary

A curious trait I have noticed in this

line is that Black lashes out with ...h6, ...g5!? and ...♘h5, and then often hesitates, refusing to take the bishop on g3, since he doesn't like the consequences of opening the h-file or allowing the recapture ♘xg3.

Game 88
A.Motylev-R.Kasimdzhanov
Wijk aan Zee 2009

1 e4 d6 2 d4 ♘f6 3 ♘c3 g6 4 ♗g5 ♗g7 5 ♕d2 h6 6 ♗h4 g5 7 ♗g3 ♘h5 8 0-0-0 c6 9 ♘ce2!

This strange move contains some powerful logic behind it. The Pirc player typically loves to bang out the moves ...♕a5, ...c6, ...b5 and ...b4 when White castles queenside. 9 ♘ce2!? denies Black ...♕a5 and also the plan ...b5 and ...b4 doesn't seem so logical for Black anymore, since there is nobody to hit on c3.

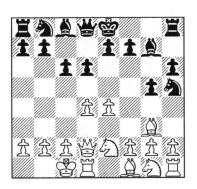

9...♕b6!

Kasimdzhanov goes immediately after b2, probably planning ...c5 and

...♘c6. Instead, 9...b5?! 10 h4 and then 10...♘xg3 11 ♘xg3 g4 12 ♘h5 looks unpleasant for Black, but after 10...g4 11 ♗h2 ♘d7 12 f3 I don't trust Black's position, which has been jarred a bit by all those kingside pawn moves.

10 e5!

An improvement over 10 h4 ♘xg3 11 ♘xg3 ♗e6 12 ♘h5 ♗f8 13 ♔b1 ♖g8 14 hxg5 hxg5, but even here I prefer White, who can play for central pawn breaks, J.Leino-J.Paasikangas Tella, Finnish League 2001.

10...dxe5

Others:

a) 10...♘xg3 11 ♘xg3 dxe5 12 ♘h5 ♗f8 13 dxe5 ♗e6 14 h4 and Black finds himself behind in development.

b) Nor does closing the game help: 10...d5 11 h4 ♗f5 12 ♔b1 g4 13 ♘f4 ♘xg3 14 fxg3 ♘d7 15 ♗d3 ♗xd3 16 ♕xd3 e6 17 ♘xe6! with a strong attack.

11 ♗xe5 ♘f6 12 h4 ♘bd7 13 hxg5 ♘e4

The only move.

14 ♗xg7!

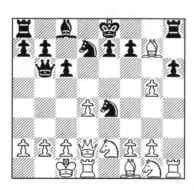

Motylev gets a lot of goodies for the queen.

14...♘xd2 15 ♖xd2 ♖g8 16 gxh6 ♘f8 17 h7?

What is the rush? The pawn may be stronger than the knight and White should delay h7 with 17 ♘g3! cutting off ...♗f5. Then if 17...♕a5 18 a3 ♗e6 19 ♘f3 0-0-0 20 h7 ♘xh7 21 ♖xh7 with a much better version than the game continuation.

17...♘xh7 18 ♖xh7 ♕a5!

Black confuses matters with an alert tactic. He threatens a2 and also ...♕f5! winning back a piece.

19 d5?!

He was better off giving up his kingside pawns rather than the one on a2, which gives Black counterplay: 19 ♘c3! ♕f5! 20 ♗d3 ♕g5 21 ♗e5 ♕xg2 22 ♘ge2 ♕xf2 23 ♖h2 with a clear initiative to White.

However, 19 a3?? falls for Black's trap: 19...♕f5! 20 ♖h8 ♖xh8 21 ♗xh8 ♕xf2 22 ♖d1 f6! 23 ♗g7 ♕e3+ 24 ♔b1 ♔f7 picking up the stray bishop.

19...♕xa2 20 ♘c3 ♕a5

He shouldn't allow White's knight to remain on c3 when he can force it back with 20...♕a1+! 21 ♘b1 ♗f5 22 ♖h5 0-0-0 23 ♗c3 ♗g6 24 ♖e5 ♖xd5 25 ♖dxd5 cxd5 26 ♖xd5! ♕a4 27 ♘a3 ♕f4+ 28 ♖d2 ♖d8 when White may have a hard time winning if all the rooks come off the board.

21 ♘f3 ♗f5 22 ♖h4! ♖d8 23 ♖a4

Now White should be winning comfortably.

23...♕b6 24 ♗e5 f6 25 ♗g3 ♖g4 26 ♘d4 ♗d7 27 ♗e2

Far simpler was 27 dxc6! bxc6 28 ♖a6 ♕b4 29 ♘xc6 ♗xc6 30 ♖xd8+ ♔xd8 31 ♖xc6 and White's pieces win without trouble.

27...♖xg3!

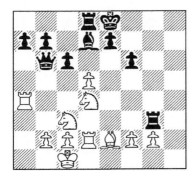

That was a monster bishop. Eliminating it increases Black's chances for survival.

28 fxg3 c5 29 ♘e6 ♗xe6 30 dxe6 ♖xd2 31 ♔xd2 ♕xe6 32 ♖xa7 ♕d6+ 33 ♔c1 ♕xg3 34 ♗f3 ♕e1+ 35 ♗d1 ♕g3 36 ♗f3 ♕e1+ 37 ♘d1 b6 38 ♖b7 ♕a5 39 ♔b1 c4 40 ♘c3 ♔f8 41 ♖b8+ ♔g7 42 ♖c8 ♕b4 43 g4

To Black's frustration, the position is a bit like turning on the kitchen light in the morning and watching cockroaches scatter into the shadows behind the fridge before you can catch any of them! White's pieces are too nimble and too well coordinated for the lone queen to do much about them. White's winning plan:

1. Double attack the c4-pawn with rook and bishop; and

2. If Black responds with ...b5, then gang up on the b-pawn and win it.

Black's queen is clumsily placed on b4. She gets in the way of ...b4.

The easiest way to do this would be 43 ♗g4! (threatening 44 ♗e6!) 43...♔f7 44 ♗e2 b5 45 ♗h5+ ♔g7 46 ♗e8 wins.

43...♔h6 44 ♖c6 ♔g5 45 ♗e2

There goes c4.

45...♔h4 46 ♖xc4

The game is essentially over. White has constructed an unbreakable blockade on e4, making Black's passed e-pawn worthless. It is just a matter of time before White reloads and b6 falls. White then slowly moves his queenside herd forward, vigilant for perpetual check.

46...♕a5 47 ♖e4 ♕c5 48 ♖e6 ♔h3 49 ♔a2 ♕b4 50 ♖e3+ ♔h2 51 ♖e4 ♕d6 52 ♗c4 ♔g3 53 ♔b3 ♕d7 54 ♗e6 ♕c6 55 ♗d5 ♕c7 56 ♗c4 ♕d7 57 ♗e2 ♔f2 58 ♘d1+ ♔g3 59 ♘e3 ♔f2 60 ♗c4 e5 61 ♔a2 ♕a4+ 62 ♔b1 ♕a5 63 ♘d5 b5 64 ♗d3 ♕d8 65 ♘c3

There goes b5.

65...♔f3 66 ♘xb5 ♕b6 67 b3 ♕c5 68 ♔b2 ♕b6 69 ♘c3 ♕c5 70 ♗e2+ ♔g2 71 b4

Head 'em up, move 'em out! Nothing can stop the cattle drive to the eighth rank.

71...♕c6 72 ♗d3 ♔g3 73 b5 ♕b7 74 ♖b4 ♕e7 75 ♘d5! 1-0

76 b6 follows.

Summary

9 ♘ce2! is a hidden (played only in two games so far) and powerful idea which may totally mess up your Pirc opponent. In fact, I will bet you a quarter (a shilling if you live in the UK) your opponent will be unable to find 9...♕b6! and play the automatic 9...b5?! instead. Please send your quarters and shillings to Everyman Chess and ask them to mail me a check of the total amount to my home address.

Game 89
K.Spraggett-L.Defrance
Metz 2007

1 e4 d6 2 d4 ♘f6 3 ♘c3 ♘bd7

I admit to a canine-like affection for this line, the Black Lion, a Philidor coming out of a Pirc move order. Most Philidorians (by now you probably have realized my strange compulsion for making up random words!) are positional players who revel in behind-the-lines manoeuvring games. We do our best to avoid this with our next move!

4 g4!

The Lion's Mouth. As a Lion player on the black side, this is the one line

which makes me very uneasy! White lunges forward and threatens to deport the knight back to g8 next move with 5 g5.

4...h6

Prudent. Black slows down g5. We will also examine 4...e5?! in due course.

5 h3 e5

I sometimes hit back in Sicilian style with 5...c5, and after 6 ♘ge2 b5!? 7 ♘xb5 ♘xe4 8 ♗g2 ♗b7 9 0-0 a6 10 ♘bc3 ♘xc3 11 bxc3 ♗xg2 12 ♔xg2 g6 13 dxc5 ♘xc5 14 ♕d4 ♖g8 15 ♖b1 ♗g7 16 ♕d5 ♖c8 White's piece activity and Black's superior pawn structure balance each other out, M.Parligras-C.Lakdawala, Internet blitz 2010.

6 ♘ge2 c6

6...b5!? is also possible, but after 7 a3 c6 8 ♗g2 ♗e7 9 f4 ♗b7 10 0-0 in M.Prusikin-R.Forster, Swiss League 2008, White had an ominous kingside build-up. Black would be very brave or very stupid to castle into this one!

7 a4

Slowing down Black's queenside expansion.

7...a6

Others:

a) 7...♗e7 8 ♗g2 g5?! (White benefits more from f5 than Black from f4) 9 ♘g3 ♘f8 10 ♘f5 ♘g6 11 ♗e3 ♗xf5 12 exf5 ♘h4 13 0-0 ♕c7 14 ♗h1 h5 15 d5! with a clear strategic advantage for White. This prompted Akobian to sac soon with 15...hxg4 16 hxg4 ♕d7 17 a5 c5 18 ♘e4 ♘xf5?! 19 ♘xf6+ ♗xf6 20 gxf5 ♕xf5 21 ♗g2, but Black didn't achieve sufficient comp for the piece in S.Kudrin-V.Akobian, Tulsa 2008.

b) 7...b6 slowly preparing ...a6, ...♖b8 and ...b5 is also possible. Then 8 ♗e3 ♗b7 9 ♗g2 ♕c7 10 0-0 a6 11 ♕d2 gave White quite a harmonious set-up in P.Herb-M.Schrepp, German League 1998.

c) Next game we see 7...a5.

8 ♗g2 ♖b8 9 a5 b5

He seeks activity at the cost of slightly weakening his a-pawn.

10 axb6 ♕xb6 11 b3 ♗e7 12 ♗e3 ♕c7 13 ♘g3 g6

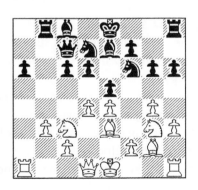

This is one of Black's biggest problems in this line. He almost always needs to weaken with ...g6 to keep a white knight out of f5.

14 ♕d2 h5!

This and his next two moves begin a strategic plan to undermine White's space on the kingside and generate counterplay.

15 g5 ♘h7 16 h4 f6! 17 gxf6 ♘dxf6 18 f3 0-0 19 ♘ge2

Neither king looks terribly safe!

19...♖f7 20 ♕d3!

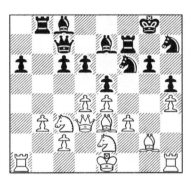

A strong prophylactic move:

1. Spraggett reasons that Black's best shot at counterplay lies in achieving the ...d5 break;

2. The white queen lies in wait for that move ready to pounce on g6 if it is ever played;

3. The queen hits a6. Why is this important? Because White plans ♗h3! and eventually swaps on c8, removing Black's defender of a6; and

4. Should Black dodge the exchange with something like ...♗b7, then White takes control over the powerful h3-c8 diagonal.

20...♘f8 21 ♗h3! ♘6d7 22 f4!

Ignoring the threat to his h-pawn.

22...exd4

If he is going to be attacked then at least be paid for it with a pawn! I would grab it with 22...♗xh4+ 23 ♔d2 exd4 24 ♗xd4 ♗f6 25 ♕g3.

23 ♗xd4 ♘c5?!

Again, I would grab the h-pawn and dare White to mate me.

24 ♗xc5!

Stronger than 24 ♕g3 ♗xh3 25 ♖xh3 ♘ce6 26 ♗f2 ♔h7 27 0-0-0 ♗f6.

24...dxc5 25 ♗xc8 ♖xc8 26 e5!

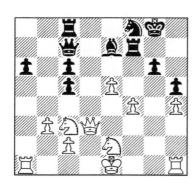

Multipurpose:

1. Opening a pathway to g6;

2. Clearing e4 for a knight; and

3. Blunting Black's dark-squared bishop along the long diagonal.

26...♖d8 27 ♕xa6!?

Many players wouldn't bother with such a pawn and allow themselves to get distracted from the attack on the black king. Kevin Spraggett was the only titled player in Montreal, where I grew up. I used to play in a Friday night blitz tournament with him participating. In my many battles (as a 15-year

old versus the then IM Spraggett!) I noticed just how unapologetically greedy he was! This left a deep impression on me, and to this day I follow my teacher's path and play like an avaricious Wall Street banker! The more noble among us would play 27 ♕e4.

27...♘e6 28 0-0!

White plans to win, not on attack, but on superior pawn structure.

28...♘d4

He rejects 28...♗xh4 29 ♘e4 ♗e7 30 ♕c4 ♕d7.

29 ♘xd4 ♖xd4 30 ♘e2 ♕d7! 31 ♖f2 ♖d1+ 32 ♖xd1 ♕xd1+ 33 ♔h2 ♕e1 34 ♔g2 ♗xh4 35 ♖f1 ♕d2 36 ♕c4

The initiative is with Black; the structure with White.

36...♔g7

He avoids a queen trade and ends up swapping a few moves later under worse circumstances. Black is slightly worse in the ending after 36...♕d5+! 37 ♕xd5 cxd5 38 ♖a1, but my feeling is that he should hold it.

37 ♕e4 ♕d5 38 ♘c3

Too late. Now Black must live with a

compromised structure.

38...♕xe4+?

A bitter wind follows this decision to meekly submit to a difficult ending. Better to repeat with 38...♕d2+ and see how White proceeds.

39 ♘xe4 ♖d7 40 ♔f3 ♗e7 41 ♖a1

This is going to be rough for Black, as his pawns stink and the white knight, with the powerful outpost on e4, outguns Black's bishop. Moreover, White's rook controls the a-file and is ready to go after the queenside pawns and, basically, Black looks busted.

41...♔f7 42 ♖a6 ♖d1

If Black goes passive with 42...♖c7 then White makes progress with 43 ♖a8 ♔e6 44 ♖h8!.

43 ♖xc6 ♖f1+ 44 ♔e3 ♖e1+ 45 ♔d3 ♖d1+ 46 ♔e2 ♖c1 47 e6+! ♔f8 48 ♖c8+ ♔g7 49 ♖e8! ♗f6 50 ♔d2 ♖f1 51 e7!

The e-pawn costs Black a piece.

51...h4??

51...♗xe7 52 ♖xe7+ ♔f8 53 ♖c7 ♖xf4 54 ♘xc5 and Black's passers are halted with ease.

52 ♖g8+ 1-0

Summary

As a Lion player, out of all of White's options 4 g4 scares me the most.

Game 90
J.Degraeve-S.Buscara
Le Touquet 2007

1 e4 d6 2 d4 ♘f6 3 ♘c3 ♘bd7 4 g4! h6 5 h3 e5 6 ♘ge2 c6 7 a4 a5

Black halts any further White queenside expansion. The downside is that he loses the option of expanding with the traditional ...c6 and ...b5.

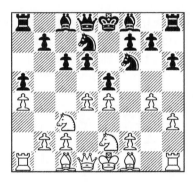

8 ♗g2 ♕c7

After 8...♗e7 9 ♗e3 ♘h7 (Black tries to eliminate the dark-squared bishops) 10 0-0 ♗g5 11 f4 exf4 12 ♗xf4 ♗xf4 13 ♖xf4 ♕b6?! (threatening nothing; taking on b2 self-traps the queen) 14 ♔h1 0-0 15 ♕d2! ♘df6 16 ♘g3 ♗d7 17 ♖af1 ♕d8 18 e5 ♘e8 19 ♘ce4 ♗e6 20 exd6 ♘xd6 21 ♘c5 ♗c4 22 ♖e1 ♘f6 23 ♘f5 Black still had to be careful of White's kingside build-up in R.Damaso-A.Strikovic, Internet blitz 2004.

9 0-0 g6 10 ♗e3 ♗g7

Be aware that the Philidor is a flexible formation and the resulting positions may look more like Pirc than traditional Philidor positions with a bishop on e7. Let's assess:

1. After ♕d2, Black won't be able to castle without playing ...h5 or ...g5;

2. White is ready for f4; and

3. Black's king is somewhat stuck and faces danger whichever direction he goes.

Conclusion: Black stands worse. If so, then the question of where Black went wrong arises. As a Philidor player, I sometimes wonder if the entire opening is just inherently in White's favour. Of course, don't tell this to those guys who write those Lion books or I will get some angry mail in response!

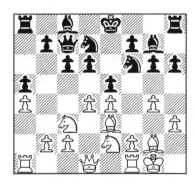

11 ♕d2 b6?

Strategically suspect. A d5 push weakens Black's b5-square. He should play 11...h5! 12 g5 ♘h7 13 ♖ad1 0-0.

12 f4

It's not bad to maintain the tension, but 12 d5!, striking at the heart of Black's problems, also favours White after 12...cxd5 13 ♘b5 ♕b8 14 f4!. If then 14...d4?! White blows open the centre with 15 ♗xd4 exd4 16 ♘exd4! ♗b7 17 e5! 0-0 18 exf6 ♘xf6 19 ♘c6 ♗xc6 20 ♗xc6 ♖a6 21 ♖ae1 when Black is in deep trouble, with a pawn about to fall and a totally immobilized rook on a6.

12...♗a6 13 ♖f2 0-0-0!

I don't blame him. The kingside looks distinctly unsafe.

14 fxe5 dxe5 15 d5! c5?

Strategic suicide. He had to maintain the tension with 15...♘c5! 16 ♗xc5 bxc5 17 ♕e3 ♖he8 18 ♖af1 ♖d6 19 ♕xc5 cxd5 20 ♕xc7+ ♔xc7 21 exd5 e4 22 ♘b5+ ♗xb5 23 axb5 e3 24 ♖f4 ♔b6 25 c4 ♘d7! 26 b3 ♗f6 when, despite White's three connected passers, Black has compensation for the pawn in the form of:

1. A grip on the dark squares;

2. An active king, which may infiltrate if a few more pieces come off the board; and

3. A strong blockade on c5 and d6.

Still, *Rybka* gives White the edge.

16 ♘g3 ♘b8 17 ♗f1!

Handing out the eviction notice to Black to clear out of the light squares.

17...h5?

A blunder losing material. Black should play 17...♘e8 18 ♗xa6+ ♘xa6 19 ♘b5 ♕d7 20 ♕e2 ♔b7 21 c3 with an awful, but materially equal position.

18 ♗xa6+ ♘xa6 19 ♗g5! h4 20 ♘f1 ♕e7 21 ♘e3 ♘c7 22 ♖af1 ♘ce8

What a tangled picture of hopelessness. Black's forces strain to cover their endangered comrade on f6. Meanwhile, White is left unopposed in the other sector and does as he pleases.

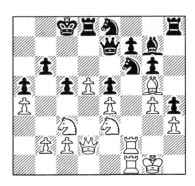

23 ♕e2!

Running roughshod through the light squares on the queenside. Also crushing is 23 ♘c4! ♔b7 24 ♗xf6! ♗xf6 25 d6 ♕e6 26 ♘d5.

23...♔b7 24 ♕b5 ♖c8 25 ♘c4 1-0

Summary

Achieving g4 in one shot and then fianchettoing on g2 is a very good plan for White, who essentially gets a Fianchetto line against the Philidor with a useful extra move, since White usually plays g4 later in that line anyway.

> ### Game 91
> **A.Motylev-A.Czebe**
> Mainz (rapid) 2008

1 e4 d6 2 d4 ♘f6 3 ♘c3 ♘bd7 4 g4 e5?!
A radical and possibly dubious idea.

Black refuses to comply with ...h6 and doesn't consider g5 a threat. Instead, he immediately counters in the centre in an attempt to overextend White.

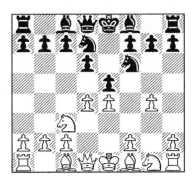

5 g5 ♘g8

It's hard for me to believe that Black gets away with ...♘f6 and ...♘g8 in an open position, essentially spotting White two tempi, like one of those odds games from Morphy's time. Granted, the two tempi are the pawn moves g4 and g5, but hey, they are free!

Instead, after 5...exd4 6 ♕xd4 ♘g4 White has two promising lines:

a) 7 ♗e2 ♘ge5 8 ♗e3 ♘c5 9 ♕d2 ♗e6 10 b3 a5 11 f4 ♘c6 12 f5 ♗d7 13 ♘f3 ♗e7 14 ♗c4 0-0 15 ♖g1 ♔h8 16 0-0-0 and White's attack clearly looks nastier than Black's, A.Skripchenko-M.Esposito, Besancon 2006.

b) 7 f4 (White isn't satisfied with simply kicking Black around and plays to trap the knight on g4) 7...h6 8 ♗e2 ♘c5 and now, instead of 9 f5?! played in J.Schlenker-L.Trabert, German League 2000, White has 9 ♕d1! hxg5 10 ♗xg4 gxf4 11 ♗xc8 ♕h4+ 12 ♔e2

Ixc8 13 ♘f3 when Black has insufficient compensation for the piece.

6 ♘f3

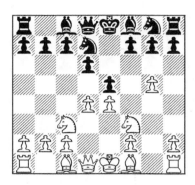

6...h6

Trying to clear f6 for a knight, but he falls even further behind in development.

After 6...c6 7 ♗c4 b5 (7...exd4 8 ♕xd4 ♕b6 may be Black's best chance for survival) 8 ♗b3 a6 (acting like he has all the time in the world) 9 dxe5 dxe5 10 ♗xf7+! ♔xf7 11 ♘xe5+ ♔e8 12 ♕h5+ g6 13 ♘xg6 hxg6 14 ♕xg6+! ♔e7 15 ♗f4 ♕e8 16 ♗d6+ ♔d8 17 ♗c7+! ♔e7 18 ♕xc6 Ia7 19 g6! threatened ♘d5 mate as well as ♕d6 mate and Black collapsed quickly in M.Bosiocic-J.Pribyl, Rijeka 2008.

7 ♗c4

f7 is the soft spot in Black's position.

7...c6

7...♘b6 8 ♗b3 exd4 9 ♕xd4 c5 10 ♕d3 ♗g4 11 Ig1 ♗xf3 12 ♕xf3 c4 13 ♗a4+ ♘xa4 14 ♘xa4 looks awful for Black, who has yet to develop a piece on the 14th move in an open position!

8 dxe5 dxe5

8...b5 9 ♗xf7+ ♔xf7 10 e6+ ♔xe6 11 ♘d4+ ♔f7 12 ♘xc6 ♕b6 13 ♕d5+ ♔e8 14 g6! is also crushing.

9 ♗xf7+!

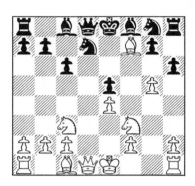

Rybka, chock full of antioxidants today, wholeheartedly approves of this sac. Punishment for Black's violations of development arrives.

9...♔xf7 10 ♘xe5+ ♘xe5!

No choice (besides resignation!). At least Black's move gives him the initiative, or perhaps just the temporary illusion of taking the initiative. Moving his king leads to a bloodbath after:

a) 10...♔e7 11 ♘g6+.

b) 10...♔e6 11 ♕g4+! ♔xe5 12 ♗f4+ ♔d4 13 ♗e3+ ♔e5 14 0-0-0! mates.

11 ♕xd8 ♗e7 12 ♕c7 ♘f3+ 13 ♔d1!

Seeing that his king will be safer on the queenside. Such scattered positions where you are up heavy material, but your opponent creates threats to your king are notoriously hard to navigate. Black does have some practical chances if White plays aimlessly.

13...hxg5 14 ♗e3 ♘f6 15 ♔c1 ♗e6 16 ♗c5 Ihe8 17 ♕xb7!

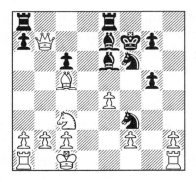

As I have mentioned before, I am a big fan of chessboard greed when a player is able to get away with it.

17...♖ab8 18 ♕c7 ♖bc8 19 ♕a5 ♗d8 20 ♕xa7+

For over a quarter century now, my father-in-law, John, ends all family meals with the declaration "Deeelicious!" I'm certain Motylev was thinking something similar as he ate this pawn for his second helping. White creates a passed a-pawn which Black must worry about for the rest of the game.

20...♘d7 21 ♖d1 ♘fe5 22 ♗d6 ♔g8 23 ♗xe5 ♘xe5 24 ♖xd8!

A good practical investment of material to regain some control over the dark squares. White foresees that his king will be very comfortable on b2 as long as he eliminates Black's most dangerous piece.

24...♖cxd8 25 ♕c5 ♗f7 26 b3 g4 27 ♘e2 ♘f3 28 ♘g3 ♖e5 29 ♕b6 ♖ee8 30 ♔b2 ♘e5 31 ♕c5 ♖d2 32 ♔c3!

The king participates to evict the intruder.

32...♖dd8 33 a4

The threat is to tie Black down with the forward march of the a-pawn.

33...♘d7 34 ♕g5!

Time to show Black who is boss. Target: g7. White finally goes on the offensive with a direct attack.

34...♘f6 35 ♖e1 ♖d7 36 ♘f5 ♗d5 37 ♘xg7!

37...♖xg7

Alternatively:

a) 37...♘h7 fails to 38 ♕g6 ♗f7 39 ♕xg4.

b) 37...♘xe4+ 38 ♖xe4 ♖xe4 39 ♘e6+ ♔f7 40 ♕f5+ ♔e7 41 ♘c5 picks off a full rook.

38 ♕xf6 ♖f8 39 ♕d6 ♖f3+ 40 ♖e3 ♗f7 1-0

Time control reached, and time to resign.

Summary

Black's refusal to play 4...h6 costs him too much time. Black hopes the free g4-g5 leads to overextension, but this is an overoptimistic assessment, as Black is far more likely to get a kick in the rear end from handing over the two tempi.

> ## Game 92
> **V.Anand-Z.Azmaiparashvili**
> Benidorm (rapid) 2003

1 e4 d6 2 d4 ♘f6 3 ♘c3 e5

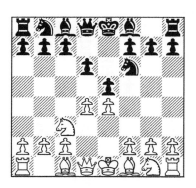

The Lion's Yawn! Black prevents some of the more dangerous white lines at the cost of castling privileges.

Instead, after 3...c6 4 f3 (let's stick with this and avoid the theoretical move 4 f4) 4...e5 5 ♗e3 ♗e7 6 ♕d2 ♘bd7 7 ♘ge2 b5 8 g4 ♘b6 9 b3 0-0 there's a sharp position. White's only

edge may lie in the fact that he has not committed to castling on either wing, I.Novikov-V.Priehoda, Austrian League 1994.

4 ♘ge2

White's options are:

a) 4 ♘f3 which transposes to the mainline Philidor. I suggest you stay away from this one. It's a good bet that your Philidor-loving opponent will either know the theory deeper, or understand the positions better than you do.

b) 4 dxe5 is thematic, but my guess is that most Veresovers are attackers, not endgame milkers! After 4...dxe5 5 ♕xd8+ ♔xd8 White has a choice between 6 ♗g5, 6 ♗c4 and 6 ♘f3. White must have a slight edge, but the resulting positions are notoriously difficult to win.

4...♗e7 5 f3

There we go. White sets up in a partial Veresov pattern of ♗e3, g4 and castle queenside. It doesn't make sense to play ♗g5 in such positions since you will be vulnerable to tactics like ...♘xd5 and ...♘xe4. Also, the dark-squared bishop is your good bishop and you don't want to exchange it either for Black's knight on f6 or his bishop on e7.

5...0-0!?

Boldly castling into it. It may be wiser to delay:

a) 5...h5!? restraining g4 makes some sense, but it also weakens Black's kingside: 6 ♗e3 ♘bd7 7 ♕d2 c6 8 a4 g6 9 g3 0-0 10 ♗g2 ♖e8 11 0-0 a5 12 h3! ♗f8 13 f4 exd4 14 ♗xd4 ♘c5 15 ♗xc5 dxc5 16 ♖ad1 ♗e6 17 ♕e3 ♕b6 18 e5 ♗f5 19 ♕f2 ♘h7 20 g4! hxg4 21 ♘g3 gxh3 22 ♘xf5 hxg2 23 ♕xg2 with a strong attack in V.Anand-A.Strikovic, Villarrobledo (rapid) 2006.

b) 5...c6 6 ♗e3 0-0 7 ♕d2 b5 8 g4 ♘bd7 9 ♘g3 exd4 10 ♗xd4 ♘e5 11 ♗e2 ♖e8 12 g5 ♘fd7 13 f4 ♘c4 14 ♗xc4 bxc4 15 ♘f5 ♗f8 16 0-0-0 with mutual chances, although I still favour White's kingside build-up over Black's open b-file, A.Brkic-R.Wukits, Oberwart 2003.

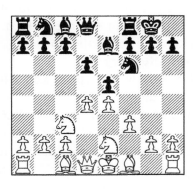

6 ♗e3 c5?!

Not all new ideas are good ones. Closing the centre favours White since he has the faster attack. Better to keep things fluid with 6...c6.

7 d5 ♘h5

After 7...a6 White may choose to take the positional route and play for the queenside light squares with 8 ♕d2 b5 9 a4! b4 10 ♘d1 ♘bd7 11 b3 ♘e8 12 ♘b2 and then slowly build up on the kingside.

8 ♕d2 g6

Or 8...h6 9 0-0-0 ♗g5 10 ♗xg5! hxg5

(10...♕xg5?? would be desirable for Black if it were not for the pesky variation 11 ♕xg5 hxg5 12 ♘b5!, which threatens 13 ♘c7 as well as the d6-pawn) 11 g4 ♘f4 12 h4! and White's attack rolls while Black hasn't even started on the other wing.

9 0-0-0 ♕a5 10 g4 ♘g7 11 ♘g3 a6

If Black gets desperate with 11...b5!? 12 ♘xb5! ♕xa2 13 ♕c3! ♘a6 14 ♔d2! ♘b4 15 ♘a3! (threat: 16 ♗c4) 15...♘xd5 16 exd5 ♕xd5+ 17 ♗d3 Black doesn't have enough for the piece.

12 h4 f6 13 g5!

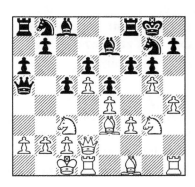

An instructive moment. Anand ensures that his theatre of action stays open for business. It would be easy to mindlessly toss in 13 h5?, but then 13...g5 closes the kingside.

13...f5 14 f4!

Ditto.

14...b5 15 h5!

From this point Black tries to stamp out the raging forest fire with the water in his canteen! The a2-pawn is meaningless and White doesn't bother with ♔b1.

15...b4 16 ♘b1 fxe4 17 fxe5 ♘d7

Alternatively:

a) 17...dxe5? 18 d6 ♗d8 19 hxg6 hxg6 20 ♗c4+ ♗e6 21 ♗xe6+ ♘xe6 22 ♕d5 wins the house.

b) 17...♘xh5 18 ♘xh5 gxh5 19 e6 ♕xa2 20 ♖xh5 and h7 falls, as will the black king soon after.

18 e6 ♘e5 19 hxg6

Threat: 20 ♕h2.

19...♘g4

19...♘f3 doesn't keep the queen off the h-file either: 20 ♕g2 hxg6 21 ♕h3.

20 ♗e2 ♖f3

Or 20...♘xe3 21 ♕xe3 hxg6 22 ♘xe4 ♕d8 23 ♖dg1 with ♕h3 to follow.

21 ♗xf3 exf3 22 ♖xh7 1-0

Veni, Vidi, Vishy!

Summary

I suggest you stay clear of the endgame in the Lion's Yawn and play 4 ♘ge2, followed by our familiar plan, f3, ♗e3 and ♕d2. This keeps us in familiar territory and far away from some weird specialty ending that Black wants.

Game 93
**V.Anand-
I.Morovic Fernandez**
Santiago (rapid) 2009

---

1 e4

Another move order to reach our position would be 1 d4 d6 2 e4 ♘f6 3 ♘c3 e5 4 ♘ge2 exd4 5 ♘xd4.

1...e5 2 ♘f3 d6 3 d4 exd4

The Antoshin Philidor is a tough line to crack for White. Black takes on the little centre in exchange for an ultra-solid position. In essence, this is the Fort Knox version of the Philidor.

4 ♘xd4 ♘f6 5 ♘c3 ♗e7

More lively is 5...g6 6 ♗g5 ♗g7 7 ♕d2 and then:

a) 7...0-0 8 0-0-0 ♖e8 9 f3 ♘c6 10 ♘xc6 bxc6 11 h4 ♗e6 12 h5 and both h- and b-files are open in this ultra sharp opposite-wing attack situation, S.Solovjov-A.Skurygin, Peterhof 2008.

b) 7...h6?! is less logical since 8 ♗f4! makes castling difficult without weakening further with ...g5. Then after 8...♘c6 9 ♘xc6 bxc6 10 ♗c4 in A.Reshetnikov-P.Dvalishvili, Moscow 2010, White was ready to castle on either wing, but Black was not!

6 g3

Maybe it's just a fad, but many of the world's elite players seem to prefer this move, which prepares to overprotect e4 and make Black's d5 break harder. You can also opt for a more traditional treatment of the position with 6 ♗c4 0-0 7 0-0 ♘c6 8 ♖e1 ♘xd4 9 ♕xd4 when White's extra centre and space give him the edge.

6...d5

If he doesn't play this freeing move now it will be much harder to achieve later.

7 e5 ♘g4

7...♘e4 doesn't score well for Black, but may well be playable if a draw is his goal: 8 ♘xe4 dxe4 9 ♗g2 ♕d5 10 0-0 ♘c6 11 ♘xc6 ♕xc6 12 ♖e1 ♗f5 was Z.Almasi-L.Nisipeanu,L Heviz 2008, where Black's e-pawn looks slightly more vulnerable than White's.

8 ♗g2 0-0

Liquidating the centre doesn't mean Black gets the draw: 8...♘xe5 9 ♕e2! ♘bc6 10 ♘xc6 ♘xc6 11 ♘xd5 ♗e6 12 0-0 0-0 13 ♖d1 ♗d6 14 ♗f4 ♖e8 15 ♘e3 ♕e7 16 ♗xd6 cxd6 left Black with a chronically weak and backward d-pawn, V.Anand-L.Aronian, Monte Carlo (blindfold) 2006. In fact, this game put 8...♘xe5 out of fashion.

9 f4 c5 10 ♘de2 d4 11 ♘d5 ♘c6 12 h3 ♘h6 13 0-0 ♘f5

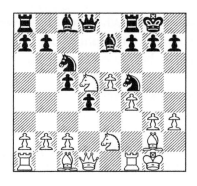

Whose pawn majority means more? Anand proves conclusively that his kingside majority packs a lot more punch, since he uses it to quickly generate threats to Black's king.

14 g4!

Unafraid to let his opponent's knight roost on h4.

14...♘h4 15 ♗h1 ♘g6!

Morovic puts heat on e5 to deter Anand from playing f5.

16 c3 dxc3?!

He shouldn't activate the e2-knight. Better was 16...♗e6 17 c4.

17 ♘exc3 ♗e6 18 ♗e3 ♗xd5 19 ♘xd5 ♖c8 20 ♖c1 b6 21 ♕e2

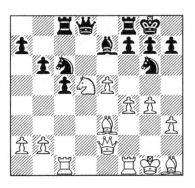

The massive oil slick approaches the Western shore. White dominates with:

1. A monster knight on d5;

2. The bishop pair in an open position;

3. Black's queen sits rather uncomfortably on d8 and soon faces White's rook on d1; and

4. Black's queenside majority is dormant and relatively useless, whereas White's pawns lurk menacingly on the other wing, ready to move forward.

Conclusion: a strategically hopeless situation for Black.

21...f6?!

The position screams out for a central counter but which one? Black gets strangled after 21...f6?!. He should try 21...♘d4! 22 ♕a6 ♗h4 23 ♖cd1 ♘e7 24 ♗xd4 cxd4 25 ♖xd4 ♘xd5 26 ♗xd5 ♕e7 27 ♕d3 ♖c7, although even here White commands the initiative, an extra pawn and the superior bishop.

22 ♖fd1 ♕e8 23 e6 f5

Otherwise White plays f5 himself, supporting his passed e-pawn.

24 g5 ♔h8 25 h4?!

Possibly a bit too bold. White offers his h-pawn to open the file.

25...♗d8?

Totally submitting to White's will. He had to gamble with 25...♘xh4!. Indeed, lines are not so clear after 26 ♖c3! ♘g6 27 ♕h5 ♗d8! 28 ♗f2 ♘ge7! and Black may just be holding on.

26 h5 ♘ge7 27 a3 ♘xd5 28 ♗xd5 ♗e7 29 ♔g2 ♗d6

It can't be disputed that White rules, but where is the concrete path to the win? Anand's energetic next few moves show the answer.

30 b4!

Destination g7. This double-purpose move clears d4 for his bishop and clears b2 for his queen.

30...cxb4 31 h6!

Black's king cover gets ripped open in a hurry.

31...♘e7

Or 31...♖g8 32 axb4 ♘xb4 33 ♗f3 ♕xe6 34 hxg7+ ♔xg7 35 ♗d4+ ♔f7 36 ♗h5+ ♔e7 37 ♗f6+ ♔d7 38 ♕b5+ ♘c6 39 ♗f3 ♕xf6 40 ♖xc6.

32 ♕b2! ♕g6

Instead, 32...♖g8 33 ♗d4 ♕g6 34 hxg7+ ♖xg7 35 ♖xc8+ ♘xc8 36 ♗b7! bxa3 37 ♗xg7+ ♕xg7 38 ♕xg7+ ♔xg7 39 ♗xc8 leaves White a rook up.

33 hxg7+ 1-0

Summary

Many of the world's best like 6 g3 against the super-solid Antoshin line of the Philidor. Who are we to argue?

Chapter Ten
Schmid Benoni and Czech Benoni

1 d4 ♘f6 2 ♘c3 c5 3 d5

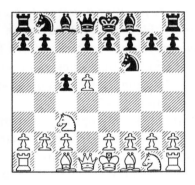

The Schmid Benoni, 3...g6 4 e4 d6, is just a Benoni with White's pawn on c2 rather than c4. I recommend the annoying 5 ♘f3 ♗g7 6 ♗b5+ line. As you will see in the coming games, Black must make a concession no matter which way he blocks the check. White can count on these factors for an edge:

1. The d5-pawn offers more space.

2. You are a move up over the normal Benoni since you didn't waste a tempo on c4.

3. Unlike a normal Benoni, Black has yet to play ...e6. Doing so may make his d6-pawn vulnerable.

4. White's e5 break looks more potent than Black's ...b5 break, which often doesn't do much to worry White.

5. White's extra central space may translate into a kingside attack with simple moves like ♗f4, ♕d2 and ♗h6.

6. Black often has a problem of what to do with his c8-bishop and sometimes plays ...♗g4 and ...♗xf3. This hands White the bishop pair.

Instead, the Czech Benoni, 1...c5 2 d5 e5 3 e4 d6, is a bit like the Fort Knox of the Benoni set-ups.

Black hopes his solid but passive central pawn-wall will lead him into a protracted manoeuvring game. White again has space and Black has deprived himself of both the ...e6 and ...c6 pawn breaks. This leaves only the ...f5 break at his disposal. White can either play for f4 with ambitions on the kingside, or just build up on the queenside with moves like a4 and later a5, followed by b4 at some point. This isn't the most intimidating set-up for Black, but he hopes to suck you into a long, drawn-out affair. Have faith in your space! It isn't so easy to play Black in such a passive position.

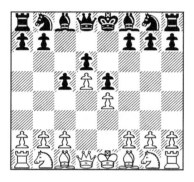

Game 94
M.Tal-P.Benko
Bled/Zagreb/Belgrade
Candidates 1959

1 e4

Our move order could be 1 d4 ♘f6 2 ♘c3 c5 3 d5 g6 4 e4 d6 5 ♘f3 ♗g7 6 ♗b5+.

1...c5 2 ♘f3 g6 3 d4 ♗g7 4 d5 d6 5 ♘c3 ♘f6

The Schmid Benoni, where the only difference between it and a normal Benoni is that White's pawn remains on c2 rather than c4. Other differences and similarities?

1. White saves a tempo on c4.

2. In a regular Benoni, Black normally trades his e-pawn for White's c-pawn. This creates queenside versus kingside pawn majorities and a potentially sharper game. In the Schmid Benoni, the structure remains more symmetrical with White holding more space due to his d5 wedge.

3. Just as in the Benoni proper, White mostly plays for the generally more effective e5 pawn break while Black plays for the ...b5 break;

4. Black hasn't played ...e6 yet and may even later play the pawn to e5. If and when Black plays ...e6, White must make a crucial decision to capture on e6, which you play if you feel you can pressure his backward pawn on d6. However, retain the central pawn tension if you feel that Black will eventually achieve the freeing ...d5 break after the exchange on e6.

Instead, 5...a6 stops our next move but also ruins Black's normal plan of ...♘a6-c7 to slowly prepare the ...b5 pawn break. After 6 a4 ♘f6 7 ♗e2 0-0 8 0-0 ♗g4 9 ♘d2!? (White can also play for the bishops: 9 ♖e1 ♗xf3 10 ♗xf3 9...♗xe2 10 ♕xe2 ♘bd7 11 ♘c4 ♘b6 12 ♘e3! (the side with space should keep pieces on the board) 12...♖e8 13 ♖d1! (discouraging the ...e6 break) 13...♕c7 14 f3 ♖ad8 15 a5 ♘c8 16 ♘c4 ♘d7 17 ♗f4 ♘a7 18 ♘a4 ♘b5 Black found himself without much counterplay against White's space plus in U.Andersson-A.Zapata, Wijk aan Zee 1987.

6 ♗b5+

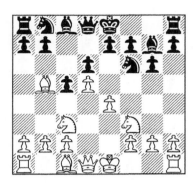

This annoying check throws Black a bit out of sync.

6...♘bd7

The most natural block, but it does deny Black the plan ...♘a6 and ...♘c7. The ...b5 break is the key to Black's counterplay, and now it will be harder to achieve.

In the next couple of games, we examine 6...♗d7 and 6...♘fd7.

7 a4

7 0-0?! doesn't make sense, since Black's reply either forces ...b5 or makes White cough up the bishop pair: 7...a6 8 ♗xd7+ ♘xd7 when Black looks good with a bishop pair and some freedom due to the last exchange, D.Balko-V.Vodicka, Tatranske Matliare 2007.

7...0-0 8 0-0 a6 9 ♗e2 ♖b8

Instead, 9...b6 stops a5. The plan is to slowly prepare the ...b5 break, but after 10 ♖e1 ♘e8 11 ♗f4 ♘c7 12 ♕d2 ♖b8 13 ♗h6 b5 14 ♗f1 b4 15 ♘d1 a5 16 ♗xg7 ♔xg7 17 ♘e3 it was advantage White in B.Abramovic-L.Popov, Stara Pazova 2007, who controls c4 and

has essentially closed off the queenside, Black's realm of counterplay. Moreover, Black's dark-squared defender has been eliminated and White may build for a kingside attack, with Black's only chance for counterplay being to engineer a timely ...e6 break.

10 ♖e1

Tal isn't attracted to the strategic plan 10 a5 and plays directly for mate.

10...♘e8 11 ♗f4 ♘c7

Last chance for White to throw in a5.

12 ♗f1!?

Sorry, not interested.

12...b5 13 ♕d2!?

Avoiding 13 axb5 ♘xb5 14 ♘xb5 axb5 15 c3 which reduces the number of attackers.

13...♖e8 14 h3 ♘f6!

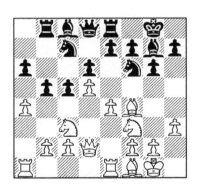

A subtle and instructive move. Black returns the merchandise to the store for a full refund. The knight retraces its steps to f6, its work done on d7;

1. A knight on f6 puts more heat on d5, which inhibits White from his planned e5 pawn break; and

2. Benko knows his opponent! He adds a defender to his king to prepare for the coming storm.

15 ℤad1 ♗d7 16 e5!?

What the ...!? I really don't understand the mind of an absolute tactician. Why didn't Tal simply throw in 16 axb5 first before the e5 pawn break? Why does he give up a pawn on the queenside? Sorry about all these questions. I realize that the annotator is supposed to offer answers not annoy the reader with questions. But really, I don't get it!

16...b4!

Winning material on the queenside.

17 ♘e4

Could this move be the reason Tal avoided 16 axb5? White eliminates a defender on f6 and gets to lift his rook at the cost of a pawn.

17...♘xe4

Correctly avoiding the line 17...♘fxd5? 18 ♗c4! ♘xf4 19 ♕xf4 ♘e6 20 ♗xe6 ♗xe6 21 exd6 where Black finds himself under heavy pressure in the centre.

18 ℤxe4 ♗xa4 19 ♗h6!

The assault begins.

19...♗h8

Avoiding the cheapo 19...♗xc2?? 20 ℤh4! and Black must give up a piece to avoid mate.

20 ℤde1 f6?!

A central counter, but the wrong one! Black should open it up with 20...dxe5!. Principle: meet a wing attack with a central counter. Indeed, after 21 c4 f6! I have my doubts about Tal's compensation for the material. When I was a kid, some of Tal's rivals would gnash their teeth and point out such lines in Tal's games, in an attempt to show that Tal's play was unsound. My answer to that is: so what if he was unsound? As chess players we all know how difficult it is to face a gifted tactician or attacker who plays a tricky but probably unsound line. Gambling is part of chess and we don't all have to be scientists at the board!

21 e6

Creating a coffin-like effect around Black's king.

21...f5 22 ♖h4!

Tal's playbook only had one page, and on that page two words: 'Scare people!'

22...♗xb2??

Enjoying a light snack before being lead to the gallows! Absolutely essential was 22...♗f6! 23 ♘g5 ♗b5 24 g4! ♗xf1 25 ♖xf1 f4 26 ♕d3 (with tricks on h7) 26...♗xg5 27 ♗xg5 ♖f8 28 ♖h6 ♘e8 29 h4 ♘f6 30 ♕h3 ♕e8 and Black absorbs the first wave of the attack and lives to tell about it. Even here, though, *Rybka* prefers White a pawn down, which usually spells doom for the material-up side.

23 ♗f8!

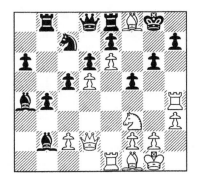

A deadly clearance of h6 for the queen's entry. Tal is in his element. I imagine at this point he was as happy as Santa on Prozac!

23...♖xf8 24 ♕h6 ♖f7

The only move. Possibly at this point, Benko may have had these thoughts: "Why, oh why did I allow Tal e6?"

25 exf7+ ♔xf7 26 ♕xh7+ ♗g7 27 ♖h6

I remember a Korchnoi quote where he trash talked about how Tal was a weak calculator who relied mainly on intuition in his attacks! To play devil's advocate on Korchnoi's behalf, *Rybka* points out that Tal rejects the more accurate line 27 ♘g5+! ♔f6 28 ♖h6 ♕e8 29 ♘e6 ♗xh6 30 ♘xc7 ♕d7 31 ♖e6+ ♔g5 32 ♕xg6+ ♔f4 33 ♕g3 mate.

27...♕g8 28 ♕xg6+ ♔f8 29 ♘g5! ♕xd5

29...♗xh6 30 ♘h7+ wins the queen.

30 ♖h8+! 1-0

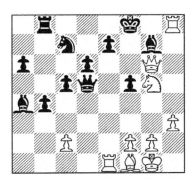

It looks like he calculated just fine to me! It's mate next move.

Summary

The disruptive 6 ♗b5+ creates problems for Black to overcome no matter how he blocks the check.

> *Game 95*
> **G.Kasparov-A.Beliavsky**
> 9th matchgame,
> Moscow 1983

1 d4 ♘f6 2 ♘f3 c5 3 d5 d6 4 ♘c3 g6 5

e4 ♗g7 6 ♗b5+ ♗d7

Black's bishop is awkwardly placed here, but it also has its plusses. Black hopes to gain time with ...♘a6 and ...♘c7.

7 a4 0-0 8 0-0 ♘a6 9 ♖e1 ♘b4!?

This move, a novelty at the time, could be a factor in Black's future troubles. I'm not sure what the knight really does on b4. Normally Black plays 9...♘c7 10 ♗f1 ♖b8 11 h3 a6 12 ♗f4 (the e5 break is coming) 12...♘h5 13 ♗h2 ♘e8 (Black is under pressure in the line 13...b5 14 axb5 ♗xb5 15 ♘xb5 axb5 16 e5 dxe5 17 ♘xe5) 14 e5 dxe5 15 ♘xe5 ♘d6 when White has a comfortable edge, and may proceed with either 16 a5 or even 16 g4!? as he did in M.Rychagov-K.Kulaots, Rakvere 2000.

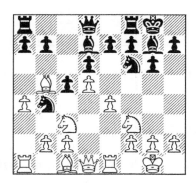

10 h3 e6 11 ♗f4!

11 dxe6 allowed Black to equalize after 11...♗xe6 12 ♘g5 a6 13 ♗f1 d5! in J.Eslon-A.Goldin, Oviedo 1993. The moral: don't play dxe6 if it allows Black the freeing ...d5 break.

11...e5

Now the position looks like a Closed Ruy Lopez.

The complications of 11...exd5?! clearly favour White after 12 ♗xd6 dxe4 13 ♗xf8 ♔xf8 14 ♘xe4 ♗xb5 15 axb5 ♕xd1 16 ♖axd1 ♘xc2 17 ♖e2 ♘xe4 18 ♖xc2 b6 19 ♖e2 f5 20 g4 ♗f6 21 ♖d7 and Black can't survive.

12 ♗g5 ♗c8

The sign of a flexible mind. The loss of time has little significance since it's a blocked position. Now that his pawns are fixed on dark, Beliavsky preserves his good, light-squared bishop.

13 ♘d2 h6 14 ♗h4 g5?!

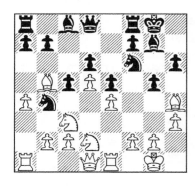

This rash, pseudo-attacking move weakens f5. If Black plays ...f5 himself, White simply takes, opening up e4 for his knights. But it's hard to criticize Beliavsky for the move. There is a Buffalo Springfield song which goes: "There's something happening here. What it is ain't exactly clear." Somehow Black's game has soured and he already experiences difficulties, but looking over the past moves I am unable to pinpoint any error or even inaccuracy on Beliavsky's part other than his strange ninth move. Kasparov once claimed to possess a sixth sense in chess. Well, here it is! He gets a close to winning position without any perceivable error on Black's part.

It may be marginally better to proceed in Lopez fashion and play for ...f5, beginning with 14...a6 15 ♗f1 b6 16 ♘cb1! (threatening c3) 16...a5 17 ♘a3 ♖b8 18 ♘b5 ♕d7 19 c3 ♘a6 20 ♘c4 ♘e8 (granted, Black is now ready for ...f5, but in doing so he has punctured his queenside and misplaced several of his pieces) 21 ♕b3 f5 (achieving his thematic break at a very high cost of puncture wounds on b5 and c4) 22 exf5 gxf5 23 ♖ad1, although I still prefer White and don't place much faith in Black's kingside attack.

15 ♗g3 g4!?

After 15...♘e8 16 ♗e2! (exploiting ...g5?! and the light-squared weaknesses it created) 16...f5 17 exf5 ♗xf5 18 ♘de4 ♘f6 19 ♗g4! ♘xg4 20 hxg4 ♗g6 21 ♘b5 ♗xe4 22 ♖xe4 the position clarifies in White's favour:

1. White owns e4;

2. Black's g7-bishop is in bad shape, with most of his pawns on the same colour;

3. White controls the light squares; and

4. White can make progress slowly on the queenside, while Black's kingside attack has come to a standstill.

16 hxg4 ♘xg4 17 f3 ♘f6 18 ♗h4 ♔h8 19 ♘e2!

Heading for g3 and preparing to give the b4-knight the boot with c3.

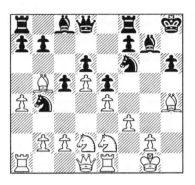

19...♖g8 20 c3 ♘a6 21 ♘g3 ♕f8 22 ♘df1

Heading for f5. Most players think of (C)asparov as some sort of human/computer hybrid, like one of the Borg Collective aliens. (My favourite was Sevenofnine, who was one hot Borg spacebabe!) In games like this, one is occasionally reminded that Kasparov is not all calculation and tactics, and sometimes he displayed superb positional skills as well.

22...♘h7 23 ♘e3 ♗f6

At least this is something. He gets rid of his bad bishop and clears the g-file.

24 ♗xf6+ ♘xf6 25 ♘gf5 ♘h5 26 ♔f2!

Preparing to attack down the h-file and reminding his opponent that Black isn't the only one doing the attacking.

26...♗xf5 27 ♘xf5 ♘f4 28 g3 ♘h3+ 29 ♔e2 ♖xg3?

Freaking out. The sac is totally unsound. I guess Beliavsky was in no mood to suffer a lingering death. Black was in pretty sorry shape strategically.

He should play more rationally and grovel with 29...♘g5 30 ♕d2 ♖g6 31 ♖h1 f6 32 ♖h5 ♖d8 33 ♘h4 ♖g8 34 ♖h1 ♘f7 35 ♔f2 ♘c7 36 ♗e2 b6 37 ♘f5 ♖g6, although it's just a matter of time before Black cracks.

30 ♘xg3 ♕g7 31 ♖g1!

The death of hope! With this simple move, Kasparov spurns greed and returns some (but not all!) of the material to take the air out of Black's attack.

31...♖g8 32 ♕d2 1-0

Black's attack has come to a dead halt. Games like this sometimes give one the impression that a top-notch GM like Beliavsky isn't such a great player. Having analysed with Beliavsky, I can assure the reader that this is merely an optical illusion! One time Alex Beliavsky, John Watson and I analysed a game I had just lost to GM Chernin at the National Open in Las Vegas. I was absolutely dazzled by Beliavsky's ability to come up with three or four plans in any given position. Watson said to me later something like: "Beliavsky and Chernin are just

scary strong, and Kasparov beats players like this – often in blowouts!"

Summary

Beliavsky's idea 9...♘b4 may soon turn the game into a kind of Closed Ruy Lopez, but one probably in White's favour.

> ### Game 96
> ### A.Fominyh-E.Hossain
> Dhaka 2004

1 d4 ♘f6 2 ♘f3 c5 3 d5 d6 4 ♘c3 g6 5 e4 ♗g7 6 ♗b5+ ♘fd7

Somewhat artificial, and it moves a defender away from the kingside, but once again, Black keeps the ...♘a6-c7 option open.

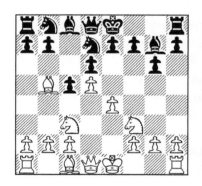

7 a4 0-0

After 7...♘a6 8 0-0 ♘c7 9 ♗c4 0-0 10 ♖e1 a6 11 ♗f4 ♖b8 12 a5 b5 13 axb6 ♘xb6 14 ♗f1 ♗g4 15 h3 ♗xf3 16 ♕xf3 ♘d7 17 ♘d1 ♘e5 (17...♗xb2?! 18 ♘xb2 ♖xb2 19 ♗h6 threatens the rook on f8 and also ♕c3) 18 ♕g3 f5 19 c4 e6 20

♗g5 ♕d7 21 f4 ♘f7 22 exf5 exf5 23 ♖e7 White has some initiative, but Black may still be okay at this point since he has a target on b2 and his position is relatively solid, F.Vallejo Pons-A.Kovacevic, Mallorca 2000.

8 ♗f4 ♘a6 9 0-0 ♘c7 10 ♗c4

10 h3!? a6 (if 10...♘xb5!? 11 axb5 Black has no useful freeing pawn breaks and White still has a touch of a bind) 11 ♗c4 ♖b8 12 a5 b5 13 axb6 ♖xb6 14 ♘a4 ♖b4 15 ♕e2 ♘b6 (15...♗xb2!? looks risky for Black) 16 ♘xb6 ♖xb6 17 c3 ♗d7 18 ♖fd1! ♕e8 19 e5 ♗b5 and White had achieved his thematic central break and also had the better pawn structure in N.Murshed-W.Sariego, Cienfuegos 1991.

10...♘b6

Not really gaining time since he must move the b6-knight again. The idea is to free the c8-bishop and swap it off for White's f3-knight.

11 ♗e2 ♗g4 12 ♖e1 ♗xf3

Freedom? Sure, but at the price of the bishop pair.

13 ♗xf3 ♘c4 14 ♗e2!

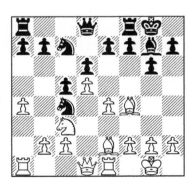

A well-calculated dare.

14...♘e5

Black can't accept with 14...♘xb2? 15 ♕d2 ♘e8 16 ♖a2! ♕a5 17 ♘b1 b6 18 e5! ♕xd2 19 ♗xd2 ♗xe5 20 ♗c3 ♘xa4 21 ♖xa4 a5 and his three pawns for the piece don't make the cut, since White constructs a firm blockade on the queenside light squares.

15 ♗g3 a6 16 f4 ♘d7 17 ♗g4!

An assessment:

1. White controls the bishop pair;

2. White's e5 break will arrive with more force than Black's ...b5; and

3. Black must watch for tricks on e6 and e7.

Conclusion: clear advantage for White.

17...♖b8 18 e5 b5 19 ♗h4!

Applying enormous pressure on e7.

19...f6!

This ugly move is best in this difficult position. Black's options are not so tempting:

a) 19...dxe5?? 20 d6 wins a piece.

b) 19...b4?? 20 exd6 and the threat to take on e7 wins.

c) 19...♘b6?! 20 exd6 ♛xd6 21 ♗xe7 ♛xf4 22 d6 when Black loses material.

20 exd6 exd6 21 ♗e6+ ♚h8 22 ♘e4 ♘b6 23 a5 ♘c8 24 f5!

The squeeze is on.

24...♘xe6

Reluctantly evicting the e6-squatter and giving White a huge passed pawn. Keeping the bishop alive too long endangered Black's king.

25 fxe6 ♖b7 26 ♛d2 g5 27 ♗f2 h6 28 ♖ad1 f5

If Black tries to prevent the coming sac, he gets reduced to total inertia after 28...♖c7 29 ♘xc5! (anyway!) 29...dxc5 30 d6 ♘xd6 31 ♛xd6 ♛c8 32 ♗g3 ♖c6 33 ♛d5 ♛e8 34 e7 ♖g8 35 ♛f5 ♖c8 36 ♖d7.

29 ♘xc5!

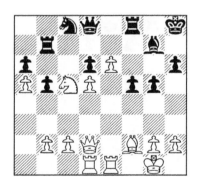

Sac'ing a knight in exchange for two deep passers is a bargain.

29...dxc5 30 ♗xc5 ♛c7

Black can forget about a blockade here: 30...♘d6?? fails miserably to 31 ♛b4.

31 ♛b4!

Engineering d6 is far more impor-

tant than taking the rook and allowing a blockade.

31...♖e8 32 d6

Yipes! Now that is what I call passed pawns! Even my dim-witted Commodore 64 computer would understand perfectly well that the pawns mean more than Black's piece!

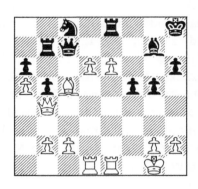

32...♘xd6

No choice.

33 ♖xd6 ♛c8 34 ♗d4! ♖be7

34...♛xc2 35 ♗xg7+ ♖xg7 36 e7 ♚h7 37 ♖xa6 ♛d3 38 ♛c5 offers Black very little hope.

35 ♛c5

Simplifying into an easily won ending. Also strong was 35 c3! and the e6-pawn is untouchable in view of 35...♖xe6?? 36 ♖dxe6 ♖xe6 37 ♖xe6 ♛xe6 38 ♛f8+.

35...♗xd4+

Or 35...♛xc5 36 ♗xc5 ♗xb2 37 ♖c6 ♖b7 38 ♖d1 ♖bb8 39 ♖d5 f4 40 ♖xa6 with total control.

36 ♛xd4+ ♚h7 37 ♛e5 ♚g6 38 c3

Black is down a pawn, his sedentary pieces are hopelessly tied up by the e6-

pawn, a6 is weak and his king in mortal danger. Conclusion: Black can safely resign.

38...♖d8

If instead 38...♕a8 39 ♕d4 ♕a7 40 ♖b6 threatens 41 ♕d6, and a6 falls.

39 ♖ed1 ♖xd6 40 ♖xd6 b4 41 h3 bxc3 42 bxc3 ♕c7 43 g4!

Black's dream of king safety falls by the wayside. White's king is remarkably secure from perpetuals due to the dominant centralization of his major pieces.

43...fxg4 44 hxg4 ♕a7+ 45 ♖b6! ♕a8 46 ♖b8! ♕a7+

If 46...♕c6 47 ♖g8+ ♔h7 48 ♕h8 mate.

47 ♔g2 1-0

Summary

6...♘fd7 fails to equalize for Black. In fact, I believe all three blocks promise White a nagging edge in the coming middlegame.

Game 97
G.Dizdar-M.Sinanovic
Pula 1998

1 d4 c5 2 d5 e5

The Czech Benoni. Black plugs up the position in anticipation of a protracted battle along closed lines. It has a solid but passive reputation. One of its defects is that Black loses both the ...e6 and ...c6 pawn breaks against the advanced white d-pawn.

3 e4

If you also play formal queen's pawn openings, then by all means plunge into 3 c4. Then after 3...d6 4 ♘c3 ♗e7 5 ♘f3 ♗g4 6 e4 ♗xf3!? 7 ♕xf3 ♗g5 (one of Black's obsessions in this line is to swap off his bad bishop for our good one on c1, but he does so at a loss of time) 8 ♗xg5 ♕xg5 9 ♘b5! ♕d8 10 ♕g4! g6 11 ♗d3 a6 12 ♘c3 ♘d7 13 g3! (we are ready for f4; White's space and the fact that he is the only one who has a pawn break gives him the advantage, and note too that our bad bishop is actually quite wonderful, halting both ...f5 and ...b5 pawn breaks from Black) 13...h5 14 ♕e2 h4 15 0-0-0 ♕g5+ 16 ♔b1 0-0-0 17 a3 ♘gf6 18 b4 ♔c7 19 ♔a2 ♖a8 20 ♖b1 hxg3 21 hxg3 ♘h5 22 ♕c2 ♖hb8 23 ♗e2 ♘hf6 24 ♖b2 ♔d8 White had all the play in P.Peev-W.Hug, Stary Smokovec 1974.

3...d6 4 ♘c3

I'm recommending this move only because you are a Veresov player! If you are comfortable in a queen's pawn opening, then it's not too late for 4 c4. This is the way I normally play it: for instance, 4...♗e7 5 ♘f3 (one of Black's main obsessions in this line is to swap his bad bishop on e7 for our good one on c1, so we stop him) 5...♘f6 (5...♗g4 would soon transpose to Peev-Hug, shown above) 6 ♘c3 0-0 7 ♗d3 ♘bd7 8 h3! ♘e8 9 g4 a6 10 a4, which Spassky thinks is White's best set-up against Czech Benoni. I began building for an attack on the kingside and won after a fishy knight sac on f5 (!) in C.Lakdawala-I.Ivanov, North American Open 2001.

4...♗e7 5 ♘f3 ♘f6 6 ♗e2 0-0 7 0-0 ♘e8

Black will either try for a ...♗g5 swap or play for the plan ...g6, ...♘g7 and eventually ...f5.

8 ♘d2 ♗g5

For sale: one slightly-used bad bishop. Black tries to unload his worst piece. Instead, 8...g6 prevents White's bishop swap on g4 when 9 ♘c4 ♗g5 10 a4 ♘d7 11 a5 ♗xc1 12 ♕xc1 ♕e7 13 ♕e3 ♖b8 14 ♘b5 a6 15 ♘c3 f5 16 f4 ♘g7 was S.Tatai-P.Votruba, Forli 1989. Now White should have played 17 ♖ae1 when he is better coordinated for the central fight.

9 ♗g4!

We can pull that trick too! White swaps off his bad bishop à la Black!

9...♗xd2

Or 9...♘d7 10 ♘c4 ♗xc1 11 ♕xc1 a6 12 a4 b6 13 f4! ♕c7 (13...exf4 14 ♗xd7! ♗xd7 15 ♕xf4 ♕b8 16 e5 is also in White's favour) 14 ♗xd7! ♗xd7 15 fxe5

dxe5 and White's powerful passed d-pawn assures him of the advantage, D.Zilberstein-R.Wong, Berkeley 1999.

10 ♗xd2 ♗xg4 11 ♕xg4 ♘d7

Black hopes his knights can keep up with White's bishop and knight team in the closed position.

12 a4 ♘ef6 13 ♕e2 ♕e7 14 ♘b5

Creating a slight weakness and re-deploying the knight to c4.

14...a6! 15 ♘a3 b6 16 ♘c4 ♘e8

16...b5? 17 ♘a5 only helps White.

17 b4!

Beginning an assault down the b-file.

17...♕d8

17...f5? is false counterplay after 18 exf5 ♖xf5 19 bxc5 bxc5 20 f4! e4 21 ♖ab1 ♖xd5 (Black is even worse off strategically after 21...♖f8?! 22 ♘e3) 22 ♘e3!, which wins the exchange.

18 ♖fb1 ♖b8 19 ♘e3

Hits a6 and keeps ...f5 in check.

19...♕c8 20 ♘f5 ♕b7 21 ♖a3!

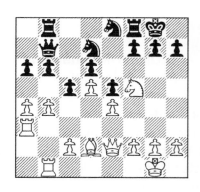

With a double purpose: it prepares ♖b3, with pressure down the b-file, and the rook may swing over to the king-

kingside if White chooses to go for a direct attack.

21...cxb4?!

He should avoid the temptation to take c5 for his knight and continue grovelling with 21...♕c7.

22 ♗xb4 ♘c5?

A miscalculation, but Black looks pretty bad also after 22...♕c7 23 ♘e7+ ♚h8 24 ♘c6 ♖c8 25 a5 b5 26 c4 bxc4 27 ♖c3.

23 ♘xd6!

It's that simple. White cuts the legs out from Black's c5-knight's support.

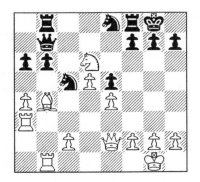

23...♘xd6 24 ♗xc5 ♕c7 25 ♗xd6 ♕xd6 26 ♖c3 b5 27 axb5 axb5 28 g3

He has all day to win the b-pawn and covers against back-rank cheapos.

28...b4 29 ♖c6 ♕d7 30 ♖c4 f5

A second pawn drops, since 30...♕d6 31 ♕e1 wins it anyway.

31 ♖cxb4 ♖xb4 32 ♖xb4 f4 33 ♖b3!

Careful defence, which denies Black any chances of mates associated with ...f3.

33...♕f7 34 ♔g2 h5 35 h3 ♕g6 36 ♖d3 1-0

Summary

The Czech Benoni is favoured mostly by positional players who want a totally closed game at the cost of space and passivity.

Game 98
A.Karpov-A.Klimas
Sao Paulo (simul) 2003

1 d4 c5 2 d5 e5 3 e4 d6 4 ♘c3 g6?!

Since Black often plays ...g6 when he develops his bishop to e7, he figures he may as well play it right away in King's Indian style. Black can play for ...♗g7, or the familiar Czech Benoni obsession of ...♗h6 in a bid to eliminate his bad bishop. In my opinion, the move is too slow and White has at least two effective methods of dealing with it.

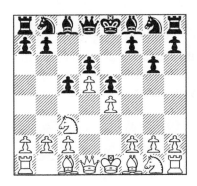

5 h4!

This excellent thrust gives Black problems to solve. You have at your disposal a more aggressive option as well in 5 f4! with immediate confrontation:

a) 5...♗g7 6 ♘f3 ♗g4 7 ♗b5+! ♘d7 8 fxe5 ♗xe5 9 ♗xd7+! ♗xd7 10 ♘xe5 dxe5 11 0-0 with clear strategic superiority for White in K.Chernyshov-A.Egyed, Salgatarjan 2003:

1. Development lead;

2. Open f-file with a potential for attack;

3. Space; and

4. A protected passed pawn on d5.

b) 5...♘d7 6 ♘f3 ♗g7 7 ♘b5! coerced Black into the embarrassing 7...♚e7 in G.Vallifuoco-G.Gasser, Italian League 1995.

5...♗g7

Allowing the pawn to keep moving forward. If Black responds with 5...h5 then 6 ♘h3! ♘h6 7 ♘g5 (the point of Karpov's play; it will be very difficult for Black to play ...f6 to eject the g5 knight) 7...a6 8 a4 b6 9 ♗c4 ♗g7 10 ♕e2 ♘d7 11 ♗d2 ♕e7 12 f3 ♘f6 13 ♘d1 0-0 14 ♘f2 ♘h7 15 g4 hxg4 16 fxg4 f5 17 ♘xh7 ♚xh7 18 g5 ♘f7 19 h5 and White's attack was under way in A.Karpov-A.Paterek, Radom (simul) 2000.

6 h5 g5 7 ♗b5+ ♘d7 8 h6!

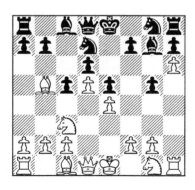

Engaging in a cunning bit of Karpovery! Is it just me or does Karpov's strategic play in general confuse you too? Of all the World Champions, I find his play most difficult to understand, where East is West, and North is often South! Karpov, unlike most strategists, tends to weave intricate, counterintuitive tactics in with his strategic ideas.

8...♗f6

The immigration authorities round up the bishop and deport him from his home on g7. Capture of the h-pawn leads to disaster for Black after:

a) 8...♗xh6?! 9 ♖xh6! ♘xh6 10 ♕h5 ♘g8 11 ♗xg5 ♕c7 12 ♘f3 which offers White enormous compensation for the exchange; Black can barely move.

b) If 8...♘xh6? 9 ♘f3 f6 10 ♘xg5! fxg5 11 ♖xh6 ♗xh6 12 ♕h5+ ♚e7 13 ♕xh6 Black gets destroyed.

c) 8...♗f8 keeping a watchful eye on h6, is possible, though: 9 ♘f3 g4 10 ♘h2 ♘xh6 11 ♘f1 ♕f6 12 ♘g3 a6 13 ♗e2 ♖g8 14 a4 and at least Black has a pawn (for now!) to console him of the fact that he has a rancid position.

9 ♕h5

This makes things rather awkward for Black, who can't develop naturally with ...♘e7 without dropping his g-pawn. I would probably go for 9 a4 a6 10 ♗e2, intending ♗g4 to take control over f5, and the kingside light squares in general.

9...a6

9...♘e7? 10 ♘f3 picks up g5.

10 ♗xd7+ ♗xd7 11 ♘f3 g4 12 ♘g5

♗xg5 13 ♗xg5 ♕b6 14 0-0-0

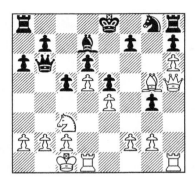

Just like that, Black is busted. White is ready to open lines on the kingside.

14...♘e7 15 ♗xe7!?

Oh no! South is North! This is what I was talking about. Karpov's move is a really strange decision. Why give up the powerful dark-squared bishop? Everyone else in the world would play 15 f4! prising open lines.

15...♔xe7 16 ♕g5+ ♔f8 17 ♕e3!?

Another odd move. Why not 17 ♕f6 ♖g8 18 ♖h5 with paralysing pressure?

17...♖g8 18 f4!

Okay, good. Now he plays more normally, opening lines.

18...♖e8 19 ♖h5 f6 20 ♖f1 ♔e7 21 ♕g3?!

Keep in mind it's a simul game. Karpov misses a breakthrough with 21 fxe5! dxe5 (21...fxe5? 22 ♖g5 threatens to check on g7) 22 d6+! ♕xd6 23 ♘d5+ ♔d8 24 ♖xf6.

21...♔d8 22 ♕h4 ♔c8 23 a3!

Now this just looks like a random move, but he foresees the coming ...c4 and ...♕e3+, and plans to hide his king

over on a2. Instead, 23 ♕xf6 is met by 23...♖ef8 24 ♕e7 exf4 with counterplay.

23...♗b5 24 ♖f2

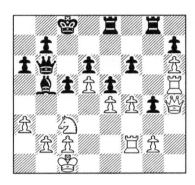

24...c4?!

24...g3! 25 ♖f3 c4! (threatening 26...♕g1+) 26 ♕h1 exf4 27 ♖f5 ♖g6 28 ♖5xf4 ♕d4 gets some counterplay, but White still stands better due to his superior pawn structure.

25 ♖f5 ♕e3+ 26 ♔b1 ♖g6 27 ♖e2?

I wonder if this was a clock simul and Karpov was running low? 27 ♖f1! exf4 28 ♖5xf4 keeps Black tied down.

27...♕g1+ 28 ♔a2 ♖f8?

Missing the tricky 28...g3! which secures f6 tactically, since 29 ♖xf6?? is met with 29...♕h2! when, suddenly, White is quite lost.

29 fxe5 dxe5 30 ♕g3!

Karpov sees the threat: ...g3! followed by ...♕h2!.

30...♖xh6 31 ♕e3?

31 ♖h5! ♖g6 32 ♘xb5 axb5 33 ♖xh7 is in White's favour.

31...♕h1??

I'm assuming the rest of the game

was a mad time scramble because the blunder ratio skyrockets from this point on! White would have to fight for the draw after 31...♕xe3! 32 ♖xe3 ♗d7.

32 ♖d2??

Both sides miss 32 ♕c5+ picking up the rook on f8.

32...♔b8 33 g3 ♖h3? 34 ♘e2?

Somehow I find all these blunders rather refreshing. If the great Karpov is capable of this much confusion (albeit with 5 seconds on his clock!), then maybe we all have a shot at the World Championship title one day! Correct was 34 ♘xb5! axb5 35 d6!.

34...♖h6 35 d6 ♗d7 36 ♖f2 ♕h5 37 ♖d1 ♕g6 38 ♘c3 ♖h5 39 ♘d5 ♗e6? 40 ♘c7! 1-0

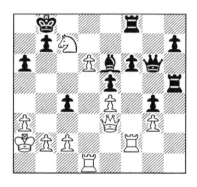

41 ♕b6 arrives with deadly effect.

Summary

4...g6 tries to mix Czech Benoni with King's Indian ideas, but here it looks too slow. You may choose to play strategically the way Karpov did with 5 h4! or you may try the confrontational 5 f4! as mentioned in the notes.

1 d4 ♘f6

The move order 1...c5 2 d5 e6 3 ♘c3 ♘f6 4 e4 transposes to our game.

2 ♘c3 e6 3 e4 c5?

The things people come up with to dodge the Veresov! This is some weird Benoni. Black should enter the French with 3...d5.

4 d5 exd5?

Black should resign himself to 4...d6 5 ♗b5+!. Now White sacs a pawn no matter how Black responds. In both cases Black ends up with vulnerable double isolanis on the e-file:

a) 5...♘bd7 6 dxe6 fxe6 7 e5! dxe5 8 ♘f3 a6 9 ♗c4 was R.Dautov-Ma.Tseitlin, Bad Zwesten 1997, won by White.

b) 5...♗d7 6 dxe6 fxe6 7 e5! dxe5 8 ♘f3 and again White won in D.Dzhangirov-V.Minakov, Kiev 2005.

5 e5!

This move is the problem for Black,

who would be in good shape after the routine 5 exd5 d6.

5...♕e7

Alternatively:

a) 5...♘g8 6 ♕xd5 ♘e7 7 ♕e4 ♘bc6! (Black gets annihilated if he tries 7...d5?? 8 exd6 ♕xd6 9 ♘b5 ♕b6 10 ♗f4 ♗f5 11 ♕f3) 8 ♘b5! (it's not often you get the pleasure of threatening a mate in one on the eighth move!) 8...♘g6 9 ♘f3 ♕b6 10 ♗c4 ♘d8 11 h4! h5 12 ♗e3 ♘e6 13 0-0-0 and positions don't get more wretched than Black's after only thirteen moves in M.Turov-D.Berczes, Budapest 2005.

b) 5...♘e4 6 ♘xd5 (White threatens 7 ♕e2) 6...c4 7 ♕d4 ♕a5+ 8 c3 ♘xf2! is a clever try in a desperate situation.

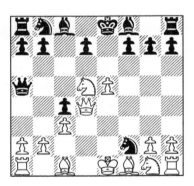

However, now comes 9 ♕xc4 with a triple threat: ♕xc8, ♘c7+ and ♔xf2. C.Lakdawala-B.Baker, San Diego (rapid) 2008, concluded 9...♕c5 10 ♗e3 (good enough, but I missed the simpler 10 ♕xc5! ♗xc5 11 b4 ♘xh1 12 bxc5 and Black can't cover c7 because 12...♔d8 is met with 13 ♗g5+) 10...♕xc4 11 ♗xc4 ♘g4 12 ♗g5! (c7 can't be covered)

12...f6 13 exf6 gxf6 14 ♘xf6+ ♘xf6 15 ♗xf6 1-0.

6 ♕e2 ♘g8 7 ♘xd5 ♕d8 8 ♘f3 h6 9 ♘f6+

Flashy, but it may have been better to simply develop with 9 ♗f4 intending to castle queenside. I just don't see a way for Black to continue playing.

9...♔e7

The equivalent of resignation. The remainder is a bloodbath, but 9...gxf6 10 exf6+ ♘e7 11 ♗f4 d5 12 ♗xb8 ♖xb8 13 ♕e5! also looks rather nasty.

10 ♕e4 g6

If 10...gxf6?? 11 exf6+ ♔xf6 12 ♕e5+ ♔g6 13 ♗d3+ f5 14 ♕xf5+ ♔g7 15 ♕g6 mate.

11 ♗c4 ♗g7 12 ♕d5 ♕f8 13 ♗e3

One can only admire Black's determination to continue playing. Some players have a very high pain threshold. **13...♔d8 14 ♗xc5 ♘e7 15 ♕e4 ♘a6? 16 ♗xa6 1-0**

Summary

3...c5? stinks! Black gets the Benoni from Hell.

Chapter Eleven
1...♘c6 and Owen's Defence

1 d4 ♘c6

In our final chapter, we examine a couple of odds and ends.

Black is trying to confuse you with 1...♘c6?!, an alternate reality Alekhine on the other side of the board. However, unlike the Alekhine which is sound, 1...♘c6 should land Black in trouble. The only path to the advantage is to vigorously chase the knight with 2 d5! and 3 f4. Not only is Black short on

space, his knight on g6 later becomes a target for White's pawn storm with h4-h5, or g4 and f5. You should castle queenside with confidence that your attack arrives first.

Owen's Defence, 1...b6, a kind of Larsen's Opening a move down, isn't so hot for Black either, but I would treat this one with more respect, mainly because people who play it are usually specialists in this type of unfixed pawn structure and are likely more familiar with it than White, who faces it very rarely. You should grab space with e4 and ♗d3, and then you can decide if you want to continue in queen's pawn style with c4, or play it more conservatively with ♘d2 and c3. In either case, you should attain a comfortable edge due to your central control.

Another goofy Black attempt to try to confuse you is 1...e5?, the Englund

Gambit. After 2 dxe5 ♞c6 3 ♞f3 Black has tried:

a) 3...♕e7 4 ♞c3! (just return the pawn for a great position) 4...♞xe5 5 e4 c6 and Black's game looks utterly ridiculous, M.Kopylov-R.Holzinger, Internet blitz 2004.

b) 3...d6 4 ♗g5! (the simplest) 4...f6 5 exf6 ♞xf6 6 e3 ♗e7 7 ♗c4 left Black without the slightest compensation for the pawn in P.Tregubov-M.Kersten, La Courneuve 2002.

Game 100
C.Ionescu-O.Yewdokimov
Bern 1992

1 d4 ♞c6?!

Provocation! As if living in a parallel universe, Black throws a queenside mirror-Alekhine at us. I'm going to be brave here and take a stand by penalizing 1...♞c6 with a '?!'. Unlike the Alekhine, which is sound, I have grave doubts about the playability of Black's opening. If Black plays ...♞c6 against 1

d4, he should do it on the second move with 1...d5 2 c4 (overlooking 2 ♞c3!) 2...♞c6, which is a Queen's Gambit Chigorin, a Veresov a move down.

2 d5!

Onward. We boot the cheeky knight around. Of course, there is nothing wrong with either:

a) 2 e4 d5 3 ♞c3 which we have already examined, but here Black also has 2...e5, which we haven't looked at. So play this way at your peril!

b) 2 ♞f3 d5 3 c4 and Black has managed to sidestep some of the more dangerous lines of the Chigorin by inducing White into ♞f3.

2...♞e5 3 f4!

Cutting down on Black's options. This is more accurate than 3 e4 d6! 4 f4 ♞d7 5 ♞f3 c6 6 c4 ♞c5 7 ♞c3 ♞f6 8 ♕c2 (White may be in danger of overextension in the line 8 e5!? ♞fe4 9 ♞xe4 ♞xe4) 8...g6, which gave Black a pleasant version of a King's Indian Four Pawns Attack in P.Soln-Z.Mestrovic, Bled 1999.

3...♞g6 4 e4 e5

This is nothing but a transposition. Most play 4...e6 5 dxe6 which leads to the game position. Instead, after 4...d6 5 c4! White gets a favourable version of the King's Indian Four Pawns Attack, with Black's knight misplaced on g6: for instance, 5...♘f6 6 ♘c3 c6 7 ♘f3 ♗g4 (7...e6 8 dxe6 fxe6 9 g3 looks good for White, who will continue with the plan: ♗d3, ♕e2, ♗e3 and 0-0-0) 8 h3 ♗xf3 9 ♕xf3 10 f5 ♘e7 left Black in an awful tangle in I.Jelen-Z.Mestrovic, Ljubljana 1997.

5 dxe6 fxe6

We are trained as kids to capture towards the centre. You may also get 5...dxe6!? if your opponent is a peace-loving member of a hippy commune! Black's idea is similar to the Lion's Yawn line of the Philidor: swap queens at the cost of castling privileges. And just as in the Lion's Yawn line, we should play to our temperament and decline a queen swap:

a) 6 ♗d3! ♗c5 7 ♘f3 ♘f6 8 g3 ♘g4 9 ♖f1 ♘e3 10 ♗xe3 ♗xe3 11 ♘bd2 ♕e7 12 ♕e2 ♗c5 13 e5! (grabbing space and clearing e4 for a piece) 13...♗d7 14 c3 ♗c6 15 ♗e4! (principle: when your opponent has the bishop pair, swap one of them off) 15...♗xe4 16 ♕xe4 0-0-0 17 b4!? ♗b6 18 a4 f5 19 exf6 ♕xf6 20 a5! ♕xc3 21 ♔e2 ♖xd2+ 22 ♘xd2 ♖d8 23 ♖fd1 ♗d4 24 ♖ac1 ♕b2 25 ♖c2 ♕a3 26 ♘f3 1-0 C.Garcia Palermo-O.Yewdokimov, Madrid 1994.

b) Just in case we have an anomaly among our Veresov readers, and some of you don't mind trying to squeeze one out in the ending, here is a good example of how to do it: 6 ♕xd8+ ♔xd8 7 ♘f3 ♗c5 8 ♗d3 ♘8e7 9 g3 f6 10 ♔e2 ♗d7 11 ♗e3 ♗xe3 12 ♔xe3 ♘c6 13 a3 ♔e7 14 ♘c3 a6 15 ♗c4 b5 16 ♗a2 ♖ae8 17 ♖hd1 ♔d8 18 ♖d2 ♔c8 19 ♖ad1 ♘f8 20 ♘e2 e5 21 f5 g6 22 g4 gxf5 23 gxf5 h6 24 b4 ♖h7 25 c3 (25 c4!) 25...♖ee7 26 c4! (he blew a tempo, but now he gets the right idea) 26...♗e8 27 cxb5 axb5 28 ♘c3 and Black is about to drop a pawn, I.Cosma-A.Labarthe, St Chely d'Aubrac 2002.

6 ♘f3 ♗c5

6...♘f6? has been played eight times so far by Black. Result in my database: eight straight blows to the head for Black! After 7 ♗d3 ♗c5 8 e5 ♘d5 9 ♗xg6+ hxg6 10 ♕d3 ♘e7 White owns g5 and is ready for ♘d2-e4, followed by ♗d2 and 0-0-0 with a huge position, V.Ruban-V.Matychenkov, Smolensk 1991.

7 ♗d3 ♘h6 8 g3

White has powerful central control, and if left alone, would continue with

♘c3, ♗d2, ♕e2 and 0-0-0, when Black's knights serve as targets for White's pawn storm on the kingside.

8...♘g4

After 8...0-0 9 ♕e2 b6 (9...a6 is seen in our next game) 10 ♘c3 ♗b7 11 ♗d2 a6 12 ♖f1 b5 13 e5 ♗xf3 14 ♖xf3 ♘f5 15 ♖f1 ♗b4 16 0-0-0 ♗xc3 17 ♗xc3 in M.Matthiesen-T.Hjorth, Danish League 2009, there were big issues for Black:

1. White's space;

2. White's attack looks faster; and

3. White's bishops outgun the Black knights.

9 ♖f1!

Nobody has tried 9 ♕e2?! ♘f2 10 ♖f1 ♘xd3+ 11 cxd3 0-0 12 ♗e3 ♗xe3 13 ♕xe3 d5 and with good reason. Black looks fine.

9...d6

Resisting temptation. 9...♘e3?! picks off the bishop pair at the cost of losing even more time: 10 ♗xe3 ♗xe3 11 ♘c3 ♕e7 12 e5! and the threat of ♗xg6+ followed by ♕d3 leaves Black in serious difficulties, T.Lindestrom-T.Flindt, Esbjerg 2007.

10 ♕e2 0-0 11 ♘c3 ♘e7 12 ♘g5 ♘h6

Sidestepping 12...♘f6?? 13 e5.

13 e5!

Black's position already looks critical.

13...♘ef5 14 g4 ♘d4 15 ♕e4 g6 16 ♕g2

I don't blame him for dodging the complications of 16 ♘xh7!? ♕h4+ 17 ♔d2! ♘hf5! 18 ♘xf8 ♕xg4. The computers still like White, but we humans could mess things up in such a situation.

16...dxe5 17 ♕h3! ♔g7 18 fxe5 ♗e7

18...♖xf1+ 19 ♔xf1 ♗e7 20 ♘ce4 ♘c6 21 ♗f4 ♘b4 22 ♖d1 also looks horrible for Black, whose king is swarmed by white attackers.

19 ♖xf8 ♗xf8 20 ♕xh6+!

Not much of a queen sac since he regains it with interest very soon, but still very cool!

20...♔xh6 21 ♘xe6+ g5 22 ♘xd8 ♘f3+ 23 ♔f2 ♘xe5

White's last challenge is how to extricate his extra but stranded knight from d8?

24 ♗e4 ♗c5+

24...♘xg4+ 25 ♔g2 ♘f6 26 ♗xb7
♗xb7+ 27 ♘xb7 does the job.
**25 ♔g2 ♗xg4 26 h4! ♗e7 27 ♘xb7 ♖f8
28 ♘d5 1-0**

Summary

The Alekhine is a perfectly good opening, but not when you do the queenside version starting with 1 d4 ♘c6?!.
Black's game looks shaky after 6...fxe6.

Game 101
A.Onischuk-I.Shkuro
Ukrainian Team
Championship 2009

---

1 d4 ♘c6?!

J'accuse! As I mentioned last game, I
don't believe this gives Black equality.
**2 d5 ♘e5 3 f4 ♘g6 4 ♘f3 e6 5 dxe6
fxe6 6 e4 ♗c5 7 ♗d3 ♘h6 8 ♕e2 0-0 9
g3 a6**

An interesting idea. Black reasons
that White is bound for queenside castling, so why not accelerate things in
that sector with ...a6 and ...b5, rather

than the meek ...b6 fianchetto?
10 ♘c3 b5 11 e5!

Thematic and strong:

1. White clears e4 for his knight;

2. The bishop on d3 now aims directly at Black's king; and

3. White takes space, which also
means his chances of a successful kingside attack go up.
**11...♗b7 12 ♘e4 ♗b6 13 ♗d2 ♘f5 14
0-0-0 h6 15 ♖hf1**

A little more refined than the cave-
man route, which also gives White the
advantage after 15 h4 ♘ge7 16 g4 ♘d4
17 ♘xd4 ♗xd4 18 g5 ♘f5 19 ♖h3. Still, I
prefer Onischuk's path. There is no reason to rush things and give Black the
f5-square blockade.
15...c5

Allowing White to enter d6, but
Black had to take action on the queenside or he gets rolled up on the other
wing if he waits too long.
16 ♘d6!

Correctly rejecting 16 g4?! c4! when
Black gets counterplay.
16...♗d5

White's space takes on alarming
proportions after 16...♘xd6?! 17 exd6
♕e8 18 ♘e5 ♘xe5 19 fxe5 c4 20 ♖xf8+
♕xf8 21 ♖f1 ♕e8 22 ♗e4 ♗xe4 23
♕xe4 ♖b8 24 g4! and Black suffocates.
17 c4!

This slows Black's queenside play,
despite the open b-file and looks superior to 17 ♗xf5 exf5 18 ♗e3, maintaining the powerful outpost on d6 at the
cost of some light-square control.

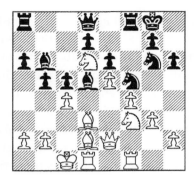

17...bxc4 18 ♘xc4 ♘fe7

He worried about White's g4, f5, and got out of the way.

19 h4 ♘f5

Wasn't he here just a moment ago? Black has no counterplay and fishes around for a plan.

20 ♖g1 ♘ge7 21 g4 ♘d4 22 ♘xd4 cxd4 23 ♖gf1!

The f5 break is ready. Note that White avoids tricks like 23 ♖df1?! ♗xc4! 24 ♗xc4 d3.

23...♖b8 24 ♔b1 ♗c5 25 f5 ♘c6 26 g5

Onischuk prefers direct attack to the technical route: 26 f6 ♕c7 27 ♗f4 ♘b4 28 fxg7 ♘xd3 29 gxf8♕+ ♗xf8 30

♕xd3 ♕xc4 31 ♕xc4 ♗xc4 32 ♖f2 d3 and White should convert eventually.

26...exf5 27 gxh6 ♕xh4 28 hxg7 ♖f7

White managed to eliminate Black's pawn cover around the king. Since the g7-pawn shields Black's king down the g-file, White must find a way to line up his major pieces on the h-file, which isn't so easy since Black controls h1.

29 ♘d6 ♗xd6

29...♗a3 30 b3 doesn't bother White.

30 exd6 ♗e4 31 ♖f4 ♗xd3+

31...♕h7 32 ♔a1 ♗xd3 33 ♕xd3 puts up more resistance.

32 ♕xd3 ♕f6?!

Black doesn't realize the importance of fighting for control over the h-file with 32...♕h5.

33 ♖h1 ♖xg7?

The only way to continue playing was the line 33...♖b5 34 ♖h8+ ♔xg7 35 ♖fh4 ♕g6 36 ♖8h5, but Black won't survive for long.

34 ♖xf5 ♕e6

34...♕g6 35 ♖h6 ♕g2 36 ♕c4+ mates.

35 ♕h3! 1-0

At long last, the queen realizes her dream to become mayor of the h-file!

Summary

9...a6 is an interesting idea, which attempts to accelerate Black's attack on the queenside. The trouble is: it isn't accelerated enough! White still looks faster on the kingside and I suspect the entire line is shaky for Black.

Game 102
G.Kamsky-P.Blatny
New York (rapid) 2004

1 d4 b6

Owen's Defence, named after the 19th Century Vicar John Owen, who quite possibly turned to the spiritual life as a result of receiving so many beatings in his line as Black! I'm kidding. Actually Owen once defeated Paul Morphy with 1...b6, and my database shows he scored an impressive 45% with the line against some of the toughest opposition of his era. Owen may have been the very first hypermodern. In his day, everyone automatically responded to 1 e4 with 1...e5 and 1 d4 classically with 1...d5. With Owen's Defence, Black, in hypermodern fashion, gives up the centre in the hope of attacking it from the wings. This was a truly radical idea for a chess player in the 19th Century.

2 e4 ♗b7 3 ♗d3 ♘f6

If they play 3...f5? take the bait! In-

deed, after 4 exf5! ♗xg2 5 ♕h5+ g6 6 fxg6 ♗g7 (avoiding the trap 6...♘f6?? 7 gxh7+ ♘xh5 8 ♗g6 mate, first seen in G.Greco-NN, Europe 1620; it's not often that an annotator gets to put a Greco game as a reference!) 7 gxh7+ (Bauer gives the line 7 ♕f5 ♘f6 8 ♗h6!! ♗xh6 9 gxh7 ♔f8 10 ♕g6 ♗c1 11 ♕xg2 ♗xb2 12 ♘e2 and Black has no defence to ♖g1 next) 7...♔f8 White has more than one good move:

a) 8 ♘f3! (*Rybka*'s choice) 8...♘f6 9 ♕g6 ♗xf3 10 ♖g1 ♖xh7 11 ♕g3! ♗e4 12 ♗xe4 ♘xe4 13 ♕f3+ ♔g8 14 ♕xe4 ♘c6 15 d5 ♘a5 16 ♗e3 c5 17 ♘c3 and White is ready to castle queenside with a winning attack, F.Rosenberger-A.Kessler, Polch 1993.

b) 8 ♘e2! also looks good for White, as the h7-pawn is stronger than Black's knight: for example, 8...♘f6 9 ♕h4 ♗xh1 10 ♗g5 ♗d5 11 ♘bc3 ♗f7 12 0-0-0 d5 13 ♗h6 e6 14 ♘f4 ♗xh6 15 ♕xh6+ ♔e7 16 ♕g7 ♘h5 17 ♘g6+ 1-0 G.Hechl-K.Kranawetter, Faaker 2003.

4 ♕e2!

The most accurate move which shuts down....♗a6. Instead, 4 ♘d2 e6 5 ♘gf3 c5 6 c3 cxd4 7 cxd4 ♗a6! 8 ♗xa6 ♘xa6 isn't so bad for Black, who has removed White's best attacker.

4...♘c6!

In the spirit of Owen, and the most accurate move.

5 c3 e5

Finally, Black stakes out a piece of the centre with a pawn.

6 ♘f3

White decides to maintain central pawn tension for a while. Alternatively, 6 d5 ♘e7 7 ♘f3 ♘g6 8 0-0 ♗c5 9 c4 0-0 10 ♘c3 a5 11 g3 d6 12 ♘a4 ♗c8 13 ♔g2 h6 14 ♘xc5 dxc5 15 b3 ♘e8 16 ♗b2 f6 17 ♘d2 and advantage White, who had space, a bishop pair and the only viable pawn breaks in P.Smirnov-E.Bacrot, Canada de Calatrava (rapid) 2006.

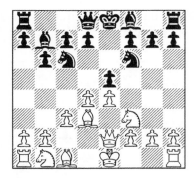

6...d6

Instead, 6...exd4?! 7 e5 ♘d5 8 ♗e4 ♘de7 9 0-0! dxc3 10 ♘xc3 ♕c8 11 ♖d1 gave White massive compensation for the pawn in J.Friedel-F.Barrios, Toronto 2009. Black is far behind in development in this Scotch-like position and unlikely to survive.

7 0-0 ♘d7

7...♗e7 8 d5 ♘b8 9 c4 0-0 10 ♘c3 ♘bd7 11 ♗c2 reaches a favourable Old Indian-style position where Black's bishop on b7 fianchettoes into a wall on d5, E.Gleizerov-M.Franic, Zagreb 2010.

8 a4!? a5

An attempt to halt White's space

grab on the queenside. Others:

a) 8...♗e7 9 d5 ♘cb8 10 a5 favours White, who made considerable progress on the queenside, even though the wily Blatny eventually managed to win in A.Shabalov-P.Blatny, New York 2004.

b) Black can also try the risky plan of abandoning the centre to White in exchange for the b4-square: 8...exd4!? 9 cxd4 ♘b4 10 ♗c4 ♗e7 11 ♘c3 0-0 12 ♗f4.

9 d5 ♘e7 10 ♗b5!

Taking full advantage of the punctures in Black's queenside.

10...h6

10...g6 11 ♘bd2 ♗g7 and White plays similar to the game, with b4, bxa5, ♘b3 and a5.

11 ♘bd2

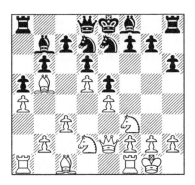

Possible plans:

1. b4 and ♘b3. If Black plays ...axb4; cxb4, White gets a passed a-pawn soon with a timely a5; and

2. b4 and bxa5. If Black recaptures with his rook, then White responds with ♘b3 and a5, blasting open the

queenside, his theatre of operations. However, if Black recaptures with ...bxa5 then White plays for the typical King's Indian plan of ♘b3, c4, ♗a3, either rook to c1 and c5.

11...♘g6 12 b4 ♗e7 13 bxa5 ♖xa5

13...♘f4 chases White's queen to where she wants to go: 14 ♕c4 ♖xa5 15 ♘b3 ♖a8 16 a5.

14 ♘c4 ♖a7 15 ♗e3 0-0

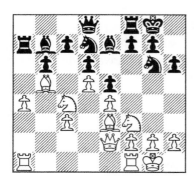

White's queenside attack clearly moves faster than anything Black has to offer on the other wing.

16 a5 ♘c5

I'm truly shocked that mess meister Blatny didn't go on a fishing expedition starting with 16...f5!? 17 exf5 ♖xf5 18 ♕d3 ♖xf3!? 19 gxf3 ♘h4. *Rybka*, of course, has nothing but disdain for Black in this line, but at least it's complicated.

17 ♗xc5 ♘f4 18 ♕c2 bxc5 19 a6 ♗a8!?

Condemning the bishop and rook to life sentences without parole on cell blocks a7 and a8! Clearly Blatny didn't like his prospects in the ending after 19...♗c8 20 ♘a5 ♖xa6 21 ♗xa6 ♗xa6

22 ♘c6 ♗d3 23 ♕xd3 ♘xd3 24 ♘xd8 ♖xd8 and it's a 99.999% probability that Kamsky, the granddaddy of technicians would win this one.

20 ♘a5 ♕c8!

Threatening to swing the queen into g4.

21 g3 ♘h3+

Or 21...♕g4 22 ♘d2 and it's hard to believe Black's attack can be anything but a failure without the help of his rook and bishop on the queenside.

22 ♔h1 f5 23 ♘c6!!

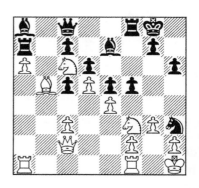

An amazing strategic decision which allows Black to dump his horrible bishop. On top of everything, this also frees Black's rook because now it has access to a8. Kamsky's deep point:

1. The bishop covers the b7-square, which Kamsky now uses to infiltrate;

2. Black's a7-rook can move but does it want to? White's a-pawn sits two squares from queening, so the rook really isn't going anywhere;

3. White opens the a2-g8 diagonal which he soon uses to good effect for a light squared attack; and

4. Black's rook and bishop were tied down, but White had also invested his a1-rook, his bishop and a5-knight to ensure Black didn't free himself with ...c6. So the reality was, Black wasn't as tied down as he looked because White expended a lot of energy keeping his opponent tied up!

23...♗xc6 24 dxc6 f4 25 ♕e2 ♕g4 26 ♗c4+ ♔h7 27 ♖ab1

The point of his previous play. ♖b7 is coming and diverts more black force away from the kingside.

27...♖fa8

Sad, but Black's attack is at a dead end after 27...♖aa8 28 ♖b7 ♗d8 29 a7 h5 30 ♘g1 f3 31 ♕d3 h4 32 ♘xh3 ♕xh3 33 ♖g1.

28 ♖a1?!

Over-caution. Welcome to my world GM Kamsky! He should dive off the cliff with 28 ♖b7! h5 29 ♖xa7 ♖xa7 30 ♖b1 ♖a8 31 ♖b7 ♖f8 32 a7 fxg3 33 fxg3 ♖xf3 34 a8♕ and Black has no good way to proceed, in which case an extra queen may come in handy for White!

28...♖f8 29 ♕d1!

Nice, clearing e2 for the bishop.

29...♕h5 30 ♗e2 ♕g6 31 ♕d5 ♖b8 32 ♖a2 ♖b6?!

32...h5 33 ♘g1 fxg3 34 fxg3 ♘xg1 35 ♔xg1 h4 36 ♔g2 and Black still suffers from the eternal prisoner a7.

33 ♗c4 ♕h5?

Losing instantly, but Black's position was hopeless after both:

a) 33...♖b8 34 ♖b2! ♕g4 35 ♘g1 ♖ba8 36 ♖b7.

b) 33...♖a8 34 a7 ♔h8 35 ♘d2 ♔h7 36 ♗a6! ♖xa7 37 ♗c4! wins.

34 ♕g8+ 1-0

Summary

Don't underestimate the tricky Owen's. If you play correctly against it, you can probably land in a good version or simulation of one of the following openings: French, Colle, Old Indian, Ruy Lopez, Queen's Gambit Accepted or Scotch! The trick is to remember 4 ♕e2!. Don't allow that bishop swap on a6 or your advantage evaporates.

Game 103
E.Najer-P.Blatny
Pardubice 2007

1 e4 b6 2 d4 ♗b7 3 ♗d3 g6

The Hippopotamus. This offshoot could also be classified as a Modern. After the double fianchetto, Black plans ...e6, ...d6, ...♘e7, ...♘d7, ...a6 and ...h6 on virtually any white set-up counting on his flexibility. In my experience

against it, White's best is to take a King's Indian route and grab as much space as possible with pawns on c4, d4, e4 and even f4. When Black strikes back later in the centre (usually with ...e5), White simply ends up in a King's Indian at least one tempo ahead of book lines.

4 c4

If you feel uncomfortable playing it King's Indian style, you can also keep it closer to a king's pawn opening with 4 ♘f3 ♗g7 and then:

a) 5 0-0 d6 6 ♖e1 e6 7 ♘bd2 (White refrains from 7 c4) 7...♘e7 8 c3 ♘d7 9 ♘f1 0-0 10 ♘g3 c5 11 ♗e3 ♕c7 12 ♕d2 ♖fe8 13 ♖ad1 ♖ad8 sees White complete development in an orthodox, Fred Reinfeld-approved way, much like a 150 Attack against Modern. Now he goes directly after Black's king: 14 ♗h6 c4 (closing the centre can't help Black's defensive chances, but how to open it?) 15 ♗c2 f6 16 h4 e5 17 h5 and Black began to feel the heat on the kingside in R.Izoria-R.Naranja, New York 2008.

b) It's not too late for 5 c4 d6 6 ♘c3 ♘d7 7 0-0 e6 8 ♗e3 ♘e7 9 ♕d2 h6 10

♖fd1 g5 11 ♖ac1 a6, as in J.Peters-P.Blatny, Los Angeles 2003, and now 12 d5 offers White a typically good King's Indian, mainly because the bishop on b7 is misplaced and ineffective.

4...♗g7 5 ♘e2!?

Very ambitious. White is willing to part with one of his bishops if he can take even more space with f4 later on. More normal is 5 ♘f3.

5...♘c6! 6 ♗e3 ♘b4

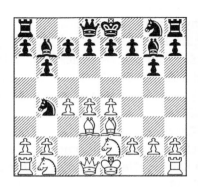

Blatny's point. White's massive space advantage will be tempered somewhat by Black getting the bishop pair, which also helps free his position. Still, I think White's space means more than Black's bishops.

7 ♘bc3 ♘xd3+ 8 ♕xd3 e6 9 0-0-0

Black isn't well placed to attack on the queenside, so White castles that wing.

9...d6 10 f4

Playing to blow Black away, no matter where he decides to castle.

10...♘e7 11 g4!?

Clearly shyness is not one of Najer's weaknesses!

11...h5

Black would like to hit back in the centre with something like 11...f5?!. The problem is the game opens too quickly in White's favour after 12 gxf5 gxf5 13 d5 ♕d7 14 ♖hg1 ♗f6 15 ♘d4.

12 g5 ♕d7 13 d5 0-0-0 14 ♗d4!

Either eliminating Black's bishop pair or forcing Black to block things up with ...e5, which would harm his bishop pair!

14...e5

Black has very little play after 14...♗xd4 15 ♘xd4 ♔b8 16 ♖hf1.

15 fxe5 dxe5 16 ♗e3 c5

To halt White's c5 break.

17 a3!

No worries, he plays for the b4 break.

17...♔b8 18 b4 ♖c8?

Black is already in big trouble. This leaves a big target on c5. Black doesn't get enough for the pawn after 18...cxb4 19 axb4 ♘c6 20 ♕b1 ♘d4 21 ♘xd4 exd4 22 ♗xd4 ♗xd4 23 ♖xd4 ♕g4 24 h4 ♕g2 25 ♖dd1 ♖c8 26 ♕d3, but he had to try this anyway.

19 bxc5 bxc5 20 ♔c2 ♖hd8 21 ♖hf1 ♕e8 22 ♖b1 ♔a8 23 ♖b5

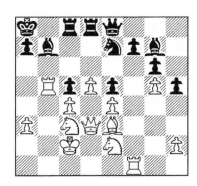

A strategic disaster for Black. White's advantages:

1. Pressure down the b-file;

2. Pressure on c5;

3. Pressure down the f-file and f7; and

4. The insecure black king.

23...♗f8 24 ♘c1 ♘c6!?

We can't blame Black for wanting to muck up the game a bit.

25 dxc6

Good enough. White has a simpler put-away with 25 ♖xb7!:

a) 25...♔xb7 26 dxc6+ ♖xc6 27 ♘d5 and the minor pieces dominate.

b) 25...♘d4+ 26 ♗xd4 cxd4 27 ♖fxf7 ♗c5 28 ♘b3 ♗b6 29 c5 forces mate.

25...♗xc6 26 ♕e2!

Avoiding 26 ♘d5 ♗xb5 27 cxb5 c4.

26...♗xb5 27 ♘xb5!

Refusing to recapture with the pawn and allow ...c4!.

27...a6 28 ♘c3 ♖c7 29 ♘b3 ♖b8 30 ♖f6! ♖c6 31 ♕f2 ♗e7

31...♖xf6 32 ♕xf6 hits c5 and a6.

32 ♖xc6 ♕xc6 33 ♕xf7 ♕b6 34 ♘d2

34 ♕d5+! ♔a7 35 ♘xc5 wins faster.

34...♕b2+ 35 ♔d3 ♖d8+ 36 ♘d5 ♕xa3+ 37 ♔e2 ♗d6 38 ♕xg6 ♕b2 39 ♕xh5

The g-pawn moves faster than Black's a-pawn.

39...a5 40 ♕f7 a4 41 ♘c7+

Or 41 g6 (this variation allows Black two queens at the cost of his king!) 41...a3 42 g7 a2 43 g8♕ ♖xg8 44 ♕xg8+ ♔a7 45 ♕f7+ ♔a8 46 ♕e8+ ♔a7 47 ♕d7+ ♔a8 48 ♕c6+ ♔a7 49 ♕xd6! a1♕ 50 ♕xc5+ ♔b7 51 ♕c7+ ♔a8 52 ♕c8+ ♕b8 53 ♘c7 mate.

41...♗xc7 42 ♕xc7 ♖h8 43 ♕c6+ ♔b8 44 ♕xa4 ♖xh2+ 45 ♔d3

White's king finds a cosy nook.

45...♔c8 46 ♕e8+ ♔c7 47 ♕e7+ ♔b8 48 ♕d6+ ♔b7 49 ♕d5+ ♔b8 50 ♕xc5 ♕a1 51 g6 ♖g2 52 g7 1-0

Summary

Against the Hippopotamus, you can go King's Indian style with c4, or play it like a 150 Attack against Modern with the plan ♘f3, c3, ♘bd2, 0-0, ♖e1, ♘f1, etc.

1 e4 b6 2 d4 ♗b7 3 ♗d3 e6?!

Believe it or not, I think this very natural move is an error, which leads to a bad French or bad Queen's Indian. Better are 3...♘f6 or 3...g6, as tried by Blatny in our last two games.

4 ♘f3 c5 5 c3 ♘f6 6 ♕e2!

I have incredibly exciting news for you. We've reached the Colle versus the Queen's Indian set-up a full move up for White since he achieved e4 in one shot! Hey, you don't look all that excited, but you should be. You should probably put the book away and contemplate what I told you for an hour or so and then come back.

Greetings! Good to see you again! I'm certain you've now realized during your contemplative retreat that a Colle is nothing more than a Semi-Slav a move up, and since we got in e4 in one move, we've reached a very sharp Semi-

Slav a full two moves up. That is worth a lot.

6...d5

This leads to a sorry French for Black, who lacks counterplay, but if he avoids 6...d5, he gets squeezed: 6...cxd4 7 cxd4 ♘c6 8 a3 ♗e7 9 ♘c3 ♘a5 10 ♗f4 0-0 11 0-0 d6 12 b4 ♖c8 13 ♘b5 ♘c6 14 ♖ac1 ♖e8 15 ♖fd1 ♘h5 16 ♗e3 a6 17 d5! exd5 18 exd5 ♘b8 19 ♖xc8 ♗xc8 20 ♘a7! ♗f6 (20...♗b7 21 ♘c6 ♘xc6 22 dxc6 ♗xc6 23 ♘d4 ♗a4 24 ♕xh5) 21 ♕c2 ♗g4 22 ♘c6 ♕d7 23 ♗xh7+ ♔h8 24 ♗e4 left White a pawn up with a dominant position, R.Antonio-K.Yang, Olongapo City 2010.

7 e5 ♘fd7

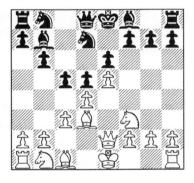

This is the French Black should avoid at all costs. It's almost a compilation of all the problems Black gets in the Advance Variation and the ...♘f6 Tarrasch:

1. Black has a terrible bishop on b7;

2. Black can't engineer ...f6 because he fianchettoed away the defender of e6, and so he remains cramped for life;

3. White's unchallenged e5 point promises a kingside attack; and

4. Black's only plan may be to seal the queenside and then castle queenside.

8 0-0

White can also hold back kingside castling to leave an h4 option open: 8 ♘bd2 ♘c6 9 a3 ♗e7 10 h4 h6 11 b4, as in M.Pap-D.Nestorovic, Belgrade 2001.

8...♗e7 9 ♘bd2 0-0

I would try 9...a5, an attempted debadification (Don't look this word up, I just made it up! And the spell check keeps telling me I misspelled it!) of his bishop! 10 g3 (10 ♖e1 ♗a6 11 c4!? is another plan) 10...♗a6 11 ♗xa6 ♘xa6 12 h4 h6 13 ♘h2 cxd4?! 14 cxd4 ♘b4 15 ♕g4 ♗f8 16 a3 h5 17 ♕d1 ♘d3 18 ♘df3 ♘xc1 19 ♖xc1, but Black hasn't yet solved the problem of king safety and he still lags far behind in development, G.Pelle-L.Castaignet, French League 2002.

10 ♖e1 a5 11 ♗b1!

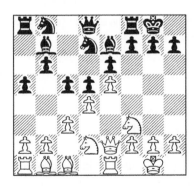

Debadification denied! White doesn't mind contorting to retain his powerful attacker.

11...♗a6 12 ♕d1 ♘c6 13 ♘f1 ♖e8 14 ♘e3

Thinking about heading out to g4 later on.

14...cxd4 15 cxd4 ♗b4 16 ♗d2

Asrian rejects 16 ♕c2!? g6 17 ♗d2 ♖c8 18 ♕d1 when White has induced the weakening ...g6 but it cost him two moves. I think it's worth the time and would play it this way as White.

16...♘f8 17 ♘g4 ♗e7 18 g3!

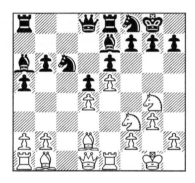

Plan:

1. Play h4;

2. White may use the g5-square to provoke pawn weaknesses in Black's camp; and

3. White may go for h5-h6, creating dark-squared weakness around Black's king.

18...♘b4 19 ♗c1

Covering d3.

19...♗b5!

A good move. Black foresees that White must eventually play a3, after which Black plays ...♘c6, with the idea ...a4 and ...♘a5 with an invasion on c4 and b3. Instead, 19...♖c8 20 a3 ♘c6 21

h4 ♗b5 22 h5 sees White rolling on.

20 h4 ♖a7 21 ♘g5 ♕c8

Black is ready to counterattack on the c-file with ...♖c7 and ...♘c2. White must eject the knight now, even it if weakens his queenside somewhat.

22 a3 ♘c6 23 ♗e3 a4 24 ♕f3 ♗d8

Forced since 24...♗xg5? 25 hxg5! allows White to eventually engineer a deadly sac on f6. He will probably first pile up heavy pieces on the h-file before the sac.

25 ♗a2 ♕d7 26 ♖ac1 ♘a5 27 ♖c3 ♗c4 28 ♗b1 ♘b3 29 ♖d1 ♕b5!

Excellent defence by Eliseev after his less-than-stellar opening play. Black threatens ...♗e2 and puts more pressure on White's queenside, whereas 29...b5?! 30 h5 h6 31 ♘xh6+ gxh6 32 ♘h3 ♘h7 33 ♗xh6 looks very tough for Black to defend.

30 ♗d3

A concession, swapping off his beloved good bishop due to the cheapo threat on e2, but White has problems making progress after 30 ♖e1 ♘a5! 31 ♗c1 ♘b3! 32 ♗e3 ♘a5.

30...♘a5 31 ♗c1 ♗xd3

31...♘b3? doesn't draw: 32 ♗xc4 dxc4 33 ♘e3! ♘xc1 34 ♖dxc1 ♗xg5 35 hxg5 and if he snaps up the b-pawn he loses with 35...♕xb2?? 36 ♘xc4 ♕a2 37 ♘d6 ♖d8 38 ♖c7.

32 ♖dxd3 ♘c4 33 ♕e2 ♖b7 34 ♖c2 ♕a5!

The queen's work is done and it's time for ...b5 and ...b4 to open lines on the queen's wing.

35 h5

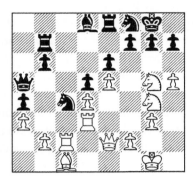

Finally, after taking great care in securing his queenside.

35...b5?

A critical decision and the wrong one. Black had to halt the pawn, even if it created a sac target with 35...h6 36 ♘h3 ♘h7. Now White has three plans of attack:

a) 37 ♘xh6+ gxh6 38 ♗xh6 with full compensation for the piece.

b) 37 ♗xh6 gxh6 38 ♘xh6+ ♔h8 again with compensation.

c) Keep building and look to sac later on with 37 ♖f3.

In all of these lines, though, Black too has his chances.

36 h6 g6??

The strain of the defence proved too much for Black. 36...f6 was the only move. Then after 37 hxg7 fxg5 38 gxf8N! (my philosophy: underpromote whenever possible! I advise this for two reasons: it's cool and it annoys your opponent!) 38...♖xf8 Black's king looks pretty shaky, but at least he is still breathing.

37 ♕f3

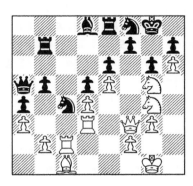

Black can resign. He has no answer to the brutal threat of 38 ♘f6+.

37...♕e1+

37...♔h8 38 ♘f6 ♖ee7 39 ♘xd5! destroys Black's position.

38 ♔h2 ♗xg5 39 ♗xg5 f5

Absolute desperation.

40 ♘f6+ ♔f7 41 ♖d1 ♕a5 42 ♘xe8 ♔xe8 43 b3!

All that remains is to open lines for his rooks to enter.

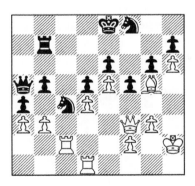

43...axb3 44 ♕xb3 ♔d7

The pawn is immune, as Black can't allow White's rooks in: 44...♕xa3? 45 ♕xa3 ♘xa3 46 ♖c8+ ♔f7 47 ♖a1 b4 48

♔g2! (zugzwang!) 48...b3 49 ♖xa3 b2 50 ♖aa8 ♘d7 51 ♖h8 mates.

45 ♖a2 ♕a4 46 ♖b1 ♔c7 47 ♕b4 ♕xb4 48 axb4 ♘d7 49 ♖a6 ♖b6 50 ♖ba1 ♘b8 51 ♖a8 ♖b7 52 ♗e7 ♔c6 53 ♗c5 g5 54 ♗a7! 1-0

A rook enters Black's camp.

Summary

A move-up Colle rules! You get a favourable version of either the French or Queen's Indian.

Game 105
I.Ibragimov-R.Tomasic
Djakovo 1994

1 d4 ♘f6 2 ♘c3 e6 3 e4 ♗b4?!

Finally, we have an attempt to confuse White and take the game out of theory. Black ends up with a position similar to the slightly dubious Pin Variation of the Sicilian, but an even worse version than that line, since he hasn't even achieved ...c5. Better to transpose to the French with 3...d5.

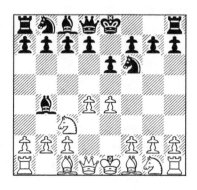

4 e5 ♘d5 5 ♕g4!

Superior to 5 ♗d2 ♘xc3 6 bxc3 ♗e7 7 ♕g4 ♔f8 8 ♗d3 c5 9 ♘e2 d6 when I still prefer White, but his advantage is not as large as in our main game, L.Day-H.Jung, Ontario 1997.

5...♔f8

The best among several bad choices:

a) 5...0-0 6 ♗h6 g6 7 ♗xf8 ♔xf8 8 a3 ♗xc3+ 9 bxc3 ♘xc3 was A.Ong-J.Badenhorst, correspondence 2005, and now White missed 10 ♕h3! double attacking c3 and h7.

b) 5...g6 6 a3! (taking advantage of the fact that ...c5 hasn't been played, which deprives Black of the ...♕a5 option) 6...♗xc3+ 7 bxc3 c5 8 dxc5 (after 8 c4! ♘e7 9 ♘f3 Black haemorrhages on the dark squares) 8...♕a5 9 ♗d2 ♕xc5 and the dark squares will become a big problem for Black very soon, P.Leisebein-U.Gohla, correspondence 2000.

c) 5...♘xc3 6 ♕xg7 ♖f8 7 a3 ♗a5 8 b4! and if Black tries to keep the extra piece he gets fried after 8...♗b6? 9 ♗g5 f6 10 ♗xf6 ♖f7 11 ♕g8+ ♖f8 12 ♕g5 ♖xf6 13 exf6 d6 14 f7+!.

6 ♗d2 ♘c6

After 6...c5 7 ♘f3 ♘c6 8 dxc5 ♘xc3 9 bxc3 ♗xc5 10 ♗d3 ♕c7 11 ♕g3 d6 12 ♗f4 ♕a5 13 0-0 the game opens up with Black essentially a rook down.

7 ♘f3 d6 8 ♗d3 ♗d7 9 0-0 ♗xc3

He can hang on to the bishop with 9...dxe5 10 dxe5 ♘xc3 11 bxc3 ♗e7 12 ♖fe1 h5 13 ♕f4, but then it's hard to say how Black completes development.

10 bxc3 dxe5 11 dxe5

Assessment:

1. White leads in development;

2. The e5-pawn chokes Black;

3. White, who has the bishop pair, has them pointing ominously in the direction of Black's king;

4. Black's rook sits bottled up and out of the action on h8;

5. Only White can make use of the open d-file; and

6. White's broken pawns on the queenside don't give Black much comfort as he contemplates his woes from numbers 1-5!

Conclusion: the opening has been an utter disaster for Black.

11...♘de7 12 ♖ad1 ♘g6 13 ♗g5 ♕e8

Naturally, not 13...♘gxe5?? 14 ♘xe5 ♘xe5?? 15 ♕b4+.

14 ♖fe1

The e5-pawn is a huge problem for Black.

14...♘ce7 15 h4 ♘d5?!

He needs to push back with 15...h6 16 ♗c1 h5.

16 h5 ♘ge7

It's suicide to allow White's pawn to h6, but 16...h6 doesn't save Black either after 17 hxg6 hxg5 18 ♘xg5 fxg6.

17 h6 ♘g6 18 c4 ♘c3 19 hxg7+ ♔xg7 20 ♗f6+ ♔g8 21 ♗xg6 fxg6

Or 21...hxg6 22 ♗xh8 ♔xh8 23 ♕h4+ ♔g8 24 ♖d3 and ♘g5 follows.

22 ♖d3 ♘xa2 23 ♖ed1

Threatening 24 d7 and d8R.

23...h5

He finds a method of defending against both threats at the cost of dismembering his kingside pawn structure.

24 ♕g5 ♖h7 25 ♘h4 ♘b4 26 ♖xd7! 1-0

It's mate in seven moves.

Summary

3...♗b4?! just leads to a position similar to a bad version of the Pin Variation of the Sicilian for Black.

Index of Variations

The Veresov: 3...♘bd7 4 f3!?

1 d4 ♘f6 2 ♘c3 d5 3 ♗g5 ♘bd7 4 f3 c6
    4...h6 5 ♗h4 e6 (5...c6 – 15)
      6 e4 ♗e7 7 e5 ♘h5 8 ♗xe7 ♕xe7
        9 g3 – 11
        9 ♘h3 – 13
    4...c5 5 dxc5 e6 (5...♕a5 – 28)
      6 b4 ♗e7
        7 ♖b1 – 23
        7 e4 – 26
    4...e6 – 19; 4...♕b6 – 6
5 e4 dxe4 6 fe4 e5

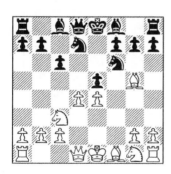

7 dxe5
    7 ♘f3
      7...♕a5 – 38
      7...h6 – 40
      7...♕b6 – 42
7...♕a5 8 ♗xf5 gxf6 9 e6 fxe6 10 ♕g4
    10...♘b6 – 31

    10...♕g5 – 34
    10...♘e5 – 36

The Veresov: 3...♘bd7 4 ♕d3

1 d4 ♘f6 2 ♘c3 d5 3 ♗g5 ♘bd7 4 ♕d3 c6
    4...e6 5 e4 dxe4 6 ♘xe4 ♗e7
      7 ♘xf6+
        7...♗xf6 – 55
        7...♘xf6 – 60
    4...h6 – 58
    4...g6 5 f3 ♗g7 6 e4
      6...dxe4 – 62
      6...h6 – 64
    4...c5
      5 0-0-0 – 66
      5 ♘f3 – 69

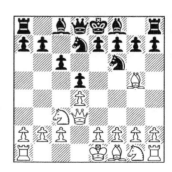

5 e4
    5 ♘f3

5...b5 – 45
5...g6 – 47

5...dxe4 6 ♘xe4
6...e6 – 51
6...♘xe4 – 53

The Veresov: Other Defences

1 d4 ♘f6 2 ♘c3 d5 3 ♗g5 ♗f5
3...c5 4 ♗xf6 gxf6 5 e3 (5 e4 – 86)
5...♘c6 6 ♕h5 cxd4
7 exd4 e6 8 ♘f3
8...♗b4 – 89
8...♗d7 – 92
8...f5 – 96
3...c6 4 ♕d3
4...b6 – 97
4...b5 – 99
3...g6 4 ♕d2 ♗g7
5 ♗h6 – 101
5 f3 – 102
3...h6 4 ♗xf6 exf6 5 e3
5...c6 – 104
5...♗b4 – 107

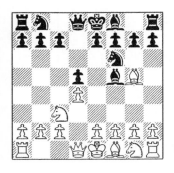

4 f3 ♘bd7
4...♗g6 – 81
4...c6 – 83

5 ♘xd5

5 ♕d2 – 79
5...♘xd5 6 e4
6...f6 – 72
6...h6 – 75

Veresov versus French: Lines with ...♘f6

1 d4 ♘f6 2 ♘c3 d5 3 ♗g5 e6 4 e4 dxe4
4...♗e7 5 e5 ♘fd7 6 h4
6...♗xg5 – 118
6...0-0 – 121
4...♗b4 5 exd5
5...exd5 – 124
5...♕xd5 – 128

5 ♘xe4 ♗e7

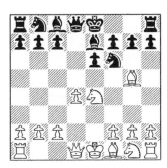

6 ♗xf6
6...♗xf6 – 110
6...gxf6 – 114

Veresov versus French: Lines without ...♘f6

1 d4 d5 2 ♘c3 e6 3 e4 dxe4
3...♗b4 4 exd5 exd5 5 ♗d3
5...♗e6 – 131
5...c6 – 134
5...♘c6 – 139

5...♞f6 – 140

5...♞e7 – 142

3...♞c6 4 ♞f3 ♞f6 5 exd5 exd5 6 ♝b5

6...♝g4 – 158

6...♝e7 – 161

4 ♞xe4 ♞d7

4...♝d7 5 ♞f3 ♝c6 6 ♝d3 ♞d7 7 0-0 ♞gf6 8 ♞ed2 ♝e7 9 ♞c4

9...♝d5 – 151

9...0-0 – 154

5 ♞f3 ♞gf6 6 ♝d3 c5 7 ♞xf6+ ♞xf6 8 ♝e3

8...♞d5 – 144

8...♛c7 – 147

1 d4 d5 2 ♞c3: Second Move Alternatives

1 d4 d5 2 ♞c3 ♝f5

2...♞c6 3 e4 dxe4 4 d5 ♞e5 5 ♝f4 ♞g6 6 ♝g3

6...a6 – 169

6...f5 – 171

2...c5 3 e4

3...cxd4 – 173

3...dxe4 – 176

2...g6 3 e4 dxe4 4 ♞xe4 ♝g7 5 ♞f3

5...♞d7 – 179

5...♞h6 – 182

2...e5 – 185

3 f3 e6 4 e4 ♝g6

5 ♝d3 – 163

5 ♞ge2 – 166

Veresov versus Caro-Kann

1 d4 d5 2 ♞c3 ♞f6

2...c6 3 ♝g5 ♝f5 4 e3 ♛b6 5 ♜b1 e6 6 ♝d3

6...♝xd3 – 200

6...♝g6 – 204

3 ♝g5 c6

3...♝f5 4 ♝xf6

4...exf6 – 194

4...gxf6 – 198

4 e3 ♞bd7 5 f4 g6

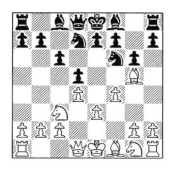

6 ♝d3 – 189

6 ♞f3 – 192

Veresov versus Dutch

1 d4 f5 2 ♞c3 d5

2...♞f6 3 ♝g5 e6 4 e4 fxe4 5 ♞xe4 ♝e7 6 ♝xf6 ♝xf6 7 ♛h5+ g6 8 ♛h6

8...♗xd4 – 222
8...♘c6 – 224

3 ♗g5
   3 e4 – 209
   3 ♗f4 – 212

3...g6
   3...♘f6
      4 ♕d2 – 215
      4 f3
         4...♘c6 – 217
         4...c5 – 219

4 f3 ♘f6 5 ♕d2
   5...♗g7 – 227
   5...♘c6 – 229
   5...♗e6 – 230

Modern, Pirc and Philidor

1 d4 d6 2 e4 ♘f6
   2...g6 3 ♘c3 ♗g7 4 ♗g5
      4...h6 – 234
      4...a6 – 237
      4...♘c6 – 239
      4...c6 – 242

3 ♘c3 ♘bd7
   3...g6 4 ♗g5 ♗g7 5 ♕d2 h6
   6 ♗h4 g5 7 ♗g3 ♘h5 8 0-0-0
      8...♘c6 – 244
      8...c6 – 247
   3...e5 4 ♘ge2
      4...♗e7 – 258
      4...exd4 – 260

4 g4 h6
   4...e5 – 255

5 h3 e5 6 ♘ge2 c6 7 a4
   7...a6 – 250
   7...a5 – 253

Schmid Benoni and Czech Benoni

1 d4 c5
   1...♘f6 2 ♘c3 e6 3 e4
      3...c5 – 278
      3...♗b4 – 296

2 d5 ♘f6
   2...e5 3 e4 d6 4 ♘c3
      4...♗e7 – 273
      4...g6 – 275

3 ♘c3 g6 4 e4 d6 5 ♘f3 ♗g7

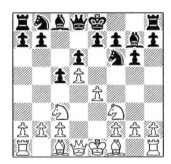

6 ♗b5+
   6...♘bd7 – 264
   6...♗d7 – 267
   6...♘fd7 – 270

1...♘c6 and Owen's Defence

1 d4 ♘c6
   1...b6 2 e4 ♗b7 3 ♗d3
      3...♘f6 – 286
      3...g6 – 289
      3...e6 – 292

2 d5 ♘e5 3 f4 ♘g6 4 e4 e6 5 dxe6 fxe6
6 ♘f3 ♗c5 7 ♗d3 ♘h6
   8 g3 – 281
   8 ♕e2 – 284

Index of Games

Akshayraj.K-Swiercz.D, Gaziantep 2008 28
Anand.V-Azmaiparashvili.Z, Benidorm (rapid) 2003 258
Anand.V-Morovic Fernandez.I, Santiago (rapid) 2009 260
Apicella.M-Vaisman.V, French Championship, Angers 1990 173
Aronian.L-Annakov.B, Moscow 1995 175
Arutinian.D-Kashlinskaya.A, Olomouc 2009 97
Asrian.K-Eliseev.A, Moscow 1996 296
Bareev.E-Onischuk.A, Elista Olympiad 1998 214
Bellin.R-Lie.K, Gausdal 1996 200
Berges.D-Delorme.A, Fouesnant 1999 38
Bosch.J-Ftacnik.L, Hamburg 2009 93
Bosch.J-Kabatianski.A, Dutch League 2009 47
Bricard.E-Todorov.O, St Affrique 2000 191
Bromann.T-Molvig.H, Borup 2009 64
Buyakhin-Botvinnik.M, USSR 1968 181
Chekhov.S-Sokolovsky.V, Voronezh 2009 107
Chernyshov.K-Kosteniuk.A, Moscow 2001 196
Chernyshov.K-Panchenko.A, Zalakaros 2003 184
Conquest.S-Sokolov.A, Portuguese Team Championship 2006 58
Cottegnie.F-Scarani.A, correspondence 2002 34
Dao.T-Babu.N, Udaipur 2000 217
Degraeve.J-Buscara.S, Le Touquet 2007 255
Dizdar.G-Sinanovic.M, Pula 1998 277
Duckworth.M-Lakdawala.C, US G/60 Championship, Commerce 1998 206
Feygin.M-Roobol.M, Dutch League 2007 239
Fier.A-Lima.D, Vitoria 2006 100
Fischer.R-Petrosian.T.V, 9th matchgame, Buenos Aires 1971 160
Fominyh.A-Hossain.E, Dhaka 2004 274
Gelfand.B-Nikolic.P, Munich 1994 211

Grachev.B-Lakdawala.C, Internet blitz 2007 .... *178*

Grischuk.A-Brynell.S, German League 2002 .... *118*

Hammer.J-Menacher.M, Balatonlelle 2005... *69*

Hasangatin.R-Tishin.D, Alushta 2005 .... *202*

Hasangatin.R-Trombik.K, Karvina 2006.. *194*

Hector.J-Bromann.T, Stockholm 2002 .... *128*

Hector.J-Evdokimov.A, Helsingor 2008.. *90*

Hector.J-Fridh.A, Swedish Championship, Malmo 1986.................................. *79*

Hector.J-Howell.D, St Helier 2005... *104*

Hector.J-Koneru.H, Wijk aan Zee 2003... *55*

Hector.J-Moberg.K, Swedish Team Championship 2001 .... *62*

Hector.J-Sprenger.J, Hamburg 2003 .... *60*

Ibragimov.I-Tomasic.R, Djakovo 1994 .... *300*

Ionescu.C-Yewdokimov.O, Bern 1992 .... *285*

Kamsky.G-Akobian.V, US Championship, Saint Louis 2009 .... *146*

Kamsky.G-Blatny.P, New York (rapid) 2004.. *290*

Karpov.A-Klimas.A, Sao Paulo (simul) 2003.. *279*

Kasparov.G-Beliavsky.A, 9th matchgame, Moscow 1983 .... *271*

Kasparov.G-Gurevich.M, Sarajevo 2000.. *114*

Khachian.M-Abrahamyan.T, Los Angeles 2010... *15*

Khachian.M-Donchenko.A, Moscow 1995 .... *23*

Khachian.M-Koniushkov.I, Moscow 1996 .... *53*

Khachian.M-Kostin.A, Pardubice 1996 .... *13*

Khachian.M-Miller.I, US Open, Los Angeles 2003... *51*

Khachian.M-Strikovic.A, Cannes 1996 .... *81*

Khachiyan.M-Dolinskij.B, Moscow 1996 .... *168*

Kobalia.M-Nguyen Ngoc Truong, Al Ain 2008.. *163*

Korchnoi.V-Vaganian.R, Skelleftea 1989 .... *134*

Kozul.Z-Brkic.A, Zagreb 2006.. *45*

Krivonogov.A-Yanin.P, Novgorod 1998.. *229*

Krug.K-Tiemann.C, Dresden 2008.. *42*

L'Ami.E-Luch.M, Maastricht 2007 .... *153*

Lakdawala.C-Baker.B, San Diego (rapid) 2007 .... *221*

Lakdawala.C-Baker.B, San Diego (rapid) 2010 .... *75*

Lakdawala.C-Barquin, San Diego (rapid) 2010... *105*

Lakdawala.C-Lozano.M, San Diego (rapid) 2010 .... *72*

Lakdawala.C-Sevilliano.E, San Diego (rapid) 2010 .... *124*

Leko.P-Topalov.V, Frankfurt (rapid) 1999... *246*

Magem Badals.J-Matamoros Franco .C, Ubeda 1996 .... *142*

Mamedyarov.S-Dukaczewski.P, Bled Olympiad 2002 .... *84*

McKenzie.C-Rey.S, correspondence 1995 .... *98*

Motylev.A-Czebe.A, Mainz (rapid) 2008 .... *257*

Motylev.A-Kasimdzhanov.R, Wijk aan Zee 2009 .... *249*

Mrkvicka.J-Sicker.R, correspondence 1998 .... *187*

Nabaty.T-Lerner.K, Elkana 2007 .... *26*

Najer.E-Blatny.P, Pardubice 2007 .... *293*

Nakamura.H-Akobian.V, Montreal 2008 .... *149*

Nakamura.H-Becerra Rivero.J, US Online League 2009 .... *19*

Nakamura.H-Kis.L, Philadelphia 2006 .... *244*

Nestorovic.N-Pezelj.S, Zlatibor 2007 .... *40*

Onischuk.A-Shkuro.I, Ukrainian Team Championship 2009 .... *288*

Peters.J-Lakdawala.C, Southern California State Championship 2008 .... *156*

Polgar.J-Rivas Pastor.M, Salamanca 1989 .... *140*

Popov.V-Neiksans.A, Pardubice 2000 .... *226*

Raetsky.A-Bojic.Z, Zurich 2003 .... *282*

Reprintsev.A-Kachar.V, Moscow 1999 .... *103*

Réti.R-Tartakower.S, Vienna 1919 .... *11*

Richter.K-Rogmann.G, Berlin 1937 .... *6*

Rublevsky.S-Chepukaitis.G, St Petersburg 2001 .... *236*

Savchenko.S-Babar.M, Bad Wiessee 2000 .... *232*

Sergienko.S-Mukhin.A, Voronezh 1999 .... *231*

Shabalov.A-Zlotnikov.M, Mashantucket 1999 .... *241*

Short.N-Beliavsky.A, Dortmund 1995 .... *139*

Smeets.J-De Jager.J, Dutch League 2010 .... *110*

Sokolov.I-Weick.B, Mainz (rapid) 2003 .... *219*

Spassky.B-Gilquin.G, Corsica (rapid) 1997 .... *171*

Spraggett.K-Defrance.L, Metz 2007 .... *252*

Steinitz.W-Winawer.S, Paris 1867 .... *131*

Tal.M-Benko.P, Bled/Zagreb/Belgrade Candidates 1959 .... *268*

Tal.M-Champion.W, Boston (simul) 1988 .... *224*

Vaganian.R-Adamski.J, Copenhagen 2006 .... *66*

Varga.Z-Lengyel.B, Budapest 1994 .... *165*

Veresov.G-Smolianow, Minsk 1963 .... *87*

Vogler.T-Balzar.A, German League 1991 .... *31*

Vorobiov.E-Rychagov.A, Aghios Kirykos 2009 .... *121*

Yilmazyerli.M-Song.R, Singapore 2007 .... *36*

a complete repertoire
based on Nc3 and Nc6

Cyrus Lakdawala

a ferocious
opening repertoire

Christoph Wisnewski

play 1...Nc6!
a complete chess opening repertoire for Black

EVERYMAN CHESS
www.everymanchess.com

Contents

Bibliography   *4*

Preface: Why 1...♘c6?   *6*

Part One: Black vs. 1 e4 – Nimzowitsch Defence   *8*

1   1 e4 ♘c6: Rare Second Moves for White   *10*

2   1 e4 ♘c6 2 d4 d5 3 exd5 ♕xd5   *24*

3   1 e4 ♘c6 2 d4 d5 3 e5 f6   *51*

4   1 e4 ♘c6 2 d4 d5 3 ♘c3 e6   *61*

5   1 e4 ♘c6 2 ♘f3 ♘f6   *74*

Part Two: Black vs. 1 d4 – Chigorin Defence   *94*

6   1 d4 d5 2 ♘f3 ♘c6 and other Rare Second Moves   *96*

7   1 d4 d5 2 c4 ♘c6 3 ♘c3 ♘f6 (4 ♗g5; 4 cxd5)   *127*

8   1 d4 d5 2 c4 ♘c6 3 ♘c3 ♘f6 4 ♘f3 dxc4   *140*

9   1 d4 d5 2 c4 ♘c6 3 ♘f3 ♗g4 (4 ♕a4; 4 e3; 4 ♘c3)   *159*

10   1 d4 d5 2 c4 ♘c6 3 ♘f3 ♗g4 4 cxd5 ♗xf3   *174*

11   1 d4 d5 2 c4 ♘c6 3 e3 and 3 cxd5   *186*

Part Three: Black vs. 1 c4 – 1...♘c6   *213*

12   1 c4 ♘c6 – Rare White Second Moves   *214*

13   1 c4 ♘c6 2 ♘c3 e5 (3 e3; 3 g3)   *224*

14   1 c4 ♘c6 2 ♘c3 e5 3 ♘f3 ♘f6   *236*

Part Four: Black vs. 1 ♘f3 – 1...♘c6   *257*

15   1 ♘f3 ♘c6   *258*

Index of Complete Games   *264*

Bibliography

Books

1...Sc6! aus allen Lagen, H.Keilhack & R.Schlenker (Schachverlag Kania 2003)
Colle, London and Blackmar-Diemer Systems, T.Harding (Batsford 1979)
Dangerous Weapons: The French, J.Watson (Everyman 2007)
The Dynamic Réti, N.Davies (Everyman 2004)
The Main Line French: 3 ♘c3, S.Pedersen (Gambit 2001)
Modernes Skandinavisch, M.Wahls (Chessgate 1997)
Nunn's Chess Openings, J.Nunn, G.Burgess, J.Emms & J.Gallagher (Gambit/Everyman 1999)
Pirc Alert, L.Alburt & A.Chernin (CIRC 2003)
Play the Open Games as Black, J.Emms (Gambit 2001)
Secrets of Opening Surprises Vol. 3, J.Bosch (New in Chess 2005)
Die Tschigorin-Verteidigung, V.Bronznik (Schachverlag Kania 2001)

Chess Software and Journals
BlitzIn
ChessBase 8.0
Crafty 19.01
Junior6

MegaBase 2006
Chess Informants 1-97
New in Chess Yearbooks

1000 Opening Traps, K.Müller & R.Knaak (ChessBase 2006)

Albin Counter-Gambit, L.Henris (ChessBase 2003)

Colle-System, D.Oleinikov (ChessBase 2003)

Dutch Defence A90-A99, B.Schipkov (ChessBase 2004)

English Opening 1 c4 e5 (A20-A29), M.Marin (ChessBase 2003)

French with 3 ♘c3, K.Neven (ChessBase 2000)

Modern Chess Openings 1...♘c6!?, I.Berdichevsky & A.Kalinin (Convekta 2005)

Nimzovich Defense Ultimate CD, H.Myers (ChessCentral 1999)

Philidor Defence, A.Bangiev (ChessBase 2001)

Queen's Gambit Accepted D20-D29, B.Schipkov (ChessBase 2001)

Die Tschigorin-Verteidigung, M.Breutigam (ChessBase 2000)

Websites

www.chessclub.com

www.chesslab.com

www.chesslive.com

www.chesspublishing.com

www.chessvibes.com

www.chessville.com

www.kenilworthchessclub.org

Preface: Why 1...♞c6?

Young players expose themselves to grave risks when they blindly imitate the innovations of masters without themselves first checking all the details and consequences of these innovations. – Alexander Alekhine

I have come across many quotes during my sixteen-year chess career, but I have never seen a quote more to the point than the one mentioned above. Don't get me wrong, losing a game without really knowing why happens more than you would expect. But if such a game goes like "hey, I am ± according to blah-blah-blah" (Move 16) followed by "hmm, what exactly is happening here" (Move 20) and "I resign, good game" (Move 25), there is hardly anything that is more frustrating. Luckily, I was spared that kind of experience in my youth, but if I told you that this was due to my superior opening skills, if questioned I would have to admit that I was overstating it a little. In fact, my opening skills were virtually non-existent, and while playing intuitively is OK if you are a kid looking for fun at the chess board, an ambitious player actually needs a different approach.

That said, I gladly caught at the offer of my club mates to lend one or two of their books, in order to build up a suitable opening repertoire for Black where I would actually understand what I was doing. But as soon as I took a look at their libraries, my head started to spin: which opening system to choose? More than 350 pages on just one line in a book written by Kindermann & Dirr about the French Winawer, a wide range of different Sicilians, not to mention the various Open Games. And what to play against 1 d4 ? To cut a long story short, I felt lost – until **1...♞c6!** stepped to the plate.

What this book has to offer
I know that many players were looking forward to reading this book, and it is likely that I will disappoint at least a few with my compilation of recommended

lines and ideas. But I hope that you will eventually reconcile with my ideas, as they are the result of more than six years of refining in thousands of games on and off the internet and thus are fondly covered. And to commend my findings to you some more, I have also tried to explain my choices, where appropriate, giving reasons why I neglected certain lines.

Following my recommendations will provide you with a coherent repertoire against all the main openings White can play. But before getting too excited, there are a few things I want you to keep in mind: the opening repertoire presented in this book is no panacea; neither will you learn it by just skimming over the pages; nor will you then exclusively give your opponents an easy wipeout. There will be a great deal of work involved, but once you have mastered the ideas your score with Black should considerably improve. How I can guarantee that? I can't. But looking at my tremendous improvement after picking up 1...♘c6, I certainly like your chances. And who knows... if you are still looking for an opening system for White, you could adopt the ideas from this book by playing 1 a3!?.

How this book is organized

Avid readers will notice that, while I do my best to keep up the 1...♘c6 spirit, some lines I recommend actually transpose into different opening systems, the ...e5 English in Part 3 (Chapters 12-14) of this book probably being the most prominent example. It contradicts the predominant unorthodox flavour of 1...♘c6, but this is exactly what I want. While the Chigorin Defence, which I will be covering in Part 2 (Chapters 6-11), may already be acknowledged as a viable opening system, the Nimzowitsch Defence still struggles with a shadowy existence. It's time to change that, and this is where our journey begins...

Part One

Black vs. 1 e4: The Nimzowitsch Defence

The Nimzowitsch Defence, **1 e4 ♘c6,** may by a long way be the 'weirdest' opening system covered in this book. Moving the queen's knight on move one may indeed seem bizarre, but it surely does have its merits. As you may notice over the course of this book, there are hardly any motifs that are typical for 1...♘c6, but instead general game plans, each depending on the actual opening line. Therefore, I will provide you with a short overview of possible objectives before each game, though of course I will also try to give you a few general impressions. To start with, let us look at some basic ideas of the Nimzowitsch Defence.

No early commitment

There are two things every player should pursue in the opening phase: development and partial control of the centre. Developing the queen's knight complies with both aspects and has the additional benefit of not presenting White with a target he can shoot at. It is now his turn to dictate the rhythm, something many players are uncomfortable with. This often results in improper set-ups, and how those are to be treated will be examined in Chapter 1.

Clash in the Centre!

The most principled answer to the Nimzowitsch Defence is **2 d4**, immediately trying to seize the centre and therefore effectively forcing Black to strike back with **2...d5**. White has different alternatives to respond to this counterstroke, the most straightforward being 3 exd5. The idea is to enforce c2-c4 and d4-d5 on a long-term basis, gaining space in the process; but at the moment, thanks to his slight lead in development, Black can exhibit significant counterplay against the white d-pawn. White is not able to solve all his problems adequately, as we will see in Chapter 2.

Kingside attack!

Another frequently played system after

2 d4 d5 is initiated by **3 e5**. White seizes more space in the centre, which seems additionally to be justified by the fact that Black, in contrast to the Advance French or the Advance Caro-Kann, cannot attack the white d-pawn with ...c7-c5 (or ...c6-c5). However, given the closed character of the position, there are other plans Black can employ. Many times attacking on the kingside is a key idea, which is often surprising to White players as a black kingside attack is something you don't see too often after 1 e4. When it comes to strategy, the whole system is quite instructive, and to get an idea of what I'm talking about I invite you to examine Chapter 3 in more detail.

Tricky Transposition

As you will notice, transpositions play an important role in this book. As a result, many games derive from a different move order; so wherever necessary, I have adjusted the move order for the sake of convenience.

The move **3 ♘c3** is a problem to many Nimzowitsch devotees. White is ready and willing to temporarily sacrifice a pawn with 3...dxe4 4 d5 ♘e5 5 ♗f4 ♘g6 6 ♗g3 – the resulting variations are sharp and quite dangerous for Black. This line is one good reason for

many players to abandon the Nimzowitsch Defence altogether.

But there is no need to despair: Black can play **3...e6!?**, transposing into a rather exotic line of the French Defence. Numerous new ideas have been recently introduced, so Black players shouldn't be reluctant to use it. Detailed coverage can be found in Chapter 4.

Activity versus Structure

The most sensible and (for Black) most dangerous way to meet the Nimzowitsch Defence is definitely with **2 ♘f3**. White develops a piece and adds pressure to the centre without presenting the d-pawn as a possible target. Many things have been tried, from passive (2...d6) to dubious (2...d5?!) to incorrect (2...f5?), but in my opinion it's clear as daylight: if White refuses to put a pawn on d4, it is the e-pawn that needs to be attacked! **2...♘f6** is the move that promises very interesting positions. Usually White is provided with more space and the healthier pawn structure, but in return Black gets the pair of bishops and half-open files to play with. The whole system is relatively unexplored and leaves more than enough room to act out your creativity. Anyway, some exciting ideas can be found in Chapter 5.

Chapter One

1 e4 ♞c6: Rare Second Moves for White

Trying to establish the Nimzowitsch Defence, **1 e4 ♞c6**, as an accepted opening system has always been like tilting at windmills.

Many reactions have crossed my path during the last four years: amusement to commiseration to sheer disgust, but delicate handling was rarely one of them. Most of the time even diligent players do not prepare more than one line against the Nimzowitsch Defence, and many players do not consider it even to be a viable system. This often leads to a certain sloppiness, with players thinking

that the opening can be played arbitrarily – a faulty premise, as I would like to show you in this chapter, in which we take a look at White's rare second moves.

White plays 2 c4?!

The position after **1 e4 ♞c6 2 c4?!** can also derive from the English Opening (via the move order 1 c4 ♞c6 2 e4), although you will not encounter it regularly either way. The idea, if there is one, is to get a good grip on d5, but the drawback of this approach is evident:

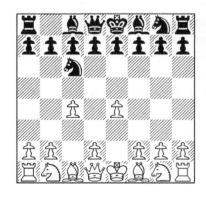

After **2...e5**, among other things the

dark squares become chronically weak, with d4 literally deteriorating to a 'black hole'. This should be duly exploited, and our first game is a nice illustration of how to do just that.

Game 1
T.Redlicki-M.Wodzislawski
Malbork 2000

1 e4 ♘c6 2 c4?! e5 3 ♘c3

3 ♘f3 ♗c5 4 ♘c3 usually transposes to the text. Note that the common fork trick 4 ♘xe5?? does not work here because of 4...♘xe5 5 d4 ♗b4+.

3...♗c5

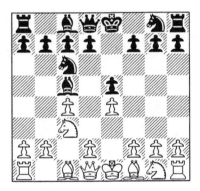

4 d3

Instead:

a) 4 ♘f3 d6 5 d3 ♘ge7, intending ...0-0 and ...f7-f5, is a plan suggested by British GM John Emms. This was perfectly carried out in the game P.Petek-J.Krajnak, Decin 1996, which continued 6 ♗e3 0-0 7 ♗e2 (Black should not fear 7 ♗xc5 dxc5 as his control over d4 will be everlasting, while a white knight hopping to d5 can be easily kicked out

by ...c7-c6) 7...♘d4 8 0-0 f5 9 exf5 ♘exf5 10 ♗xd4 ♗xd4 11 ♘xd4 ♘xd4 and Black exploited the weakness of the d4-square, just according to plan.

A game I watched between two unknown players on the Internet Chess Club revealed the true potential of Black's plan:

b) After 4 g3 d6 5 ♗g2 ♘ge7 6 ♘ge2 0-0 7 0-0 f5 (Black should not wait too long before initiating his assault; after 7...♗e6 8 d3 ♕d7 9 ♔h1 f5 10 f4 Black was only slightly better in V.Tarasova-I.Paulet, European Girls Championship, Chalkidiki 2001) 8 d3 f4!, a rather typical pawn sacrifice was the prelude to a dangerous attack. The game concluded 9 gxf4 ♗g4 10 f5 (if 10 fxe5 dxe5 and White also has difficulties coming to grips with his situation, as Black's initiative on the kingside is very dangerous) 10...♘d4 11 ♗e3 ♘f3+ 12 ♔h1 (after 12 ♗xf3 ♗xf3 13 ♗xc5 ♘xf5!, intending 14...♕g5 or 14...♕h4, is decisive) 12...♘xf5! 13 exf5 ♕h4 14 h3 ♗xh3 15 ♗xf3 ♗g4+ 16 ♔g1 ♗xf3 0-1.

4...d6 5 ♗e3

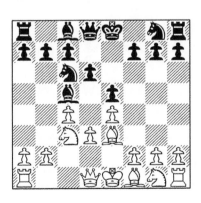

5...♗b6

5...♘ge7 is also a perfectly valid move, following the same idea introduced in the note to White's fourth move. In the game Ed.Lasker-L.Evans, Havana 1952, White tried 6 ♗e2 0-0 7 ♘f3 ♘d4 8 a3 a5 9 ♗xd4 exd4 10 ♘a4, and now Black left his bishop where it was and played 10...♘g6 – a strategy that paid off, as after 11 ♕d2 ♗d7 12 ♘xc5 dxc5 13 ♕g5 ♕xg5 14 ♘xg5 f5 15 g3 h6 16 exf5 ♗xf5 17 ♘e4 ♖ae8 18 f3 ♗xe4 19 fxe4 ♘e5 the black knight was superior to the white bishop.

6 ♘f3

6 ♘d5 is premature as it allows Black to trade more potential defenders of d4. After 6...♗a5+ 7 ♗d2 (7 ♘c3 is again answered by 7...♘ge7 followed by ...0-0 and ...f7-f5) 7...♗xd2+ 8 ♕xd2 ♘ge7 9 ♘f3 0-0 10 ♗e2 ♗g4 11 0-0 ♗xf3 12 ♗xf3 ♘xd5 13 cxd5 ♘d4 Black has a clear advantage due to his far superior knight.

6...♘ge7 7 ♘d5 ♗a5+ 8 ♘d2 0-0 9 g4?!

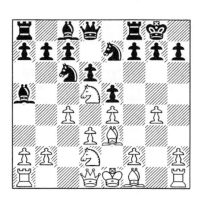

White understandably tries to prevent Black from playing ...f7-f5, but he does so at a high price. On the other hand, 9 ♗e2 f5 10 ♗g5 (10 f3 cannot

stop Black either: 10...♘xd5 11 cxd5 ♘e7 12 0-0 c6 13 dxc6 ♘xc6 and the d4-square will be exploited sooner or later, after which White is left with his puny bishop on e2) 10...h6 11 ♗xe7 ♘xe7 gives Black carte blanche to play on the kingside.

9...♘xd5 10 cxd5 ♘d4 11 ♗g2 c6

11...♕h4 looks tempting, but doesn't lead anywhere at the moment. White can play 12 h3 ♗d7 13 0-0 and it is not evident how Black should proceed.

12 dxc6 bxc6 13 0-0 ♗xd2! 14 ♗xd2 ♕b6

But now 14...♕h4 would have been good. After 15 f3 (or 15 h3 h5) 15...♖b8 16 ♗c3 ♗e6 White is virtually a piece down because of his poorly-placed bishop g2. The text move does no harm though.

15 ♗c3 ♘e6 16 ♖e1 ♗a6 17 ♕d2 ♖ab8 18 ♖e3 c5 19 b3 ♘f4 20 ♗f1 ♗c8

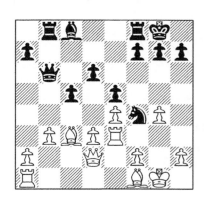

White is without any play, so Black can calmly shuffle his pieces.

21 ♖g3 ♗e6 22 ♕e1 ♖b7 23 h4

Desperately seeking counterplay, but the result is just overextension.

23...♕d8 24 h5 ♕h4 25 f3 ♕e7 26 ♗d2

g5?!

Although not evident yet, the drawbacks to this move will soon show. Retaining control of the dark squares with 26...♕g5 is better: White cannot really loosen the grip, while Black can quietly improve his position. After 27 ♕f2 (27 ♕c1 allows 27...f5!, cracking the white pawn chain) 27...f6 he can choose between attacking on the kingside by opening the h-file with ...g7-g6, and playing on the queenside with ...♖a8 and rushing his a-pawn forward.

27 ♔h2 ♖a8 28 ♖g1 f6 29 ♗xf4 gxf4

29...exf4 seemed more logical, but then White can try to break free with 30 d4!?. After 30...cxd4 31 ♖d1 ♖c8 32 ♖xd4 the weak d6-pawn should provide White with sufficient counterplay.

30 ♕h4?!

Returning the favour. White had to retain the possibility of g4-g5 with 30 h6. Then after 30...a5 31 ♕h4 a4 32 g5 f5 33 ♗h3 fxe4 34 dxe4 axb3 35 axb3 White would have had definite counterplay.

30...h6

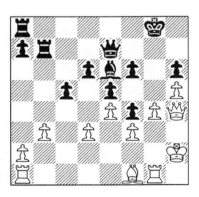

Now the door is closed, and Black can turn his attention to the queenside again.

31 ♗h3 ♔h7 32 ♖g2 a5 33 ♖b2 a4 34 ♖ab1 axb3 35 axb3 ♖ab8 36 ♕e1 ♖b4 37 ♕c3 ♕f7 38 ♕d2 ♔g7 39 ♕c3 ♗xb3 40 d4

Desperation, but what else is there to do?

40...exd4?!

Black starts to lose the thread. The reason he did not play 40...cxd4 41 ♕d2 ♖4b7, followed by ...♗e6, is beyond my understanding.

41 ♕d2 ♖8b6 42 ♕xf4 c4 43 ♖g2 ♖4b5 44 ♖bg1 ♖g5 45 ♕d2 ♖bb5?

45...d3 46 f4 ♖c5 47 g5 fxg5 48 fxg5 ♔h8! was the only way to maintain the advantage. Now White strikes back.

46 f4 ♖gc5 47 ♕xd4 ♔h7 48 g5 hxg5 49 e5 ♕d5 50 ♕f2 ♖c7 1-0

And Black resigned in view of 51 exf6.

It is hard for me to believe that it is actually possible to lose a game from a position like the one after move 19, but I am confident that you will not share this fate. Pursue the strategy outlined and you will be amply rewarded.

White plays 2 d3

I admit that I have not been fully able to uncover the secret why anyone would want to play **2 d3**. If I were jaunty I would claim that this move is highly prophylactic and that it pays tribute to the fact that Black is ready to jump at the centre with ...d7-d5. But more realistically, it seems that White is merely trying to lure Black into a

Reversed Philidor after **2...e5**. My excuses to all Philidor aficionados out there, but this is a demand I am more than happy to fulfil. The only thing I am willing to concede is that, with his extra move, White can equalize more easily.

> ## Game 2
> ### M.Autenrieth-T.Kabisch
> West German Junior
> Championships, Dortmund 1982

1 e4 ♘c6 2 d3

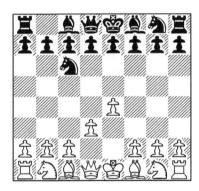

2...e5

For those who don't like to play against the Philidor, I recommend 2...♘f6 3 ♘f3 d5 4 e5 ♘d7 5 d4 ♘b6, which transposes to Game 20 in Chapter 5 (see the note to White's 4th move), the only difference being that the white queen's knight still is on b1 instead of c3.

3 ♘f3

According to Emms, 3 f4!? is 'the only way for White to make things exciting'. Yet, after 3...♘f6 4 ♘c3 (4 ♘f3

exf4 5 ♗xf4 d5 6 e5 ♘h5 7 ♗g5 ♗e7 8 ♗xe7 ♕xe7 is also better for Black, while 4 fxe5 ♘xe5 5 ♘f3 ♘xf3+ 6 ♕xf3 d5 is at least a quick equalizer) 4...♗b4 5 fxe5 ♘xe5 6 ♘f3 ♕e7 7 ♗f4 ♘g6 8 ♗g5 d5 the black position was favourable in V.Vorotnikov-M.Berkovich, Moscow 1990.

3...♘f6 4 ♗e2

Instead, 4 g3 aims at a King's Indian set-up (after 4 ♘c3 Black naturally plays 4...d5 with no problems), but Black can obtain a good position with 4...d5 5 ♘bd2 (if 5 exd5 ♕xd5! 6 ♗g2 ♗g4 7 h3 ♗h5 8 g4 ♗g6 9 0-0 0-0-0 10 ♘c3 ♕e6 left Black with a good game in J.Heissler-D.Werner, German League 1997) 5...♗c5 6 ♗g2 0-0 7 0-0 ♖e8 8 c3 dxe4 9 dxe4 a5, followed by ...b7-b6 and ...♗c8-b7.

4...d5 5 ♘bd2

After 5 exd5 Black should play 5...♕xd5,

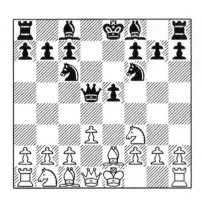

when White can choose between two sensible moves:

a) 6 ♘c3 ♗b4 is a kind of reversed Ruy Lopez, Steinitz Defence. This line is not very popular for good reasons:

Black had no problems due to his firm control of the centre after 7 ♗d2 ♗xc3 8 ♗xc3 0-0 in J.Hansen-H.Hjort, Vejle 1974.

b) 6 0-0 circumvents the pin but also gives Black time to establish control over the central dark squares. After 6...♗c5 7 ♘c3 ♕d6 8 ♗g5 ♗g4 9 h3 ♗xf3 10 ♗xf3 0-0-0 Black is not worse.

5...♗c5 6 0-0 0-0 7 c3 a5

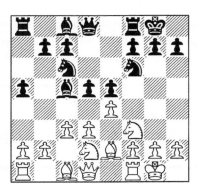

8 a4

Alternatively:

a) 8 b3 is another common move, but the bishop is needed on its current diagonal as well. Following 8...♖e8 9 a3 h6 10 ♗b2 dxe4 11 dxe4 ♘h5, the weak squares in the white camp cannot be denied.

b) A.Groszpeter-P.Lukacs, Budapest 1981, saw a different plan: 8 ♕c2 ♕e7 9 ♘b3 ♗b6 10 ♗g5. Black reacted well with 10...dxe4 11 dxe4 h6 12 ♗h4 ♕e6 13 ♘bd2 ♘h5 14 ♖fe1 ♘f4 15 ♗f1, but now instead of the committal 15...g5, Black should have played 15...♖e8 and slowly improved his position.

c) 8 ♘xe5 would be nice if it worked, but 8...♘xe5 9 d4 ♘xe4 leaves

Black ahead.

8...h6 9 ♕c2 ♗e6 10 h3 ♕d7 11 ♖e1 ♖ad8 12 ♗f1 ♖fe8

After centralizing all his pieces, Black is obviously better.

13 ♘b3 ♗b6 14 ♗e3 ♗xe3 15 ♖xe3 b6 16 ♘bd2 d4!

Once again, occupying the d4-square is the key idea.

17 ♖ee1

17 cxd4 ♘xd4 18 ♘xd4 ♕xd4 19 ♕xc7 does not work. After 19...♖c8! 20 ♕a7 ♕xb2 21 ♖d1 ♖c2 the black pieces are pouring in.

17...♘h5 18 ♖ec1 ♖e7 19 cxd4 ♘xd4 20 ♘xd4 ♕xd4 21 ♘f3 ♕d6 22 d4

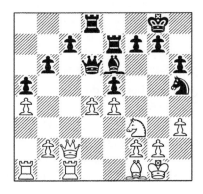

For the moment it seems that White is solving his problems, but Black stays ahead.

22...exd4 23 ♘xd4 c5 24 ♘f3

Or 24 ♘xe6 ♕xe6 and White has to choose between surrendering the e-pawn or the d-file.

24...♕f4 25 ♗e2

25 ♖d1 allows 25...♖xd1 26 ♕xd1 (if 26 ♖xd1 ♗xh3) 26...♖d7 (but not 26...♕xe4?? 27 ♕d8+) 27 ♕e2 ♘f6 28 ♖e1 ♖d8 with a commanding position.

25...♖ed7 26 ♖d1 ♘f6 27 e5 ♘d5 28 g3 ♘b4! 29 ♖xd7 ♖xd7 30 ♕xc5 ♕e4 31 ♕e3 ♕xe3 32 fxe3 ♗xh3

After a few tactical finesses Black has reached a technically won endgame. Nevertheless, precise play is required.

33 ♖c1 ♖e7

33...♘d3! 34 ♖c8+ ♔h7 35 b3 ♗e6 would have been even better.

34 ♖c4 ♗e6

34...♗d7, forcing 35 b3 (35 ♖c7? runs into 35...♘d5) 35...♗e6 36 ♖c3 ♘a2! 37 ♖d3 ♘c1, is another improvement. Now White manages to achieve just enough counterplay.

35 ♖d4 ♗d5 36 ♔f2 ♗xf3 37 ♔xf3 ♖xe5 38 ♗c4 ♘c6 39 ♖d6 ♖c5 40 ♗d5 ♘b4 41 ♗b3 ♘c6 42 ♗d5 ♘e5+ 43 ♔e4 ♘c4 44 ♖d8+ ♔h7 45 b3 f5+ 46 ♔d4 ♘a3 47 ♗g8+ ♔h8

Or 47...♔g6 48 ♖d6+ ♔g5 49 ♖xb6.

48 ♗e6+ ♔h7 49 ♗g8+ ½-½

Fair enough. As long as White can only scrape a draw when Black shows technical deficiencies, I will not complain. And if your opponent is incidentally a Philidor expert, deliberately playing 2 d3 in order to get his favourite opening with an extra move, you can still choose the set-up recommended in the note to Black's second move.

White plays 2 f4?!

We will now continue our toil with obscure opening schemes by looking at **2 f4?!**. Again, even after extensive creative thinking I could not come up with a good reason why this move should be played at all, so I will limit myself to showing you how it is best handled.

> ### Game 3
> ### J.Koller-M.Lammers
> German Junior Championships, Willingen 2004

1 e4 ♘c6 2 f4?!

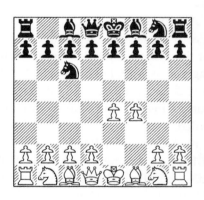

2...d5 3 exd5

Instead:

a) After 3 e5 the position shows a structural resemblance to positions in Chapter 3, one difference being that Black has saved the move ...f7-f6. That said, 3...♘h6 still seems logical, but 3...d4! is even better.

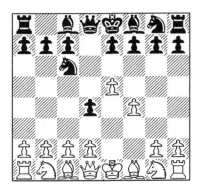

For example:

a1) After 4 ♘f3 Black can move his queen into a safe position with 4...♕d5!. The game F.Pearson-W.Faxon, Framingham 1993, continued 5 ♘a3 (5 g3 is strongly met by 5...♘b4!, the ideas being ...♕e4+, ...♘xc2+ and ...d3, which cannot all be coped with at once) 5...♗g4 (5...♕e4+ 6 ♗e2 ♕xf4 is too greedy: after 7 ♘b5 ♔d8 8 d3 ♕f5 9 0-0 White has more than enough compensation for the pawn) 6 ♗e2 (now if 6 ♗c4?! ♕e4+ 7 ♕e2 ♗xf3 8 gxf3 Black can take the f4-pawn) 6...e6 7 0-0? (7 d3 is better, but after 7...♘h6 8 h3 ♗h5 9 g4 ♗g6, followed by ...f7-f6, Black still enjoys an advantage) 7...♗xa3 8 bxa3 d3! 9 cxd3 ♗xf3 10 ♗xf3 ♕d4+ 11 ♔h1 ♕xa1 and White could have resigned with a clear conscience.

a2) 4 ♗c4 prevents 4...♕d5, but does not solve White's development problems. Black, on the other hand, can play 4...♘h6 5 ♘f3 ♗g4 6 0-0 e6 7 d3 ♘f5 and once again a knight is superior to a bishop, A.Razumovski-V.Sukho-

rukov, Russian Cup, Smolensk 1997.

a3) 4 d3 ♘h6 5 ♘d2 (after 5 g3 the Israeli GM Gadi Rechlis showed in a blitz game against an unknown player how the position should be handled: 5...♗g4 6 ♘f3 f6 7 exf6 exf6 8 ♗g2 ♗b4+ 9 ♔f2 0-0 and Black is clearly better) 5...♗g4 6 ♘gf3 ♘f5 7 ♘e4 e6 8 ♗e2 ♗e7 9 0-0 ♕d7 10 h3 ♗xf3 11 ♗xf3 0-0-0 and White has problems with his dark squares.

b) 3 ♘c3 just provokes 3...d4 4 ♘b1 (instead, V.Petrov-O.Attia, Paris 1995, continued 4 ♘ce2 e5 5 ♘f3 and now Black uncorked the spectacular 5...f5!? 6 d3 ♗d6 7 fxe5 ♗xe5 8 ♘xe5 ♘xe5 9 ♗f4 ♘g6 10 ♕d2 ♘f6 11 exf5 ♗xf5 and this time the white light-squared bishop has a rather miserable existence) 4...e5 5 ♘f3 (5 d3 weakens the dark squares once more; Black is better either after 5...♗b4+ 6 c3 dxc3 7 ♘xc3 ♘f6 or 7 bxc3 ♗d6) and Black can even hang on to the pawn with 5...exf4 6 d3 g5.

3...♕xd5 4 ♘c3 ♕d6

This is the most sensible square for the queen, retaining maximum mobil-

ity while having a look at the f-pawn.
5 ♞f3

5 ♗b5 ♗d7 6 d3 ♞f6 7 ♞f3 a6 8 ♗c4 ♞d4 9 ♞g5 e6 10 ♞ge4 ♞xe4 11 ♞xe4 ♕b6 12 c3 ♞f5 13 d4 ♗c6 14 ♗d3 ♗e7 led to a comfortable game for Black in X.Arroyo Valera-A.Heredia Tarrats, Sants 2001.

5...♗g4 6 ♗c4

Unpinning the knight with 6 ♗e2 was probably the better choice. 6...0-0-0 7 d3 (7 0-0 ♞d4 8 ♞e5 ♞xe2+ 9 ♞xe2 ♗h5 10 ♕e1 f6 11 ♞f3 e6 12 d4 ♗xf3! 13 ♖xf3 f5 left the white bishop restrained in J.Petro-P.Dudas, Miskolc 1997) 7...♕c5 8 ♞e4 ♕b6 9 ♞e5 was played in A.Norris-J.Sherwin, British League 1999, and now 9...♞xe5 10 fxe5 ♗f5 would have been only slightly better for Black.

6...0-0-0 7 d3

7 ♗xf7?! ♕xf4 8 ♗b3 ♞d4 is nothing White should be aiming at.

7...♞d4 8 ♞e4

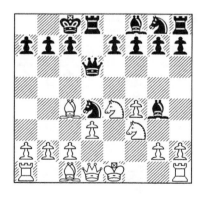

8...♕b6?!

But this is the wrong place for the queen. 8...♕b4+! is clearly better as 9 c3? runs into 9...♞xf3+ 10 gxf3 ♕xc4! 11

fxg4 ♖xd3 and Black is a healthy pawn up, while 11 dxc4 ♖xd1+ 12 ♔xd1 ♗xf3+ simply loses.

9 ♞eg5 ♞h6 10 h3 ♗xf3 11 ♞xf3 ♞hf5 12 ♞xd4?!

Failing to rise to the occasion with 12 ♞e5!, when Black suddenly has difficulties protecting his only weakness, the f7-pawn. After 12...♞g3 (if 12...♞d6 then 13 ♗xf7 and it is hard to prove enough compensation for the pawn) there follows 13 ♖f1 ♞df5 (if 13...♞xf1 14 ♔xf1 and Black can't defend f7) 14 ♕f3 ♞xf1 15 ♔xf1 ♞h6 16 ♗xf7 with good play for the exchange. Certainly this was the lesser of two evils for White when compared to the course of the actual game, where Black is now back in control.

12...♕xd4 13 ♕e2 e6 14 c3 ♕b6 15 ♕f3 h5 16 a4 a5 17 d4 ♗e7 18 g3 c5!

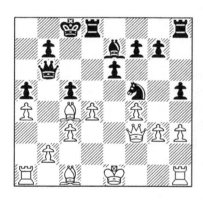

With a useful lead in development it certainly makes sense to open the position.

19 dxc5 ♗xc5 20 ♗d3 ♖xd3! 21 ♕xd3 ♗f2+ 22 ♔f1 ♞xg3+ 23 ♔g2 ♞xh1 24 ♔xh1

Being up in material and development, Black is winning.

24...♕c6+ 25 ♔h2 h4 26 ♕e2 ♗g3+ 27 ♔g1 ♖d8 28 ♗d2 ♕d5 29 ♗e1 ♕f5 30 ♕c4+ ♔b8 31 ♗xg3 hxg3 32 ♔g2 ♖d2+ 33 ♔xg3 ♕g6+ 34 ♔f3 ♕g2+ 35 ♔e3 ♕f2+ 36 ♔e4 ♖e2+ 0-1

White plays 2 ♗b5

Improbable as it may sound, **2 ♗b5** is not as wacky as it looks. The main idea is to lure Black into playing 2...e5, after which White can gratefully transpose into the Ruy Lopez with 3 ♘f3, something Black is obviously not inclined to do. Instead, he should try to exploit the one drawback of 2 ♗b5 – the neglection of the g2-pawn! This is done best with **2...d5!**, asking for **3 exd5 ♕xd5** when Black is attacking both the bishop and the g-pawn.

This would leave White to choose between the alternatives 4 ♗xc6+ and 4 ♗f1 – an almost satirical situation. Therefore, he should look for third move alternatives, but those are thin on the ground. Anyway, Black has nothing to worry about.

Game 4
E.Gafner-V.Zolotukhin
Alushta 2005

1 e4 ♘c6 2 ♗b5

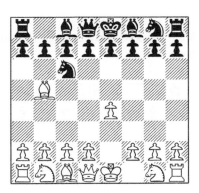

2...d5! 3 ♘c3

Instead, 3 ♗xc6+?! gives the bishop pair away for no reason; the temporary defect in Black's pawn structure after 3...bxc6 does not justify this course of action; for example, 4 e5 (4 exd5?! cxd5 is even worse, as it repairs the black pawns again) 4...c5 and Black reaches a favourable version of a French Defence.

As noted above, 3 exd5 ♕xd5 shows the defect of 2 ♗b5. White has nothing better than 4 ♗xc6+ (4 ♗f1?! leaves Black two tempi up, which is completely out of the question; while 4 ♘c3? ♕xg2 5 ♕f3 ♗h3! is a motif worth remembering) 4...♕xc6 and the pair of bishops promises a small advantage.

3...dxe4 4 ♕e2

Instead:

a) 4 ♘xe4 ♕d5! 5 ♕e2 ♗f5 6 ♘g3 was played in J.Plaskett-J.Speelman,

Gibraltar 2003, and now Black should have simply collected a pawn with 6...♗xc2.

b) 4 ♗xc6+ bxc6 5 ♘xe4 was subject of H.Schueler-C.Wisnewski, Hamburg 2003; then after 5...♘f6 6 ♘xf6+ exf6 the pair of bishops compensates for the crippled pawn structure.

4...♗d7 5 ♘xe4 ♘d4 6 ♗xd7+ ♕xd7 7 ♕d3 e5

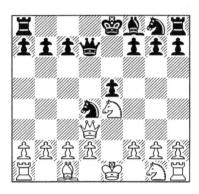

Black has comfortably equalized, with the position not being too sterile to play for a win.

8 c3 ♘e6 9 ♕xd7+ ♔xd7 10 ♘f3 ♗d6 11 d3 f5 12 ♘xd6?!

Although it is usually tempting to trade a knight for a bishop, this time White should have avoided it. 12 ♘eg5 would have maintained the balance.

12...cxd6 13 ♗e3 f4 14 ♗d2 g5 15 0-0-0 ♘f6 16 c4 g4 17 ♘h4 ♘d4 18 ♖he1 g3?!

But this is too optimistic. Black is trying to play for tricks but in the end is unsuccessful. Instead 18...♖hg8 19 ♗c3 ♖g5! would have left Black in control as the white knight cannot get back into play.

19 hxg3 ♘g4 20 ♖f1 fxg3 21 fxg3 ♖af8

22 ♔b1 ♘f2 23 ♗h6 ♘xd1 24 ♗xf8 ♘e3 25 ♖f6

Now White is even better, but this is not the last time the tables turn...

25...♘g4 26 ♗g7

Here 26 ♖xd6+ would have been possible as 26...♔c7 27 ♗g7 ♖g8 is met by 28 ♗xe5.

26...♘xf6 27 ♗xh8 ♘g4 28 ♘f3 ♘f5 29 ♔c1 h6 30 d4?! e4 31 ♘e1 ♘xg3 32 d5 h5 33 ♔d2 h4 34 ♗d4 a6 35 ♘c2 ♘h5 36 ♗e3 ♘e5 37 b3 b5 38 cxb5 axb5 39 ♗g5??

39...h3?

39...♘f3+! would have been better as 40 gxf3 loses to 40...h3.

40 gxh3 ♘f3+ 41 ♔e3 ♘xg5 42 ♘d4?

42 h4! would have drawn here.

42...♘f6 43 h4 ♘xd5+ 44 ♔e2 ♘f4+ 45 ♔f1 ♘f3 46 ♘xf3 exf3 47 a4 bxa4 48 bxa4 ♔e6?

Missing the important 48...♘h3! after which White will not be able to go after Black's d-pawn in time.

49 ♔f2 ♔f5 50 ♔xf3 ♘d5 51 a5 ♘c7 52 h5 ♔g5 53 ♔e4 ♔xh5 54 a6?

The final blunder. Instead, 54 ♔f5 followed by ♔f6 and ♔e7 would have drawn.

54...♔g6 55 a7 ♔f7 ½-½

According to *MegaBase 2006* this game ended in a draw, but now Black is simply winning as White cannot trade pawns.

White plays 2 ♘c3

I will conclude this chapter with the most sensible of all second move alternatives, **2 ♘c3**. Because of its close relationship to Chapter 4, I recommend **2...e6** as the move to play. Now White's best choice is indeed to transpose to Chapter 4 with 3 d4. Apart from that there are only a few alternatives worth mentioning, and it is no surprise that Black is not seriously put to the test by any of them.

Game 5
F.J.Dos Santos-C.Dolezal
Carilo 2005

---

1 e4 ♘c6 2 ♘c3 e6

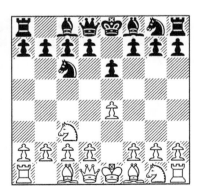

3 g3

The main line 3 d4 d5 is covered in

Chapter 4. White has also tried:

a) 3 ♗c4 is not a serious attempt to prevent ...d7-d5 after 3...♘f6.

b) 3 ♘f3 d5 4 exd5 exd5 5 d4 transposes to Stern-Alexopoulos (Game 17) also in Chapter 4.

c) Finally, 3 f4 has similar drawbacks to 2 f4 (as in Koller-Lammers): 3...d5 4 e5 d4 5 ♘e4 b6!? 6 ♗b5 ♗b7 7 d3 ♕d7 8 ♘f3 0-0-0 resulted in a space advantage for Black in A.Carvalho-S.Rocha, Portuguese League 1994. White tried to generate some play with 9 c3 dxc3 10 ♕a4 cxb2 11 ♗xb2, but 11...a6!, with the idea 12 ♗xa6 ♘xe5, leaves White empty-handed.

3...d5 4 ♗g2 d4 5 ♘b1

5 ♘ce2 d3 6 cxd3 ♕xd3 7 ♘f4 ♕d8 8 ♘ge2 e5 9 ♘d5 ♗g4 again features the exploitation of the d4-square, while after 8 ♘f3 e5 9 ♘d5 ♘f6 the white knight is politely shown the door.

5...e5

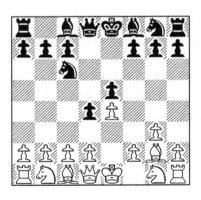

Black has already obtained a notable space advantage.

6 d3 ♗e6 7 a3 ♕d7 8 h3 ♗d6 9 ♘e2 h5 10 f4 f6 11 f5

Desperately trying to close the position, but the attempt will fail miserably.

11...♗f7 12 ♞d2 0-0-0 13 ♞f3 g6

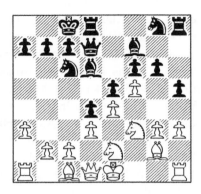

With natural moves Black is cracking open the position.

14 ♞h4 ♞ge7 15 0-0

Directly heading into the storm is hardly advisable. 15 fxg6 ♞xg6 16 ♞f5 ♗f8 would have been the lesser evil, when there is at least some time for White to catch breath.

15...♖dg8 16 ♗d2

16 fxg6 ♞xg6 17 ♖xf6 is just suicide: after 17...♞xh4 18 gxh4 ♗e6 the attack is decisive.

16...gxf5 17 exf5 e4! 18 ♗xe4 ♞d5 19 ♔h2 ♗e5 20 ♗xd5 ♗xd5 21 ♞f4 ♞e7 22 ♞fg6 ♞xg6 23 fxg6

Or 23 ♞xg6 h4! and the white king will be hunted down.

23...♖xg6! 24 ♗f4

It is questionable if White rejected 24 ♞xg6 h4 25 ♖f5!? because of 25...hxg3+ 26 ♔g1 ♖xh3 27 ♖h5 ♔d8!.

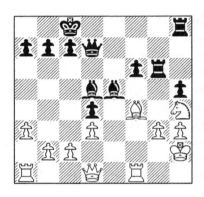

24...♖xg3?!

But that is one spectacular move too many. 24...♖g7 would have preserved the attack, whereas now there is nothing more than a draw.

25 ♔xg3 ♖g8+ 26 ♔h2 ♛f5! 27 ♛d2

27 ♞xf5 ♖g2+ 28 ♔h1 ♖f2+ 29 ♔g1 ♖g2+ also results in a draw by perpetual.

27...♛g5 28 ♛f2 ♛xh4 29 ♛xh4 ♖g2+ 30 ♔h1 ♖g4+ 31 ♔h2 ♖g2+ 32 ♔h1 ♖g4+ ½-½

Summary

The games in this chapter show that the Nimzowitsch Defence has to be taken seriously; any attempt to face it without a proper strategy is doomed to fail. That said, you will hardly ever encounter any of the lines examined herein. But if you actually do, I just have two words for you: happy hunting!

1 e4 ♘c6 *(D)* **2 ♘c3**

     2 c4 e5 *(D)* – *Game 1*
     2 d3 e5 – *Game 2*
     2 f4 d5 – *Game 3*
     2 ♗b5 d5 – *Game 4*
2...e6 3 g3 d5 *(D)* – *Game 5*

      1...♘c6   *2...e5*   *3...d5*

Chapter Two

1 e4 ♘c6 2 d4 d5
3 exd5 ♕xd5

Practice shows that the position after **2 d4 d5 3 exd5 ♕xd5**, which can also arise via the move order 1 e4 d5 2 exd5 ♕xd5 3 d4 ♘c6, is quite popular. Therefore this is a good starting point for a few strategic elucidations. The move 3 exd5 features a clash of ideas: in an ideal world White would try to gain more space with c2-c4 and d4-d5, but in reality he first has to think about taking care of his d-pawn.

White plays 4 ♗e3

There is only one real advantage to **4 ♗e3**, in that White circumvents the pin of his king's knight. However, there are many disadvantages outweighing this, the most important one probably being that after **4...e5 5 ♘c3 ♗b4** the bishop cannot help resolve the pin on the queen's knight. Because of that White is often left with doubled c-pawns, a structural deficit (see diagram) which has helped to decide numerous games.

5 c4 is the only way to avoid this

destiny, but then instead of doubled pawns there are now weak squares Black can aim at, as our next game illustrates.

Game 6
W.Grund-R.Broemmel
German League 2003

---

1 e4 ♘c6 2 d4 d5 3 exd5
Instead:
a) 3 ♗e3? is a desperate attempt to

steer the game into a position typical for the Blackmar-Diemer Gambit. However, the knight on c6 once more stands Black in good stead; for example, 3...dxe4 4 f3 ♘f6 5 c3 e5! 6 ♗b5 exd4 7 ♗xd4 ♗d7 8 ♗xf6 ♕xf6 9 ♕e2 0-0-0 10 fxe4 ♘e5 11 ♗xd7+ ♖xd7 12 ♘f3 ♘d3+ 13 ♔f1 ♘f4 and White resigned in H.Schuhmacher-C.Wisnewski, Kiel 2004.

b) 3 ♗b5 only makes sense if the pin can be exploited, but this is not the case here. After 3...dxe4 none of the following options are really convincing:

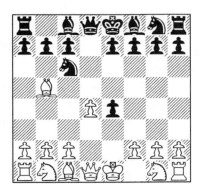

b1) 4 ♗xc6+?! is completely harmless. After 4...bxc6 5 ♘c3 ♘f6 6 ♗g5 ♗f5 7 ♘ge2 ♘d5! 8 0-0 h6 9 ♗e3 e6 White had no compensation for the pawn in H.Borges-V.Van Riemsdijk, Sao Paulo 1993.

b2) 4 ♘c3 e5! 5 d5?! (retrieving the pawn with 5 dxe5 led to complete equality after 5...♕xd1+ 6 ♘xd1 ♗d7 in I.Totos-F.Kiss, Hungarian Girls Championship 1994) 5...a6 6 ♗a4 b5 7 ♘xb5 axb5 8 ♗xb5 ♘ge7 9 dxc6 ♕xd1+ 10 ♔xd1 has been the subject of many games. For example, 10...♘f5 11 ♘e2

(11 c4 as played in D.Romito-W.Maly, correspondence 1999, is merely a further weakening of the position: after 11...♘d4! White will have a hard time defending himself as the black pieces quickly join the attack) 11...♗c5 12 ♔e1 (12 ♘c3 seems to be a promising move, but 12...♘d6 13 ♗e3 ♗d4 14 ♗e2 ♗xc3 15 bxc3 ♗e6, intending to win the c6-pawn with ...♗e6-d5, offered Black good chances in A.Ponelis-R.Sicker, correspondence 1990) 12...♗e6 13 a3 (13 ♗d2 looks like a more natural way to prevent ...♗b4; however, the game A.Reichmann-S.Pickard, correspondence 1990, showed that there are also disadvantages: 13...♘d6 14 ♘c3 0-0 15 b3 f5! 16 a4 f4 17 f3 e3 18 ♗c1 ♗b4 19 ♗b2 ♘xb5 20 axb5 ♖xa1+ 21 ♗xa1 ♖d8 and White was busted) 13...0-0 14 c4 ♖fd8 and Black had a dangerous initiative in L.Schuler-A.Eger, correspondence 1984. The game concluded 15 g3 ♗b4+ 16 ♔f1 (or 16 ♘c3 ♘d4! 17 ♖b1 ♘c2+ 18 ♔e2 ♗g4+ and Black is winning) 16...♘h4! 17 ♘g1 (other lines are winning as well, e.g. 17 ♗g5 ♗h3+ 18 ♔g1 ♘f3 mate, or 17 gxh4 ♗h3+ 18 ♔g1 ♖d1 mate, or 17 ♘c3 ♗h3+ 18 ♔e2 ♗xc3 19 bxc3 ♗g4+ etc) 17...♖d1+ 18 ♔e2 ♖e1 mate.

b3) 4 d5 a6 5 ♗a4 (even worse than before; but 5 ♗xc6+ bxc6 6 dxc6 ♕xd1+ 7 ♔xd1 ♗g4+ 8 f3 exf3 9 gxf3 0-0-0+ 10 ♔e1 ♗f5 11 ♘a3 e5 12 ♘c4 f6 led to a stable advantage for Black in R.Furdzik-M.Ardaman, Internet blitz 1997) 5...b5 6 dxc6 (6 c4 is well met by 6...♘b4!) 6...♕xd1+ 7 ♔xd1 bxa4 8 ♘c3 and now Black could have gotten a significant advantage in G.Simango-V.Afriany, Thessaloniki Olympiad 1988, had he played 8...e5, intending to capture the c6-pawn with ...♘e7 and ...♘xc6.

3...♕xd5

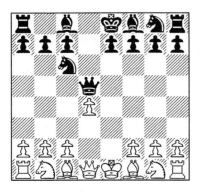

4 ♗e3

4 ♘c3 will be looked at in the next game, while 4 ♘f3 is the subject of Games 8-12. White has also tried:

a) 4 c3 is a bit toothless. After 4...e5 5 ♗e3 (5 ♘f3 ♗g4 6 ♗e2 0-0-0 transposes to Game 10) 5...♘f6 6 ♘f3 ♗g4 7 ♗e2 0-0-0 8 dxe5 (8 c4?! ♕a5+ 9 ♗d2 ♗b4 10 d5 ♗xf3 looks like a position from Game 10, but with a key difference: here the black knight is already on f6, effectively giving Black an extra tempo) 8...♕xd1+ 9 ♗xd1 ♘xe5 10 0-0 ♘xf3+ 11 ♗xf3 ♗xf3 12 gxf3 ♘d5 Black enjoyed an endgame advantage in F.Zamudio-M.Tempone, Boca 1996.

b) 4 ♘e2 is not as innocuous as it looks; the idea is to circumvent the pin on the d1-h5 diagonal. After 4...e5 5 ♘bc3 ♗b4 6 ♗d2 ♗xc3 7 ♗xc3 exd4 8 ♘xd4 ♘xd4 9 ♕xd4 ♕xd4 10 ♗xd4 the bishop pair guarantees a long-lasting advantage for White. But if Black does

not play 4...e5, the knight is misplaced on e2. I recommend 4...♗f5 5 ♘bc3 ♕d7, and now 6 d5 ♘b4 7 ♘d4 0-0-0 8 ♗c4 e5 9 ♘xf5 ♕xf5 is good for Black.

4...e5

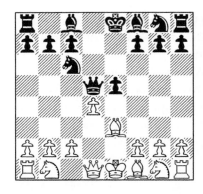

5 c4

Instead:

a) 5 dxe5 ♕xd1+ 6 ♔xd1 ♘xe5 is obviously better for Black.

b) 5 ♘f3 transposes to a position covered in Game 8.

c) 5 ♘e2?! does not avoid the pin after 5...♗g4! as 6 f3? fails to 6...♗xf3!, for example 7 ♘bc3 (7 gxf3 ♕xf3 forks bishop and rook) 7...♗b4 8 ♗d2 (or 8 ♕d2 ♗xe2 9 ♘xd5 ♗xd2+ 10 ♔xe2 ♗xe3 11 ♘xc7+ ♔d7 12 ♘xa8 exd4 with a winning advantage for Black) 8...♗xc3 9 ♘xc3 ♗xd1 10 ♘xd5 0-0-0 and Black has a clear advantage according to H.Myers. Relatively best (after 5...♗g4!) is 6 ♘bc3 ♗b4 7 dxe5 ♕xe5 with the initiative.

d) 5 ♘c3 ♗b4 shows the disadvantage of playing 4 ♗e3, in that the bishop cannot help to resolve the pin, and other ways of coping with it are not as effective:

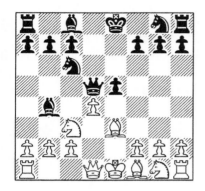

antarian, Voroshilovgrad 1989, continued 7 dxe5 ♘ge7 8 ♗c4 ♗e6 9 ♗xe6 ♖d8! 10 ♗xf7+ ♔xf7 11 ♕c1 ♗xc3+ 12 bxc3 ♕xc3+ 13 ♔f1 ♘f5 with a dangerous initiative for Black) 7 bxc3 ♘f6 8 c4 ♕d6 9 d5.

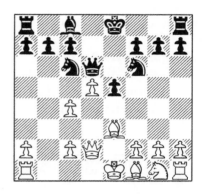

d1) 6 ♘ge2?! leads to 5 ♘ge2 after 6...♗g4!.

d2) 6 a3 ♗xc3+ 7 bxc3 leaves White with an immobile centre. Following 7...♗f5 8 ♘f3 ♕a5 9 ♗d2 (9 ♕d2 led to a disaster in M.Spaans-J.Van Arkel, correspondence 1986: 9...0-0-0 10 ♗c4 ♘f6 11 0-0 exd4 12 ♗xd4 ♘xd4 13 ♘xd4 c5 and then 14 ♕g5? cxd4 15 ♗d3 ♖d5 with an extra piece, whereas on 14 ♘b3 ♖xd2 15 ♘xa5 ♖xc2 White would 'only' have been a pawn down) 9...♕a4! 10 ♘xe5 ♘xe5 11 dxe5 0-0-0 12 ♗d3 ♗xd3 13 cxd3 ♕xd1+ 14 ♖xd1 ♖xd3 Black had a nice game in Will-C.Crouch, London 1974.

Instead, 8 c4 was tried in A.Khadzhynov-V.Jashchenko, Ukrainian Championship 2002, but after 8...♕a5+ 9 ♗d2 ♕a4 10 dxe5 (or if 10 c3 ♕xd1+ 11 ♖xd1 exd4 and Black was just a pawn up in S.Ludwig-S.Kuemin, Pizol 1997) 10...0-0-0 11 ♘f3 ♗xc2 12 ♕c1 f6 Black had a clearly better position.

d3) 6 ♕d2 ♗xc3 (6...exd4?? loses to 7 ♘xd5 dxe3 8 ♕xb4, but 6...♕a5 is another possibility: R.Akhundov-N.Kal-

Now if you were to compare the position with those examined in Chapter 11, you would think that 9...♘e7 is the right move. It is playable, as the game E.Keogh-M.O'Cinneide, Kilkenny 1997, showed: after 10 f3 (better is 10 ♘e2 as played in F.Adamek-M.Spal, Klalovy 1996, though Black should have no problems after 10...♘g4) 10...0-0 11 ♗d3 c6 12 dxc6 ♕xc6 13 ♘e2 ♗e6 Black had a solid positional advantage.

But the enterprising 9...♘d4!? is even more interesting. The game T.Thorhallsson-R.Forster, Bermuda 1999, continued 10 f3 (accepting the pawn with 10 ♗xd4 is dangerous, as either 10...exd4 11 ♕xd4 0-0 12 ♗e2 ♖e8 or 11 ♘f3 0-0 12 ♘xd4 ♖e8+ 13 ♗e2 ♘e4 provides Black with good attacking chances) 10...0-0 11 g4?!, and now following 11...♕a3! White would have hit on problems as the knight can no longer be harassed with c2-c3 and the threat of 12...♕xe3+ has to be dealt with as well. After 12 ♗d3 c6 the white position is about to crumble.

5...♕a5+ 6 ♗d2

6 ♘c3 exd4 7 ♗xd4 ♘xd4 8 ♕xd4 abandons the bishop pair for no reason.

6...♗b4 7 d5 ♗xd2+ 8 ♘xd2

Or 8 ♕xd2 ♕xd2+ 9 ♔xd2 (if 9 ♘xd2 ♘b4 is annoying) 9...♘d4 with a comfortable position for Black.

8...♘d4

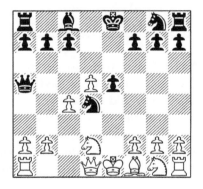

9 a3

9 ♗d3, preventing the c8-bishop from going to f5, seems to make more sense. But Black is also fine here; for example, 9...♘f6 10 ♘e2 ♗g4 11 0-0 (11 f3? just drops a pawn to 11...♗xf3!) 11...♗xe2 (11...e4?! 12 ♘xe4 ♘xe4 13 f3 ♕c5 as in Cu.Hansen-N.Fries Nielsen, Danish Championship 1981, is too ambitious since 14 ♔h1! wins material) 12 ♗xe2 0-0. White has a bishop versus a knight (for example after 13 ♘b3 ♘xb3 14 ♕xb3 ♕b6), but I have always been fond of such endgames, especially with

the white pawns being fixed on the light squares.

9...♗f5 10 ♖c1 ♕b6!

The queen's task on a5 is done. It is now time to assign her another one.

11 ♕a4+ ♔f8 12 b4 ♕h6

12...♕g6, eyeing c2 and g2, would have been better. But the position is still far from bad for Black.

13 ♖c3 ♘f6 14 ♘gf3 a6 15 b5 ♘e4 16 ♘xe4 ♗xe4 17 ♗e2 ♗xf3 18 ♗xf3 ♘xf3+ 19 gxf3 ♕d6 20 0-0 h5 21 c5 ♕xd5 22 ♖d1 ♕e6 23 c6

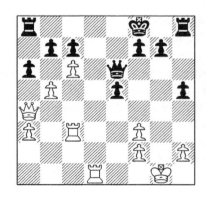

23...bxc6?

Black probably did not play 23...b6!? because of 24 ♖d7, but after 24...♖h6 25

♖xc7?! ♕h3! 26 ♕b4+ ♔g8 27 f4 ♕g4+ 28 ♖g3 (but not 28 ♔f1? ♕d1+ 29 ♔g2 h4 and wins, for example 30 ♖d7 ♖g6+ 31 ♖g3 h3+! 32 ♔xh3 ♕f1+ 33 ♔h4 ♖h6+ with a devastating attack, or 30 f5 h3+! 31 ♖xh3 ♖xh3 32 ♔xh3 ♕f3+ 33 ♔h4 axb5 etc) 28...♕d1+ 29 ♔g2 h4 30 ♖d7 ♕c1 he would have been more than compensated with attacking chances against the white king. Whereas now his position becomes difficult.

24 ♖xc6 ♕e8 25 ♖xc7

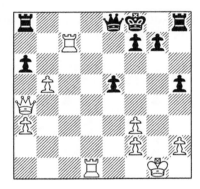

25...♕xb5?

The losing move; Black might still have defended with 25...axb5 26 ♕e4 ♖h6 27 ♖dd7 ♖f6.

26 ♕e4 ♖b8 27 ♖dd7

27 ♕f5! would have won immediately. But all the same, with the white rooks having penetrated the seventh rank, the game is technically over.

27...♕b1+ 28 ♔g2 ♕xe4 29 ♖xf7+ ♔e8 30 fxe4 g5 31 ♖ce7+ ♔d8 32 ♖a7 ♔e8 33 ♖fe7+ ♔f8 34 ♖xe5 ♖h6 35 ♖f5+ ♔e8 36 ♖xg5 ♔f8 37 h4 ♖b3 38 ♖c5 ♖g6+ 39 ♔h2 ♖e6 40 ♖c8+ ♖e8 41 ♖xe8+ ♔xe8 42 ♖xa6 1-0

Too bad that one move was enough

to spoil a better position. But that should not lure you from coming to the conclusion that 4 ♗e3 is just scanty.

White plays 4 ♘c3!?

The pawn sacrifice with **4 ♘c3!?** is treated as an orphan in most publications, even though it is highly dangerous if it's not given some respect. After **4...♕xd4 5 ♕e2** White can accelerate his development by attacking the black queen, and Black has to be very careful not to go to the dogs. In my opinion, the best possible treatment was seen in the following game.

Game 7
J.Canal Oliveras-
M.Narciso Dublan
Terrassa 1994

---

1 e4 ♘c6 2 d4 d5 3 exd5 ♕xd5 4 ♘c3!?

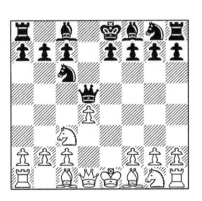

4...♕xd4 5 ♕e2

The only sensible way to prevent the queen from being traded off.

a) 5 ♗d3 is met by 5...♘b4! as 6 ♗b5+ c6 7 ♕xd4 allows 7...♘xc2+ followed by 8...♘xd4.

b) 5 ♗e3 does not offer enough for the pawn. After 5...♕xd1+ 6 ♖xd1 ♗f5 7 ♘b5 ♖c8 Black is safe.

5...e6!

Shutting in the light-squared bishop, but a pawn up you have to compromise a little bit. The natural-looking 5...♗g4?! is dangerous after 6 f3 and then:

a) 6...♗h5 7 ♗e3 ♕b4 8 0-0-0 e6 (Black does not have the time for 8...a6? 9 ♘d5 ♕a5 10 ♗b6! and White wins, or 9...♕d6 10 ♘b6 ♘d4 11 ♖xd4 ♕xb6 12 ♖d5! winning a piece) 9 ♖d5! ♘f6 10 ♖b5 ♘d4 11 ♗xd4 ♕xd4 12 ♖xb7 and White has won his pawn back. But not 12 ♖xh5?, winning two pieces for the rook, as after 12...♘xh5 13 ♕b5+ c6 14 ♕xh5 ♕e3+ 15 ♔d1 ♕f2 16 ♘h3 0-0-0+ 17 ♗d3 ♕xg2 Black picks up too many pawns.

b) 6...♗d7 7 ♘b5 (7 ♗e3?! is harmless: Black managed to erect a safe position after 7...♕b4 8 0-0-0 ♘f6 9 ♘h3 e6 10 ♘f4 0-0-0 11 ♘b5 ♕a5 12 ♔b1 a6 13 ♘d4 ♘xd4 14 ♗xd4 ♗d6 in P.Juslin-K.Kiik, Naantali 1999) 7...♕b6 8 ♗e3

♕a5+ 9 ♗d2 and Black has nothing better than to repeat moves with 9...♕b6, as 9...♕b4 10 ♕e5! ♗xb5 11 ♗xb5+ c6 12 ♗xc6+ ♘xc6 13 ♕xa5 ♘xa5 14 ♗xa5 is good for White.

6 ♘b5

6 ♗e3 ♕d8 is a motif known from the Steinitz Variation in the Scotch Opening. After 7 ♖d1 ♗d6 8 ♘b5 (8 ♕g4 ♘f6 9 ♕xg7 ♖g8 10 ♕h6 ♖g6 11 ♕h4 ♕e7 results in Black leading in development, the main idea being ...♗d7 followed by ...0-0-0) 8...♕e7 9 ♘xd6+ cxd6 Black has a safe position.

6...♕d8 7 ♗f4 ♗b4+!

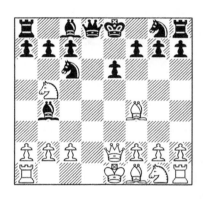

7...♗d6? is now bad: 8 ♗xd6 (not 8 ♖d1?! e5) 8...cxd6 9 0-0-0 and the d-pawn is doomed due to 9...d5 10 ♖xd5! ♕xd5 11 ♘c7+, winning the queen.

8 c3 ♗a5 9 ♖d1

9 ♘f3 is too slow. With 9...a6 10 ♘a3 ♘f6 11 ♘c4 0-0 12 ♘xa5 ♘xa5 13 ♖d1 ♕e7 14 ♕e5 ♘d5! Black could consolidate his position in D.Geiselman-S.Wrinn, correspondence 1997. The game continued 15 ♗c1 (15 ♖xd5? founders on 15...♘c6!) and after 15...♖d8 White has nothing for the pawn.

9...♕e7 10 ♘f3 ♘f6 11 g3 a6 12 ♘bd4 ♘xd4 13 ♘xd4 c5 14 ♘b3 ♗c7 15 ♗xc7 ♕xc7 16 ♗g2 ♗d7 17 0-0 0-0

Black has managed to repel the attack and remains a pawn up.

18 ♖d2 c4 19 ♘d4 e5 20 ♘c2 ♗f5 21 ♖e1 ♖ad8 22 ♘b4 ♗g4 23 f3 ♖xd2 24 ♕xd2 ♗e6 25 ♕e3 a5 26 ♘c2 ♗f5 27 ♘a3 ♖e8 28 ♗f1 ♘d5 29 ♕d2 ♘b6 30 ♖d1 ♕c6 31 ♗e2 ♕c5+ 32 ♔g2 h6 33 ♕d6 ♕e3 34 ♕d2 ♕c5 35 ♕d6 ♕e3 36 ♕d2 ♕xd2 37 ♖xd2 ♗e6 38 ♖d6 ♘a4 39 ♘xc4 ♗xc4 40 ♗xc4 ♘xb2 41 ♗d5 ♖e7 42 ♖d8+ ♔h7 43 ♖b8 ♘d1 44 ♗e4+ g6 45 ♖xb7 ♖xb7 46 ♗xb7 ♘xc3

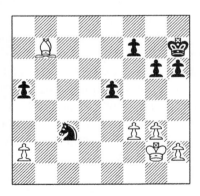

Black has simplified into a winning

endgame, as once more the knight dominates the bishop. A theme worth remembering!

47 a3 ♘b5 48 a4 ♘d6 49 ♗d5 ♔g7 50 ♔f2 f5 51 ♔e3 ♔f6 52 ♔d3 g5 53 ♔e3 f4+ 54 gxf4 gxf4+ 55 ♔d3 ♔e7 56 ♗g8 ♔d7 57 ♗d5 ♔c7 58 h3 ♔b6 59 ♗e6 ♔c5 60 h4 ♔b4 61 ♗d7 ♘b7 0-1

So 4 ♘c3!? can be played successfully after all, although it does take a bit of inside knowledge. I have seen many players suffer humiliating defeats following 5...♗g4?!, and that is simply not necessary.

White plays 4 ♘f3

As a result of the previous games the only sensible option left is the natural **4 ♘f3**. Black is at a crossroads now, as he can choose between the rock-solid **4...e5** and the riskier **4...♗g4**. I will actually cover both, as it will not hurt to be able to react differently to different (tournament) situations.

As the consequences of **4...e5** are less complicated, we might as well start our investigation at this point. Its advantages can be summed up quickly: not only does it renew the attack on d4, it also frees the path for the dark-squared bishop and therefore saves the queen from being harassed, as **5 ♘c3** is met by **5...♗b4**. The most logical course of action is **6 ♗d2 ♗xc3 7 ♗xc3 e4 8 ♘e5 ♘xe5 9 dxe5 ♘e7** when we have arrived at the critical position of 4...e5.

Some players may not feel comfortable in this position, as they have to face a pair of bishops in an open position.

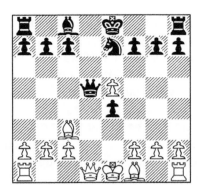

But this dogmatic view is one which should be quickly set aside – the knight can be a powerful piece too, and the great Nimzowitsch himself showed that Black has nothing to worry about.

Game 8
S.Tarrasch-A.Nimzowitsch
Bad Kissingen 1928

---

1 e4 ♞c6 2 d4 d5 3 exd5 ♛xd5 4 ♞f3 e5

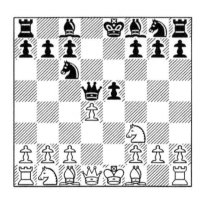

This game was actually A.Nimzowitsch-S.Tarrasch, and according to *ChessBase* started 1 e3!? e5 2 ♞c3 d5 3 d4 exd4 4 ♛xd4 ♞f6 5 e4,

reaching the same position with reversed colours.

The more enterprising 4....♝g4 will be covered in Games 9-12.

5 ♞c3

Other moves:

a) 5 dxe5?! is not a serious alternative. After 5...♛xd1+ 6 ♚xd1 ♝g4 7 ♝f4 ♞ge7 8 ♝d3 0-0-0 9 ♚e2 ♞g6 10 ♝xg6 ♞d4+! 11 ♚e3 ♝xf3 12 ♝d3 ♝xg2 13 ♖g1 ♝c6 Black had a clearly better position in J.Juntunen-Se.Ivanov, Oulu 2002.

b) 5 ♝e3 could also occur via 1 e4 ♞c6 2 d4 d5 3 exd5 ♛xd5 4 ♝e3 e5 5 ♞f3. But there is a reason the knight should not be put on f3 here: 5...♝g4 6 ♞c3 ♝b4 7 dxe5 ♝xc3+ 8 bxc3 ♝xf3 9 gxf3 ♛xe5 and the pair of bishops did not compensate for the totally crippled pawn structure in S.Fabian Nagy-L.Szabadi, Hungary 1997, while 6 ♝e2 exd4 (a more enterprising try is 6...♝xf3!? 7 ♝xf3 e4 8 ♝e2 0-0-0 9 c3 f5 with counterplay according to M.Wahls) 7 ♞c3 ♛h5 8 ♞xd4 ♝xe2 9 ♛xe2 ♛xe2+ 10 ♞cxe2 ♞ge7 11 0-0-0 0-0-0 was just equal in W.Besel-A.Bandza, Giessen 1995.

c) 5 c4 could transpose to Game 6 after 5...♛a5+. But even better is 5...♛e4+ 6 ♝e3 exd4 7 ♞xd4 ♝b4+ 8 ♞c3 ♞ge7, for example 9 ♝e2 ♛xg2! 10 ♝f3 ♛g6 11 ♞db5 0-0 and White can hardly take on c7 as 12 ♞xc7 ♝xc3+ 13 bxc3 ♖d8 14 ♛e2 ♞e5! leads to a very dangerous attack.

5...♝b4 6 ♝d2

6 dxe5 is similar to 5 dxe5. After 6...♛xd1+ 7 ♚xd1 ♝g4 8 ♝f4 0-0-0+ 9

♗d3 ♘ge7 10 ♔c1 ♗xc3 11 bxc3 ♘d5 12 ♗g5 ♖de8 Black had a good game in F.Heritier-C.J.Roos, correspondence 1995.

6...♗xc3 7 ♗xc3 e4

7...exd4?! 8 ♘xd4 ♘xd4 9 ♕xd4 ♕xd4 10 ♗xd4 only helps White.

8 ♘e5

8 ♘d2 is too passive. 8...♘f6 9 ♘c4 (if 9 ♗c4 ♕g5 and White has problems protecting his kingside properly) 9...♗e6 10 ♘e3 (or 10 ♕d2 0-0 11 ♖d1 ♖ad8 12 ♕f4 ♕d7 13 ♘e3 ♘e7 14 ♗e2 ♘ed5 and it was White who had to struggle for equality in G.Saidy-Kaplan, Puerto Rico 1969) 10...♕d7 11 d5 (11 ♗b5 a6 12 ♗a4 0-0 13 ♗xc6 ♕xc6 14 ♗b4 was played in E.Rozentalis-M.Petrov, Athens 2003, and now with 14...♖fd8 Black would not have had any problems) 11...♘xd5 12 ♗xg7 ♖g8 13 ♘xd5 ♗xd5 14 ♗c3 0-0-0 and Black had a very nice game in L.Mazi-M.Semri, Ljubljana 1998.

8...♘xe5 9 dxe5 ♘e7

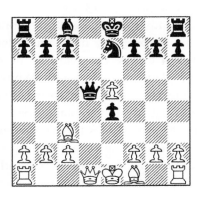

We have come to the actual starting position of this line as already mentioned in the introduction. Now White

is at a crossroads.

10 ♗e2

The other pathways are:

a) 10 ♕xd5 ♘xd5 usually transposes to the text and is only significant if White plays 11 ♗a5. Nevertheless, this sideline has to be taken very seriously, as the game S.Kishnev-T.O'Donnell, Budapest 1991, shows: 11...b6 12 0-0-0 ♗b7 13 ♗d2 0-0-0 14 ♗e2 h6 15 ♖he1 ♖he8 16 c4 ♘e7 17 ♗h5 ♖f8 18 ♗b4 and the bishops' potential fully emerged. Better is 11...♗g4!, and after 12 c4 ♘b6 13 h3 ♗e6 14 b3 0-0-0 15 ♔e2 ♖he8 16 ♔e3 ♗f5 17 ♗c3 ♘d7 18 e6 ♖xe6 19 ♗xg7 (as in E.Prie-A.Haik, Lyon 1995) 19...♘c5 would have promised Black good play.

b) With 10 ♕e2 White tries to go for the e-pawn, but Black does not really need to worry about that. For example, 10...♗e6 11 ♖d1 ♕c6 12 ♕b5 (after 12 ♖d4 ♘f5! 13 ♖xe4 0-0-0 14 f3 ♕d5 15 g3 h5 16 ♗h3 ♕xa2 17 0-0 h4 18 g4 ♘e7 19 b3 ♘d5 Black was better in I.Veinger-J.Klinger, Munich 1987) 12...♕xb5 13 ♗xb5+ c6 14 ♗e2 ♘d5 15 ♗d2 (15 ♗d4?! allows 15...♘f4 16 ♗f1 0-0 17 g3 ♗g4! 18 ♖d2 ♗f3) 15...0-0-0 16 0-0 (16 ♗g5 ♖d7 17 ♖d4 does not win a pawn as after 17...♖e8 18 ♖xe4 ♗f5 White cannot hold onto his own e-pawn) 16...♖d7 is nothing that Black should fear.

10...♗e6 11 ♕xd5 ♘xd5 12 ♗d2 0-0 13 0-0 ♖fe8 14 c4

Keilhack recommends 14 ♗c4 ♘e3!? 15 ♗xe3 ♗xc4 16 ♖fd1 ♖xe5 17 ♖d7, but clearly this is not something White is looking for.

14...♞e7 15 f4 exf3 16 gxf3

16 ♖xf3 would not have damaged the pawn structure so much, but due to the isolated pawn on e5 Black should still have the more comfortable game. For example, 16...♖ad8 17 ♗c3 ♗g4 18 ♖f2 ♗xe2 19 ♖xe2 ♞c6 and it is difficult for White to protect his e-pawn on a long-term basis.

16...♞f5

Looking at this position I cannot emphasize enough how important it is to be able to play confidently with a knight against a bishop. And not only for this position. The knight is an excellent piece to play with!

17 ♖f2 ♖ad8 18 ♗f1 ♖d7 19 ♖e1 h6 20 ♗c3 ♖ed8 21 ♖c2 ♞d4 22 ♖f2 ♗f5 23 ♖c1 ♞e6 24 f4 ♞c5 25 ♖f3 ♞a4 26 ♗e1 ♖d1 27 ♖xd1 ♖xd1 28 ♔f2 ♖b1 29 b3 ♞c5 30 ♖e3 ♖b2+ 31 ♖e2 ♞d3+ 32 ♔e3 ♖b1 33 ♗h3 ♗xh3 34 ♔xd3 ♗f1 35 ♔c2 ♖a1 36 ♔b2 ♖xa2+ 37 ♔xa2 ♗xe2

Usually opposite-coloured bishops give the defending side hope of a draw even a pawn down, but here the deficiencies of the white pawn structure are an additional disadvantage.

38 ♔b2 ♔h7 39 c5 ♔g6 40 ♔c1 ♔f5 41 ♔d2 ♗b5 42 ♔e3 ♗c6 43 ♗d2 g6 44 b4 ♔g4 45 ♔f2 h5 46 ♗c1 ♔h3 47 ♔g1 b6 48 cxb6 cxb6 49 f5 gxf5 50 ♗d2 ♔g4 51 ♔f2 f4 52 ♗c3 ♔f5 53 ♔e2 ♔e4 54 ♗e1 ♔xe5 55 ♗c3+ ♔e4 56 ♗e1 ♔d4 57 ♗f2+ ♔c4 58 ♗e1 ♗e4 59 ♗d2 ♔b3 60 ♔f2 f3 61 ♗e1 f5 62 ♔e3 ♔a4 63 ♔f2 b5 64 ♔e3 a5 65 bxa5 b4 0-1

In short, I like 4...e5. If I ever need a draw in a serious game, I would prefer 4...e5 over 4...♗g4 any day.

The Main line: 4 ♞f3 ♗g4

As I already indicated at the beginning of this chapter, the main line after **4 ♞f3 ♗g4** can be characterized by different plans on both sides: White is heading for a static long-term advantage (in the form of a notable space advantage), while Black is trying to make use of his current dynamic short-term advantage (in the form of his lead in development and more active pieces). The resulting complications are usually favourable to Black, but there are numerous skirmishes which need a thorough examination.

White plays 5 ♘c3

Having regard to all the points just mentioned, the move **5 ♘c3** does not really fit in. The knight blocks its own c-pawn, and without c2-c4 White will never be able to enforce d4-d5 under favourable circumstances. Black, on the other hand, can combine his counter-play in the centre with a possible king-side attack – a dangerous combination as we will see in our next game.

Game 9
G.Noakes-T.Menzel
Correspondence 1998

---

1 e4 ♘c6 2 d4 d5 3 exd5 ♕xd5 4 ♘f3 ♗g4 5 ♘c3

The main move, 5 ♗e2, is the subject of Games 10-12.

5...♕h5!

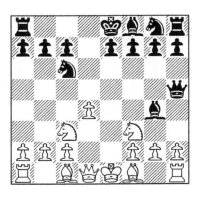

Before continuing, let's look at possible alternatives for Black:

a) 5...♕f5?! is a different approach, two ideas being ...♘b4 (attacking c2) and ....♗xf3 (crippling the pawn structure). Yet, I was not able to refute the simple 6 d5 ♘e5 (6...♘b4 7 ♗b5+ c6 8 dxc6 bxc6 9 ♗a4 ♖d8 10 ♕e2 is just bad) 7 ♗b5+ c6 8 dxc6 bxc6 9 ♘xe5! ♕xe5+ 10 ♗e3 ♗d7 (after 10...♗xd1 11 ♗xc6+ ♔d8 12 ♖xd1+ ♔c8 13 ♗xa8 White has more than enough play and material for the queen) 11 ♕f3 with a clear advantage for White in R.Ginther-M.Turcan, correspondence 1998.

b) 5...♗xf3 is another popular option, but I cannot reconcile myself to this idea. After 6 ♘xd5 ♗xd1 7 ♘xc7+ ♔d8 (7...♔d7? is worse as the king is more vulnerable to checks: 8 ♘xa8 ♗xc2 9 d5 ♘d4 10 ♗e3 e5 11 dxe6+ ♘xe6 12 ♗b5+ ♔c8 13 ♗xa7 and White wins) 8 ♘xa8 ♗xc2 9 d5! ♘d4 (or 9...♘b4 10 ♗e3 ♗e4 11 ♖c1 ♘xa2 12 ♖c7 ♗xd5 13 ♗xa7 e5 14 ♗b5) 10 ♗e3 e5 11 dxe6 ♗b4+ 12 ♗d2 ♗xd2+ 13 ♔xd2 fxe6 (13...♗g6 14 ♖c1 ♘c6 was played in K.Kirby-K.Blevins, Winston-Salem 1996, and now 15 ♗a6! would have been decisive) 14 ♖c1 ♘f6 15 ♖xc2 ♘xc2 16 ♔xc2 ♔e7 17 ♗c4 ♖xa8 18 ♖e1 ♖c8 19 ♖xe6+ ♔d7 20 ♔d3 White has a stable endgame advantage (analysis by Wahls).

c) 5...♕a5?! is usually reached via 1 e4 ♘c6 2 ♘f3 d5 3 exd5 ♕xd5 4 ♘c3 ♕a5 5 ♘f3 ♗g4 and is a pet line of the Russian IM Nikolai Vlassov. In his analysis he states that 6 ♗b5 0-0-0 7 ♗xc6 bxc6 8 ♕e2! ♔b7 (8...♖xd4 is no improvement: after 9 h3 ♗xf3 10 ♕xf3 White wins the pawn back and leaves Black with a scattered pawn structure) 9 b4! ♕f5 10 b5 ♗xf3 11 gxf3 e6 12 bxc6+ ♔xc6 is the critical position. Black even managed to gain the upper hand in L.Kviatkowski-N.Vlassov, Polanica Zdroj 1993, following 13 ♕a6+?! ♔d7 14 ♕a4+ c6 15 ♖g1 ♕xf3 16 ♗e3 ♗d6 17 ♖b1 ♞e7 18 ♖b7+ ♔e8. However, I could not find a way to cope with 13 ♖g1! which brings the rook into action and slightly changes the move order, winning a precious tempo. Black must prevent 14 ♖g5 at all cost, but after 13...h6 14 ♖b1 there is no satisfactory way to prevent 15 ♕a6+ followed by ♕a6-a4 and ♖b1-b7; for example, 14...♔d7 (if 14...♖xd4 15 ♖b5! ♕f6 16 ♖b8 and the black king can only escape under large concessions) 15 ♖b5 ♕h3 16 ♗f4 c6 17 ♖b7+ ♔e8 18 ♗c7 ♖a8 19 d5! and the white attack is devastating.

6 ♗e2

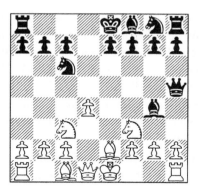

6 ♗b5 0-0-0 7 ♗xc6 bxc6 is similar to the previous note, the crucial difference being that White cannot play b2-b4 with tempo. For example, 8 ♕d3 ♗xf3 9 gxf3 e6 10 ♕a6+ ♔d7 11 ♗d2 ♕xf3 12 ♖g1 ♞f6 13 ♞e2 (surprisingly, if 13 ♕xa7 ♞g4 the white king is in more danger than the black one: after 14 ♞d1 ♞xh2 White cannot prevent the knight

from going decisively to f3) 13...♞e4 14 0-0-0 g6 and Black was OK in K.Kjolner-Po.Nielsen, Copenhagen 1991.

6...0-0-0 7 0-0

7 ♗e3 is naturally met by 7...e5!, and if 8 d5 (8 h3 ♞f6 9 0-0 exd4 10 ♞xd4 ♗xe2 11 ♞cxe2 ♗c5 12 c3 ♞d5 is better for Black), then Black has the pleasant choice between 8...♞f6 9 0-0 e4 10 ♞d4 ♞xd4 11 ♗xd4 ♗xe2 12 ♕xe2 ♕xe2 13 ♞xe2 ♞xd5 and 8...♗b4 9 0-0 ♗xc3 10 bxc3 e4 11 ♞d4 ♗xe2 12 ♕xe2 ♕xe2 13 ♞xe2 ♖xd5, winning the d5-pawn in both lines.

7 h3 wants to shake off the pressure at once, but after 7...♗xf3 8 ♗xf3 ♕g6 9 d5 ♞e5 the d-pawn has a precarious future. Nor does 9 ♗e3 e5 10 ♗xc6 bxc6 solve all the problems (but not 10...♕xc6?!, allowing 11 ♕g4+ followed by 12 dxe5).

7...e5 8 h3 ♞f6!

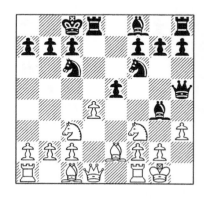

Offering a piece which White can hardly accept.

9 d5

a) 9 ♗e3 transposes to 7 ♗e3, covered in the note to White's 7th move.

b) 9 hxg4?! ♘xg4 takes up the gauntlet, but the arising complications favour Black:

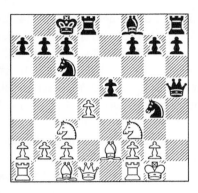

b1) 10 ♘b5 a6 11 a4 takes advantage of the fact that the knight is impervious to 11...axb5 12 axb5, as 12...♘xd4 13 ♖a8+ ♔d7 14 ♘xe5+! wins and 12...♘b8 takes the heat off d4. However, Black can play 11...♘xd4 12 ♘bxd4 ♖xd4! when White has nothing better than 13 ♗d2 (or 13 ♗d3 e4 14 ♖e1 ♗c5! 15 ♘xd4 ♗xd4 with a winning attack, while 14 ♗f4 is countered by 14...♗d6!) 13...e4 14 ♘h4 e3! 15 g3 exf2+ 16 ♔g2 (if 16 ♖xf2 ♗c5! 17 ♔f1 ♘xf2 18 ♗xh5 ♘xd1 leads to a better endgame for Black) 16...♗c5 and Black, now with three pawns for the sacrificed piece, still has an attack.

b2) 10 ♘h4 is a desperate try to confront the attackers, but d4 is also a matter of concern. For example, 10...f5 11 f3 (11 g3 ♘xd4 is good for Black) 11...♘f6 12 ♕e1 ♘xd4 13 ♗d3 ♗c5 14 ♗e3 e4! 15 fxe4 ♘g4 and Black has a deadly attack.

b3) The critical move is 10 d5, but after 10...f5! (planning ...e5-e4) 11 ♗g5

(other moves do not help either, as Wahls showed in his compelling analysis: 11 ♕d2 ♗e7 12 ♘b5 a6 13 ♗d3 ♖xd5 14 ♗xf5+ ♕xf5 15 ♕xd5 axb5 16 ♕xb5 ♖f8 17 ♗e3 ♕h5 when the threat 18...♖xf3 is decisive, or 11 ♘b5 a6 12 ♗g5 ♘e7 13 d6 axb5 14 dxe7 ♖xd1 15 ♖axd1 ♗xe7 16 ♗xe7 e4 17 ♘h4 ♖e8 18 ♖d5 ♖xe7 19 ♗xg4 ♕xg4 20 ♘xf5 ♖d7 and Black has a winning position) 11...e4 12 ♗f4 ♗d6 13 ♕d2 (if 13 ♗xd6 ♖xd6 14 ♘h4 ♕xh4 15 ♗xg4 fxg4 and White cannot prevent the invasion on the h-file, while after 13 ♘h2 ♗xf4 14 ♘xg4 ♘e5! 15 g3 fxg4 Black again has a winning attack, e.g. 16 ♕d4 ♖d6!, or 16 ♘xe4 ♖xd5!, or 16 gxf4 ♘f3+ 17 ♗xf3 exf3 and mate is unavoidable) 13...exf3 14 ♗xf3 (if 14 gxf3 ♘h2! 15 dxc6 ♘xf3+ 16 ♗xf3 ♕xf3 17 cxb7+ ♔b8 18 ♘e2 ♕g4+ 19 ♔h1 g5 and Black wins) 14...♘ce5 15 ♗xg4 ♕xg4 16 ♗xe5 ♗xe5 this time Black has a bishop, which is clearly superior to the white knight.

9...♗xf3 10 ♗xf3 ♕g6

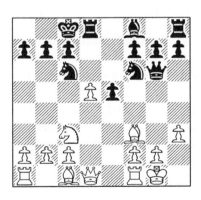

11 ♗e3

The best move among many. Instead:

a) 11 dxc6?! ♖xd1 12 cxb7+ ♚b8 13 ♖xd1 ♝c5 does not offer enough compensation for the queen.

b) 11 ♖e1 ♝b4 12 ♝d2 ♘d4 13 ♖xe5 ♘xf3+ 14 ♕xf3 ♕xc2 15 ♕f4 (15 ♖e2 ♕g6 results in a comfortable position for Black) 15...♝xc3 16 ♝xc3 ♘xd5 17 ♕g4+ ♚b8 18 ♕xg7 ♘xc3 19 bxc3 was played in H.May-Donner, Austria 1966, and now 19...♖hg8 20 ♕f6 (not 20 ♕xf7? ♖gf8) 20...♕xc3 would have given Black a slight endgame advantage.

c) 11 ♝d2 ♘d4 12 ♖c1 ♕f5! eliminates the pair of bishops, while simultaneously keeping an eye on d5.

11...♚b8! 12 ♕e2

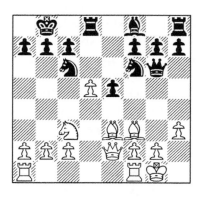

Again, other moves do not promise much:

a) 12 ♖e1 ♝b4 13 ♝d2 ♘d4 is the same as 11 ♖e1 examined above, with the extra move ...♚b8 for Black.

b) 12 ♘b5? e4 13 dxc6 ♖xd1 14 ♝xa7+ ♚a8 15 cxb7+ ♚xb7 16 ♝xd1 c6 buries any hopes White might have had.

c) 12 ♘e2? ♘b4 loses the pawn on d5, as 13 c4 ♘c2 14 ♖c1 ♘xe3 15 fxe3 e4 is even worse.

d) 12 a3 prevents the black knight and bishop from going to b4 but loses time. Black can play 12...♘e7 13 ♖e1 (13 ♘b5 a6 14 d6 is met simply by 14...cxd6 15 ♝a7+ ♚a8 16 ♝b6 ♖d7 and Black is a pawn up) 13...♘f5 14 ♝c1 (14 ♝d2 allows 14...♘d4 15 ♖xe5 ♘xf3+ 16 ♕xf3 ♕xc2 and if 17 ♖e2 ♕g6 when Black should not be worse) 14...♝c5 15 ♘a4 ♝d6 16 c4 ♘h4 17 g3 (or 17 c5 e4!) 17...e4 and Black has a huge attack.

12...♘d4?

12...♘b4! was the road to success. The best White can do is 13 ♖ac1, but after 13...e4 14 ♘xe4 ♘fxd5 Black is OK.

13 ♝xd4 exd4 14 ♘b5 ♝c5

14...a6 15 ♘xd4 ♘xd5 is no improvement, as after 16 ♖ad1 Black has problems completing his development.

15 ♕c4 ♝b6 16 a4 a5 17 ♘xd4 ♝xd4 18 ♕xd4 ♕xc2 19 b4

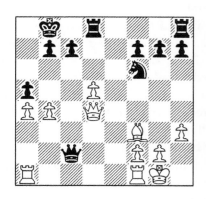

The white attack will soon be irresistible.

19...axb4 20 ♖fc1 ♕f5 21 ♕xb4 ♘xd5 22 ♕b5 ♕d7 23 ♖ab1 ♕xb5 24 ♖xb5 c6 25 ♖xc6 ♘c7 26 ♖b1 1-0

What a pity. Black came this close to equality, but just one move screwed up his efforts. However, with proper preparation this will not happen again, and the fact that White has far more pitfalls to avoid should be an added consolation.

White plays 5 ♗e2 0-0-0 6 c3

After rejecting 5 ♘c3, it is now time to look at the lines resulting from **5 ♗e2 0-0-0**. With his last move Black uttered the intention to take the d-pawn, a threat to which White can react in different ways. The value of **6 c3** depends solely on its interpretation.

The ideas behind the move are clear: White protects his central pawn, thus parrying the threat of 6...♗xf3 7 ♗xf3 ♕xd4. If allowed, he would like to complete his development with 7 0-0, 8 ♗e3 and 9 ♘bd2, followed by c3-c4 or b2-b4. Obviously Black cannot tolerate this, so stabbing at d4 with **6...e5!** is the logical continuation.

Now **7 c4!** is the only sensible way for White to avoid getting into difficulties. Moving the c-pawn twice in a row

seems bizarre, but with a pawn on e5 the black queen can no longer switch to the kingside via the fifth rank, which is quite powerful as we will see in Game 11. In addition to that, the d-pawn can now safely advance to d5 without being picked on by a possible ...e7-e6. However, providing Black with an additional tempo to attack the centre puts White in a slippery situation, and he can only struggle for a draw, as we'll see in our next game.

Game 10
V.Klyuner-J.Koscielski
Duisburg 2000

1 e4 ♘c6 2 d4 d5 3 exd5 ♕xd5 4 ♘f3 ♗g4 5 ♗e2 0-0-0 6 c3 e5

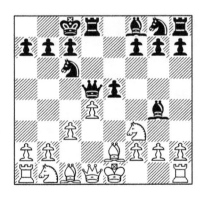

7 c4

Many other moves have been tried, but with only moderate success:

a) 7 ♗e3 ♘f6 has already been discussed in Game 6 (see the note to White's 4th move).

b) 7 h3 ♗xf3 8 ♗xf3 e4 9 ♗e2 f5 10 ♗f4 h6 11 ♘d2 g5 12 ♗c4 ♕d7 13 ♗h2

♘f6 14 ♘b3 f4 and the black pawns were rolling down the board in A.Huellen-T.Meier, Olpe 2005.

c) 7 0-0? exd4 8 cxd4 ♘xd4 9 ♘xd4 ♗xe2 10 ♕xe2 ♕xd4 11 ♗e3 was played in S.Rosta-I.Gosztola, Hungarian Team Championship 1992, and now instead of 11...♕d3, White would not have had any compensation after 11...♕e5.

d) 7 dxe5 allows Black to choose between 7...♕xd1+ 8 ♗xd1 ♘xe5 9 0-0 ♘xf3+ 10 ♗xf3 ♗xf3 11 gxf3 ♖d3 12 ♗e3 ♘f6 with a stable endgame advantage in A.Lazar-P.Kovacic, Bled 1998, and 7...♕e4 8 ♕b3 (8 ♘bd2 ♗xf3 9 gxf3 ♕xe5 is out of the question, while 9 ♘xe4?! is not good either because of 9...♖xd1+ 10 ♗xd1 ♗xe4) 8...♗xf3 9 gxf3 ♕xe5 10 ♕xf7 ♘f6 with the initiative.

7...♕a5+ 8 ♗d2

6 ♗e3 e5 7 c4 ♕a5+ 8 ♗d2 comes to the same thing and was in fact the course of this game.

8...♗b4

8...♕b6? is a trap many players have fallen victim of – White wins after 9 c5! ♗xc5 10 dxc5 ♕xb2 11 ♗c3 ♖xd1+ 12 ♔xd1.

9 d5 ♗xf3

9...e4 is not good. White is better after 10 ♘g5 ♗xe2 11 ♕xe2 ♘d4 12 ♕d1 ♘h6 13 0-0 ♗xd2 14 ♘xd2 ♕b6 15 ♘dxe4 (analysis by Wahls).

10 ♗xf3 ♗xd2+ 11 ♘xd2 ♘d4 12 0-0

12 a3 seeks to expand on the queenside. In R.Lehtivaara-K.Tikkanen, Finnish Team Championship 1994, Black seized the moment to play in the centre

with 12...f5, and after 13 0-0 e4 14 ♗e2 ♘f6 15 b4 ♕a6 16 ♖e1 he should have continued 16...♕d6 followed by ...c7-c6, which would have given him the advantage.

12...♕b4!

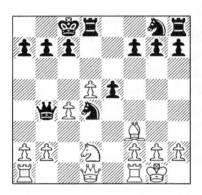

Now 12...f5?! is dubious, due to 13 ♘b3 ♘xb3 14 axb3 ♕b6 15 ♕c2 and c4-c5 proves to be rather inconvenient.

13 b3?!

After 13 ♖e1! it was long thought that Black can take the pawn with 13...♕xb2, but in fact after 14 ♖b1 ♕xa2 the move 15 ♖xe5! is very strong. Wahls only gave 15...♘xf3+ 16 ♘xf3 ♕xc4 with complicated play (which he backed up with a few variations), but White can do better with 16 ♕xf3! when Black has serious problems, one example being 16...♕xd2 17 d6! c6 (or 17...b6 18 ♕a8+ ♔d7 19 ♕xa7) 18 ♕f5+ ♔b8 19 ♕d7!! and White wins. Therefore, the right way to continue is 13...♘f6 (instead of 13...♕xb2) with the idea 14 ♖xe5 ♘xf3+ 15 ♘xf3 ♕xc4 which results in a nice position for Black.

13...f5 14 a3 ♕d6 15 b4 e4 16 ♗e2 ♘f6

The white pawns on the queenside have been successfully fixed as the d5-pawn needs to be protected. Therefore Black is better.

17 ♘b3 ♘xe2+ 18 ♕xe2 ♘g4 19 g3 ♕h6 20 f4 g5?

20...exf3! was obviously better. Following 21 ♖xf3 ♖he8 22 ♕c2 (or 22 ♕d2 ♕xd2 23 ♘xd2 ♖e2 24 ♘f1 g6 with a clear endgame advantage) 22...♖e4! Black has at least a slight advantage, for example 23 ♖xf5 ♖de8 24 ♖af1 ♖xc4! (but not 24...♖e2? which loses to 25 ♕xe2! ♖xe2 26 ♖f8+ ♔d7 27 ♖1f7+ ♔d6 28 ♖d8+ ♔e5 29 ♖e8+ ♔d6 30 ♖xe2 etc). Instead Black just collapses and loses quickly.

21 ♘d4 gxf4 22 ♖xf4 ♖hg8 23 ♘xf5 ♕g5 24 ♖af1 ♖de8 25 ♖xe4 ♖xe4 26 ♕xe4 ♔b8 27 ♕f4 ♕h5 28 h4 ♕e8 29 ♘d4 a6 30 ♘e6 1-0

White plays 6 c4

6 c4 is the most consequential attempt to realize the plan I outlined in the introduction to this chapter. White reaches for space in the centre and forces the black queen to abandon her central post. Various moves have been tried here, but 6...♕a5+ and 6...♕f5 are certainly the most attractive options.

6...♕f5 has the merit that the queen retains an active position, without being forced to move again after 7 h3 ♗xf3 8 ♗xf3. The only thing Black has to look out for is the threat of 9 ♗g4, but this can be easily countered by 8...♘f6, when White will experience difficulties keeping his fragile centre together as 9 ♗xc6?! ♕e6+! 10 ♗e3 ♕xc6 drops a pawn.

The only sensible continuation is **7 0-0**. Now Black should refrain from grabbing the d-pawn with 7...♗xf3?! 8 ♗xf3 ♖xd4 as White gets good attacking chances after 9 ♕a4!. Instead, the quiet **7...♘f6** is simple and good. In his book *Modernes Skandinavisch*, German GM Matthias Wahls claims that after 8 ♗e3 e5 9 d5 e4 10 ♘d4 ♘xd4 11 ♗xd4 ♗d6 12 ♘c3 it is White who has the better prospects, but I can't share this opinion. Our next game will feature the more common **6...♕a5+**, but I'd also like to support my theory that 6...♕f5 is a viable alternative.

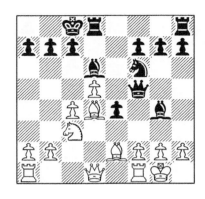

Game 11
B.Schramm-P.Muehlig Versen
Schloss Schney 2002

1 e4 ♘c6 2 d4 d5 3 exd5 ♕xd5 4 ♘f3 ♗g4 5 ♗e2 0-0-0 6 c4

6...♕a5+

As I said above, 6...♕f5 is a decent alternative. Now 7 ♗e3 transposes to the text, while 7 0-0 ♘f6!?, although being dismissed by Wahls, leads to a good game for Black. After 8 ♗e3 (8 d5? heads for disaster after 8...e6 9 ♗d3 ♗xf3! 10 gxf3 ♕h3 as 11 dxc6 loses to 11...♗d6 12 f4 ♘g4) 8...e5 9 d5 e4 10 ♘d4 (10 ♘h4? is bad due to 10...♕h5 11 ♗xg4+ ♘xg4 12 h3 ♘ce5!; while on 10 ♘fd2 ♘e5 Black has an advantage in space, and White cannot grab a pawn with 11 ♗xa7? as after 11...b6 12 ♗xg4 ♕xg4! the bishop is doomed) 10...♘xd4 11 ♗xd4 ♗d6 12 ♘c3.

Wahls claims that White has better prospects for an attack on the enemy king, but the game M.Lazic-N.Sulava, St Affrique 2002, proved him wrong:

12...♗xe2 13 ♕xe2 ♘g4 14 h3 ♘h2! 15 ♖fd1 ♘f3+ 16 ♔f1 (16 ♔h1? runs into 16...♘xd4 17 ♖xd4 ♕e5) 16...♖he8 17 ♗e3 ♘h2+ 18 ♔e1 ♕g6 and Black was on top. If instead 18 ♔g1, then 18...♕e5 is possible and White has to defend very accurately; for example 19 ♕c2 ♘f3+ 20 gxf3 exf3 21 ♔f1 g6! and the threat of 22...♕h2! is difficult to meet, or 19 c5 ♘f3+ 20 ♔f1 ♕h2 21 ♕c2 ♘h4 22 cxd6 ♘xg2! 23 ♔e2 ♘xe3 24 ♔xe3 ♖xd6 and with two pawns for the piece the attack is far from over.

7 ♗d2 ♕f5 8 ♗e3

Instead:

a) 8 0-0!? was dismissed rather too quickly by Wahls, who claimed a clear advantage for Black after 8...♘xd4 9 ♘xd4 ♖xd4. Things are not that clear, though, as it is not easy to see what actually happens after 10 f3. It takes guts to play 10...♕c5 11 b4 ♖xd2+ 12 bxc5 ♖xd1 13 ♖xd1 ♗d7, when Black is an exchange down, but is in possession of two bishops and two pawns (should he manage to consume the pawn on c5). After 14 ♘d2 e5 15 ♘b3 ♘e7 the position is highly unclear.

Black's idea is to exchange the white knight to win the c5-pawn. After that the two bishops and two pawns should provide more than enough chances in this unbalanced position. But those who do not like these complications can choose 6...♕f5.

b) After 8 d5 Black can choose between 8...♘e5 9 ♘xe5 ♕xe5 10 f3 (10 ♗e3?! is dubious because of 10...♗xe2 11 ♕xe2 e6!) 10...♗h5 11 0-0 e6 12 ♗c3 ♕e3+ 13 ♔h1 with unclear play in Bardi-Jakobetz, Budapest 1986; or 8...♗xf3 9 dxc6 ♗e2 (but not 9...♗xc6?? 10 ♗g4) 10 cxb7+ ♔xb7 11 ♕xe2 e5 12 0-0 ♗c5 13 b4 ♗d4 14 ♘c3 ♘f6 15 ♖ab1 as in J.Krajcik-J.Benci, Slovakian League 1995, and now 15...♕g4 would have held the balance.

8...♗xf3 9 ♗xf3

9...♘xd4 10 ♗g4?!

The critical line is 10 ♗xd4 ♕e6+ 11 ♗e2 ♕e4! and then:

a) 12 ♘c3 ♕xd4 13 ♕xd4 ♖xd4 14 ♘b5 ♖d8 (also interesting is 14...♖d7 15 ♘xa7+ ♔b8 16 ♘b5 e6 17 0-0 ♗b4 18 ♖fd1 ♗d2!?, as in A.Nuevo Perez-C.Matamoros Franco, Seville 2000,

when Wahls gives 19 ♘c3 ♘f6 20 ♘b1 ♖hd8 21 ♘xd2 ♖xd2 with a slight advantage to Black) 15 ♘xa7+ ♔b8 16 ♘b5 e6, where Black's plan is to exploit the d4-square. A possible course of action is 17 0-0 ♗e7 18 ♖ad1 ♘h6! 19 ♗f3 ♗f6 20 b3 c6 21 ♘d6 ♗e7 22 ♘e4 ♘f5 23 ♖xd8+ ♖xd8 24 ♖d1 ♘d4 25 ♔f1 f5 and due to the activity of his pieces Black is better.

b) More dangerous is 12 0-0!?:

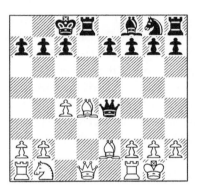

b1) I played 12...♖xd4, but was confronted with 13 ♕a4!, after which the only variation to be considered is 13...♕xe2 14 ♕xa7 ♕xb2 (the best try: 14...♖d1?? runs into 15 ♕a8+ ♔d7 16 ♕a4+ and wins; 14...e5? obviously fails to 15 ♕a8+ ♔d7 16 ♘c3 followed by ♕xf8; while 14...♖d6, planning ...♖a6, loses to 15 ♕a8+ ♔d7 16 ♘c3, as after 16...♕xb2 17 ♘b5 ♘f6 18 ♕xb7 Black cannot parry both 19 ♕xc7+ and 19 ♘xd6) 15 ♘a3 (here 15 ♕a8+ ♔d7 16 ♕xf8 ♕xa1 17 ♕xg7 is no good, since after 17...♘f6! 18 ♕xh8 ♕xa2 followed by ...♕xc4, Black is just two pawns up!) 15...♖d3 16 ♕a8+ ♔d7 when W.Polischtschuk-C.Wisnewski, German League 2007, continued 17 ♖fd1?!

♖xd1+ ♖xd1+ 18 ♖xd1+ ♔e6 19 ♕xf8 c6!
20 h3 ♔f6 21 ♖d3 ♕c1+ 22 ♔h2 ♕f4+
and a draw was agreed. However, 17
♘b5! again is much stronger, when
17...♘f6 18 ♕xb7 e5 (or 18...♘e8 19 c5!
threatening 20 c6+ ♔e6 21 ♘xc7+) 19 c5!
♗xc5 20 ♕xc7+ ♔e6 21 ♕xc5 doesn't
look too promising for Black.

b2) 12...♕xd4 13 ♕a4! e6 (Karsten
Müller's suggested improvement on
13...♕xb2? 14 ♕xa7 e6 15 ♗f3 ♘f6 16
♘c3! ♕xc3, as in G.Shahade-M.Fierro
Baquero, Paget Parish 2001, when 17
♕xb7+ ♔d7 18 ♗c6+ would have led to
a quick end either after 18...♔e7 19
♕xc7+ ♘d7 20 ♖fd1 or 18...♔d6 19
♖ad1+ etc) 14 ♘c3 ♗d6 (14...♕b6 is also
possible) 15 ♘b5 ♕e5 16 ♘xd6+ cxd6
17 ♗f3 ♔b8 18 ♖fe1 ♕c5 19 b4 ♕c7 20
♖ac1 ♘e7 21 c5 ♖c8 22 ♖e3 ♘d5 23
♗xd5 (if 23 ♖a3 ♕b6! is an improbable
defence; for example 24 cxb6 ♖xc1+ 25
♗d1 ♘xb6 and if 26 ♕xa7+? ♔c7
threatens both 27...♖xd1 mate and
27...♖a8) 23...exd5 24 h3 dxc5 25 bxc5
♕c6 and Black defended in P.Carroll-
F.Rahde, correspondence 2004.

10...♘c2+ 11 ♕xc2 ♕xg4 12 0-0

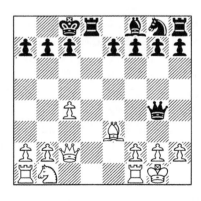

12...♘f6?!

12...a6 is a simple move which
keeps the a-pawn. After this, White has
absolutely no compensation for the
pawn.

13 ♗xa7 b6 14 c5 ♕e4?

Admitting his faulty play. Black
had to try 14...♔b7 15 cxb6 cxb6 16
♗xb6 ♔xb6, but playing without any
shelter for the king is a daunting task.

**15 ♕xe4 ♘xe4 16 cxb6 e6 17 bxc7
♔xc7 18 f3 ♗c5+ 19 ♗xc5 ♘xc5 20 ♘a3
♘d3 21 b3 ♖d5 22 ♘c4**

Here Black could have resigned
with a clear conscience.

**22...♖a8 23 a3 ♔c6 24 ♖fd1 ♔b5 25
♖d2 ♘c5 26 ♖xd5?!**

26 ♖c2 looks better, the idea being
to play b3-b4.

**26...exd5 27 ♘d2 ♖e8 28 ♔f1 ♖e3 29
♖e1 ♖d3 30 ♔e2 ♖c3 31 ♖b1 d4 32 ♔d1
d3?**

Allowing White to exchange rooks
just capitulates. More resilient is
32...♖e3 when Black can play on.

**33 ♖c1 ♖xc1+ 34 ♔xc1 ♔c6 35 ♔b2
♔b5 36 ♔c3 f6 37 ♘e4 ♘e6 38 g3 ♘c7
39 ♔xd3 ♔a5 40 ♘c3 ♘e6 41 b4+ ♔b6**

42 a4 ♘g5 43 ♔e3 ♘f7 44 f4 ♘d6 45 a5+ ♔a6 46 ♔d4 ♘f5+ 47 ♔c5 h5 48 ♘d5 h4 49 gxh4 ♘xh4 50 ♔c6 ♘f5 51 ♘c7+ ♔a7 52 b5 g5 53 b6+ ♔b8 54 ♘a6+ 1-0

White plays 6 ♗e3

Our final game in this chapter deals with the natural **6 ♗e3**. This time it's the bishop that protects the d-pawn, providing maximum flexibility as White can still choose whether to play c2-c3 or c2-c4, and whether to put his queen's knight on c3 or d2. Nevertheless, Black can now either transpose to Game 10, or even choose another option discussed in the following game – a clear sign that the whole 3 exd5 system is flawed.

Game 12
N.Vujmilovic-G.Rumiancev
Pula 1990

---

1 e4 ♘c6 2 d4 d5 3 exd5 ♕xd5 4 ♘f3 ♗g4 5 ♗e2 0-0-0 6 ♗e3

6...♘f6

With 6...e5 Black can transpose to Game 10 after 7 c4 ♕a5+ 8 ♗d2 ♗b4, as the alternatives are nothing to be worried about:

a) 7 ♘c3 quickly leads to a comfortable game for Black after 7...♕a5 8 ♘xe5 ♗xe2 9 ♕xe2 (9 ♘xc6?! ♗xd1 10 ♘xa5 ♗xc2 11 ♖c1 ♗d3 was better for Black in A.Iodo-N.Polyakova, Serpukhov 2003) 9...♘xe5 10 dxe5 ♕xe5 11 0-0 ♘f6, since 12 ♗xa7? ♕xe2 13 ♘xe2 b6 works as usual.

b) After 7 c3 Black should not play 7...exd4 8 cxd4 since White unnecessarily gets attacking chances. Instead, he should choose 7...e4 8 ♘fd2 ♗xe2 9 ♕xe2 f5 when his kingside initiative is developing fast. The game J.Schubert-A.Wimmer, Niederbayern 1999, continued 10 0-0 ♕f7 11 b4 ♗e7 12 ♘b3 g5 13 ♘a3 h5 14 ♖fd1 f4 15 ♗c1 ♕f5 16 ♖e1 ♘f6 17 ♘d2 g4 with a huge attack. Note that 18 ♘xe4 is answered by 18...♗xb4! 19 cxb4 ♘xd4.

c) 7 dxe5 ♕xd1+ 8 ♗xd1 ♘xe5 9 ♘bd2 ♘xf3+ 10 ♗xf3 ♘f6 is a bit dry, but Black can play instead 7...♗xf3 8 ♗xf3 ♕xe5 9 ♘d2 ♗c5 10 ♗xc6 (10 ♕e2?! is best met by 10...♗xe3 11 ♕xe3 ♕xe3+ 12 fxe3 ♘b4! with good play for Black in A.Mihailidis-T.Gelashvili, Korinthos 2002) 10...♗xe3 11 ♗xb7+ ♔b8 12 fxe3 ♕xe3+ 13 ♕e2 ♕xe2+ 14 ♔xe2 ♔xb7 when the endgame is not as dull.

7 0-0

7 ♘bd2 is a prophylactic move which tries to strengthen control over d4. But after 7...♕f5!, the white pieces are clumsily positioned. White has to

choose between the following moves:

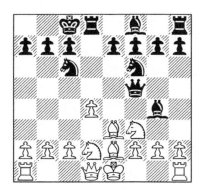

a) 8 h3?! is too slow. Black gets a good game after 8...♗xf3 9 ♘xf3 e5.

b) 8 c4 seems natural, supporting d4-d5 in case of the typical ...e7-e5. But after 8...e5 9 d5 ♘b4! we see another advantage to 7...♕f5. White has nothing better than 10 0-0 (if 10 ♖c1 Black plays 10...e4! and is rewarded with a nice position after 11 ♘d4 ♕g6 12 f3 ♗d7) 10...♘c2 11 ♘h4 (11 ♖c1 is no better, as I painfully experienced in C.Wisnewski-A.Neffe, German League 2003: after 11...♘xe3 12 fxe3 ♗c5 13 ♖c3 h5! Black has excellent attacking chances) 11...♗xe2 12 ♘xf5 (12 ♕xe2? is answered by 12...♕g4!) 12...♗xd1 13 ♖axd1 ♘xe3 (but not 13...g6?? because of 14 ♗g5) 14 fxe3 g6 15 ♘g3 ♘g4 16 ♖xf7 ♘xe3 17 ♖e1 ♗c5 18 ♔h1 ♖df8 with a stable endgame advantage.

c) Finally, after 8 0-0 Black can equalize with 8...e5 9 ♘xe5 ♘xe5 10 dxe5 ♗xe2 11 ♕xe2 ♕xe5 12 ♘c4 ♕e6 13 ♖fe1 ♘d5 14 ♗d2 (14 ♗xa7? loses the bishop again to 14...♕xe2 15 ♖xe2 b6 16 ♘e5 ♖e8!) 14...♕xe2 15 ♖xe2 ♗c5.

7...♕h5!?

There are a few alternatives, but I do not like any of them:

a) 7...e5?! doesn't work too well here, as after 8 c4 White is an important move up on Game 10 (Klyuner-Koscielski).

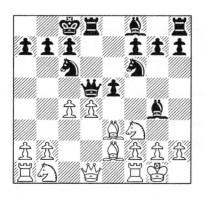

B.Heim-D.Willing, Eberbach 1980, continued 8...♕a5 9 d5 e4 10 ♘fd2 (10 ♘g5 is even better: after 10...♗xe2 11 ♕xe2 ♘e5 12 ♗d4 Black cannot avoid material losses) 10...♘e5 11 ♘c3 ♕b4 12 ♗d4, and now Black collapsed with 12...♗d6? 13 ♘b5 (13 ♗xe5 or 13 a3 would have won instantly) 13...♗xe2 14 ♕xe2 a6 15 ♗c3 ♕c5 16 b4 ♕b6 17 ♗d4 and White won. But 12...♗xe2 13

♕xe2 ♖e8 is only relatively better (not 13...♗d6? 14 a3 again), as after 14 a3 ♕e7 15 ♘cxe4 White, among other things, is a pawn up.

b) 7...♕f5?! does not promise much either. After 8 c4 e5 (8...♗xf3? 9 ♗xf3 is bad, as the motif from Game 11 does not work here: 9...♘xd4 10 ♗xd4 e5 11 ♕b3 or if 9...♘e5 10 ♗xb7+ ♔xb7 11 ♕b3+ followed by 12 dxe5) 9 d5 e4 (not 9...♘b4? 10 a3 ♘c2 11 ♗d3 e4 12 ♗xc2 ♕h5 13 ♘bd2 exf3 14 ♘xf3 and White is a pawn up, while after 9...♗xf3 10 ♗xf3 e4 11 ♗e2 ♘e5 12 ♘c3 a6 13 h3 the pair of bishops provides White with an advantage) 10 ♘fd2 ♗xe2 (or 10...♘e5 11 ♘c3 a6 12 ♗d4 and again Black will have difficulties protecting his e-pawn) 11 ♕xe2 ♘b4 (if 11...♘e5 12 ♘c3 ♗d6 13 ♗xa7 ♘eg4 14 h3 ♕e5 15 g3 and White easily shakes off the attack, or 12...a6 13 ♗d4 with well-known problems for Black) 12 ♘c3 ♘c2 (or 12...a6 13 ♗d4! ♘c2 14 ♗xf6 and White wins the e-pawn) 13 ♖ad1 and again Black will be unable to save e4. Trying to launch an attack would not be crowned with success either, for example 13...♘xe3 14 ♕xe3 ♗d6 15 ♕xa7 ♗xh2+ 16 ♔xh2 ♕h5+ 17 ♔g1 ♘g4 18 ♖fe1 e3 19 ♖xe3! and Black has nothing.

c) 7...e6?! is too tame. Black needs to initiate counterplay, as the game F.Hedke-N.Michaelsen, German Championship, Bad Wildbad 1993, showed: 8 h3 ♗h5 9 c4 ♕d7 10 ♘bd2 h6 11 a3 g5 12 b4 ♗xf3 13 ♘xf3 g4 14 hxg4 ♘xg4 15 b5 ♘e7 16 ♕a4 ♔b8 17 ♘e5 ♘xe5 18 dxe5 ♘c8, and now 19 c5!

would have given White a huge advantage.

d) Finally, 7...♗xf3 8 ♗xf3 ♕b5 has been suggested by Wahls, but the simple 9 ♘c3! promises White good play,

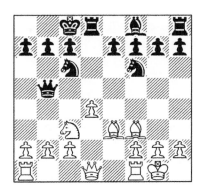

one example being the game B.De Schepper-V.Baci, correspondence 2000, which continued 9...♕xb2 10 ♘e4 ♘xe4 11 ♗xe4 ♕c3 12 ♕f3! ♕c4 (12...♘xd4 is no improvement, since White can obtain a good position with simply 13 ♕xf7) 13 ♖ab1 g6 14 ♖xb7! ♔xb7 15 ♗xc6+ ♔c8 (if 15...♕xc6 16 ♖b1+ wins) 16 ♗b7+ ♔d7 17 d5 f5 18 ♗c6+ ♔c8 19 ♗xa7 ♗g7 20 ♖b1 and Black resigned as mate is unavoidable.

8 h3

8 ♘bd2 only has independent value after 8...e5 9 dxe5 (9 h3 transposes to the text), but this proved to be ineffective in S.Del Rio Angeles-A.Minasian, Ubeda 2001, which continued 9...♘xe5 10 ♖e1 ♗d6 11 ♘xe5 ♗xe5 12 ♗xg4+ ♕xg4 13 c3 ♖d7 14 ♕xg4? ♗xh2+! 15 ♔xh2 ♘xg4+ 16 ♔g3 ♘xe3 17 ♖xe3 ♖xd2 and Black even gained the upper hand.

8...e5!?

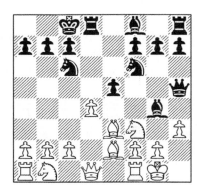

Offering an interesting piece sacrifice.

9 hxg4

9 ♘bd2! is supposed to refute the whole line according to Wahls. While I tend to agree that White is generally better, the variations after 9...♗xf3 10 ♗xf3 are very complicated; for example:

a) 10...♕f5?! unfortunately does not work: 11 ♗xc6 exd4 (11...bxc6 is hopeless, as White gets a good game after simply 12 dxe5 ♕xe5 13 ♕e2; for example 13...♗d6 14 ♕a6+ ♔d7 15 ♘f3 ♕b5 16 ♕xa7 ♕xb2 17 ♖ad1 and White has nice attacking chances, or 13...♔b7 14 ♘c4 and Black will have big problems preventing the knight from going decisively to a5) 12 ♘b3! (12 ♘f3?! allows 12...dxe3! 13 ♗xb7+ ♔xb7 14 ♕xd8 exf2+, followed by 15...♘e4 with the initiative) 12...bxc6 13 ♘xd4. A.Magalotti-M.Van der Werf, Denmark 1999, continued 13...♕e4 14 ♕e2 ♔b7 (not 14...♖xd4? 15 ♕a6+ and 16 ♗xd4 wins) 15 ♘b3 (15 ♕c4! instead would have been even better) 15...♕a4 16 ♖ad1 ♗d6 17 ♖d4 ♕b5 18 c4 ♕a6 19

♖fd1 and White had a commanding position.

b) 10...♕g6 11 ♗xc6 exd4 and now we have:

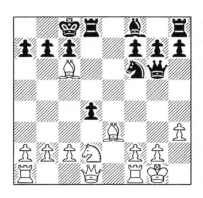

b1) 12 ♗xb7+ ♔xb7 13 ♕f3+ ♔c8! (but not 13...c6? 14 ♘b3! dxe3 15 ♘a5+ ♔b8 16 ♘xc6+ ♔c7 17 ♘xd8 ♔xd8 18 ♕a8+ ♔c7 19 ♕xa7+ with a decisive advantage, or 15...♔a6 16 ♕xc6+ ♔xa5 17 a3 and Black cannot avoid being mated; while after 13...♔b8 14 ♗f4 Black will have problems defending his weak queenside as he cannot now play 14...♕f5) 14 ♗f4 ♕f5 15 ♖fe1 ♘d5 and Black seems to have enough counterplay to compensate for his structural deficits.

b2) 12 ♘f3 bxc6 13 ♕e2 d3!? 14 cxd3 ♕xd3 15 ♕xd3 ♖xd3 16 ♘e5 ♖d5 17 ♘xf7 ♖g8 and White is slightly better due to the weakened black pawn structure.

But anyway, those who don't like this turn of events can play the alternative 6...e5 and transpose to Game 10, as described in the note to Black's 6th move.

9...♘xg4

10 ♘h4

Besides the text move, there are a few alternatives to examine:

a) 10 d5 e4! 11 ♘h4 ♘ce5 and while White won't be able to save the piece, the black attack is far from over.

b) 10 ♘bd2 looks more promising, but Black has definite compensation after 10...♘xd4 11 ♗xd4 ♖xd4!, for example 12 c3 ♖d6 (intending ...♖h6) 13 ♖e1 (if 13 ♕a4 f5 and the queen covers e8) 13...f5 (not 13...♖h6?! 14 ♘h4! f5 15 g3 g5? 16 ♗xg4 fxg4 17 ♖xe5 and White wins) 14 g3 g5 (14...♗e7!? is also interesting) 15 ♕c2 ♖f6 16 ♘f1 ♗c5 17 ♘xe5 ♗xf2+ 18 ♔g2 ♗xg3 19 ♗xg4 fxg4 20 ♘xg3 ♕h3+ 21 ♔g1 ♕xg3+ 22 ♕g2 ♕xg2+ 23 ♔xg2 h5 and Black has three passed pawns for the piece.

c) 10 c3 seeks to protect d4, but 10...f5! issues the threat of ...e5-e4, and after 11 g3 ♕h3! and White will have a very hard time defending himself; for example 12 ♗g5 e4 13 ♘bd2 exf3 14 ♘xf3 ♘ce5! wins.

10...f5!

Surprisingly, White seems unable to save himself after this move.

11 ♗xg4

If 11 g3 first, then 11...g5 12 ♗xg4 fxg4 13 ♘f5 (13 ♘g2 exd4 14 ♗c1 transposes to the game) 13...exd4 14 ♘xd4 (14 ♗c1 is the next note) 14...♘xd4 15 ♗xd4 ♖d6 and 16...♖h6 wins.

11...fxg4 12 g3 exd4 13 ♗c1 g5 14 ♘g2

14 ♘f5 is hardly better as the knight has a shaky position here; for example 14...♘e5 15 ♘d2 ♕g6 16 f4 gxf3 17 g4 d3! 18 ♘xf3 ♘xg4 19 ♘xg5 and now either 19...♗c5+ 20 ♔g2 ♘e5 21 cxd3 h6 22 ♕e2 ♖he8 23 d4 ♗xd4 24 ♘xd4 ♖xd4 (analysis by Wahls) or simply 19...♕h5 20 ♗f4 h6 wins.

14...♘e5

15 f4?

White collapses, but the position was beyond repair anyway. Wahls suggests 15 ♘e1 as a possible defence, giving 15...♘f3+ 16 ♘xf3 gxf3 17 ♖e1 ♖d6 18 ♕d3 ♗g7 19 ♗xg5 ♕xg5 20 ♘d2, but Black can instead play the immediate 15...♖d6! with a winning attack. 15 ♘d2 does not help either, as after 15...♗c5! 16 b4 ♗b6 17 ♖e1 ♖he8 Black stands much better.

15...gxf3 16 ♘e1 f2+ 0-1

Summary

Games 6 and 7 show that White has nothing better than to play 4 ♘f3, after which Black has the luxury to choose between two almost equivalent alternatives. While 4...e5 in Game 8 is the more solid option, 4...♗g4 from Games 9-12 is my recommendation if you are going for the full point. White can equalize with precise play, but it is a long way to go.

1 e4 ♘c6 2 d4 d5 3 exd5 ♕xd5 (D) 4 ♘f3

      4 ♗e3 – *Game 6*

      4 ♘c3 – *Game 7*

4...♗g4

      4...e5 – *Game 8*

5 ♗e2 0-0-0 (D) 6 ♗e3

      6 ♘c3 – *Game 9*

      6 c3 – *Game 10*

      6 c4 – *Game 11*

6...♘f6 7 0-0 ♕h5 (D) – *Game 12*

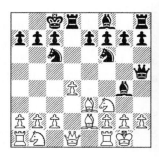

3...♕xd5   *5...0-0-0*   *7...♕h5*

Chapter Three

1 e4 ♘c6 2 d4 d5 3 e5 f6

The move **3 e5** is of such great practical relevance that I can hardly wait to instruct you how it should be treated. Many sources compare the resulting position to the Advance French or the Advance Caro-Kann, stating that the current version is even more appealing as Black's queen's knight is now blocking his c-pawn, seemingly depriving him of his only chance of counterplay in the centre. As an enthusiastic advocate I should really try to convince them of the contrary, but as long as I am scoring points against players blindly following such dogmatic statements, I will restrict myself to convincing just you.

I do agree that Black should probably not opt for 3...♗f5. This deploys the bishop prematurely and offers White a way to obtain an advantage by going right after it with 4 ♘e2!. Following 4...f6 5 f4 the game J.Te Kolste-A.Nimzowitsch, Baden Baden 1925, continued 5...e6 6 ♘g3 fxe5 7 fxe5 and now 7...♕d7 8 ♘xf5 exf5 left Black with a pawn structure which is not to my liking at least. Myers suggested 7...♕h4 as an improvement, but after 8 c3 there is no sensible way to avoid ♘b1-d2-f3, driving the queen back with a better position for White.

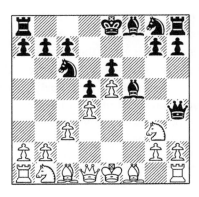

I was not able to refute this idea, but fortunately that isn't necessary. A commendable option is the immediate **3...f6**, directly attacking the white centre, to which there are different ways to react...

White plays 4 ♗d3

The move **4 ♗d3** seems a logical answer to 3...f6. As White is threatening 5 ♕h5+ there is no time to take on either d4 or e5. But Black can simply play **4...g6**,

which immediately reveals the drawbacks of 4 ♗d3. Now White needs to take care of both his d- and e-pawns and, as a consequence, is not able to reinforce his centre with f2-f4. The only sensible alternative is 5 exf6, but that does not solve all the problems as it still leaves the d-pawn unprotected. So White needs to waste further time, which Black can utilize to enforce ...e7-e5 under favourable circumstances, resulting in a comfortable position.

Game 13
L.Myagmarsuren-D.Van Geet
World Student Team
Championship, Varna 1958

---

1 e4 ♘c6 2 d4 d5 3 e5 f6 4 ♗d3

The immediate 4 exf6 ♘xf6 directly defuses the situation in the centre, but

brings Black one step closer to equality:

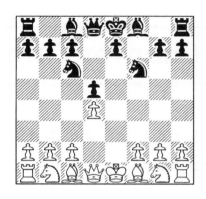

a) 5 ♘f3 allows the annoying pin 5...♗g4. Now the only way for White to successfully prevent Black from playing ...e7-e5 is by 6 ♗b5 (if 6 ♗e2 ♗xf3 7 ♗xf3 e5 8 dxe5 ♘xe5 and Black has comfortably equalized), after which T.Walseth-M.Ardaman, Internet (blitz) 1999, continued 6...♕d7 7 h3 ♗xf3 8 ♕xf3 a6 9 ♗xc6 ♕xc6 10 ♘c3 e6 11 ♗g5 ♗b4! 12 ♗xf6 0-0 13 0-0 ♖xf6 14 ♕e3 ♖af8 and Black was clearly better due to his more active pieces.

b) 5 ♗f4 is the only challenging move. Now Black should not play 5...♗g4, since after 6 ♗e2 ♗xe2 7 ♘xe2 e6 8 ♘bc3 ♗d6 9 ♘b5 ♗xf4 10 ♘xf4 he cannot play 10...e5 because of 11 ♘e6. Better is 5...♗f5, when T.Thompson-E.Cruz, World Junior Championships 1993, continued 6 c3 a6! 7 ♘f3 e6 8 ♘bd2 ♗d6 9 ♘e5 ♗xe5! 10 ♗xe5 0-0 11 h3 ♘xe5 12 dxe5 ♘e4 13 ♘xe4 ♗xe4 and Black had a very nice position.

4...g6 5 ♘f3

5 f4?! allows Black to reach a comfortable position after 5...♘xd4 6 ♗xg6+ hxg6 7 ♕xd4 ♗f5. Instead, 5 exf6 solves

the problem of the e5-pawn, but not of the one on d4. After 5...♘xf6 6 c3 (6 ♘f3 ♗g4 transposes to the text) 6...e5! 7 dxe5 ♘xe5 8 ♗e2 ♗g7 9 ♘f3 (9 f4 just weakens the kingside and Black gets a good game after 9...♘f7) 9...♘xf3+ 10 ♗xf3 0-0 Black has the clearly better position.

5...♗g4 6 exf6 ♘xf6 7 c3 ♗g7 8 h3 ♗xf3 9 ♕xf3 0-0 10 ♕e2 e5! 11 dxe5 ♘xe5 12 0-0 ♘h5

Black could have removed one bishop from the board with 12...♘xd3, but he is looking for more.

13 ♗e3 ♕h4 14 ♘d2 ♖ad8

14...♖ae8 makes more sense, introducing the rook to a vis-à-vis with the white queen.

15 ♔h2 ♘f4

All the black pieces have moved into attacking positions.

16 ♗xf4 ♕xf4+ 17 g3??

Admittedly White throws the game away rather too quickly, but after 17 ♔g1 ♖de8! the position remains extremely difficult; for example 18 ♘b3 ♖e7, followed by ...♖fe8, and Black has fun on the e-file.

17...♕xd2 18 ♕xd2 ♘f3+ 19 ♔g2 ♘xd2 20 ♖fd1 ♘e4 21 f3 ♘c5 22 ♗f1 c6 0-1

White plays 4 f4

4 f4 is the move you will most likely encounter. It seems that Black's endeavour to endanger the white centre bites on granite, and this is indeed the case for the moment. But Black can draw on another strategic idea – by moving his f-pawn White severely weakened his light squares, a fact that Black should try to exploit. The most important resource is the light-squared bishop, which has been fondly called 'the sweeper in front of the pawn chain' by Harald Keilhack.

The diagram shows the position after 4...♗f5 5 c3 e6 6 ♘f3 ♕d7 7 ♗d3 ♗e4 8 ♕e2 f5 from O.Duras-A.Nimzowitsch, Ostend 1907. The strategic implications arising are clear: Black will castle long and try to initiate an attack on the kingside. White, on the other hand, has to try to get counterplay on the queenside, but he has always to watch out for the powerful black bishop on e4. And what is more, scope for his own dark-squared bishop is virtually non-existent.

However, Black needs to be careful about implementing the correct move order. The immediate 4...♗f5?! is still dubious, as 5 ♘e2! leads to the Te Kolste-Nimzowitsch game mentioned above. More to the point is **4...♘h6!**, which is a useful move as the knight is being deployed to f5 or f7 anyway. Only after 5 ♘f3 should Black play 5...♗f5. For a nice illustration of a possible strategic course of action I urge you to sit back and enjoy the following game.

Game 14
B.Bengsch-R.Becker
Kassel 1998

1 e4 ♘c6 2 d4 d5 3 e5 f6 4 f4 ♘h6 5 ♘f3 ♗f5

6 c3

Alternatives are few and far between:

a) 6 ♗b5 ♕d7 usually transposes to the 7 ♗b5 line examined below.

b) On 6 ♗d3, carrying out the in-tended plan with 6...♗e4?! is not advisable, as after 7 ♘c3 f5 8 ♘g5! White can point his finger to the weak e6-square; for example 8...♘xd4 (8...♕d7 9 e6 ♕d8 10 ♘xh7! is completely hopeless for Black) 9 ♗e3 ♘c6 10 ♗xe4 dxe4 11 ♘d5 and the threat of 12 ♘e6 cannot be successfully parried. Instead 6...e6 usually transposes to the text.

c) After 6 ♗e3, the game T.Heinemann-C.Wisnewski, German Club Cup 2004, showed that White can go down quickly if he plays carelessly: 6...e6 7 exf6 gxf6 8 ♗e2 ♖g8 9 ♘h4 ♗e4 10 ♗h5+ ♔d7 11 0-0?? ♘f5! and White was already lost.

6...e6 7 ♗d3

Instead:

a) 7 ♗b5 is not dangerous in this line as the critical e5-square is safely covered. After 7...♕d7 8 h3 a6 (or 8...♗e4 9 ♗e3 ♗e7 10 ♘bd2 f5 11 c4?! dxc4 12 0-0 ♗d5 13 ♖c1 ♘f7 14 ♘xc4 a6 15 ♗xc6 ♗xc6 with a strategically won position in H.Schulz-C.Wisnewski, Bargteheide 2004, as Black's control over the light squares is decisive) 9 ♗e2,

Black showed a proper treatment of the position in the old game W.Von Holzhausen-B.Kostic, Berlin 1928: 9...♗e7 10 0-0 ♗e4 11 ♔h2 f5 12 ♗e3 ♘f7 13 ♘bd2 h6 14 ♘xe4 dxe4 15 ♘d2 g5 16 g4?! gxf4 17 ♗xf4 ♗g5 18 ♘c4 ♘e7 19 ♘e3 ♗xf4+ 20 ♖xf4 ♘g6 with a huge kingside initiative. The attacking scheme with ...♘f7, ...h6 and ...g5 is very instructive and should be implemented whenever possible.

b) The quiet 7 ♗e2 poses no threat to the black set-up. After 7...♗e7 8 0-0 0-0 9 ♘a3 ♗e4 10 ♘c2 ♕e8 11 ♘e3 fxe5 12 fxe5 ♕g6 Black again had good prospects on the kingside in F.Gomez-O.Castro Rojas, Colombian Championship 1977.

7...♗e4! 8 ♕e2

8 ♗xe4 dxe4 9 ♘fd2 is met simply by 9...f5, as 10 ♕b3 ♕d5 11 ♕xb7 can be smoothly answered with 11...♘xe5!, while 11 ♕xd5?! exd5 just leaves White with the worse bishop.

8...f5 9 ♘bd2 ♕d7 10 0-0 ♘f7

11 b4 ♗xd3

There was no need to swap the bishop right away, but the character of the position is not dramatically changed by that.

12 ♕xd3 ♗e7 13 ♘b3 h6 14 a4 g5 15 h3 0-0-0 16 a5 ♖dg8 17 ♘c5 ♗xc5 18 bxc5 a6 19 ♘h2 ♕e7 20 ♖f3 ♖g7 21 c4 dxc4 22 ♕xc4 ♕d7 23 ♖a4 ♘e7 24 ♖b4 c6

A beautiful sight. The white attack on the queenside has been stopped and the bishop rendered totally inoperative.

25 ♖fb3 ♘d8 26 ♖xb7? ♘xb7 27 ♕xa6 ♕xd4+ 28 ♖e3 gxf4 29 ♕a8+ ♔c7 30 ♕xh8 fxe3 0-1

Instead of 5 ♘f3 above, **5 c3** is a useful move which puts Black more to the test. White has still not committed his king's knight and Black is out of sensible waiting moves. However, Black can adopt a different set-up with **5...♗g4!**, the point being that after 6 ♗e2 Black can reply 6...♗f5!, with a similar position to the previous game. The only difference is the extra development of the white king's bishop, but that actually favours Black since the bishop is not doing much on e2 other than blocking the knight's way.

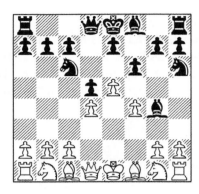

That leaves **6 ♘f3** once more, but after **6...♕d7 7 ♗e2 ♘f5** we see another way of getting the black pieces into action. Both manoeuvres offer Black excellent prospects on the kingside, as can be seen in our next game.

Game 15
M.Dupre Guegan-D.Bergez
French League 1998

---

1 e4 ♘c6 2 d4 d5 3 e5 f6 4 f4 ♘h6 5 c3 ♗g4 6 ♘f3

As already mentioned, after 6 ♗e2 Black can afford to lose a tempo with 6...♗f5, as the bishop can no longer be harassed by the white knight and the white bishop isn't doing much on e2 anyway. The game could continue 7 ♘f3 e6 8 0-0 ♗e7 9 ♘bd2 0-0 10 ♖e1 fxe5 11 fxe5 ♕e8 with good prospects on the kingside.

Instead 6 ♕b3 puts the finger on b7, but Black can react with 6...♘a5. The game Burkhanlansky-N.Mitkov, Bulgaria 1977, continued 7 ♕c2 ♕d7 8 ♗d3 g6 9 h3 ♗f5 10 ♘f3 0-0-0 11 g4 ♗xd3 12

♕xd3 ♘f7 13 ♕e2 ♕e6 14 ♘a3 h5! 15 ♖g1 hxg4 16 hxg4 ♕c6 17 ♗d2 fxe5 18 dxe5 e6 with a clearly better position for Black.

6...♕d7

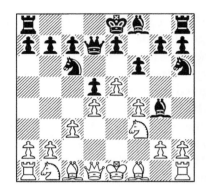

7 ♗e2

After 7 ♗e3 ♘f5 8 ♗f2 h5 9 ♘a3 h4 10 ♘c2 g5! was the correct treatment of the position in G.Sanders-M.Ardaman, Internet (blitz) 1999. The game continued 11 exf6 exf6 12 fxg5 fxg5 13 ♕e2+ ♗e7 14 0-0-0 0-0-0 and due to his space advantage on the kingside, Black was better.

7 h3?! just weakens the position. As the typical devotee of the Nimzowitsch Defence is not afraid to trade a bishop for a knight, 7...♗xf3 is the usual consequence. After 8 ♕xf3 e6 9 ♘d2 ♗e7 10 ♗d3 0-0-0 11 ♘b3 fxe5 12 dxe5 ♖df8 13 ♗b5 a6 14 ♗xc6 ♕xc6 15 ♘d4 ♕d7 16 b4 ♘f5 17 ♘xf5 ♖xf5 Black controlled the light squares in N.Cartier-D.Berges, France 1999.

7...♘f5 8 ♕d3 e6 9 b3 0-0-0 10 a4 h5 11 a5 ♗e7 12 ♗a3 ♗xf3 13 ♗xf3 fxe5 14 fxe5 ♘h4 15 ♗xe7 ♘xf3+ 16 ♕xf3 ♕xe7

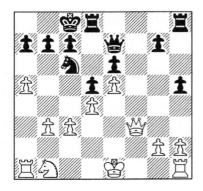

The dust has settled. Black's only problem is the misplaced knight on c6. In exchange he has a lead in development and good kingside prospects.

17 ♞d2 ♖df8 18 ♕e2 g5 19 ♖f1 g4 20 b4 ♖xf1+ 21 ♞xf1 ♖f8 22 b5 ♞b8 23 ♞d2 c5! 24 c4

Lacking alternatives, White tries to unbalance the position, but with precise play Black should gain the upper hand.

24...cxd4 25 cxd5 exd5 26 ♖c1+ ♚d8 27 ♞b3

27...♕b4+?!

27...♞d7! was simple and good. After 28 e6 (28 ♞xd4? ♕b4+ 29 ♕d2 loses

after 29...♖f1+) 28...d3! 29 ♕xd3 ♕xe6+ White is without counterplay.

28 ♕d2 ♕xd2+ 29 ♚xd2 ♖f2+ 30 ♚d3 ♖xg2 31 ♚xd4 b6 32 axb6 axb6 33 ♚xd5 ♖xh2 34 ♚e6?

Blocking the path of the e-pawn makes no sense. Instead 34 ♚d6 makes use of the knight on b3 which prevents the annoying check from behind.

34...g3 35 ♖f1 ♖f2 36 ♖xf2 gxf2 37 ♞d2

37...♚c7?

37...♞d7! was evidently better. The endgame is probably still drawn, but White has to steer clear of rocks. For example, he cannot take care of the h-pawn immediately as 38 ♚f5 h4 39 ♚g4 ♞xe5+ 40 ♚xh4 runs into 40...♞f3+!.

38 ♚f7 ♞d7 39 e6 ♞e5+ 40 ♚f6 ♞c4 41 ♞f1 ♞d6 42 ♚g5 ♞xb5 43 ♚xh5 ♚d6 44 ♚g4 ♚xe6 45 ♚f3 ♚d5 46 ♞e3+ ♚d4 47 ♚xf2 ♞a3 48 ♚e2 ♞c4 49 ♞c2+ ♚c3 50 ♚d1 b5 51 ♚c1 ♞b6 52 ♚b1 ♞d5 53 ♚c1 ♞f4 54 ♚b1 ♞e2 55 ♞e3 ♚b3 56 ♞c2 ♞c3+ 57 ♚c1 ♞e2+ 58 ♚d2 ♚b2 59 ♚d3 ♞f4+ 60 ♚d2 ♞d5 61 ♚d3 ♞f4+ 62 ♚d2 ♞e6 63 ♚d3 ♞c5+ 64 ♚d4 ♞b3+ 65 ♚d3 ♞c1+ 66 ♚d2 ♞e2 67 ♚d3 ♚b3 68 ♞a1+ ♚a2 69 ♞c2 ½-½

White plays 4 ♗b5

White's best way to confront Black's plans is with **4 ♗b5**.

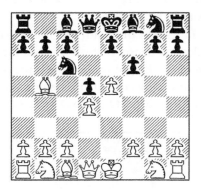

By pinning the knight White takes pressure off his centre – and what may be even more important, Black can neither play the natural 4...♗f5 because of 5 ♗xc6+! bxc6 6 ♘f3 when his pawn structure is shoddy, nor 4...fxe5 as White can sacrifice a pawn with 5 ♘f3! for a dangerous initiative.

Black has to settle for **4...♗d7**. After **5 ♘c3 fxe5 6 dxe5 e6** his position is a bit more passive than in the previous games, but it still offers enough counterplay, as our final game in this chapter illustrates.

Game 16
R.Nocci-K.H.Johnsen
Correspondence 2000

---

1 e4 ♘c6 2 d4 d5 3 e5 f6 4 ♗b5 ♗d7

Black would like to reach positions similar to those in the previous games, but the simple 4...♗f5 5 ♗xc6+ bxc6 6 ♘f3 creates a problem. Black cannot play 6...e6 as 7 ♘h4! trades off the bishop, after which the black pawn structure is just a mess.

5 ♘c3

This protects the bishop and therefore deals with the threat of ...♘xe5. Other moves are less accurate:

a) **5 ♗xc6 ♗xc6** leads to a different type of game where White tries to keep the position closed.

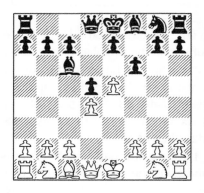

However, as his central pawns are on dark squares, a certain weakness of his light squares cannot be denied, even more so as his light-squared bishop has just been traded off. I was unable to find any practical examples, but I feel that after 6 ♘f3 ♛d7 7 0-0 0-0-0 Black must be better, as it is easier for him to initiate a kingside attack than it is for White to get some play on the queenside.

b) After 5 f4 Black could choose an inferior version of one of the previous games with 5...e6 6 ♘f3, but 5...♘xe5 6 ♗xd7+ ♘xd7 7 ♛h5+ g6 8 ♛xd5 c6 is better. After 9 ♛e6 ♘b6 10 ♘f3 ♛d5 Black has nothing to worry about, while 9 ♛e4 allows 9...e5! 10 fxe5 fxe5

11 dxe5 ♕a5+ 12 ♘c3 ♕xe5 with equality.

c) 5 ♘f3 tries to force Black into an inferior position with 5...e6, but again Black can play 5...♘xe5!, possible consequences being 6 ♘xe5 fxe5 7 ♗xd7+ ♕xd7 8 ♕h5+ g6 9 ♕xe5 ♘f6 10 0-0 ♗g7 11 c3 (11 ♖e1 does not disturb Black's development as 11...0-0 12 ♕xe7 is countered by 12...♖ae8 13 ♕b4 ♕a4! 14 ♗d2 ♖xe1+ 15 ♗xe1 ♕xc2) 11...0-0 12 ♗f4 c6 and Black will have no problems enforcing ...e7-e5.

5...fxe5 6 dxe5 e6 7 ♘f3 ♗b4 8 a3 ♗xc3+ 9 bxc3 ♘ge7 10 ♗d3

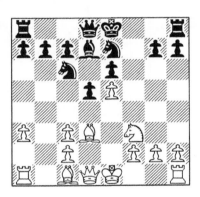

10...h6

Not 10...0-0?! 11 ♗xh7+! ♔xh7 12 ♘g5+ ♔g8 13 ♕h5 ♖f5 14 ♕h7+ ♔f8 15 f4 with a ferocious attack.

11 ♖b1 b6 12 c4 0-0 13 0-0 ♗e8?!

After the superior 13...♕e8 Black can be very happy with his position, as his only weakness (on e6) cannot be the target of attack any time soon. There fore White doesn't have anything to play against, while Black can calmly fathom his chances on the kingside.

14 cxd5 ♕xd5 15 c4 ♕a5?!

After this bold move White gets unnecessary attacking chances against the king, and although Black manages to defend with precise play, 15...♕d7, followed by ...♖d8 and/or ...♗g6, is better.

16 ♖b5 ♕a6 17 ♘h4 ♖d8 18 ♗xh6!? ♖xd3 19 ♕xd3 gxh6 20 ♕h3

20...♕a4 21 ♕xe6+ ♔h7 22 ♕g4 ♕xa3 23 ♕e4+ ♔h8 24 ♖bb1 ♕c5 25 ♖be1 ♗h5 26 g4 ♗e8 27 h3 ♘a5 28 ♖c1 h5 29 ♖c3 a6 30 ♖f3 ♖xf3 31 ♕xf3 ♕xe5 32 ♕a8 ♘g8 33 ♘f3 ♕e6 34 ♖e1 ♗c6 35 ♕xa6 ♕xc4 36 ♕xc4 ♘xc4 37 ♘e5 ♘xe5 38 ♖xe5 hxg4 39 hxg4 ♗d7 40 g5 ♔g7 41 f4 ♔f7 42 f5 ♘e7 43 f6 ♘f5 44 ♔f2 c5 45 ♖e2 c4 46 ♖d2 ♗a4 47 ♖d5 c3 48 ♖d8 c2 49 ♖c8 ♘d6 50 ♖c7+ ♔g6 51 ♔e1 ♔xg5 52 f7 ♘xf7 53 ♔d2 ♘e5 54 ♖c8 b5 0-1

Summary

Game 13 proves that 3...f6 is a viable move that cannot be refuted directly, so White has to think about how to retain control over e5. Doing this with 4 f4 weakens the light squares and is best exploited by the set-up beginning with 4...♘h6, explained in Games 14 and 15. Playing 4 ♗b5 is probably the smartest way to treat the position, but Game 16 showed that Black has no problems.

1 e4 ♘c6 2 d4 d5 3 e5 f6 *(D)* **4 f4**

       4 ♗d3 – *Game 13*

       4 ♗b5 ♗d7 *(D)* – *Game 16*

4...♘h6

       5 ♘f3 ♗f5 – *Game 14*

       5 c3 ♗g4 *(D)* – *Game 15*

3...f6

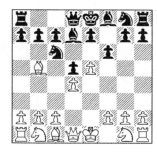
4...♗d7

5...♗g4

Chapter Four

1 e4 ♘c6 2 d4 d5 3 ♘c3 e6

If not the most frequently played move, **3 ♘c3** is certainly the most annoying. I can imagine that many players were hoping that I would cover 3...dxe4 in great detail, but if you are among them I have to disappoint you there. I admit that I was simply too lazy to deal with a line that lives virtually on the brink of refutation every day. Even more so as I have a credible alternative at my disposal, as you will see in this current chapter.

With **3...e6** Black transposes to an inconspicuous line of the French Defence that is usually reached via the move order 1 e4 e6 2 d4 d5 3 ♘c3 ♘c6. To pay tribute to its two pioneers, this variation has been named the 'Hecht-Reefschläger'. I stumbled upon it about a year after I took up the Nimzowitsch Defence and I immediately scored well with it. Combine this with a largely increasing popularity these days and we have two good enough reasons to take a closer look.

White plays 4 exd5

The position after **4 exd5 exd5** bears a close resemblance to the Exchange French, but the inclusion of ♘c3 and ...♘c6 is favourable to Black, as the only way that White can hope for an advantage is with c2-c4. But another thing is perhaps even more important: many White players underestimate the dangers lying in this seemingly quiet position – an attitude that spells brinksmanship.

Game 17
M.Stern-G.Alexopoulos
Somerset, USA 1985

---

1 e4 ♘c6 2 ♘c3 e6 3 d4 d5 4 exd5

Besides the text, various other moves have been tried. 4 e5 is seen in Game 18, while 4 ♘f3 will be covered in Game 19. Also:

a) 4 ♗b5 is quite similar to Game 4, only with the moves d2-d4 and ...e7-e6 included. After 4...dxe4 5 ♘xe4 (5 ♗xc6+ bxc6 6 ♘xe4 ♕d5 7 ♕f3 ♗b7! 8 ♗e3 0-0-0 9 ♘c3 ♗b4 10 ♕xd5 cxd5 and Black enjoyed the advantage in form of the two bishops in F.Grzesik-H.Reefschläger, German League 1984) 5...♕d5 6 ♕e2 (6 ♕d3 ♘f6 7 ♘xf6+ gxf6 8 ♘f3 ♗d7 9 c4 ♕h5 10 0-0 0-0-0 11 ♗f4 e5 favoured Black in K.Pinkas-J.Bany, Polish Team Championship 1990) 6...a6 7 ♗xc6+ ♕xc6 8 ♘f3 ♘f6 9 ♘xf6+ gxf6 10 0-0 b5!? 11 ♖d1 ♕d5 12 b3 ♗b7 13 c4 ♕e4 14 ♕xe4 ♗xe4 once more the two bishops provided an advantage for Black in C.Maier-L.Keitlinghaus, German Championship 1989.

b) 4 ♘ge2 seems to be a sensible move, protecting both d4 and c3. But 4...♗b4 shows that ...♘c6 does have its merits.

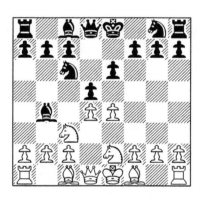

b1) Now 5 a3 ♗xc3+ 6 ♘xc3 is not possible, as after 6...dxe4 the d-pawn is hanging.

b2) 5 exd5 is also harmless; for example 5...exd5 6 a3 ♗a5 7 b4 ♗b6 8 ♘a4 ♕e7 9 ♗e3 and in F.Fronmueller-K.Pomm, German League 1988, Black already seized the advantage with

9...f5! 10 ♘xb6 axb6 11 ♘c3 ♘f6 12 ♗e2 0-0 13 0-0 ♗e6 14 ♗g5 h6 15 ♗xf6 ♕xf6 16 ♘b5 ♖f7. Now White tried to stop a further advance on the kingside with 17 f4, but after 17...♖e7 18 ♗f3 ♗f7 19 ♕d2 ♖ae8 20 ♖ad1 ♘d8! 21 ♘c3 c6 22 ♘e2 ♗g6 23 ♘c1 ♘f7 24 ♕c3 ♘d6 25 a4 ♘c4 26 ♖f2 ♖e3 Black was in complete command.

So White has to take care of his fragile centre in another way, but the alternative does not look too promising:

b3) 5 e5 f6 and the knight is misplaced on e2; for example:

b31) 6 ♘f4 ♕e7 7 ♗b5 fxe5 8 ♗xc6+ bxc6 9 ♕h5+ ♕f7 10 ♕xf7+ (if 10 ♕xe5 ♘f6 11 0-0 0-0 White can hardly prevent Black from preparing ...e6-e5, as 12 ♖e1 is met by 12...♘e4!) 10...♔xf7 11 dxe5 ♘h6 12 ♘d3 ♗e7 13 ♘a4 ♘f5 14 f4 ♗a6 15 ♗d2 ♗b5 16 ♘dc5 ♗xa4! 17 ♘xa4 c5 and Black achieved a nice position in H.Lopez Silva-L.Rojas, Chilean Championship 2002.

b32) 6 f4 ♘h6 bears a close resemblance to the positions examined in Chapter 3. The treatment here is about the same, for example 7 g3 (freeing the bishop with 7 ♘g3 has too many disadvantages: R.Kammer-W.Reimer, German League 1990, continued 7...0-0 8 a3 ♗a5 9 b4 ♗b6 10 ♘ce2 fxe5 11 fxe5 ♕h4 12 ♗xh6 ♕xh6 13 ♕d3 ♗d7 and now 14 c3 ♘xe5! 15 dxe5 ♗f2+ 16 ♔d1 ♗a4+ is a rather abrupt end, while after 15 ♕c2 ♘c4 16 ♕c1 ♕f6 17 a4 a5 18 b5 e5 White had also had enough) 7...0-0 8 ♗g2 ♗d7 9 0-0 ♖e8! 10 ♗f3 ♗g6 11 a3 ♗a5 12 ♘a4 ♗b6 13 ♘xb6 axb6 14 ♗e3

♕e7 and now White dropped a pawn with 15 ♗f2? fxe5 16 dxe5 ♘xe5 in M.Jorquera Cahu-D.Barria, Chilean Championship 1995, but his position was worse in any case.

4...exd5

We have reached an interesting position. White has a certain dilemma, as he is forced to commit himself in one way or another – 'zugzwang lite', as Jonathan Rowson would call it.

5 ♘f3

Instead:

a) 5 g3 looks to put pressure on d5, but Black can develop smoothly with 5...♗f5 6 ♗e3 (or 6 a3 h6 7 ♗g2 ♘f6 8 ♘ge2 ♕d7 9 0-0 0-0-0 with a comfortable position) 6...♗b4 7 ♗g2 ♕d7 8 ♘ge2 ♘f6 9 a3 ♗xc3+ 10 ♘xc3 0-0-0 11 h3 ♘e4 12 ♘xe4 ♗xe4 13 f3 ♗f5 14 ♕d2 ♕d6 15 ♗f4 ♖he8+ 16 ♔f2 ♕g6 and stood better in W.Posch-J.Smolen, Austrian League 2005.

b) 5 ♗b5 might actually be the most sensible move as it gives Black no real target. The game could continue 5...♗b4 6 ♘ge2 (6 ♗xc6+ bxc6 7 ♗d2 ♘f6 8 ♘f3 ♗g4 9 ♕e2+ was played in

J.Birinyi-Z.Sipka, Fuzesabony 1994, and now 9...♕e7 would have equalized) 6...♘ge7 7 0-0 0-0 8 ♗g5 (8 ♖e1 ♖e8 9 a3 ♗d6 10 ♗f4 was also completely equal in A.Jurkovic-D.Del Rey, Vila de Salou 1995) 8...f6 9 ♗f4 ♘f5 10 ♗xc6 bxc6 11 ♘a4 ♖e8 12 c3 ♗d6 13 ♗g3 h5 14 ♕d3 ♖e4 15 c4 as in L.Hansen-P.Bank, Aarhus 1994, when 15...h4 16 ♗xd6 ♕xd6 is not worse for Black.

5...♗g4 6 ♗e2 ♗b4 7 a3 ♗xc3+ 8 bxc3 ♘f6 9 h3 ♗h5 10 0-0 ♘e4 11 ♗d2 ♕d6 12 ♖e1 0-0-0!

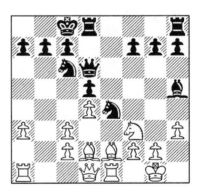

Here we see a classical theme of the Nimzowitsch Defence: hiding the king on the queenside to attack on the kingside!

13 a4 f6 14 a5 g5 15 ♘h2 ♗g6!

Black consequently avoids the exchange of pieces.

16 ♘g4 h5 17 ♘e3 ♕f4 18 ♗f3 ♘xd2 19 ♕xd2 g4!

The attack just takes care of itself.

20 ♗e2 gxh3 21 g3

Of course opening the g-file with 21 gxh3? is utter suicide.

21...h2+!

After this fine move, Black is breaking through.

22 ♔xh2

If 22 ♔g2 ♗e4+ 23 f3 ♖dg8 24 ♘f1 (24 fxe4 ♖xg3+ 25 ♔h1 ♕xe4+ 26 ♗f3 ♕xf3+ 27 ♘g2 ♖hg8 28 ♖e2 h4 is a nice finish as well) 24...♖xg3+! 25 ♘xg3 (25 ♔f2 allows the neat 25...h1N mate) 25...♕xd2 and Black wins.

22...♕xf2+ 23 ♘g2

Or 23 ♔h3 ♗e8!.

23...♗e4 24 ♖g1 ♖dg8 25 ♕f4 h4!

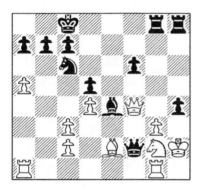

26 g4

Other moves lead to quick ends; for example 26 ♕xf2 hxg3 mate, or 26 ♗g4+ ♖xg4! 27 ♕xg4+ f5 28 ♕g7 hxg3 mate, or 26 gxh4 ♖xg2+ 27 ♔h3 ♖h2+ 28 ♕xh2 ♖xh4 mate.

26...♕xe2 27 ♖af1 ♖xg4

Only time trouble saved White from 27...h3.

28 ♖f2

28 ♕f2 is still answered by 28...h3! 29 ♘f4 ♖g2+! 30 ♘xg2 hxg2+ etc.

28...♖xf4 29 ♖xe2 ♖g4

White could have resigned here to save at least some dignity.

30 ♖e3 ♖hg8 31 ♖e2 h3 32 ♔xh3 ♖g3+

33 ♔h2 ♖3g5 34 ♖e3 ♖xg2+ 35 ♖xg2 ♖xg2+ 36 ♔h3 ♖xc2 37 ♖g3 ♘xa5 38 ♖g8+ ♔d7 39 ♖g7+ ♔d6 40 ♖f7 ♖xc3+ 41 ♔h4 ♔e6 42 ♖f8 b5 43 ♖e8+ ♔f5 44 ♖a8 ♗g2 0-1

As you can see, 4 exd5 is completely harmless. And the prospect of playing for a win without any real danger should whet everyone's appetite.

White plays 4 e5

Similarly to the popular viewpoint introduced in Chapter 3, here **4 e5** also seems a sensible move: White grabs some space and makes use of the fact that his d-pawn cannot be jostled by the black c-pawn. With 3 ♘c3 e6 interposed it even appears White has reached a favourable version of the previous chapter as the black light-squared bishop is now shut in.

This poses the question of how Black should continue. 4...f6 still seems playable, as 5 f4 founders on 5...fxe5 6 fxe5 ♕h4+. But White can successfully stay in control of e5 with 5 ♗b5!. Then 5...fxe5 runs into 6 ♘f3! with a white knight coming to e5, so Black's best answer is 5...♗d7. This is recommended by French Defence expert John Watson in his book *Dangerous Weapons: The French*, but I don't much like this approach.

My recommendation would be **4...♘ge7**.

Black opts for smooth development and wants to expose a disadvantage of 3 ♘c3 – White's inability to protect the d-pawn with c2-c3. 5 ♘f3 protects the d-pawn in another way, but after 5...♘f5 (intending ...f7-f6) White can no longer bolster up his centre with f2-f4. Which leaves the immediate 5 f4, but this can cause difficulties along the g1-a7 diagonal, as the next game illustrates.

1 e4 e6 2 d4 d5 3 ♘c3 ♘c6 4 e5 ♘ge7 5 f4

Instead:

a) 5 ♗g5 tries to impede the knight's journey to f5.

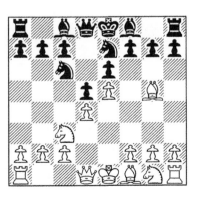

Black has two ways to react:

a1) 5...♕d7 looks like a bughouse move, but as the c8-bishop is leaving home via the c8-a6 diagonal in any case, unpinning the knight in such a fashion is quite feasible. After 6 ♘f3 b6 7 ♗e2 (7 ♗b5 a6 8 ♗a4 h6 9 ♗f4 b5 10 ♗b3 a5 11 a4 b4 12 ♘e2 ♗a6 13 h4 ♘f5 14 c3 h5 15 ♗c2 ♘ce7 16 ♗d3 ♗xd3 17 ♕xd3 ♘g6 18 ♗g5 ♗e7 19 ♗xe7 ♔xe7 20 ♕d2 ♖ab8 left Black with good prospects on the queenside in S.Ottens-C.Dammer, Cologne 1991, while 7 a3 ♗b7 8 ♗b5 a6 9 ♗d3 ♘a5 10 b3 c5 11 ♘a4 ♕c7 12 ♗e3 c4 13 ♗e2 ♘f5 14 b4 ♗c6 15 ♘c3 ♘b7 16 g4 ♘xe3 17 fxe3 ♗e7 18 0-0 b5 19 ♕b1 a5 gave the same result in N.Kolev-V.Minchev, Bankia 1992) 7...♗b7 8 0-0 ♘a5 9 b4 ♘c4! 10 ♘d2 h6 11 ♘xc4 dxc4 Black enjoyed a nice position in Gatto-Cordara, Finale 1977.

a2) 5...h6 forces White to decide what to do with the bishop. After 6 ♗xe7 (if 6 ♗h4 g5! does not weaken the position at all; S.Sisnovic-R.Hauser, Austrian League 1996, continued 7 ♗g3 ♘f5 8 ♘ge2 ♗g7 9 ♕d2 ♕e7 10 f4 a6 11 a3 f6 12 0-0-0 b5 – note that with the centre being closed and fixed, Black can attack on both wings – 13 ♘a2 a5 14 ♗f2 b4 15 a4 ♗d7 16 b3 gxf4 17 ♘xf4 fxe5! 18 ♘g6 ♕f6 19 ♘xh8 exd4 20 ♗d3 ♗xh8 21 ♖de1 ♘e3 22 ♖e2 e5 and the black pawn mass quickly decided the game) 6...♘xe7 7 ♘f3 ♘f5 8 ♗d3 g6 9 ♘e2 c5 10 c3 ♕b6 11 ♕b3 ♕c7 12 dxc5 ♗xc5 and Black equalized easily in D.Wilde-C.Wisnewski, Büsum 2004.

b) 5 ♘f3 develops the knight without protecting the e5-pawn with f2-f4, something Black should attempt to exploit with 5...♘f5 followed by ...f7-f6.

White usually tries to combat this plan with different set-ups:

b1) 6 g4?! is a bit careless, as the pawn will quickly become a target after 6...♘h4 7 ♘xh4 ♕xh4. The game R.Müller-D.Porth, German League 1996, continued 8 ♗e3 ♗b4 9 ♕f3 h5! 10 ♗h3 hxg4 11 ♗xg4 f5 12 exf6 gxf6 13 ♕g3 ♗d6 14 ♕g2 ♗d7 15 ♘b5 0-0-0 and Black had a nice position with good prospects on the kingside.

b2) 6 ♗e2, when Black should not play 6...f6?! as after 7 g4 ♘h6 8 exf6 gxf6 9 h3 he cannot play the freeing ...e6-e5 in the near future. Instead, 6...♗e7 7 0-0 0-0 8 g4 ♘h4 9 ♘xh4 ♗xh4 10 f4 f6 was played in K.Jell-M.Grundherr, German League 1990, which continued 11 exf6 ♗xf6 12 ♗e3 g5! 13 fxg5 ♗xg5 14 ♖xf8+ ♔xf8 15 ♕d2 h6 16 ♗f3 ♔g7 17 ♘e2 e5! and the white king was in more danger than his black colleague.

b3) 6 ♗b5 is a typical way to fight for control of e5. Now 6...♗d7 7 ♗g5

(after 7 0-0, in V.Piber-G.Gara, Harkany 2001, Black took advantage of the closed centre and initiated a kingside attack: 7...a6 8 ♗a4 h6 9 a3 g5! 10 g4 ♘fe7 11 b4 ♘g6 12 ♗b3 ♗e7 13 ♘e2 h5 14 h3 hxg4 15 hxg4 ♘a7 16 ♔g2 ♗b5 17 ♖h1 ♖xh1 18 ♔xh1 and now 18...♔d7!? would have provided Black with good attacking chances on the kingside) 7...♗e7 8 h4 was played in J.Polgar-E.Rozentalis, Groningen 1993. The game continued 8...h5?! 9 ♕d2 a6 10 ♗f1 b6 11 0-0-0 g6 12 ♕f4 with a White advantage, but I do not see what is wrong with 8...f6!?. After 9 exf6 gxf6 10 ♗f4 (or 10 ♗c1, but then 10...h5 gives Black a more favourable position to the one in the actual game) Black can play 10...♗d6, followed by ...♕e7 and ...0-0-0 with a good position.

5...♘f5 6 ♘f3 b6

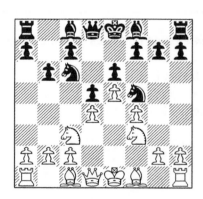

7 ♗b5

White has also tried:

a) 7 ♘e2 is a prophylactic move seeking to maximize the strength of the white centre. But Black can still get enough counterplay after 7...♗a6 8 c3 ♕d7, for example 9 ♕a4 ♘b8 10 ♕c2

♗e7 11 ♘g3 ♗xf1 12 ♖xf1 as played in M.Strange-C.Nielsen, Farum 1993, when 12...♘xg3 13 hxg3 c5 would have been fully satisfactory for Black.

b) 7 ♗d3? is even worse than it looks, since 7...♘fxd4 8 ♘xd4 ♘xd4 9 ♗xh7? ♕h4+! 10 g3 ♕xh7 11 ♕xd4 ♕xc2, among other things, loses a pawn.

c) 7 a3 prevents ...♗b4, but serves no other purpose. After 7...♗e7 8 ♗b5 ♗d7 9 g4 ♘h4 10 ♗xc6 ♗xc6 11 ♕e2 ♕d7 12 ♗e3 a5 13 ♕f2 ♘xf3+ 14 ♕xf3 a4! 15 0-0 0-0-0 16 b3 ♔b7 17 b4 ♗b5 18 ♖f2 ♕c6 19 ♘xb5 ♕xb5 Black eliminated any counter-chances on the queenside in M.Bonfioli-H.J.Hecht, Lenzerheide 1964.

7...♗d7

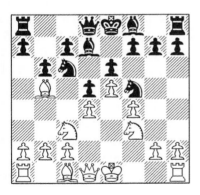

8 g4?!

This weakens the kingside, but it is hard to suggest improvements. 8 0-0? is a trap surprisingly many players fall victim of: 8...♘cxd4! 9 ♘xd4 ♘xd4 and Black is a pawn up since 10 ♕xd4?? ♗c5 loses the queen. And 8 ♘e2? is no better as it runs into 8...♘xe5.

8...♘h4 9 ♗xc6 ♗xc6 10 0-0 h5! 11

♘g5?!

11 g5 ♘f5 was a necessary, albeit humiliating concession.

11...hxg4 12 ♗e3 ♘f5 13 ♗f2 ♕d7 14 ♕xg4 0-0-0

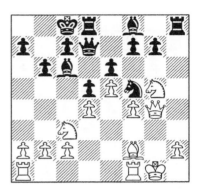

With his king brought to safety on the queenside, Black can now concentrate on his attack on the kingside.

15 a3 ♖h6 16 ♕e2 ♗b7 17 b4 ♕e8 18 ♘d1 ♗e7 19 ♘f3 ♕a4 20 ♘c3 ♕c6 21 ♕d2 ♖h3 22 ♔g2 ♖dh8 23 ♖h1 g5 24 ♘e2 g4 25 ♘fg1 ♖3h7 26 ♘c3 ♗h4 27 ♘d1 ♗xf2 28 ♘xf2 ♕xc2 29 ♕xc2 ♘e3+ 30 ♔g3 ♘xc2 31 ♖d1 ♗a6 32 ♘xg4 ♖g7 0-1

White plays 4 ♘f3

As closing the centre doesn't have a big impact, **4 ♘f3** is the only option left to protect the d-pawn. It turns out that this move is also the best choice, as it maintains the tension in the centre and forces Black to make a decision.

In the absence of sensible alternatives, **4...♘f6** is the best move. After **5 e5 ♘e4 6 ♗d3** nearly all theoretical sources on this matter (including the aforementioned book by Watson) give only 6...♗b4, concluding that White has a stable advantage. Without presenting further lines for the moment, I want to point out that I agree with this assessment.

But I think that Black has an interesting alternative in **6...f5!?**.

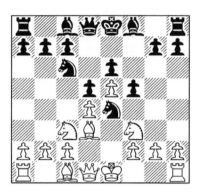

As White can hardly allow the black knight to stay on e4, 7 exf6 ♘xf6 is a logical consequence. After 8 0-0 ♗d6 9 ♗g5 0-0 10 ♖e1 the key idea is revealed with 10...♘b4. This attacks the bishop and enables Black to play ...c7-c5 without giving White the opportunity to strengthen his centre with c2-c3. The resulting position might still be slightly better for White, but in my opinion Black has good chances of counterplay. In any case, the following game shows that White needs to play precisely to claim an advantage.

Game 19
F.Lopez Gracia-
A.Ansola Marquinez
Zaragoza 1998

---

1 e4 ♘c6 2 ♘c3 e6 3 d4 d5 4 ♘f3 ♘f6 5

e5

Before going on, we need to look at several other moves:

a) 5 exd5 exd5 is harmless as usual.

Black doesn't have to fear any of the various continuations:

a1) 6 ♗f4 a6 7 ♘e5 looks active, but just helps Black to improve his position: 7...♗d6 8 ♘xc6 bxc6 9 ♗xd6 cxd6 10 ♕d3 0-0 11 ♗e2 ♕b6 12 ♖b1 a5! 13 0-0 ♗a6 14 ♕d1 ♗xe2 15 ♘xe2 ♖fe8 resulted in a nice position for Black in V.Di Fonzo-F.Castaldo, Milan 2003.

a2) 6 ♗e2 ♗b4 7 0-0 (7 a3 ♗xc3+ 8 bxc3 ♗g4 transposes to Game 17) 7...0-0 8 ♗g5 ♗xc3 9 bxc3 ♕d6 led to a comfortable game for Black in J.Hengelbrock-W.Beilfuss, German League 1989.

a3) 6 ♗b5 ♗d7 7 0-0 (or 7 ♗g5 ♕e7+! 8 ♕e2 0-0-0 9 ♗xf6 ♕xf6 10 ♘xd5 ♕d6 11 ♗xc6 ♗xc6 12 ♘e3 ♗xf3 13 ♕xf3 ♕xd4 and Black was slightly better in H.Tiemann-F.Schober, correspondence 1988), when Black can play 7...♗d6 8 ♖e1+ ♘e7 9 ♗g5 c6 10 ♗xf6 gxf6 11 ♗d3 ♕c7 12 h3 0-0-0. In M.Ebeling-J.Kekki, Helsinki 1993,

White tried to exploit the doubled f-pawns with 13 ♘h4 ♘g6 14 ♘f5, but Black managed to create counterplay down the g-file after 14...♘f4 15 ♘e2 ♘xd3 16 ♕xd3 ♖dg8 17 ♘eg3 ♖g5 18 ♕f3 ♗xf5 19 ♘xf5 ♖hg8.

b) 5 ♗d3!? is a move that has to be treated with respect and accurate play:

b1) 5...dxe4?! 6 ♘xe4 ♘xe4 7 ♗xe4 is no good, as the black pieces are just misplaced in this position.

b2) 5...♗b4?! leads to a variation covered in many opening sources dealing with 3...♘c6 in the French. After 6 e5 ♘e4 7 ♗d2 ♘xd2 8 ♕xd2 f6 9 a3 White gets the advantage as both the following black moves are insufficient for equality:

b21) 9...♗xc3 10 ♕xc3 fxe5 11 dxe5 ♗d7 (11...0-0 12 h4!? ♕e7 13 ♕d2 ♗d7 14 ♕e3 ♗e8 15 c3 ♗h5 16 ♘d4! ♘xd4 17 cxd4 ♕f7 18 ♖c1 c6 19 f3 ♗g6 20 ♗e2 left Black without counterplay in J.Hjartarson-E.Rozentalis, Tilburg rapid 1994) 12 0-0-0 ♕e7 13 h4 0-0-0 14 ♖h3 a6 15 ♖g3 ♘a7 16 ♕b4! c5 17 ♕b6 ♘b5 18 c4 ♘c7 19 ♕d6 ♕xd6 20 exd6 ♘e8 21 ♘e5 ♘xd6 22 ♖xg7 and White

was on top in S.Janovsky-T.Schütz, Dortmund 1990.

b22) 9...♗e7 10 exf6 ♗xf6 11 ♗b5 0-0 (after 11...♗d7 12 0-0 0-0 13 ♖fe1 ♖e8 14 ♘e2 ♘b8 15 ♗xd7 ♕xd7 16 ♘f4 ♘c6 17 c3 ♖e7 18 ♖e2 ♖ae8 19 ♖ae1 Black could not enforce ...e6-e5 in A.Mallahi-S.Ghane Gardeh, Iranian Championship 2001; or if 11...♕d6 then White should probably should try 12 0-0 0-0 13 ♗xc6 ♕xc6 14 ♖fe1 when Black will have problems with his light-squared bishop and/or his weak e-pawn, while 13...bxc6 14 ♘a4 just transposes to Mencinger-Soln) 12 ♗xc6 bxc6 13 ♘a4 ♕d6 14 0-0 e5 15 dxe5 ♗xe5 16 ♘xe5 ♕xe5 17 ♖fe1 ♕f6 18 c3 ♗f5 19 ♘c5 and due to the superior pawn structure and minor piece, White enjoyed a slight advantage in V.Mencinger-P.Soln, Finkenstein 1994.

b3) 5...♘b4!? is the right answer; for example, 6 e5 ♘xd3+ 7 ♕xd3 (7 cxd3 is not as dangerous, the point being that 7...♘d7 8 ♗g5 ♗e7 9 ♗xe7 ♕xe7 10 ♘b5 can be met by 10...♕b4+), and now:

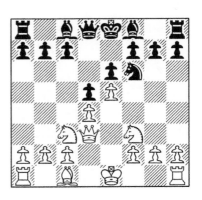

b31) 7...♘d7 8 ♗g5 ♗e7 (8...f6?! 9

exf6 ♘xf6 10 0-0 ♗e7 11 ♘e5 0-0 12 ♖ae1 c5 13 ♖e3 c4?! led to a disaster after 14 ♕d1 b5? 15 ♘c6 ♕c7 16 ♘xe7+ ♕xe7 17 ♘xd5 in H.Sislian-O.Steffens, German League 1997) 9 ♗xe7 ♕xe7 10 ♘b5! ♘b6 11 ♕c3 leaves White in better shape.

b32) 7...♘g8!? looks crooked, but seems possible since the closed character of the position makes it difficult for White to exploit his lead in development. After 8 0-0 (8 b4 ♘e7 9 ♘e2 ♗d7 10 0-0 ♘c8 11 ♗g5 ♗e7 12 ♗xe7 ♕xe7 13 a4 ♘b6 14 ♕b3 ♘c4 15 ♕c3 a5 was fine for Black in M.Krakops-S.Dizdar, Werfen 1993) 8...♗e7, a game between *YACE 0.99.56* and *Monarch 2002-04* continued 9 b3 b6 10 ♖d1 ♗d7 11 a4 h5 12 ♘b5 a6 13 ♘c3, and now 13...g5!? 14 ♗a3 g4 15 ♗xe7 ♘xe7 16 ♘g5 ♘g6 would have led to a position in which Black is not worse.

c) 5 ♗g5 ♗e7 leaves White a choice between three moves:

c1) 6 ♗d3 is met by 6...♘xe4 7 ♘xe4 dxe4 8 ♗xe7 ♕d5! as played in B.Rogulj-V.Kovacevic, Croatian Team Championship 2005, when 9 ♗c5 exd3

10 ♕xd3 b6 is good for Black.

c2) 6 e5 ♘e4 and then:

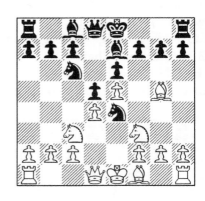

c21) 7 ♘xe4?! dxe4 8 ♗xe7 ♕xe7 completely surrenders the centre. In E.Van den Doel-S.Ernst, Nijmegen 1992, White tried 9 ♘d2 ♘xd4 10 ♘xe4 ♘c6 11 ♕g4, but after 11...♕b4+! 12 c3 ♕xb2 13 ♖d1 ♗d7 14 ♖d2 (or 14 ♕xg7 0-0-0 and White will have serious problems getting his king into safety) Black could have played 14...♘xe5! with a slight advantage after 15 ♖xb2 ♘xg4 16 ♖xb7 ♗c6 17 ♗b5 ♗xb5 18 ♖xb5 0-0.

c22) 7 ♗d2 loses precious time. Black should immediately attack the centre with 7...f6!, for example 8 exf6 ♗xf6 9 ♘xe4 dxe4 10 ♘g5 ♕xd4 and Black was better in M.Mueller-U.Teich, German League 1987.

c23) 7 ♗xe7 ♕xe7 8 ♗d3 ♕b4 9 ♗xe4 (9 a3?! ♘xc3 10 axb4 ♘xd1 11 ♔xd1 ♘xb4 just leaves Black a pawn up, while after 9 0-0 ♘xc3 10 bxc3 ♕xc3 11 ♖b1 ♕a3! 12 ♕d2 ♕e7 13 c3 ♘a5 14 ♘g5 h6 15 ♘h3 ♗d7 16 ♘f4 0-0-0 White had a hard time proving any compensation in B.Lengyel-L.Majzik, Budapest 1998) 9...dxe4 10 a3 ♕xb2 11 ♘xe4 and now Black can equalize with 11...♕b5!, for example 12 ♞ed2 ♞a5 13 c4 ♕d7 (but not 13...♞xc4? losing a piece to 14 ♕e2) 14 0-0 b6 15 ♖c1 ♗b7 16 ♞b3 ♕a4!, as in P.Keres-A.Lein, USSR Championship, Baku 1961.

c3) 6 ♗xf6 ♗xf6 and now:

c31) 7 e5 aims for an advantage in space again, but Black has sufficient counterplay after 7...♗e7 8 a3 (8 ♕d2 a6!? 9 0-0-0 b6 10 h4 ♗b7 11 ♕f4 looks suspicious as White seems to have good prospects on the kingside; but the game M.Zelic-V.Kovacevic, Solin 1996, showed that Black has resources too: 11...♕d7 12 ♖h3 h6 13 ♗e2 ♗f8 14 ♞d2 0-0-0 15 ♞f1 ♔b8 16 ♖f3 f6! 17 exf6 gxf6 18 ♕xf6 ♗g7 19 ♕g6 ♗xd4 and Black was more than OK) 8...0-0 9 ♕d2 f6 10 exf6 ♗xf6 11 h4 e5! 12 dxe5 ♞xe5 13 ♞xe5 (if 13 ♕xd5+?! ♕xd5 14 ♞xd5 ♞xf3+ 15 gxf3 ♗xb2 is obviously better for Black) 13...♗xe5 14 ♕xd5+ ♕xd5 15 ♞xd5 ♗xb2 16 ♖b1 ♗d4 (16...♖e8+ is more ambitious, keeping the game alive either after 17 ♔d2 ♗e5 or 17 ♗e2 ♗e5 18 0-0 c6 19 ♞e3 ♗d4 with compensation for the sacrificed pawn) 17

♞xc7, as played in V.Juergens-M.Thesing, Dortmund 1992; now 17...♗xf2+ would have more or less forced White to repeat moves with 18 ♔d2 ♖b8 19 ♞a6 ♖a8 20 ♞c7.

c32) 7 ♗b5 keeps the tension in the centre. Black's best option is 7...0-0 8 0-0 (8 ♗xc6 bxc6 9 0-0 c5 10 exd5 cxd4! 11 ♞e4 exd5 12 ♞xf6+ ♕xf6 13 ♕xd4 ♕xd4 14 ♞xd4 was played in M.Furlan-N.Praznik, Bled 1995, when 14...c5 would have provided Black with the better game, for example 15 ♞c6 ♖e8 and the knight is not of much use) 8...♞b8!? 9 ♖e1 b6. The game G.Fish-C.Wisnewski, German Club Cup 2007, continued 10 exd5 exd5 11 ♞e5, but after 11...♗e6 12 ♕f3 ♕d6 13 ♗d3 c6 Black had nothing to worry about.

5...♞e4 6 ♗d3

6 ♞e2 again gives Black time to attack the centre with the typical 6...f6. After 7 exf6 (7 ♞g3 fxe5 8 dxe5 ♗e7 9 ♗d3 ♞c5 10 ♗b5 0-0 11 0-0 ♗d7 12 ♗xc6 bxc6! 13 ♞d4 ♕e8 14 c4 was G.Garcia-G.Russek Libni, Granma 1987, and now 14...♕g6 would have been better for Black) 7...♕xf6 8 ♞g3 e5! was played in J.Heissler-M.Schaefer, German League 1989, which continued 9 ♗b5 (9 dxe5 ♞xe5 10 ♕xd5? runs into 10...♗b4+ 11 c3 ♞xf3+ 12 gxf3 ♞xc3, while if 10 ♞xe4 dxe4 11 ♞xe5 ♕xe5 the activity of Black's pieces and his advantage in space compensate for the long-term weakness of the isolated e-pawn) 9...exd4 10 ♕xd4 ♕xd4 11 ♞xd4 ♞xg3 12 hxg3 ♗d7 13 ♞xc6 ♗xc6 14 ♗xc6+ bxc6 15 ♗e3 ♗b4+ 16 c3 ♗a5 17 0-0-0

♝b6 and Black's chances in the end-game were not worse.

6...f5!? 7 exf6 ♞xf6

8 0-0

8 ♝g5 ♝d6 9 0-0 0-0 10 ♖e1 ♞b4! shows the key idea of this chapter. By attacking the bishop on d3 Black gains the time he needs to attack the white centre with ...c7-c5, after which it will be easier for him to enforce ...e6-e5. Surprisingly, besides a few blitz games of mine there are no practical examples, but I urge you to try it! For White, 9 ♝b5!? is a possible improvement, but after 9...0-0 10 ♝xc6 bxc6 11 0-0 c5 Black now has two c-pawns at his disposal. Then 12 ♝xf6 ♛xf6? 13 dxc5 ♝xc5 14 ♞xd5! is a little trap, but after just 12...♖xf6 Black is fine.

8...♝d6 9 ♞e2 e5! 10 dxe5 ♞xe5 11

♞xe5 ♝xe5 12 ♝f4 ♝xf4 13 ♞xf4 0-0

Black has comfortably equalized.

14 h3 ♛d6 15 ♛d2 c6 16 ♖fe1 ♝d7 17 ♖ad1 ♖ae8 18 c3 ♖xe1+ 19 ♖xe1 ♖e8 20 ♖xe8+ ♝xe8 21 ♛e3 ♝d7

21...♝f7 is a better place for the bishop, leaving d7 for the knight.

22 ♞e2 b6 23 f4 c5 24 ♛e5 ♛xe5 25 fxe5 ♞e4?

Underestimating the power of the white knight in the endgame. Now Black is constantly driven back.

26 ♞f4 ♝c6 27 ♝xe4 dxe4 28 h4 ♚f7 29 ♚f2 ♝d7 30 ♚e3 ♝f5 31 c4 g6 32 ♞d5 ♚e6 33 ♚f4 h6 34 g4 ♝xg4 35 ♚xg4 ♚xe5 36 ♞e7 ♚d4 37 ♞xg6 ♚xc4 38 ♞e5+ ♚d4 39 ♞f7 ♚d3 40 ♞xh6 e3 41 ♞f7 e2 42 ♞e5+ ♚c2 43 ♞f3 ♚xb2 44 h5 c4 45 h6 c3 46 h7 c2 47 h8♛+ ♚xa2 48 ♛c3 1-0

Summary

Transposing into the French is not a bad idea after all; it is quite likely that White will be lured into unknown territory where careless play is immediately punished, as Game 17 nicely illustrated. Keeping the position closed with 4 e5 is probably the line you will encounter most, so I recommend memorizing the ideas from Game 18. White's best choice is 4 ♘f3, but Game 19 showed that Black does not need to stand back.

1 e4 ♘c6 2 d4 d5 3 ♘c3 e6 *(D)* **4 ♘f3**

       4 exd5 exd5 – *Game 17*

       4 e5 ♘ge7 *(D)* – *Game 18*

4...♘f6 5 e5 ♘e4 6 ♗d3 f5 *(D)* – *Game 19*

     3...e6   *4...♘ge7*   *6...f5*

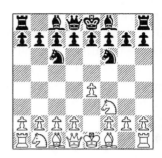

Chapter Five

1 e4 ♘c6 2 ♘f3 ♘f6

In my experience, **2 ♘f3** is the move most responsible for players abandoning the Nimzowitsch Defence. And it is quite cunning indeed: by developing his king's knight White increases his influence in the centre without presenting his d-pawn as a possible target. Now Black could give in with 2...e5 which transposes to the Open Games, but then there would be no reason not to play 1...e5 in the first place. There has to be something else, and in fact there is.

Choosing between the respectable number of sensible second move alternatives is by no means an easy task. Except for 2...d6, which I dismissed as too passive, I have tried virtually everything; but nothing impressed me as much as **2...♘f6**. The resulting positions are highly unbalanced, which is perfectly suited my style of play. And hopefully this chapter will show that it will suit yours too.

White plays 3 ♘c3

The passive move **3 ♘c3** is often used by players who shun the complications arising from the more forcing lines resulting from 3 e5 ♘g4. Black could now simply transpose into the Four Knights Game with 3...e5, but apart from that being a sin against principles, the more thematic **3...d5** offers greater chances to create the unbalanced positions required to play for the full point. White can equalize with precise play, but being the only one striving for a win should be comforting enough for any Black player.

> *Game 20*
> **R.Jiganchine-S.Wright**
> Richmond, Canada 1999

1 e4 ♘c6 2 ♘f3 ♘f6 3 ♘c3

The quiet alternative 3 d3 was covered in Game 2.

3...d5

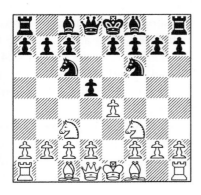

4 exd5

And here 4 d3?! dxe4 5 dxe4 ♕xd1+ 6 ♔xd1 ♗g4 7 ♗e2 0-0-0+ 8 ♔e1 e5 is just better for Black.

Instead, after 4 e5, Black has a few possibilities I would like to mention:

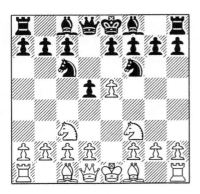

a) 4...♘g4?! can be quickly dismissed after 5 d4 ♗f5 6 h3 ♘h6 7 ♗b5.

b) 4...♘e4 5 ♘e2 mostly transposes to a line usually reached via 1 e4 ♘f6 2 ♘c3 d5 3 e5 ♘e4. I could easily devote a whole chapter to examining this variation, but as this line finally made me give up Alekhine's Defence after nine years' practice, I will not recommend it.

c) 4...d4 is another line related to the Alekhine. It is not my cup of tea, but as it is solid, I do not want to withhold it from you: 5 exf6 (5 ♘xd4 ♘xd4 6 exf6 exf6 and 5 ♘e2 ♘g4 are not to be taken seriously) 5...dxc3 and now:

c1) 6 bxc3 gxf6 (6...exf6?! is not to be recommended; White reached a better position after 7 ♗b5 ♕d5 8 ♕e2+ ♗e6 9 0-0 ♗d6 10 ♘d4 0-0 11 ♗xc6 bxc6 12 ♘xe6 fxe6 13 d3 in I.Reyes Acevedo-J.Ramirez Gonzalez, St Feliu 1994) 7 d4 (7 ♗b5 ♕d5! 8 c4 ♕e4+ 9 ♕e2 ♗f5 10 d3 ♕xe2+ 11 ♔xe2 ♗d7 12 ♗e3 a6 13 ♗xc6 ♗xc6 14 g3 0-0-0 15 ♖hb1 e5 left Black in complete control in D.Vega-D.Levadi, Eastpointe 1993) 7...♗g7 8 ♗e2 ♗f5 9 ♗e3 0-0 10 0-0 e5 11 d5 ♘e7 12 c4 ♕d6 13 ♕d2 ♖fd8 14 ♖fd1 ♗g6 15 ♘h4 f5 16 ♘xg6 hxg6 17 ♗h6 b6 18 h4 ♔h7 19 ♗xg7 ♔xg7 20 ♕c3 f6 and Black reigned over the dark squares in H.Ewin-H.Deuster, Braunfels 1998.

c2) 6 fxg7 cxd2+ 7 ♕xd2 ♕xd2+ 8 ♗xd2 ♗xg7 9 0-0-0 ♗g4 10 ♗e2 (10 ♗b5!?) 10...0-0-0 and although Black is by no means worse, there is just not enough action for my taste.

d) 4...♘d7!? is my favourite choice. After 5 d4 (here 5 e6 again bears resemblance to Alekhine's Defence, but compared to the original line 1 e4 ♘f6 2 ♘c3 d5 3 e5 ♘fd7 4 e6, the moves ♘f3 and ♘c6 have been inserted – a factor which favours Black: for example, after the typical 5...fxe6 6 d4 g6 7 h4 ♗g7 8 h5 e5! 9 dxe5 ♘dxe5 10 ♕xd5 ♘xf3+ 11 ♕xf3 ♘d4 Black has a significant advantage) 5...♘b6 we have reached the starting point of a line regularly played by American FM Miles Ardaman.

Now White has a number of options:

d1) 6 ♗g5 tries to hamper Black from developing, but in the end Black is OK, as Ardaman has showed in numerous blitz games under his handle "ChessDoc" on the Internet Chess Club; for example, 6...♗g4 7 ♗b5 ♕d7 8 0-0 (or 8 h3 ♗xf3 9 ♕xf3 a6 10 ♗xc6 ♕xc6 11 0-0 ♕g6! 12 ♗f4 e6 13 ♕e2 c5 14 ♗e3 ♘c4) 8...a6 9 ♗e2 f6 10 ♗f4 0-0-0 11 a4 e6 12 ♖e1 ♗b4 13 h3 ♗h5 14 exf6 gxf6 15 g4 ♖dg8 16 ♗g3 ♗f7 17 ♕d2 h5 and Black has a tremendous attack.

d2) 6 h3 is fittingly met by 6...h6!, creating an escape route to h7 for the black bishop. White can try to prevent this with 7 ♗d3, but after 7...♘b4 8 0-0 ♘xd3 9 ♕xd3 e6 10 ♘e2 ♗d7 11 ♘f4 a6 Black had good prospects on the queenside in L.Bonet-A.Panchenko, Berga 1996.

d3) 6 ♗b5 ♗g4 7 he ♗xf3 8 ♗xc6+ bxc6 9 ♕xf3 e6 10 ♕g3 was played in K.Pulkkinen-T.Paakkonen, Finnish Team Championship 1999, but then 10...♘d7 11 0-0 c5 12 dxc5 ♘xc5 13 ♗e3 ♘d7, intending a second ...c5, threatening ...d4 and ...♕b8, is good for Black.

d4) 6 ♗e2 ♗f5 7 ♘h4 (after the committal 7 0-0 Black can opt for a kingside attack with 7...e6 8 ♗f4 ♗e7 and ...g7-g5; but note that this is only possible due to the closed nature of the position) 7...♗e4!? 8 ♗e3 (or 8 ♘xe4 dxe4 9 ♗e3 e6 10 g3 ♕d5 11 ♘g2 0-0-0 with a nice game) 8...e6 9 ♘f3 ♗g6 10 0-0 ♗e7 11 ♘e1 0-0 12 f4 f6 13 ♘f3 fxe5 14 fxe5 ♘b4 15 ♖c1 c5 16 a3 ♘c6 and the position was almost too good to be true in J.Servitja Perez-A.Jerez Perez, Barcelona 1994.

4...♘xd5

5 ♗c4

Or:

a) 5 ♗b5 ♘xc3 6 ♗xc6+ (6 bxc3 allows 6...♕d5 7 ♕e2 ♗g4 or 7 c4 ♕e4+ 8 ♕e2 ♕xe2+ 9 ♔xe2 ♗d7 with equality) 6...bxc6 7 bxc3 ♕d5! 8 h3 ♕e4+ 9 ♔f1 (if 9 ♕e2 ♕xc2) 9...e5 with a slight advantage for Black.

b) 5 g3 ♗g4 6 ♗g2 e6 7 h3 ♗h5 8 0-0 ♗e7 gave Black an easy game in J.Houska-C.Wisnewski, German League 2004.

c) 5 d4 features a funny line: 5...♘xc3 6 bxc3 ♗g4 7 d5 ♘e5!?, inviting White to play 8 ♘xe5 (on 8 ♗e2 Black can safely play 8...♕d6) 8...♗xd1 9 ♗b5+ c6 10 dxc6, and now after 10...♗e2!! White collapsed with 11 ♔xe2? ♕d5! in R.Goldenberg-F.Chevaldonnet, Bordeaux 1982. Instead 11 ♘d3 is necessary, though after 11...♗xd3 12 cxd3 b6 13 c7+ ♕d7 14 ♗xd7+ ♔xd7 15 ♗f4 e5! 16 ♗g3 ♗d6 Black still has a good game.

5...♘b6 6 ♗b3 ♗f5

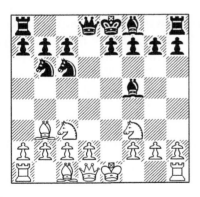

The game has finally transposed to a line from Alekhine's Defence, usually reached by 1 e4 ♘f6 2 ♘c3 d5 3 exd5

♘xd5 4 ♗c4 ♘b6 5 ♗b3 ♘c6 6 ♘f3 ♗f5 – a harmless line, if I might say so.

7 0-0

7 a4 a5 8 d4 e6 hardly makes a difference.

7...e6 8 d4 ♗e7 9 ♗f4

The immediate 9 d5 is unable to get anything out of the position either; for example 9...exd5 10 ♘xd5 ♘xd5 11 ♕xd5 ♕xd5 12 ♗xd5 0-0 13 ♖e1 ♗f6 14 c3 ♘d8 15 ♗f4 c6 16 ♗b3 ♘e6 and the game was equal in I.Almasi-K.Kaunas, Hungary 1992.

9...0-0 10 d5

The calm 10 ♖e1 should be answered by 10...♘a5, eliminating the bishop.

10...exd5 11 ♘xd5 ♘xd5 12 ♕xd5

Trying to keep the queens on board is dangerous. Instead after 12 ♗xd5?! ♗xc2! 13 ♕xc2 ♕xd5 14 ♗xc7 ♖ac8 15 ♗f4 ♘d4 16 ♕d3 ♘xf3+ 17 ♕xf3 ♕xf3 18 gxf3 Black had a significant endgame advantage in B.Niedermaier-D.Seyb, Nuremburg 2002.

12...♕xd5 13 ♗xd5 ♖fd8 14 ♗b3 ♗d6 15 ♗xd6 ♖xd6

Of course this position is dead level.

But the rest shows an aspect of the game you should always remember: a strong player, you draw with him; a weak player, you beat him with your superior technique.

16 ♖ad1 ♖ad8 17 c3 ♗d3 18 ♖fe1 ♘a5 19 ♘e5 ♘xb3 20 ♖xd3 ♖xd3 21 ♘xd3 ♚f8 22 ♘e5 ♘c5 23 ♘f3 ♘a4 24 ♖b1 ♘xb2 25 ♚f1 ♖d1+ 26 ♖xd1 ♘xd1 27 c4 ♘c3 28 a3 ♘b1 29 a4 a5 30 ♚e2 ♘c3+ 31 ♚d3 ♘xa4 32 ♚d4 ♚e7 33 c5 f6 34 ♚c4 ♘b2+ 35 ♚b5 a4 36 ♚b4 ♘d3+ 37 ♚xa4 ♘xc5+ 0-1

Rare 5th and 6th moves

The position after **3 e5 ♘g4 4 d4 d6 5 h3 ♘h6**

can be seen as the starting position of the system I present in this chapter. The inventor, Spanish GM Marc Narciso Dublan, has called it 'El Columpio'. This translates into 'The Swing', and if you look at the route g8-f6-g4-h6 taken by the knight, it seems indeed that it swings around the board.

To give you a first impression, I would like to present a game I played shortly after I picked up 'El Columpio'.

Ten moves into the game one could think that things have gone wrong for Black, but I invite you to look a little further...

Game 21
M.Kraemer-C.Wisnewski
Kiel 2003

1 e4 ♘c6 2 ♘f3 ♘f6 3 e5 ♘g4 4 d4 d6

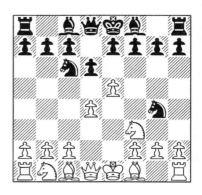

5 h3

Other moves:

a) 5 ♗f4, from M.Müller-C.Wisnewski, Kiel (rapid) 2003, is not as dumb as it looks. Black has to play quite accurately in order to exploit it. 5...dxe5 6 ♘xe5 ♕xd4 7 ♕xd4 ♘xd4 8 ♗d3 and now 8...g5! 9 ♗g3 ♗g7 10 ♘xg4 ♗xg4 is the most precise way to take hold of the position.

b) 5 e6 is similar to 6 e6 (the subject of the next game), but without the black knight being driven back, it is not as powerful. After 5...fxe6 6 ♘g5 ♘f6! 7 ♗c4 d5 8 ♗b5 ♕d6, ...e6-e5 must be prevented at all cost. White may have a certain amount of compensation for the pawn after 9 f4 (9 0-0 allows 9...e5 10 dxe5 ♕xe5 11 ♖e1 ♕d6 and White has hardly anything) 9...a6 10 ♗a4 (or 10 ♗e2 ♘d8!?, intending ...♕b6 followed by ...c5 and ...♘c6 with play against d4) 10...g6 11 0-0 ♗g7, but no more than that.

5...♘h6

6 ♘c3

6 exd6, 6 ♗b5 and 6 e6 will be covered in subsequent games. Other possible alternatives:

a) 6 ♗xh6?! regularly transposes to other lines and therefore will not be covered separately.

b) After 6 ♗d3 ♗f5 is the simplest route to equality; for example, 7 ♗xf5 (7 ♗xh6 is met by 7...♗xd3) 7...♘xf5 8 e6?! fxe6 9 0-0 ♕d7 10 ♖e1 g6 11 g4 ♘h6 12 ♘g5 ♘d8 13 ♘d2 ♗g7 14 ♘df3 ♘hf7 15 c3 e5 and Black even enjoyed an advantage in R.Myhrvold-C.Wisnewski, Modum 2003.

c) 6 ♗c4?! is dubious, as after 6...dxe5 7 d5 ♘a5 is possible. Instead 7 ♗xh6 gxh6 8 ♘xe5 was played in D.Escobar-M.Narciso Dublan, Spanish Junior Championships 1992, but after

8...♘xe5 9 dxe5 ♕xd1+ 10 ♔xd1 ♖g8 11 g4 (11 g3? loses a pawn to 11...♖g5 12 ♖e1 ♗xh3) 11...h5 12 f3 ♖g5 13 e6 (or 13 ♖e1 hxg4 followed by ...♗g7), 13...♗xe6 would leave White seeking even a spark of compensation.

6...a6!?

Black needs to parry the threat of 7 exd6 ♕xd6 8 ♘b5.

6...dxe5!? 7 d5 is a highly complicated alternative that requires detailed knowledge of possible lines. Here 7...♘b8?! 8 ♘xe5 looks suspicious, as after 8...♘f5 9 ♗b5+ ♘d7 White has the pleasant option of 10 ♘e4!, threatening 11 ♘c5 or even 11 ♘g5. Instead, 7...♘d4!? has been suggested by Narciso Dublan,

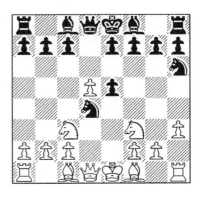

when play can continue 8 ♘xe5 (8 ♘xd4 exd4 9 ♕xd4 – not 9 ♗xh6?! dxc3! – 9...♘f5 10 ♕e5 f6!? 11 ♕e4 ♘d6 12 ♕e3 g6 13 ♗d2 ♗g7 14 0-0-0 0-0 is OK as Black is about to play ...e7-e5, qualifying the weakness of the e6-square) 8...♘hf5 and then:

a) 9 ♗c4 f6 10 ♘f3 (10 ♘g4 e5! equalizes, but after 10 ♘d3 e5? does not work because of 11 dxe6 ♗xe6 12

♗xe6 ♘xe6 13 0-0 and Black experiences problems on the e-file; better is 10...♘d6 11 ♗b3 and only then 11...e5) 10...e5 11 dxe6 ♗xe6 with equality.

b) 9 ♘b5!? ♘xb5 10 ♗xb5+ c6 is razor sharp.

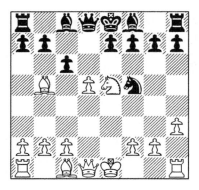

Many of the following lines were given by Narciso Dublan, who is a very imaginative and creative player. You could do worse than to study his games in this whole line. 11 ♗a4 (11 dxc6? ♕a5+ and 11 ♗c4?! ♘d6 favour Black, while 11 ♘xc6!? bxc6 12 ♗xc6+ ♗d7 13 ♗xa8 ♕xa8 is unclear) 11...♕d6! 12 ♘xc6 (here 12 ♘f3 b5 13 ♗b3 ♗b7 14 ♕d3 g6 is unclear, while 12 ♘c4? ♕b4+ and 12 ♗f4? ♕b4+ are not) 12...♗d7 13 ♕f3 ♘h4 14 ♕e4 ♕g6! 15 ♕xh4 ♕xg2 16 ♖f1 ♕xd5 17 ♘b4 ♕e6+ 18 ♗e3 ♗xa4 19 0-0-0 ♖c8 and after all those complications, Black is a pawn up.

c) 9 g4 f6! 10 gxf5 (10 ♘c4?! allows 10...♘h4! 11 ♘d2 e5) 10...fxe5 11 ♕h5+ ♔d7 12 ♗d3 ♕e8 13 ♕g4 ♔d8 14 ♗e3 g6 15 ♗xd4 ♗xf5 16 ♗xf5 gxf5 17 ♕h4 (17 ♕xf5 exd4 18 ♕e5 ♖g8 19 ♕xd4 ♕h5 and ...♖g5, ...♕f3 and ...♗g7 are all ideas justifying the pawn sacrifice) 17...exd4 18 ♕xd4 ♖g8 and in this totally weird position Black is not worse according to Narciso Dublan. What can I say... You will have fun at the board, that's for sure!

7 ♗g5!?

This move is quite annoying and puts Black to the test. 7 exd6 ♕xd6 will be looked at in Game 23. Instead, 7 ♗xh6 gxh6 8 ♕e2!? is an interesting idea from German FM Hanno Sislian. In H.Sislian-C.Wisnewski, Bargteheide 2004, I intuitively began the right treatment with 8...dxe5 9 dxe5 ♘d4! 10 ♘xd4 ♕xd4 11 ♖d1 ♕c5 12 ♘d5, but now misplayed the position with 12...♗d7?!, when White got a strong initiative following 13 b4 ♕c6 14 ♕e3. The correct move was 12...♗e6, and after removing the knight from d5 Black should have no problems.

7...♗f5 8 g4 ♗g6 9 ♗g2 ♕d7

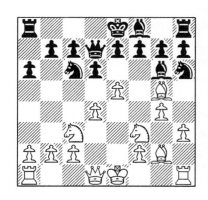

10 0-0

I played the exact position again about one year later, and the game M.Szelag-C.Wisnewski, German League 2004, showed that the black set-up is indeed playable. After 10 ♕e2 d5 11 ♖d1

♘g8 12 ♘h4 e6 13 f4?! ♗e7 14 ♗xe7 ♕xe7 15 ♕f2 ♗xc2 16 ♖d2 ♘b4 Black had gotten rid of all possible problems.

10...d5! 11 ♕d2 e6

Closing the centre helps Black to re-group before coming from behind.

12 a3 ♘g8 13 b4 f6!? 14 ♗f4 ♗e4!?

This manoeuvre brings back memories of Chapter 3. It helps to know your systems!

15 exf6 ♘xf6 16 ♘e5 ♘xe5 17 dxe5 ♗xg2 18 ♔xg2 ♘g8

This is the second time the knight has returned to g8, but each time it was for a reason.

19 ♗e3 h5 20 f4 0-0-0

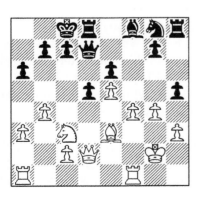

Now the black king is safe and Black can prepare for his final assault on the kingside.

21 ♗d4 ♘h6 22 ♕e2 hxg4 23 hxg4 ♗e7 24 ♖h1 ♖df8 25 ♖af1 ♕e8 26 ♔g3 ♕g6 27 ♗f2 ♔b8 28 ♖fg1 ♗h4+! 29 ♖xh4 ♘f5+ 30 ♔h3 ♘xh4 31 ♗xh4 ♕h7 32 ♕e1 ♖xf4 33 ♖h1 ♕xc2 0-1

White plays 6 e6

Sacrificing a pawn with **6 e6** is not completely unfounded. It is usually followed by 7 ♗xh6 (or vice versa) as White opts for attacking chances on the kingside. After **6...fxe6 7 ♗xh6 gxh6,**

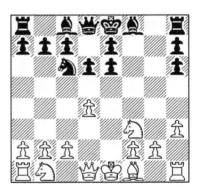

White normally plays **8 ♘h4**, immediately trying to exploit the weakness of the h5-e8 diagonal, when Black has to be careful; for example 8...♗g7 9 ♕h5+ ♔d7? (relatively better is 9...♔f8, but I still prefer White here) 10 d5! and Black is lost either after 10...exd5 11 ♕g4+ or 10...♗xb2 11 dxe6+ ♔xe6 12 ♕f5 mate!

The key manoeuvre in this position is the bizarre-looking **8...♕d7!**, a move serving multiple purposes. The most important point is to answer 9 ♕h5+

with 9...♔d8, followed by ...♕e8, intending to transfer the queen to help defend the kingside; but the now vacant d8-square can also be used as an escape route for the knight after a possible d4-d5 (in response to ...e6-e5). All in all I think this beautiful idea provides Black with excellent chances, as you will see in our next game.

Game 22
M.Homuth-C.Wisnewski
Luetjenburg 2003

---

1 e4 ♘c6 2 ♘f3 ♘f6 3 e5 ♘g4 4 d4 d6 5 h3 ♘h6 6 e6 fxe6

7 ♗xh6

Instead:

a) 7 ♗d3?! is an inaccuracy that can be exploited by 7...♘b4, when White has nothing better than to play 8 ♗e2 ♘f7 9 c3 ♘c6 10 ♗d3 ♕d7, transposing to 7 c3.

b) 7 c3 shows a different idea, playing on the b1-h7 diagonal. But again 7...♕d7! is the right move, and now 8 ♗d3 ♘f7 9 ♕c2 (9 ♘g5 ♘xg5 10 ♗xg5

was played in Cardenas-M.Narciso Dublan, Spain 1992, when 10...♔d8!, intending ...♕e8, would have been better for Black) 9...g6 and then:

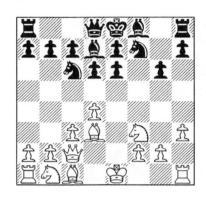

b1) 10 h4 e5 11 h5 (or 11 d5 ♘cd8 12 h5 ♕g4!) 11...♕g4! 12 hxg6 (if 12 ♖h4 ♕xg2 13 ♗e4 gxh5 the queen cannot be harmed as any knight move would allow ...♕g1+) 12...hxg6 13 ♖xh8 ♘xh8 and Black has a notable advantage.

b2) 10 ♘g5 ♘xg5 11 ♗xg5 e5 12 d5 ♘d8 13 h4 e6 14 c4 (14 dxe6 ♘xe6 15 ♗f6 is rebuffed with 15...♗g7, while 14 h5 is met by 14...exd5 15 hxg6 e4) 14...♕g7! 15 ♘c3 ♘f7 16 ♘e4 ♗e7 and Black is in complete control.

7...gxh6 8 ♗c4

White has also tried:

a) 8 ♘h4 ♕d7! once more shows the key idea of this line. After 9 ♕h5+ ♔d8 10 c3 ♕e8 11 ♗e2 ♗g7 12 ♘d2 ♕xh5 13 ♗xh5 ♗f6 White had no compensation for the pawn in Trias-J.Ramirez, Catania 1990.

b) 8 ♘e5 ♘xe5 (but not 8...dxe5?! 9 ♕h5+ ♔d7 10 dxe5 ♗g7 11 f4 with attacking chances for White, while 10...♕e8?? leads to mate after 11 ♕d1+

♘d4 12 ♕xd4+ ♚c6 13 ♕c4+ ♚b6 14 ♕b4+ ♚c6 15 ♕b5 or 13...♚d7 14 ♕d3+ ♚c6 15 ♕b5) 9 dxe5 and once more 9...♕d7! 10 ♕h5+ ♚d8 11 ♘c3 ♕e8 saves the day. In D.Fox-K.Krug, Wolfsberg 2004, Black reached a safe and sound position after 12 ♕f3 ♗g7 13 exd6 exd6 14 0-0-0 ♕c6 15 ♕xc6 bxc6 16 ♘e4 ♚e7.

8...♗g7

9 c3

9 0-0 e5 would be good for Black, if White didn't have the possibility of 10 ♘g5! hxg5 11 ♕h5+ ♚d7 12 ♕g4+ ♚e8 13 ♕h5+ with a surprising perpetual check. And this time 9...♕d7?! doesn't work either: after 10 ♖e1 e5?! 11 dxe5 ♘xe5? 12 ♘xe5 ♗xe5 13 ♕h5+ ♚d8 14 ♖xe5! dxe5 15 ♘c3 ♕e8 16 ♖d1+ ♗d7 17 ♗f7 Black resigned in U.Gebhardt-R.Schober, Giessen 1996. The correct move is 9...0-0! as White cannot afford to take on e6; i.e. 10 ♖e1 ♚h8! 11 ♗xe6 ♗xe6 12 ♖xe6 ♖xf3! 13 gxf3 (or 13 ♕xf3 ♘xd4) 13...♗xd4!, threatening both 14...♗xb2 and 14...♕g8+ which cannot be parried by White at the same time.

9...♕d7 10 0-0 e5

This does not spoil everything, but there was a better move in 10...0-0! with ideas similar to those in the previous note. After 11 ♖e1 ♘d8 there is little that White can do to prevent Black from consolidating with ...♚h8 and preparing ...e6-e5 afterwards.

11 dxe5 ♘xe5 12 ♘xe5 ♗xe5 13 ♕h5+ ♚d8 14 f4 ♗f6 15 ♘d2

White could have won back his pawn with 15 ♕xh6 (as well as on the previous move), but after 15...♕f5 Black becomes very active.

15...♕f5 16 ♕f3 ♗d7!

Completing development and correctly sensing that Black can afford to return the pawn.

17 ♕xb7 ♕c5+ 18 ♚h1 ♗c6 19 ♕b3 a5! 20 a4 ♕a7 21 ♖ad1 ♖b8 22 ♗b5 ♕c5

Through skilful manoeuvring Black is improving his position step by step.

23 ♕e6 ♕d5! 24 ♕xd5 ♗xd5

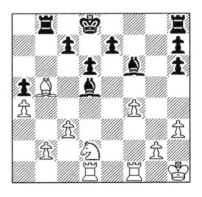

With queens off the black king is safe, so Black can direct his attention to his two bishops.

25 ♘f3 c6 26 ♗d3 ♖xb2 27 c4 ♗f7 28 ♖b1 ♖xb1 29 ♖xb1 ♚c7 30 ♚g1 ♖b8 31 ♖xb8 ♚xb8 32 ♚f2 ♚c7 33 ♚e3 ♚b6 34

♗xh7 ♗xc4 35 g4 ♔c5 36 h4 ♗g7 37 g5
♗b3 38 ♘d2 ♗xa4 39 ♘e4+ ♔b4 40 f5
hxg5 41 hxg5 ♗c2 42 f6 exf6 43 gxf6
♗xf6! 44 ♘xf6 ♗xh7 45 ♘xh7 ♔c3 46
♘g5 d5 47 ♘e6 a4 48 ♘f4 a3 0-1

White plays 6 exd6

From a positional point of view, **6 exd6**
is the clearest attempt to prove that the
black king's knight is simply misplaced
on h6. Since either 6...exd6 or 6...cxd6 is
strongly met by 7 d5, **6...♕xd6** is practically forced.

Following **7 ♘c3 a6** (the threat of 8
♘b5 followed by 9 ♗f4 had to be parried) we reach the following position:

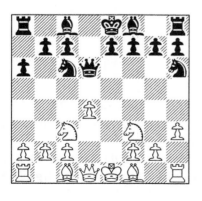

Connoisseurs of the Scandinavian
Defence will notice a similarity to the
3...♕d6 variation, only this time the
black knight has been developed to h6
instead of f6. The idea, of course, is to
transfer the knight to f5 from where it
will exert pressure on d4. White may
be able to get a slight advantage, although precise play is needed, as our
next game illustrates.

Game 23
Rodriguez-M.Narciso Dublan
St Cugat 1993

**1 e4 ♘c6 2 ♘f3 ♘f6 3 e5 ♘g4 4 d4 d6 5
h3 ♘h6 6 exd6**

Inserting 6 ♗xh6 gxh6 and then
playing 7 exd6 ♕xd6 gives a few different situations, as Black can now play
...♗g7 at any certain moment:

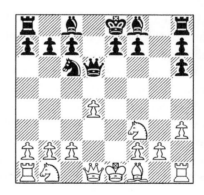

a) 8 ♘c3 a6 9 ♗d3 (9 ♘e4 ♕g6
would be similar to the text, while if 9
♗c4 ♗g7 10 0-0, then Black can safely
take the pawn as White has no compensation after 10...♘xd4 11 ♘xd4
♕xd4 12 ♕e2 ♕e5 13 ♕f3 0-0) 9...♗g7

10 ♘e4 was played in O.De la Riva Aguado-J.Ramirez Gonzalez, Terrassa 1994, and now 10...♕b4+ was the simplest way to continue.

b) 8 c3 ♗f5 (here Black should refrain from 8...♗g7 9 ♘bd2 0-0 10 ♗d3 e5?! 11 ♘c4, when the game D.Sebastian-R.Stuermer, German Junior Championships 1996, continued 11...♕e7 12 dxe5 b5?! 13 ♘e3 ♘xe5 14 ♘xe5 ♗xe5 and now after 15 ♗xb5 ♖b8 16 ♕e2 Black would not have had enough play for his pawn; instead 12...♘xe5 13 ♘cxe5 ♗xe5 14 ♘xe5 ♕xe5+ 15 ♕e2 ♖e8 would be the emergency brake, though it is only White who can play for the full point) 9 ♘a3 (9 ♗d3?! ♗xd3 10 ♕xd3 ♕g6! 11 ♕xg6 hxg6 or 11 ♕f1 ♕c2 is comfortable for Black; as is 9 ♕b3 ♕e6+! 10 ♕xe6 ♗xe6 11 ♗b5, P.Herweh-C.Mehne, Baden 1996, and now 11...♗d5) 9...0-0-0 10 ♘c4 ♕f6 (10...♕f4!? is also interesting) 11 ♕a4 h5 12 ♘ce5 ♘xe5 13 ♘xe5 ♔b8 14 ♗c4 ♖g8! 15 g3 (it is not immediately evident that 15 ♘xf7? is bad, but after 15...♖xg2! 16 ♘xd8 ♗d3!! 17 ♖f1 ♗xf1 18 0-0-0 ♗xc4 19 ♕xc4 ♕g6! and 20...♗h6+ wins; White's best option is 16 ♖f1 ♖c8 17 ♘e5 ♗xh3 18 0-0-0 ♖xf2 when Black is just a healthy pawn up) 15...e6!, and now White blundered in J.Lacasa Diaz-D.Bosch Porta, Barcelona 1992, with 16 ♘c6+? (although after 16 ♘d7+ ♖xd7 17 ♕xd7 ♗h6 Black would have had serious compensation for the exchange) when 16...bxc6 17 ♗a6 ♗d3! 18 ♕b3+ (or 18 ♗xd3 ♕f3 19 ♗a6 ♕xh1+ 20 ♔e2 ♕e4+) 18...♗b5 19 a4 ♕f3 20 axb5 ♕xh1+ 21 ♔e2 (or 21 ♔d2

♗h6+) 21...♕e4+ 22 ♔f1 c5 would have given Black a winning advantage.

6...♕xd6

7 ♘c3

7 g4!?, as played in L.Busquets-J.Ramirez Gonzalez, Spain 1992, should be answered by 7...f5!? 8 g5 ♘f7 9 ♘c3 a6, when Black can go for ...g6, ...♗g7 and ...e5.

7 ♘a3!? is annoying in so far as, after 7...a6 8 ♘c4, Black can hardly avoid the repetition of moves with 8...♕d5 9 ♘e3 ♕d6 10 ♘c4; but at least he does not have to worry about 10 ♗d3 ♘b4 or 10 ♗e2 ♘f5.

7...a6! 8 ♘e4?!

8 d5 ♘e5 9 ♗f4 ♘d3+! 10 ♗xd3 ♕xf4 and 8 ♗c4 ♘f5 9 d5 ♘e5 10 ♗f4 ♘d3+! 11 ♕xd3 ♕xf4 12 0-0 ♘d6 13 ♗b3 ♗f5 both lead to an equal game. However, 8 ♗e2! (from V.Vehi Bach-M.Narciso Dublan) offers White a chance to reach a better position if Black plays 8...♘f5 9 d5 ♘e5 10 ♘xe5 ♕xe5 11 0-0. Narciso Dublan suggests 8...g6!? as an improvement, intending ...♗g7, ...0-0 and only then playing ...♘f5.

8...♕g6 9 ♗d3

If 9 ♘g3 then 9...♘b4!, while 9 ♘c5 is effectively met by 9...e5! 10 ♕e2 ♗xc5 11 dxc5 0-0.

9...♘b4! 10 g4

After 10 0-0 Black can take the pawn with 10...♗xh3 as 11 ♘h4 is met by 11...♕g4.

10...♘xd3+ 11 ♕xd3 f5!

12 gxf5

12 ♘eg5 can be answered by 12...fxg4! 13 ♕xg6+ hxg6 and now 14 ♘e5 ♘f5! 15 c3 (or 15 ♘xg6 ♖h6 16 ♘xf8 ♘xd4!) 15...gxh3 16 ♘xg6 ♖h6 17 ♘xf8 ♔xf8 18 ♘xh3 ♖h5 and Black is better.

On 12 ♘e5, Keilhack gives 12...fxe4 13 ♘xg6 exd3 14 ♘xh8 ♗e6 15 cxd3 0-0-0(?) as better for Black, but after 16 ♗g5! I do not see how Black can pick up the knight; for example 16...g6 17 ♔d2 ♗g7 18 ♖he1 ♖d6 (18...♔d7 runs into 19 d5) and there is no piece left to take the white knight, as the bishop is tied to the protection of the black knight. However, slightly adjusting the move order with 15...g6 helps, as now 16 ♗g5 ♗g7 17 ♔d2 ♔d7 saves a pre-

cious tempo and Black is better (if 18 ♖he1 ♘g8!).

12...♗xf5 13 ♘fg5 0-0-0

Finally Black has obtained a decisive advantage.

14 ♗f4 e5! 15 ♗xe5 ♗b4+ 16 c3

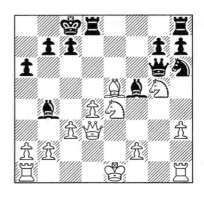

16...♗e7?!

16...♕xg5! must be better, as after 17 ♘xg5 ♗xd3 18 cxb4 ♖d7 the bishop on e5 is the only trump card White has with his shattered pawn structure. After 19 b3 (19 0-0-0?! is inferior as it allows Black to relocate his bishop to d5 by 19...♗c4 20 b3 ♗d5) 19...♘f5 20 0-0-0 ♗b5 Black is clearly on top, as once he has won back his pawn (and he certainly will) the white structure will be deficient.

17 h4?!

After 17 ♕e3!? it is not clear how Black should proceed.

17...♘g4 18 ♕c4 ♘xe5 19 dxe5 ♖he8

Instead 19...h6! is more precise, for example 20 h5 hxg5 21 hxg6 ♖xh1+ 22 ♔e2 ♖xa1.

20 ♖g1 ♗xe4 21 ♕xe4 ♗xg5 22 ♕g4+

Or 22 ♕xg6? ♗d2+.

22...♔b8 23 ♕xg5? ♖xe5+! 0-1

White plays 6 ♗b5

The move **6 ♗b5** gives the black set-up its toughest test. Then after **6...a6 7 ♗xc6+ bxc6** we have reached the most critical position to be found in this chapter:

By swapping his light-squared bishop for Black's queen's knight, White has reduced the pressure on his pawn centre and is also equipped with the better pawn structure. As a rule of thumb, with his two bishops Black should try to open up the position. The typical counterstroke is now ...c6-c5, which not only opens the h1-a8 diagonal but also attacks the white centre. But most of the time (even more so if White decides to eliminate the other knight as well) it is the dark-squared bishop who is the hero of the day – and Black shouldn't be afraid to sacrifice material (up to an exchange) to broaden its horizons.

The ensuing variations are highly complicated and only have a few practical examples, but they give ample scope to play for a full point, as the next game illustrates.

> ### Game 24
> ### J.Sprenger-H.Keilhack
> ### Correspondence 1996

1 e4 ♘c6 2 ♘f3 ♘f6 3 e5 ♘g4 4 d4 d6 5 h3 ♘h6 6 ♗xh6

Playing this move prematurely deprives White of numerous options. The immediate 6 ♗b5 a6 leads to a different type of position:

a) 7 ♗a4?! is dubious; for example, 7...b5 8 ♗b3 dxe5 9 d5 e4! 10 ♘g5 ♘a5 11 0-0?! ♗b7 12 ♘c3 ♘xb3 13 axb3 b4 14 ♘cxe4 ♕xd5 and Black won a pawn in A.Fabregas Fonanet-M.Narciso Dublan, Barcelona 1992. 11 ♘xe4 is better, but after 11...♘f5 12 0-0 ♘xb3 (just not 12...g6?? 13 ♕e1 and White picks up the knight as Black has to take care of 14 ♘f6 mate!) 13 axb3 ♗b7 14 c4 e6 White still has a tough game to follow.

b) 7 ♗xc6+ bxc6 is the critical variation:

b1) 8 ♘c3 e6 usually transposes to 8 0-0. The only significant attempt to avoid these lines is 9 ♗g5!?, as played in G.Langhanke-A.Korn, German League 2004. Now the correct answer is 9...♕d7!?, for example 10 ♗xh6 (if 10 0-0 Black can play 10...♘f5 with ideas similar to those after 8 0-0 ['b2'] below) 10...gxh6 11 ♘e4 ♗g7 12 ♕d2 (or 12 0-0 c5!) 12...c5! with counterplay, for example 13 ♕f4 cxd4 14 ♘f6+ ♗xf6 15 ♕xf6 ♖g8 or 13 dxc5 dxe5 14 0-0-0 ♕xd2+ 15 ♖xd2 ♗b7. Instead, 9...♗e7?! was played in the actual game, but after 10 ♗xh6 gxh6 11 ♕d2 Black, unless ready to be a pawn down for nothing, would have been forced to play 11...dxe5 (11...♗f8? 12 ♘e4 ♗g7 13 ♕f4! is completely hopeless) 12 ♘xe5 ♗g5 13 ♕d3 ♗b7 14 0-0 and now the black pawn structure is a bit too tatty.

b2) 8 0-0 e6 (I was fond of 8...g6 for quite a long time, but during my preparation for this book I noticed a hole in the analysis of Narciso Dublan: after 9 ♘c3 ♘f5 10 ♖e1 he gives 10...♕d7, but 11 ♘e4! buries the whole line; the simple threat is 12 exd6 followed by 13 ♘f6+ and there is nothing sensible Black can do about that), and now:

b21) After 9 ♗g5, similarly to 8 ♘c3 e6 9 ♗g5, Black should react with 9...♕d7 10 ♗xh6 gxh6 11 ♘bd2 ♗g7 12 ♘e4 c5!.

b22) 9 ♘c3 ♘f5!? 10 g4 ♘e7 11 ♘e4 ♕d7, followed by ...♗b7 and sooner or later ...c5, provides Black with sufficient counterplay.

b23) 9 ♗xh6 gxh6 10 ♘c3 ♗g7 11 ♘e4 ♗b7 12 ♖e1 once more features 12...c5! 13 dxc5 (on 13 exd6 Black can choose between 13...♗xe4!? 14 ♖xe4

♕xd6, when the dark-squared bishop compensates well for the inferior pawn structure, and 13...cxd4 14 ♘xd4 0-0 15 ♕g4 cxd6 16 ♖ad1 ♔h8 17 ♘xd6 ♕xd6 18 ♘xe6 ♕xe6 19 ♖xe6 ♗c8 when Black has a rook and two bishops for the queen in open terrain, or if 14 dxc7 ♕xc7 15 ♘xd4 0-0-0 16 c3 ♖hg8 with attacking chances according to Narciso Dublan) 13...dxe5 14 ♕e2 ♕d5! 15 ♖ad1 ♕xa2 and this time it is White who has to look for adequate compensation.

6...gxh6 7 ♗b5 a6 8 ♗xc6+

8 ♗a4 was played in M.Sawadkuhi-C.Wisnewski, Bargteheide 2004. The game continued 8...b5 9 ♗b3 dxe5 10 d5 e4 11 ♘fd2 ♘d4 12 ♘c3 (12 ♘xe4 ♗g7 13 ♘bc3 transposes) 12...♗g7 13 ♘dxe4 0-0 14 ♘g3 and now 14...♖b8!?, with the idea 15 0-0 ♖b6 to get the rook into play via the sixth rank, would have been very interesting.

8...bxc6

9 ♕e2

Besides this move, White has a variety of alternatives. Let's take a look:

a) 9 ♘c3 ♖g8?! was played in P.De Laat-C.Tanis, correspondence 1996, but

I do not like the black set-up. The game continued 10 g3 ♕d7 11 ♕d3 ♖b8 12 0-0-0 ♕f5 13 ♕e2 (13 ♘e4 is a worthy alternative) 13...♗e6, and now instead of 14 g4 White should have played 14 ♘h4! ♕g5+ 15 ♔b1 when I honestly cannot imagine how Black might generate any counterplay. More to the point is 9...♗g7, and then after 10 0-0 0-0 11 ♘e4 (or 11 ♖e1) Black should play 11...♗e6 (but not 11...♔h8 12 ♖e1 ♖g8?? 13 ♘eg5! and Black is suddenly lost!) 12 ♖e1 ♕c8 when we reach an unclear position. White has an advantage in space and the superior pawn structure, but in return Black has two bishops and two half-open files to play with. I would advance my a-pawn next to try to pick on the white b-pawn, and/or play ...♔h8 followed by ...♖g8. To my knowledge there are no practical examples yet, so you are free to let your creativity take its course!

b) 9 0-0 ♗g7 10 ♖e1 0-0 11 ♘c3 is merely a transposition to 'a'.

c) 9 ♕d3 is an interesting move, taking control over the usually important f5-square. Now the game H.Diek-R.Schlenker, Germany 1993, continued 9...♗g7 10 ♘bd2 a5?! (the 'calm' 10...0-0 is the right move for those who do not want ultimately to burn their bridges behind them; after 11 0-0 ♗e6 Black has a passive, though solid position) 11 ♕c3 0-0 12 0-0 ♔h8 13 ♕xc6 ♖a6 14 ♕e4 ♖g8, and now the move 15 ♕e3?! is a bit too convenient for Black. Instead of releasing control over f5, White could have played 15 c4!?, preventing d5 and therefore denying the

a6-rook from joining his friends on the kingside. Black could then try to upset the centre with 15...c5!? but his compensation is far from obvious.

Instead, 9...♖b8!? from S.Kowalczyk-Y.Gerritse, Hengelo 1998, is my favourite. The resulting positions are so full of possibilities that I cannot possibly list them all. However, I shall try to give you at least a small impression: 10 ♕c3 (10 b3?! unwarily weakens the a1-h8 diagonal and gives Black time to work on the centre; for example, 10...♗g7 11 ♕e4 c5! 12 dxc5 ♕d7 or 11 0-0 dxe5 12 dxe5 ♕xd3 13 cxd3 ♗f5 14 d4 h5 and the two bishops compensate for the inferior pawn structure) 10...♖g8 11 ♖g1 (after 11 ♕xc6+ ♗d7 12 ♕xa6 ♖xb2 13 ♕d3 ♖xg2 14 ♘bd2 ♕a8! or 12 ♕c3 ♖xg2 13 ♘bd2 ♕c8! 14 0-0-0 ♕b7, Black again gets sufficient counterplay). Now Black lost the thread after 11...♗b7?! 12 ♘bd2 ♗g7 13 0-0-0 ♕d7 14 ♕d3 ♕e6 15 ♕xh7 ♔f8 16 b3 and collapsed after 16...c5 17 dxc5 dxc5 18 ♕d3 a5? 19 ♘e4 c4 20 ♕d8+ 1-0. But 11...♗g7! offers plenty of practical chances; for example:

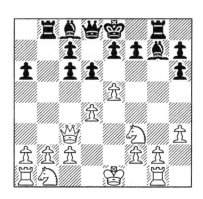

c1) 12 ♕xc6+ ♕d7! 13 ♕c3 (if 13 ♕xd7+ ♗xd7 14 b3 c5! 15 c3 cxd4 16 cxd4 dxe5 17 ♘xe5 ♖b4 or 17 dxe5 ♖b5 and Black regains the pawn) 13...c5! 14 dxc5 (14 ♘bd2 cxd4 15 ♕xd4 dxe5 must be better for Black) 14...dxe5 and now 15 ♘bd2 (15 ♘xe5? loses to 15...♕f5) 15...e4 16 ♘e5 ♕d5 17 f4 exf3 18 ♘dxf3 (or 18 gxf3 ♔f8 19 f4 ♗xe5! 20 ♖xg8+ ♔xg8 21 fxe5 ♕h1+) 18...♖b5, and once again the two bishops make the difference.

c2) 12 ♘bd2 c5 13 dxc5 dxe5 14 0-0-0 e4 15 ♘e5 ♕d5 16 ♘dc4 ♕xc5 17 ♕d4 ♕xd4 18 ♖xd4 ♗b7 and the bishops rule the board. Instead, 17 ♕d2 looks good at first sight, but after 17...♗e6 18 ♘d7 ♕xc4! 19 ♘xb8 ♗xb2+ 20 ♔xb2 ♕xa2+ 21 ♔c3 ♕a3+ (21...♕c4+ 22 ♔b2 ♕a2+ is a safety net) 22 ♔d4 ♖g5! Black gets a devastating attack.

9...♖g8!

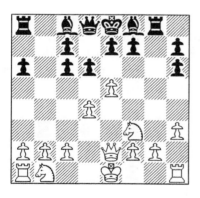

A bold heart is half the battle! And indeed, from now on a furious fight ensues, and it is impossible to fully analyse all the potential implications. Nevertheless, I will do the best I can to offer you the most important ideas.

10 ♘c3

10 g3 is best met by 10...♖b8 11 b3 (11 c3?! looks natural but is dubious, as it ties the queen to b2 and denies the queen's knight access to c3; after 11...dxe5 12 ♘xe5 ♕d5 or 12 dxe5 ♕d5! 13 ♘a3 c5 14 ♖d1 ♕c6 15 ♕d3 ♗b7 16 ♘c4 ♕e4+ 17 ♕xe4 ♗xe4 18 ♔e2 e6 the black pawn structure is damaged, but this is compensated by the pair of bishops and the option to play on the half-open b- and g-files again). Now 11...c5!? is recommended by Keilhack, leading to an unclear position after 12 dxc5 dxe5 13 ♘c3 ♕d7 14 ♖d1 ♕c6 15 ♘d5 f6; for example 16 ♕c4 (or 16 b4 ♖g6 17 ♘h4 ♖xb4! 18 ♘xg6 hxg6 and with two bishops, one pawn and a more or less repaired pawn structure, Black has definite compensation for the sacrificed exchange; but not 16...♗g7 17 c4 e6? 18 ♘xe5! fxe5 19 ♕h5+ ♔f8 20 ♕f3+ ♔e8 21 ♘f6+ and White wins) 16...♖g6!, protecting f6 and intending to chase the knight on d5 away with ...e7-e6. But 13 ♕e4!? is a problem; for example 13...♖g6 14 ♘xe5 ♗g7 15 ♘xg6 ♗xa1 16 ♘e5 when I do not like Black's position. Therefore, I recommend 11...♕d7!?, after which White does not have anything better than to transpose to the previously mentioned line after 12 ♘c3 c5 13 dxc5 dxe5 14 ♖d1 ♕c6, as 12 ♕e4 c5! 13 ♕xh7 ♖g6 14 ♘h4 is met by 14...♕c6! with a good game for Black.

10...♖xg2

Looking for the greatest possible complications, but in my opinion this move does not live up to its expectations. Perhaps more accurate is

10...♗e6!? 11 0-0-0 ♕b8 with counterplay on the half-open b-file.

11 ♘e4

If White tries to get his pawn back with 11 ♕e4, Black can play 11...d5 12 ♕xh7 ♕d7, intending ...♕f5.

And 11 ♘h4 ♖g8 12 ♕e4 is successfully answered by 12...e6! when White cannot take either pawn: 13 ♕xh7 (13 ♕xc6+ ♗d7 14 ♕e4 ♖b8 is similar) 13...♖g7 14 ♕e4 ♖b8! 15 0-0-0 (or 15 b3 f5! 16 exf6 ♕xf6 and Black is much better) 15...♕g5+ 16 ♖d2 d5 17 ♕g4 ♕xg4 18 hxg4 ♖xg4 and with the queens off the board and an extra pawn, Black must be better.

11...♗e6

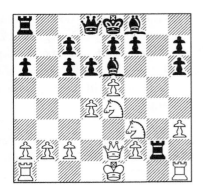

12 0-0-0

If 12 ♘h4 ♖g8 13 f4 dxe5 14 f5 ♗d5 15 dxe5 (or 15 0-0-0) 15...♗xe4 16 ♕xe4 ♕d5 and Black has weathered the storm.

With 12 ♘g3 White tries to trap the rook, so Black must initiate counterplay quickly by 12...♕b8 and then:

a) 13 c3 ♕b5! 14 ♘h4 (or 14 ♕xb5 axb5 15 ♘h4 ♖xg3 16 fxg3 dxe5 17 dxe5 ♗g7 18 ♘f3 ♖xa2 19 ♖xa2 ♗xa2 with two bishops and two pawns for the

exchange) 14...♗c4 15 ♕d2 ♖xg3 16 fxg3 dxe5 and Black has sufficient compensation.

b) 13 0-0-0!? ♕b5! 14 ♕e3 ♖b8 15 b3 ♕a5 16 ♔b2 ♗d5 17 ♔a1 (or 17 c4 ♗xc4 18 ♘h4 ♖xg3 19 fxg3 ♗e6 with unclear play) 17...♗g7 18 c4 ♖xf2! 19 ♕xf2 ♕c3+ 20 ♔b1 (20 ♕b2? ♕xb2+ 21 ♔xb2 ♗xf3 is good for Black) 20...♗xf3 21 ♖df1 ♗xh1 22 ♕xf7+ ♔d7 23 ♕xg7 ♗e4+ 24 ♘xe4 ♕d3+ 25 ♔b2 ♕xe4 and Black is slightly better.

c) 13 b3! is the critical move. Keilhack claims an unclear position after 13...c5 14 ♔f1 ♖xg3 15 fxg3 cxd4, but I am not yet entirely convinced. More practical tests are needed for an accurate evaluation.

12...♕b8!

Being a pawn up, Black seeks simplification with ...♕b5.

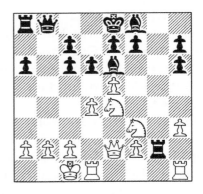

13 c4

13 ♘c3?! is another way to prevent ...♕b5, but Black can react appropriately: 13...♕b4!?, and now for example 14 a3 ♕b6 15 ♘h4 ♖g7 16 f4 ♖b8 17 b3 ♕a5 18 ♔b2 ♖g3! with a strong attack.

13...♕b4 14 ♘h4?!

Instead, 14 exd6 (14 d5?! cxd5 15 cxd5 is answered by 15...♗f5 16 ♖d4 ♕b5!) would have been the most dangerous move according to Keilhack. Indeed, Black must be careful:

a) 14...♗xc4? leads to instantaneous exitus after 15 ♘e5!! ♗xe2 (or 15...♗e6 16 d7+ ♗xd7 17 ♘f6+!) 16 d7+ ♔d8 17 ♘c5! and Black cannot avoid mate.

b) 14...♕xc4+? is bad: 15 ♕xc4 ♗xc4 16 d7+ ♔d8 17 ♘e5 ♗d5 18 ♘c5 ♖a7 19 ♖hg1 and Black gets squeezed.

c) After 14...cxd6 15 ♘h4, Keilhack gives 15...♖g7 (15...♗xc4? runs into 16 ♕e1! ♕xe1 17 ♖dxe1 followed by 18 ♘xd6+) 16 d5 cxd5 17 cxd5 ♖c8+ (or 17...♗c8 18 f4 ♖a7 19 ♔b1 ♖c7 20 ♖c1 ♖xc1+ 21 ♖xc1 ♔d8 22 ♕c2 ♕b7 23 f5 with attacking chances) 18 ♔b1 ♗d7 19 ♘f6+ ♔d8 20 ♘xd7 ♔xd7 21 ♕xa6 and if 21...♕xh4 22 ♖c1! ♖c5 23 ♕b7+ ♔d8 24 ♕b8+ ♔d7 25 ♕xf8 with a slight advantage for White. But 15...♖g5! is a far superior move. White can hardly accept this sacrifice, as 16 ♘xg5 hxg5 17 ♘f3 ♗xc4 nets another pawn, in addition to repairing Black's pawn structure.

14...♗xc4 15 ♕e3?!

15 ♕d2 was White's best option. But still, after 15...♕xd2+ 16 ♘xd2 ♗d5 17 ♘xg2 ♗xg2 18 ♖hg1 (or 18 ♖h2 ♗d5) 18...♗xh3 Black has more than adequate compensation for the exchange.

15...♖g7

15...♖g6!? is also interesting, as 16 ♘xg6 hxg6 again repairs the pawn structure. With his two bishops and two pawns for the exchange, Black enjoys a nice advantage once more. Keilhack rejected this move due to 17 exd6

cxd6 18 a3 ♕b8 19 h4!, but 19...h5 stops any ambitions White might have had.

Nevertheless, the text move suffices – here Black can already be choosy.

16 ♘f5 ♖g6 17 b3 ♗d5 18 ♘h4 dxe5! 19 ♘xg6 hxg6 20 ♖he1 a5!

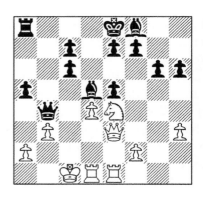

Launching the final wave of attack. Black can also play 20...♗g7 21 ♘c5 ♗f6 22 ♘e4 (not 22 dxe5? ♗g5) 22...♗xe4 23 ♕xe4 0-0-0! 24 ♕xc6 ♕a3+ 25 ♔b1 exd4 now with three pawns for the exchange.

21 dxe5

21 ♘c3 is unable to stop the attack, for example 21...a4! 22 bxa4 (both 22 ♘xd5 cxd5 23 dxe5 e6 and 22 ♘xa4 ♕a3+ 23 ♔b1 ♖xa4! 24 bxa4 ♕xa2+ 25 ♔c1 ♕a1+ 26 ♔c2 ♕xa4+ 27 ♔c1 ♕a1+ 28 ♔c2 ♕a2+ 29 ♔c1 e6 lead to a decisive advantage for Black) 22...♕a3+ 23 ♔c2 ♗xa2 and Black is breaking in.

21 ♔b2 is the only way to avoid being squashed in an instant, but after 21...a4 22 ♕c3 ♕xc3+ 23 ♘xc3 axb3 24 ♘xd5 cxd5 25 ♔xb3 e6, the black pawns are just too strong.

21...♕a3+ 22 ♔b1 a4 23 ♕f3 axb3 24 ♘f6+ exf6 25 exf6+ ♗e7! 0-1

Summary

2 ♘f3 is the most cunning move against the Nimzowitsch Defence. Many players were banging their heads against a wall while trying to find a way to counter it, eventually giving the Nimzowitsch up in the process. 'El Columpio' is a nice attempt to unbalance the position, and while Black was not seriously put to the test in Games 20-23, Game 24 shows the critical move order. There haven't been too many practical examples, but I think that Black shouldn't be afraid to face the consequences.

1 e4 ♘c6 2 ♘f3 ♘f6 *(D)* **3 e5**

       3 ♘c3 d5 – *Game 20*

3...♘g4 4 d4 d6 *(D)* **5 h3**

       5 exd6 – *Game 21*

5...♘h6 6 ♗b5

       6 ♘c3 a6 – *Game 21*

       6 e6 fxe6 – *Game 22*

       6 exd6 ♕xd6 – *Game 23*

6...a6 7 ♗xc6+ bxc6 *(D)* – *Game 24*

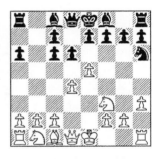

    2...♘f6   *4...d6*   *7...bxc6*

Part Two

Black vs. 1 d4: The Chigorin Defence

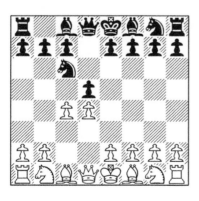

In my opinion, the only opening sys-tem besides the Chigorin Defence that enables the Black player to play confi-dently for the full point is the King's Indian Defence. I have played both, but I favour the Chigorin for the following reason: in the King's Indian, the strate-gic implications are often clear to both players; many lines have even been completely dissected, giving the White player the advantage of knowing ex-actly what he is up against. As a result, room for creativity has been signifi-cantly reduced. The Chigorin Defence, on the other hand, offers unusual types of positions, often to the extent that 1 d4 players have a hard time coping with them.

But what are the exact ideas behind the Chigorin Defence anyway?

Down with playing schemes!

The so-called Queen's Pawn Games originating from **1 d4 d5 2 ♘f3** enjoy great popularity, especially at club level. Be it the Torre Attack, the Cata-lan, the Colle or the London System, the chance to play similar positions with clear-cut plans against almost all possible set-ups is attractive to many players.

Against the Chigorin Defence, **2...♞c6**, those players are in for a rude awakening. The special set-up of the black pieces has to be treated accordingly, and bone-headed adherence to a system can quickly end in disaster, as numerous examples in Chapter 6 will show.

Dealing with overextension

The Chigorin Defence is often marked by a fierce battle for the centre. In many cases White will gain space by pushing his pawns, while Black will try to initiate counterplay by zeroing in on the advanced forces. In addition to that, seizing space is not totally free. White usually needs to sacrifice a pawn, and winning it back takes time – which Black can use to consolidate his

position, as we will see in Chapters 7 and 8.

There's also strategy involved!

To many players the Chigorin Defence has a somewhat swashbuckling reputation, but there is more to it than that. Ambushes, skirmishes and scuffles are not the only actions the Chigorin Defence allows. You will see as well that Black can exploit weaknesses in the enemy pawn structure, as the games in Chapters 9 and 10 will show.

Initiative versus Material

Willingness to snatch the initiative is mandatory for a Chigorin player, and there are certain situations in which you are bound to sacrifice material. However, as the games in Chapter 11 demonstrate, you will be more than compensated by a lead in development and attacking chances.

Chapter Six

1 d4 d5 2 ♘f3 ♘c6 and Other Rare Second Moves

One could argue that **1 d4 d5** has no place in a book about 1...♘c6, but ultimately the difference is purely semantic. Granted, you will not enjoy coverage of lines such as 1 d4 ♘c6 2 d5, but as I am encouraging you to play the Chigorin Defence anyway, there is absolutely no reason to give White an opportunity to circumvent it – even more so because, after 1 d4 d5, there is absolutely no sensible way to avoid it. Okay, there are a few moves besides 2 ♘f3 and 2 c4 White can play, but those are hardly dangerous, as we will see in our first game in this chapter.

<hr>

Game 25
R.Schlindwein-V.Bukal Jr
Austrian League 2000

<hr>

1 d4 d5 2 ♗f4

Other moves usually transpose to lines covered elsewhere:

a) 2 e4 is the trademark of the

Blackmar-Diemer community. The simplest way for Black to react is 2...♘c6!, returning to the 1 e4 ♘c6 2 d4 d5 lines in Chapters 2-4.

b) 2 ♘c3 should be answered by the system-compatible 2...♘c6.

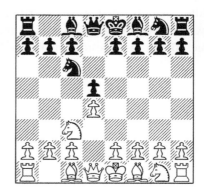

Note that with the knight on c3 our plans are a little bit different here, as ...e7-e5 often puts d5 in the pillory. Let's look how the game could evolve: 3 ♗g5 (3 e4 e6 again transposes to Chapter 4, while 3 ♗f4 ♗g4 can be compared with 1 d4 d5 2 ♘f3 ♘c6 3

♗f4 ♗g4 examined in Games 32-35, the difference being that the knight on c3 hampers any counterplay White might have against the d5-pawn) should be met by 3...♗f5 (I do not recommend 3...♗g4 here, as after 4 f3 ♗h5 5 e4 Black cannot play 5...e6) 4 e3 ♕d7, intending ...0-0-0. This gives added protection to the d5-pawn and allows Black eventually to think about ...f7-f6 followed by ...e5 or ...g5, depending on White's response.

c) 2 ♗g5 ♘c6 3 e3 f6 4 ♗h4 (4 ♗f4?! e5 is already very good for Black due to his unchallenged presence in the centre) 4...♘h6 most likely transposes to Game 27. However, 3 c4!? is not so bad. After 3...dxc4 4 e3 White tries to make use of the fact that Black cannot advance his e-pawn. Now 4...f6!? probably results in a mixture of different systems, so the simplest way to react seems to be 4...♕d5!? 5 ♘f3 e6, when White will have a hard time regaining his pawn under favourable circumstances.

2...♗g4!

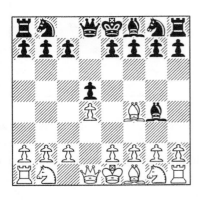

2...♘c6?! is inaccurate, as 3 e3 trans-

poses to the London System, with the Chigorin player being lured out of known territory.

3 c4

3 ♘f3 ♘c6 transposes to 1 d4 d5 2 ♘f3 ♘c6 3 ♗f4 ♗g4, covered in Games 32-35.

If instead 3 f3 ♗h5 4 e3 e6 5 ♗d3, Black can go for a Chigorin-style set-up with ...♗d6 and ...♘f6, or play the more aggressive 5...♘f6 6 ♗g3 ♗e7 7 ♘e2 c5 as in K.Bondick-D.Serrano, Internet (blitz) 2004. The idea is to show that by playing 3 f3 White has weakened his e-pawn. The game continued 8 dxc5?! (White would do better to eat humble pie with 8 c3 ♘c6) 8...♗xc5 9 ♗f2 ♘c6 10 0-0 0-0 11 a3 a6 12 ♘bc3 b5 and Black had the initiative.

3...♘c6 4 f3

Here White should have transposed to Games 34-35 with 4 ♘f3 e6 5 e3. Instead, he opts for a dubious pawn sacrifice which is easily refuted by Black.

4...♗h5 5 cxd5 ♕xd5 6 ♘c3?! ♕xd4 7 ♘d5 0-0-0!

8 ♕xd4 ♘xd4 9 ♖c1 ♖xd5 10 ♖xc7+ ♔d8

White is fishing for compensation, but he doesn't get any.

11 ♖xb7 ♞c2+ 12 ♔f2 e5 13 ♖b8+ ♔c7 14 ♗xe5+ ♖xe5 15 ♖xf8 f6 16 ♖a8 ♔b7 17 ♖d8 ♔c7 18 ♖a8 ♔b7 19 ♖d8 ♗e8

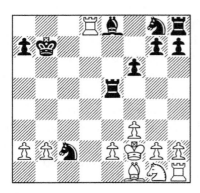

20 f4 ♖e7 21 e4 ♞b4 22 ♗c4 ♖xe4 23 a3 ♖xc4 24 ♖xe8 ♞d3+ 25 ♔f3 ♖c8 26 ♖xc8 ♔xc8 27 ♞e2 ♞e7 28 b4 ♖d8 29 ♖b1 ♔b7 30 h4 ♞f5 31 g4 ♞xh4+ 32 ♔e3 ♞g2+ 33 ♔e4 g5 34 fxg5 fxg5 35 ♔f5 h6 36 ♔g6 ♖d6+ 37 ♔g7 ♞e5 0-1

White cut a poor figure here, but that is what you get if you stray too far from known paths. The game also shows that you shouldn't be afraid of not getting your intended positions, while the number of transpositions to familiar systems is noteworthy.

For the rest of this chapter we will deal with **2 ♞f3**, a move especially popular at club level. After **2...♞c6**, there are various systems White can choose from.

White plays 3 ♗g5

3 ♗g5 is a move with a certain degree of originality. The idea is to hamper Black's development on the kingside. Now 3...♞f6?! 4 ♗xf6! results in a better pawn structure for White: if Black plays 4...gxf6, a white queen on h5 can be very annoying (an idea which is actually taken up by Black in Chapter 9, Game 45), while after 4...exf6 the pawn majority on the queenside provides White with a long-term endgame advantage.

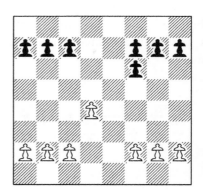

However, there are reasons why this move is not commonly played. Disregarding the fact that it is just not to everyone's taste, there are also concrete positional adversities. Black can solve all his problems with **3...f6!**.

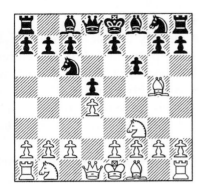

After **4 ♗f4** we have a position similar to 1 d4 d5 2 ♘f3 ♘c6 3 ♗f4, (Games 32-35). The difference is that the f-pawn is on f6 instead of f7, but this favours Black, as it supports the advance ...e7-e5. Black will soon be on top, as we will see in our next game.

Game 26
O.Springer-D.Koenig
Passau 1999

1 d4 d5 2 ♘f3 ♘c6 3 ♗g5 f6! 4 ♗f4

4 ♗h4 is the subject of Game 27.

4...♗g4

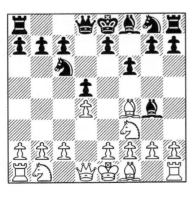

White's wasted tempo with ♗c1-g5-f4 means that he is now defending the black side of a Veresov (i.e. 1 d4 d5 2 ♘c3 ♘f6 3 ♗g5 ♗f5 4 f3 with reversed colours).

5 ♘bd2

Numerous other moves have been seen as well:

a) 5 e3? obviously loses a piece to 5...e5 6 ♗g3 e4.

b) 5 h3 just forces Black to do what he was planning to do anyway: 5...♗xf3 6 exf3 e5 7 dxe5 fxe5 8 ♗e3 ♘f6 and Black has occupied the centre, resulting in a comfortable game.

c) 5 c4 e5! (5...dxc4!? 6 d5 e5 is also interesting; A.Morozevich-L.Van Wely, Monte Carlo blindfold 2005, continued 7 ♗c1 ♘b4 8 e4 c6 9 a3 ♘d3+ 10 ♗xd3 cxd3 11 dxc6 bxc6 12 0-0 ♗c5 and Black was clearly better) 6 dxe5 (Black is fine after 6 cxd5 ♗xf3 7 dxc6 ♗xc6 8 dxe5 ♕xd1+ 9 ♔xd1 0-0-0+ or 7 ♕xd4 ♘c6) 6...♗b4+ (better than 6...♗xf3 7 exf3 fxe5 8 cxd5 exf4 9 dxc6 ♕xd1+ 10 ♔xd1 0-0-0+ 11 ♔c2 ♗c5 12 cxb7+ ♔xb7 13 ♘c3 which resulted in a White advantage in M.Olea Perez-P.Glavino Rossi, Ribadedeva rapid 1999) 7 ♗d2 ♗xd2+ 8 ♘bxd2 fxe5 9 cxd5 ♕xd5 10 ♕a4 and a draw was agreed in G.Henriksen-G.Gross, Kiekrz 1995. After 10...♘f6 11 e4 ♕c5 the position offers chances for both sides, as the potential weakness of the isolated e5-pawn is compensated by active piece play.

d) The harmless 5 c3 can be met by 5...e5 6 dxe5 ♗xf3 7 exf3 fxe5 8 ♗e3 ♘f6, but 5...e6 is good as well, for example 6 ♕b3 ♖b8 7 h3 ♗h5 8 ♘bd2 ♗f7

9 ♗h2 ♗d6 10 e4 ♗xh2 11 ♖xh2 ♘ge7 12 0-0-0 0-0 13 h4 b5! and Black quickly initiated an attack on the queenside in the game E.Heyken-C.Wisnewski, German League 2004.

5...♘xd4!

Alternatively:

a) 5...e6 is a solid choice too; for example, 6 c3 (6 e3?! is not as bad as before, but still not to be recommended: 6...e5 7 dxe5 fxe5 8 ♗g5 ♗e7 or 8 ♗g3 e4 9 h3 ♗h5 and now 10 ♗h4 is possible, but Black is more than OK after 10...♗e7 11 ♗xe7 ♘gxe7 12 g4 ♗g6 13 ♘h4 0-0) 6...♗d6 7 ♗xd6 (7 ♗g3 f5 actually transposes to Game 33) 7...♕xd6 8 e4 ♘ge7 9 exd5 exd5 10 ♗d3 0-0-0! 11 0-0 g5 and Black developed a dangerous kingside initiative in O.Valaker-S.Heim, Bergen 2001.

b) 5...♕d7 is the other Veresov move. The game C.Arduman-P.Claesen, Istanbul Olympiad 2000, continued 6 c3 0-0-0 7 h3 ♗xf3 8 ♘xf3 e5!? 9 dxe5 ♕f5 10 e3 fxe5 11 g4 ♕e6 12 ♗g3 ♗d6 13 ♕a4 ♘ge7 14 0-0-0 ♖hf8 15 ♗e2 e4 16 ♘d4 ♕h6 17 g5 ♕xg5 when a draw was agreed, although this line is

certainly not my cup of tea.

6 ♗xc7?

After this terrible move Black obtains complete control of the centre as well as the pair of bishops. 6 ♘xd4 was necessary, although Black is also able to keep his game up with 6...e5 7 h3 (7 ♗xe5?! fxe5 followed by 8...♘f6 is clearly better for Black, while 7 ♗e3 exd4 8 ♗xd4 c5 seizes more and more space) 7...♗h5 (7...♗c8?! is bad, as K.Lerner-S.Lejlic, Berlin 1997, showed: 8 e4! exf4 9 ♕h5+ g6 10 ♕xd5 ♕xd5 11 exd5 ♗d7 12 0-0-0 and the two bishops could not compensate for the structural defects of the pawn structure), and now:

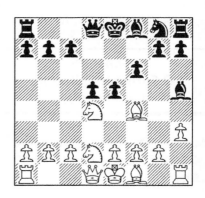

8 ♘e6 (if 8 ♘2b3 then 8...exf4 9 ♘e6 ♕d6? runs into 10 ♕xd5!, but 8...c6 9 ♗h2 exd4 10 ♕xd4 ♗d6 11 ♗xd6 ♕xd6 12 0-0-0 ♘e7 is OK for Black) 8...♕d6 9 ♘xf8 exf4 10 ♘c4 (or 10 ♘xh7 ♖xh7, and although Black's position looks plucked, the advantage in space cannot be denied) 10...♕c6 (but not 10...♕b4+? 11 c3 ♕xc4 12 ♘e6 ♔f7 13 ♘xf4! ♕xf4 14 ♕xd5+ ♔g6 15 g4 and Black could have resigned in G.Kuhn-M.Trescher,

Stade 1992) 11 ♘a5 ♕b6 12 ♕xd5 (after 12 ♘b3 ♗f7 13 ♘xh7 ♖xh7 14 ♕d3 ♖h5 15 ♕f3 a5! 16 ♖b1 a4 17 ♘c1 ♖h4 18 g3 fxg3 19 ♕xg3 g5 20 ♗g2 ♘e7 Black enjoyed a tremendous advantage in M.Galyas-G.Kallai, Budapest 2000) 12...♕xb2 13 ♖d1 ♕c3+ 14 ♕d2 (if 14 ♖d2 ♕a1+ 15 ♖d1 ♕c3+ invites a draw, though White still can decline with 16 ♕d2; or Black can play 14...♔xf8 15 ♘xb7 ♗f7 16 ♕c5+ ♕xc5 17 ♘xc5 ♗xa2) 14...♕xd2+ 15 ♖xd2 ♔xf8 16 ♘xb7 (16 ♖d7?! is dubious as Black can untangle himself with 16...b6 17 ♘c6 ♖c8 18 ♘xa7 ♗e8!) 16...♖b8 17 ♖d8+ ♖xd8 18 ♘xd8 ♗f7 19 ♘xf7 ♔xf7 and Black seems to be better, although there is still plenty to play for.

6...♕xc7 7 ♘xd4 e5 8 ♘4f3

Instead, 8 h3 ♗d7 9 ♘4b3 d4 10 e3 dxe3 11 fxe3 ♗c6 12 ♕g4 ♘h6 13 ♕e6+ ♗e7 14 0-0-0 was played in V.Todorovic-M.Yeo, Belgrade 2003, and now 14...♗d7 would have been the simplest way to maintain the advantage.

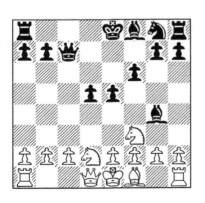

8...♗c5?!

Although Black is still better after

this move, there was no need to abandon the pair of bishops. 8...0-0-0! would have been better: not only is d5 now protected, it also prevents e2-e4.

9 ♘b3 ♘e7 10 h3 ♗h5 11 g4?!

After 11 e3 0-0 12 ♗e2 ♗d6 the Black advantage would not have been as big.

11...♗g6 12 c3 h5

12...♗b6 13 e3 0-0 14 ♘h4 ♗f7 saves the bishops from being traded off and asks the question whether White can complete his development before Black opens the position with ...♖d8 and ...d5-d4.

13 ♘xc5 ♕xc5

14 ♕a4+?

The final mistake. White had to take g4 out of the line of fire.

14...b5! 15 ♕a6 hxg4 16 ♘d2 gxh3 17 e3 ♖b8 18 a4 b4 19 ♘b3 ♕b6 20 ♗b5+ ♔f7 21 c4 ♕xa6 22 ♗xa6 h2 23 f3 ♗d3 24 ♘d2 ♘f5 25 ♔f2 ♖h3 26 ♖ac1 ♘g3 27 ♔g2 ♘xh1 28 ♖xh1 ♖hh8 29 ♖xh2 ♖xh2+ 30 ♔xh2 dxc4 31 ♘xc4 ♗xc4 32 ♗xc4+ ♔e7 33 b3 ♖c8 34 ♗d5 f5 35 ♔g3 g5 36 f4 gxf4+ 37 exf4 ♖c3+ 38 ♔h4 exf4 39 a5 ♔f6 0-1

With 4 ♗f4 inadequate, the only sensible alternative is **4 ♗h4**. Indeed, it makes much more sense to keep the bishop on the h4-d8 diagonal, as it would pin the f-pawn should Black play ...e7-e5. On the other hand its scope is limited on the rim, and Black can try to exploit its misplacement by playing **4...♘h6!**, seeking to trade the knight for the bishop after ...♘f5. A proper treatment of the position will be the subject of our next game.

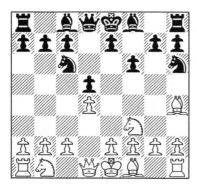

Game 27
D.Ter Minasjan-H.Jurkovic
Schwarzach 1999

---

1 d4 d5 2 ♘f3 ♘c6 3 ♗g5 f6 4 ♗h4 ♘h6! 5 e3

Instead:

a) 5 c4 has to be handled with care. The game J.Dreesen-K.Büchmann, Kiel 2001, continued 5...e5?! 6 ♘xe5 ♘xe5 7 dxe5 ♘f5 and now White could have won a pawn with 8 cxd5! ♘xh4 9 ♕a4+ followed by 10 ♕xh4. The right answer is 5...e6,

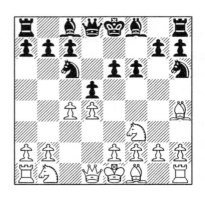

when things develop similar to the main game; for example:

a1) 6 cxd5 exd5 7 ♘c3 ♘f5 8 ♗g3 h5 9 ♗f4 g5 10 ♗c1 saves the bishop but leaves Black with a significant advantage in space after 10...g4 11 ♘g1 ♗e6.

a2) 6 e3 ♘f5 7 ♗g3 (7 ♗d3?! is dubious because of 7...dxc4! 8 ♗xc4 h5! 9 h3 g5 10 ♗g3 ♘xg3 11 fxg3 ♗d6 and Black is clearly better; 8 ♗xf5 is even worse, as after 8...exf5 followed by 9...♗e6 White will have a hard time getting his pawn back) 7...h5 8 h3 (8 ♗d3 dxc4 transposes to the previous line) 8...♘xg3 9 fxg3 ♗d6 and again Black is better.

a3) 6 ♘c3 ♘f5 7 ♗g3 h5 8 h4 (trying to make a play with 8 ♘b5?! backfires after 8...♗b4+ 9 ♘d2 ♗a5 when White has to take care of his bishop and his d-pawn) 8...♘xg3 9 fxg3 ♗d6 with the usual advantage for Black in this type of position.

b) 5 c3 ♘f5 6 ♗g3 h5 7 ♗f4 g5 8 ♗c1 g4 9 ♘g1 e5 10 e3 ♗e6 had a funny resemblance to note 'a1' above in A.Kireev-I.Krush, Moscow 2002.

5...♘f5

6 ♗d3

6 ♗b5 g5!? 7 ♗g3 h5 8 h4 ♘xg3 9 fxg3 g4 10 ♘fd2 ♕d6 11 ♔f2 ♗h6 12 ♘f1 occurred in a game I played on the Internet Chess Club. Now 12...♗d7 would have led to a big advantage, with the pawn structure and the pair of bishops being two important factors.

Another game went 6 ♗g3 h5 7 ♘h4? (a desperate try to oppose the enemy pawns; but in any case after 7 ♗d3 ♘b4! 8 ♗xf5 ♗xf5 9 ♘a3 c6 10 0-0 e6 11 ♘h4 ♗e4 12 f4 g6 Black is obviously better) 7...♘xh4 8 ♗xh4 g5 9 ♗e2 gxh4 10 ♗xh5+ ♔d7 11 c4 e6 12 cxd5 ♗b4+ 13 ♘c3 exd5, which was simply not enough for White in P.Martynov-C.Wisnewski, Internet blitz 2001.

6...♘xh4 7 ♘xh4 g6 8 c4 e5!

Finally Black can upset the white centre.

9 cxd5 ♕xd5 10 ♘c3 ♗b4 11 dxe5

11 0-0 ♗xc3 12 bxc3 ♕d6 results in a position similar to one covered in Chapter 10 (see Game 52). Again there are no practical examples available, but the fact that White cannot fall back upon two bishops here is something

that should positively influence the assessment towards Black.

11...♗e6!? 12 ♕d2

12 exf6? loses to 12...0-0-0 13 ♗e2 (or 13 ♗c2 ♕c4) 13...♕e4 and Black wins a piece.

12...♘xe5 13 ♘xd5 ♗xd2+ 14 ♔xd2 ♗xd5 15 f4 ♘xd3 16 ♔xd3 0-0-0

The white king is caught in the crossfire of the black pieces and can only be saved by making material concessions.

17 ♔c3 ♖he8 18 ♖he1 ♗e4 19 ♖e2

White cannot prevent Black from entering as 19 ♖ad1 is countered by the simple continuation 19...♖xd1 20 ♖xd1 g5! 21 ♘f3 ♗xf3 22 gxf3 ♖xe3+ and Black is winning easily

19...♖d3+ 20 ♔c4 ♖e6 21 ♖d1 ♖c6+ 22 ♔b4 a5+ 23 ♔b5 ♖b6+ 24 ♔xa5 ♗c6 25 e4 ♖b5+ 0-1

All in all, 3 ♗g5 does not cause any serious problems. In fact quite the opposite, as Black is effectively forced to play a move which helps him accomplish his main goal: the implementation of ...e7-e5.

White plays 3 e3

From a psychological point of view, the Colle System is an opening system the Chigorin player should be especially happy to face. The reason behind this claim has a whiff of irony: as stereotypical play will result in quick equality, the only hope for White to obtain an advantage is to adopt a playing style that is completely contrary to a 'normal' treatment of the Colle.

But that does not mean that **3 e3** should be treated lightly.

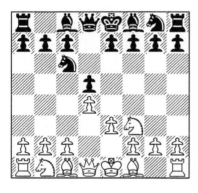

After **3...♗g4 4 ♗b5!? e6 5 ♗xc6+ bxc6 6 c4** Black has to be very careful.

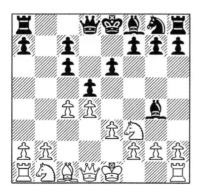

With his last move White is prepar-

ing to pick on the doubled c-pawns. 6...♘ge7 is certainly not attractive as it blocks the bishop and ends in an awkward set-up. The Croatian GM Nenad Sulava has mastered this line and it takes precise play to enfeeble it. The most reliable method has been shown by the Swedish GM Stellan Brynell.

> ## Game 28
> ### N.Sulava-S.Brynell
> European Team
> Championship, Plovdiv 2003

1 d4 d5 2 ♘f3 ♘c6 3 e3 ♗g4

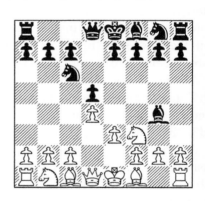

4 ♗b5!?

The only way to fight for an advantage. Other moves are harmless:

a) 4 c4 e6 transposes to Game 47 in Chapter 9.

b) 4 ♗d3 is naturally met by 4...e5 with equality.

c) After 4 ♗e2 Black should develop in a traditional way with 4...e6 5 0-0 ♘f6 6 ♘bd2. The game T.Svensen-C.Wisnewski, Oslo 2002, continued 6...♗d6 7 c4 0-0 8 a3 a5 9 ♕c2 ♖e8 10 h3

♗f5 11 ♗d3 ♗xd3 12 ♕xd3 and after 12...e5 the game was equal.

d) 4 c3 e5 5 dxe5 ♘xe5 6 ♘bd2 ♘f6 7 ♗e2 was played in A.Cremerius-S.Lessing, Leverkusen 2005, and now instead of losing a pawn after 7...♗d6?! 8 ♘xe5 ♗xe2 9 ♕xe2 ♗xe5 10 ♘f3 ♗d6 11 ♕b5+, Black should have played 7...♘xf3+ 8 ♘xf3 ♗d6 with a comfortable game.

e) After 4 ♘bd2 Black should be content with 4...e6 (4...e5?! 5 h3 ♗xf3 6 ♘xf3 e4 7 ♘d2 ♘f6 8 c4 led to a French-type position in V.Dydyshko-J.Furhoff, Berlin 1997 – something I wouldn't want to aim at; while 4...♘f6 5 ♗b5 e6 6 h3 ♗xf3 7 ♘xf3 ♗d6 8 c4 dxc4 9 ♕a4 ♕d7 was played in M.M.Ivanov-A.Karpatchev, Stuttgart 2005, and now after 10 ♕xc4 a6 11 ♗xc6 ♕xc6 12 ♕xc6+ bxc6 13 ♗d2 White could have obtained the advantage due to his superior pawn structure) 5 c3 ♗d6 6 ♗d3 f5, which is a superior version of Game 33 as the dark-squared bishop is on c1 rather than g3.

4...e6 5 ♗xc6+

Alternatives again prove to be less promising:

a) 5 ♘bd2?! ♘ge7 6 c3 a6 7 ♗d3 e5 was equal in N.Sulava-C.Wisnewski, Cappelle la Grande 2001.

b) 5 c4 ♘ge7 6 cxd5 exd5 7 ♘bd2 a6 8 ♗a4 ♕d6 (8...g6, followed by ...♗g7 and ...0-0, is a solid alternative) 9 0-0 0-0-0 10 a3 g5 11 b4 was played in M.Krysztofiak-M.Nemeth, European Junior Championships 2000, when 11...h5!? (planning ...h4-h3) would be quite unclear.

c) Finally, 5 h3 ♗xf3 6 ♕xf3 ♘ge7 was just equal in J.Visser-J.Van den Bosch, Utrecht 1945.

5...bxc6 6 c4

Here 6 h3 ♗xf3 7 ♕xf3 ♕f6 8 ♕d1 ♗d6 9 ♗d2 ♘e7 10 0-0 0-0 11 a3 c5 favoured Black in C.Caylor-M.O'Sullivan, correspondence 1997.

6...♗xf3!

6...dxc4?! is inadvisable: 7 ♕a4 ♗xf3 8 gxf3 ♕d5 9 ♘d2 ♘f6 10 e4 ♕b5 11 ♕xc4 ♕xc4 12 ♘xc4 left White with a clear advantage in C.Wisnewski-H.Hebbinghaus, Kiel 2006.

7 gxf3 c5!

Resolving the doubled c-pawns just in time.

8 cxd5 exd5 9 ♕c2 ♕d6 10 dxc5 ♕xc5 11 ♕a4+ c6 12 ♗d2 ♘f6

12...♗d6?! 13 ♗c3 ♘e7 was tried in N.Sulava-M.Geenen, Monaco 2003, but after 14 ♗xg7 ♖g8 (14...♕c1+ 15 ♕d1 ♕xd1+ 16 ♔xd1 ♖g8 17 ♗f6 ♖g2 18 ♔e2 is not enough either) 15 ♗c3 ♘f5 16 ♘d2 ♖g2 17 ♘b3 ♕b6 18 ♘d4 Black was driven back step by step.

13 ♘a3 ♕b6 14 ♖c1 ♖c8 15 ♘c2!? ♕xb2 16 ♔e2

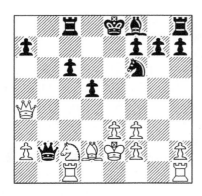

16...♕b5+?!

16...♗c5! was an excellent alternative and is the move I would recommend in this position. White can now win the pawn back with 17 ♘d4 ♕b6 (not 17...♗xd4? 18 ♖b1 and the queen is trapped) 18 ♖b1 ♕c7 19 ♕xc6+ ♕xc6 20 ♘xc6 0-0, but after 21 ♘a5 d4 Black has nothing to worry about.

17 ♕xb5 cxb5 18 ♘d4 ♖xc1 19 ♖xc1 ♔d7 20 ♘xb5 a6 21 ♘d4

Compared with the previous note, White now has the better chances. Black manages to hold steady, but this is most certainly not the type of position you would want to have as Black.

21...♗d6 22 ♘f5 ♖b8 23 ♗c3 ♘e8 24 ♘xg7 ♘xg7 25 ♗xg7 ♖b4 26 f4 ♖a4 27 ♖c2 ♔e6 28 ♗c3 ♖a3 29 ♗d4 ♖a4 30 ♔f3 f5 31 ♖b2 ♖b4 32 ♖c2 ♖c4 33 ♖b2 ♖b4 34 ♖d2 ♖a4 35 ♔g3 ♗e7 36 ♖b2 ♖b4 37 ♖xb4 ♗xb4 38 ♔h4

38 ♔f3, intending ♔e2-d3 and f2-f3 and e3-e4, makes no progress as Black simply holds his position, when it is impossible for White to break through.

38...♗e7+ 39 ♔h5 ♔f7 40 a4 ♗d8 41 ♔h6 ♔g8 42 f3 ♗e7 43 ♗e5 ♗d8 44

♔h5 ♔f7 45 ♗c3 ♗e7 46 h3 ♗d8 47 ♗e1 ♗e7 48 ♔h6 ♔g8 49 ♗a5 ♗f6 50 ♗b6 ♗e7 51 ♗a5 ♗f6 52 ♗e1 ♗d8 53 ♔h5 ♔f7 54 ♗h4 ♗b6 55 ♗f2 ♗d8 56 ♗e1 ♗e7 57 ♔h6 ♔g8 58 h4 ♗d8 59 h5 ♗e7 60 ♗c3 ♗d8 61 ♗d4 ♗e7 62 ♗a7 ♗d8 63 ♗c5 ♗f6 64 ♗b6 ♗e7 65 ♗d4 ♗d8 66 ♗c3 ♗e7 67 ♗e5 ♗d8 68 ♗d4 ♗e7 69 e4 dxe4 70 fxe4 fxe4 71 f5 ♗h4 72 f6?

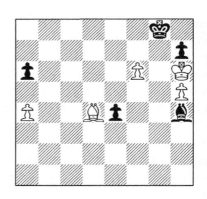

But this is gross. White is digging his own grave.

72...♔f7! 73 ♔xh7 ♗g5 74 h6

Or 74 ♗f2 ♗d2 75 ♗h4 e3 76 ♗g5 a5 77 h6 ♗c1 78 ♗h4 ♗a3 79 ♗g3 ♗b4 80 ♔h8 e2 81 ♔h7 e1♕ 82 ♗xe1 ♗xe1 83 ♔h8 ♗d2 84 h7 ♔f8 85 f7 ♗c3 mate.

74...♗d2 75 ♔h8 e3 76 h7 e2 77 ♗f2 ♗c3 0-1

And in view of 78 ♗h4 e1♗ (sic!) 79 a5 ♗f2 80 ♗g5 ♗fd4 White resigned.

It is unlikely that you will encounter the idea introduced in this game very often. Most Colle players are creatures of habit who unreel their playing scheme without keeping a close eye on their opponent's actions... something you shouldn't do against the Chigorin.

White plays 3 g3

Fianchettoing the king's bishop with **3 g3 ♗g4 4 ♗g2** is characteristic of the Catalan way of life. White feigns quiet development only to attack the black centre by surprise, the intention being to exploit the h1-a8 diagonal by means of c2-c4.

The usual counterstroke ...e7-e5 does not make sense here. The e-pawn is needed to strengthen d5, even more so as the c-pawn is currently blocked by the queen's knight. But control of e5 still plays an important role, since the white player will frequently try to use it as an outpost for one of his knights. Don't worry though, the situation is not as bad as it looks. And in order to substantiate this statement I even offer you two different ways to react to 3 g3.

The first features a set-up with **4...♕d7** and ...0-0-0, intending an attack on the kingside.

The Ukrainian IM Valerij Bronznik dismisses this idea as probably too risky, but I beg to differ. Please allow yourself to be convinced by the following game.

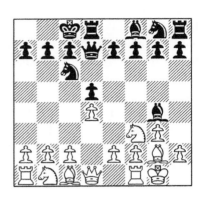

Game 29
L.Spassov-T.Thiel
Badalona 1993

1 d4 d5 2 ♘f3 ♘c6 3 g3 ♗g4 4 ♗g2 ♕d7

4...e6 will be examined in Games 30 and 31.

5 c4

Not the only move to have been played in this position:

a) 5 ♘e5 is harmless as Black can easily defend the d5-pawn. For example, 5...♘xe5 6 dxe5 e6 7 c4 c6 8 0-0 ♘e7 and now 9 ♘c3 dxc4 10 ♕c2 ♘d5 11 ♘e4 b5 is even better for Black.

b) 5 0-0 is too calm, since Black can successfully build up a kingside attack: 5...0-0-0 6 c3 (6 ♘bd2 f6 7 c3 e5 8 b4 e4 9 ♘e1 h5 10 f3 exf3 11 exf3 ♗f5 12 ♘b3 g5 13 a4 ♕h7 14 b5 ♘b8 15 a5 ♗d6 was played in M.Lehmann-A.Raetsky, Samnaun 2004, when Black is better as his attack is more menacing) 6...f6 7 b4 h5 8 ♕a4 (or 8 ♘bd2 g5 with a strong initiative in I.Radulov-S.Lorenz, Bad

Mergentheim 1989) 8...h4 9 b5 ♘b8 10 ♖d1 hxg3 11 fxg3 e5 12 ♖e1 a6 (or just 12...e4) 13 ♗a3 e4 14 ♘fd2 ♕xb5 with a clear advantage for Black in I.Fancsy-T.Ruck, Hungarian Junior Championships 1994.

c) 5 c3 ♗h3 6 0-0 ♗xg2 (6...h5?! is a bit too optimistic: 7 ♗xh3 ♕xh3 8 ♘g5 ♕d7 9 e4 and White is better) 7 ♔xg2 0-0-0 8 b4 f6 9 ♘bd2 e5 10 b5 e4 11 bxc6 exf3+ 12 ♘xf3 ♕xc6 left Black comfortable in J.Mellado Trivino-A.Pascual Arevalo, Barbera 1995.

d) After 5 h3 ♗f5 there are again several alternatives:

d1) 6 ♗f4?! 0-0-0 7 ♘bd2 f6 gave Black an excellent game in V.Ianov-T.Ruck, Koszeg 1996.

d2) 6 a3 has surprisingly led to numerous White victories; but what surprises even more is that nobody has played the simple 6...♘f6 7 b4 ♘e4, which puts a halt to any queenside actions by White, as deploying the queen's knight to d2 runs into ...♘e4-c3.

d3) 6 ♘e5!? ♘xe5 7 dxe5 0-0-0 8 ♘c3 e6 9 e4 dxe4 10 ♕xd7+ ♖xd7 11 ♘xe4

was seen in B.Villamayor-J.Gonzales, Phillipines Championship 2001, which continued 11...f6 12 ♗f4 ♖d4 13 ♘d2 ♗xc2 14 ♖c1 ♗d3 15 exf6 ♖d7 16 ♗e4, and now after 16...♗xe4 17 fxg7 ♗xg7 18 ♘xe4 ♗xb2 it would have been for White to prove enough compensation for the pawn.

d4) 6 g4 ♗g6 7 ♘h4 ♗e4! 8 f3 ♗g6 9 ♘xg6 hxg6 10 ♗f4 e6 11 ♗g3 ♗d6 12 ♗f2 ♘ge7 13 ♘d2 g5 14 c3 ♘g6 and Black's control of the dark squares accounted for his advantage in O.Issel-R.Jenal, Saarlouis 2001.

d5) 6 c3 plans to advance on the queenside with b2-b4, but Black can strike back in the centre with 6...0-0-0 7 b4 f6 8 ♘bd2 e5!. The game M.Rufener-S.Kuemin, Swiss League 1998, continued 9 b5 ♘ce7 10 dxe5 ♕xb5 11 ♕b3 ♕d7 12 ♗a3 ♘c6 13 ♗xf8 ♖xf8 14 exf6 ♘xf6 15 ♘d4 ♘e4 16 ♘xf5 ♘xd2 17 ♕xd5 ♕xf5 18 ♕xf5+ ♖xf5 19 ♗xc6 bxc6 20 ♔xd2 ♖d8+ (20...♖xf2 would have been good as well) 21 ♔e1 ♖c5 22 ♖c1 ♖a5 23 ♖c2 ♖ad5 24 ♔f1 ♖d2 25 ♖xd2 ♖xd2 26 f4 ♖xa2 with a slightly better endgame for Black.

d6) 6 c4 e6 7 ♘c3 is best met by 7...♗b4 8 0-0 (8 ♕b3 0-0-0 9 ♗f4 dxc4 10 ♕xc4 ♕d5! 11 ♕xd5 exd5 12 ♖c1 ♗e4! 13 a3 ♗xc3+ 14 ♖xc3 f6 was equal in P.Johansson-O.Valaker, Gausdal 2002) 8...♗xc3 9 bxc3 ♗e4!? 10 cxd5 (10 ♖e1 0-0-0 11 ♗f1 ♘ge7 12 ♘d2, as in S.Bromberger-M.Lyell, Banyoles 2005, is a complicated way to get rid of the e4-bishop without trading it for the one on g2; now 12...♗g6 13 ♗g2 e5 would have been at least equal) 10...exd5 11 ♕b3

0-0-0 and Black had no problems in M.Drasko-D.Kosic, Herceg Novi 1999.

If instead 7 0-0 ♘f6 8 ♘c3 then 8...♗e4!? is again interesting. R.Bilinskas-A.Gavrylenko, Wisla 2000, continued 9 ♘e5 ♘xe5 10 dxe5 ♗xg2 11 ♔xg2 d4 12 ♘b5 ♕c6+ 13 ♔g1, and after 13...♕xc4 14 exf6 ♕xb5 15 ♕xd4 gxf6 16 ♕xf6 ♖g8 the position is unclear.

5...e6

5...dxc4 brings about complications which favour White: 6 d5 ♗xf3 7 ♗xf3 ♘e5 (or 7...0-0-0 8 ♘c3 ♘e5 9 ♗g2 e6 10 ♕d4 ♘c6 11 ♕xc4 ♘b4 12 0-0 exd5 13 ♕b3 ♘f6 14 ♖d1 c6 15 ♗e3 ♔b8 16 ♕a4 ♘a6 17 b4 ♗xb4 18 ♖ab1 with a very dangerous attack in T.Darcyl-A.Garbarino, Pehuaj 1983) 8 ♗g2 e6 9 ♕d4 ♘c6 10 ♕xc4 exd5 11 ♕xd5 ♗b4+ 12 ♘c3 ♕xd5 13 ♗xd5 ♘ge7 14 ♗g2 0-0-0 15 ♗d2 ♘d4 16 0-0-0 ♖he8 (not 16...♗xc3?! 17 bxc3 ♘xe2+? 18 ♔b2 and the knight is trapped) 17 ♖he1 and White was slightly better in V.Zaitsev-A.Raetsky, Russian Team Championship 1999.

6 0-0 0-0-0 7 ♘c3 dxc4 8 ♕a4 ♔b8 9 ♖d1

9 ♗e3 ♗xf3 10 ♗xf3 is an idea from V.Loginov-M.Dubois, Bad Wörishofen 2000. But Black can simply play 10...♘xd4 11 ♕xc4 ♘xf3+ 12 exf3 ♘f6 13 ♖fd1 ♘d5 14 ♖ac1 c6 and White has hardly any compensation for the pawn.

9...♗xf3 10 ♗xf3 ♘b4

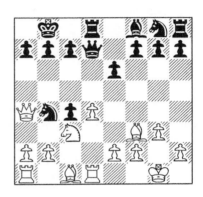

11 ♕a5

11 ♕xd7?! is obviously nothing for White: 11...♖xd7 12 e3 ♘f6 13 ♗e2 ♘d3 14 ♗xd3 cxd3 15 ♖xd3 c5 16 ♖d1 ♗e7 (16...cxd4 17 ♖xd4 ♖xd4 ½-½ was G.Sosonko-L.Fressinet, Cannes 1996) 17 dxc5 ♖xd1+ 18 ♘xd1 ♖d8 19 ♘c3 ♗xc5 resulted in a good endgame for Black in D.McMahon-T.Thiel, Badalona 1993.

11...b6!

Much better than 11...♘f6 12 a3 ♘bd5 13 e4 b6 14 ♕a6 ♘xc3 15 bxc3 ♕c6 16 a4 which led to a dangerous attack in V.Loginov-P.Wells, Harkany 1994.

12 ♕e5 ♘f6 13 ♗g2 h6 14 ♕f4 ♘fd5 15 ♕d2 f5

Black is still a pawn up, controls the centre and has a lead in development. What more could you want?

16 f3?! ♘f6

16...♘e3! would have been more to the point.

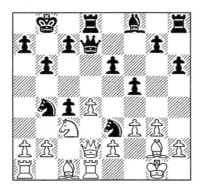

After 17 ♕xe3 ♘c2 18 ♕e5 (pseudo-active; but if 18 ♕d2 ♘xa1 and there is no sensible way to attack the knight on a1; or 18 ♕f2 ♘xa1 19 e4 e5 20 ♗e3 exd4 21 ♖xd4 ♕xd4!? 22 ♗xd4 ♖xd4, followed by ...♗c5 and the rooks are better as the knight still can't be won) 18...♗d6 19 ♕b5 ♕xb5 20 ♘xb5 ♘xa1 21 ♖d2 (21 ♘xd6 cxd6 22 ♖d2 b5 leaves no white piece to pick up the knight at a1) 21...♗b4 the knight can escape, for example 22 ♘c3 e5 23 e3 exd4 24 exd4 and now 24...♖xd4! is possible as after 25 ♖xd4 ♗c5 26 ♗e3 ♘c2 27 ♖d7 ♗xe3+ 28 ♔f1 ♗c1 Black is several pawns up.

17 ♖b1 c5 18 e3 cxd4 19 exd4 ♘d3 20 ♘e2 e5 21 ♕c2 exd4

21...♕c8 would have maintained the advantage.

22 ♕xc4 ♘xc1 23 ♖bxc1 d3 24 b4 ♖c8 ½-½

This game illustrates why the whole idea of 4...♕d7 is so popular. Although it has been cut down by other popular sources, I don't see why this line shouldn't be fully playable. You should try it!

The other, more solid alternative is **4...e6**. Black wastes no time before bolstering his centre, and prepares ...♗d6 in order to increase his control over e5. After **5 0-0 ♘f6** White has two different set-ups to choose from.

The above diagram shows what I call the 'Anti-Catalan set-up'. Instead of going directly for the centre with 6 c4 and 7 ♘c3, White fianchettoes his queen's bishop with **6 b3**, trying to assume complete control of e5. The most promising formation against this plan seems to be a 'Stonewall' set-up similar to that in the Dutch Defence.

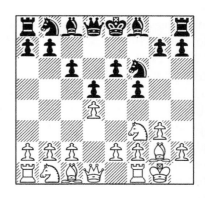

The first diagram shows a typical 'Stonewall' deriving from the Dutch Defence, the second diagram features its equivalent from the Chigorin Defence. You will quickly notice that the two positions have a lot in common. Black has a compact centre, a firm grip on the light squares and a slight advantage in space on the kingside; the only drawback is the weakness of his dark squares, particularly e5. Other than that, Black's intentions are clear: Attack! Attack! Attack!

Game 30
O.Jovanic-B.Kovacevic
Zadar 2000

---

1 d4 d5 2 ♘f3 ♘c6 3 g3 ♗g4 4 ♗g2 e6 5 0-0 ♘f6 6 c4

6 b3 transposes to the text after 6...♗d6 7 c4. Instead, 6 c3 is harmless: Black equalized after 6...♗d6 7 ♕b3 ♖b8 8 ♗g5 h6 9 ♗xf6 ♕xf6 10 ♘bd2 0-0 11 e4 ♗xf3 12 ♗xf3 dxe4 13 ♗xe4 e5 in M.Krasenkow-C.Wisnewski, German League 2005.

6...♗d6

7 ♘e5 is a threat that has to be taken seriously. Hence 6...♗e7?! is already a mistake, since after 7 ♘e5!,

Black experiences problems on the h1-a8 diagonal, as the following examples illustrate:

a) 7...♘xe5 8 dxe5 ♘d7 9 cxd5 exd5 (or 9...♘xe5 10 ♗f4 ♘g6 11 ♗xc7! ♕xc7 12 ♕a4+ ♔f8 13 ♕xg4 and White won a pawn in C.Lingnau-P.Dittmar, German League 1987) 10 ♕xd5 ♗xe2 11 ♖e1 c6 was played in G.Schlichtmann-F.Polenz, Bad Zwesten 1999, and now 12 ♕e4 ♗h5 13 e6! would have given White a nice advantage.

b) 7...♗h5 8 ♘c3 0-0 9 cxd5 exd5 (9...♘xd5 10 ♘xc6 bxc6 results in a wretched pawn structure for Black) 10 ♗g5 ♘xe5 11 dxe5 ♘d7 12 ♗xe7 ♕xe7 13 ♕xd5 and White was a pawn up in Vogel-Welling, Wijk aan Zee 1983.

c) 7...h5 is a creative approach from P.Kemp-M.Goldberg, St Helier 1999. The idea is 8 ♘xg4 hxg4 with counterplay down the h-file, but White can simply play 8 ♘c3 and only after 8...0-0 then 9 ♘xg4 hxg4 10 cxd5 and White has the better position.

7 b3

7 ♘c3 is the subject of the next game.

7...0-0 8 ♗b2 ♘e4 9 ♘e1

A thoughtful move, preparing f2-f3 and ♘e1-d3. After 9 ♘c3 Black can again opt for a 'Stonewall' set-up with 9...f5! as the d-pawn is indirectly protected; i.e. 10 cxd5 exd5 11 ♘xd5 ♗xg3! 12 hxg3 ♕xd5, and now the bishop on b2 is temporarily out of the game.

9...♗h5 10 ♘d2 f5

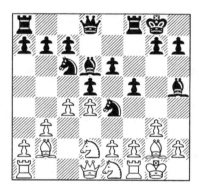

Because of the factors mentioned in the introduction to this game, Black is already better.

11 ♘d3 a5!

Black's main idea is to play on the kingside, but preventing possible counterplay on the queenside takes precedence.

12 ♘f3 a4 13 c5

13 cxd5 exd5 14 bxa4?! is an extra pawn of no value. White will not be able to hold onto it after 14...♘e7 followed by ...♕d7, and then Black will enjoy a healthy advantage due to his better pawn structure.

13...a3!

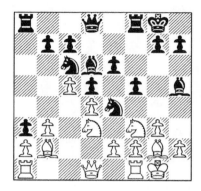

14 ♗c1

14 cxd6 axb2 15 ♘xb2 ♕xd6 is no alternative.

14...♗e7 15 ♗e3

15 e3?! provides more protection for the centre, but entombs the dark-squared bishop.

15...b6?!

The immediate 15...♗f6! is better when, as opposed to the text, White does not have any chances for counterplay on the b-file.

16 b4 bxc5 17 bxc5 ♗f6 18 ♕c2

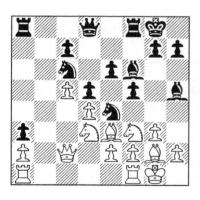

18...♕e7

18...♗xf3! would have been the logical conclusion, picking up the d4-pawn. After 19 exf3 (or 19 ♗xf3? ♗xd4 and White can resign with a clear conscience) 19...ᐱxd4 20 ♗xd4 ♗xd4 21 ♖ae1 (if 21 fxe4?! fxe4 22 ᐱf4 ♗xa1 23 ♖xa1 ♕f6 24 ♖d1 c6 and Black has a rook and a massive pawn centre for the knight and the bishop, securing a big advantage) 21...ᐱc3 22 ᐱf4 e5!? 23 ᐱe6 ♕f6 24 ᐱxf8 ♕xf8 would leave Black with a monster bishop on d4 and a pawn armada, giving him more than enough compensation for the exchange.

19 ♖ab1 g5?!

Black is still dreaming of a kingside attack, but after opening the b-file White's chances of a counterattack are getting real. Instead 19...♖fb8, neutralizing any play on the b-file and keeping the pressure on d4, would have maintained the advantage.

20 ᐱfe5 ♗xe5 21 dxe5 ᐱa5 22 ♗d4 ᐱc4 23 ♖b4 g4

Black is getting stuck on the kingside, whereas White can build up a battery on the b-file.

24 ♖fb1 ♖a5 25 ♖b8 ♗e8 26 ♖1b4 ♗c6 27 ♕c1 ♕g5 28 ᐱf4

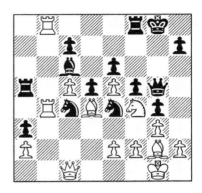

The tables have turned. Now it is White who is in pole position.

28...♕h6 29 ♗xe4 fxe4 30 ♖xf8+ ♔xf8 31 ᐱxe6+?!

This allows Black to escape with precise play. 31 ♗e3 was called for, when after 31...ᐱxe3 32 ♕xe3 we have a rare case of a 'good' white knight versus a 'bad' black bishop.

31...♕xe6 32 ♖b8+ ♗e8

Moving the king does not help. Either 32...♔g7?? 33 ♕g5+ ♔f7 (33...♕g6 34 e6+ mates in an even more beautiful way) 34 ♕g8+ ♔e7 35 ♕f8+ ♔d7 36 ♖d8 mate or 32...♔f7 33 ♕f4+ ♔g6 34 ♖f8 is winning for White.

33 ♕f4+ ♔g8 34 ♕g5+ ♔f8 35 c6

Repeating moves with 35 ♕f4+ was apparently not in White's interest.

35...h6 36 ♕h5 e3 37 ♖xe8+ ♕xe8 38 ♕xh6+ ♔g8?

38...♔f7! was necessary, when White does not have anything better than perpetual check after 39 ♕f6+ (or just 39 ♕h5+ ♔e7 40 ♕g5+ ♔f7 41 ♕h5+) 39...♔g8 40 e6 exf2+ 41 ♗xf2 (not 41 ♔g2?? f1♕+! 42 ♔xf1 ♕f8 and Black wins) 41...♕f8 42 ♕g6+ ♕g7 43 ♕e8+

♔h7 44 ♕h5+ ♔g8 45 ♕e8+ etc.
39 e6 exf2+ 40 ♔f1

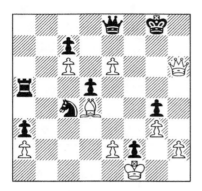

40...♘d2+

40...♘e3+ does not help either, as the black rook is simply too far away. After 41 ♗xe3 ♖b5 42 ♕g5+ ♔h7 (42...♔f8 43 ♕f6+ ♔g8 44 ♗h6 leads to mate) 43 ♕h4+ ♔g8 44 ♕xg4+ ♔h7 45 ♔xf2 White has more than enough pawns for the exchange.
41 ♕xd2 ♖b5 42 ♕g5+ 1-0

Although White managed to prevail in the end, the previous game shows why the plan with **6 c4 ♗d6 7 ♘c3** is much more common.

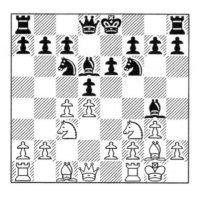

With his centre being immediately pressurized Black has no time to adopt the set-up from the previous game, since 7...♘e4?! just loses a pawn after 8 cxd5 exd5 9 ♕b3!. However, Black is flexible enough to shift gear.

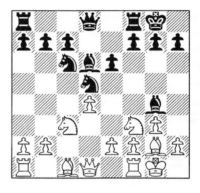

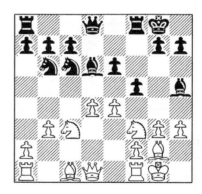

First you see the position after the typical **7...0-0 8 cxd5 ♘xd5!**. The main idea is to lure White into building a seemingly strong pawn centre, so that Black can blast it afterwards. Another common idea is ...f7-f5, to force the knight's path to the strategically important d5-square. A nice illustration is the following game by the Greek Chigorin expert Spyridon Skembris.

Game 31
Y.Razuvaev-S.Skembris
Porto San Giorgio 1998

1 d4 d5 2 ♘f3 ♘c6 3 g3 ♗g4 4 ♗g2 e6 5 0-0 ♘f6 6 c4 ♗d6 7 ♘c3 0-0

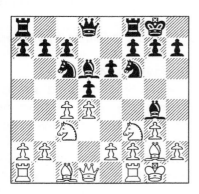

As noted above, 7...♘e4?, intending to reach the Stonewall set-up from the previous game, does not work here. White can simply play 8 cxd5 exd5 9 ♕b3! winning a pawn.

8 cxd5

8 c5? is very comfortable for Black as it takes all pressure off d5. After 8...♗e7 9 ♗f4 h6! Black can safely relocate his bishop to the b1-h7 diagonal and take a tighter grip on e4.

And 8 ♗g5 is consequently met by 8...dxc4, when 9 ♕a4 h6 10 ♗c1 (or 10 ♗xf6 ♕xf6 and Black has nothing to worry about) 10...♘d5 11 ♕xc4 ♘a5 12 ♕d3 ♘b4 13 ♕d1 ♘c4 14 b3 ♘b6 is similar to the game, with control over d5 to be secured by ...f7-f5.

8...♘xd5!

We have now reached the key posi-

tion of this section. Black invites his opponent to build a strong pawn centre in order to undermine it afterwards. Instead, 8...exd5?! 9 ♗g5 would give White a comfortable position with sufficient play against d5.

9 h3 ♗h5 10 e4 ♘b6

11 g4?!

Understandably White wants to resolve the pin of his knight, but the price is a further weakening of his position. 11 b3, in order to develop the bishop at b2 (11 ♗e3 runs into 11...♘c4 and is nothing for White), is a more regular move. However, Black can meet this with the typical 11...f5!, when M.Todorcevic-G.Mohr, Ljubljana 1989, continued 12 e5 ♗e7 13 ♘e2 ♘d5 with the initiative.

11...♗g6 12 ♕e2 f5! 13 ♗g5?

13 gxf5 was necessary. The resulting position after 13...♗h5!? is very complicated, for example 14 ♖d1 (if 14 ♗e3?! exf5 15 e5 f4! 16 exd6 fxe3 17 dxc7 exf2+ 18 ♕xf2 ♕xc7 and Black must be better) 14...exf5 15 e5 ♗b4 16 a3 (16 d5 ♘e7 17 d6 cxd6 18 exd6 ♘c6 19 ♗f4 ♕d7 is also unclear) 16...♗e7 17 d5 ♘a5

with unclear play.

13...fxg4!!

Not really a queen sacrifice since accepting it has dire consequences: 14 ♗xd8? gxf3 15 ♕e3 (or 15 ♗xf3 ♞xd4) 15...fxg2 16 ♔xg2 ♗f4 17 ♕d3 ♖axd8 and White will be steamrollered by the black pieces.

14 hxg4 ♞xd4 15 ♞xd4 ♕xg5 16 e5

16 ♞xe6? loses to 16...♕e5 .

16...♕xe5 17 ♕xe5 ♗xe5 18 ♞xe6 ♖f6

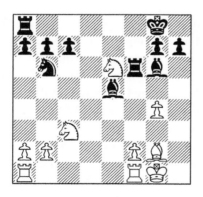

By the end of the opening phase, Black has managed to obtain an extra pawn and the pair of bishops.

19 ♞c5 ♗d4

19...♖f4 would have been better, as

after 20 g5 ♖g4 21 ♞xb7 ♖xg5 Black is still in command.

20 ♞b3 ♗xc3 21 bxc3 ♖f4 22 ♗xb7 ♖xg4+ 23 ♔h2 ♖f8 24 f3 ♖c4 25 ♞d4 ♖xc3 26 ♖ac1 ♖d3 27 ♞c6 ♖d2+ 28 ♔g3 ♞d5 29 ♖f2 ♖xf2 30 ♔xf2 ♖e8 31 ♖c5 ♞f4 32 ♔g3

White has managed to create sufficient counterplay, so Black decides to repeat moves.

32...♞h5+ 33 ♔f2 ♞f4 34 ♔g3 ½-½

White plays 3 ♗f4

The London System with **3 ♗f4** is by far the most popular of all third move alternatives. Indeed, it seems to be especially suited to playing against the Chigorin Defence, as White puts a hammer lock on e5 while conducting his usual playing scheme. Now Black is not able to enforce the freeing ...e7-e5 immediately, so a more subtle approach is needed: **3...♗g4 4 e3 e6.**

The diagram shows the common developing scheme Black should employ against the London System. The light-squared bishop is posted to g4, from where it can help to support ...e6-

e5 by taking care of the white knight. But more important is understanding how Black should react if White, after ...♗f8-d6, chooses to trade the dark-squared bishops.

Many players are reluctant to take the bishop with the c-pawn, even though this approach has its virtues. The doubled d-pawns are no weakness; quite the opposite, as they serve several purposes:

1) The possible advance ...e6-e5 becomes more significant as Black can retake on e5 with a pawn, resulting in a strong centre.

2) Black gains good prospects on the half-open c-file, plus the possibility of launching a useful minority attack with ...b7-b5-b4 should White play c2-c3 (see the preamble to Game 48 for a more detailed description of these ideas).

3) After ...c7xd6, the advance c2-c4 becomes less important, as Black can afford to play ...d5xc4 without having to fear being outnumbered in the centre.

It is now time to look at a sample game illustrating how the ideas outlined above can be implemented.

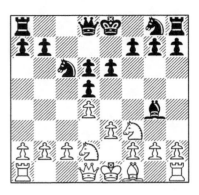

Game 32
V.Guddahl-C.Wisnewski
Oslo 2002

---

1 d4 d5 2 ♘f3 ♘c6 3 ♗f4 ♗g4 4 e3 e6 5 ♘bd2

Instead:

a) 5 c4 is the subject of Games 34 and 35.

b) 5 ♗b5 should automatically trigger 5...♘e7, and now one of my games on the Internet Chess Club continued 6 ♘bd2 a6 7 ♗e2 ♘g6 8 ♗g3 ♗d6 9 ♗xd6 ♕xd6 10 h3 ♗xf3 11 ♘xf3 0-0 12 0-0 f5! 13 g3 e5 14 dxe5 ♘gxe5 15 ♘xe5 ♘xe5 and already there is a clear advantage for Black.

c) After 5 ♗e2 ♗d6 6 ♗g3 (the immediate capture 6 ♗xd6 cxd6 will transpose to the text sooner or later) Black should play 6...♘h6!? 7 c4 ♘f5 with a comfortable game.

d) 5 c3 is the classical set-up for the Queen's Pawn Game.

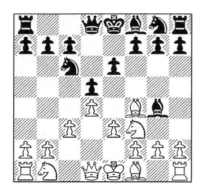

Once again Black employs the idea mentioned in the introduction: 5...♗d6 6 ♗xd6 (6 ♗g3 f5 7 ♘bd2 transposes to the next game, Hort-Wisnewski) 6...cxd6 7 ♘bd2 ♘ge7 (7...e5?! is dubious as it would allow White to equalize after 8 dxe5 dxe5 9 ♗b5) 8 ♗e2 (here 8 e4?! e5! 9 exd5 ♘xd5 10 dxe5 dxe5 leaves White to worry about his position, while 8 ♗d3?! e5 9 dxe5 dxe5 10 ♗e2 ♕b6 is better for Black, or if 9 ♗e2 ♕b6 10 ♕b3 ♕xb3 11 ♘xb3 e4 and the doubled d6-pawn plays an exceptionally good role, controlling the squares e5 and c5) 8...0-0 9 0-0, and now Black can choose between playing on the kingside with ...f7-f5 and playing on the queenside with ...b7-b5-b4.

5...♗d6 6 ♗xd6

On 6 ♗g3 Black should play 6...♘h6!? 7 ♗e2 (after 7 c4 ♘f5 8 ♗xd6 ♘xd6 the knight is misplaced on d2) 7...f5 8 ♘e5 (or 8 c4 ♘e7, intending ...c7-c6, and if 9 ♘g5!? ♕d7 10 f3 ♗h5 11 ♕b3 ♖b8 is fine) 8...♘xe5 9 ♗xe5 (after 9 dxe5 ♗e7 the bishop on g3 lives a sad life) 9...♗xe5 10 dxe5 c6 11 ♘f3 (11 f4? drops a pawn to 11...♕b6)

11...♕c7 12 ♕d4 ♘f7 13 ♖g1 ♖g8 14 0-0-0 was R.Marcolin-P.De Souza Haro, Sao Caetano 1999, and now Black could have won a pawn with 14...♗xf3 15 gxf3 ♕xe5.

6...cxd6 7 c4

7 ♗e2 ♘ge7 8 0-0 0-0 9 h3 ♗xf3! 10 ♗xf3 b5 11 c3 ♖b8 12 a4 was played in A.Adorjan-A.Morozevich, Alushta 1994, and now 12...b4 would be comfortable for Black.

7...dxc4 8 ♗xc4 ♘ge7 9 0-0 0-0

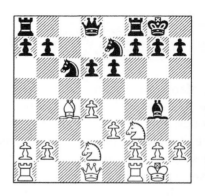

We have reached the key position of the game. There are certain similarities to the Exchange Slav, but one important difference: instead of being on d5, the black d-pawn is on d6. This is a big advantage for Black as the pawn controls e5 and c5, squares which are often used as outposts by white knights. And what's more, ...e6-e5 is always in the wind – although Black is usually more interested in playing on the queenside.

10 h3 ♗h5 11 a3

After 11 ♖c1 it makes sense to oppose the rook on the c-file with 11...♖c8, but I think that 11...♕b8!? is preferable. Then the other rook can go to c8, while the queen's rook can be transferred via a7, once Black has advanced his pawns.

11...a5

This temporarily weakens b5, but preventing White from advancing on the queenside is more important.

12 ♕a4

12 a4?! is no alternative, as it irreparably weakens b4. And 12 b3 is met by 12...♕b8 with the same plan as in the note to White's 11th move.

12...♕b8 13 ♖ac1 ♕a7 14 ♕b5?! d5 15 ♗d3 a4!

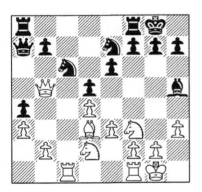

Fixing the b-pawn. Now all that is left to do is to neutralize the pressure on the c-file.

16 ♕c5 ♕b8 17 ♕c2 h6 18 ♗b5 ♖c8 19 ♗xc6 ♖xc6 20 ♕d3 ♖b6 21 ♕c3 ♘c6 22 ♘e5 ♕d6 23 ♘xc6 ♖xc6 24 ♕d3 ♖ac8 25 ♖xc6 ♕xc6

Black has finally managed to get the c-file under his control. Now the game concludes quickly.

26 ♘b1 ♗g6 27 ♕d2 ♕c2 28 ♕xc2

28 ♕b4 ♗d3 29 ♖e1 b5 is only a marginal improvement.

28...♖xc2 29 ♘c3 b5! 30 ♘d1?

Or 30 ♘xb5? ♗d3.

30...♗d3 31 ♖e1 ♖c1 0-1

...as 32...♗c2 wins a piece.

The next game features a different approach. White protects his d-pawn with **5 c3**, retaining the possibility of playing e4 in one move. But after **5...♗d6 6 ♗g3** Black can take steps against this idea immediately:

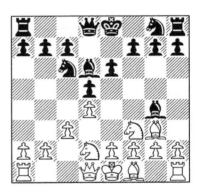

The move that is most appropriate to meeting e2-e4 is **6...f5!?**. The plan is quite similar to the one introduced in Jovanic-Kovacevic (Game 30), but this time the black d-pawn is not under as much pressure, which makes the whole idea even more attractive. The only thing Black has to take care of is that White cannot exploit the weak e5-square, but that's not too difficult at all.

Game 33
V.Hort-C.Wisnewski
German Championship,
Altenkirchen 2005

---

1 d4 d5 2 ♘f3 ♘c6 3 ♗f4 ♗g4 4 ♘bd2

e6 5 c3 ♗d6

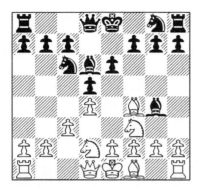

6 ♗g3

White can also play one of the following moves:

a) 6 ♗xd6 cxd6 7 e3 (7 e4 ♘f6 8 ♗d3 0-0 9 0-0 e5 was good for Black in Joehnk-Wisnewski, Bargteheide 2007) 7...♘ge7 was covered in the previous game (see the note with 5 c3).

b) 6 ♘e5 is a bit overzealous. After 6...♗xe5 7 dxe5 (7 ♗xe5 ♘xe5 8 dxe5 c6 leaves Black with the better pawn structure) 7...♘ge7 8 ♕b3 (if 8 h3 ♗h5 9 g4 ♗g6 10 e3 h5 and the white position gives an overextended impression) 8...0-0 9 ♗g3 (9 ♕xb7 ♖b8 10 ♕a6 ♖xb2 is nothing White could possibly fancy) 9...♘g6 10 f4 ♖b8 Black has a nice position, ...b7-b5-b4 being one of many ideas.

c) 6 e3 ♘ge7 (not 6...e5? 7 dxe5 ♘xe5 8 ♗xe5 ♗xe5, as in V.Gansvind-I.Kudriashova, Moscow 2000, when 9 ♕a4+ ♗d7 10 ♕b3 ♗d6 11 ♕xd5 would have won a pawn) 7 ♗e2 ♘g6 8 ♗g3 (8 ♗xd6 cxd6 9 0-0 0-0 10 h3 ♗xf3 11 ♘xf3 ♖b8 was good for Black in R.Schoengart-H.Porth, Hamburg 2005) 8...0-0 9 0-0 f5 and Black had good

prospects on the kingside in R.Wilczek-R.Baumhus, German League 1999.

6...f5!? 7 e3

7 ♕a4 was an idea in Janssen-C.Wisnewski, Internet (blitz) 2002, but after 7...f4 8 ♗h4 ♘ge7 9 e3 fxe3 10 fxe3 ♕d7 11 ♗b5 ♘f5 12 ♗f2 0-0 Black was clearly better.

7...♘h6!

A multi-purpose move: not only protecting the bishop but also enabling the knight to go to f5, should Black manage to play ...f5-f4. But what is most important is that with ...♘h6-f7 Black can put additional control over the weak e5-square, a key idea in this system.

8 ♕b3

8 ♗b5?! was correctly dismissed by A.Finkel – after 8...0-0 9 ♗xc6 bxc6 10 c4 c5! Black has the better chances.

8...♖b8 9 ♗xd6

Finkel suggested playing 9 c4 without trading bishops first, but after 9...♗xf3! 10 ♘xf3 0-0 11 cxd5 (11 ♗xd6 admits the necessity to get rid of the bishop, but the other bishop is no better; for example 11...♕xd6 12 c5 ♕e7 13 ♗b5 ♘d8! and given the solid black pawn structure, the bishop rams his head against a stone wall) 11...♗b4+ 12 ♔d1 exd5 13 ♖c1 ♔h8!? 14 ♗xc7 ♕xc7 15 ♕xb4 f4 Black has sufficient counterplay for the sacrificed pawn; for example 16 ♘e5 ♘g4! 17 ♘xg4 ♕c8 18 ♕d2 ♕xg4+ 19 ♔c2 (or 19 ♕e2 ♕e6) 19...♕g6+ 20 ♔b3 ♖be8 with ongoing pressure.

9...cxd6 10 c4 ♗xf3! 11 gxf3

11 ♘xf3 ♕a5+ 12 ♘d2 dxc4 13 ♗xc4 d5 14 ♗e2 f4!, followed by ...0-0 and ...♘f5, requires very precise play from White in order to defend himself properly.

11...dxc4 12 ♗xc4 d5 13 ♗b5

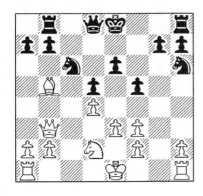

13...0-0

I don't know why I didn't play the natural 13...f4!. Maybe I was afraid of 14 ♕a4?!, but after 14...0-0 15 ♗xc6 bxc6 16 ♕xc6 ♖xb2 17 ♕xe6+ ♔h8 White will not be able to find a safe place for his king.

14 f4 ♘a5 15 ♕b4 a6 16 ♗e2 ♘c6 17 ♕a3 ♖c8 18 ♘f3 ♕a5+?!

Hastily trying to secure the draw; instead with 18...♘f7! Black still could play for a better result.

19 ♕xa5 ♘xa5 20 ♘e5 ♘f7 21 ♘d7 ♖fe8 22 ♘c5 ♘d6 23 ♗d3 ♖e7 24 ♔e2 ♔f7 25 ♖hc1 ♖ec7

Black's pieces are perfectly placed, but the position is too sterile to get anything out of it.

26 b3 ♘c6 27 ♔d1 a5 28 a3 ♘b8 29 ♘a4 ♘d7 30 ♖xc7 ♖xc7 31 ♖c1 ♖xc1+ 32 ♔xc1 b6 ½-½

Our final two games in this chapter mark a White strategy that is a mixture between the quiet London realms and a more aggressive line of action against the black centre. After **5 c4 ♗b4+ 6 ♘c3** we arrive at the following position:

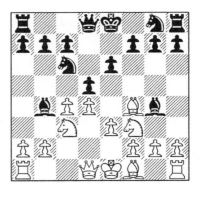

The idea of this set-up is simple: by playing ♖a1-c1 and taking on d5 in due time, White wants to play along the half-open c-file and/or initiate the kind of minority attack known from the Orthodox Queen's Gambit Declined (see the preliminary notes to Game 48 for more information). Here Black has two valid options to choose from. The first one, seen in the next game, is **6...♘ge7**, with the idea of transferring the knight to g6 from where it supports a possible ...e6-e5 and ...f7-f5-f4. And of course it also attacks the bishop on f4, a fact which White shouldn't completely ignore.

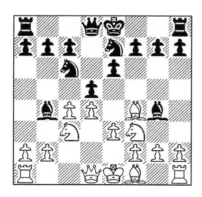

Game 34
P.Nemecek-R.Rybak
Correspondence 1999

1 d4 d5 2 ♘f3 ♘c6 3 ♗f4 ♗g4 4 e3 e6 5 c4 ♗b4+ 6 ♘c3 ♘ge7

Black's second option, 6...♘f6, will be discussed in the subsequent game.
7 ♖c1

Alternatively:

a) 7 h3 ♗xf3 8 ♕xf3 ♗xc3+ 9 bxc3 0-0

10 ♗d3 dxc4 11 ♗xc4 ♘d5 12 ♖c1 (or 12 ♗xd5 exd5 13 0-0 ♘a5 with good play on the light squares) 12...♘a5 13 ♗d3 ♘xf4 14 ♕xf4 c5 and Black was in control in R.Christ-C.Wisnewski, Büsum 2004.

b) 7 a3 ♗xc3+ 8 bxc3 0-0 9 h3 was played in S.Saljova-T.Fomina, European Women's Championship 2001, and now 9...♗xf3! 10 ♕xf3 dxc4 11 ♗xc4 ♘d5 is the same position as in Christ-Wisnewski, the negligible difference being that the white a-pawn is on a3 instead of a2.

7...0-0

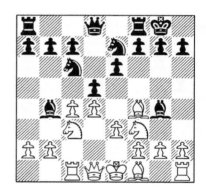

8 ♗d3

8 a3 ♗xc3+ 9 ♖xc3 should be answered by 9...♘g6 10 ♗g3 (10 h3 ♗xf3 11 ♕xf3 ♘xf4 12 ♕xf4 ♘e7 13 ♗d3 ♘g6 14 ♕g3 dxc4 15 ♖xc4 c6 was comfortable for Black in M.Saucey-H.Renette, Avoine 1999) 10...f5 11 h3 (or 11 cxd5 exd5 12 ♗b5 f4! 13 exf4 ♕e7+ 14 ♖e3 ♕f6 with an unclear position according to Bronznik, while 13 ♗xc6? loses to 13...fxg3 14 ♗xb7 ♖b8 15 ♗c6 ♘h4) 11...♗xf3 12 ♕xf3 f4! 13 exf4 ♘xd4 14 ♕g4, as in V.Malakhatko-S.Kapnisis, Athens 2003, when Black should have

played 14...♕f6 with a big advantage.

8...♘g6 9 h3

On 9 ♗g3 Bronznik gives 9...e5 10 cxd5 ♕xd5 11 0-0 ♗xc3 12 bxc3 e4 13 c4 ♕f5, but after 14 ♗b1! (instead of 14 ♗c2 ♘b4) it is difficult to meet 15 ♕b3. Therefore, I suggest 9...dxc4 10 ♗xc4 ♗d6 as in A.Yermolinsky-Z.Rahman, Stratton Mountain 2000, which continued 11 ♗b5 ♘ce7 12 0-0 ♘f5 13 ♗e2 ♘xg3 14 hxg3 c6 15 ♘e4 ♗c7 16 ♘c5 ♖b8 17 ♕c2 ♕e7 and Black was not worse.

9...♗xf3 10 ♕xf3 dxc4 11 ♗xc4 ♘xd4!

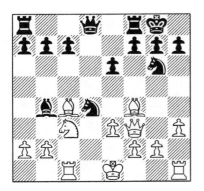

12 ♕xb7

After 12 exd4?! ♕xd4 Black wins back the piece with interest, and if White gets too greedy with 13 ♗xc7 ♕xc4 14 ♕xb7? he will be punished by 14...♖ac8 15 ♗g3 ♖fd8 16 ♕xa7 ♕d3.

12...♘xf4 13 ♕xb4

H.Schüssler-J.Hector, Swedish Championship 1986, saw 13 exf4 ♖b8 14 ♕e4 (if 14 ♕xa7 ♕d6 15 0-0 ♗c5 16 ♕a6 ♕xf4) 14...♗a5 15 b3 ♕f6 and now 16 ♕e5? ♕xe5+ 17 fxe5 ♘b5 18 ♗xb5 ♖xb5 19 0-0 ♖xe5 netted Black a pawn. If instead 16 ♕e3 ♗b6 17 ♕e4, Black can choose whether he wants to repeat

moves with 17...♗a5 or play 17...♘f5!?.

13...♘xg2+ 14 ♔f1 ♘xe3+!

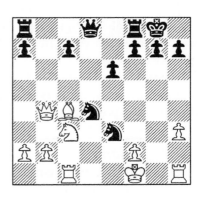

This move is not mentioned by Bronznik in his first edition of *Die Tschigorin-Verteidigung*, but it is simply winning as the game shows:

15 fxe3 ♕f6+ 16 ♔e1 ♖ab8 17 ♕a4 ♕g5 18 ♘d1 ♕g3+ 19 ♔f1 ♕f3+ 20 ♔g1 ♖xb2! 21 ♘xb2 ♕xe3+ 22 ♔g2 ♕d2+ 23 ♔f1 ♕xc1+ 24 ♘d1 ♕d2 25 ♘f2 ♘f5 26 ♔g2 ♕g5+ 27 ♘g4 ♖d8 28 ♗e2 h5 0-1

All in all I like the implications of 6...♘ge7, but Black's other option, **6...♘f6**, is certainly not worse.

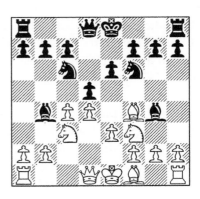

Black has two main ideas in this system. One is to play the thematic ...e6-e5, which can be additionally supported by ...♕d8-e7; the other is to swap the dark-squared bishop for the knight on c3 to get the light squares under control (by ...♘c6-a5). The following game well illustrates a proper treatment of the position.

Game 35
S.Giardelli-C.Boissonet
Buenos Aires 1991

---

1 d4 d5 2 ♘f3 ♘c6 3 ♗f4 ♗g4 4 e3 e6 5 c4 ♗b4+ 6 ♘c3 ♘f6 7 ♖c1

Playing along the c-file is again the most popular choice. But before continuing, let's take a look at possible alternatives:

a) 7 a3 immediately resolves the pin, forcing Black to trade his bishop instead of his knight. However, Black is flexible enough and can change to another plan: 7...♗xc3+ 8 bxc3 0-0 9 ♗e2 ♘e4 10 ♕c2 and now 10...♘a5! 11 cxd5 exd5 leaves Black in command of the light squares. After 12 0-0 (12 c4?! is problematic due to 12...♗f5!) 12...c6 13 ♖fc1 b5 14 a4 a6 15 h3 ♗f5 16 ♗d3 ♘c4 Black had a firm grip on the position in Sorkin-C.Wisnewski, Internet (blitz) 2002.

b) 7 h3 was played in P.Cramling-R.Vera, Malaga 2000, and Black gained the advantage after 7...♗xf3! 8 ♕xf3 ♕e7 9 cxd5 ♗xc3+ 10 bxc3 ♕a3! 11 e4 exd5 12 exd5 ♘xd5 13 ♗d2 0-0-0 14 ♗e2 ♕b2 even though a draw was

agreed at this point.

c) 7 ♗e2 is as dubious as 7 ♗d3. In either case Black can play 7...dxc4 8 ♖c1 (if 8 ♗xc4 ♘d5 9 ♗xd5 ♕xd5!? 10 0-0 ♗xc3 11 bxc3 0-0-0 once more allows Black to control the light squares) 8...♗xc3+ 9 bxc3 (9 ♖xc3 ♘d5 10 ♖xc4 ♘xf4 11 exf4 leaves White with a weak isolated d-pawn) 9...b5 and Black was a pawn up in P.Zangiev-R.Jenetl, Krasnodar 1998.

d) 7 ♕b3 is best answered by 7...a5!, and now 8 a3 a4 9 ♕c2 ♗xc3+ 10 bxc3 leads to the usual play on the light squares after 10...0-0 11 cxd5 exd5.

7...♘e4

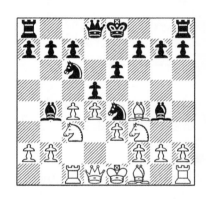

8 cxd5

8 ♕b3 again triggers 8...a5! 9 cxd5 (9 ♘e5? is bad due to 9...a4 10 ♕c2 ♘xe5 11 ♗xe5 a3 and White is in serious trouble) 9...a4 10 ♕c2 exd5 followed by ...♗xc3+ and better play for Black.

8 h3 ♗xf3 9 ♕xf3 ♕e7 has not been seen in too many games as yet. Nevertheless, it is White who has to be careful, one example being U.Krause-C.Wisnewski, Luetjenburg 2003, which continued 10 ♗d3? ♗xc3+ 11 bxc3 ♕a3!

and White lost material. In their book *Win with the London System*, Johnsen and Kovacevic claim a White advantage after 10 cxd5 exd5 11 ♕d1, referring to the game Kir.Georgiev-D.Pirrot, Bad Wörishofen 2003, which continued 11...0-0 12 ♗e2 ♘d8 13 0-0 ♗xc3 14 bxc3 ♘e6 15 ♗h2 ♖fd8 16 c4. But as we will see later, Black went wrong on his 12th move. The right course of action is 12...♗xc3 13 bxc3 ♘a5 with good play on the light squares (see Chapter 11 for more information).

8...♕xd5!?

8...exd5 is perfectly playable as well, but the text move is more active.

9 ♗d3 e5!

Simple and good.

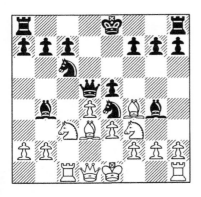

10 dxe5?!

10 ♗xe4 was necessary, when

10...♕xe4 11 ♗xe5 ♘xe5 12 dxe5 ♗xc3+ 13 ♖xc3 ♖d8 would have been roughly equal.

10...0-0-0 11 ♗xe4 ♕xe4 12 ♕e2 ♗xc3+ 13 bxc3

Not 13 ♖xc3?? ♕b1+ and mates.

13...♖he8 14 h3 ♘xe5! 15 ♗xe5

15 hxg4?? loses to 15...♘d3+.

15...♗xf3 16 ♕xf3 ♕xf3 17 gxf3 ♖xe5

White's pawn structure is completely crippled. With the proper technique Black has the game in the bag.

18 ♖g1 g6 19 ♖g4 ♖a5 20 a4 ♖d6 21 ♖h4 ♖f6 22 ♔e2 b6 23 ♖xh7 ♖xa4 24 e4 ♖c4 25 h4 ♗c5 26 ♔e3 b5 27 f4 a5 28 h5 gxh5 29 e5 ♖fc6 30 ♖xf7 b4 31 c4 b3 32 ♖f8+ ♔b7 33 ♖e8 a4 34 f5 a3 35 f6 a2 36 f7 b2 37 ♖c3 b1♕ 38 f8♕ ♕e1+ 39 ♔d3 ♖d5+ 40 cxd5 ♖xc3+ 41 ♔d4 ♕d2+ 42 ♔e4 ♕e2+ 0-1

Summary

Despite beginning the game with 1...d5, Black cannot be prevented from getting 'his' positions, as we have seen in Game 25. The move 2 ♘f3 is especially popular at club level, so examining this chapter in detail is advisable. No matter whether you have to face the Colle (Game 28), the Catalan (Games 29-31) or the London System (Games 32-35) – just follow the outlined strategies and you will score your fair share of points.

1 d4 d5 2 ♘f3
>   2 ♗f4 ♗g4 – *Game 25*

2...♘c6 (D) 3 ♗f4
>   3 ♗g5 f6
>>   4 ♗f4 ♗g4 – *Game 26*
>>   4 ♗h4 ♘h6 – *Game 27*
>   3 e3 ♗g4 – *Game 28*
>   3 g3 ♗g4 4 ♗g2 e6
>>   4...♕d7 – *Game 29*
>>>   5 0-0 ♘f6 6 c4 ♗d6 (D)
>>>   7 b3 – *Game 30*
>>>   7 ♘c3 – *Game 31*

3...♗g4 4 e3
>   4 ♘bd2 e6
>>   5 c3 ♗d6 – *Game 32*
>>   5 e3 ♗d6 – *Game 33*

4...e6 5 c4 (D) ♘f6
>   5...♘ge7 – *Game 34*

6 ♘c3 ♗b4 – *Game 35*

2...♘c6

6...♗d6

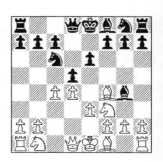

5 c4

Chapter Seven

1 d4 d5 2 c4 ♘c6
3 ♘c3 ♘f6 (4 ♗g5; 4 cxd5)

It is safe to assume that **3 ♘c3** is a red rag to many Chigorin players. If I were to give you a characterization of this move based on its public image, I would have to describe it as both frequently played and scoring exceedingly well. Two trends that ought to be stopped, particularly with regard to the fact that 3 ♘c3 is not as dangerous as many make it out to be.

Since 3...dxc4 4 d5 often leads to a type of position many Chigorin players are uncomfortable with, Black is well advised to look for more suitable options. For that reason I recommend **3...♘f6**, after which the game usually transposes to the main line by 4 ♘f3 dxc4 (see the next chapter). But first, we have to deal with possible alternatives.

White plays 4 ♗g5
Given that attacking the centre plays a crucial role in the Chigorin Defence, it is hard to condemn **4 ♗g5** at first sight.

By going after the black knight, White increases the pressure he was already putting on d5 with his third move. Unfortunately, this Chigorinesque style of play does not get rewarded, as Black has a smooth counter in the form of **4...♘e4!?**.

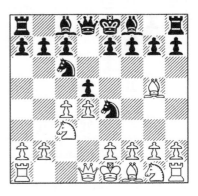

The most natural response to the sally of the bold knight is to get rid of it immediately. While doubling the black pawns at the same time may additionally justify this, there are certain drawbacks to this course of action. Firstly, since the black knight has left the stage, the bishop on g5 serves no real purpose and is vulnerable to attacks similar to those seen in the previous chapter. And what may be even more important, the transformation of the pawn structure helps Black to apply even more pressure on the white centre.

Game 36
M.Dorn-D.Flassig
Germany 2001

---

1 d4 d5 2 c4 ♘c6 3 ♘c3 ♘f6 4 ♗g5 ♘e4!? 5 ♘xe4

5 cxd5 is the subject of Game 37.

Instead, **5 ♗h4** keeps the h4-d8 diagonal under control and prevents the e-pawn from moving.

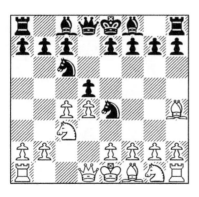

Let's take a closer look at possible answers:

a) 5...g5 is rather reckless:

a1) 6 ♗g3 favours Black after 6...h5!? 7 cxd5 (not 7 ♘xd5? e6! when both 8 ♘xc7+ ♕xc7 9 ♗xc7 ♗b4+ and 8 ♘c3 ♘xc3 9 bxc3 h4 10 ♗e5 f6 are winning for Black) 7...♘xc3 8 bxc3 ♕xd5 9

h4 (after 9 ♗xc7 ♕d7! White can only decide between losing the bishop or playing 10 d5 ♗g7 11 ♖c1 ♕xc7 12 dxc6 ♕xc6 with an overwhelming position for Black) 9...♕a5 10 ♕d2 g4 and Black has the freer development.

a2) 6 cxd5 ♘xc3 7 bxc3 ♕xd5 8 ♗g3 e5! is unclear according to Bronznik. It is difficult to expand on this assessment as there are so many possibilities. But to give you just one example, after 9 ♘f3 exd4 10 ♘xd4 ♗g7 11 e3 ♗e6 12 ♗xc7 0-0 Black's lead in development and piece activity compensate for the sacrificed pawn.

a3) 6 ♗xg5!? is White's best option, when 6...♘xg5 7 cxd5 e5 8 dxe5 (8 dxc6 exd4 9 cxb7 ♗xb7 10 ♕a4+ ♕d7 11 ♕xd7+ ♔xd7 12 0-0-0 c5 led to an unclear position in A.Romero Holmes-V.Gallego, Spanish Championship 1997) 8...♘xe5 is more or less forced. Now 9 h4 was played in P.Lukacs-H.Bartels, Copenhagen 1987, when 9...♘e6 10 dxe6 ♗xe6 would have given Black at least some compensation for the pawn. But before playing the position after 9 f4 ♗d6 10 fxe5 ♗xe5 11 ♕d3 I would rather go to the dentist.

b) 5...g6 has been suggested by M.Breutigam. Indeed, after 6 ♘xd5 ♗e6 7 ♕b3 (7 f3?! ♗xd5 8 cxd5 e6! is clearly good for Black, while 7 e3 ♗xd5 8 cxd5 ♕xd5 is just a bit better) 7...♘xd4 8 ♕d3 (not 8 ♕xb7?? ♗xd5 9 exd5 ♘c5 and the queen is trapped) 8...♗xd5 9 ♕xd4? c5! White is lost. Unfortunately, he can simply play 6 e3, after which Black has difficulties creating sufficient counterplay.

c) 5...♘xc3!? is my personal favourite. Black collects a pawn and waits for White to show whether he has anything in return – by no means an easy task, as 6 bxc3 dxc4 7 e4 ♘a5! (but not 7...b5?! when 8 a4 ♗a6 9 axb5 ♗xb5 10 ♘f3 g6 11 ♗xc4! ♗xc4 12 ♕a4 ♕d7 13 ♕xc4 led to a good game for White in P.Lukacs-S.Maksimovic, Vrnjacka Banja 1987) 8 ♗xc4 ♘xc4 9 ♕a4+ ♕d7! 10 ♕xc4 dashes against 10...♕g4, attacking both the bishop and the e4-pawn. Instead, White should try to speed up his development, but even after 7 ♘f3 b5 8 a4 c6 his compensation is murky at best.

5...dxe4

6 d5

6 e3?! is already dubious. Similarly as in the previous chapter, Black can play 6...f6 7 ♗h4 (7 ♗f4? is even worse: after 7...e5! 8 dxe5 ♗b4+ 9 ♔e2 ♗e6 Black's lead in development is decisive; F.Rudyak-C.Wisnewski, Internet blitz 2003, continued 10 b3 fxe5 11 ♗g3 ♕f6 and in view of 12...♖d8 White quickly threw in the towel) 7...e5 8 d5 ♘e7 9 ♘e2 (9 a3, in order to prevent ♗b4+, is similar to the text after 9...♘f5 10 ♗g3

h5 11 h3 ♘xg3) 9...♘f5 and now A.Huss-M.Rüfenacht, Switzerland 1987, saw 10 ♗g3 h5 11 h3 ♗b4+ 12 ♘c3 ♗xc3+ 13 bxc3 ♘xg3 14 fxg3 f5 when the white pawn structure was severely crippled.

6...e6! 7 ♗xd8

7 dxc6? is asking for trouble. Black quickly moves into attack mode with 7...♕xg5 8 ♕a4 ♖b8! and now 9 e3 (9 ♕xa7?? ♗b4+ 10 ♔d1 ♕d2 mate and 9 cxb7+?? ♗d7 10 ♕c2 ♕a5+ 11 ♔d1 ♗a4 12 b3 ♖d8+ 13 ♔c1 ♗a3 are just two ways to a quick end) 9...bxc6 leaves White in search of a way to survive the coming assault.

7...♗b4+ 8 ♕d2 ♗xd2+ 9 ♔xd2 ♘xd8

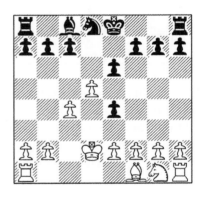

10 e3?!

White fails to acknowledge the vital importance of dealing with the e4-pawn. 10 f3 was called for, although Black can still comfortably choose between 10...exd5 11 cxd5 ♗f5 12 ♔e3 exf3 13 exf3 c6 with equality and 12...0-0!? 13 ♔f4 ♗g6 14 fxe4 f6 15 ♘h3 ♘f7 with play for the sacrificed pawn.

10...0-0 11 f4

In H.Fraas-A.Buckel, German League

1988, White tried 11 ♘e2, but fell behind as well after 11...exd5 12 cxd5 c6 13 dxc6 ♘xc6 14 ♘c3 ♖d8+ 15 ♔c2 ♗e6.

11...b6 12 g3 ♗b7 13 ♗g2?

If there was a way to play on it was with 13 dxe6 ♘e6, although White is certainly worse. Now the game is over.

13...exd5 14 ♖c1 c5 15 g4 f5 16 gxf5 ♖xf5 17 ♗h3 ♖f6 18 b3 ♖d6 19 ♔e1 d4 20 exd4 cxd4 21 ♖d1 e3 0-1

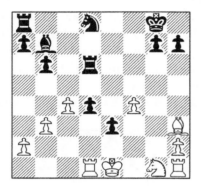

Since a direct assault on the centre usually proves to be ineffective, White should opt for a 'stabilize-first-occupy-later' strategy. However, the bishop on g5 needs to be taken care of as well, which gives Black the time he needs to organize his forces to get a grip on the light squares.

Game 37
A.Ornstein-S.Brynell
Swedish Championship,
Malmo 1986

1 d4 d5 2 c4 ♘c6 3 ♘c3 ♘f6 4 ♗g5 ♘e4!? 5 cxd5

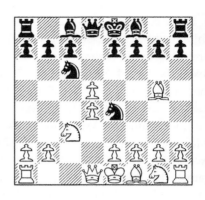

5...♘xc3 6 bxc3 ♕xd5 7 ♘f3

Retreating the bishop with 7 ♗f4? is inadvisable. D.Fleischmann-E.Almada, Uruguay 1983, continued 7...♕a5 8 ♕d2 e5 9 dxe5 ♗f5! 10 ♘f3 ♖d8, when White collapsed with 11 ♘d4?? ♘xd4 12 cxd4 ♗b4, but his position was hopeless anyway.

7...♗g4

Since controlling the light squares is the key idea in this line, 7...♗f5 seems logical. Nevertheless, Bronznik right-fully dismisses this move, giving 8 ♕b3 0-0-0 9 e3 ♕a5 10 ♗b5 ♗e6 11 ♗c4 ♗xc4 12 ♕xc4, G.Kluger-P.Voiculescu, Bucharest 1954, and 8...♗e4 9 ♕xd5 ♗xd5 10 ♘d2 f6 11 e4 ♗f7 12 ♗e3, W.Nautsch-E.Fischer, Dresden 2002, with an advantage for White in both variations. One could be tempted to fall back on 8...e6 with ideas similar to those in the game, but after 9 e3 it is not possible to prevent White from pushing his pawns.

8 ♕b3 e6!

Strictly playing for control of the light squares. 8...♗xf3 is inferior, since 9 gxf3 ♕xg5? does not work because of

10 ♕xb7!, while 8...0-0-0 9 ♕xd5 ♖xd5 10 e4 is everything White was hoping for.

9 e3

Instead, 9 ♕xd5 exd5 is obviously nothing, while 9 ♕xb7 ♖b8 10 ♕a6 ♗d6 leaves Black with enough compensation for the pawn. I wish I could shed more light on this, but lacking practical examples I can only provide you with a sample of my analysis: 11 ♗d2 0-0 12 ♘g5 (in order to push the e-pawn to e4) 12...f6 and now 13 e4 is met by 13...♘xd4! 14 ♕d3 (14 cxd4? leads to a devastating attack after 14...♕xd4 15 ♖c1 ♗b2!) 14...♕b7! with unclear play.

9...♗d6

9...♗xf3? is still bad: after 10 gxf3 ♕xf3 (or 10...♕xg5?? 11 ♕xb7 as before) 11 ♖g1 it is White who takes command.

10 ♗e2 0-0 11 ♗h4 ♕e4?!

11...♘a5! was the right move, after which Black would have been successful in putting a stop to White's central ambitions.

12 ♗g3 e5 13 0-0 ♗e6?

Neglecting the b7-pawn for too long. Now the game concludes swiftly.

14 ♕xb7 ♗d5 15 ♕b1 ♕g4 16 h3 ♕g6 17 ♕xg6 hxg6 18 c4 ♗e4 19 c5 1-0

The result of this game is the only blemish to this line. All in all, Black does not have to be afraid of 4 ♗g5.

White plays 4 cxd5

Relatively few players will choose **4 cxd5** on purpose. The majority will recognize a faint resemblance to the Grünfeld Defence (1 d4 ♘f6 2 c4 g6 3 ♘c3 d5) and treat the position accordingly – a situation from which the Chigorin player will benefit:

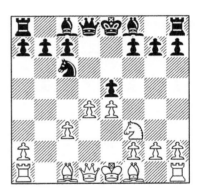

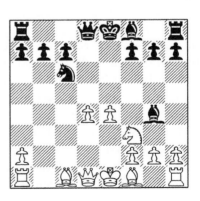

Indeed, after **4...♘xd5 5 e4 ♘xc3 6**

bxc3 e5 7 ♘f3?! the central configuration remotely resembles a Grünfeld-like structure, but the arrangement of the black pieces makes the difference. Even with precise play, White will quickly fall behind.

1 d4 d5 2 c4 ♘c6 3 ♘c3 ♘f6 4 cxd5 ♘xd5 5 e4

Here 5 ♘f3!? is an interesting alternative which is definitely worth closer examination:

a) 5...♗g4? is a common mistake. Although g4 is usually the right place for the bishop, it is not in this particular line. After 6 e4 ♘xc3 7 bxc3 e5 8 d5 ♘b8 (or 8...♗xf3 9 ♕xf3 ♘a5 10 ♕g3 ♕d6 11 ♗e3 with a clear advantage) 9 ♕a4+ ♘d7 (9...♗d7 loses to 10 ♕b3 b6 11 ♘xe5 ♕e7 12 ♗f4 f6 13 d6! cxd6 14 ♕d5 winning the rook on a8) 10 ♘xe5 ♕f6 11 ♗e2!! White already gets a winning advantage, for example 11...♕xe5

(or 11...♗d6?? 12 ♗xg4 ♕xe5 13 ♗xd7+ ♔d8 14 ♗d2 1-0 P.Cramling-C.Landenbergue, Biel 1987) 12 ♗xg4 ♖d8 (12...0-0-0 13 0-0 ♗c5 14 ♖b1 ♖he8 15 ♖xb7! ♕d6 16 ♗f4 ♕xf4 17 ♕a6 was a nice finish in Z.Gyimesi-F.Patuzzo, World Junior Championships 1995) 13 0-0 ♗c5 14 ♗xd7+ ♖xd7 15 ♗a3 ♗xa3 16 ♕xa3 and White was a pawn up for nothing in H.Woestmann-J.Rehfeldt, German League 1989.

b) 5...♗f5 is no help either. Bronznik recommends 6 e3 e6 7 ♗b5 claiming an advantage for White, with which I agree.

c) Although White has tried to prevent the thematic ...e7-e5, Black should play **5...e5!** anyway.

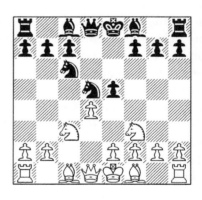

This temporarily sacrifices a pawn, but Black gets sufficient counterplay:

c1) 6 ♘xe5 ♘xc3 7 ♘xc6 (V.Antoshin-P.Voiculescu, Helsinki 1956, saw 7 bxc3 ♘xe5 8 dxe5 ♕xd1+ 9 ♔xd1 ♗f5 10 e3 0-0-0+ 11 ♔e1 and now 11...g6 12 ♗c4 ♗g7 would have been unclear; or if 10 f3 0-0-0+ 11 ♔e1 ♗c5 12 e4 ♗e6 13 ♗g5 ♖d7 and it is difficult for White to finish his development)

7...♘xd1 8 ♘xd8 ♘xb2 9 ♗xb2 (but not 9 ♘xf7?? as 9...♗b4+ 10 ♗d2 ♗xd2+ 11 ♔xd2 ♔xf7 is winning for Black) 9...♔xd8 provides equal chances in the upcoming endgame.

c2) After 6 dxe5 precise play is needed. 6...♘xc3?! 7 ♕xd8+ ♔xd8 8 bxc3 ♗g4 9 ♗f4 ♗a3 10 ♖b1 does not provide enough compensation for the pawn, J.Ulko-C.Wisnewski, Internet (blitz) 2001, being one example. Instead, Bronznik recommends 6...♗b4!?, giving the following variations: 7 ♗d2 ♘xc3 8 ♗xc3 (or 8 bxc3 ♗c5 when Black's lead in development and White's damaged pawn structure compensate for the sacrificed pawn) 8...♗xc3+ 9 bxc3 ♕e7 10 e3 (10 ♕d5 ♗e6 is unclear) 10...♕c5 (or 10...♘xe5 11 ♘xe5 ♕xe5 12 ♕d4 with equality) 11 ♕d2 ♗g4 once again with compensation for the pawn.

5...♘xc3 6 bxc3 e5

7 ♘f3?!

By keeping the tension in the centre White already gets into trouble. Here 7 d5 is necessary and will be discussed in the next game.

7 ♗b5 is rarely played, and with good reason. Black obtains a good game after 7...exd4 when White can choose between 8 ♗xc6+ bxc6 9 ♕xd4 (9 cxd4 loses a pawn to 9...♗b4+ 10 ♔f1 ♗c3) 9...♗a6 10 ♗f4 ♕xd4 11 cxd4 0-0-0 12 0-0-0 ♗a3+ 13 ♔c2 ♖he8 14 f3 ♔d7 as in A.Kriesch-P.Daus, Bad Zwesten 1998; or 8 cxd4 ♗b4+ 9 ♔f1 0-0 (here 9...♗c3?! is not so good; White has definite compensation for the pawn either after 10 ♖b1 ♕xd4 11 ♕c2 or 10...♗xd4 11 ♗a3) and Black stands well in both cases.

7...exd4! 8 cxd4 ♗g4

9 d5

Instead:

a) 9 ♗e3? is utterly terrible: 9...♗b4+ 10 ♗d2 (or 10 ♔e2 ♗c3) 10...♗xf3 11 gxf3 ♕xd4 and Black is more than just a pawn up.

b) 9 ♗c4 does not help either, as the simple 9...♗b4+ 10 ♔f1 0-0 leads to a very comfortable game for Black.

c) Finally, after 9 ♗b5 ♗b4+ 10 ♗d2 ♗xf3 11 ♗xc6+ bxc6 12 gxf3 ♕xd4 13 ♖b1 ♗xd2+ 14 ♕xd2 ♕xd2+ 15 ♔xd2 it is White who has to fight for the draw.

9...♗b4+ 10 ♗d2

On 10 ♔e2 P.Motwani gives 10...♕e7! with the idea 11 dxc6 ♕xe4+ 12 ♗e3 ♖d8 13 ♕b3 ♖d2+ and Black has a winning advantage.

10...♗xf3 11 gxf3

11 ♕xf3?! ♗xd2+ 12 ♔xd2 0-0 is obviously better for Black, as the white king is stranded in the centre where he will quickly become a target.

11...♗xd2+ 12 ♕xd2 ♕f6!

13 ♖c1 ♘e5 14 ♕e3

Trying to hold on to the pawn is dangerous. After 14 ♗e2 ♘xf3+ 15 ♗xf3 ♕xf3 16 0-0 0-0 17 ♖xc7 ♖ae8! 18 ♖e1 ♕g4+ Black will take the pawn on e4, when the weak position of the white king will secure a lasting advantage.

14...♘xf3+ 15 ♔e2 ♘e5 16 f4

16 ♖xc7 is too risky. Black gets good attacking chances after 16...0-0.

16...♘g4 17 ♕g3 ♕b2+ 18 ♔f3 h5

18...f5! is more direct: 19 ♖xc7 (19 exf5? 0-0-0 is completely hopeless for White) 19...♕a3+ 20 ♔g2 ♕xa2+ 21 ♔h3 0-0 and again Black is much better; for instance 22 ♗c4 ♕d2 23 ♖f1 ♔h8 24

exf5 h5 and White still has problems.

19 ♗e2

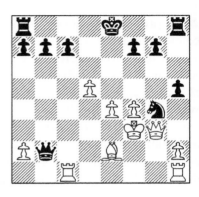

19...♖h6?

In an overwhelming position, Black starts losing the thread. 19...f5! would have led to a winning position, e.g. 20 e5 (or 20 exf5 0-0-0 and the game will not last much longer) 20...♕d2 21 ♗b5+ c6 22 ♗c4 (22 dxc6 loses the bishop to 22...♕d5+) 22...h4 23 ♕e1 (23 ♕g1 is answered by 23...g5!) 23...♘xh2+ 24 ♖xh2 ♕xh2 with a decisive material advantage.

20 ♕e1 ♖f6 21 ♕c3 ♕b6 22 ♕c5 0-0-0 23 h3

White has managed to shake off the pressure.

23...♘e5+ 24 ♔e3 ♘g6 25 ♕xb6 axb6 26 ♖hf1 ♘h4?

The final mistake, although by this stage it is hard to suggest anything better.

27 ♗xh5 ♘g2+ 28 ♔f3 ♘h4+

28...♘xf4 29 ♗g4+ ♔b8 30 e5 is probably what Black had missed.

29 ♔g3

Having regained the pawn, White now has a commanding position.

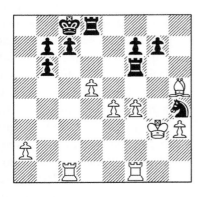

29...♖h6 30 ♗xf7 ♘g6 31 e5 ♘e7 32 f5 ♘xd5 33 ♖fd1 ♘e3 34 ♗e6+ ♖xe6 35 ♖xd8+ ♔xd8 36 fxe6 ♘d5 37 ♔g4 ♔e7 38 ♔f5 c6 39 ♖g1 ♔f8 40 e7+ ♘xe7+ 41 ♔e6 ♘d5 42 ♔d7 c5 43 ♖f1+ 1-0

With 7 ♘f3?! brought into disrepute, the only alternative to oppose the idea of a Black counterstroke in the centre is **7 d5**. After this move the centre is no longer under pressure, and White even enjoys a certain advantage in space. But there are also drawbacks to this kind of action:

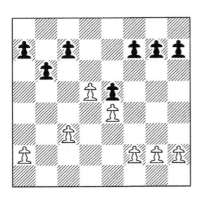

An examination of the pawn structure reveals that Black has a good grip on the dark squares. And there is more than just that: with a rather fixed centre, wing attacks are much more attractive; and while Black will have no difficulties initiating a kingside attack with ...f7-f5, any White ambitions on the queenside can be easily stopped by ...b7-b6.

Game 39
J.Laurent-D.D.Popescu
Creon 1999

---

1 c4 ♘c6 2 d4 d5 3 ♘c3 ♘f6 4 cxd5 ♘xd5 5 e4 ♘xc3 6 bxc3 e5 7 d5

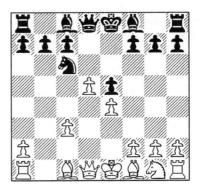

7...♘b8

Rerouting the knight to a more suitable location. 7...♘e7?! does not live up to expectations, as the knight simply does not belong here. White can easily get an advantage, for instance 8 ♘f3 ♘g6 9 ♗b5+ ♗d7 10 ♕b3 b6 11 h4 ♗d6 12 h5 ♘e7 13 h6 g6 14 ♗g5 with complete control over the dark squares in D.Justo-N.Giffard, Evry 2001.

8 ♘f3

8 f4 is an ambitious, albeit double-

edged way to treat the position. S.Lputian-M.Sibilio, Nereto 1999, continued 8...♗c5 9 ♘f3 exf4 10 ♗xf4 c6 11 ♗c4 (11 c4 strengthens the centre, but after 11...0-0 the dark squares remain incredibly weak, not to mention the white king who will not succeed in finding a safe haven) 11...0-0 12 d6, and now 12...♕f6! 13 ♕d2 ♕g6 14 ♗d3 ♖e8 (not 14...♗xd6?? 15 e5) 15 ♗c2 (15 0-0-0 loses as Black can now take the pawn: 15...♗xd6 16 e5 ♗a3+ 17 ♔b1 ♗f5 with a decisive advantage) 15...♘d7 16 0-0-0 ♘b6 would have resulted in a comfortable position for Black. The centre is relatively fixed while the white queenside is wide open, inviting the black pieces to attack.

8...♗d6 9 ♗b5+

9 ♗e2 is the most popular alternative. After 9...0-0 10 0-0 ♘d7 11 ♗e3 ♕e7 12 ♘d2 ♗c5 13 ♘c4 ♗xe3 14 ♘xe3 ♘c5 the game steered into calm waters in A.Botsari-F.Wohlers Armas, Dortmund 1988.

An interesting try to spice things up is the enterprising 10...f5!?,

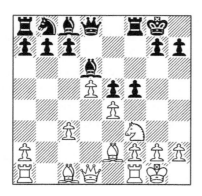

which I played on the Internet

Chess Club. A game against a player nicknamed "PudelsKern" continued 11 ♘g5?! (11 exf5 ♗xf5 leads to an unclear position: in exchange for the isolated pawn, Black has more active pieces and nice play on the half-open f-file, but more practical tests are needed) 11...f4 12 ♘e6 (12 ♘f3 ♘d7 would have given Black two precious tempi) 12...♗xe6 13 dxe6, and after 13...♕e7 14 ♕b3 b6 15 a4 ♘c6 16 ♕d5 ♘a5 17 f3 ♖ad8 18 ♔h1 ♖f6 19 ♖d1 ♕xe6 Black encircled and captured the pawn. The way White was denied any queenside activity is especially noteworthy.

9...♘d7

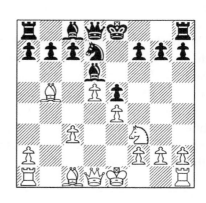

10 0-0

Besides this move, White has several other options:

a) 10 ♕b3 peers hard at b7, but Black can still play 10...0-0 11 ♗xd7 ♗xd7! as after 12 ♕xb7 ♕f6! his pieces become tremendously active. The game A.Lesiege-I.Miladinovic, Montreal 2000, continued 13 ♕b1 ♕g6 14 0-0 ♗h3 15 ♘e1 (both 15 ♘h4 ♕h5 16 ♕d3 ♕xh4 17 gxh3 f5! and 16 gxh3 ♕xh4 17 ♔g2 f5 provide Black with excellent attacking chances) 15...f5 16 ♕d3 ♗g4 17 exf5 ♕h5! 18 h3 (18 f3 allows 18...e4! 19 fxe4 ♕xh2+ 20 ♔f2 ♖xf5+! 21 exf5 ♖e8 with a mating attack) 18...♗e2 19 ♕e4 ♗xf1 20 ♔xf1 ♕xf5 and Black converted his positional advantage into a material one.

c) 10 ♗e3 is another common move.

After 10...0-0 11 ♕b3 (11 0-0 ♕e7 transposes to the text) 11...♔h8 12 ♗xd7 ♗xd7 13 ♕xb7 ♖b8 Black gets a strong initiative; for example 14 ♕a6 (or 14 ♕xa7 ♕f6, threatening to win the queen with ...♖b8-a8 and ...♖f8-b8, 15 ♗g5 ♕g6 16 ♗e3 f6 17 ♗h4 ♗c5! 18 ♕xc5 ♕xg2 19 ♖g1 ♕xf3 20 ♕e3 ♕h5 21 ♗g3 ♖b2 with a hopeless position for White; no better is 18 ♕d3 ♗b5 19 c4 ♕xg2 20 ♖g1 ♗xc4! and if 21 ♕xc4 ♕xf3 22 ♕xc5 ♕xe4+ and ...♕xh4) 14...♗b5 15 ♕a5 ♕d7 16 h3 a6 17 ♘d2 ♗d3 18 c4 ♗b4 19 ♕xa6 f5! and now Powell-P.Grimsey, correspondence 1980, concluded 20 exf5 ♕xf5 21 ♕e6 ♕e4 22 ♕g4 ♖f4! 23 ♕g3 ♗xd2+ 0-1 as mate is unavoidable.

c) 10 ♗g5 is meant to provoke a weakness before taking its usual place on e3. Nevertheless, Black can realize his plans and build up a kingside attack after 10...f6 11 ♗e3 0-0 12 0-0 ♘c5 13 ♘d2 f5 14 f3 (14 exf5 ♗xf5 was necessary, when we have an unclear position similar to the one described in the notes to White's 9th move) 14...♕e7 (or immediately 14...f4!?) 15 ♕c2 a6 16 ♗e2 f4 17 ♗f2 ♕g5 18 ♔h1 ♖f6 19 ♖g1 ♖h6 20 g4 ♗d7 21 ♘b3 ♘xb3 22 axb3 ♖h3 23 ♔g2 ♕h6 24 ♖h1 ♖f8 25 c4 ♗xg4! 26 c5 ♖xf3! 27 h4 ♖xf2+ 0-1 was A.Rashas-S.Wrinn, correspondence 1990. Note once more how White was without any counterplay.

10...0-0 11 ♗e3

Now 11 ♕b3 is met simply by 11...♘c5, followed by 12...f5 with the usual attacking prospects.

11...♕e7 12 ♕c2 ♘c5

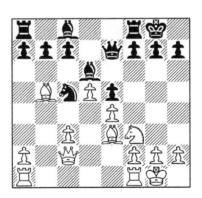

The opening phase is nearly complete and Black can be happy, as he reigns over the dark squares.

13 ♖fe1 a6 14 ♗e2 ♔h8 15 c4 ♗d7 16 a4 a5 17 ♘d2 b6

Now the queenside is fixed White is without any counterplay. Time to look at the other side of the board!

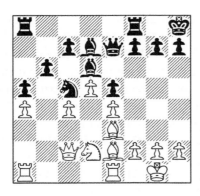

18 ♘b1 ♘b7 19 ♖f1 ♗c5 20 ♗d2

Now Black's attack develops quickly. Admittedly White does not put up too much resistance. Continuing the redeployment of the knight with 20 ♘c3 would certainly have been better, not fearing 20...♗xe3 21 fxe3 ♘c5 22 ♖f3 since doubling rooks on the f-file would at least have promised some counterplay. Additionally, after

20...f5 21 exf5 ♗xf5, then 22 ♗d3 would have been possible as the key e4-square is under control.

20...f5!

21 ♗d3

21 exf5? ♗xf5 leaves White at the mercy of the black bishops.

21...f4 22 ♔h1 ♕h4 23 g3 ♕h3 24 f3 fxg3 25 ♗e1 ♗f2! 26 ♖xf2 gxf2 27 ♗xf2 ♖xf3 28 ♗f1 ♕xf1+ 0-1

Summary

White's attempts to seize control of d5 are not successful. Neither 4 ♗g5 (Games 36-37) nor 4 cxd5 (Games 38-39) is able to leave a lasting impression. Quite the opposite is the case, as White needs to be attentive that he is not strategically out-played.

1 d4 d5 2 c4 ♘c6 3 ♘c3 ♘f6 *(D)* **4 cxd5**
>   4 ♗g5 ♘e4 *(D)*
>>   5 ♘xe4 dxe4 – *Game 36*
>>   5 cxd5 ♘xc3 – *Game 37*

4...♘xd5 5 e4 ♘xc3 6 bxc3 e5 *(D)* **7 d5**
>   7 ♘f3?! exd4 8 cxd4 ♗g4 – *Game 38*

7...♘b8 – *Game 39*

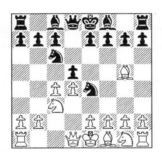

3...♘f6   4...♘e4   6...e5

Chapter Eight

1 d4 d5 2 c4 ♞c6
3 ♞c3 ♞f6 4 ♞f3 dxc4

As we saw in the previous chapter, after **3 ♞c3 ♞f6** taking immediate action against d5 is not successful. Therefore, White is advised to slacken off a bit – the move **4 ♞f3** is sensible, as it develops a piece and protects d4.

4 ♞f3 is much more dangerous for Black, as the thematic 4...♝g4? presents a problem. After 5 cxd5 ♞xd5 6 e4 ♞xc3 7 bxc3 e5 8 d5 ♞b8, White can play 9 ♛a4+! ♞d7 (9...♝d7 10 ♛b3 is equally bad) 10 ♞xe5 ♛f6, and now 11 ♝e2! is an important resource.

Without giving all the substantiating variations again (for these see the first note to Game 38 in the previous chapter), let me just tell you that Black is already lost.

Therefore, Black needs a different approach, and the best way to treat the position is with **4...dxc4**, after which, White has various ways to react.

White plays 5 ♛a4

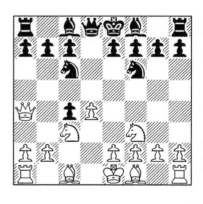

After **5 ♛a4** we have reached a position that can also arise via the

Queen's Gambit Accepted, the move order being 1 d4 d5 2 c4 dxc4 3 ♘f3 ♘f6 4 ♕a4+ ♘c6 5 ♘c3. As a rule of thumb it is usually not recommendable to bring the queen out so early, but playing 1...♘c6 I have long abandoned such dogmatic views.

The implications of 5 ♕a4 are evident. White gets his queen into an active position, pinning the black knight and attacking the c-pawn. In an ideal world White would just regain his pawn, play e2-e4 and delight in a stable centre, so Black has to think of appropriate countermeasures. Being quite common in the Chigorin Defence, 5...♗g4, intending to play against the white d-pawn, seems a good way to continue; but the fact that, after 6 e3, the white knight is not pinned forces Black to play 6...♗xf3 in order to parry the threat of 7 ♘e5. Compared with the positions after 3 ♘f3 ♗g4 4 ♕a4 ♗xf3 5 gxf3 e5 in Chapter 10, we see that here after 7 gxf3 the white centre is not in any imminent danger. The pair of bishops is therefore the deciding factor which should convince Black to refrain from playing this variation.

Another popular move is 5...e6. This shuts in the light-squared bishop but also allows the dark-squared bishop to get out of his closet. Confronted with the threat of 6...♗b4, after which it would be more difficult for White to win back the pawn, the game usually continues 7 ♕xc4 ♘b4 8 ♕b3 c5, but in my opinion Black just doesn't get enough play here.

Instead, my recommendation is the interesting **5...♘d5!?**, with the idea of relocating the knight to the more useful b6-square, from where it supports the extra pawn. As a result many players will regain the pawn at once with 6 ♕xc4, but Black has two good responses in 6...♘bd4 and 6...♘b6; the former being for lovers of a quick draw, the latter for a more energetic approach.

The most critical continuation seems to be **6 e4**, spurning the opportunity to win back the pawn and opting for a strong centre instead. The resulting positions are not clear, but I certainly like Black's chances.

Game 40
T.Engqvist-M.Sadler
Isle of Man 1995

---

1 d4 d5 2 c4 ♘c6 3 ♘c3 ♘f6 4 ♘f3 dxc4 5 ♕a4

5 e3, 5 d5 and 5 e4 are the subject of the subsequent games in this chapter.

The remaining option, 5 ♗g5, is rarely played.

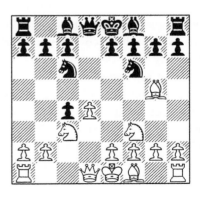

Black can try to prop up c4 with 5...a6 6 d5 (6 a4?! is bad as it denies further access to a4, which makes ...♘a5 unconditionally possible) and now after 6...♘a7!? 7 e4 ♘b5 (7...b5!? is another option) 8 ♕a4 (if 8 ♗xc4 ♘xc3 9 bxc3 ♘xe4, or 8 ♕c2 ♘xc3 9 bxc3 b5 10 a4 ♗b7) 8...♗d7 9 ♕xc4 ♘xc3 10 bxc3 h6 11 ♗f4 (or 11 ♗h4 b5 12 ♕d3 c6), as in V.Ivanchuk-W.Arencibia, Havana 2005, and now 11...b5 12 ♕d3 e6 is unclear according to R.Dautov.

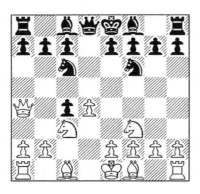

5...♘d5!?

Other moves do not promise much:

a) 5...♗d7 is too passive. After 6 ♕xc4 e6 7 e4 ♘b4 8 ♕b3 c5 9 ♗e2 cxd4 10 ♘xd4 ♘c6 11 ♗e3 White was better in V.Akobian-G.Small, Las Vegas 2002.

b) Although 5...e6 enjoys a certain popularity, it is definitely not my cup of tea. Confining his light-squared bishop to quarters, Black never seems able to get rid of his passive position. One example is 6 ♕xc4 ♘b4 7 ♕b3 c5 8 dxc5 ♗xc5 9 a3 ♘c6 10 g3 ♘a5 11 ♕c2 ♕b6 12 e3 ♗e7 13 b4 ♘c6 14 ♘a4 ♕d8 15 ♗g2 ♗d7 16 0-0 ♖c8 17 ♕b3 0-0 18 ♗b2, I.Stohl-Y.Meister, Slovakian Team

Championship 1994. The position might be solid, but with nothing to play for, Black is in for a dull experience at best.

c) 5...♗g4 is a 'normal' move in the Chigorin, and the fact that 6 ♘e5 ♗d7 7 ♕xc4 ♗e6 8 ♕b5 a6 9 ♘xc6 axb5 10 ♘xd8 ♔xd8 11 ♘xb5 ♖xa2 12 ♖xa2 ♗xa2 was good for Black in A.Alekhine-E.Book, Warsaw Olympiad 1935, seems additionally to justify it. But White can play 6 e3 ♗xf3 7 gxf3 and now 7...a6 (7...♘d7 8 ♕xc4 ♘b6 9 ♕e2 ♕d7 10 f4 e6 11 ♗g2 was better for White in T.Petrosian-W.Golz, Copenhagen 1960) 8 ♕xc4 e5 from M.Abatino-S.Skembris, Cutro 1999, is not too convincing after 9 d5 ♘b4 10 ♕b3 ♘bxd5 (10...♘fxd5? is bad because of 11 ♗c4 c6 12 a3 b5 13 ♗e2) 11 ♗c4 ♗b4 12 e4 ♘xc3 13 ♗xf7+ ♔f8 14 ♕xb4+ ♔xf7 15 ♕xc3 resulting in an advantage for White.

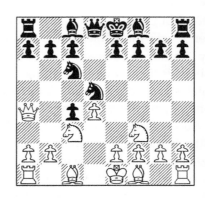

6 e4

The main alternative is 6 ♕xc4 (6 ♘e5 fails to frighten Black after 6...♘b6 7 ♘xc6 ♕d7), when Black has two choices:

a) 6...♘db4 is for lovers of an easy

draw. White has nothing better than 7 ♕b3 ♘xd4 8 ♘xd4 ♕xd4 9 ♗e3 ♗e6 10 ♕a4+ ♗d7 11 ♕b3 ♗e6 12 ♕a4+ with a draw by repetition.

b) 6...♘b6 is the enterprising alternative.

Now it is White who has to choose:

b1) 7 ♕b3 ♗g4 8 d5 ♗xf3 9 gxf3 ♘d4 10 ♕d1 e5 11 e3 ♘f5 12 f4 ♗b4 13 e4 ♘d6 14 ♗g2 was played in V.Bukal-L.Hansen, Sitges 1999, and 14...exf4 would have led to an unclear game.

b2) After 7 ♕d3 Black should not be afraid to sacrifice a pawn with the typical 7...e5!. S.Conquest-M.Dlugy, New York 1984, continued 8 ♘xe5 (or 8 dxe5 ♗g4 9 ♗f4 and in this unclear position a draw was prematurely agreed in M.Drasko-S.Marjanovic, Sarajevo 1985; inadvisable is 8...♕xd3, as played in Y.Lavrenov-T.Bosschem, Antwerp 2003, since after 9 exd3 ♘b4 10 ♔d2 ♗f5 11 ♘b5 0-0-0 12 ♘bd4 ♗g6 13 a3 c5 14 axb4 cxd4 15 ♖xa7 ♗xb4+ 16 ♔c2 it is difficult for Black to find enough compensation for the pawn) 8...♘b4!? (8...♕xd4 9 ♘xc6 ♕xd3 10 exd3 bxc6 was a bit better for White in

S.Reshevsky-L.Portisch, Tel Aviv Olympiad 1964) 9 ♕b1 (9 ♕d1 ♕xd4 10 ♕xd4 ♘c2+ 11 ♔d1 ♘xd4 also promises Black a nice game either after 12 e3 ♘e6 13 ♔c2 ♗d6 14 ♘c4 ♘xc4 15 ♗xc4 ♗d7 or 12 ♗e3 ♘e6 13 g3 ♗d6 14 ♘d3 ♘c4) 9...♕xd4 10 ♘f3 ♕d6 11 e4 ♗g4 12 a3 ♗xf3 13 gxf3 ♘c6 14 ♘b5 ♕e7 15 ♗e3 (or 15 ♗f4 ♘e5) 15...0-0-0 and Black had a good game.

6...♘b6 7 ♕d1 ♗g4 8 d5

8 ♗e3?! ♗xf3 9 gxf3 e6 left Black a pawn up in R.Cruz-R.Sanguineti, Buenos Aires 1963.

8...♘e5

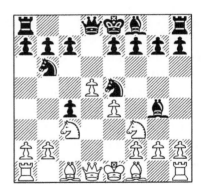

9 ♗f4

Instead:

a) 9 ♕d4 is active, but not to be recommended: 9...♘xf3+ 10 gxf3 ♗xf3 11 ♖g1 ♕d6 12 ♕e3 (after 12 e5 ♕d7 the d-pawn is doomed) 12...♘h5 13 f4 (or 13 ♗d2 e5 14 dxe6 fxe6 15 ♕g5 ♗g6 16 ♘b5 ♕d7 17 ♗h3 a6 18 ♘c3, as in R.Markus-S.Mannion, Calvia Olympiad 2004, when 18...♗d6 19 f4 0-0 20 0-0-0 ♖ae8 is unclear according to Huzman) 13...e6 14 ♖g5 g6 15 ♕d4 ♖g8 16 ♗xc4 h6 17 ♖e5 (or 17 ♖g2 0-0)

17...0-0-0 18 ♗e3 ♗g7 19 ♗b3 exd5 20 exd5 ♖ge8 21 ♘e4 ♕d7 22 a4 ♕f5! and White resigned in C.Crouch-C.Duncan, Hampstead 1998.

b) 9 ♗e2 is no improvement: 9...♗xf3 10 gxf3 e6 11 f4 ♘d3+ 12 ♗xd3 cxd3 13 dxe6 (or 13 ♕xd3 exd5 14 exd5 ♗d6 and due to the disrupted white pawn structure Black has a clear advantage) 13...fxe6 14 ♕h5+ g6 15 ♕e5 d2+! 16 ♔e2 was G.Rey-J.Berry, San Francisco 1999 (16 ♗xd2 ♕xd2+ 17 ♔xd2 ♘c4+ 18 ♔e2 ♘xe5 19 fxe5 0-0-0 is also good for Black), and now 16...♕d7! 17 ♗xd2 (17 ♕xh8? does not work because of 17...0-0-0 18 ♔f3 ♗b4 19 ♕e5 ♘c4 20 ♕f6 ♖f8 21 ♕h4 ♗xc3) 17...♕xd2+ 18 ♔xd2 ♘c4+ 19 ♔e2 ♘xe5 20 fxe5 0-0-0 and Black is clearly better.

9...♗xf3 10 gxf3 ♕d6 11 ♗g3

Regaining the pawn with 11 ♗xe5 ♕xe5 12 ♗xc4 runs into trouble after 12...0-0-0, as Black can open the position to his advantage with ...e7-e6.

11...g5!

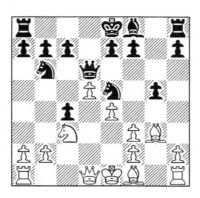

An excellent move which prevents the e5-knight from being molested by f3-f4.

12 h4 ♗g7!?

Sacrificing a pawn for the initiative. But 12...gxh4 13 ♖xh4 ♗g7 would also have been good as 14 f4 ♘g6 15 f5 ♕b4! 16 fxg6 ♕xb2 causes serious problems for White.

13 hxg5 ♕b4 14 ♖b1 0-0-0 15 f4 ♘c6 16 ♕c1 ♘d4

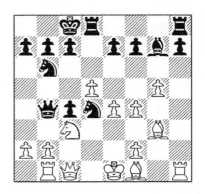

Black is clearly the winner of the opening phase. He is fully developed, while White is struggling to find a safe place for 'her majesty'.

17 ♗h3+

After 17 ♗g2 Black should try to open the position with 17...h6!?, searching for attacking lanes towards the white king.

17...♔b8 18 ♔f1 f5?!

Again Black should have opened the position with 18...h6!. After 19 ♔g2 e6 20 dxe6 fxe6 21 g6 ♕c5 the position remains difficult for White.

19 gxf6 exf6 20 ♗e6?!

Now it is White who misses an opportunity. 20 ♕e3 looks promising as now the black knight is in trouble. After 20...c5 (20...f5 21 e5 c5 22 ♗g2 leaves White with a very nice centre) 21 f5+

♔a8 22 ♗g4 White manages to stabilize his centre and put a halt to the black attack.

20...f5! 21 exf5 ♕f8

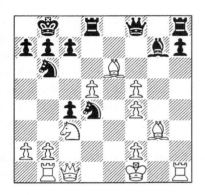

22 ♖h5 c6 23 f6 ♗xf6 24 f5+ ♔a8 25 ♗c7

25 dxc6 bxc6 26 ♘e4 ♗g7 with an unclear position would have been a better choice. Now Black is in command.

25...♖e8 26 dxc6 bxc6 27 ♗xb6 axb6 28 ♘e2?!

Here White should play 28 ♘e4 ♘xe6 29 fxe6 ♖xe6 30 ♕xc4, when 30...♕f7 31 ♕a6+ ♕a7 32 ♕c4 ♕f7 would probably have led to a draw by repetition.

28...♘xe6 29 fxe6 ♕b4?!

29...♖xe6 30 ♕xc4 ♕f7 would have been better when, compared with the previous note, Black has the more active minor piece.

30 ♕e3 ♖e7 31 ♘d4?

31 a3 would have prevented all the threats. After 31...♕b3 32 ♕xb3 cxb3 33 ♘f4 White is over the worst.

31...♗xd4?

But Black returns the favour. 31...c3!

would have been strong, since 32 ♘e2 (32 ♘xc6? is countered by 32...♕c4+, and 32 ♕xc3 ♕xd4 33 ♕xc6+ ♔b8 34 ♖d5 ♖c7! is also bad) 32...♖he8 33 ♕f4 ♕xf4 34 ♘xf4 cxb2 is clearly better for Black. Now the game quickly runs dry.

32 ♕xd4 ♖he8 33 a3 ♕b3 34 ♕c3 ♖xe6 35 ♕xb3 cxb3 36 ♖xh7 ♖e2 37 ♖h3 ♖c2 38 ♖xb3 ♖ee2 39 ♖f3 ♖xb2 40 ♖xb2 ♖xb2 41 ♖c3 ♔b7 42 ♔g2 c5 43 ♔f3 ♔c6 44 ♔e3 ♔d5 45 f4 ♖h2 46 ♖d3+ ♔c4 47 ♖d6 b5 48 ♖a6 ♖a2 49 ♖a5 ♖a1 50 f5 ♖f1 51 ♔e4 b4 52 axb4 cxb4 53 ♖a8 b3 54 ♖c8+ ♔b4 55 ♔e5 b2 56 ♖b8+ ♔c3 57 f6 b1♕ 58 ♖xb1 ♖xb1 59 f7 ♖f1 60 ♔e6 ♔d4 61 ♔e7 ♔e5 62 f8♕ ♖xf8 63 ♔xf8 ½-½

White plays 5 e3

5 e3 has its pros and cons.

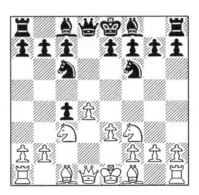

On the one hand it shuts in the dark-squared bishop and leaves White with less control over the centre (compared to 5 e4); on the other hand, the d-pawn is now well protected, which allows for smooth development should Black not react quickly. One example is 5...♗g4 6 ♗xc4 when again we have reached a position from the Queen's Gambit Accepted, but this time with an odd-looking knight on c6.

More to the point is the thematic **5...e5!**, which is not really a pawn sacrifice, as after either 6 ♘xe5 ♘xe5 7 dxe5 ♕xd1+ 8 ♘xd1 ♗b4+ or 6 dxe5 ♕xd1+ 7 ♘xd1 ♘g4 Black is getting more than good play. Instead, 6 ♗xc4 exd4 7 exd4 ♗d6 leads to a position with an isolated d-pawn, something not all White players are comfortable with. However, **6 d5** is the most logical move, effectively forcing **6...♘e7 7 ♗xc4 ♘g6**. Then 8 h4!? is an interesting attempt to barge against the knight on g6, but the developing scheme you will most likely face continues 8 e4 a6 9 0-0 ♗d6, after which Black has excellent prospects on the kingside.

Game 41
B.Korsus-C.Wisnewski
German League 2000

---

1 d4 d5 2 c4 ♘c6 3 ♘c3 ♘f6 4 ♘f3 dxc4 5 e3 e5!

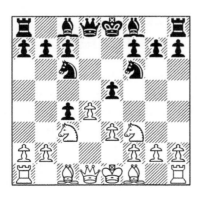

6 d5

Or:

a) After 6 ♘xe5 ♘xe5 7 dxe5 ♕xd1+ 8 ♘xd1 I recommended 8...♘g4?! in an earlier publication, making a hasty judgment that Black can equalize this way. However, deeper analysis has now convinced me that Black is actually in trouble after 9 f4, as the knight does not feel that safe anymore on g4. Fortunately, 8...♗b4+ is better; for example 9 ♗d2 (or 9 ♘c3 ♘e4) 9...♗xd2+ 10 ♔xd2 ♘e4+ 11 ♔e1 ♗e6 and Black was not worse in P.Meister-J.Cavendish, London Lloyds 1990. Thanks to Bert Corneth for pointing that out to me.

b) 6 dxe5 ♕xd1+ 7 ♘xd1 ♘g4, on the other hand, allows Black to easily get a good position.

c) 6 ♗xc4 exd4 7 exd4 ♗d6 8 0-0 0-0

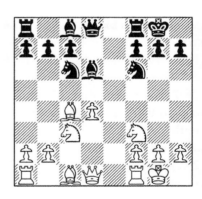

is another frequently played position (in fact a quiet line of the Queen's Gambit Accepted: 1 d4 d5 2 c4 dxc4 3 e3 e5 4 ♗xc4 exd4 5 exd4 ♗d6 etc), in which chances are roughly balanced. For example:

c1) 9 ♗g5 h6 10 ♗h4 ♗g4 11 h3 (11

♗e2?! ♗xf3 12 ♗xf3 ♘xd4 13 ♗xb7 ♖b8 14 ♘d5 ♗e5 15 ♖e1 ♕d6 16 f4 ♖xb7 17 ♖xe5 ♘xd5 18 ♕xd4 was played in H.Pihlajasalo-N.Shalnev, Helsinki 1996, and now Black could have won a pawn with 18...♘xf4! 19 ♕xf4 ♖b4) 11...♗xf3 12 ♕xf3 ♘xd4 13 ♕xb7 ♘f5 14 ♗xf6 ♕xf6 15 ♕f3 ♖ab8 16 b3 ♕e5 17 g3 ♘d4 was equal in F.Berkes-R.Rabiega, German League 2003.

c2) 9 h3 h6 10 a3 (on 10 ♖e1 Black should not be afraid of 10...♗f5 11 d5, when R.Vaganian-G.Souleidis, German League 2003, continued 11...♘e7 12 ♘d4 ♗g6 13 ♘db5 a6 14 ♘xd6 ♕xd6 15 ♕f3 ♘f5 16 ♗f4 ♕c5 17 ♗b3 ♖fe8 18 ♘a4 ♕b4 19 ♗e5, and now 19...♘d4 would have equalized) 10...♗f5 11 ♖e1 (11 b4 a6 12 ♗b2 ♕d7 is also fine for Black) 11...a6! 12 d5 again poses no threat: after 12...♘e7 13 b4 ♘g6 14 ♗b2 ♖e8 15 ♕d4 ♖xe1+ 16 ♖xe1 ♕f8! 17 ♗c1 ♖e8 the game was completely equal in P.Van der Sterren-J.Piket, Linares 1995.

6...♘e7 7 ♗xc4 ♘g6

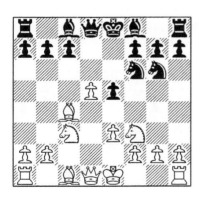

8 0-0

Besides this move, White has several alternatives:

a) 8 e4 a6 will most likely transpose to the game.

b) 8 ♗b5+!? avoids the events from the text, but after 8...♗d7 9 ♕b3 ♖b8 10 0-0 ♗d6 Black gets an easy position. The game P.Lukacs-O.Staudner, Austrian League 2002, continued 11 ♗xd7+ ♕xd7 12 ♘d2 0-0 13 ♘de4 ♘xe4 14 ♘xe4 f5 15 ♘g5 ♖f6 16 g3 h6 17 ♘e6? c6 18 e4 cxd5 19 exd5 ♘f8 20 ♘xf8 ♖fxf8 and a draw was agreed. However, I do not see what was wrong with 18...fxe4! when the white knight seems to be lost.

c) After 8 ♕a4+ Black must avoid stereotypical play with 8...♗d7?! 9 ♕b3 ♗d6 10 ♕xb7 ♖b8 11 ♕a6 as it is hard to prove any compensation for the pawn. Better is 8...♘d7! and after 9 0-0 ♗d6 10 e4 0-0 11 ♗e3 ♘f6 Black had no problems in J.Hampel-V.Lainburg, Dresden 2001.

d) 8 ♕c2?!, with the idea of castling in the opposite direction, was employed in B.Sitarek-B.Gibbons, correspondence 1985. But after 8...♗d6 9 ♗d2 0-0 10 0-0-0 a6 11 h4 ♗g4! 12 ♖dg1 b5 13 ♗b3 ♘e7 14 ♘g5 h6 15 ♘ge4 ♘xe4 16 ♘xe4 c5! 17 dxc6 ♖c8 Black got excellent attacking chances.

e) 8 h4, intending to poke the knight on g6, is a popular alternative which must be examined: 8...♗d6 9 h5 ♘f8 (9...♘e7?! is not as good; after 10 h6 g6 11 e4 ♗g4 12 ♕a4+ ♗d7 13 ♕c2 0-0 14 ♗g5 ♘e8 15 0-0-0 White had the better position in V.Smyslov-J.Rogers, London Lloyds 1988) 10 h6 g6 11 e4 ♘8d7 12 ♗g5 a6 13 a4 (preventing Black from advancing on the queenside with ...b7-b5; instead 13 ♘d2 0-0 14 g3 was played in A.Beliavsky-A.Morozevich, German League 2000, and after 14...♗e7 15 f4 b5 16 ♗b3 ♗b7 17 ♕f3 c5! Black obtained sufficient counterplay) 13...0-0 14 ♕e2 ♗e7! 15 ♖d1 ♘e8 16 ♗c1 ♘d6 17 ♗d3 ♗f6 18 ♘d2 (on 18 ♗e3 ♗h8!?, intending ...f7-f5, is interesting) 18...♘c5 and having successfully regrouped, Black was not worse in A.Khalifman-A.Morozevich, Yalta (rapid) 1995.

8...a6 9 a4?!

This move prevents ...b7-b5, but that is not Black's main idea in this set-up.

9...♗d6 10 e4 0-0

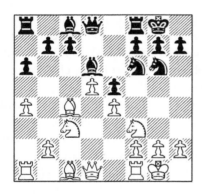

We have reached the starting point of this line. Here White has tried many things to stop Black from advancing on the kingside.

11 ♘e1

With this move White wants to prevent ...♘h5 and redeploy his knight to e3 via c2. The problem is that it loses precious time. Instead, 11 g3?! takes control of f4, but in return weakens the light squares. After 11...♗h3 12 ♖e1 h6 Black is ready to execute a kingside attack with ...♘g4 followed by ...f7-f5.

11 ♗g5 cannot stop Black either; for example 11...h6 12 ♗d2 (12 ♗xf6?! ♕xf6 just helps Black) 12...♗d7 13 ♕e2 ♖b8 14 a5 ♘h5 15 g3 f5 16 exf5 ♗xf5 with the initiative.

11...♗c5 12 ♘c2 ♕e7 13 ♗e2 ♖d8

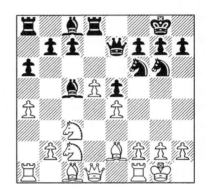

Playing on the kingside is not the only plan Black can follow.

14 ♗e3 c6 15 ♗xc5 ♕xc5 16 ♘e3 ♘f4

The d5-pawn is now under serious pressure.

17 ♖c1?

White collapses. 17 ♗f3 was necessary, but after 17...♗e6 the white centre is still in grave danger.

17...♘xe4!!

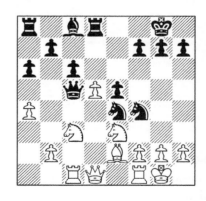

18 ♕e1

If instead 18 ♘xe4? then the reply 18...♕xc1! 19 ♕xc1 ♘xe2+ 20 ♔h1 ♘xc1 21 ♖xc1 cxd5 reveals the point of the combination.

18...cxd5

With two healthy extra pawns for Black, the game is over.

19 b4 ♕xb4 20 ♘xe4 ♘xe2+ 21 ♕xe2 ♕xe4 22 ♕b2 b5 23 axb5 axb5 24 ♖fe1 d4 25 ♘c2 ♕f4 26 ♖cd1 ♗e6 27 ♘b4 ♗c4 28 f3 f6 29 ♖e4 ♕f5 30 ♘c6 ♖d7 31 ♘b4 h6 32 h4 ♖a4 33 ♘d3 ♖a2 34 ♕b1 ♖a3 35 ♘b4 ♖b3 0-1

White plays 5 d5

Our next game features **5 d5 ♘a5 6 e4**, where White builds up a strong centre and secures an advantage in space, while hoping to regain his pawn sooner rather than later. But the advanced white d-pawn is currently lacking support, a factor Black should try to exploit with a brisk ...c7-c6 and/or ...e7-e6.

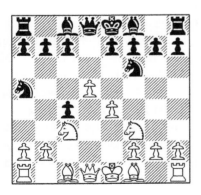

For a proper treatment of the position I kindly invite you to have a look at our next game.

Game 42
U.Adianto-W.Arencibia
Cap d'Agde (rapid) 1998

1 d4 d5 2 c4 ♘c6 3 ♘c3 ♘f6 4 ♘f3 dxc4 5 d5 ♘a5

6 e4

Instead:

a) 6 ♕a4+ will be the subject of Game 43.

b) 6 b4? cxb3 7 axb3 is met by 7...e6, when 8 ♖xa5? loses to 8...♗b4.

c) 6 ♗g5 still is not good enough. Following 6...h6 7 ♗xf6 exf6 8 e3 (White can win the pawn back with 8 ♕a4+ c6 9 0-0-0 ♗d7 10 dxc6 ♘xc6 11 ♕xc4, but after 11...♖c8 he is in trouble) 8...♗d7 9 ♗e2 b5 10 0-0 ♗b4 11 ♘d4 a6 White had no compensation for the pawn in B.Zueger-Ye Rongguang, World Team Championship, Lucerne 1989.

6...c6 7 ♘e5

7 dxc6?!, from Lont-C.Wisnewski, Internet (blitz) 2001, was not convincing. After 7...♕xd1+ 8 ♔xd1 (or 8

♞xd1? ♞xc6 9 ♗xc4 ♞xe4 and Black is a pawn up) 8...♞xc6 9 ♗xc4 ♗g4 Black was the winner of the opening phase. And 7 b4? still fails to 7...cxb3 8 axb3 e6!. After 9 dxe6 ♕xd1+ 10 ♔xd1 ♗xe6 11 ♖xa5? ♗b4 White resigned in L.Sokolin-C.Wisnewski, Internet (blitz) 2001.

7...e6 8 dxc6 ♕xd1+ 9 ♔xd1 ♞xc6 10 ♞xc6 bxc6 11 ♗xc4

We have reached the critical position for this line. Black has an isolated pawn on c6 and a bad bishop on c8. Is this worth being sought after?

11...♞g4!

Yes! By attacking the weakest spot in the white camp, Black manages to alter the course of the game.

12 ♔e1

12 ♔e2? seems to make more sense, but after 12...♞e5! White is forced to trade his light-squared bishop, as abandoning the f1-a6 diagonal could involve dire consequences; i.e. 13 ♗d3 (not 13 ♗b3? ♗a6+ and the king becomes a puppet of the black pieces) 13...♞xd3 14 ♔xd3 and the two bishops are responsible for Black being better.

12...♗c5 13 ♗e2!

On 13 f3 ♞e5, followed by ...♞g6 and ...e5, would result in a nice game for Black.

13...e5

But not 13...♗xf2+? 14 ♔f1 or 13...♞xf2? 14 ♖f1 both of which lose material.

14 ♗xg4 ♗xg4 15 ♗e3 ♗xe3 16 fxe3 0-0-0

White has managed to liberate himself by trading pieces, but Black still has the more active game. It is White who has to fight for the draw.

17 h3 ♗h5

I would have ordered the bishop to a more active post with 17...♗e6. Now White holds the balance more easily.

18 g4 ♗g6 19 ♔e2 h5 20 ♖ac1 hxg4 21 hxg4 ♖xh1 22 ♖xh1 ♔c7 23 ♖h2 ♖b8 24 ♔f3 ♖d8 25 ♖c2 ♖h8 26 ♔g3 ♖h1 27 ♞b5+ ♔b6 28 ♞d6 f6 29 ♖d2 ♖g1+ 30 ♔f3 ♖f1+ 31 ♔g2 ♖e1 32 ♔f2 ♖h1 33 ♔g2 ♖e1 ½-½

Since 6 e4 has not usually been crowned with success, the only critical line to look at is **6 ♕a4+ c6 7 b4**, which tries to exploit the exposed position of the black knight.

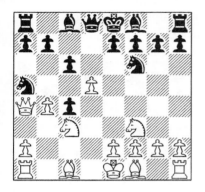

White will win a piece in the process, but in exchange Black gets two pawns and a massive pawn centre which will soon start to roll down the board. White has a hard time stopping them, the next game being one example.

Game 43
D.Justo-C.Wisnewski
Internet Chess Club (rapid) 2002

---

1 d4 d5 2 c4 ♘c6 3 ♘c3 ♘f6 4 ♘f3 dxc4 5 d5 ♘a5 6 ♕a4+ c6

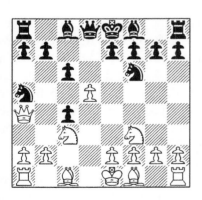

7 b4

7 dxc6 is harmless: after 7...♘xc6 8 ♘e5 (or 8 e4 e6 9 ♗xc4 ♗d7) 8...♗d7 9 ♘xd7 ♕xd7 10 ♕xc4 e5 Black doesn't have any problems.

7...b5

Forced, since 7...cxb3? 8 axb3 b6 9 dxc6 is good for White. The previously mentioned idea of 8...e6 (intending 9 ♕xa5 ♕xa5 10 ♖xa5? ♗b4) is no good this time, because 9 b4! b5 (9...♘c4 10 dxc6 b5 11 ♕xb5 ♘b6 12 e4 also left Black in bad shape in K.Kaunas-P.Lasinskas, Birstonas 2002) 10 ♕xa5 ♕xa5 11 bxa5 b4 12 ♘a4 exd5 13 ♗b2 gives White a superior version of the game. Black does not have enough compensation for the piece here.

8 ♕xa5 ♕xa5 9 bxa5 b4 10 ♘a4

Alternatively:

a) 10 ♘d1 (the other way for the knight to retreat) 10...cxd5 and now:

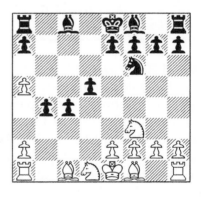

a1) 11 ♗f4 seeks to prevent ...e7-e5, but Black can react appropriately with 11...♘e4, intending ...f7-f6 and then ...e7-e5; for example 12 ♘d2 ♘xd2 13 ♔xd2 (or 13 ♗xd2 e5) 13...f6.

a2) 11 ♘e5 e6 12 f3 ♗d6 13 ♗f4

♗b7! (13...♘h5?! runs into 14 ♘xf7!) 14 ♘xf7 ♗xf4 15 ♘xh8 ♔e7 provides Black with excellent compensation for the exchange.

a3) 11 g3 e6 12 ♗g2 ♗e7 13 ♘e5 ♗a6 14 ♘c6 ♖c8 15 ♘xe7 ♔xe7 16 ♖b1 ♖b8 17 ♘e3 was good for White in M.Granados Gomez-A.Garcia Cano, Sant Cebria 1998. But 11...♗f5, as suggested by Breutigam, is definitely an improvement.

b) 10 dxc6!? returns the piece, hoping to be able to exploit weaknesses in the pawn structure after 10...bxc3 and:

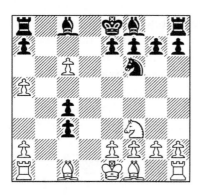

b1) 11 ♖b1?! ♗a6 12 ♘e5 0-0-0! and suddenly White is in danger. G.Meins-R.Rabiega, German Championship 2000, continued 13 ♘xf7 (if 13 ♗e3? c2 14 ♖c1 e6! 15 ♖xc2 ♗b4+ 16 ♗d2 ♖xd2 17 ♖xd2 ♘e4 or 15 ♗d2 ♘e4 wins) 13...c2 14 ♖b8+ ♔xb8 15 ♘xd8 e5 and Black had a clear advantage.

b2) 11 e3 ♗a6 12 ♘e5 ♘d5 (12...♖c8 13 ♖b1 e6 14 ♗xc4 ♗xc4 15 ♘xc4 ♗c5 16 ♖b5 ♘e4 17 f3 a6 was tried in O.Misch-G.Heisel, German League 1998, but after 18 ♖b3 ♘f6 19 ♗a3 ♗xa3 20 ♘xa3 Black is struggling for equal-

ity) 13 ♗a3 (13 ♘xc4?! ♘b4 14 ♖b1 e6 gives Black the better chances) 13...e6 14 ♗xf8 ♖xf8 15 ♘xc4 with unclear play (analysis by Bronznik).

10...cxd5

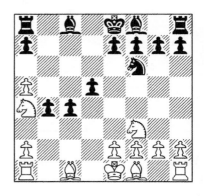

11 a3

Instead:

a) In G.Kane-J.Silman, San Francisco 1977, White tried to control e7-e5 with 11 ♗e3 e6 12 ♗d4 (12 ♘c5? runs into 12...♘g4 13 ♗d4 e5!), but again 12...♘e4!, followed by ...f6 and ...e5, would have solved any problems Black might have had.

b) 11 ♘e5 was another attempt in Pohl-Plath, correspondence 1989, but after 11...e6 12 ♗f4 ♘h5 13 ♗e3 ♗d6 14 ♗d4 f6, the idea ...e6-e5 strikes again!

c) 11 ♗g5?! does nothing to prevent Black from occupying the centre, and after 11...♘e4 12 ♗e3 e6 13 ♘d2 ♘xd2 14 ♔xd2 ♗d7 15 ♘c5 ♗b5 Black was clearly better in A.Alonso Roselli-S.Zehnter, World Junior Championships 2005.

11...b3

Now Black has two connected passed pawns, but for the moment

White can safely blockade them – something which needs to be changed! **12 ♗b2 ♗f5 13 e3 e6 14 ♘d4 ♗g6 15 f3 ♗e7 16 ♘c6 ♗d6 17 ♘c3 ♔d7 18 ♘d4**

18...♗c7?!

18...a6!? is an attractive alternative. Then the a5-pawn is fixed and b5 is no longer accessible to the white knights, which makes ...e6-e5 a real threat. White can try to exploit the newly accrued weakness on b6, but Black can stay on top; for example, 19 ♘a4 ♗c7 20 ♘c5+ ♔e7 21 ♗c3 e5 and the pawns are starting to roll. The immediate 18...e5! is possible, too.

19 a6 ♗b6 20 ♘a4

20...♖he8?!

I should have protected the bishop with 20...♖ab8, but I simply missed a move in my calculations.

21 ♔d2?!

At the time I didn't fear 21 ♘xb6+! axb6 as I thought I could just pick up the a6-pawn. It was only after the game that I realized ...♖xa6 is always answered by ♘xb3!.

21...♔d6 22 ♘b5+ ♔c6 23 ♘d4+ ♗xd4

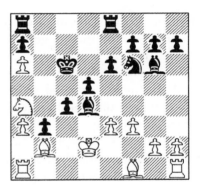

24 exd4?!

24 ♗xd4 would have been better, as the originally planned 24...♔b5 25 ♘b2 ♔xa6 would have been countered by 26 ♘xc4! dxc4 27 ♗xc4+ ♔b7 28 e4 with the better position for White. Of course Black could play 24...e5, but after 25 ♗b2 it is not so easy to advance the pawns further. White might undermine them with e3-e4 at an opportune moment; for example 25...♖ad8 26 ♖c1 ♔b5 27 ♘c3+ ♔xa6?! 28 e4!, or even 27...♔a5 28 a4 d4 29 e4! dxc3+ 30 ♔xc3 returning a piece to eliminate the pawn mass, when 30...♗xe4! 31 fxe4 ♘xe4+ 32 ♔c4 ♘d2+ 33 ♔c5 ♘e4+ leads to an unexpected draw by perpetual check.

24...♞d7 25 f4 ♔b5 26 ♞c5?

This just capitulates. 26 ♞c3+ was necessary, despite the fact that Black gets a third pawn for the piece with 26...♔xa6 and an excellent position. **26...♞xc5 27 dxc5 ♔xc5 28 ♖c1 f6 29 a4 ♖ac8 30 ♗a3+ ♔b6 31 ♔c3 ♔a5 32 ♗b4+ ♔xa4 33 ♖a1+ ♔b5 34 ♗e2?? d4+ 35 ♔xd4 ♔xb4 0-1**

White plays 5 e4

The immediate building of a strong centre with **5 e4** is the most common plan employed in the Chigorin Four Knights. The 'only' thing left for White to do is regain the pawn, but there's the rub. Actually achieving this costs precious time – time Black can use to organize counterplay.

The only sensible reply is **5...♗g4**, pinning the knight and thereby putting pressure on d4. Now 6 d5 is quite possible, especially as the apparently typical 6...♞a5? loses to 7 ♕a4+. But after 6...♞e5 7 ♗f4 ♞g6 8 ♗e3 e5 9 ♗xc4 a6 we get a position similar to that in Korsus-Wisnewski (Game 41) which is not to every White player's taste. The most popular way to continue is **6 ♗e3**, and after **6...e6 7 ♗xc4 ♗b4 8 ♕c2 0-0 9 ♖d1** it is Black who has to make a choice.

(see following diagram)

9...♕e7, intending ...e6-e5, is considered to be the main line, but I don't like the implications of that. **9...♗xf3!? 10 gxf3 ♞h5**, on the other hand, is a plan that should immediately appeal to you. Black, while pointing his finger at the now weakened f4-square, hacks the

kingside to pieces, leaving White to wonder what to do with his king. There is nothing more for me to say – just that the overall results (62% for Black) of the games in *MegaBase 2006* speak volumes.

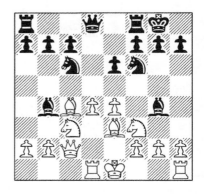

Game 44
E.Magerramov-M.Al Modiahki
Dubai 2000

1 d4 d5 2 c4 ♞c6 3 ♞c3 ♞f6 4 ♞f3 dxc4 5 e4 ♗g4 6 ♗e3

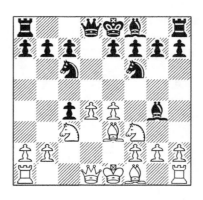

6 d5 is also seen from time to time. Black must be careful not to play the

'typical' 6...♘a5? 7 ♕a4+ c6 8 b4 cxb3 9 axb3 e6 10 b4 which loses a piece. Instead, 6...♘e5 is the correct move, and then:

a) 7 ♗e2 is harmless. The game E.Jelling-J.Fries Nielsen, Danish Championship 1988, continued 7...♗xf3 8 gxf3 e6 9 ♕d4 ♘fd7 10 f4 ♗c5 11 ♕d1 and now 11...♘d3+! 12 ♗xd3 cxd3 13 dxe6 fxe6 14 ♕xd3 0-0 would have been good for Black.

b) 7 ♗xc4 is equally benign.

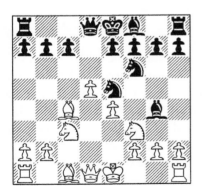

After 7...♘xc4 8 ♕a4+ ♘d7 9 ♕xc4 e5 Black is at least equal. R.Wade-V.Korchnoi, Buenos Aires 1960, continued 10 ♗g5 f6 11 ♗e3 ♗xf3 12 gxf3,

and now Black could have improved upon his game with 12...a6! followed by ...♗d6.

c) 7 ♗f4 ♗xf3 8 gxf3 ♘g6 (8...♕d6 and 8...♘fd7 are alternatives worth mentioning) 9 ♗g3 e5 10 dxe6 ♕xd1+ 11 ♖xd1 fxe6 and Black is OK after either 12 ♗xc4 e5 or 12 ♗xc7 ♖c8 13 ♗g3 e5.

d) 7 ♕d4!? is dangerous if not treated accordingly; for example, 7...♘xf3+ 8 gxf3 ♗xf3 9 ♖g1 e6 and now 10 ♖g3 ♗h5 11 ♗xc4 or the immediate 10 ♗xc4 provides White with a dangerous initiative. 9...e5! is a better move, though. After 10 ♕xe5+ ♕e7 11 ♕xe7+ ♗xe7 White doesn't have the time to take the c-pawn because of his hanging e-pawn, while on 12 ♗g2 ♗xg2 13 ♖xg2 ♗b4 14 f3 ♖g8 15 ♗d2, as in O.Touzane-A.Dunnington, Cannes 1995, Black would have been better after 15...0-0-0 as White's compensation for the pawn is far from evident.

6...e6 7 ♗xc4 ♗b4

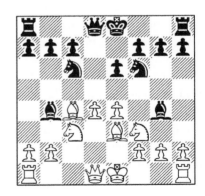

8 ♕c2
Instead:

a) 8 e5? is utterly terrible. After 8...♘d5 9 ♗xd5 ♕xd5 10 0-0 ♗xc3! 11 bxc3 ♗xf3 12 gxf3 ♘a5 the endgame is a perfect dream for Black.

b) 8 ♕d3!? is meant to keep both central pawns protected, but on the other hand the light-squared bishop can no longer retreat down the f1-a6 diagonal. After 8...0-0 White has tried:

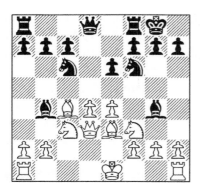

b1) 9 a3 ♗xc3+ 10 bxc3 ♗xf3 11 gxf3 ♘h5, Z.Szabo-J.Dobos, Budapest 1994, leaves White wondering where to put his king.

b1) 9 ♗b5, when Bronznik suggests 9...♗xc3+ 10 bxc3 ♗xf3 11 gxf3 ♘e7, but it is not clear to me why Black should trade both bishops here. Instead, 9...♗xf3 10 gxf3 ♘e7 was played in P.Neuman-G.Kuba, Pula 2003, and now 11 0-0-0 a6 12 ♗c4 b5 13 ♗b3 ♘g6 14 ♔b1 e5 15 d5 ♗d6 shows a point of not trading the dark-squared bishop, while the original game continued 15 ♘d5 ♘xd5 16 ♗xd5 ♖b8 17 ♖hg1 ♕f6 with a good game for Black.

b2) 9 ♘d2 gets the knight under shelter, but simultaneously relinquishes control in the centre. Then

9...e5 10 d5 ♘e7 11 f3 ♗d7 12 0-0 a6!?, followed by ...♘g6 and ....♗d6, offers Black good chances on the kingside, comparable to Game 41 (Korsus-Wisnewski).

8...0-0 9 ♖d1

9 0-0-0?! is dubious. After 9...♗xc3 10 bxc3 ♕e7 11 h3 ♗xf3 12 gxf3 ♖fb8! 13 ♗d3 b5! 14 e5 ♘d5 15 ♗xh7+ ♔h8 16 ♗e4 b4 17 ♗xd5 (if 17 c4 b3! 18 axb3 ♘a5) 17...exd5 18 ♔d2 ♘a5 19 ♔e2 ♘c4 Black had attacking chances in A.Shirov-A.Morozevich, Amsterdam 1995.

9...♗xf3!? 10 gxf3 ♘h5

11 e5

This opens the b1-h7 diagonal and makes e4 available for White's pieces, but it also weakens d5, f5 and the d-pawn. Then again, if 11 0-0 ♕h4 12 ♘e2 e5 13 d5 ♘d4! and Black takes control of the dark squares.

11...♘e7 12 0-0 c6! 13 ♗g5

13 ♘e4 ♘d5 14 ♘g3 ♘hf4 15 ♔h1 was played in M.Kopylov-C.Wisnewski, German League 2003, and now 15...♔h8, intending ...f7-f5, would have given Black the advantage.

13...h6 14 ♗c1 ♘d5 15 ♘e2 ♕h4 16

♕e4 ♗e7 17 ♗d3 f5! 18 exf6 ♕xf6

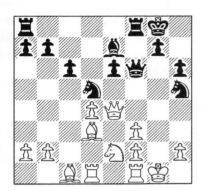

The white pawn structure is completely shredded. Black is clearly better.

19 ♕g4 ♕xf3 20 ♕xe6+ ♕f7 21 ♕e4 ⓝhf6 22 ♕g2 ♔h8 23 ♗g6 ♕e6 24 ⓝg3 ⓝh7! 25 ♗b1 ⓝg5 26 ♖de1 ♕h3

Keeping the queens on the board with 26...♕g4!? made more sense.

27 f4 ♕xg2+ 28 ♔xg2 ⓝh7 29 a3 ♗f6

30 ⓝf5 ♖ad8 31 ♔g3 ♖d7 32 ♖e2 ♖fd8 33 ♖fe1 ⓝf8 34 ♗d2 ♔g8 35 ♔f3 ⓝc7 36 ♗b4 ⓝd5 37 ♗c5 b6

This is the weakness White needed to initiate sufficient counterplay.

38 ♗xf8 ♔xf8 39 ♖e6 ⓝe7 40 ⓝxh6 ♗xd4 41 ⓝf5 ♗f6 42 b3 c5 43 a4 ♔f7 44 h4 ⓝxf5 45 ♗xf5 g6 46 ♗b1 ♖d1 47 ♖6e2 ♗xh4 48 ♖xd1 ♖xd1 49 ♗c2 ♖d6 50 ♖e3 g5 ½-½

Summary

This chapter shows that Black shouldn't be afraid of the so-called 'main line' 3 ♘c3. Early white queen moves need not be feared, as Games 40 and 43 illustrate. 5 e3 provides Black with a position that is easy to play, whereas White often struggles to find an appropriate plan. Game 44 shows a relatively new idea to combat the white set-up, and Black's results have been more than adequate.

1 d4 d5 2 c4 ♘c6 3 ♘c3 ♘f6 4 ♘f3 dxc4 *(D)* **5 e4**

       5 ♕a4 ♘d5 – *Game 40*

       5 e3 e5 – *Game 41*

       5 d5 ♘a5 *(D)*

             6 e4 c6 – *Game 42*

             6 ♕a4+ c6 – *Game 43*

5...♗g4 *(D)* – *Game 44*

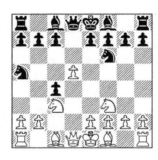

    4...dxc4   *5...♘a5*   *5...♗g4*

Chapter Nine

1 d4 d5 2 c4 ♘c6
3 ♘f3 ♗g4 (4 ♕a4; 4 e3; 4 ♘c3)

Developing the king's knight with **3 ♘f3** is quite logical, as it protects the d-pawn and makes it more difficult for Black to play ...e7-e5. As a consequence, Black should respond **3...♗g4**, proceeding against the knight and therefore helping to enforce ...e7-e5 after all. Now the most popular move is 4 cxd5 (which will be the subject of the next chapter), but White does have other moves at his disposal as well.

White plays 4 ♕a4

The line that breaks the first ground is an invention of the great Alexander Alekhine himself. **4 ♕a4** bears comparison to the idea we encountered in Game 40, but this time it is more dangerous as the threat of 5 ♘e5 is imminent. All in all White opts for quick development, and is ready and willing to sacrifice the d-pawn in the process.

After **4...♗xf3** both ways of retaking the bishop have been tried, with the uncompromising 5 exf3 being the more popular and more dangerous one. But before going into more detail about this, let's take a look at how to play against **5 gxf3**.

Game 45
P.Etchegaray-V.Bukal Sr
Cannes 1997

1 d4 d5 2 c4 ♘c6 3 ♘f3 ♗g4 4 ♕a4

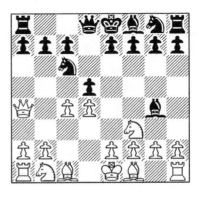

4 ♘e5?! is similar to the idea with

4...♘e4!? I introduced in Chapter 7. However, the absence of a knight on f6 means it is less effective: 4...♘xe5 5 dxe5 dxc4 6 ♕a4+ ♕d7 7 ♕xc4 0-0-0 8 ♘c3, and now the most accurate treatment seems to be 8...♗e6 9 ♕e4 ♗f5 10 ♕c4 e6 with a small advantage for Black due to the favourable pawn structure.

4...♗xf3 5 gxf3

5 exf3 is seen in the next game.

5...e5!

Instead:

a) 5...e6 6 ♘c3 is a bit too passive for my taste:

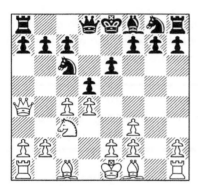

a1) 6...♕h4 does not have the same effect as in the game. After 7 e3 dxc4 (7...0-0-0 8 ♗d2 ♘ge7 9 f4 f6 10 b4! e5 11 cxd5 exd4 12 dxc6 dxc3 13 ♗xc3 ♘d5 14 ♕xa7 led to a decisive attack in L.Lengyel-A.Sydor, Polanica Zdroj 1966) 8 ♗xc4 ♗d6? 9 ♘b5 (actually White could have thrown in 9 ♗a6! already) 9...♘f6 10 ♘xd6+ cxd6 11 ♗a6! bxa6 12 ♕xc6+ ♔e7 White was better in Z.Kozul-G.Mohr, Ljubljana 1994.

a2) 6...♘ge7 7 ♗g5! makes it difficult for Black to complete his develop-

ment adequately: 7...♕d7 8 0-0-0 h6 (if 8...0-0-0 9 cxd5 exd5 10 h4, intending 11 ♗h3, gives White a nice advantage) 9 ♗h4 g5 10 ♗g3 f5 11 e3 ♗g7 12 cxd5 exd5 13 h4 ♘d8 (or 13...0-0-0 14 ♘b5 and Black is lost) 14 ♘b5 ♖c8 15 hxg5 hxg5 16 ♖xh8+ ♗xh8 17 ♕xa7 and White was a pawn up in E.Bukic-M.Cander, Slovenian Championship 1991.

a3) 6...♕d7 7 e3 (7 ♗g5 is not that strong this time, as Black can play 7...h6! 8 ♗h4 ♘xd4 9 ♕xd7+ ♔xd7 10 0-0-0 ♘f5, but not immediately 7...♘xd4? 8 ♕xd7+ ♔xd7 9 0-0-0 when White has a good game) 7...♘ge7 opts for a set-up which is good against 5 exf3. But here White's centre is stable, which allows for queenside action: 8 ♗d2 g6 9 b4! ♗g7 10 b5 ♘d8 11 ♖c1 0-0 12 ♕b3 and White had the advantage in W.Schmidt-D.Bischof, Dortmund 1992.

a4) 6...♘f6 7 ♗g5 ♗e7 (7...dxc4 8 0-0-0 ♗e7 9 ♕xc4 ♘d5 10 ♗xe7 ♘cxe7 11 ♔b1 ♘xc3+ 12 ♕xc3 ♘d5 was unclear in L.Portisch-V.Smyslov, Portoroz 1971; but simply 8 e3 is better, when I do not like Black's position) 8 e3 ♘d7 9 cxd5 ♘b6 10 ♕d1 ♘xd5 11 ♗xe7 ♕xe7 12 f4 provided White with a small advantage in L.Lengyel-V.Kozomara, Sarajevo 1965.

a5) 6...♗b4 7 cxd5 exd5 (7...♕xd5?! 8 ♕xb4 ♘xb4 9 ♘xd5 exd5 10 ♔d1 was clearly better for White with the bishop pair in G.Raptis-P.Kazantzidis, Kavala 2000) 8 a3 ♗xc3+ 9 bxc3 ♘ge7 10 ♖b1 ♖b8 11 ♗f4 and again the pair of bishops dominates.

b) 5...dxc4 is another alternative which requires precise play: 6 e3 e5 (or 6...e6 7 ♗xc4 a6 8 ♗e2 ♘e7?! 9 f4 ♕d5 10 ♖g1 ♘f5 11 ♗d2 b5 12 ♕d1 ♘h4 13 ♘c3 ♕d7 14 ♖c1 and White was better in A.Korotylev-G.Gross, Budapest 1994; instead Black should have tried 8...♕g5!?, with 9 ♔f1 ♕h4 leading to very interesting play) 7 dxe5 and then:

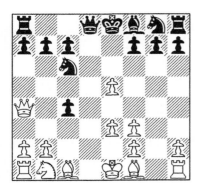

b1) 7...♕d7 8 ♗xc4 ♘xe5 9 ♕xd7+ ♔xd7 10 ♗e2 and the pair of bishops made the difference in C.Rivero-J.Hedman Senarega, Fuerteventura 1992.

b2) 7...♗b4+ 8 ♗d2 ♕e7 9 f4 ♗xd2+ 10 ♘xd2 ♕b4, as in J.Kristensen-E.Nicolaisen, Copenhagen 2001, is not good either. After 11 ♕xb4 ♘xb4 12 ♖c1 b5 (12...♘xa2? 13 ♖xc4 is disastrous) 13 a3 Black's position is beyond repair.

b3) 7...♕d5! 8 ♘c3 ♕xf3 (8...♕xe5 9 f4 ♕a5 10 ♕xc4 led to White's advantage in N.Ibraev-S.Iuldachev, Calvia Olympiad 2004) 9 ♖g1 ♕h5 (not 9...0-0-0?? 10 ♗e2 trapping the queen in W.Schmidt-B.Grabarczyk, Polish Championship 1991; surprisingly this is not the only game which has ended this way) 10 ♗g2 ♘e7 11 ♗d2 0-0-0

with unclear play in J.Demina-N.Hoiberg, Kuala Lumpur 1990.

6 dxe5 ♕h4!

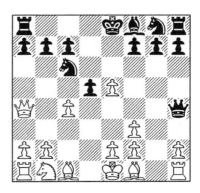

This is an excellent square for the queen, from where she exerts pressure on h2 and f2 and along the fourth rank.

7 ♗g2

Not the only move. Let's look at the alternatives:

a) After 7 e3 d4 we reach a position similar to those covered in Chapter 11 (after 3 e3 e5 4 dxe5 d4). Black has more than adequate compensation, as the d4-pawn restricts White's development: 8 ♕b3 (8 exd4? is met simply by 8...♕xd4 when Black regains the pawn, while the white kingside is in ruins) 8...0-0-0 9 f4 ♘h6 and Black has a dangerous initiative.

b) 7 ♖g1?! is just bad since 7...♕xh2 8 cxd5 ♕xg1 9 dxc6 fails to 9...b6, as in I.Dubinka-A.Segal, Rotterdam 1998.

c) 7 ♘c3 is unable to shock Black either. After 7...♗b4 8 a3 (or 8 ♗d2 d4 9 ♘d5 ♗xd2+ 10 ♔xd2 0-0-0 and Black has a good game; 9 ♘e4 is also met by 9...♗xd2+ 10 ♘xd2 0-0-0) 8...♗xc3+ 9 bxc3 ♘ge7 10 ♖b1 ♖b8 chances are roughly equal, for example 11 f4 0-0 12 ♗g2 dxc4 13 0-0 ♘g6 14 e3 ♕g4 15 h3 ♕e6 with unclear play.

7...0-0-0 8 0-0 ♗c5 9 f4 ♘h6 10 e3?!

10 h3!?, to prevent ...♘h6-g4, has to be considered. Now 10...♘d4 11 ♘c3 dxc4 12 ♕xc4 favours White, but 10...♗b6!? is interesting, preparing ...♘d4 by ensuring the bishop won't be attacked (after ...dxc4) with ♕xc4. After 11 cxd5 ♘xe5 Black has sufficient counterplay for the sacrificed pawn.

10...d4 11 ♕b3 ♘a5 12 ♕b5? dxe3! 13 ♗xe3

After 13 ♕xc5? Black's lead in development pays off: 13...♘g4 14 h3 exf2+ 15 ♖xf2 (or 15 ♔h1 ♕g3 with mate to follow) 15...b6! and the white queen can no longer protect f2.

13...♗xe3 14 fxe3 ♘g4

The black attack is decisive.

15 h3 ♘xe3 16 c5

Or 16 ♕xa5 ♕g3 with mate in four.

16...♕g3 17 ♕e2 ♘xf1 18 ♕xf1 ♘c4 19 ♘c3 ♘e3 20 ♕f3 ♕xg2+ 21 ♕xg2 ♘xg2 22 ♔xg2 ♖d2+ 23 ♔f3 ♖xb2 24 ♖g1 ♖d8 25 ♔e3 g6 26 f5 ♖c2 27 ♘e2 ♖xc5 0-1

So that's that. Having seen that the move 5 gxf3 doesn't meet the needs of White's opening strategy, let's get down to brass tacks and have a look at **5 exf3**.

Taking the d-pawn with 5...dxc4?! 6 ♗xc4 ♕xd4 allows White too great an initiative, so Black should opt for the solid **5...e6** instead. Nevertheless, with a white bishop aiming for b5, there are still a few rocks to steer clear of. For example, after **6 ♘c3** the methodical **6...♗b4?!** runs into 7 exd5 exd5 8 ♗b5, forcing 8...♗xc3+ 9 bxc3 with a big advantage for White as his bishops now rule the board with an iron hand. The immediate **6...♘e7!** is much better, as illustrated by the following game.

> ## Game 46
> ### M.Meyer-H.Langrock
> ### German League 1999

1 d4 d5 2 c4 ♘c6 3 ♘f3 ♗g4 4 ♕a4 ♗xf3 5 exf3 e6

5...dxc4?! has seen in numerous games, but it is White who gets the initiative after 6 ♗xc4 e6 (grabbing the pawn with 6...♕xd4 is very dangerous: 7 ♘c3 e6 8 0-0 ♗d6 9 ♖d1 ♕e5 10 ♗a6! with a good game for White in L.Portisch-S.Mariotti, Budapest 1975) 7 ♘c3 ♘f6 (if 7...♗d6 8 d5 exd5 9 ♗a6! ♕c8 10 ♘xd5 ♘e7 11 ♘xe7 ♗xe7 12 ♕xc6+ bxc6 13 ♗xc8 ♖xc8 14 ♗e3 and White had a significant endgame advantage in J.Barle-S.Truta, Bled 1996; while 10...♕e6+ 11 ♗e3 ♕xd5 12 ♗xb7 just wins for White) 8 0-0 ♗e7 9 ♖d1 ♘d5 10 ♘xd5 exd5 and now in L.B.Hansen-H.Porth, Bad Wörishofen 1992, instead of 11 ♗b5 as played in the game, 11 ♗a6! would have led to a decisive advantage after 11...♕c8 12 ♗b5 ♕d7 13 ♗f4.

6 ♘c3 ♘e7!

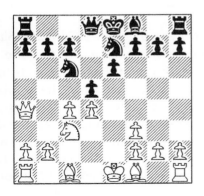

A good move, supporting the centre and thwarting any ♗b5 ideas. As already mentioned, 6...♗b4?! seems logical but it does not work very well. After 7 cxd5 exd5 8 ♗b5 ♗xc3+ 9 bxc3 the white bishops dominate the board.

7 cxd5 exd5 8 ♗e3

Instead, 8 ♗g5 ♕d7 9 ♖d1 h6 10 ♗e3 g6 is comfortable for Black.

8 ♗b5 does not pose any threat ei-

ther. Black equalized after 8...a6 9 ♗xc6+ ♘xc6 10 0-0 ♕d7 11 ♖e1+ ♗e7 12 ♗f4 0-0 in A.Constantinou-H.Leeners, correspondence 1986.

8...g6 9 ♗b5 ♗g7 10 0-0-0?!

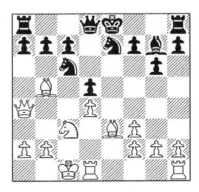

This turns out to be an unfortunate decision. White had to settle for 10 0-0 0-0 when the black advantage is only microscopic.

10...♕d7 11 h4 0-0

There is really no need to fear a white kingside attack...

12 h5 a6 13 ♗xc6 ♘xc6 14 ♕c2 b5!

...as Black's queenside attack will be a lot faster!

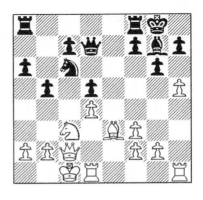

15 ♖h3 b4 16 ♘e2 b3!

Time is more important than a measly pawn.

17 ♕xb3 ♖ab8 18 ♕c2 ♘b4 19 ♕b1 c5 20 ♘c3 c4 21 ♖d2 ♘d3+ 22 ♔d1 ♖b7 23 ♔e2 ♖fb8

The moves just fly off the shelves. There is no way White can withstand the mighty force of the combined black pieces.

24 ♘d1 ♘xb2!

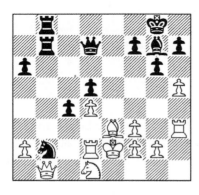

25 ♕c2

Both 25 ♘xb2 c3 and 25 ♖xb2 ♖xb2+ 26 ♘xb2 c3 are moves of true finishing quality.

25...♘xd1 26 ♕xd1 c3 27 ♖c2 ♖b2 28 ♗c1 ♕b5+ 29 ♔e1 ♖e8+ 30 ♗e3 ♖b1 31 ♖c1 ♖xc1 32 ♕xc1 ♕b2 33 ♔d1 ♖c8 34 ♕c2 ♕a1+ 35 ♔e2 ♖b8 36 ♔d3 ♖b2 37 ♕xc3 ♕f1 mate

White plays 4 e3

Understandably enough, **4 e3** is not a move with which White can throw his weight around. Granted, by strengthening the d-pawn and protecting the c-pawn White gets rid of any problems he might have had in the centre, but he also limits the scope of his dark-

squared bishop and does absolutely nothing to confront Black's presence in the centre.

Now Black has two distinct ways to continue with his e-pawn. However, I do not like the reckless 4...e5?!, as after 5 ♕b3! Black suddenly has some problems.

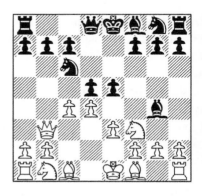

I prefer the more solid **4...e6**. Since White is not putting any pressure on the black centre there is enough time for calm development. The position after **5 ♘c3 ♘f6 6 ♗d2 ♗e7** can be compared to that in Game 48, the difference being that the dark-squared bishops have not been traded off. This situation favours Black, so White does best to force the issue with **6 h3**. The best way to react is shown in the following game.

1 d4 d5 2 c4 ♘c6 3 ♘f3 ♗g4 4 e3 e6 5 ♘c3 ♘f6

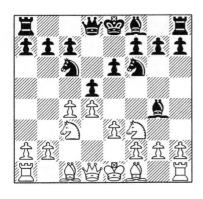

6 h3

This immediately defuses the situation, but there are other alternatives worth mentioning:

a) 6 ♗e2 ♗b4 (6...dxc4 is another safe way to equalize, for example 7 ♗xc4 ♗e7 8 0-0 0-0 9 ♗e2 ♖e8 10 a3 ♗f8 11 b4 a6 12 ♗b2 ♘d5 13 ♖c1 ♘xc3 14 ♗xc3 ♘e7, Y.Rodriguez-O.Chervet, Bern 2004; note that e3-e4 is answered by ...f7-f5! in order to gain control over d5) 7 ♗d2 (after 7 0-0 ♗xc3 8 bxc3 ♘e4, followed by ...♘a5, with control over the light squares is the correct response) 7...0-0 8 0-0 ♗xc3!? 9 ♗xc3 ♘e4 10 ♖c1 a5 11 h3 ♗xf3 12 ♗xf3 f5 with a solid position for Black in M.Taus-P.Nowak, Plzen 1996.

b) 6 ♗d2 works against ...♗b4, so Black consequently plays 6...♗e7. After 7 cxd5 exd5 8 ♗e2 0-0 9 h3 ♗h5 10 ♖c1 ♗d6 11 ♕b3 ♘a5 12 ♕a4 ♘c6 13 ♕b5?! a6 14 ♕b3 ♘a5 15 ♕c2 ♗g6 16 ♗d3 ♗xd3 17 ♕xd3 ♘c6 18 a3 ♖e8 19 0-0 ♘e7 Black had no problems in I.Peroutka-B.Vyhnalek, Nachod 1998.

6...♗xf3!?

I prefer this move to 6...♗h5, since

after 7 cxd5 exd5 White can try to seize the initiative with 8 ♗b5 ♗d6 9 g4!? ♗g6 10 ♘e5 0-0 11 ♘xc6 bxc6 12 ♗xc6 ♖b8. G.Timoshenko-A.Gross, Metz 1995, continued 13 0-0 ♖b6 14 ♗xd5 ♘xd5 15 ♘xd5 ♗e4 (15...♕h4 16 ♕f3! was not good enough for Black in A.Kolev-G.Gross, St Ingbert 1989), and now 16 ♘xb6 ♕h4 17 ♕e2! cxb6 18 f3 ♗d3 19 ♕g2 ♗xf1 20 ♔xf1 ♗b4 21 ♗d2 ♗xd2 22 ♕xd2 ♕xh3+ 23 ♕g2 ♕h6 24 ♖e1 would have given White a clear endgame advantage.

7 ♕xf3 ♗b4 8 ♗d3

8 ♗d2 is best met by 8...♗xc3 9 ♗xc3 ♘e4 with similar ideas to the note with 6 ♗e2 ♗b4 above. Instead, after 8 cxd5 exd5 9 ♗d3 0-0 10 ♗d2 a6 11 0-0 Bronznik gives 11...♖e8 12 ♖fc1 ♕d6 13 a3 ♗xc3 14 ♗xc3 ♘e4 15 ♗e1 ♖e6 16 b4 ♖f8 17 ♖ab1 f5 with counterplay, but slightly adjusting the move order by 11...♕d6!? 12 ♖fc1 ♖ae8 13 a3 ♗xc3 14 ♗xc3 ♘e4 15 ♗e1 f5, gaining two tempi on the previous line, seems even more accurate.

8...e5!

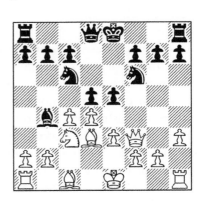

9 cxd5 ♕xd5 10 ♕xd5 ♘xd5 11 ♗d2

0-0-0 12 ♗e4!

12 ♘xd5?! is rightly dismissed by Bronznik. After 12...♗xd2+ 13 ♔xd2 ♖xd5 14 ♗f5+ ♔b8 15 ♗e4 ♖d6 16 ♗xc6 ♖xc6 White has to struggle for a draw, as 17 dxe5 allows 17...♖d8+ 18 ♔e2 ♖c2+.

12...♘f6 13 ♗f5+

After 13 ♗xc6 exd4 14 ♘e4 (14 ♗e4 dxc3 15 ♗f5+ ♔b8 16 bxc3 ♗a5 is no alternative) 14...♗xd2+ 15 ♔xd2 bxc6 16 ♘xf6 gxf6 Black is a pawn up and has the better chances, despite his pitiful pawn structure.

13...♔b8 14 a3 ♗a5 15 dxe5 ♘xe5 16 b4 ♘c4! 17 ♗c1 ♗b6 18 ♖a2 ♖he8 19 0-0 c6

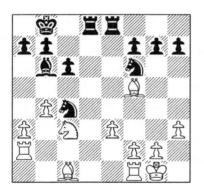

The opening phase is complete and it is time to take a look at the position. White has two bishops, but the knight on c4 is well placed and momentarily dominates the bishop on c1, and in addition to that, Black has occupied the central files with his rooks. All in all, the position is roughly equal.

20 ♗b1 ♖d7 21 ♖c2 ♖ed8 22 ♗a2 ♘e5 23 ♘a4 ♘d3 24 ♘xb6 axb6 25 f3 ♘xc1 26 ♖fxc1 ♘d5 27 ♔f2 b5!

White has managed to free himself while remaining with a now strong bishop, but Black has sufficient counterplay as the white pawns on the queenside are weak.

28 ♖d1 f6 29 ♖d4 ♘b6 30 ♖xd7 ♖xd7 31 ♔e2 ♔c7 32 f4 ♖d8 33 g4 ♖a8 34 ♖c3 ♘a4 35 ♖d3 ♘b2 36 ♖d4 ♘c4 37 ♗xc4 bxc4 38 ♖xc4 ♖xa3 39 h4 b6 40 ♔f3 ♖d3 41 f5 ♖d5 42 ♔f4 h6 43 g5 hxg5+ 44 hxg5 ♖d1 45 b5 c5 46 ♖a4 ♔b7 47 ♖a2 ♖f1+ 48 ♔e4 c4 49 ♖c2 ♖b1 50 ♖xc4 ♖xb5 51 ♔f4 ♖b1 52 ♖c2 b5 53 ♖h2 b4 54 ♖h7 ♔c6 55 ♔e4 b3 56 gxf6 gxf6 57 ♖h8 ♔c7 58 ♖h7+ ♔c6 59 ♖h8 ½-½

White plays 4 ♘c3

For those players who like to avoid the complications arising from 4 cxd5, **4 ♘c3** is the most popular move. To find out why this is the case, let's take a look at the position after **4...e6 5 cxd5 exd5 6 ♗g5 ♗e7 7 ♗xe7 ♘gxe7 8 e3**.

For the moment the position is definitely not oozing excitement. As opposed to the previous game, White has managed to trade his dark-squared

bishop for its black counterpart,

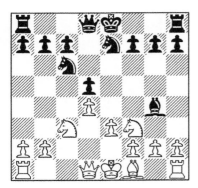

and as a result is provided with a plan that even has some chances of success: playing on the half-open c-file combined with the launch of a minority attack, hoping to procure a backward pawn on c6 that he can then besiege.

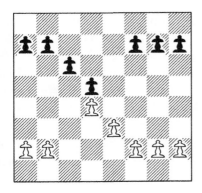

All in all, the position bears a certain resemblance to the Queen's Gambit Declined, but the set-up of the black pieces is much more dynamic here. There are times where a black attack on the kingside almost appears out of thin air, the following game being a good example.

Game 48
A.Plueg-C.Wisnewski
Hamburg 2003

1 d4 d5 2 c4 ♘c6 3 ♘f3 ♗g4 4 ♘c3

4...e6

Black must remember not to play 4...♘f6? here, as it transposes to the unsound variation 3 ♘c3 ♘f6 4 ♘f3 (or 4 cxd5 ♘xd5 5 ♘f3 ♗g4?) 4...♗g4? 5 cxd5 ♘xd5 already dismissed in Chapters 7 and 8 (see the first note to Game 38 for more details).

5 cxd5

5 ♗g5 ♗e7 6 ♗xe7 ♘gxe7 can transpose to the text after 7 cxd5 if Black plays 7...exd5, but there is an alternative in the shape of 7...♘xd5!?. After 8 e3 (8 ♘xd5 ♕xd5 9 e3 ♗xf3 10 gxf3 e5 gives Black a clearly superior version of Chapter 10) 8...0-0 9 ♗e2 ♘xc3 10 bxc3 ♘a5 (planning ...c7-c5) 11 ♕a4 b6 12 ♖d1 ♕d6 13 0-0 ♖fd8 14 ♖fe1 ♖ac8 15 ♖d2 ♗xf3 (this trade is important, as 15...c5 16 dxc5 sees the bishop unattended) 16 ♗xf3 c5 White had no coun-

counterplay in K.Hulak-M.Muse, Vinkovci 1993.

5...exd5 6 ♗g5

Here 6 ♕b3!? can be dangerous if not treated accordingly.

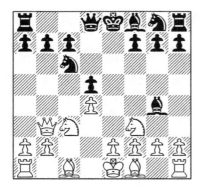

After 6...♗xf3?! 7 exf3 ♞xd4 8 ♕xb7 8...♖b8 White has 9 ♕xa7! (instead of 9 ♕a6, as given by Bronznik in the first edition of *Die Tschigorin-Verteidigung*), when S.Giemsa-O.Teschke, German League 2002, continued 9...♞c2+ 10 ♔d1 ♞xa1 11 ♗b5+ ♖xb5 12 ♖e1+ ♔d7 (12...♗e7 is not able to save the line, for example 13 ♞xb5 c6 14 ♞d4 ♕c8 15 b3 intending ♗a3 and Black is lost; while 12...♞e7!? 13 ♞xb5 f6 14 ♞xc7+ ♔f7 15 ♞e6 ♕c8 16 ♞d4 remains difficult for Black) 13 ♞xb5 ♗b4 and now the simple 14 ♗d2 would have led to a great advantage for White.

The correct answer is 6...♗b4, for example 7 ♞e5 (or 7 a3 ♗xc3+ 8 bxc3 ♗xf3 9 exf3 ♞a5 and Black can try to exploit the weaknesses in his opponent's pawn structure) 7...♞xd4! 8 ♕d1 ♞c6 9 ♞xg4 d4 and Black wins back the piece following 10 a3 ♗e7 11 ♞e4 h5, after which the game will be equal.

6...♗e7 7 ♗xe7 ♞gxe7 8 e3 0-0

9 ♗e2

9 ♗d3 is the other popular choice, which prevents Black from adopting the set-up used in the actual game, as 9...♕d6? runs into 10 ♗xh7+! ♔xh7 11 ♞g5+ ♔g6 12 ♕g4 f5 13 ♕f4 ♕xf4 14 exf4 ♞xd4 15 0-0-0 when White is clearly better. The proper response is 9...f5!? with ideas similar to those in the text; for example 10 h3 (or 10 ♕b3 ♗xf3 11 gxf3 ♖b8 12 0-0-0 b5 13 ♞e2 ♕d6 with good attacking chances for Black) 10...♗xf3 11 ♕xf3 f4!? 12 ♕g4 fxe3 13 fxe3 ♞b4 14 ♗b1 ♕d6 15 a3 ♕f6!? 16 ♞d1 (16 axb4 ♕f2+ 17 ♔d1 ♕xb2 18 ♖a2 ♕xb4 gives Black two pawns and an attack for the sacrificed piece) 16...♞bc6 and the white king was caught in the middle in E.Bukic-J.Barle, Slovenian Championship 1995.

9...♕d6!

An excellent square for the queen.

10 h3 ♗h5

10...♗xf3!? is even better. I was afraid of 11 ♗xf3 f5?! 12 ♕b3 ♖ad8 blocking the c6-knight's way, but the simple 11...♞d8 leaves Black a tempo up on the game. For example, 12 0-0 c6 13 g3 ♘e6 14 ♗g2 f5 15 ♖b1 ♔h8 16 b4 b5 17 a4 a6 18 h4 ♘c8 19 ♘e2 ♘b6 20 a5 ♘c4 and Black was better in D.Feofanov-V.Orlov, St Petersburg 2005.

11 0-0 ♘d8!

After being redeployed to e6, the knight serves a dual purpose: it keeps an eye on c5 (which is often used as an outpost in this structure) and supports the thrust ...f7-f5-f4.

12 ♖c1

12 ♘b5?! is an inferior attempt to prevent Black from consolidating his queenside: for example, 12...♕b6 13 a4?! (but 13 ♘e5 ♗xe2 14 ♕xe2 c6 15 ♘c3 ♕c7 is also comfortable for Black) 13...♗xf3! 14 ♗xf3 c6 15 ♘c3 (not 15 ♘d6? ♕c7) 15...♕xb2 with an extra pawn.

12...c6 13 ♘a4 ♘e6 14 ♘c5 ♘xc5 15 ♖xc5

Playing by numbers. White's next goal is to begin the typical minority attack with b2-b4-b5.

15...♗xf3!

By eliminating the knight Black

provides a basis for two themes quite common in the Chigorin Defence: the kingside attack and the 'good' knight versus 'bad' bishop.

16 ♗xf3 f5 17 g3 ♖f6 18 ♕b3 ♖b8 19 ♖c3 a6!

A prophylactic move, recognizing the 'threat' 20 ♕a3.

20 ♕a3 ♕d7 21 ♗g2 ♘c8 22 ♕a5 ♘d6

The knight has reached its final destination.

23 ♖c2 ♔h8 24 h4 ♖g8 25 a4 g5 26 hxg5 ♖xg5 27 ♗f3

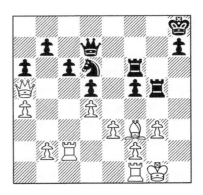

27...♘e4

Although clearly better, it is not easy for Black to improve his position. 27...f4?! is not as strong as it looks, as after 28 exf4 ♖xf4 29 ♕d2 ♕f7 30 ♗g2 the pawn shield is still intact. However, 27...h5!? is interesting: White needs to prevent 28...h4, but after 28 ♔g2 (intending 28...h4 29 ♖h1) 28...f4! 29 exf4 ♖xf4 30 ♕d2 ♕f5 Black has a strong attack, since the bishop cannot retreat to g2 this time.

28 ♔g2 ♕d6 29 ♗xe4 fxe4

Black still has a commanding position, but it seems that White can withstand the siege.

30 ♖h1 ♖f3 31 ♖h3 ♖gf5 32 ♕e1 ♖f7 33 ♖h4 ♕f6 34 ♕d2 ♖g7 35 ♖f4 ♖xf4 36 exf4 h5 37 ♕e3 a5 38 ♖c1 ♖h7 39 b3 ♔g7 40 f3 h4 41 fxe4 hxg3 42 exd5 ♖h2+ 43 ♔g1 ♕h4 44 ♕e5+ ½-½

Despite its innocent appearance, **6 ♗f4** is a whole lot niftier than 6 ♗g5. Intending to let the light-squared bishop grasp at nothing after 7 ♘e5, it usually prompts Black to play **6...♗xf3**. Then as **7 gxf3** covers the e4-square, 7...♗b4 doesn't make sense – Black should only seek to swap this bishop for the knight if he is able to get a firm grip on the light squares.

A more appropriate post for the bishop is on d6, and Black can place it there at once as, after **7...♗d6**, the d-pawn is indirectly protected by 8 ♘xd5 ♘xf4 9 ♘xf4 ♕xd4. If White renews the threat with **8 ♗g3**, then following **8...♘ge7 9 e3** we have reached the critical position for this variation.

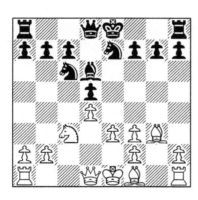

Now 9...a6 10 ♕c2 h5 11 0-0-0 h4 is assessed as 'unclear' by Bronznik. Having experimented with this line in nu-

merous games, I cannot agree with this conclusion. In fact it is quite difficult for Black to get anything going: after 12 ♗xd6 ♕xd6 13 ♗h3 the position remains difficult, and limiting the scope of the bishop with 13...g6 14 ♔b1 f5 15 f4 0-0-0 doesn't much help, as White can easily create good play on the queenside with 16 ♘a4.

A more compelling idea seems to be **9...0-0!?**, orientating the forces to the kingside in case counterplay is needed there; i.e. should White still decide to initiate his own play on the queenside. I have only found a handful of games featuring this move, but the results of my analysis are promising.

Game 49
W.Schoebel-R.Vidonyak
Passau 1997

1 d4 d5 2 c4 ♘c6 3 ♘f3 ♗g4 4 ♘c3 e6 5 cxd5

After 5 ♗f4 Black can choose between 5...♗b4, which usually transposes to Chapter 6 after 6 e3 (see Games 34 and 35), and 5...♗d6; for example, 6 ♘e5 (6 ♗g3 ♘ge7 7 e3 a6 was just equal in F.Baumbach-R.Marszalek, Warsaw 1988) 6...♗xe5! 7 dxe5 d4 8 ♘e4 ♕e7 9 a3 0-0-0 10 ♕b3 f6 and Black enjoyed a significant advantage in S.Rothman-M.Vecek, correspondence 1998.

5...exd5 6 ♗f4 ♗xf3 7 gxf3 ♗d6 8 ♗g3

8 ♘xd5 ♗xf4 9 ♘xf4 ♕xd4 10 ♕xd4 ♘xd4 led straight to equality in T.Henrichs-R.Rabiega, Altenkirchen

2005, which continued 11 0-0-0 ♖d8 12 e3 ♘e6 13 ♖xd8+ ♔xd8 14 ♘xe6+ fxe6 15 ♖g1 g6 16 ♗c4 ♔e7 17 ♖g5 ♔d6 and a draw was soon agreed.

8...♘ge7 9 e3 0-0!?

Bronznik doesn't mention this move, but I find it quite compelling. I played the more common 9...a6 for a while, but realized that Black has problems in this line. For example, 10 ♕c2 h5 11 0-0-0 h4 (Bronznik stops here, assessing the position as "unclear") 12 ♗xd6 ♕xd6 13 ♗h3 g6 14 ♔b1 f5 15 f4 0-0-0 16 ♘a4 b6 17 a3 ♔b7 18 ♖d3 ♖hg8 19 ♖c3 g5 20 fxg5 f4 21 ♖c1 and White had a significant advantage on the queenside in V.Epishin-T.Bromann, Copenhagen 2002. I tried to improve on that game with 15...♘d8 16 ♘e2 ♘e6 17 ♘c1 0-0-0, but after 18 ♘d3 g5 19 fxg5 ♘xg5 20 ♗f1 ♖df8 21 ♖c1 c6 22 a3 ♖hg8 23 ♔a2 ♖f6 24 ♕a4 ♘e4 25 ♖c2 ♕c7 26 f3 ♘d6 27 ♘e5 I still fell behind in V.Epishin-C.Wisnewski, Kiel 2004.

10 ♗d3

The most logical move. After 10 a3, then 10...♕d7 was played in Z.Izoria-A.Chibukhchian, Yerevan (rapid) 2004,

but eventually failed after 11 ♘b5 ♗xg3 12 hxg3 ♘d8? 13 ♕c2 ♘g6 14 ♕xc7 with an extra pawn. Instead, 10...f5?! was tried in Y.Seirawan-B.Finegold, US Championship 1994, but Black still hit on problems after 11 f4 ♕d7 12 ♗g2 ♕e6 13 0-0 ♘d8 14 b4 c6 15 b5. Therefore I suggest 10...a6, probably with similar play to the text after 11 ♗d3 f5 12 ♗xd6 ♕xd6 13 f4.

10...f5! 11 ♗xd6 ♕xd6 12 f4 a6 13 ♖c1 ♖ae8

The game J.Rejfir-E.Zinner, Luhacovice 1935, featured (by transposition) a different idea: 13...♔h8 14 a3 ♖f6 15 ♕f3 ♖g8 16 h4 ♖h6 17 ♘a4 ♘d8 18 ♘c5 and now, instead of dropping a pawn with 18...b6? 19 ♘xa6, Black should have played 18...a5, intending ...b6, which results in a nice position.

14 ♕f3 ♘b8

The knight has a long journey to make until he finally gets to e4, but it is worth it.

15 a3 c6 16 ♘a4 ♘d7 17 0-0 ♘f6 18 ♘c5 ♖b8 19 ♖c2 ♘e4

Black has obtained a very nice position. The bishop is completely useless, and White is far from having any initiative on the queenside. Black's next logical objective is a kingside attack.

20 ♖fc1 ♖f6 21 ♗f1 ♖h6 22 ♘d3 g5

It would have been nice if this thrust could have been additionally prepared by ...♔h8 and ...♖g8, but with a white knight threatening to go to e5, Black does not have that kind of luxury.

23 ♕d1 gxf4 24 f3

After the natural-looking 24 ♘xf4, Black plays 24...♘g6 25 f3 ♘g5 26 ♖g2 ♕e7 and then, besides the kingside attack, playing against the e3-pawn is another item on his agenda.

24...♖g6+

Now 24...♘g5 is not as effective, since after 25 ♖g2 ♖g6 26 ♘xf4 ♖g7 27 ♔f2 Black cannot easily get his other knight into action.

25 ♔h1 ♘f6 26 ♘xf4 ♖g7 27 ♗d3 ♘g6! 28 ♘xg6 hxg6

Black has successfully repaired his pawn structure and remains with the

superior minor piece.

29 ♖g2 ♔f7 30 ♕b3 ♖h7 31 ♔g1 ♕e7 32 e4

This ultimately fails, but it is understandable that White didn't want to await a slow death without counterplay.

32...fxe4 33 fxe4 ♘xe4 34 ♖xc6 bxc6 35 ♕xb8 ♖h4

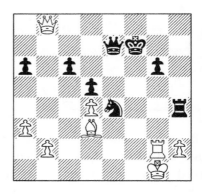

36 ♗xa6?!

This completely neglects the safety of his own king, but White's position was difficult anyway. For example, 36 ♗xe4 eliminates the powerful knight, and White can even protect his highly endangered king, but it means abandoning his d-pawn. After 36...♖xe4 37 ♖f2+ ♔g7 38 ♕g3 ♖xd4 Black has a decisive endgame advantage.

36...♘d6 37 ♖g3 ♘f5 38 ♖f3 ♖g4+ 39 ♔f1 ♕g5 40 ♕c7+ ♔g8 41 ♕c8+ ♔h7 42 ♕d7+ ♔h6 43 ♖h3+ ♘h4 44 ♖e3 ♕f4+ 45 ♔e2 ♖g2+ 46 ♔d3 ♕f1+ 47 ♔c3 ♕c1+ 0-1

Summary

3 ♘f3 is a sensible move, as long as it is followed up appropriately. 4 ♕a4 can lead to quick victories against players to whom the implications are unfamiliar, but proper ways to react can be seen in Games 45 and 46. Game 47 featured the harmless 4 e3, but the increasing popularity of 4 ♘c3 is not for nothing. Nevertheless, I am surprised that the idea from Game 49 has not been played more often, and I strongly urge you to try it.

1 d4 d5 2 c4 ♘c6 3 ♘f3 ♗g4 (D) 4 ♘c3

    4 ♕a4 ♗xf3 (D)

        5 exf3 e5 – *Game 45*

        5 gxf3 e6 – *Game 46*

    4 e3 e6 – *Game 47*

4...e6 5 cxd5 exd5 6 ♗f4

    6 ♗g5 – *Game 48*

6...♗xf3 7 gxf3 ♗d6 (D) – *Game 49*

3...♗g4   4...♗xf3   7...♗d6

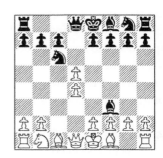

Chapter Ten

1 d4 d5 2 c4 ♘c6
3 ♘f3 ♗g4 4 cxd5 ♗xf3

As we have seen in the previous chapter, after **3 ♘f3 ♗g4**, keeping the central tension does not really benefit White. In consequence **4 cxd5** takes the bull by the horns, and a quick look reveals that 4...♕xd5? 5 ♘c3 is bad:

The d-pawn enjoys sufficient protection, which renders any black counterplay in the centre non-existent. Any black queen move will be followed up by 6 d5, after which White enjoys a tremendous advantage in space. A rather sad display was given in

A.Alekhine-V.Nenarokov, Moscow 1907: 5...♕a5 6 d5 0-0-0 7 ♗d2 ♗xf3 8 exf3 ♘b4 9 a3 ♘xd5 10 ♘a4 and significant material losses cannot be avoided.

Having witnessed this little mishap, the necessity of **4...♗xf3!** becomes evident. Now White must choose between three moves: 5 dxc6, 5 exf3 and 5 gxf3.

White plays 5 dxc6
The system after **5 dxc6 ♗xc6** is one of the few where Black is actually allowed

to keep his light-squared bishop on a long-term basis. White's intention is to build a strong pawn centre with pawns on e4 and d4; especially as, with the black queen's knight gone, pressure is taken off d4.

After **6 ♘c3**, Black has two options in 6...♘f6 and 6...e6. The first one, which usually involves a pawn sacrifice, will be briefly covered in the notes to our first game; although it is not bad, my recommendation is **6...e6**. Then the occupation of the centre with **7 e4** will be answered by **7...♗b4**, when Black's plan quickly becomes evident.

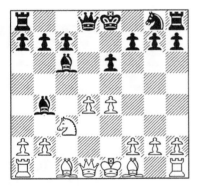

All of a sudden the white pawn centre doesn't look that strong anymore. Since opening the h1-a8 diagonal with 8 e5 is completely out of the question, the only sensible way to continue is with **8 f3** – but then **8...♕h4+! 9 g3 ♕h5** results in a further weakening.

The following ideas are simple: by playing ...0-0-0 and ...f7-f5, Black puts maximum pressure on the white centre – a strategy that is hard to meet, as we will see in our featured game.

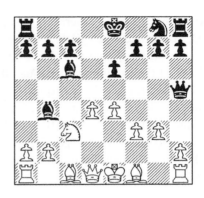

Game 50
E.Degtiarev-C.Wisnewski
German Championship,
Höckendorf 2004

---

1 d4 d5 2 c4 ♘c6 3 ♘f3 ♗g4 4 cxd5 ♗xf3 5 dxc6 ♗xc6

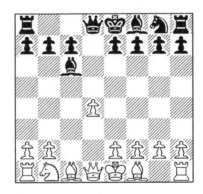

6 ♘c3

6 f3 usually transposes to the text by 6...e6 7 e4 ♗b4+ 8 ♘c3, but a few players will try to circumvent the resulting positions and play 7 ♘c3 instead. Then Black can try to exploit the slight weakness of the e1-h4 diagonal with

7...♗d6, after which the game S.Kraemer-T.Escher, German League 1993, continued 8 g3 (if 8 ♗e3 ♘e7 9 ♗f2 e5 and the game is at least equal) 8...h5 9 e4 (9 ♗g2 is not a serious alternative: 9...h4 10 ♔f2 f5 and the black bishops dominated in R.Koepcke-Y.Lapshun, Parsippany 2001) 9...h4 10 g4 a6! and Black had a good game as his bishops were out of harm's way.

6...e6

6...♘f6 is a popular alternative. Let's take a look at the possible consequences: 7 f3 e5 (7...e6 8 e4 is too passive, as there is no sensible way to put any pressure on the white centre in the near future) 8 dxe5 and now Black has two alternatives:

a) To my surprise, 8...♕xd1+?! is quite regularly played. Being a pawn down, Black needs to initiate some active play, and trading queens does not do the trick. After 9 ♔xd1 (9 ♘xd1 ♘d7 10 ♗f4 ♗b4+ 11 ♘c3 0-0 12 e4 ♖fe8 at least allowed Black to regain his pawn in M.Chetverik-H.Dusper, Harkany 1994) 9...0-0-0+ (another try is 9...♘d7, but then 10 e6 fxe6 11 e4 ♘b6 12 ♗e3

♘a4 13 ♘b5 ♘xb2+ 14 ♔c2 ♗xb5 15 ♗xb5+ c6 16 ♗xc6+ bxc6 17 ♔xb2 led to a significant endgame advantage for White in V.Karasev-V.Akopian, Dnepropetrovsk 1970) 10 ♔c2 ♘d7 11 e6 fxe6 12 e4 ♗d6 13 ♗g5 ♖de8, as in F.De la Fuente Gonzalez-L.Bass, Collado Villalba 2003, White could have played 14 ♗b5 with the better position.

b) 8...♘d7 is more suitable. Now returning the pawn immediately with 9 e6 favours Black, for example 9...fxe6 10 e4 ♗d6 11 ♗e3 ♕h4+ 12 ♗f2 ♕h6 13 ♗c4 0-0-0 and Black was clearly better in M.Brigden-A.Miles, Bristol 1982. Instead, after 9 ♗f4 things are not so clear:

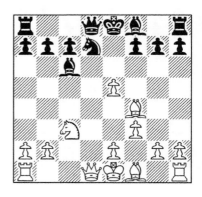

b1) 9...♕h4+?! 10 ♗g3 ♕h5 was played in L.Santolini-C.Cuartas, Reggio Emilia 1981, but after 11 f4 and 12 e3, Black's compensation for the pawn is rather shady.

b2) 9...♗b4, while common in other lines, is probably the wrong place for the bishop: 10 ♕b3 ♕h4+ (before proceeding to e7, the queen provokes g2-g3 to cut off the bishop's retreat; but that move has its merits too, as we will see soon enough, so 10...♕e7 seems to make more sense, but then after 11 0-0-0 Black will not be able to capture on e5 anytime soon) 11 g3 ♕e7 12 ♗h3 ♘c5 13 ♕c2 g5 14 ♗d2 ♕xe5 (or 14...♖d8 15 0-0-0 ♕xe5 16 ♕f5! ♕xf5 17 ♗xf5 h6 18 h4 ♖g8 19 hxg5 hxg5 20 ♖h5 with a clear advantage) 15 a3 ♗a5 (15...♗xf3 16 0-0 doesn't change anything) 16 b4 ♗xf3 17 0-0 and White went on to win in V.Babula-M.Kaminski, Lazne Bohdanec 1996.

b3) 9...♗c5 is much better: 10 ♕b3 ♕e7 (10...g5?! is not as good; after 11 ♗g3 ♕e7 12 e6! fxe6 13 ♗xc7 Black's compensation is hardly sufficient) 11 0-0-0 0-0-0 (on 11...♘xe5?! 12 ♘d5! is awkward) 12 e4 was seen in G.Dizdar-H.Porth, Hamburg 1993, and now instead of 12...g5?! Black should have played 12...♘xe5 13 ♘d5 ♗xd5 14 ♖xd5 ♖xd5 15 ♕xd5 f6 when the chances would have been equal.

b4) The aggressive 9...g5!? would be my favoured choice. S.Wehmeier-M.De Putter, Vlissingen 2000, continued 10 ♗g3 ♗g7 11 e6 fxe6 12 e4 ♘e5 13 ♕b3 ♕e7 14 ♖d1 (14 0-0-0 0-0 15 ♗c4 ♖ae8 16 ♔b1 b5! led to sharp play in E.Ibanez-W.Arencibia, Badalona 1995) 14...0-0 15 ♗e2 a6 16 0-0 ♘g6 17 ♖fe1 and now 17...♗e5 promises interesting play.

7 e4

7 e3 is a rather poor choice. After 7...♗b4 and either 8 f3 ♕h4+ 9 g3 ♕h5 10 ♗g2 0-0-0 11 a3 ♗a5 12 b4 ♗b6 13 0-0 e5 14 d5 ♘f6 15 f4 ♕xd1 16 ♖xd1 ♗d7 17 fxe5 ♘g4 (G.Ballon-G.Baches Garcia, Sitges 2003), or 8 ♗e2 ♘f6 9 0-0

0-0 10 ♗f3 ♘d5 11 ♘xd5 exd5 12 a3 ♗d6 13 b4 a6 14 ♗b2 f5 (Escher-C.Wisnewski, Internet blitz 2002), Black gets the better game. 7 a3 ♕h4 8 e3 0-0-0 is no alternative either.

7...♗b4 8 f3

8 ♕d3?! fails to meet the required standard, due to 8...♕h4! when the only way to save the pawn is 9 e5, but after 9...0-0-0 10 ♗e3 ♘e7 the white centre just aroused pity in A.Joppien-C.Wisnewski, Kiel 2003.

8...♕h4+ 9 g3 ♕h5

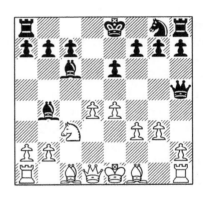

10 ♗e3

Besides the text move, White has several alternatives:

a) 10 ♗g2 0-0-0 11 ♗e3 transposes to the game, while 11 0-0 runs into 11...♖xd4!.

b) 10 ♗d3?! is rarely played, since this is not the right place for the bishop, and Black can initiate play against d4 immediately with 10...0-0-0 11 ♗e3 ♗a5!, followed by ...♗b6, as in H.Zoebisch-W.Wittmann, Austrian League 1981.

c) 10 ♗c4?! is also dubious. After 10...0-0-0 11 ♗e3 ♗c5! 12 0-0 ♘e7 White experienced severe problems in K.Schlenga-A.Bartel, German League 1991; the ideas are ...e6-e5 or ...♗xd4 followed by ...e6-e5.

d) 10 ♗e2, when Black can play similarly to the game with 10...0-0-0 11 ♗e3 (11 ♕b3?! ♖xd4 12 ♗e3 was beautifully countered by 12...♗a4!! in Rolle-Stek, correspondence 1990) 11...f5! 12 ♕b3 ♗xc3+ 13 bxc3 fxe4 14 ♕xe6+ (14 fxe4 ♕g6 just drops the e4-pawn) 14...♗d7 15 ♕xe4 ♘f6 (improving on 15...♖e8?! 16 ♕d3 ♘e7 17 c4 ♘f5 18 ♗f4! and White was better in J.Granda Zuniga-A.Morozevich, Amsterdam 1995) 16 ♕e5 ♕f7! 17 ♕a5 (not 17 0-0? ♖he8 18 ♕f4 ♕e6 and White loses a piece) 17...♘d5 and Black had a strong initiative for the pawn in J.Verdier-J.Gather, correspondence 1998; for example, if 18 ♕xa7 ♗c6 19 ♗d2 ♖he8 20 ♔f2 ♖xe2+! 21 ♔xe2 ♖e8+ 22 ♔f2 ♘e3 and Black is winning.

10...0-0-0 11 ♗g2 f5

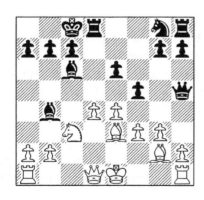

12 ♕b3

Instead:

a) 12 0-0 allows Black to exert more pressure on the white centre with

12...♘f6, when 13 e5 (13 exf5 exf5 was obviously better for Black in M.Kaabi-E.Repkova Eid, Cairo 1997) 13...♗xc3 14 bxc3 ♘d5 15 ♗d2 (15 ♕d2 ♘b6! 16 ♕e2 ♗d5 17 ♖fc1 ♘c4 18 ♖ab1 g5 left Black in complete control in H.Rau-W.Arztmann, Feffernitz 2004) 15...f4 16 ♕e2 ♕g6 17 ♕f2 fxg3 18 hxg3 h5 gave Black good attacking chances in V.Akopian-A.Reprintsev, USSR Team Championship 1990.

b) 12 ♕c2?! is even worse: 12...fxe4 13 fxe4 ♘f6 14 e5 ♘g4 15 ♗xc6 ♘xe3 and Black soon won in J.Waffenschmidt-N.Gospodinow, Neumünster 2000.

12...fxe4 13 fxe4

13 ♕xb4? runs into 13...exf3 14 ♗f1 f2+, while 13 ♕xe6+ ♔b8 14 fxe4 ♘f6 gives Black more than enough for the pawn.

13...♗xc3+ 14 ♕xc3

Or 14 bxc3 ♘f6 15 ♕xe6+ ♔b8 again with good compensation in J.F.Campos-E.Mendez Ataria, Buenos Aires 1996.

14...♘f6

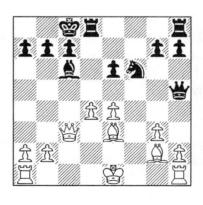

After this move the position is assessed as unclear by Bronznik. Indeed, the position is not easy to play, but in my opinion it is White who has to be more careful – the unsafe position of the king and the unstable centre being only two important factors.

15 ♖c1 ♖d7 16 ♕a3 ♗b5 17 ♖c2

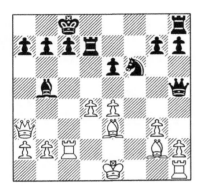

17...♗a6

Protecting the a-pawn with 17...♔b8 would have been better, after which White should probably play 18 ♕c5 ♕xc5 19 ♖xc5 ♗c6 20 ♖f1 ♗xe4 21 ♗xe4 ♘xe4 22 ♖e5 ♘d6 23 ♖xe6 when chances are roughly equal.

18 ♔d2 ♕g6 19 ♔c1 ♘xe4

Picking up the e-pawn, but now White manages to create sufficient counterplay.

20 ♗f1! ♗xf1 21 ♕xa7?

White loses the thread. 21 ♖xf1 would have been the right move, when 21...a6 22 ♖f8+ ♖xf8 23 ♕xf8+ ♖d8 24 ♕e7 ♖d7 25 ♕f8+ leads to a draw by repetition.

21...♖f7! 22 ♕a8+ ♔d7 23 ♕xb7

It was probably now that White realized that 23 ♕xh8 loses, as after 23...♗d3 24 ♖g2 e5! the white king is

unable to escape.

23..♖c8 24 d5 e5 25 ♕b3 ♘d6 26 ♕a4+ ♗b5 27 ♕a7 ♕d3 28 b3 ♕xd5 29 ♖d1

Allowing a neat finish.

29...♕xd1+

And White resigned in view of 30 ♔xd1 ♖f1+ 31 ♔d2 ♘e4 mate.

0-1

It should be pointed out that my opponent had already played this line in an earlier round of the tournament and therefore was not completely caught off guard. Looking at the difficulties he experienced in the game, there is only one conclusion: White has to get rid of the bishop, one way or another.

White plays 5 exf3?!

This move fully deserves its doubtful reputation. Without being coerced White 'produces' an isolated pawn on d4; and even though this pawn will be traded off most of the time, the devaluated white pawn structure provides Black with a long-term endgame advantage thanks to his queenside majority.

The only trump card White might have left in this position are his two bishops, but in most cases Black is successful in dissolving this factor rather quickly.

Game 51
J.Rotstein-A.Kalka
Essen 2000

---

1 d4 d5 2 ♘f3 ♘c6 3 c4 ♗g4 4 cxd5 ♗xf3 5 exf3?! ♕xd5 6 ♗e3 e5!

At first, eliminating White's biggest weakness doesn't seem to make much sense, but in return Black is rewarded

with smooth development. And what is more, after trading the central pawns Black enjoys a healthy endgame advantage due to his queenside majority.

7 ♘c3 ♗b4 8 dxe5

8 a3 is an attempt to keep a pawn in the centre. C.Burton-N.Davies, Chorley 1977, continued 8...♗xc3+ 9 bxc3 exd4 10 cxd4 ♘ge7 11 ♗d3 and now after 11...0-0-0! 12 ♕a4 ♘xd4, the complications favour Black; for example:

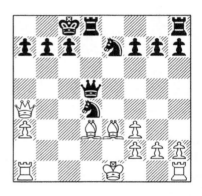

a) 13 ♕xa7 ♘xf3+ 14 gxf3 ♕xd3 15 ♕a8+ (if 15 ♖c1 ♘c6 16 ♕a8+ ♘b8 and Black is a safe pawn up) 15...♔d7 16 ♕xb7 ♖b8 17 ♕e4 ♕c3+ 18 ♔e2 ♕b2+ 19 ♗d2 ♕b5+ 20 ♕d3+ ♕xd3+ 21 ♔xd3 ♖b3+ 22 ♗c3 (22 ♔c2? ♖xf3 just loses a pawn) 22...♖hb8 and the black pieces are much more active.

b) 13 ♖d1 ♕b3! 14 ♕xb3 (if 14 ♕xa7 ♘ec6 15 ♕c5 ♖d5! 16 ♕c4 ♖hd8 and Black dominates the board; but not 15...♘xf3+?? 16 gxf3 ♖xd3 as 17 ♕f5+ picks up the rook) 14...♘xb3 15 ♗xa7 ♖d6 and Black has a tremendous endgame advantage in the shape of his passed c-pawn.

8...♕xe5 9 ♖c1 ♘ge7

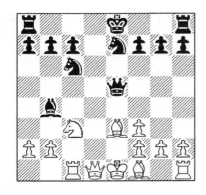

10 ♗c4

10 f4 is no real improvement: 10...♕e4 11 ♕d3 ♕xd3 12 ♗xd3 0-0-0 13 ♗c4 ♘d5 and Black was better in L.Klima-J.Jackova, Czech League 1995.

10...♘f5 11 0-0?!

11 ♕e2 saves the pawn, but after 11...♘cd4 12 ♗xd4 ♕xe2+ 13 ♔xe2 ♘xd4+ the queenside majority once more gives Black a lasting endgame advantage.

11...♘xe3 12 fxe3 ♗d6! 13 f4 ♕xe3+

After winning a pawn, winning the game is a matter of proper technique.

14 ♔h1 0-0 15 ♕g4 ♖ae8 16 ♖cd1 ♔h8 17 ♗d3 ♘d4 18 f5 ♕h6 19 h3

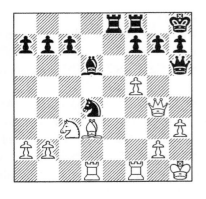

19...♖e3?

Unnecessarily complicating the position. 19...♗e5 would have maintained the advantage.

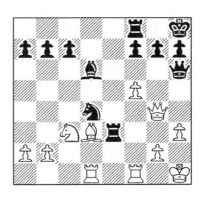

20 ♕xd4??

Immediately returning the favour. Instead, it would have been interesting to see what Black had planned after 20 ♘d5 ♖g3 21 ♕xd4 ♖xh3+ 22 ♔g1, as 22...♖h4 is now met by 23 ♕e3, shaking off the attack, while 22...♗h2+ is answered by 23 ♔f2 ♗g3+ 24 ♔e2 ♖e8+ 25 ♗e4 ♕h5+ 26 ♔d2 when Black's compensation is not evident.

20...♖xh3+ 21 ♔g1 ♖h4 22 ♕xh4 ♕xh4 23 ♖f3 ♗c5+ 0-1

White plays 5 gxf3

After **5 gxf3 ♕xd5 6 e3** Black once more has to make a choice between 6...e6 and 6...e5. Although both moves are perfectly playable, I do not like the resulting positions after 6...e6 7 ♘c3 ♕h5 8 f4 ♕xd1+ 9 ♔d1, as the early trade of queens does not go with my aggressive style. Therefore, I recommend the traditional (and most popular) **6...e5!**, when play continues **7 ♘c3**

♗b4 8 ♗d2 ♗xc3 9 bxc3, reaching a position which has to be examined in great detail.

It seems that White can be very satisfied here. He is in possession of two bishops, each one with a great potential; he has a massive pawn centre that is ready and willing to advance by c3-c4 and d4-d5, gaining more space and opening lines for his bishops; and he has two half-open files to occupy with his rooks, picking on the black pawns at b7 and g7. These strategic factors can hardly be denied – but they can also be fought against. Black's foremost concern should be to stop a possible pawn advance, and **9...♕d6!** does the trick.

Game 52
M.Konopka-M.Muse
European Cup, Clichy 1995

---

1 d4 d5 2 c4 ♘c6 3 ♘f3 ♗g4 4 cxd5 ♗xf3 5 gxf3 ♕xd5 6 e3 e5

6...e6 is more cautious. But the Chigorin Defence is not about caution, it's about rampage! So why not play that way?!

7 ♘c3 ♗b4 8 ♗d2 ♗xc3 9 bxc3 ♕d6!

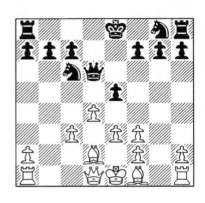

It is important for Black to fix the white centre, but 9...e4? does not work because of 10 ♗g2. Neither does 9...♘f6?!, as after 10 c4 (but not 10 e4? ♘xe4 11 fxe4 ♕xe4+) 10...♕d6 11 d5 ♘e7 12 ♖b1 b6 13 ♗b4 White was better in A.Saidy-M.Al Modiakhi, Las Vegas 2001. Finally, 9...exd4, although examined by Bronznik, is completely out of the question. Why release the tension and open the position for the pair of bishops at the same time?!

After 9...♕d6 White has to decide whether he wants to play on the b-file, the g-file or even both.

10 ♖b1

There are several adequate alternatives:

a) 10 ♖g1 ♘ge7 11 ♖b1 b6 is merely a transposition to the text.

b) 10 ♗d3 is harmless. After 10...♘ge7 11 0-0 0-0 12 ♕b1 ♘g6 13 ♕xb7?! ♘h4 14 ♗e4 f5! 15 ♕xc6 fxe4 16 ♕xd6 ♘xf3+ 17 ♔g2 cxd6 Black was clearly better in A.Mikhalev-B.Rositsan, Istanbul 2002.

c) 10 ♗g2 ♘ge7 11 ♖b1 (11 f4 exf4 12 e4 is a temporary pawn sacrifice which is quite common in this system; but in this particular line, Black can get a good game after 12...0-0 13 e5 ♕g6 14 0-0 ♘f5 15 ♗xf4 ♘h4 16 ♗g3 ♘xg2 17 ♔xg2 ♖ad8 as in V.Moskalenko-A.Morozevich, Moscow 1994) 11...b6 12 0-0 0-0 13 f4 exf4 14 e4 ♖ad8 15 e5 ♕h6 with unclear play according to Bronznik.

d) 10 f4 exf4 11 e4 ♘ge7 12 ♕f3 (12 ♗g2 returns to 10 ♗g2) 12...♘g6 13 h4 h5 again with unclear play; for example 14 e5 ♕e6 15 ♗h3 ♘xh4! (D.Bischoff-T.Schlager, Baden 2002) and now 16 ♕xf4 leads to a draw after ♕d5 17 0-0-0 ♘g6 18 ♕f5 ♕xa2 19 e6 ♕a1+.

e) 10 ♕b3 b6 11 ♗c4 has occurred in a few of my blitz games on the internet. Black can play 11...♘h6 and after 12 e4 exd4 13 ♗xh6 ♕xh6 14 ♗xf7+ ♔e7 his king is surprisingly safe. Thelen-C.Wisnewski, Internet (blitz) 2003, continued 15 ♗d5 ♖ad8 16 ♕c4 ♘e5! 17 ♕xc7+ ♔f6 18 cxd4 ♘xf3+ 19 ♔e2 ♘xd4+ 20 ♔d3 ♘e6 and the white king was in more danger than his black counterpart.

10...b6 11 ♖g1

The critical variation 11 f4!? exf4 12 e4 was introduced by Kasparov, and Black needs to be very careful here: 12...♘ge7 13 ♕f3 (13 ♗g2 transposes to 10 ♗g2 – see the note to White's 10th move) 13...0-0 (this time 13...♘g6 does not work well, as 14 e5 ♕e6 15 ♗b5 ♘ge7 16 ♗xf4 0-0 17 0-0 is just better for White) 14 ♗xf4 and now:

a) 14...♕e6 15 ♗xc7 (15 d5 is refuted by 15...♘xd5 16 ♗c4 ♖fe8 or 16 ♗h3 ♘e5! 17 ♕g3 ♘d3+ and Black wins, or if 15 ♗b5 f5! and Black strikes the white centre in due time) 15...♕xa2 16 ♖d1 (but not 16 ♗d3 ♕a5! 17 0-0 ♕xc3 18 d5 ♘e5 19 ♗xe5 ♕xe5 and Black is simply a pawn up) 16...♖ac8 17 ♗g3 f5! with attacking chances.

b) 14...♕a3!? is another possibility. After 15 ♗e2 (or 15 ♗g2 ♘g6 and now 16 ♗g3 is met by 16...f5! again, when 17 exf5 ♖ae8+ 18 ♔f1 ♘ce7 is much better for Black, or if 17 e5 ♘a5 and the bishops are not doing anything) 15...♘g6 (better than 15...f5?! 16 0-0 fxe4? 17 ♕xe4 ♕xc3 18 ♗e3 ♕a3 19 ♗d3! and White was winning in G.Kasparov-V.Smyslov, Candidates match, Vilnius 1984) 16 ♗g3 (16 ♗xc7 is too risky: 16...♖ac8 17 ♗g3 ♘ce7, when 18 0-0 ♖xc3 19 ♕h5 f5! and 18 ♖b3 ♕xa2 19 ♗d1 f5! both give Black good play, or if 18 c4 ♕a5+ 19 ♔f1 f5! with a strong initiative) 16...♕xa2 17 0-0 ♘ce7 18 ♗xc7 ♕e6 19 d5 (or 19 ♖fe1 ♖ac8 20 ♗g3 f5 and Black is afloat) 19...♕d7 is totally unclear; for example, 20 ♕g3 (or 20

♗g3 f5!) 20...f5 21 ♗b5 ♕c8 22 d6 f4 23
♕g5 ♘e5! 24 ♕h5 (24 ♕xe5 ♕g4+ leads
to perpetual check) 24...♘7g6.

11...♘ge7

12 f4

It is now too late for this idea as
Black can build up enough counterplay. 12 ♖xg7 is more interesting, although Black has enough compensation for the sacrificed pawn after
12...0-0-0 13 ♕a4 (13 ♖xf7? is too
greedy: 13...♕g6 14 ♗c4 ♘d5! and
White loses material) 13...♖he8 14 ♗b5
♔b7 15 ♖b3 exd4 16 cxd4 ♕xh2, as in
O.Cvitan-B.Maksimovic,   Yugoslav
Championship 1988.

12...exf4 13 e4 0-0-0

13...0-0 is also good; for example, 14
♕f3 ♘g6 15 e5 ♕e6 16 ♗xf4 ♕f5 17
♗d3 ♘cxe5! 18 dxe5 ♕xf4 and Black
won in E.Yepes Martinez-M.Narciso
Dublan, Terrassa 1994.

14 ♕g4+

14 ♖xg7? now loses to 14...♘xd4! 15
cxd4 ♕xd4; for example 16 ♗a6+ ♔b8

17 ♖xf7 ♕xe4+ 18 ♔f1 ♖xd2! or 18 ♗e2
♖hg8.

14...f5!

15 ♕xf4

15 exf5 is dangerous, as after
15...♖he8 16 ♗e2 (not 16 ♔d1? ♘xd4
and Black gets a ferocious attack)
16...♔b8 White has to play very precisely to maintain the balance.

15...♕a3 16 ♗c4 g6

The white king is nowhere to run.
Black has an excellent position.

**17 ♔f1 ♖hf8 18 ♖b3 ♕a4 19 ♗e6+ ♔b8
20 e5 ♘d5 21 ♕f3 ♕c4+ 22 ♔g2 ♘e3+!
23 ♗xe3 ♕xe6**

And again we have 'good' knight
versus 'bad' bishop.

**24 ♗g5 ♖d5 25 ♖gb1 ♖f7 26 ♖b5 ♖fd7
27 a4 a6 28 ♖5b3 ♔a7 29 ♗f6 g5 30
♔g1 g4 31 ♕f4 h5 32 ♕h6?**

Missing his opponent's reply, but
the position was by now hopeless
anyway.

**32...♘xe5! 33 dxe5 ♖d1+ 34 ♔g2 ♖7d3
35 ♖xd1 ♕d5+ 36 f3 ♕xf3+ 0-1**

Summary

While 5 dxc6 (Game 50) and 5 exf3 (Game 51) are simply inferior, the positions resulting after 5 gxf3 ♕xd5 6 e3 e5 are highly complicated and require deep study. I recommend that you look at these lines repeatedly from time to time, as the ideas that lie within are typical for the Chigorin Defence. Master them, and you master the whole opening.

1 d4 d5 2 c4 ♘c6 3 ♘f3 ♗g4 4 cxd5 ♗xf3 *(D)* **5 gxf3**

     5 dxc6 ♗xc6 6 ♘c3 e6 *(D)* – *Game 50*

     5 exf3 e6 – *Game 51*

5...♕xd5 6 e3 e5 *(D)* – *Game 52*

    4...♗xf3   *6...e6*   *6...e5*

Chapter Eleven

1 d4 d5 2 c4 ♘c6
3 e3 and 3 cxd5

Most games in this chapter feature the move order 2 c4 ♘c6 3 cxd5 ♛xd5, but **3 e3** is just as good, as the main line can still be reached after **3...e5 4 cxd5**. Adjusting the move order in this fashion offers White a few more options – options we are now going to examine.

White plays 3 e3 e5 4 dxe5

After **3 e3 e5**, **4 dxe5** takes up the gauntlet and accepts the (temporary) pawn sacrifice just offered to him. The resulting positions bear a close resemblance to the Albin Counter-Gambit, with White having played the inferior e2-e3 instead of the usual ♘g1-f3. The black queen's knight, on the other hand, is beautifully placed, exercising control over d4 and e5, while also ready and willing to join an eventual attack.

With **4...d4!** Black temporarily constricts White's freedom, aiming to regain his pawn with positional interest later; this is especially the case if White opts for the dubious 5 ♘f3?!. A better move is the more persistent 5 exd4, but Black still has the comfortable choice between winning his sacrificed pawn back or trying to make use of his lead in development, intending to exploit the weaknesses that have accrued in the white camp.

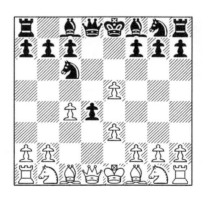

Game 53
R.Réti-E.Bogoljubow
German Championship, Kiel 1921

1 d4 d5 2 c4 ♘c6 3 e3 e5 4 dxe5

4 cxd5 ♕xd5 transposes to 3 cxd5 ♕xd5 4 e3 e5 and will be covered later (see Games 57-60). 4 ②f3 exd4 5 exd4 ②f6 transposes to a position from the English Opening, which we will examine in more detail in Chapter 13 (see Game 64).

4...d4 5 exd4

Instead:

a) 5 ②f3?! is highly unsound. After 5...♗b4+ 6 ♗d2 dxe3 7 fxe3 (7 ♗xb4 is even worse: 7...exf2+ 8 ♔e2 ♕xd1+ 9 ♔xd1 ②xb4 and White, already a pawn down, will have a hard time defending his e-pawn) 7...②ge7 8 ②c3 ②g6 9 ②d5 ♗xd2+ 10 ♕xd2 ②cxe5 Black has a clear advantage as the white pawn structure is shattered.

b) 5 a3 prevents the check on b4 but has the drawback of weakening b3. Black can play 5...a5! and then:

b1) 6 exd4 is worse than in the actual game. After 6...♕xd4 7 ♕xd4? (7 ②f3 ♕xd1+ 8 ♔xd1 ♗g4 is similar to 6 ②f3 in the text) 7...②xd4 White has to play the pitiful move 8 ♖a2 (8 ♔d1 ②b3 9 ♖a2 ♗f5 10 ②d2 0-0-0 is not desirable either) when Black's advantage after

8...♗f5 9 ②c3 0-0-0 is obvious.

b2) 6 ②f3 ♗c5 7 exd4 ♗xd4! 8 ②xd4 ♕xd4 9 ②c3 ♕xe5+ 10 ♗e2 (or 10 ♕e2 ♗e6 11 ♗e3 ②ge7 12 0-0-0 0-0 13 f4 ♕f6 14 ♕f3?! ②f5 15 ♗c5 ♖fd8 16 ♗e2? ②fd4 17 ♕f2 ♗f5 and White could resign in I.Celedon-C.Wisnewski, Internet blitz 2000) 10...②ge7 11 0-0 0-0 12 ♖e1 ♖d8 with a comfortable position in W.Weschke-M.Kahn, Baden Baden 1993.

5...♕xd4!

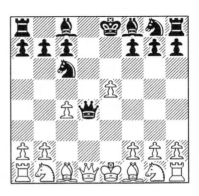

6 ♕xd4

6 ②f3?! is not convincing either. After 6...♕xd1+ 7 ♔xd1 ♗g4 8 ♗f4 0-0-0+ 9 ②bd2 ②ge7 10 a3 ②g6 11 ♗g3 ②gxe5 12 ♔c2 ②xf3 13 gxf3 ②d4+ 14 ♔c3 ②xf3 15 ②xf3 ♗xf3, White is now a pawn down with no compensation.

6...②xd4 7 ♗d3 ♗g4! 8 f3

Of course not 8 ②e2?? ♗xe2! 9 ♗xe2 ②c2+ and wins. Instead, 8 ♗e3 0-0-0 9 ②c3 was played in Muir-C.Wisnewski, Internet (blitz) 2001, and now after 9...②c6 Black could have regained the pawn with a better position.

8...♗e6 9 ♗e3 0-0-0 10 ♗xd4

10 ②e2? ②xf3+! 11 gxf3 ♖xd3 is clearly better for Black

10...♖xd4 11 ♔e2

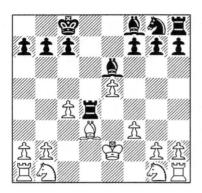

11...♞e7

Taking the pawn is also possible. After 11...♗xc4 12 ♗xc4 ♖xc4 13 ♞c3 (13 ♔d3?! is dubious: 13...♖c5 14 f4 ♖c1 15 ♔d2 ♖f1, when White's best chance is to give up a pawn with 16 ♔e2 ♖xf4) Black can play 13...♗a3!, winning at least a pawn.

12 ♞d2 ♞g6 13 ♗xg6 hxg6 14 b3 ♗f5

Preventing ♞d2-e4 and threatening 15...♗b4.

15 a3 ♗e7

Black is fully developed while the white kingside is still sleeping.

16 ♖a2 g5 17 ♔e1 ♖hd8 18 ♞e2 ♖d3

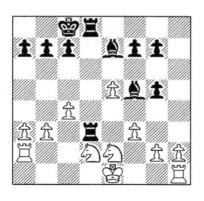

Despite being a pawn down, Black is completely dominant.

19 ♞g3 ♗g6 20 b4 ♖e3+ 21 ♔f2 ♖xe5

Now that Black has won his pawn back, the game is about over.

22 ♖e1 ♖xe1 23 ♔xe1 ♗d3 24 ♞ge4 ♖d4 25 c5 f5 26 ♞f2 ♗b5 27 ♞f1 ♗f6 28 ♖d2 ♖c4 29 ♞d1 ♖c1 30 ♔f2 f4 31 g3 ♗c3 32 ♞xc3 ♖xc3 33 ♖a2 ♗c4 34 ♖a1 ♖c2+ 35 ♔g1 ♗d5 0-1

White plays 3 cxd5 ♞xd5 4 ♞f3

4 ♞f3 seems to be an improvement on e2-e3, considering that it protects d4, does not restrict the dark-squared bishop and seems to work against ...e7-e5 – all at the same time! But these advantages are all of an imaginary nature, as the methodical advance **4...e5** is still possible (and necessary, as Black must be able to pin the queen's knight).

Tangling with the e-pawn is inadvisable, as after **5 dxe5?! ♛xd1+ 6 ♔xd1** the positional concessions are just too great. Not only can Black win the pawn back easily, his lead in development and White's inability to castle will result in a very comfortable position.

**1 d4 d5 2 c4 ♘c6 3 cxd5 ♕xd5 4 ♘f3 e5!
5 dxe5?!**

Accepting the pawn Black offered with his last move. In exchange, Black gets a quick lead in development and deprives White of his ability to castle. And even with the queens off the board, there is still enough attacking potential left. The stronger 5 ♘c3 will be covered in Games 55 and 56.

5...♕xd1+ 6 ♔xd1

6...♗g4

6...♗c5 is also possible; for example, 7 e3 (or 7 ♔e1 ♘b4 8 ♘a3 ♗e6 9 b3 0-0-0 10 e4 ♘e7 with compensation) 7...♗g4 8 ♗e2 (or 8 ♗b5 0-0-0+ 9 ♔e2?! ♘xe5 10 ♘c3 ♘f6 11 h3 ♗h5 12 g4? ♘fxg4 13 hxg4 ♗xg4 and Black won in C.Didner-S.Bouillot, French League 2002) 8...0-0-0+ 9 ♗d2 ♘ge7 10 h3 ♗xf3 11 ♗xf3 ♘xe5 and Black regained his pawn with the better position in

G.Spanier-J.Head, correspondence 1996.

7 ♗f4

After 7 h3 0-0-0+ 8 ♘bd2 ♗xf3 9 gxf3 ♘xe5 Black has won back his pawn under favourable circumstances again.

7...♘ge7 8 ♘bd2 ♘g6 9 ♗g3 0-0-0

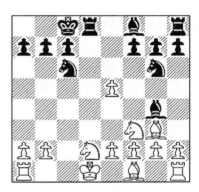

By making obvious, natural moves, Black completes his development. White already is in serious trouble.

10 ♔c1

10 a3 ♗xf3 11 gxf3 (or 11 exf3) 11...♘gxe5 regains the pawn, once more with better play for Black.

10...♗b4 11 a3 ♗xd2+ 12 ♘xd2 ♘gxe5

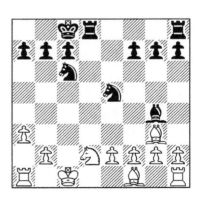

And again Black has won his pawn back, while White is still worrying about how to finish his development and bring his king into safety.

13 f3 ♗e6 14 e3 ♘d3+ 15 ♔c2

15 ♗xd3 is hardly better, for example 15...♖xd3 16 e4 ♖hd8 17 ♖d1 ♗b3 18 ♘xb3 ♖xd1+ and it is time to resign.

15...♘xb2 16 ♗b5 ♘a5 17 ♔xb2 ♖xd2+ 18 ♔c3 ♖hd8 19 ♔b4

After this, the game sees a deserving end.

19...♖b2+! 20 ♔xa5 ♖d5 21 a4 ♔b8!

Not 21...b6+ 22 ♔a6 ♔b8? which would allow 23 ♗xc7+.

22 ♗xc7+ ♔xc7 23 ♖hc1+ ♔b8 24 e4 ♖d6 25 ♗f1 ♖a6+! 0-1

In view of 26 ♗xa6 b6 mate.

After 4 ♘f3 e5, **5 ♘c3** is a more common approach to the position, and following **5...♗b4 6 ♗d2 ♗xc3 7 ♗xc3 e4** the players, for a change, struggle for control of the light squares.

White now has to choose between 8 ♘e5 and 8 ♘d2. Both continuations have one thing in common: should White be able to play e2-e3, his posi-

tion would improve dramatically.

Black mustn't allow that, and fortunately he is offered a fantastic resource in shape of the positional pawn sacrifice **8...e3!**. After 9 fxe3 Black will usually retain control over the light squares, effectively paralyzing the white kingside. For more information about concrete ideas and variations please take a closer look at the following game.

Game 55
M.Löffler-C.Wisnewski
Internet Chess Club (blitz) 2000

---

1 d4 d5 2 c4 ♘c6 3 cxd5 ♕xd5 4 ♘f3 e5 5 ♘c3 ♗b4 6 ♗d2

6 e3 will be examined in the next game.

6 a3?! is rather pointless. Black wants to take on c3 anyway, and now the a3-pawn just blocks the way of the c1-bishop. After 6...♗xc3+ 7 bxc3 e4 8 ♘d2 ♘f6 9 e3 0-0 10 c4 ♕g5 11 ♕c2 ♖e8 12 ♗b2 ♗f5 White experienced difficulties completing his development in

T.Klecker-J.Prachar, Prague 2005.

6...♗xc3 7 ♗xc3

After 7 bxc3 e4 8 ♘g1 ♘a5 9 e3 ♗d7 Black can employ the usual 'massage' of the light squares.

7...e4 8 ♘d2

The major alternative is **8 ♘e5**, but Black can play similarly to the text with **8...e3!** and then:

a) 9 f3 is an attempt to encircle and ultimately collect the e3-pawn. Black has to react quickly: 9...♘ge7 10 ♕d3 (10 ♕b3?! is not good: after 10...♕xb3 11 axb3 ♘xe5 12 dxe5 ♗e6 13 b4 ♘d5 14 g3 a6 15 ♗g2 ♘xc3 16 bxc3 0-0-0 17 0-0 ♖d2 Black had a commanding position in H.Haselhorst-N.Tolstikh, Decin 1995) 10...♘xe5 11 dxe5 ♕xd3 12 exd3 ♘d5 13 g3 (after 13 d4 ♗e6 14 ♗c4? ♘xc3 15 ♗xe6 ♘b5 16 ♗b3 ♘xd4 leads to a much better position for Black, or if 14 g3 c5 15 ♗b5+ ♔e7 16 ♔e2 c4!? 17 ♖hc1 ♖hc8 18 ♗e1 ♖c7 and Black was OK in J.Mont Reynaud-J.Watson, Cardoza 1998) 13...♗f5 14 d4 0-0-0 15 ♗c4 c5! 16 ♖c1 (16 ♗xd5?! is dubious as it allows Black to keep the pawn on e3 after 16...♖xd5 17 dxc5 ♗d3!) 16...♔b8

17 dxc5 ♗e6 18 ♗a5 ♖c8 19 ♔e2 ♖xc5 20 ♗xd5 ♖xa5 21 ♗xe6 fxe6 with equality in A.Veingold-J.Kiltti, Helsinki 1996.

b) 9 fxe3 ♘xe5 10 dxe5

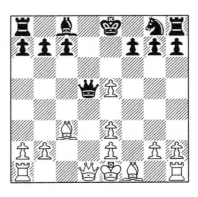

10...♘e7 (10...♗e6 is only good for a draw after 11 ♕a4+ ♗d7 12 ♕d4 ♕e6 13 0-0-0 ♘e7 14 e4 ♘c6 15 ♕c5 0-0-0 16 e3 ♕xa2 17 ♗c4 ♕a1+ 18 ♔c2 ♕a4+ 19 ♔b1, as in M.Uimonen-J.Pystynen, Finnish Team Championship 1996, and now 19...♗f5! 20 ♖xd8+ ♖xd8 21 exf5 ♖d1+ 22 ♖xd1 ♕xd1+ 23 ♔a2 ♕a4+ etc) 11 ♕xd5 ♘xd5 12 ♗d4 (12 ♗d2 saves the bishop from being harassed with ...c7-c5 but also removes the protection from the e5-pawn; after 12...♗f5 13 g3 ♗e4! 14 ♖g1 0-0-0 Black has no problems) 12...♗f5 13 g4 ♗e4 14 ♖g1 b6 15 b3 (or 15 ♔f2 c5 16 ♗c3 ♘xc3 17 bxc3 0-0-0 and the white pawn structure has a certain comedy value) 15...c5 16 ♗b2 ♘xe3 17 ♔f2 ♘d5 18 ♖d1 0-0-0 and Black was clearly better in J.Bonin-C.Wisnewski, Internet (blitz) 2000.

c) After 9 ♕d3 exf2+ 10 ♔xf2 Black can seize control over e4 with 10...♘f6. The game A.Scheffner-R.Baumhus,

German League 1988, continued 11 ♕f3 (11 ♘xc6 is answered by 11...bxc6!, rather than 11...♕xc6, allowing 12 d5) 11...♘xe5 12 dxe5 ♘e4+ 13 ♔e1 ♘xc3 14 ♕xc3 0-0 and White was the side to be sorry for.

8...e3! 9 fxe3 ♘f6

With his control over the light squares and lead in development, Black has definite compensation for the pawn.

10 ♕b3

10 ♘f3 has been tried as well, the idea being to accelerate the kingside development. But now Black can win back his pawn in a favourable way after 10...0-0 11 g3 ♘g4 12 ♗d2 ♖e8 13 ♗g2 (not 13 ♕c1? ♘xd4!! and the white position instantly implodes) 13...♘xe3 14 ♗xe3 ♖xe3.

10...♗e6 11 ♕xd5

11 ♕xb7 is answered by 11...♘xd4! 12 ♕xd5 ♘c2+ 13 ♔f2 ♗xd5 or 13 ♔d1 ♘xe3+ and Black is fine.

11...♗xd5 12 e4

12 ♖g1 tries to untangle the kingside in another way. Following 12...h5! 13 g3 (13 e4 ♘xe4 14 ♘xe4 ♗xe4 15 d5

♗xd5 16 ♗xg7 ♖g8 17 ♗c3 0-0-0 was better for Black in S.Loeffler-T.Thiel, Berlin 1993) 13...0-0-0 14 h3 ♖he8 15 ♔f2 ♖e6 16 g4 hxg4 17 hxg4 ♖h8 (17...g5!?) 18 g5 ♘e4+ 19 ♘xe4 ♗xe4 20 ♖g3 ♖h2+ provided Black with sufficient counterplay in F.Hager-H.Grabher, Austrian League 1997.

12...♘xe4 13 ♘xe4 ♗xe4 14 e3

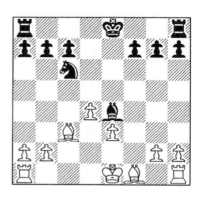

14...0-0

14...0-0-0 would have been even better, when the black rooks get access to the central files more quickly.

15 ♔f2 ♘e7 16 ♗e2 ♘d5 17 ♗d2 c6 18 ♖ac1 ♖fe8 19 ♗f3 ♖e7 20 ♖he1 ♖ae8 21 h4 f6 22 a3 ♔f7

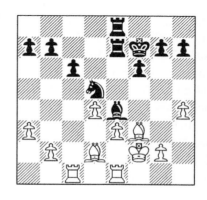

Black can calmly improve his position as White is without counterplay. The way the knight dominates the dark-squared bishop is an especially beautiful sight.

23 ♗b4 ♖e6 24 ♗h5+ g6 25 ♗g4 f5 26 ♗d1 ♘f6!

White threatened to trade off the knight with ♗b3.

27 ♗d2 ♗d5 28 ♗f3 h6 29 ♔g3 g5 30 hxg5 hxg5 31 ♖h1 ♔g6 32 ♔f2 g4 33 ♗xd5 ♘xd5 34 e4

Desperately trying to initiate some counterplay, but it is easily repulsed.

34...♖xe4 35 ♖h6+ ♔g7 36 ♖ch1? ♖e2+ 37 ♔g3 ♖xd2 38 ♖h7+ ♔f8

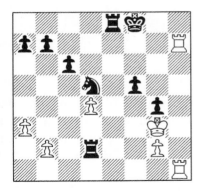

39 ♖xb7

If 39 ♖h8+ ♔e7 40 ♖e1+ ♔d7 41 ♖hxe8 f4+ 42 ♔h4 (or 42 ♔xg4 ♘f6+) 42...♖xg2 43 ♖1e2 ♖xe2 44 ♖xe2 ♘e3! wins.

39...♖e3+ 40 ♔h4 ♖xd4 41 ♔g5 ♖e7 42 ♖h8+ ♔f7 43 ♖h6 f4 44 ♖h7+ ♔e6 45 ♖h6+ ♔e5 46 ♖xe7+ ♘xe7 47 ♔xg4 ♖d3 48 ♖h5+ ♔e4 49 ♖h7 ♘d5 50 g3 ♖xg3+ 0-1

Another major issue is **5 e3**. After

5...exd4 6 exd4 we have a position that can also be reached from the Göring Gambit Declined via 1 e4 e5 2 ♘f3 ♘c6 3 d4 exd5 4 c3 d5 5 exd5 ♕xd5 6 cxd4. Then one main line continues **6...♘f6 7 ♘c3 ♗b4 8 ♗d2 ♗xc3 9 bxc3.**

The implications here are similar to those in Chapter 10. If White is able to get his central pawns going, Black is in severe danger of becoming a sitting duck. Therefore it is Black's main goal to keep the hanging pawns where they are by initiating a blockade on the light squares.

Game 56
G.Nyholm-A.Alekhine
Stockholm 1912

1 d4 d5 2 c4 ♘c6 3 cxd5 ♕xd5 4 ♘f3 e5 5 e3 exd4 6 exd4 ♘f6 7 ♘c3 ♗b4

5 ♘c3 ♗b4 6 e3 exd4 7 exd4 ♘f6 comes to the same thing, while the game took a different route entirely: 1 e4 e5 2 d4 exd4 3 c3 d5 4 exd5 ♕xd5 5 cxd4 ♘c6 6 ♘f3 ♘f6 7 ♗e2 ♗b4+ 8 ♘c3 etc.

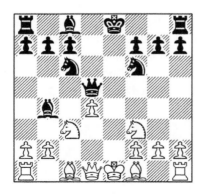

8 ♗e2

After 8 ♗d2 Black can either transpose to the game with 8...♗xc3 9 bxc3 0-0 10 ♗e2 ♘e4 (10 c4?! is refuted by 10...♖e8+ 11 ♗e2 ♕xc4 or 11 ♗e3 ♕a5+ 12 ♕d2 ♘b4!), or play 8...♕d6 as in P.Lebed-V.Chichkin, Kiev 1999, when 9 a3 ♗a5 10 ♘b5 ♕e7+ 11 ♗e2 ♗xd2+ 12 ♕xd2 0-0 13 0-0 ♗e6 left White with no positional compensation for the weak isolated d-pawn.

If instead 8 a3 ♗xc3+ 9 bxc3, then 9...♘a5! 10 ♗e2 0-0 11 0-0 b5 12 ♗f4 c6 13 ♖b1 ♘e4 14 ♕c2 ♗f5 15 ♗d3 ♖fe8 16 ♘h4 ♗g6 17 ♘xg6 hxg6 18 ♗c7 ♘c4 would be another way to play on the light squares.

8...♘e4 9 ♗d2

There is nothing else. 9 ♕d3? only helps Black: after 9...♗f5 10 ♕e3 0-0-0 11 0-0 ♘xc3 12 bxc3 ♖he8 13 ♘e5 (or 13 ♕d2 ♗xc3 14 ♕xc3 ♖xe2) 13...♗xc3 14 ♕xc3 ♘xd4 15 ♗c4 ♕xe5 Black already had a winning advantage in J.Mieses-S.Freiman, St Petersburg 1909. While 9 0-0? just gives a pawn away for nothing, since White has no compensation after 9...♗xc3 10 bxc3 ♘xc3 11 ♕c2

♘xe2+ 12 ♕xe2+ ♗e6 13 ♗a3 0-0-0.

9...♗xc3 10 bxc3 0-0 11 0-0

11 c4 tries to avoid the plan employed in the game. But after 11...♕d6 12 d5 ♘b8 followed by ...♘a6 and ...♘c5 Black can still fix the white pawns – only this time the dark squares are chronically weak.

11...♘a5! 12 ♖e1 b5 13 ♗d3 f5!

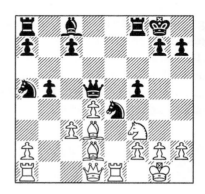

14 a4?!

14 ♘e5 was played in V.Parginos-C.Wisnewski, Internet (blitz) 2001, but Black obtained a nice position after 14...♗b7 15 f3 ♘d6 16 a4 a6 17 ♕c2 ♘ac4.

Instead, 14 ♘g5 ♘xg5 15 ♗xg5 ♗b7 16 f3 was tried in A.Waltemathe-K.Schmidt, correspondence 1986, and now instead of 16...♖ae8?? 17 ♗e7 ♖f7 18 ♗b4 1-0, Black should have played 16...♖fe8 when his position is not worse.

14...♘b3! 15 ♖a3 bxa4 16 ♖xa4 ♘bxd2 17 ♘xd2 ♘xc3! 18 ♕c2 ♕d7! 19 ♖a5 ♕xd4!

Now Black gets rewarded for his accurate play. Of course not 19...♘d5?? 20 ♖xd5 ♕xd5 21 ♗c4 or 19...♘e4?? 20

♘xe4 fxe4 21 ♗xe4 ♖b8 22 ♗xh7+ ♔h8 23 ♖h5 and White wins.

20 ♖c1 ♖d8 21 ♕b3+ ♗e6!!

Again not 21...♘d5??, which unfortunately loses after 22 ♘f3 ♕f4 23 ♖xd5! ♕xc1+ 24 ♗f1 ♗e6 25 ♖xd8+ ♖xd8 26 ♕xe6+ ♔h8 27 ♘e5.

22 ♕xe6+ ♔h8 23 ♖e5 ♕xd3 24 ♖ce1 h6?

An unnecessary weakening. Black could have consolidated with 24...♕d6, since if 25 ♕e8+ ♖xe8 26 ♖xe8+ ♕f8 or 25 ♕f7 ♖f8 26 ♖e8 ♘e4 defends.

25 ♕g6??

Returning the favour with interest, as ♖e8+ is not a threat at all. Instead, 25 ♘f3 and White is still in the game.

25...♕xd2 0-1

White plays 3 cxd5 ♕xd5 4 e3

We are about to get to the main course of this chapter. Although in my remarks to Game 47 (from Chapter 9) I condemned White for playing **4 e3**, in this position it is actually the best move. The main differences are that White can hope to gain a few tempi by pushing the queen about and, what

may be even more important, the f3-square is yet not blocked, therefore allowing the f-pawn to use it and support its neighbour in advancing to e4 at a later date.

After the practically forced **4...e5 5 ♘c3 ♗b4 6 ♗d2 ♗xc3** White must choose between 7 bxc3 and 7 ♗xc3. While the latter is tactically motivated, the former flows into rather positional waters.

7 bxc3 leaves the dark-squared bishop temporarily incarcerated, but also provides a solid centre. Black will have no chance to undermine it in the near future; he even has to be on his guard not to be overrun by the pawns: c3-c4 together with d4-d5, or f2-f3 together with e3-e4 being just two examples.

Following **7...♘f6**, Black has different ideas, depending on the opponent's reaction. If White decides to seize space by advancing his pawns with **8 c4 ♕d6 9 d5 ♘e7**, Black can bring their advance to a halt by blockading them on the dark squares, after which he has three different objectives:

1) Redeploy the king's knight to c5 via d7 or e4.

2) Blast the centre with ...c7-c6 and possibly ...b7-b5 or ...f7-f5.

3) Utilize his lead in development by initiating an attack on the white king.

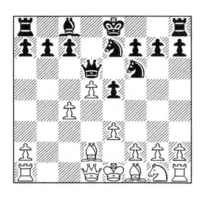

A nice illustration of all these possible ideas is implemented in the following game.

> ### Game 57
> ### S.Farago-R.Bigaliev
> Budapest 1996

1 d4 d5 2 c4 ♘c6 3 cxd5 ♕xd5 4 e3 e5 5 ♘c3 ♗b4 6 ♗d2

The alternative 6 a3 ♗xc3+ 7 bxc3 ♘f6 is similar to the text, although with the bishop still on c1 and the pawn now on a3, there are a few independent possibilities:

(see following diagram)

a) 8 f3 0-0 9 c4 (or 9 e4 ♕a5) 9...♕d6 10 d5, when Black can choose between 10...♘b8 11 e4 ♘a6 12 ♗d3 ♘c5 13 ♘e2 ♘fd7 as in E.Arlandi-O.Renet, Al-

bufeira 1999, and 10...♘e7 11 e4 ♘d7 12 ♘h3 ♘c5 13 ♘f2 f5 14 ♗e3 fxe4 15 fxe4 ♗d7 as in E.Arlandi-S.Maze, Zemplin-ska Sirava 2004, with a comfortable position in either case.

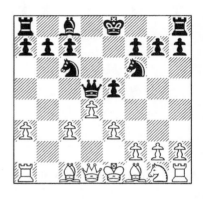

b) 8 a4 allows Black to target the a-pawn after 8...exd4 9 cxd4 ♘e4 10 f3 ♕a5+ 11 ♗d2 ♘xd2 12 ♕xd2 ♗d7.

c) 8 ♘f3 ♗g4 9 ♗e2 e4 10 ♘g1 ♗xe2 11 ♘xe2 only weakens the light squares. After 11...0-0 12 ♖b1 b6 13 ♕a4 ♘a5 14 ♖b4 c5 15 c4 ♕d8 16 dxc5 ♘d7! (or 16...♘b7!) 17 ♕c2 (17 cxb6 is answered by 17...♘c5 18 ♕xa5 ♘d3+ 19 ♔f1 ♕f6!) 17...♘xc5 Black was in command in V.Kovacevic-A.Raetsky, Geneva 2005.

d) 8 c4 ♕d6 9 d5 and again Black has a choice of retreats:

d1) 9...♘b8 10 a4 ♘a6 11 ♗a3 ♘c5 12 ♘f3 ♗g4 13 ♗e2 ♗xf3 14 ♗xf3 0-0 15 0-0 ♘fd7 16 ♗e2 a5 17 ♕c2 f5 18 ♖ab1 b6 with a nice position for Black in D.Meier-M.Jaeckle, German League 2004.

d2) 9...♘e7 10 a4 ♕b4+ (10...♘d7 11 ♗a3 ♘c5 is similar to 9...♘b8) 11 ♗d2 ♕d6 12 ♗c1 (12 ♕b1 is similar to the text) 12...♕b4+ leads to a draw by repetition. Worse is 11 ♕d2?! ♕xd2+ 12 ♗xd2 ♘e4 13 ♗b4 c5! 14 dxc6 (or 14 ♗a3 b6 15 a5 ♗a6 16 ♘f3 f6 17 axb6 axb6 18 ♗e2 0-0 19 ♘d2 ♘d6) 14...♘xc6 15 ♗a3 ♗e6, when White's queenside pawns require special care.

6...♗xc3 7 bxc3

The alternative 7 ♗xc3 is featured in Games 59 and 60.

7...♘f6 8 c4

White can also try:

a) 8 f3 is covered in the next game.

b) 8 ♘f3?! ♗g4 9 ♗e2 (relatively better is 9 h3 ♗h5 10 ♗e2 e4 11 g4 ♗g6 12 c4 ♕d6 13 ♘h4 0-0, but Black is still OK) 9...e4 10 ♘g1 ♗xe2 11 ♘xe2 0-0 12 0-0 ♘a5 and Black was in control of the light squares once more in H.Machelett-S.Brynell, German League 2000.

c) 8 ♕b3 ♕d6 and now:

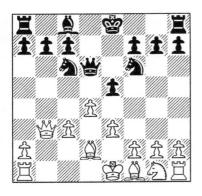

c1) 9 ♗c1 ♗e6 10 ♗a3 (10 ♕xb7 0-0 11 ♕a6 ♖fb8 12 dxe5 ♘xe5 13 ♕xd6 cxd6 and in this unclear position a draw was agreed in R.Bairachny-P.Tishin, Tula 2000) 10...♗xb3 (10...♕d7?! is a try to spice things up, but after 11 ♕xb7 ♖b8 12 ♕a6 exd4 13 cxd4 ♘b4 14 ♗xb4 ♖xb4 15 ♕a5 ♖b6 16 ♘f3 Black had no adequate compensation in K.Kluss-C.Wisnewski, Genoa 2004; while 12...♘d5 13 ♘e2 exd4 is met by 14 ♘xd4!) 11 ♗xd6 cxd6 12 axb3 0-0 was equal in Hoang Thanh Trang-A.Botsari, Istanbul Olympiad 2000.

c2) 9 ♗b5 0-0 10 ♘f3 ♗e6 11 ♕c2 e4 12 ♗xc6 ♕xc6 13 ♘e5 ♕a6 resulted in a small advantage for Black in Y.Shulman-A.Morozevich, Internet (blitz) 1999.

c3) 9 ♗d3 0-0 10 ♘e2 b6 11 0-0 ♗e6 12 ♕c2 ♖ad8 13 f4 (13 ♘g3? fails to 13...exd4 14 cxd4 ♘xd4!, while after 13 ♔h1 Black can play 13...♘a5 followed by ...c7-c5 with good play) 13...e4! 14 ♗xe4 ♘xe4 15 ♕xe4 ♗c4 16 ♕f3 f5 provides Black with enough compensation for the pawn.

c4) 9 ♘e2 0-0 10 ♘g3 is a rare developing scheme, but after 10...a6!? 11 ♗e2 ♗e6 12 ♕b2 ♖fd8 13 0-0 ♘a5 14 ♖fd1 ♘c4 15 ♗xc4 ♗xc4 16 ♗e1 e4 Black again managed to get a firm grip on the light squares in M.Franke-F.Ferster, Bad Mergentheim 2003.

An interesting alternative is 8...♕d8!?, for example 9 ♘f3 (relocating the bishop with 9 ♗c1 0-0 10 ♗a3 ♖e8 11 ♘e2 ♖b8 12 ♖d1 ♗e6 13 ♕c2 occurred in one of my games on the Internet Chess Club, but now 13...♕d5! simply was better for Black) 9...e4 10 ♘e5 ♘xe5 11 dxe5 ♘d7 (or 11...♘g4) 12 e6 fxe6 13 ♕xe6+ ♕e7 14 ♕xe7+ ♔xe7 15 ♖b1 b6 16 ♗c4 ♗b7 17 ♔e2 ♘e5 and once again the black knight is clearly superior.

8...♕d6 9 d5 ♘e7

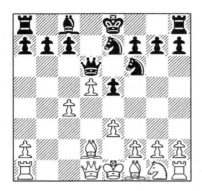

10 ♕b1

Again White has many other moves to choose from:

a) 10 ♗d3 c6 11 e4 b5! 12 cxb5 cxd5 13 ♕a4 ♗b7 14 ♗b4 ♕d7 was better for Black in M.Zivanic-C.Lupulescu, World Junior Championships 1998.

b) 10 ♕a4+ ♗d7 11 ♕b3 a5! 12 ♗c3 (12 ♕xb7? 0-0 13 ♖b1 c6 was very dangerous for White in V.Toporov-P.Tishin, St Petersburg 2001, while 12 ♗d3 e4 13 ♗c2 b5! 14 cxb5 ♘exd5 15 ♘e2 ♘b4 promised Black good chances in D.Rogozenko-J.Fries Nielsen, Hamburg 1997) 12...♘e4 13 ♕xb7 (13 ♘f3 ♘xc3 14 ♕xc3 f6 is slightly better for Black) 13...0-0 14 ♕b2 ♖fb8 15 ♕c1 ♘xc3 16 ♕xc3 ♕b4! 17 ♕xb4?! (or 17 ♘e2 f5 18 a3 ♕b2 19 ♕xb2 ♖xb2 with counterplay) 17...axb4 18 ♗d3 b3 and Black went on to win in M.Mayo Martinez-V.Gallego Jimenez, Benasque 1997.

c) 10 ♕b3 a5! 11 ♘f3 (or 11 ♗d3 e4 12 ♗c2 c6 13 dxc6 ♕xc6 and the c4-pawn is a real target) 11...♘d7 12 ♗e2 ♘c5 13 ♕b2 ♘g6 14 0-0 0-0 15 ♗c3 ♘a4

16 ♕c2 ♘xc3 17 ♕xc3 b6 18 ♘d2 f5 with a good game for Black.

10...a5 11 e4

Here 11 ♗d3 0-0 12 ♘e2 c6 13 e4 b5! 14 cxb5 cxd5 led to an advantage for Black in Y.Yakovich-N.Sulava, Bastia 1998.

11...0-0

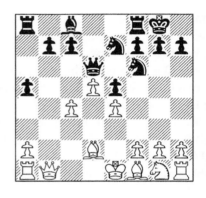

12 ♘f3

On 12 ♗d3 c6 13 ♗e3 Black cannot play the usual ...b7-b5 because of 14 c5, but after 13...cxd5 14 cxd5 ♘g4 15 ♕b6 ♕a3! 16 ♕b3 ♕xb3 17 axb3 ♘xe3 18 fxe3 ♗g4 19 h3 ♗h5 20 g4 ♗g6 21 ♔e2 ♘c8 22 ♘f3 f6 23 ♖a4 ♘d6 Black could be more than happy in L.Seres-R.Bigaliev, Budapest 1996.

Instead, 12 f3 c6 13 a4 was played in G.Giorgadze-N.Sulava, San Marino 1998, but after 13...♘d7 14 ♘h3 ♘c5 15 ♘f2 ♗d7 16 ♘d3 cxd5 17 ♘xc5 ♕xc5 18 cxd5 f5 Black again had the better chances.

12...c6 13 ♗c3

13 ♗e3 cxd5 14 cxd5 ♘g4 is similar to Seres-Bigaliev in the previous note.

13...♘g6 14 ♗d3 b5! 15 ♘d2 ♘f4 16 ♗f1 cxd5 17 cxd5 ♘g4

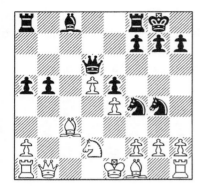

Black's initiative is compelling.

18 ♕c2

If 18 ♕xb5 ♗d7 (or 18...♗a6 19 ♕c6 ♕a3 20 ♗xa6 ♖xa6! 21 ♕xa6 ♕xc3) 19 ♘c4 ♕g6 20 ♕b1 ♖ab8 21 ♕c2 ♗b5 also leads to a huge attack.

18...♘xf2! 19 ♔xf2 ♕c5+ 20 ♔f3 ♗g4+! 21 ♔xg4 ♕f2 22 g3 h5+ 23 ♔h4 f6 0-1

As the Chigorin Defence became increasingly popular at the beginning of this decade, White players searched frantically for possible improvements. The system based on **8 f3!?** constitutes such an improvement and has to be taken very seriously.

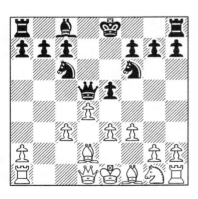

The idea is to push the pawns with e3-e4 and d4-d5, gaining space in the process and making room for the bishops. Despite being propagated by several theoreticians, I don't think that Black should allow this kind of advance. Therefore, **8...e4!** is the logical consequence, and while White tries to get rid of this thorn in his flesh, Black should attempt to make use of his slight space advantage and lead in development. A good illustration of a possible outcome is the following game.

**Game 58
H.Grünberg-C.Wisnewski**
German League 2002

---

1 d4 d5 2 c4 ♘c6 3 e3 e5 4 cxd5 ♕xd5 5 ♘c3 ♗b4 6 ♗d2 ♗xc3 7 bxc3 ♘f6 8 f3!? e4!

8...0-0 completely ignores White's idea. After 9 e4 ♕d6 10 d5 ♘e7 11 c4 Black will have a hard time creating sufficient counterplay, the game R.Dautov-I.Miladinovic, Yerevan

Olympiad 1996, being one example. There may be improvements for Black, but why take such chances?

9 c4

9 f4 0-0 10 c4 ♕d6 transposes to the text; while after 9 ♕b3 Black should play 9...♕f5, for example 10 ♕b5 (or 10 ♕a3 h5! 11 h4 ♗d7 12 ♗e2 ♕g6 13 ♔f2 ♘e7 14 ♗c4 ♘f5 when White's kingside made a fragile impression in J.Avila Jimenez-M.Peek, Barcelona 2003) 10...0-0 11 ♕xf5 ♗xf5 12 g4 ♗g6 13 g5 ♘e8 14 f4 ♘d6 and the white pawns were completely fixed in R.Janssen-M.Peek, Amsterdam 2002.

9...♕d6

10 f4

White has also tried:

a) 10 ♕b1!? which practically forces 10...♗f5 11 f4 0-0 12 ♘e2 ♖fe8 13 ♘g3, but now instead of the immediate 13...♗d7 (as in T.Radjabov-G.Antal, Budapest 2000), 13...♗g4! is an improvement I am quite proud of, the point being that 14 h3 ♗d7 15 ♗e2?! allows 15...♘xd4! 16 exd4 e3 17 ♗c3 ♕xf4 with a winning attack, or if 17 0-0 exd2. The game J.Gustafsson-

C.Wisnewski, Dresden 2001, continued 14 ♗c3 a5 15 h3 ♗d7 16 ♗e2 h5 17 ♘xh5 ♘xh5 18 ♗xh5 ♕h6 19 ♕d1 b5!? with good chances for Black.

b) 10 ♘e2 0-0 and then:

b1) 11 ♘g3?! was played in D.Tyomkin-I.Miladinovic, Verona 2000, when Black could have initiated an attack with 11...exf3 12 gxf3 ♖e8; for example, 13 d5 ♘e5 14 e4 h5!? 15 f4 (15 h4? is crushed by 15...♘d3+ 16 ♗xd3 ♕xg3+ 17 ♔e2 ♘xe4!, while if 15 ♔f2 h4 16 ♘e2 ♕c5+ 17 ♗e3 ♘xe4+ 18 fxe4 ♘g4+ or 16 ♘f5 ♗xf5 17 exf5 ♘xc4! wins) 15...♘eg4 16 e5 h4 17 ♘e2 ♕c5 and White is totally lost. Or if 13 ♗e2 ♗h3 14 d5 ♘e5 15 ♖b1 (or 15 ♔f2 c6) 15...c6!? 16 ♗b4 ♕d7 17 e4 (White has no time to advance his d-pawn as after 17 d6 ♕e6 18 c5? ♗g2 19 ♖g1 ♘xf3+ Black is just winning) 17...b5!? 18 dxc6 ♕xc6 19 cxb5 ♕b6 and Black has a strong attack.

b2) 11 f4 is better, and then 11...♖e8 12 ♘g3 ♘xd4! 13 ♗c3 (or 13 exd4 ♕xd4, when 14 ♗b4 ♕e3+ 15 ♘e2 ♗e6 16 ♕d4 ♕d3 17 ♖d1 ♕xc4 18 ♕xc4 ♗xc4 leads to an interesting endgame with Black having three pawns for the piece) 13...♘f5 14 ♕xd6 (14 ♘xf5?! ♕xd1+ 15 ♖xd1 ♗xf5 16 h3 ♖ad8 17 g4 ♖xd1+ 18 ♔xd1 ♖d8+ 19 ♔e2 ♗d7 20 ♗g2 ♗c6 was just good for Black in P.Giannoutsos-A.Botsari, Halkida 1997) 14...cxd6 (14...♘xd6 15 ♗xf6 gxf6 16 ♘h5 ♖e6 17 g4 is unclear) 15 ♘xf5 ♗xf5 16 ♗xf6 gxf6 17 g4 ♗d7 18 ♖d1 ♖ad8 19 ♖xd6 ♗xg4 20 ♖xd8 ♖xd8 21 ♖g1 ♖d1+ with a draw by repetition after 22 ♔f2 ♖d2+ 23 ♔e1 ♖d1+ (analysis by Bronznik).

10...0-0 11 ♘e2 ♗g4!? 12 h3

Not 12 ♕b1 ♖fe8 13 ♘c3? ♘xd4 14 exd4 e3 when Black has a winning initiative.

12...♗d7 13 ♖b1 a5!

A typical move which prevents the bishop from going to b4 (after a possible d4-d5).

14 ♔f2

In an earlier publication I proclaimed 14 ♖xb7?! to be dangerous for White after 14...♘b4 without giving further proof. I would like to expand on this with the following lines: 15 ♗xb4 (15 ♘c1 is met by 15...♗c6 16

♗xb4 axb4 17 c5 ♕d8! 18 ♖xb4 ♘d5 and White is lost) 15...axb4 and now:

a) 16 ♕b3 ♖a4! 17 c5 (no better is 17 g4 ♖fa8 18 ♗g2 ♗c6 19 c5 ♕d8 20 ♖xb4 ♖xa2) 17...♕a6 18 ♖xc7 (18 ♖xb4? loses to 18...♕a5) 18...♗e6 with a winning initiative.

b) 16 ♕d2 ♖a4! 17 c5 ♕d5 18 ♖xc7 (or 18 ♖xb4 ♖xa2 19 ♕c1 ♕h5 with excellent compensation) 18...♖xa2 19 ♕xb4 ♕a8! 20 ♕b7 ♕a5+ 21 ♔f2 ♗e6 and Black has a dangerous attack for the two pawns.

14...b6 15 ♗c3 ♘b4 16 ♘c1 ♖fe8

Black can be happy with his position. The e4-pawn proves to be very annoying.

17 ♗e2 ♕e7 18 ♖e1 b5!

To get access to d5 in this position, sacrificing a pawn is a small price to pay.

19 ♗xb4 axb4 20 ♕b3 ♖a4 21 cxb5 ♖ea8 22 ♖d1 h5 23 ♕c4

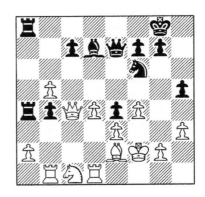

23...♘g4+?

Trying to go for the kill, Black misses a defending resource. Better is 23...♕d6, when Black is a pawn down, but White can hardly move any of his pieces. The idea is to bring the knight to d5 (and optionally to c3) and/or capture the b5-pawn. All in all the position is unclear, but I would take the black pieces any day.

24 hxg4 ♕h4+ 25 g3?

25 ♔g1 hxg4 26 ♕d5!, enabling 27 ♕h5 after 26...g3, was the move I missed. Black can fudge with 26...♗e6 27 ♕g5 ♕g3, but nothing more.

25...♕h2+ 26 ♔e1 b3! 27 ♕xb3

If 27 ♕xc7 ♖xa2! 28 ♘xa2 ♖xa2 mates.

27...♖a3

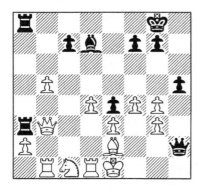

28 gxh5?

The last chance was 28 ♕c4, when 28...♕xg3+ 29 ♔d2 ♕xe3+ 30 ♔c2 ♖8a4 31 ♖b4 ♗xb5! 32 ♕xc7 ♖xb4 33 ♕c8+ is a draw, or if 32...♖xa2+ 33 ♖b2 ♖xb2+ 34 ♔xb2 ♕a3+ 35 ♔c2 ♗xe2 36 ♕c8+ ♕f8 37 ♕xf8+ ♔xf8 38 ♘xe2 ♖a2+ 39 ♔c3 ♖xe2 40 gxh5 and White survives.

28...♖xb3 29 ♖xb3 ♕xg3+ 30 ♔d2 ♗g4 31 ♖e1 ♕h2 32 ♔d1 ♕xh5 33 ♗xg4 ♕xg4+ 34 ♖e2 g6 35 ♖c3 ♖a5 36 ♖b3 ♔g7 37 ♔c2? 0-1

Becoming aware of 37...♖xa2+, White immediately resigned.

At long last I'd like to take a look at the line that is supposedly the most dangerous for Black in the Chigorin Defence. After **7 ♗xc3** the dark-squared bishop, usually a child of sorrow in many different systems, nestles on the a1-h8 diagonal creating various threats. This makes use of the fact that after **7...exd4** White can play **8 ♘e2!**.

When Breutigam published his *ChessBase* CD on the Chigorin back in 2000, the piece sacrifice begun by 8...♗g4 9 f3 ♘f6 10 ♘xd4 0-0-0!? was still playable, but over time resources have been found that refute the whole idea. Fortunately, **8...♘f6 9 ♘xd4 0-0** has managed to hold on to the present day. Before delving into the ambitious 10 ♘b5, let's look at other options first.

Game 59
F.Lamprecht-C.Wisnewski
German League 2005

1 d4 d5 2 c4 ♘c6 3 cxd5 ♕xd5 4 e3 e5 5 ♘c3 ♗b4 6 ♗d2 ♗xc3 7 ♗xc3 exd4 8 ♘e2

8 ②f3?! is the wrong square for the knight, as it allows the pin after 8...♗g4. Then after 9 ♗e2 0-0-0 White has nothing better than 10 ②xd4 ♗xe2 11 ♕xe2 ②xd4 (or 11...♕xg2 12 0-0-0 ②ge7 13 ♖hg1 ♕xh2) 12 ♗xd4 ♕xg2 13 0-0-0 ②e7 14 ♖hg1 ♕c6 15 ♔b1 ②f5 with advantage for Black in Wu Shaobin-Wu Wenjin, Wuxi 2005.

8...②f6!

Instead, 8...♗g4?! is a piece sacrifice that came into fashion in the late nineties of the last century. But today, as the variation has been heavily analysed, the complications see White as the winner after 9 f3 and then:

a) 9...②f6 10 ②xd4 0-0-0 (or equally 9...0-0-0 10 ②xd4 ②f6) 11 ♕a4 ♕g5 (11...♖he8?! is answered by 12 ②xc6 ♖xe3+ 13 ♔f2 ♖xf3+ 14 ♔g1 ♕c5+ 15 ♗d4 ♕xc6 16 ♕xc6 ♖xf1+ 17 ♖xf1 bxc6 18 ♗xf6 gxf6 19 h3) 12 ②xc6 ♕xe3+ 13 ♗e2 ♖he8 14 ♕c2! bxc6 15 ♗xf6 followed by 16 fxg4 and Black had no compensation for the piece in S.Helms-N.Gospodinow, German League 2002.

b) 9...♗xf3 10 gxf3 ♕xf3 11 ♗xd4 with the following possibilities:

b1) 11...♕xh1 12 ♗xg7 ♕xh2 13 ♕a4 was clearly better for White in F.Peredy-H.Kleinhenz, Liechtenstein 2000.

b2) 11...②f6 12 ②g3 ②xd4 13 exd4 left Black with no compensation in G.Spiess-T.Escher, German League 2003.

b3) 11...0-0-0 12 ♖g1 ②xd4 13 exd4 ②f6 14 ♗g2 ♕h5 15 ♕b3 and White stayed on top in L.Krutwig-S.Horstmann, Essen 2002.

b4) 11...②xd4 12 ♕xd4 ♕xh1 13 ♕xg7 0-0-0 14 ♕xh8 ♕xh2 15 ♕g7 ♕h4+ 16 ♕g3 ♕b4+ 17 ♔f2 ②f6 (or 17...♕xb2 18 ♖c1 ♕b6 19 ♕h3+ ♔b8 20 ♕xh7 ②f6 21 ♕h4) 18 ♗h3+ ♔b8 19 ♕f4 and White went on to win in I.Khenkin-A.Czebe, Liechtenstein 1998.

9 ②xd4 0-0

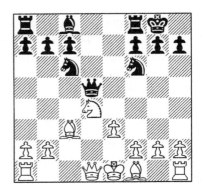

10 ②xc6

The critical 10 ②b5 is the subject of the next game. Other moves are no better than the text:

a) 10 ♕f3?! ②xd4 11 ♕xd5 (if 11 ♗xd4 ②e4! 12 a3?! c5 13 ♗c3 ②xc3 14 bxc3 ♕b3 and the white queenside is in ruins, or 12 ♖c1 ♕a5+ 13 ♗c3 ②xc3 14

♖xc3 ♕xa2 and Black is a pawn up for nothing) 11...♘c2+! 12 ♔d2 ♘xd5 13 ♔xc2 ♗f5+ 14 ♗d3 ♗xd3+ 15 ♔xd3 ♖fd8 with active play in M.Tyrtania-R.Rabiega, Berlin 2000.

b) 10 ♕b3 ♘xd4 11 ♗xd4 (11 ♕xd5?! transposes to 10 ♕f3?! above) 11...♕d6 12 ♖d1 c5 13 ♗c3 ♕e7 14 ♗c4 b6 (or 14...♘e4 15 0-0 b6 16 ♗d5 ♖b8 17 f3 ♘xc3 18 ♕xc3 ♗b7 19 e4 and a draw was agreed in R.Dautov-A.Morozevich, German League 2000) 15 0-0 ♗b7 16 ♗xf6 ♕xf6 17 ♖d7 ♗c8 18 ♖d2 ♖e8 with equality in H.Kunze-C.Wisnewski, Bad Bocklet 2002.

c) 10 ♗e2 ♘e4 (10...♕xg2?! is too greedy: 11 ♗f3 ♕g6 12 ♘xc6 bxc6 13 ♕d4 ♕f5 14 ♗xc6 ♖b8 15 ♖g1 ♔h8 16 0-0-0 ♖b6 17 ♕d8! ♕c5 18 ♖g5! ♘d7 19 ♖xd7 ♗xd7 20 ♕e7! and Black resigned in S.Kishnev-R.Rabiega, German League 2001; better is 13...♗e6 and if 14 0-0-0 Black can play 14...♗xa2 15 ♖hg1 ♕b1+ 16 ♔d2 ♕xd1+ 17 ♗xd1 ♖fd8, but the position remains difficult after 18 ♔c2 ♖xd4 19 ♗xd4) 11 0-0 (or 11 ♘xc6 ♕xc6 12 ♗d4 ♕g6 followed by ...c7-c5 with a good game in P.Andreasen-T.Bromann, Danish League 2001) 11...♘xc3 12 bxc3 ♕c5 13 ♕b3 ♖b8 14 ♖ad1 was played in Se.Ivanov-L.Madebrink, Sweden 2001, when 14...♗d7 would have been equal.

10...♕xc6 11 ♕f3

Instead:

a) 11 ♖c1 ♖e8 12 ♗d4 ♕d6 13 ♗e2 (or 13 ♗c4 ♕b4+ 14 ♕d2 ♕xd2+ 15 ♔xd2 ♘e4+ 16 ♔e2 c5 17 ♗c3 ♘xc3+ 18 ♖xc3 b6 with equality) 13...b6 14 0-0 (14 ♗f3 ♘e4 15 ♕c2 ♗b7! was also fine for

Black in M.Richter-M.Breutigam, German League 2000, as 16 ♕xc7? would lose to 16...♖ac8) 14...c5 15 ♗c3 ♕e6 16 ♗f3 ♘e4 17 ♗xe4 ♕xe4 and Black had no problems in M.Richter-I.Miladinovic, St Vincent 2000.

b) 11 ♕d4 ♗e6 12 ♕h4 was tried in L.Verat-L.Dubois, Clichy 2000, but after 12...♖fd8 13 ♕g3 (if 13 ♗xf6 gxf6 14 ♕xf6 ♕c2 15 ♕c3 ♕xc3+ 16 bxc3 ♖d6 gives Black sufficient counterplay for the pawn) 13...♗f5 14 ♕g5 ♗g6 15 ♗b5 ♕e4 Black was even a little bit better.

11...♕xf3 12 gxf3 ♘d5 13 ♗d4 ♗e6

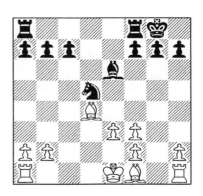

14 ♖c1

Or:

a) 14 0-0-0 was played in I.Rausis-C.Wisnewski, Bad Bocklet 2002, and now instead of 14...♖fd8, the immediate 14...c5! would have equalized.

b) 14 ♖g1 f6 (14...g6?! unnecessarily weakens the dark squares; White got a good position after 15 ♖c1 ♖fd8 16 h4 ♖d7 17 h5 ♘e7 18 hxg6 fxg6 19 a3 ♘f5 20 ♗e5 in S.Giessmann-C.Wisnewski, German Championship 2004) 15 a3 a5 16 ♖c1 ♖ac8 17 ♔d2 ♖fd8 18 e4 c5 19 ♖xc5 ♖xc5 20 ♗xc5 b6 21 exd5 (or 21

♗e3 ♘xe3+ 22 ♔xe3 ♖d1) and here a draw was agreed in B.Gulko-S.Brynell, Copenhagen 2000.

14...c6 15 a3 f6 16 ♗c4 ♘c7 17 ♗e2 ♖fd8 18 0-0 ♗b3 19 ♔g2

The position still offers enough room to play on, but...

½-½

As I have already pointed out, **10 ♘b5** is the most ambitious attempt to cause problems for Black. The position after **10...♕g5 11 ♘xc7 ♗g4 12 ♕b3 ♖ad8 13 ♕xb7 ♖d6** shows the implications of this line.

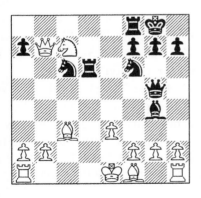

In exchange for the two pawns

Black has a significant lead in development, but in order not to lose momentum a radical approach is required. The position is highly complicated with possibilities for both sides. I'd like to give you a few ideas by examining the following game.

Game 60
M.Socko-C.Foisor
Athens 2004

---

1 d4 d5 2 c4 ♘c6 3 cxd5 ♕xd5 4 e3 e5 5 ♘c3 ♗b4 6 ♗d2 ♗xc3 7 ♗xc3 exd4 8 ♘e2 ♘f6 9 ♘xd4 0-0 10 ♘b5 ♕g5

10...♕xd1+ is too benign. After 11 ♖xd1 ♘e8 12 ♗c4 Black lacked prospects in M.Lindinger-E.Maahs, Hamburg 1999.

11 ♘xc7

Choosing the most complicated way. Other moves promise less:

11 ♕f3?! was smoothly countered by 11...♗g4 12 ♕g3? (12 ♗xf6 was necessary) 12...♘e4 13 ♕xc7 a6 14 ♕xb7 ♕d5 15 ♘c7 ♘d4!! in S.Batyrov-C.Wisnewski, Bad Bocklet (blitz) 2002;

while the plain 11 ♗xf6 ♕xf6 12 ♘xc7 is met by 12...♗g4!, e.g. 13 ♕xg4 ♕xb2 14 ♖d1 ♕c3+ 15 ♖d2 ♘e5 and Black picks up the knight on c7.

But 11 h4 is a cunning move, to which there are two ways to react:

a) 11...♕g6?! eyes g2, but has the disadvantage that White can develop his f1-bishop with tempo: 12 ♘xc7 ♗g4 13 ♗d3! ♕h6 (after 13...♗xd1 14 ♗xg6 ♖ac8 15 ♗f5 ♖xc7 16 ♖xd1 Black is already fighting a losing battle) 14 ♕a4 ♖ac8 (or 14...♖ad8 15 ♗c2 ♗c8 16 ♖d1 and Black had nothing for the pawn in R.Cifuentes Parada-I.Miladinovic, Dos Hermanas 2000), when White can play 15 ♘b5 and now 15...♖fe8 (15...♗d7 saves the bishop, but after 16 0-0 there is no compensation in sight) 16 ♗xf6 ♖xe3+ 17 ♔f1! (but not 17 fxe3? ♕xe3+ 18 ♔f1 ♕xd3+ 19 ♔f2 ♘e5 20 ♗xe5 ♖c2+ 21 ♕xc2 ♕xc2+ 22 ♔g3 ♕d3+! and Black is better after 23 ♔h2 ♕xb5 or 23 ♔xg4 f5+ 24 ♔f4 ♕e4+ 25 ♔g3 ♕xe5+ and ...♕xb5) 17...♕xf6 18 ♕xg4 ♖d8 (or 18...♖xd3 19 ♕xc8+) 19 ♗e2 ♕xb2 20 ♖e1 when White keeps the extra piece.

b) 11...♕h6! sees another crossroads:

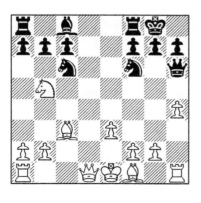

b1) 12 ♕f3?! again allows Black to play 12...♗g4 13 ♕g3 ♖ad8 14 ♗c4 (if 14 ♗xf6 ♕xf6 15 ♕xg4 ♕xb2 16 ♖d1 ♘b4! and Black gets a dangerous attack) 14...♗e6! 15 ♗xe6 fxe6 16 0-0 (taking the c7-pawn is good for Black after either 16 ♘xc7 ♘e4 17 ♕xg7+ ♕xg7 18 ♗xg7 ♖xf2 or 16 ♕xc7 e5 intending 17 ♗xe5 ♖f7) 16...♘e4 17 ♕g4 ♘xc3 18 ♘xc3 ♖f7 and in exchange for his devalued pawn structure, Black has good prospects on the half-open f-file.

b2) 12 ♗e2 ♖d8 13 ♕c2 ♘d5 14 0-0-0 (14 ♗d2?! saves the bishop from being traded, but Black gets a good game after 14...a6 15 ♘a3 ♕f6 or 15 ♘c3 ♘db4 16 ♕e4 f5 17 ♕b1 ♘e5; while 14 ♖d1 ♗e6 15 a3 ♗d7 gave Black a comfortable position in D.Rogozenko-A.Morozevich, Istanbul Olympiad 2000), and now Bronznik gives 14...♗e6 15 g4 (or 15 a3 a6 16 ♘d4 ♘xc3 17 ♕xc3 ♘xd4 18 ♖xd4 c5!) 15...♘db4 16 ♗xb4 ♘xb4 17 ♖xd8+ ♖xd8 18 g5 ♕g6 19 ♕xg6 ♘xa2+ 20 ♔b1 hxg6 with a complicated endgame, for example 21 ♘xc7 ♗b3 22 ♘b5 ♘b4 23 ♘d4 (but not 23 ♘xa7? ♗c2+ 24 ♔c1 ♗e4 and Black wins) 23...♗d5 24 ♖c1 ♗e4+ 25 ♔a1 ♖d5 26 ♖c8+ ♔h7 27 ♖c3, when 27...♖a5+ 28 ♖a3 ♖c5 29 ♖c3 ♖a5+ is a draw by repetition.

b3) 12 ♘xc7 ♗g4 13 ♕b3 (13 ♕d6 ♖ad8 14 ♕g3 was played in G.Dizdar-M.Ivanov, Austrian League 2004, when Black continued with the methodical 14...♖d7 15 ♗c4 ♖fd8, but fell behind after 16 ♘d5 ♖xd5 17 ♗xd5 ♖xd5 18 ♗xf6 ♕xf6 19 ♕xg4; instead 14...♘e4! would have been the correct response, and after 15 ♕xg4 ♘xc3 16 bxc3 ♕d6 17 ♗e2 ♘e5 Black regains the piece with sufficient compensation for the pawn due to his greater activity) 13...♖ad8 14 ♕xb7 is similar to the main game, but with the moves h2-h4 and ...♕h6 inserted. This actually favours Black more than White, as can be seen in the following analysis: 14...♘e4 15 ♗b5 (not 15 ♗c4?! ♘xc3 16 bxc3 ♖d7 and White cannot extricate the knight) 15...♗d7 and now to show the number of pitfalls lurking in this line, I would like to give you a few sample variations:

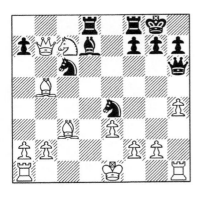

b31) 16 ♖c1? is met by 16...♕d6! when both ...♖b8 and ...♘c5 threaten to win the queen which is still tied to the knight on c7.

b32) 16 ♗c4? fails to 16...♘xc3 17 bxc3 ♕d6, now with the triple threats of ...♖b8, ...♘a5 and ...♗c8.

b33) 16 ♘d5?! ♘d6 17 ♕a6 ♘b8 18 ♘f6+ gxf6 19 ♕xd6 ♗xb5 20 ♕xf6 ♕xf6 21 ♗xf6 ♖d7 22 ♖h3 ♖c8 23 ♖g3+ ♔f8 was clearly better for Black in C.Marcelin-S.Conquest, French League 2001.

b34) 16 ♗e2 ♕g6 17 ♗f3 (17 0-0?! ♘xc3 18 bxc3 ♘d4! is as surprising as it is forceful; for example, 19 ♗f3 ♘xf3+ 20 ♕xf3 ♗c6 21 ♕g3 ♕xg3 22 fxg3 ♖c8 23 ♘a6 ♗b5 and Black wins; better is 21 e4 ♗xe4 22 ♕g3 but after 22...♕c6 the knight is still in grave danger) 17...♘c5 18 ♕b5 and now Bronznik suggests 18...♘b4!? 19 ♕c4 ♘c2+ 20 ♔e2 ♘xa1 21 ♖xa1 with unclear play. But I like 18...♘e5!? even better, for example 19 ♕e2 ♕d6 20 ♗xe5 ♘d3+ 21 ♔f1 ♘xe5 22 ♘b5 ♗xb5 23 ♕xb5 ♘xf3 24 gxf3 ♖b8 25 ♕e2 ♕f6 and despite being two pawns down, Black has sufficient compensation as his forces are well coordinated while the white pieces are incredibly not.

11...♗g4 12 ♕b3 ♖ad8

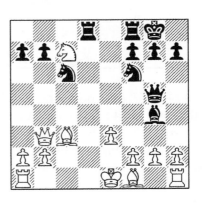

13 ♕xb7

13 h3 wants to eliminate possible mating threats on d1. The game G.Flear-I.Miladinovic, Athens 1999, continued 13...♗c8 14 ♕b5 ♕g6 15 ♗xf6 (15 ♖c1 was suggested as an improvement by Miladinovic, but after 15...♘e4! White has to be careful, for instance 16 ♕b3 ♕f5 17 ♕c2 ♖d2! and

Black is winning), and now 15...♕xf6 (instead of 15...gxf6 as played in the game) 16 ♘d5 (or 16 ♗c4 ♕g6) 16...♕e5 17 ♘f4 ♕d6 18 d3 ♘b4 would have led to active play according to Bronznik, for example 19 ♖d1 ♗d7 20 ♕c4? ♗f5 21 ♔e2 ♘xd3 22 ♘xd3 ♖c8 23 ♕b3 ♗e6 and Black will invade the second rank.

13...♖d6!?

The major alternative is 13...♕c5, when White has several different moves at his disposal:

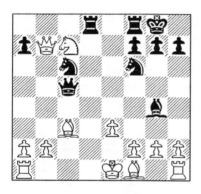

a) 14 ♕b5?! does not work as well as in the text, as 14...♕d6 simultaneously threatens 15...♕xc7 and 15...♕d1+. White's best option seems to be 15 f3 ♕xc7 16 ♗xf6 gxf6 17 fxg4 but after 17...♖fe8 Black has a dangerous initiative, despite being two pawns down.

b) 14 ♘a6?! ♕d6 15 ♕b3 (no better is 15 f3 ♗c8, for example 16 ♕b3 ♖fe8 17 ♔f2 ♖xe3! as White gets mated after 18 ♔xe3 ♘g4+! 19 fxg4 ♖e8+ 20 ♔f3 ♗xg4+! 21 ♔xg4 ♖e4+ 22 ♔h3 ♕h6+ 23 ♔g3 ♕e3) 15...♘e4 16 f3 was played in P.Wiebe-C.Wisnewski, Kiel (rapid) 2004, but after 16...♕h6! 17 ♕c2 ♗xf3 18 ♗b5 ♕xe3+ 19 ♔f1 ♖d2 20 ♕xd2 ♘xd2+

21 ♗xd2 ♕xd2 22 gxf3 ♕xb2 White had to resign.

c) 14 h3 should also be answered by 14...♗c8 15 ♕b3 ♘e4 with compensation for the two pawns.

d) 14 ♗b5 ♖d6 15 ♘a6 ♕d5 16 0-0 ♗c8 17 ♕c7 ♕xb5 18 ♕xd6 ♘e4 19 ♕f4 ♘xc3 20 bxc3 ♗xa6 resulted in a roughly equal position in L.Van Wely-I.Miladinovic, FIDE World Championship, Groningen 1997.

e) 14 ♕b3 returns the queen to safety, but neglects development. After 14...♘e4 15 ♗b5 ♖d7 (15...♕d6?! 16 ♕d5!) White has to be very careful:

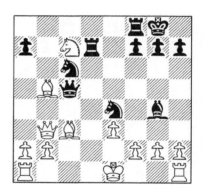

e1) 16 ♘a6?! ♕f5 17 0-0 is surprisingly punished by 17...♗f3! and White is lost; for example: 18 gxf3 (if 18 ♗xc6 ♕g4 mates, while after 18 ♖fc1 ♗xg2 19 ♔xg2 ♕xf2+ 20 ♔h1 ♕f3+ 21 ♔g1 ♖d6 or 19 f4 ♗h3 20 ♕c2 ♖d2! White cannot avoid being mated for much longer) 18...♖d6! 19 ♖fd1 (or 19 ♖fc1 ♕h3 20 ♗f6 ♘d2) 19...♖g6+ 20 ♔f1 ♕xf3 21 ♕c2 ♖g2 22 ♔e1 (or 22 ♖d2 ♖xh2 and mates) 22...♖xf2 23 ♕xe4 ♕xe4 24 ♔xf2 ♕f5+ 25 ♔g1 ♕xb5 with a decisive advantage for Black.

e2) 16 h3 ♕f5 17 ♕c2 (better is 17 0-0 and if 17...♗xh3? 18 ♗xc6, while 17...♗f3! 18 gxf3 ♕xh3 19 ♘d5 ♘g3 20 fxg3 ♕xg3+ 21 ♔h1 ♕h3+ leads to a draw by perpetual check; but not 19 fxe4?! ♖d6 20 ♘e6 ♖xe6 21 ♕xe6 ♕xe6 22 f3 f5! when Black gets good attacking chances according to Bronznik) 17...♘xc3 18 ♕xc3 ♖xc7 19 ♗xc6 ♕c8 20 hxg4 ♖xc6 21 ♕d3 (not 21 ♕d2? ♖d8 22 ♕b4 ♖c1+ 23 ♔e2 ♖c2+ 24 ♔f1 ♖dd2 regaining both pawns with interest) 21...♖c1+ 22 ♖xc1 ♕xc1+ 23 ♕d1 ♕xb2 and Black, having already won back one of the pawns, had excellent compensation in O.Kniest-A.Liebau, correspondence 2000.

14 ♕b5!?

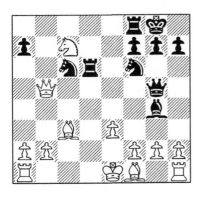

Although discovered independently by other chess players as well, according to my games database (more than five million games) this move was first employed by my clubmate Patrick Wiebe in a game we played back in 2002. But before we take a look at this, let's see how to treat the alternatives:

a) After 14 ♘b5?! ♖e6 many games have featured 15 ♘d4?, when Black

plays 15...♖xe3+! with a winning attack, for example 16 fxe3 ♕xe3+ 17 ♘e2 ♘e4 18 ♕xc6 ♖d8 19 ♕xe4 ♕xe4 20 ♖d1 ♖xd1+ 21 ♔xd1 ♗xe2+ 22 ♗xe2 ♕b1+ and White resigned in A.Martin-C.Wisnewski, Internet (blitz) 2003.

b) 14 h4 ♖fd8! 15 ♗e2 ♕g6 16 ♗xf6 (or 16 ♗xg4 ♕xg4 17 0-0 ♕d7 18 ♗xf6 gxf6 and White cannot save his knight) 16...♗xe2! 17 ♗xd8 ♕c2 and mates.

c) 14 h3!? is an interesting try that has not been tested in any serious game as yet. The idea is to force Black to make a decision about his bishop. Bronznik gives 14...♖b8 15 ♕a6 ♗h5 16 ♕a4 ♖bd8, but after 17 g4 it is not clear to me how Black is compensated for his two sacrificed pawns. Instead 15...♗f5 looks better, with the idea of ...♘e4 and ...♕h4, now that 14 h3 has weakened g3 and therefore enables ...♘xg3 after g2-g3. The safest way for White to respond seems to be 16 ♘b5 ♖e6 17 ♘c7 with a draw by repetition (!), but in any case Black should not be afraid to make his stand here.

14...♕g6

14...♗f5!? is an interesting alternative suggested by Bronznik in the second edition of *Die Tschigorin-Verteidigung*. I remember analysing this position for about three hours with the Danish expert theoretician S.Pedersen, and while we came to the conclusion that Black has definite compensation for the two pawns, the position is so rich in possibilities that it is simply not possible to give it an adequate coverage. But one advantage of this omission is that you are not deprived of the fun you will have when analysing this position for yourself!

15 ♗e2

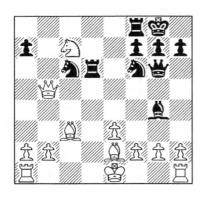

15...♗xe2?!

Interposing 15...♖b8! makes more sense. After 16 ♕c4 (if 16 ♗xg4, then rather than accept the queen, Black should play 16...♕xg4 17 ♕f1 ♘b4! or 17 f3 ♕xg2 18 ♕f1 ♖xb2! 19 ♕xg2 ♖xg2, regaining the sacrificed material and remaining with the better position) 16...♗xe2 17 ♕xe2 ♕xg2 Black is virtually a move up on the text, as the rook is usually better placed on b8 than on f8. All the same, it doesn't seem to make a big difference here, but it many lines this kind of additional resource could be decisive.

16 ♕xe2 ♕xg2 17 ♕f1 ♕f3 18 ♖g1 g6

I don't understand why Black didn't play 18...♖fd8. Perhaps she feared 19 ♕e2 ♕h3 20 ♗xf6 ♖xf6 21 ♕g4, but after 21...♕xg4 22 ♖xg4 ♘e5! Black gets more than sufficient counterplay. Then again, even after the text move the position is more difficult to play for White, and Black has definite compensation for the pawn.

19 ♘b5 ♖e6 20 ♕e2 ♕f5 21 ♖d1 ♘e4 22 ♘c7

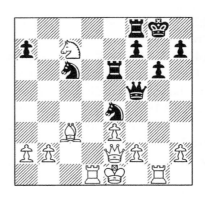

22...♘xc3?!

Now White manages to consolidate her position, but there was no need to capture the bishop at this point. I would prefer 22...♖e7!? here, for example 23 ♘b5 (if 23 ♘d5 ♖d7 24 ♘f4, then 24...♘xc3 25 bxc3 ♖xd1+ 26 ♕xd1 ♖b8 leaves Black with a dangerous initiative) 23...♖fe8 24 ♘d6 (or 24 ♘d4 ♘xd4 25 ♗xd4 ♘g5!? with decent chances on the light squares) 24...♘xd6 25 ♖xd6 ♘e5 26 ♖g3 ♕b1+ 27 ♕d1 ♕xa2 and Black has evened out the material.

23 bxc3 ♖e5 24 f4 ♖a5 25 c4 ♖b8 26 ♘d5 ♔f8 27 ♔f2 ♕h3 28 ♖g2 ♘e7 29 ♘xe7?!

The immediate 29 ♔g1! would have been a better choice. The white knight on d5 is much better, so why not profit from a possible trade by improving the pawn structure?

29...♕h4+ 30 ♔g1 ♕xe7 31 ♕d2 ♖a3

Now Black manages to create enough counterplay by attacking the numerous white pawn islands.

32 ♖e2 ♔g8 33 ♕d6 ♕xd6 34 ♖xd6

♖b1+ 35 ♔f2 ♖c1 36 ♖c6 ♖a4 37 c5 ♖a5 38 ♖c8+ ♔g7 39 c6 ♖a6 40 c7 ♖ac6 41 ♔f3 ♖xc7 42 ♖xc7 ♖xc7

The endgame is completely equal, but White, probably disgusted by her earlier poor technique, manages to lose this one.

43 ♖d2 ♖c3 44 a4 ♖c4 45 ♖d4 ♖c2 46 h3 ♖a2 47 ♖c4 h5 48 ♖d4 a5 49 ♖c4 ♔f6 50 ♖e4 ♖a1 51 ♔g3 ♔g7 52 ♖d4 ♔h6 53 ♖c4 ♖a3 54 ♔f3 h4 55 ♔g4 ♖xe3 56 ♔xh4 f5 57 ♖d4 ♖b3 58 ♖c4?? ♖b4 59 ♖c7 ♖xf4+ 60 ♔g3 ♖xa4 61 h4 ♖g4+ 62 ♔h3 a4 63 ♖a7 ♖b4 64 ♔g3 ♖b3+ 65 ♔g2 a3 66 ♖a8 ♔h5 67 ♖a6 ♖b4 68 ♖xa3 ♖xh4

It is really time to resign.

69 ♖a6 ♖b4 70 ♔f3 g5 71 ♖a5 ♖b3+ 72 ♔f2 ♔g4 73 ♖c5 ♖b2+ 74 ♔f1 f4 75 ♖a5 ♔h4 76 ♖f5 ♖b4 77 ♖c5 g4 78 ♖c2 ♖b1+ 79 ♔g2 f3+ 80 ♔f2 ♖h1 81 ♖c4 ♖h2+ 82 ♔g1 ♖a2 83 ♖c1 ♔h3 84 ♖f1 ♔g3 85 ♖b1 ♖g2+ 86 ♔h1 ♖h2+ 87 ♔g1 f2+ 0-1

Summary

The games in this chapter have shown that you shouldn't be afraid to sacrifice a pawn or two as you get compensated in many ways, be it a lead in development (Games 53-54), a positional advantage (Games 55-56) or simply a dangerous initiative (Game 60). But what may be even more important, you don't have to worry about being strategically outplayed either, as Games 57-59 demonstrated.

1 d4 d5 2 c4 ♘c6 3 cxd5

> 3 e3 e5 – *Game 53*

3...♕xd5 *(D)* **4 e3**

> 4 ♘f3 e5

>> 5 dxe5 – *Game 54*

>> 5 ♘c3 ♗b4 *(D)*

>>> 6 ♗d2 ♗xc3 7 ♗xc3 e4 – *Game 55*

>>> 6 e3 exd4 7 exd4 ♘f6 – *Game 56*

4...e5 5 ♘c3 ♗b4 6 ♗d2 ♗xc3 7 ♗xc3

> 7 bxc3 ♘f6

>> 8 c4 ♕d6 – *Game 57*

>> 8 f3 e4 – *Game 58*

7...exd4 8 ♘e2 ♘f6 9 ♘xd4 0-0 10 ♘b5

> 10 ♘xc6 – *Game 59*

10...♕g5 *(D)* – *Game 60*

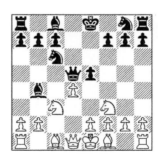
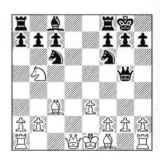

3...♕xd5   *5...♗b4*   *10...♕g5*

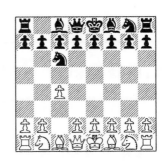

Part Three

Black vs. 1 c4: 1...♘c6

I have to tell you, the English Opening is a bit of a nuisance to the 1...♘c6 player. White refuses to occupy the centre with any pawns but opts for piece development instead, effectively trying to play Black at his own game!

Therefore, a change of gear is needed. and I recommend transposing to the 1...e5 English. Normally 1...♘c6 is hardly associated with main lines, but I think that the resulting positions will be to your liking.

Take the game into uncharted territory!
Even if the game will most likely transpose to 1 c4 e5, there are still a few independent options to entice the English adherent away from his known territory, resulting in positions that perfectly fit the style of the 1...♘c6 player. We will take a closer look at these options in Chapter 12.

Swim against the stream!
It is not always necessary to adhere to common assessments of certain opening lines. As I would like to show you in Chapter 13, systems that are supposedly known to be dubious can actually be faithful companions. Once again I can only say: know your systems, and you will be amply rewarded.

The class conflict: knight(s) versus bishop(s)
As you have already seen in my examination of the Chigorin Defence, parting with the pair of bishops does not necessarily result in a worse position; Black is usually provided with positional compensation in the form of a weakened enemy pawn structure and/or sufficient counterplay in the centre. More examples can be found in Chapter 14.

Chapter Twelve

1 c4 ♘c6: Rare Second Moves for White

As I have already indicated, playing 1...♘c6 against the English Opening has little independent value. After **1 c4 ♘c6** very few players will accept the invitation to transpose to the Chigorin Defence with 2 d4; most of the time you will encounter the typical **2 ♘c3**. Black could then play 2...♘f6, once more hoping to reach the Chigorin Defence after 3 d4 d5, but there is no reason to believe that White players will fall for this bait if they already have declined it on the previous move. And what is even more important: White could play 3 e4, when 3...e5 would reach an inferior version of Chapter 1, as Black has already committed his king's knight to f6 while White is not obligated to develop his own to f3 (which incidentally would lead to Game 68 in Chapter 14). Therefore, Black has nothing better than **2...e5**, which is subject of Chapters 13 and 14.

However, there are a few players who deliberately choose other second moves, the most sensible being 2 g3 and 2 ♘f3, which we will now examine in more detail.

White plays 2 g3

As you may notice over the course of this part of the book, a frequent Black plan in the English Opening is to trade the dark-squared bishop for White's queen's knight in order to get a better grip on the light central squares. Some White players do not like to play such positions and therefore choose **2 g3**, in order to reach their familiar fianchetto systems while denying Black that possibility.

However, Black has an opportunity to ginger things up with **2...d5!**, making use of the fact that White has both neglected to bring d5 under his control and temporarily weakened the h1-a8 diagonal. After **3 cxd5 ♕xd5 4 ♘f3 ♘f6 5 ♘c3** (or 5 ♗g2) **5...♕h5!?** Black intends ...♗h3 to exchange the light-squared bishops. This has been played in only a handful of games so, besides the great potential lying within this line, it is quite probable that you will take your opponent by surprise – something that usual works out well.

> ## Game 61
> ## C.Laqua-C.Wisnewski
> German League 2006

1 c4 ♘c6 2 g3 d5

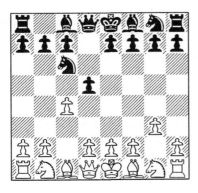

3 cxd5

3 ♘f3?! is a peculiar attempt to reach the Réti Opening; peculiar as ...♘c6 serves Black especially well here. M.Lindinger-C.Wisnewski, Bargteheide 2006, continued 3...dxc4 4 ♗g2 ♖b8! 5 ♕c2 b5 6 b3 ♗b7 7 0-0 (7 bxc4 would have regained the pawn, but after 7...♘d4 8 ♕c3 b4 9 ♕b2 e6 Black is still better, or if 8 ♕d1?! ♘xf3+ 9 exf3 ♕d4 10 ♘c3 ♕xc4 wins it back again) 7...cxb3 8 axb3 e6 9 ♗b2 ♘f6 10 ♖c1 ♗d6 and White had no compensation for the pawn.

3...♕xd5 4 ♘f3 ♘f6 5 ♘c3

After 5 ♗g2 Black should play

5...♕h5!? as well, when White can react differently:

a) 6 h3 has pros and cons. On the one hand, White simultaneously prevents ...♗g4 and ...♗h3; on the other, he can no longer castle without further weakening his position with g3-g4. Meanwhile Black has to be careful not to get his queen trapped. After 6...e5 7 g4 (7 d4 exd4 8 ♘xd4 ♘xd4 9 ♕xd4 ♗c5 is at least equal, while if 7 d3 ♗b4+ 8 ♗d2 ♗xd2+ 9 ♕xd2 ♗d7 or 8 ♘c3 e4 9 ♘g5 exd3 10 ♕xd3 0-0 and Black has no problems) 7...♕g6 8 d3 (if 8 ♘h4 ♕h6 9 ♘f3 ♘d7 leads to comfortable play for Black) 8...♗b4+! is again the key idea to provide the queen with much needed breathing space: 9 ♗d2 ♘d7, and once Black has regrouped his forces, the extended white kingside will be the main target.

b) 6 ♕b3 is another way to prevent ...♗h3, but Black can easily shift gears: 6...e5 7 d3 ♗c5 8 ♘c3 ♗b6 9 h3 ♘d4 10 ♘xd4 exd4 11 ♕b5+ ♕xb5 12 ♘xb5 a6 and Black got a good position in M.Niesel-D.Suhl, German League 1991.

5...♕h5!?

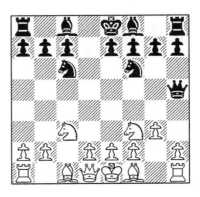

6 d3

There are a few alternatives, but none of them is too appealing:

a) 6 d4?! is dangerous only for White as the d-pawn quickly loses support. Luckhaus-D.Suhl, Würzburg 1987, continued 6...♗g4 7 d5 ♗xf3 8 exf3 0-0-0 9 ♗e2, and now Black could have picked up the pawn with 9...♘xd5! 10 f4 ♕g6 11 ♘xd5 ♕e4.

b) 6 ♗g2 ♗h3 7 0-0 0-0-0 is the kind of position Black is dreaming of, his ideas being ...♘f6-g4 and ...♘c6-d4 with a strong attack against the white king.

c) 6 h3 is similar to 5 ♗g2, when 6...e5 7 d3 ♗b4 8 ♗d2 (for 8 ♗g2 e4 see the note to White's 5th move) 8...0-0 results in a nice position for Black

6...♗h3 7 ♗xh3 ♕xh3 8 ♕b3 0-0-0! 9 ♗e3

9 ♕xf7? is too greedy. After 9...e6 the queen is mouse-trapped and can only be freed at a high price: 10 ♘g5 ♕g2 11 ♕xe6+ ♖d7 12 ♖f1 ♘d4 and Black collects the rook on a1.

9...e6

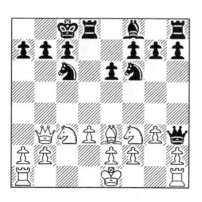

We have reached a roughly level

position. But maybe more importantly, this is no typical position for the English Opening. There is a good chance that White players will mistreat it, as my opponent did in this game.

10 ♘g5?!

Post-mortem analysis with my opponent showed that, sad as it may seem, White should probably seek to trade queens, beginning with 10 ♕a4 ♕g4, but the position still leaves more than enough room for Black to play. 10 0-0-0, on the other hand, allows Black to remove the white bishop with 10...♗g4!.

10...♕h5 11 ♕a4 ♘d5 12 g4?!

Not being familiar with the position, my opponent already slides downhill.

12...♕g6 13 h4 ♘xe3 14 fxe3 h6 15 ♘f3

15 ♘ge4 is effectively met by 15...f5!.

15...♗c5

16 ♔d2

16 d4 was not to my opponent's liking, but was probably still the better choice. I would have played 16...♗b4 17 ♖g1 e5! 18 0-0-0 ♗xc3 19 bxc3 ♕e4

20 ♖d3 exd4 21 cxd4 ♖d5 with a firm grip on the light squares.

16...f5! 17 ♖hg1 ♕f6 18 g5 hxg5 19 ♖xg5 ♘e5 20 ♖f1

Against 20 ♘xe5 ♕xe5 21 ♕f4 I planned 21...♗d6! 22 ♕xe5 ♗xe5, when it is extremely difficult for White to defend the h-pawn.

20...♘g4

21 ♘d1

21 ♖xg4 fxg4 22 ♕xg4 was White's only hope to complicate Black's task. Now the game resolves itself quickly.

21...♖xh4 22 ♕c4 ♘xe3! 23 ♕xh4 ♘xf1+ 24 ♔e1 ♘e3 25 ♘c3 ♗b4 26 ♔d2 ♘d5 27 ♕c4 ♖d6 28 e4 fxe4 29 ♕xe4 ♘xc3 30 bxc3 ♕xc3+ 31 ♔e2 ♕c2+ 32 ♔e3 ♗c5+ 33 ♔f4 ♕f2 34 ♖xg7 ♖d4 35 ♖g8+ ♔d7 36 ♖g7+ ♔e8 37 ♖xc7 0-1

The next game features a different approach. Instead of allowing Black to commence action on the kingside, White calmly continues his development with **3 ♗g2**, knowing that taking on c4 is no serious option for Black. However, after **3...d4**, for a change it is Black who is grabbing some space. The game usually continues **4 ♘f3 e5 5 d3 ♘f6 6 0-0 ♗e7** when we have reached (by transposition) a variation of the Réti Opening.

This position also resembles a reversed Classical Modern Benoni, and while it is already unlikely that your opponent will actually play the Modern Benoni (or the Réti for that matter) and be familiar therefore with the correct treatment, this is one of the few positions where being a move down actually benefits Black! That is because, in the Benoni, the d4-square plays an important role for the fianchettoed bishop – which in the reversed position means the d5-square, but with the black c-pawn still back on c7 (instead of the usual c5) this feature is put into perspective.

Nevertheless, the plans usually employed in the Benoni are not significantly altered here. White will still aim to advance on the queenside, while Black tries to break through in the centre and play ...e5-e4 under favourable circumstances. Check out the next game for a proper handling of the position.

Game 62
A.Serebro-R.Bairachny
Ukrainian Championship,
Donetsk 1993

1 c4 ♘c6 2 g3 d5 3 ♗g2 d4 4 ♘f3 e5 5 d3 ♘f6 6 0-0 ♗e7 7 b4

Instead:

a) Attacking the centre with ...e7-e6 is a standard plan in the Modern Benoni. But here, since the d5-square is not weak (with the c-pawn still on c7), Black is more inclined to answer 7 e3 with 7...dxe3.

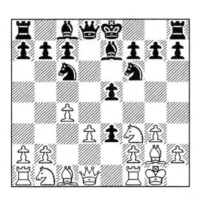

After 8 fxe3 (or 8 ♗xe3 ♘g4 9 ♘c3 0-0 10 ♕e2 ♘xe3 11 fxe3 ♗g4 12 h3 ♗e6 with a comfortable position), Black can disrupt the white pawn structure with 8...e4 9 dxe4 ♕xd1 10 ♖xd1 ♗g4! (10...♘xe4?! 11 ♘d4 gives White unnecessary chances on the long diagonal). The game S.Gelzenleichter-K.Brandenberg, Bad Wiessee 1999, continued 11 ♘c3 (11 h3 ♗xf3 12 ♗xf3 ♘e5

13 ♗g2 ♘xc4 14 e5 ♘xe5 15 ♗xb7 ♖d8 is roughly equal) 11...♗xf3 12 ♗xf3 ♘e5 13 ♗e2 c6 14 a3 a5 15 ♖b1 a4 16 b4 axb3 17 ♖xb3 ♖a7 18 ♗d2 ♘fd7 19 a4 ♘c5 20 ♖b2 0-0 and Black had definite compensation for the pawn.

b) 7 ♘a3 is another common idea, as White reroutes the knight to c2 in order to support a possible queenside pawn advance. In return, Black looks for ways to enforce ...e5-e4 under favourable circumstances: 7...0-0 8 ♘c2 ♖e8 9 ♖b1 a5 10 b3 (not 10 a3?! a4! and the white queenside is fixed) 10...♘d7 11 a3 f5 12 b4 axb4 13 axb4 ♗f6 14 b5 ♘e7 15 ♘b4 ♘c5 provided Black with the better chances in B.Pingas-F.Quiroga, Potrero de los Funes 1995.

7...e4!

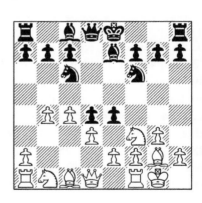

7...♗xb4?! 8 ♘xe5! is just what White wants.

8 dxe4 ♗xb4 9 e5

Black is put more to the test by 9 ♗b2!?, and then:

a) 9...♘xe4?! just runs into 10 ♘xd4.

b) 9...♗c5 has been tried in numerous games, but White gets an easy advantage with 10 ♘bd2 ♕e7 11 ♘b3

♘xe4 12 ♘fxd4 ♘xd4 13 ♘xc5! ♘xc5 14 ♕xd4, V.Salov-R.Hübner, Barcelona 1989, being one of many examples.

c) 9...♗e6 is better. White temporarily wins a pawn, but in return Black can safely complete his development, while the scattered white pawns remain weak. Play continues 10 e5 ♘d7 (10...♘g4?! is the wrong place for the knight; after 11 ♘xd4 ♘xd4 12 ♗xd4 ♕d7 13 ♗b2 0-0-0 14 ♕b3 c5 15 a3 ♗a5 16 ♘c3 ♘xe5 17 ♘e4! ♗xc4 18 ♘d6+! or 17...♘c6 18 ♘xc5 White had a decisive advantage in A.Zakharov-V.Doroshkievich, Lvov 1986) 11 ♘xd4 ♘xd4 12 ♕xd4 c6 and then:

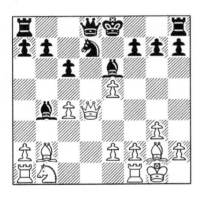

c1) 13 ♘a3 0-0 14 ♖fc1 ♕a5 15 ♘c2 ♗c5 16 ♕e4 ♘b6 17 ♘d4 ♗xd4 18 ♕xd4 ♖fd8 19 ♕e4 ♕c5 20 e3 ♘xc4 and Black regained his pawn in R.Keene-P.Griffiths, British Championship, Coventry 1970.

c2) 13 a3 ♗c5 14 ♕f4 ♕b6 15 ♗c3 ♕b3 16 ♕f3 ♕xc4 17 ♘d2 ♕g4 18 ♘e4 and a draw was agreed in S.Shestakov-A.Vaulin, Moscow 1996.

c3) 13 ♘c3!? has not been played yet, but the prospect of a knight on e4

seems appealing, an additional point being that 13...♘b6 and 13...♘c5 are refuted by 14 ♘d5!. Nevertheless, it seems that after 13...♕a5 14 ♘e4 0-0-0!? Black has enough compensation for the pawn due to his active pieces. Two sample variations are 15 ♘d6+ ♔b8 16 ♖ab1 ♘b6 17 a3 ♗c5 18 ♕f4 ♖d7 and 15 a3 ♗c5 16 ♕c3 ♕xc3 17 ♗xc3 ♗xc4 18 ♖fd1 ♗d5 19 ♘d6+ ♗xd6 20 exd6 ♗xg2 21 ♔xg2 f6 both with highly unclear play. Practical tests are needed.

9...♘e4

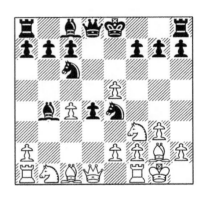

10 ♕c2

Now 10 ♗b2 is not as effective: 10...♗c5 11 ♘bd2 (or 11 ♘xd4 ♗xd4 12 ♗xd4 ♕xd4 13 ♕xd4 ♘xd4 14 ♗xe4 ♘xe2+ 15 ♔g2 ♘d4 16 ♘c3 c6 and Black is not worse) 11...♘c3 12 ♗xc3 dxc3 13 ♘e4 ♕xd1 14 ♖fxd1 c2 15 ♖d2 ♗b4 16 ♖xc2 ♗f5 17 ♘h4 ♗xe4 18 ♗xe4 ♘d4 19 ♖b2 ♗c3 20 ♖ab1 ♗xb2 21 ♖xb2 ♖b8 and Black had the slightly better position in D.Vigorito-A.Cherniack, Marlborough 1999.

10...♘c5 11 a3

11 ♗g5 is smoothly countered by 11...♕d7 12 ♖d1 ♕f5! 13 ♕xf5 ♗xf5 14

♗f4 (14 ♘xd4?! runs into 14...♘xd4 15 ♖xd4 ♘e6 16 ♗xb7 ♖b8 17 ♗c6+ ♔f8 18 ♗e3 ♘xd4 19 ♗xd4 ♖d8 20 e3 h5 and the black rook swings into action via h6) 14...0-0-0 15 ♘g5 ♖d7 16 ♗d5 ♘d8 17 ♗d2 ♗xd2 18 ♘xd2 h6 with the advantage in D.Barash-R.Shabtai, Ramat Hasharon 1990.

11...♗a5 12 ♖d1 ♗g4 13 ♗e3 ♘e6

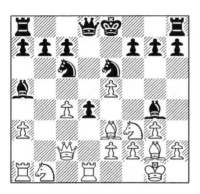

With the d4-pawn enjoying full support, Black is better.

14 h3 ♗h5 15 ♘h4 ♗b6 16 ♔h2 ♕e7! 17 ♘f5 ♕c5 18 ♗xc6+ ♕xc6 19 ♘xd4?!

Getting rid of this pawn was probably what White was aiming at for the whole game, but Black has other strengths too.

19...♗xd4 20 ♗xd4 0-0-0 21 ♗b2

21 ♗e3 is marginally superior, as 21...♖xd1 22 ♕xd1 ♕xc4 is 'only' clearly better for Black.

21...♖xd1 22 ♕xd1 ♕b6 0-1

Oops!

White plays 2 ♘f3

The idea behind **2 ♘f3** is identical to that of 2 g3 most of the time: leaving the queen's knight at home for the

moment, thus depriving Black of certain options. However, it is my opinion that, after **2...e5**, White should actually transpose to Chapter 14 with 3 ♘c3, as his other options are impractical. But you can convince yourself by looking at the following game.

Game 63
R.Wiedner-H.Grabher
Austrian League 1996

---

1 c4 ♘c6 2 ♘f3 e5 3 d4

3 d3 and 3 e3 usually transpose to Chapter 14 after 3...♘f6 4 ♘c3, while 3 e4 ♗c5 was dealt with in the first game of this book.

Instead, 3 g3 e4 4 ♘h4 is a trademark of Israeli GM Jacob Murey. Black must now suppress his urge to punish this bizarre idea. Instead, if he manages to keep his pawn on e4, the knight will be a sad sight on h4. After 4...♘f6, White has two possibilities:

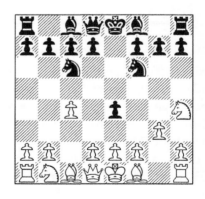

a) 5 ♗g2 should be answered by 5...d5!?. L.Cherner-W.Simpson, correspondence 1997, continued 6 cxd5

♕xd5 7 ♘c3 ♕e5 8 ♕a4 (better is 8 d3 ♗b4 9 0-0 ♗xc3 10 bxc3 0-0 when the position is roughly equal; or if 10...g5 11 d4 ♕a5 12 d5!) 8...♕d4! and the threat of 9...g5 proved troublesome.

b) 5 ♘c3 ♗b4 6 ♗g2 ♗xc3 7 dxc3 (7 bxc3 is problematic as the c-pawns are now weak; for example 7...0-0 8 d3 exd3 9 exd3 ♖e8+ 10 ♗e3 d5! with a good game for Black, or 8 0-0 d6 and it is difficult for White to get his knight back into action) 7...h6 8 ♘f5 0-0 9 ♘d4, and while White has managed to relocate his knight, in the meantime Black has pressed ahead with development. After 9...♘e5 10 b3 ♖e8 11 0-0 d6 12 ♕c2 a6! 13 ♕d1 (13 ♗xe4?! ♘xe4 14 ♕xe4 ♘xc4 is good for Black) 13...♗d7 14 h3 b5 Black had a nice initiative on the queenside in P.Walczak-K.Turecki, Polish Junior Championship 2001.

3...exd4 4 ♘xd4 ♗c5

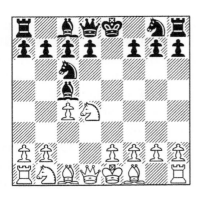

5 ♘c2?!

This retreat is common in some other lines, but here White doesn't have the time to reach a favourable set-up. Other options are:

a) 5 ♘xc6 ♕f6 is a well-known motif

from the Scotch Opening. After 6 e3 ♕xc6 Black has no worries.

b) 5 ♘f5 is a waste of time that is not justified by the slight weakening of the dark squares. After 5...g6 6 ♘g3 ♘f6 7 e4 (7 ♗g5? is met by 7...♗xf2+ 8 ♔xf2 ♘g4+ 9 ♔e1 ♕g5; while 7 e3, in order to close the g1-a7 diagonal, shuts in the bishop and leaves Black with an easy game after 7...d5), it is White who has to be very careful. For example, 7...d6 8 ♗e2 (8 ♗d3 ♘g4 9 0-0?? ♕h4 is an illustration of typical carelessness) 8...♘d4 9 ♗d3 ♘g4 and it is Black who is playing on the dark squares.

c) 5 ♘b3 is also harmless: 5...♗b4+ 6 ♗d2 ♗xd2+ 7 ♕xd2 ♘f6 8 ♘c3 0-0 9 e3 (9 e4 grabs more space but limits the scope of the remaining bishop; after 9...d6 Black doesn't have any problems) 9...d6 10 ♗e2 ♖e8 11 0-0 ♘e4 12 ♘xe4 ♖xe4 with equality in V.Arbakov-V.Rodchenkov, Tula 2002.

d) Finally, 5 e3 ♘ge7 6 ♗e2 0-0 7 0-0 d6 8 ♘c3 a6 9 b3 ♗d7 10 ♗b2 ♘f5 was comfortable for Black in F.Van der Klashorst-C.Kruijf, Haarlem 1997.

5...♕h4! 6 e3 ♘f6 7 ♘c3 d6

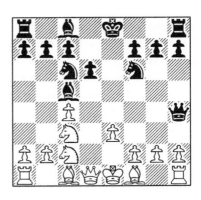

A closer look at the position reveals that it is White who has to fight for equality here.

8 g3 ♕g4

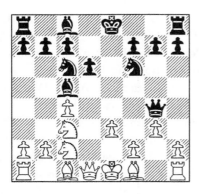

9 h3

9 ♗e2!? is probably better. After 9...♕g6 10 ♘d5 ♘xd5 11 cxd5 ♘e5 12 b4 ♗b6 13 ♗b2 White is still a bit worse, but at least he has managed to developed to a certain degree.

9...♕g6

9...♕xd1+ 10 ♔xd1 (on 10 ♘xd1 ♗f5 is quite annoying) 10...♗e6 is also a good choice if you like to play without queens.

10 ♘b5?!

White had to try and complete his development at any cost. Therefore 10 ♗g2 was necessary, although the position remains difficult. For example 10...0-0 11 ♘d5 (or 11 0-0 ♗f5 12 ♘e1 ♖fe8; while 12 ♘d4 just loses a pawn to 12...♗xd4 13 exd4 ♗d3) 11...♘xd5 12 cxd5 ♘e5 13 0-0 ♗f5 14 ♘d4 ♗e4 and Black is better.

10...♗f5! 11 ♘cd4 ♗xd4 12 ♘xd4

12 ♘xc7+? ♔d7 13 ♘xa8 ♖xa8 is no good, as White cannot afford to take the bishop: 14 exd4 ♗c2! and Black wins.

12...e4 13 ♖g1 0-0 14 ♘xc6 bxc6 15 b3 d5 16 c5 d4!

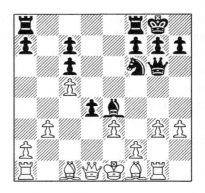

This move can hardly be called a sacrifice, as White is not really allowed to accept it.

17 f3

After 17 exd4 ♖fe8 18 ♗e3 ♘d5 19 ♕d2 ♗f3 20 ♗e2 ♗xe2 21 ♕xe2 ♖e4, followed by ...♖ae8, Black regains the pawn with a clearly better position, while 17 ♕xd4 ♖ad8 18 ♕c4 ♗f3 underlines the chronic weaknesses in the white camp.

17...♗c2 18 ♕xd4 ♖ad8 19 ♕c4 ♖fe8

All the black pieces are well centralized – merely for the price of a pawn.

20 ♔f2 ♘e4+! 21 ♔e1

21 fxe4 ♕f6+ picks up the rook on a1.

21...♖d1+ 22 ♔e2 ♗d3+ 23 ♔xd1 ♗xc4 24 ♗xc4 ♖d8+ 25 ♔e1 ♕f6 0-1

Summary

If White decides not to play 2 ♘c3, then 1...♘c6 proves to be quite effective. White will quickly be facing unfamiliar positions (as in Games 61 and 62); and even if he plays sensibly, care is still required at all times – Game 63 is a good example of that.

1 c4 ♘c6 *(D)* **2 g3**

    2 ♘f3 e5 3 d4 exd4 4 ♘xd4 ♗c5 *(D)* – *Game 63*

2 g3 d5 *(D)* **3 ♗g2**

    3 cxd5 ♕xd5 – *Game 61*

3...d4 – *Game 62*

    1...♘c6   *4...♗c5*   *2...d5*

Chapter Thirteen

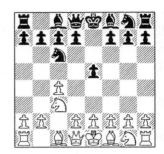

1 c4 ♘c6 2 ♘c3 e5 (3 e3; 3 g3)

After **1 c4 ♘c6 2 ♘c3 e5** we are at the beginning of the 1...e5 English. It is fair to say that 1...♘c6 is mostly employed by offbeat players, but those of you who fit this description will find out that playing main lines is not so bad after all – not as long as there isn't too much theory involved and the plans are easy to understand.

Normally, the best way to get to grips with a new opening system is to look at the lines one by one, sorted by popularity, starting with the most and ending with the least popular. However, in this case I will make an exception, as I find the English Four Knights to be the most suitable way for White to get an advantage, and we'll come to that later. First of all, it is important to know what to do against White's other third moves.

White plays 3 e3

As we have already discovered, adjusting move orders can play an important

role in the English Opening. After **3 e3**, usually a later ♘f3 will take the game into the Four Knights, which is covered in the next chapter. Hence **3...♘f6** is the simplest way for Black to react, inviting the transposition to Games 71-73 with 4 ♘f3. However, White has two other sensible moves to be considered, the first one being **4 d4**. The position after **4...exd4 5 exd4 d5** bears a close resemblance to that in Game 56 (Nyholm-Alekhine) from Chapter 11, but Black can even do better, as we will see in our next game.

Game 64
M.Roskam-W.Vermeulen
Utrecht 2005

1 c4 ♘c6 2 ♘c3 e5 3 e3 ♘f6 4 d4

Instead, 4 ♘f3 transposes to Chapter 14 (Games 71-73), while 4 a3 is the subject of the next game.

4...exd4 5 exd4 d5

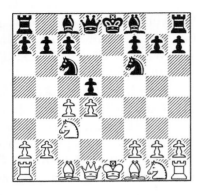

6 ♘f3

Instead:

a) The game N.Scheiderup-J.Pedersen, Harstad 1998, showed one possible way to deal with 6 ♗g5: 6...♗e7 7 ♘f3 ♗g4 8 ♗e2?! dxc4 9 ♗xc4 (or 9 d5 ♗xf3 10 ♗xf3 ♘e5 and White is a pawn down for nothing) 9...♗xf3 10 ♕xf3 ♘xd4 and Black altered the situation to his (material) advantage.

b) 6 cxd5 only makes sense if followed up aggressively. C.Von Bardeleben-H.Süchting, Barmen 1905, continued 6...♘xd5 7 ♗b5 ♗b4 8 ♘ge2 0-0 9 0-0 ♘ce7 10 ♗g5 c6 11 ♗d3, and now the simple 11...♗e6, followed by ...♕d7, would have given Black a clear positional advantage as White has nothing to counterbalance his isolated pawn on d4.

6...♗g4

Black can also try to transpose to Nyholm-Alekhine (Game 56 in Chapter 11) with 6...♗b4 7 cxd5 ♕xd5 8 ♗e2. The only fashionable way to avoid this is 7 ♗g5, when Black should respond 7...0-0, with the idea 8 cxd5 ♕e8+ 9 ♗e2 ♘xd5 10 ♗d2 ♗e6 11 0-0 ♖d8 12 ♗b5

♘de7 13 ♘e4 ♗xd2 14 ♕xd2 ♘f5 and Black had a clear positional advantage due to the isolated d-pawn in P.Stoma-A.Zontakh, Kazimierz Dolny 2001. But this is just for die-hard fans, as the text move is surely good enough.

7 ♗e2?!

After this move White temporarily loses the c-pawn, and getting it back wastes time which Black can use to build up the final assault. Instead, 7 cxd5 bears a close resemblance to 6 cxd5 and was treated similarly in S.Hiemstra-M.Nieuwenbrook, Hengelo 1999, after 7...♘xd5 8 ♗b5 ♗b4. The game continued 9 ♕e2+ ♘de7 10 ♗xc6+ bxc6 11 a3 ♗d6 12 b4 0-0 13 0-0 ♘f5, and with the isolated d-pawn and the doubled c-pawns cancelling each other out, the two bishops are the deciding factor to declare this position better for Black.

7...dxc4 8 0-0 ♗d6 9 ♕a4 0-0 10 ♕xc4 ♗xf3 11 ♗xf3 ♘xd4 12 ♗xb7 ♖b8 13 ♗a6 ♖e8 14 ♖b1 ♘g4!

15 h3 ♘e5 16 ♕a4 ♕h4 17 ♕d1

17 ♗e3 seems better at first sight, but Black has 17...♘ef3+! 18 ♔h1 (if 18

gxf3 ♕xh3 mates) 18...♖xe3! and wins.
**17...♖bd8 18 ♗e3 ♘ef3+ 19 ♔h1 ♖xe3
0-1**

The move order employed in the following game, **4 a3** (instead of 4 d4), only enjoys independent value if the king's knight is developed to e2, from where it can be redeployed to the queenside as in the Sicilian Taimanov. But Black doesn't need to fear this approach, as the great Garry Kasparov himself demonstrated in the following game.

Game 65
L.Van Wely-G.Kasparov
Tilburg 1997

---

1 c4 ♘c6 2 ♘c3 e5 3 e3 ♘f6 4 a3 g6

5 b4
Instead:
a) 5 d4 seizes the centre, to which Black should react with 5...exd4 6 exd4. For the moment, Black can safely ignore the opponent's supremacy in the centre as White cannot capitalize on it.

After 6...♗g7 (6...d5 is similar to Game 64, but with the moves a2-a3 and ...g7-g6 inserted, a condition that certainly favours White) 7 d5 ♘e7 8 ♗e2 d6 9 ♗f4 0-0 10 h3 ♘f5 11 ♘f3 ♖e8 12 0-0 ♘e4 13 ♘xe4 ♖xe4 14 ♗g5 ♗f6 15 ♗d3 ♖e8 16 ♗xf6 ♕xf6 17 b4 ♗d7 18 ♖c1 ♘d4 19 ♘xd4 ♕xd4, Black came up from behind in S.Conquest-J.Howell, Oakham 1994. The alternative 7 ♘f3 pays deference to this, but ultimately fails to impress. Black has to make a choice:

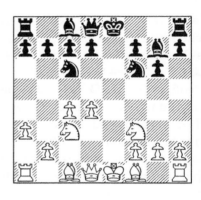

a1) 7...d5!? 8 ♗g5 0-0 gambits the pawn for a dangerous initiative (8...h6 is a fail-safe device; after 9 ♕e2+ ♔f8 10 ♗e3 ♔g8 11 cxd5 ♘xd5 12 ♘xd5 ♕xd5 13 ♕b5 a draw was agreed in F.Vallejo Pons-V.Kramnik, Linares 2003). A prominent example is F.Bistric-E.Bareev, Bosnian Team Championship 1999, which continued 9 ♘xd5 ♗g4 10 ♗e2 ♗xf3 11 ♗xf3 ♖e8+ 12 ♔f1 h6 13 ♗e3 ♘xd5 14 ♗xd5 ♕f6 15 ♗xc6 ♕xc6 16 ♖c1 ♖ad8 17 d5 ♕f6 18 ♖c3 c6 19 ♖d3 ♕xb2 and Black regained the pawn with the advantage.
a2) 7...d6 is also possible. For exam-

ple, 8 ♗e2 (8 d5 gains space, but again weakens the dark squares in the centre; after 8...♘e7 9 ♗d3 0-0 10 0-0 ♖e8 11 h3 ♗f5 12 ♘d4 ♗xd3 13 ♕xd3 ♘d7 14 ♗e3 ♘c5 15 ♕c2 ♗xd4!? 16 ♗xd4 ♘f5 17 ♖ad1 ♕h4 18 ♗xc5 dxc5 19 ♘b5 ♖e7 Black obtained an active position in R.Behling-H.Schwing, German League 1997) 8...0-0 9 0-0 d5! 10 cxd5 ♘e7 11 ♗g5 ♘exd5 12 ♗c4 c6 13 ♕b3 ♗e6! and Black was OK in V.Beim-M.Boehm, Bad Wiessee 1997.

a3) Finally, 7...0-0 8 d5 ♘e5! 9 ♘xe5 ♖e8 10 ♗e2 ♖xe5 11 0-0 ♘e4 12 ♘xe4 ♖xe4 13 ♗d3 ♖e8 14 ♖b1 d6 15 ♗f4 was completely equal in G.Lebredo-J.Diaz, Havana 1975.

b) 5 ♘f3 ♗g7 6 d3 is a completely different set-up, and one of the few where Black should accept the invitation to play a reversed Sicilian. After 6...0-0 7 ♗e2 d5 8 cxd5 ♘xd5 9 ♕c2 ♖e8 10 0-0 ♘xc3 11 bxc3 b6!? 12 e4 ♗b7 13 ♗g5 ♕d6 14 ♖fd1 ♘a5 15 ♘d2 h6 16 ♗h4 ♗f6 17 ♗g3 ♕e7 18 ♘b3 ♘xb3 19 ♕xb3 h5 20 f3 c5 Black enjoyed better prospects in I.Papaioannou-S.Skembris, Greek Championship 1999.

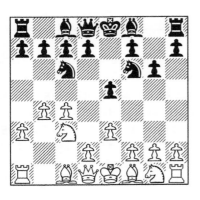

5...♗g7 6 ♗b2 0-0 7 d3

7 ♘f3?! e4 8 ♘g5 h6! 9 ♘h3 d5 shows one downside of the white set-up. In N.Syrigos-S.Logothetis, Greek Team Championship 1999, White tried another formation: 7 ♕c2 ♖e8 8 ♘ge2 d6 9 ♘g3 ♗e6 10 ♗d3, but after 10...♕e7 11 0-0 d5 12 cxd5 ♘xd5 13 ♘xd5 ♗xd5 14 ♘e4 ♘d8 15 ♖ac1 ♖c8 16 ♕c5 ♕d7 17 ♗b5 (17 ♕xa7? is bad due to 17...♘e6 18 ♘c5 ♘xc5 19 ♕xc5 ♗xg2 20 ♔xg2 ♕xd3) 17...c6 18 ♕d6 ♖c7 19 ♕xd7 ♖xd7 20 ♘c5 ♖de7 21 ♗c4 ♗xc4 22 ♖xc4 ♘e6, Black had nothing to worry about.

7...♖e8 8 ♕c2 d5!

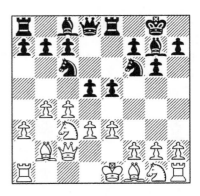

The time is ripe to strike in the centre!

9 cxd5 ♘xd5 10 ♘xd5

On 10 ♘f3 Black can play 10...a5 (the immediate 10...♘d4!? leads only to a forced draw: 11 exd4 ♘xc3 12 dxe5 ♗xe5 13 ♘xe5! ♖xe5+ 14 ♔d2 ♘e4+ 15 ♔e1 ♘c3+ 16 ♔d2 etc; but not 13 ♗e2? ♘xe2 14 ♗xe5 ♘d4! or 14 ♘xe5 ♘d4! and wins) 11 b5 ♘d4! 12 exd4 ♘xc3 13 dxe5 ♗xe5 14 ♘xe5 ♖xe5+ 15 ♔d2 when the idea of 10...a5 comes to light after 15...♕g5+ 16 ♔xc3 ♖c5+ and mates.

10...♕xd5 11 ♘e2

11 ♘f3 should again be met by 11...a5.

11...f5!

A fine move, allowing the queen to retreat to f7 and build a battery with the bishop on e6, which is especially important as this keeps an eye on b3.

12 ♘c3 ♕f7 13 ♘a4?!

Heading directly to c5, but now the white king is stuck in the centre. Instead, 13 ♗e2 would have enabled White to castle, but then after 13...♗e6 the knight cannot get to c5 anymore.

13...♗e6 14 ♘c5 ♗d5

Now the white bishop is tied to g2.

15 b5

15 e4 and 15 ♘xb7 are also effectively met by 15...♘d4!.

15...♘d4!!

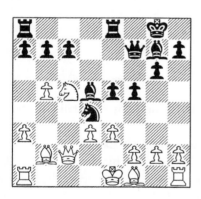

A typical sacrifice, but admirable nevertheless. Black will get a strong attack.

16 exd4 exd4+ 17 ♗e2

17 ♔d1 is refuted simply by 17...b6; while if 17 ♔d2 ♕e7, threatening

18...♗h6+, is deadly.

17...♗xg2 18 0-0-0 ♗xh1 19 ♖xh1 ♕d5!

With loose pieces everywhere, the black queen does well to join the action.

20 ♖e1

Of course not 20 ♖g1? ♖xe2!.

20...♖e5! 21 ♕b3

21 ♘b3 is answered by 21...♖e7 22 ♕c5 (if 22 a4 ♖ae8 and White cannot break the pin on the bishop) 22...♕xc5 23 ♘xc5 ♖e5 24 ♘b3 (or 24 ♗xd4 ♖xe2) 24...♖ae8 25 ♔d1 ♖xb5 transposing to the game.

21...♕xb3 22 ♘xb3 ♖ae8! 23 ♔d1

If 23 ♘xd4 ♖5e7 24 ♔d2 ♖d7 wins.

23...♖xb5 24 ♗f3 ♖xe1+ 25 ♔xe1 c6

Of course not 25...♖xb3?? 26 ♗d5+.

26 ♗d1 a5!

This effective manoeuvre decides the game.

27 ♗xd4 a4 28 ♗xg7 ♔xg7 29 ♘d2 ♖e5+ 30 ♗e2 b5 31 ♔d1 ♖d5 32 ♔c2 g5 33 ♗f3 ♖d6 34 h3 ♔g6 35 ♘b1 h5 36 ♘c3 g4 37 ♗g2 ♔f6 38 hxg4 hxg4 39 d4 ♔g5 40 ♔d3 ♖h6 41 ♔e2 f4 42 ♗e4 ♖h3! 43 ♔d2 ♖h2 44 ♔e1 g3 45 fxg3 fxg3 46 ♔f1

Or 46 ♗xc6 ♖c2 47 ♘e4+ ♔f4, threatening 48...♖xc6 and 48...♖c1+ followed by 49...g2.

46...♖f2+ 47 ♔g1 b4! 48 axb4 a3 49 d5 ♔f4! 50 ♗g6 cxd5 51 ♘xd5+ ♔g5 0-1

In view of 52 ♗b1 ♖b2 53 ♘c3 ♖xb1+! 54 ♘xb1 a2 etc.

White plays 3 g3

Amongst all the third move alternatives, **3 g3** is by far the most popular as it usually provides clear-cut plans depending on Black's reaction. However, I think Black has a suitable antidote up his sleeve with **3...♘f6 4 ♗g2 ♗c5**. This is dismissed by M.Marin on his *Chess-Base* CD on the 1...e5 English; in his opinion White can play e2-e3 followed by ♘g1-e2, reaching a favourable formation as the dark-squared bishop is supposedly biting on granite.

But things are not that easy. First of all, there is the question of the right move order. The immediate **5 e3** can be answered by **5...d5!**,

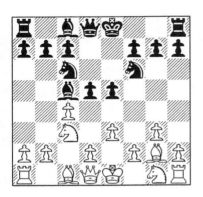

which offers a pawn for decent play on the light squares. Marin refers to the game D.Rogozenko-M.Parligras, Ru-

manian Championship 1999, in which White implemented a new idea: **6 cxd5 ♘b4 7 d4 exd4 8 exe4 ♗e7 9 ♘ge2** and after 9...♗f5 10 0-0 ♘c2 11 g4 ♗g6 12 f4!? White indeed soon gained the upper hand. But there is no need for Black to enter this dangerous line. Instead, he can safely castle, **9...0-0**, intending to capture on d5 afterwards and then build up against the isolated d-pawn. A nice illustration of how to do this was given by the British GM Julian Hodgson.

Game 66
D.Bunzmann-Ju.Hodgson
German League 1999

1 c4 ♘c6 2 ♘c3 e5 3 g3 ♘f6 4 ♗g2 ♗c5

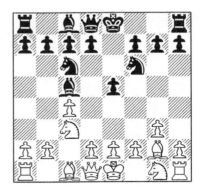

5 e3?!

5 a3 is considered in the next game.

5 d3 is a different, albeit harmless set-up. If Black finds the correct move order, he has nothing to worry about: 5...a6 6 ♘f3 (White would like to play 6 ♗g5 but this currently runs into 6...♗xf2+) 6...d6 7 0-0 (again 7 ♗g5 does

not achieve anything as 7...h6 8 ♗xf6 ♕xf6 9 ♘e4 ♗b4+ saves the bishop) 7...h6 8 a3 0-0 9 b4 ♗a7 10 ♗b2 ♗e6 11 ♘d2 d5 12 cxd5 ♘xd5 13 ♖c1 ♘xc3 14 ♗xc3 ♗d5 15 ♗xd5 ♕xd5 16 ♕b3 ♖ad8 17 a4 ♕xb3 18 ♘xb3 ♖d5 and Black stopped all possible queenside activities in M.Vujadinovic-J.Van Esbroeck, correspondence 1999. Instead, 11 ♖c1 ♕d7 allows Black to reach the set-up we will take a closer look at in the next game. Here 12 e3 ♗h3 13 d4 ♗xg2 14 ♔xg2 exd4 15 exd4 d5! 16 c5 ♖fe8 (16...♖ae8, intending ...♗b8 and a subsequent ...c6, is even more precise) 17 ♕d3 was played in D.Mirzagaliamova-K.Ambarcumova, Russian Junior Championships 1999, and now with 17...♖e7, followed by ...♖ae8, Black could have reached a comfortable position.

5...d5! 6 cxd5

The other sensible capture is 6 ♘xd5 ♘xd5 and then:

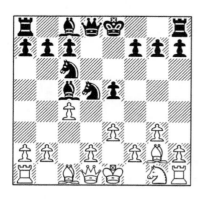

a) 7 ♗xd5 7 ♘b4 8 ♗e4 ♘d3+ 9 ♗xd3 (or 9 ♔e2 ♘xc1+ 10 ♖xc1 f5 11 ♗g2 0-0 12 f4 e4 with a great position; not 9...♘xf2? 10 ♔xf2 ♗xe3+, hoping

for 11 ♔xe3?! ♕d4+ 12 ♔f3 ♗g4+! 13 ♔xg4 ♕xe4+ 14 ♔h3 ♕xh1 with a better position for Black, as after 11 ♔g2 ♗b6 12 d3 f5 13 ♗f3 0-0 14 ♘h3 Black had no adequate compensation in V.Makhianov-A.Fomin, Tula 2001) 9...♕xd3 10 ♕e2 ♕g6 11 d4 ♗b4+ (Tomescu suggests 11...♗e7 as an improvement) 12 ♗d2 ♗xd2+ 13 ♕xd2 ♕c6! 14 f3 exd4 15 ♕xd4 0-0 16 ♔f2 ♗e6 17 ♘e2 and a draw was agreed in I.Almasi-V.Tomescu, Budapest 1997.

b) 7 cxd5 ♘b4

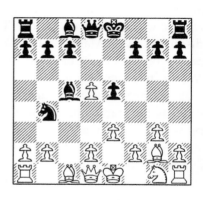

8 ♕b3 (8 d3 c6!? 9 a3 ♘xd5 10 ♘f3 ♕e7 11 0-0 ♗b6 12 b4 0-0 13 ♗b2 f6 14 ♘d2 was equal in Z.Izoria-A.Kogan, Bastia rapid 2005; while 8 a3?! ♘d3+ 9 ♔e2 ♗g4+! 10 f3 ♕xd5 11 ♕c2 0-0-0 12 ♘h3 ♖he8 13 b4 ♗b6 14 ♖b1 ♖e6 15 ♖g1 ♗f5 16 g4 ♘xc1+ 0-1 J.Graf-F.Braga, German League 1989, was close to an execution) 8...c6! and White can hardly accept the pawn as 9 dxc6 bxc6 gives Black excellent attacking chances, the game T.Reschke-P.Kopp, Bruchkoebel 1993, being a powerful illustration: 10 a3 ♘d3+ 11 ♔e2 ♗a6! 12 ♗xc6+ ♔e7 13 ♗b5 ♖b8 14 a4 ♕a5! 15

♕c3 ♗b4 16 ♕c6 ♘xc1+ 17 ♕xc1 ♖xb5!
18 axb5 ♕xb5+ 19 ♔f3 ♗b7+ 20 e4 ♖c8
21 ♕f1 ♗xe4+! 22 ♔xe4 ♖c4+ 23 ♔e3
♗xd2+! 24 ♔xd2 ♕xb2+ 25 ♔e3 ♕d4+
26 ♔e2 ♕e4+ 27 ♔d2 ♖d4+ 28 ♔c1
♕c6+ when White might consider himself fortunate to be beaten in such a
glamorous fashion.

6...♘b4

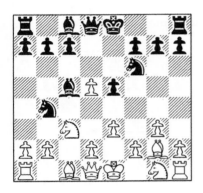

7 d4

Alternatively:

a) 7 ♘e4?! was tried in J.Cortes
Mambiona-C.Vargas Drechsler, Barcelona 1997, but after 7...♘xe4 8 ♗xe4 f5 9
♗g2 ♘d3+ 10 ♔f1, 10...e4 is just terrible
for White.

b) 7 d3 ♘bxd5 8 a3 c6 9 ♕c2 ♗d6
was equal in K.Lippmann-C.Wisnew-
ski, Kiel 2001.

c) 7 a3 ♘d3+ 8 ♔e2 ♗g4+ 9 f3 ♗f5
and Black has excellent compensation.

7...exd4 8 exd4 ♗e7 9 ♘ge2 0-0

This is the best way to continue –
not only to achieve equality, but also to
play for a win! Instead, 9....♗f5 was
long thought to be a safe route to a
draw after 10 0-0 ♘c2 11 ♖b1 ♘b4 12
♖a1 ♘c2, but 11 g4 ♗g6 12 f4!? im-

proved on this for White in
D.Rogozenko-M.Parligras, Rumanian
Championship 1999. The game continued 12...♘xa1 (12...♘xg4 is no better: 13
f5 ♗d6 14 ♕xc2! ♗xh2+ 15 ♔h1 ♕h4 16
♗g5 ♕xg5 17 ♗h3 ♗h5 18 ♗xg4 ♗xg4
19 ♔xh2 and White has a winning advantage) 13 f5 ♘xg4 (Rogozenko suggested 13...♗d6!? 14 ♗f4 ♘xg4 15 fxg6
hxg6) 14 ♘g3 ♘xh2 15 ♔xh2 ♗d6 16
♘ce4 ♕h4+ (16...0-0 17 ♗g5 ♗xg3+ 18
♔xg3 f6 19 fxg6 fxg5 20 ♕xa1 is also
good for White) 17 ♗h3 ♕xe4 18 ♖e1
♕xe1 19 ♕xe1+ ♔f8 20 fxg6 hxg6 21
♔g2 and White won a few moves later.

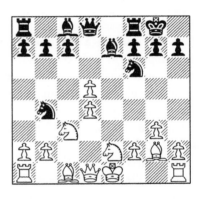

10 0-0 ♘bxd5 11 ♕b3

11 ♘f4 is another attempt to solve
the problems of the isolated d-pawn.
Black should respond 11...♘xf4 12 ♗xf4
♗d6 (12...c6 is fruitless as it allows 13 d5
cxd5 14 ♘xd5 ♘xd5 15 ♕xd5 ♕xd5 16
♗xd5 and White is better due to his
more active bishops) 13 ♗e5 (13 ♗g5 h6
14 ♗xf6 ♕xf6 15 ♖c1 ♖b8 16 ♕a4 a6 17
♘d5 ♕d8 18 ♖c3 ♗d7 19 ♕c2 ♗c6 led to
a good game for Black in H.Quelle-
M.Loehr, German League 1996) 13...c6
14 ♕b3, as in M.Balduan-M.Loehr,

German League 1996, and now 14...♝xe5 15 dxe5 ♞g4 16 ♖fe1 ♕e7 would have been good for Black.

11...c6 12 ♝g5 h6 13 ♝xf6 ♞xf6 14 d5 c5!

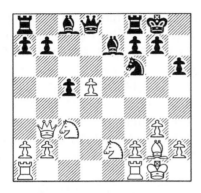

This move shows a fine understanding of the position – the d5-pawn is not as strong as it looks. Black now continues with excellent technique, improving his position step by step.

15 ♖ad1 ♝d6 16 ♞b5 a6 17 ♞xd6 ♕xd6 18 a4 b5! 19 ♞c3

Not 19 axb5 axb5 20 ♕xb5? ♝a6.

19...♝d7 20 ♕c2 ♖fe8 21 axb5 axb5 22 ♖a1 ♖xa1 23 ♖xa1 ♕e5 24 ♖d1 b4 25 ♞a2 ♕e2

26 ♕c1 ♞e4 27 ♖f1 ♞d2 28 ♕xc5 ♞xf1 29 ♝xf1 ♕e1

It doesn't matter but 29...♞xf1+! 30 ♔xf1 ♝h3+ mates at once.

30 ♕xb4 ♝h3 31 ♕c4 ♖a8 32 ♞c1 ♕xf1+ 33 ♕xf1 ♝xf1 34 ♔xf1 ♖a1 0-1

A true masterpiece!

With the preliminary **5 a3** White accounts for the developments in the previous game.

Not only are sallies to b4 prevented once and for all, the possibility of harassing the bishop with b2-b4 is also an attractive option. Now the black bishop needs a safe haven on the g1-a7 diagonal, so moving the a-pawn is necessary. I prefer **5...a6** to 5...a5 since the latter weakens the b5-square, and I don't think that b2-b4 needs to be prevented anyway. Following **6 e3 d6 7 ♞ge2** Black should take the time to play **7...h6** as well, to prevent the possibility of 8 d4 exd4 9 exd4 ♝a7 10 ♝g5. Then after **8 0-0 0-0**, White can choose between different set-ups, but Black's plan usually remains the same: playing ...d6-d5 to fix the white pawns on the dark squares in order to attack them at a later date. One example of how the black idea can be implemented is the following game.

Game 67
J.Stanke-C.Wisnewski
Hamburg 2003

---

1 c4 ♘c6 2 ♘c3 e5 3 g3 ♘f6 4 ♗g2 ♗c5 5 a3 a6 6 e3 d6 7 ♘ge2 h6

It is important to play the correct move order. The immediate 7...0-0?! allows 8 d4 exd4 9 exd4 ♗a7 10 ♗g5, showing the point of a timely ...h7-h6; while after 8...♗a7 9 d5 ♘e7, Black although not worse, does not get his desired positions.

8 d4 exd4 9 exd4 ♗a7 10 h3 0-0 11 0-0 ♖e8

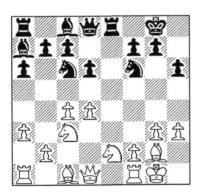

12 ♗e3

12 b4 is the alternative set-up. Black does best to build his play around the e4-square: 12...♗f5 13 ♗b2 ♘e4!? and now 14 ♘d5 (14 ♘xe4 ♗xe4 15 ♗xe4 ♖xe4 reveals the true weakness of the white pawns, or if 15 d5 ♗xg2 16 ♔xg2

♘e5 and Black is better) 14...♘e7 15 ♘e3 ♗h7 16 ♘f4 c6! 17 ♔h2 d5 18 c5 ♗b8 with a clear advantage in A.Jochens-C.Wisnewski, Kiel (rapid) 2004.

12...♗f5 13 b4 ♕d7 14 g4 ♗h7 15 ♘g3 ♔h8!

A multifunctional move, freeing the g8-square for the knight, the bishop or the rook.

16 ♕d2 ♖ab8 17 ♖fe1 ♘e7 18 ♖e2 d5! 19 c5 c6

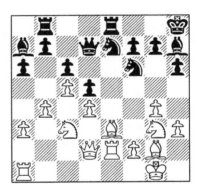

The current pawn structure is what Black is looking for in this line. As we will see, the white pawns will become weak in the endgame. But before that, Black's dark-squared bishop, once redeployed to b8, is a monster in many cases, so White does best to eliminate it as soon as possible.

20 ♖ae1 ♖bd8 21 ♗f4 ♘g6 22 ♗e5 ♘g8

Black's position looks passive, but it is rock solid. In the actual game, White is driven back step by step.

23 ♗d6 ♘h4 24 ♖xe8 ♖xe8 25 ♖xe8 ♕xe8 26 ♕e3 ♕d8 27 ♗f1 ♗b8 28 ♗xb8 ♕xb8 29 f4 f5!

Note how the white pawns, which

secured an advantage in space for a long time, are now picked upon.

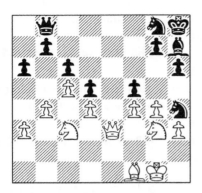

30 ♗e2 ♞f6 31 ♕e5 ♕c8 32 ♞h5 ♞g6 33 ♕e3

White should have tried to make the best of a bad job with 33 ♕xf5 ♕xf5 34 gxf5 ♞h4 35 ♞xf6 gxf6 36 ♗g4 ♞xf5 37 ♗xf5 ♗xf5 and a drawish endgame. **33...♕f8 34 ♞xf6 ♕xf6 35 gxf5 ♞e7! 36**

♗g4 h5 37 ♗xh5 ♞xf5 38 ♕e8+ ♗g8 39 ♞e2 ♞xd4 40 ♞xd4 ♕xd4+ 41 ♔g2 ♕xf4

42 ♗g4 ♕g5 43 ♕d7 ♕d2+ 44 ♔g3 ♕e3+ 45 ♔h4??

It was not necessary to let the game end so abruptly, but after 45 ♗f3 d4 the extra pawn should decide in any case. **45...♕f2+ 0-1**

Summary

Set-ups with 3 e3 are rarely played – and with good reason, as Games 64 and 65 show. The best White can do is transpose to the Four Knights in the next chapter. 3 g3 from Games 66 and 67 is by far the more popular choice; you will encounter this line quite often. But many White players are in danger of underestimating Black's possibilities in my recommended set-up, and that's where the writing is on the wall.

1 c4 ♘c6 2 ♘c3 e5 *(D)* **3 g3**

    3 e3 ♘f6

        4 d4 exd4 5 exd4 d5 – *Game 64*

        4 a3 g6 *(D)* – *Game 65*

3...♘f6 4 ♗g2 ♗c5 *(D)* **5 a3**

    5 g3 – *Game 66*

5...a6 – *Game 67*

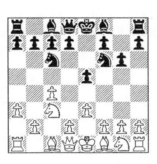

     2...e5   *4...g6*   *4...♗c5*

Chapter Fourteen

1 c4 ♘c6 2 ♘c3 e5
3 ♘f3 ♘f6

While not being the most popular of all systems, the English Four Knights, which we reach via **1 c4 ♘c6 2 ♘c3 e5 3 ♘f3 ♘f6**, is certainly one of the most uncompromising. The usual intention is to transpose into various positions similar to those in the Sicilian Defence where the extra move will certainly not hurt. At some occasions picking up that gauntlet might be justified, but there is no need to do your opponent that kind of favour. I will therefore recommend a more conservative approach which has served me well over the past few years. But enough of the talking, let's look now at the numerous formations the White player has at his disposal.

White plays 4 e4

The position after **4 e4** bears a certain resemblance to Chapter 1, but there are a few noteworthy differences. First of all, Black has already committed his king's knight to f6, effectively depriving himself of ...f7-f5 which has proven to be quite successful. But what may be even more important is that Black cannot exploit the weakness of the d4-square so easily, since 4...♝c5 now runs into 5 ♘xe5 ♘xe5 6 d4 which is favourable to White, as I will show below. Therefore a more subtle approach is needed, and the move that offers the best chances is **4...♝b4**.

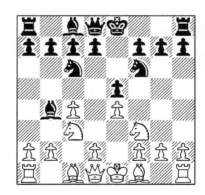

This move puts more pressure on the white centre by challenging the white knight, but the main intention is simply to develop the bishop before playing the consolidating ...d7-d6, only then seeking to exploit the weakness of the dark squares (in particular d4). After **5 d3 d6** there are two distinct possibilities between which White may choose. With 6 ♗e2 White opts for quick development, intending to play f2-f4 as soon as possible. 6 g3 has the same idea but is a bit slower. The proper reaction to both moves is the subject of our next game.

Game 68
M.Rohde-P.Wolff
Boston 1994

---

1 c4 ♘c6 2 ♘c3 e5 3 ♘f3 ♘f6 4 e4 ♗b4

This time 4...♗c5?! is unfortunately dubious after 5 ♘xe5! and then:

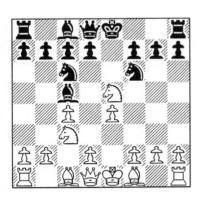

a) 5...♗xf2+ 6 ♔xf2 ♘xe5 7 d4 with a clear advantage, as Black cannot exploit the exposed position of the white king.

b) 5...0-0!? is an interesting pawn sacrifice, but in my opinion Black does not have enough compensation to con-

sider it a serious alternative. After 6 ♘f3 ♖e8 7 d3 d5 8 cxd5 ♘xd5 9 ♗e2 White had a safe position besides his extra pawn in A.Nimzowitsch-F.Yates, Dresden 1926.

c) 5...♘xe5 6 d4 ♗b4 (6...♗xd4 7 ♕xd4 only centralizes the queen, while 6...♗d6 is met by 7 c5! with a good game for White) 7 dxe5 ♘xe4 8 ♕d4 ♘xc3 (8...♘c5 does not work well; White can easily obtain an advantage after 9 ♗d2 0-0 10 0-0-0 b6 11 ♘e4!, when 11...a5? 12 ♗g5 ♕e8 13 ♘f6+! gxf6 14 ♗xf6 ♕e6 15 ♕f4 was completely hopeless for Black in R.Cifuentes Parada-J.Gatica, Santiago 1991) 9 bxc3 and now all moves prove deficient:

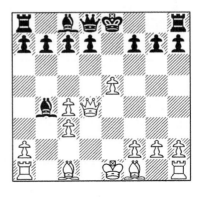

c1) 9...♗a5?! 10 ♗a3 d6 11 exd6 0-0 12 0-0-0 cxd6 13 ♕xd6 ♕xd6 14 ♗xd6 ♖e8 15 ♔b2 ♗d7 16 ♗d3 was played in V.Korchnoi-R.Hübner, Solingen 1973; but begging for a draw is hardly something I would like to do in my spare time.

c2) 9...c5?! 10 ♕e3 ♗a5 11 ♗a3 (Black was OK after 11 ♗d2 ♕e7 12 ♗d3 0-0 13 0-0 d6 14 exd6 ♕xd6 in

K.Budt-R.Soelter, Enningerloh 1965) 11...♕e7 (11...b6 shuts in the bishop, allowing White to rule the board after 12 ♗e2 0-0 13 ♗f3 ♖b8 14 0-0 ♖e8 15 ♖ad1 ♕h4 16 ♗d5 ♗b7 17 f4 in A.Meymuhin-A.Zvidra, correspondence 2000) 12 ♗xc5 ♗xc3+ 13 ♕xc3 ♕xc5 14 ♖d1 0-0 (or 14...b6 15 ♗e2 ♗b7 16 0-0 ♖d8 17 e6!) 15 ♖d5 ♕c6 16 ♗d3 and Black has serious problems.

c3) 9...♗e7 10 ♕g4

10...g6 (if 10...♔f8 11 ♕e4! is the best way to continue, and then 11...♗c5 12 ♗e2 ♖b8 13 0-0 b6 14 ♗f4 ♗b7 15 ♕d3, followed by ♖ad1 and/or ♕g3, is better for White according to Carsten Hansen; while after 11...d6 12 ♗e3 dxe5 13 ♖d1 ♕e8 14 ♕xe5 ♗d6 15 ♕h5 ♗e5, the game V.Karavaev-S.Emilianov, Krasnodar 2003, continued 16 ♗e2! ♗xc3+ 17 ♔f1 ♗e6 18 f4 ♕c6 19 ♔f2 g6 20 ♕h4 ♔g7? 21 f5! with a decisive advantage for White) 11 ♗h6 d6 12 ♕e4 ♕d7 (12...♗f5 can be met by 13 ♕xb7 ♖b8 14 ♕xa7) 13 ♗d3 dxe5 14 0-0! f6 15 f4 ♕c6 16 ♕xc6+ bxc6 17 fxe5 f5 was played in S.Conquest-A.Khalifman, Hastings 1995 (17...fxe5?! 18 ♗g7 ♖g8 19 ♗xe5 is

just sad for Black), and now after 18 g4! ♗e6 (or 18...fxg4 19 ♗e4 ♗b7 20 ♖ad1) 19 gxf5 gxf5 20 ♗xf5 ♗xc4 21 ♖f3 White's advantage presents itself in the form of the e5-pawn.

5 d3 0-0

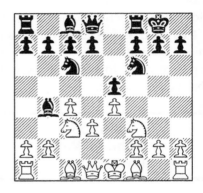

6 ♗e2

6 g3 is the other popular choice. Summarizing briefly, I can say that attempts to nag at the white centre with ...a7-a6 and ...b7-b5 have proved insufficient. But an effective plan can be devised by employing familiar ideas from Chapter 1 – the occupation of d4 and the implementation of ...f7-f5. R.Cifuentes Parada-V.Epishin, Groningen 1997, continued 6...d6 7 ♗g2 h6 8 0-0 ♗c5 9 h3 ♘d4 10 ♘xd4 ♗xd4 11 ♔h2 ♘h7!? 12 ♕e2 c6 13 ♗e3 ♕b6 14 ♖ae1 ♗d7 15 ♕d2 ♖ae8 16 f4 ♗xe3 17 ♖xe3 exf4 18 gxf4 f5! after which Black had a good game.

6...d6 7 0-0 ♗xc3!

Trading a bishop for a knight is once more the key to a successful strategy.

8 bxc3 ♘d7 9 ♘e1 ♘c5 10 f4 exf4 11 ♗xf4 f5 12 exf5 ♗xf5

The opening phase is complete, and Black is better due to his favourable pawn structure.

13 ♘c2 ♕e7 14 ♕d2 ♖ae8 15 ♖ae1 ♘e5 16 ♘b4 ♕d7 17 ♗xe5 dxe5!?

This devalues the pawn formation, but also grants a more direct access to the backward pawn on d3. For those who are unwilling to play with an isolated pawn, 17...♖xe5 is a solid alternative.

18 ♕e3 ♕d6 19 ♗f3 c6 20 d4 ♘d7

This shows another point of the plan begun with 7...♗xc3 – the white centre is immobile, so trading pawns on e5 is hardly an option.

21 c5 ♕g6 22 ♗e2 exd4 23 ♕xd4 ♔h8 24 ♗d3 ♖xe1 25 ♖xe1 a5 26 ♗xf5 ♕xf5 27 ♘d3 h6 28 h3 ♖f7 29 ♔h2 ♔h7 30 ♖e3 ♘f6 31 ♖f3 ♕d5!

For the second time Black is unafraid of creating an isolated pawn. The white pawns are just too weak.

32 ♕xd5 cxd5 33 ♖f5 ♖c7 34 ♖e5 ♔g6 35 ♖e6 ♔f7 36 ♖b6 ♘e4 37 ♖b5 a4 38 c4 dxc4 39 ♘e5+ ♔e8 40 ♘xc4 ♖xc5

Black finally picks up a pawn and converts it with excellent technique.

41 ♖b4 b5 42 ♘e3 ♘d6 43 ♔g3 ♔d7 44 ♔f4 ♔c6 45 h4 ♘c4 46 ♘f5 ♘e5 47 ♔e4 ♘d7 48 ♘xg7 ♖c2 49 ♘f5 ♖xa2 50 ♘d4+ ♔c5 51 ♖xb5+ ♔c4 52 ♖b1 ♘c5+ 53 ♔e5 ♘d3+ 54 ♔e4 ♖xg2 55 ♘f5 ♖g4+ 56 ♔e3 ♔c3 57 ♘d6 ♘b2 58 ♘b5+ ♔c2 59 ♖h1 ♘c4+ 60 ♔f3 h5 61 ♖h2+ ♔b3 62 ♖h1 ♔c2 63 ♖h2+ ♔d3 64 ♔f2 ♖f4+ 65 ♔e1 ♖e4+ 66 ♔d1 ♘e3+ 67 ♔c1 ♖c4+ 68 ♔b1 ♖b4+ 69 ♖b2 ♖xh4 70 ♘c7 ♘d1 71 ♖g2 ♘c3+ 72 ♔b2 ♖b4+ 0-1

White plays 4 a3

Here **4 a3** is more than just a waiting move.

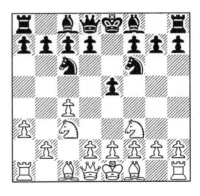

Not only does it prevent 4...♗b4, it also discourages Black from playing 4...♗c5, as after 5 b4 the bishop would have to retreat again, since 5...♗d4 6 ♘xd4 ♘xd4 7 e3 is hardly an option.

Avoiding a reversed Open Sicilian (after 4...d5) is a matter of principle, but how else should this position be treated? An aggressive method would be 4...e4, but after the rather forced 5 ♘g5 ♕e7 6 d3 exd3 the move 7 e4! poses problems for Black, which I at least have been unable to solve satisfactorily. But fortunately this is not necessary: Black has the interesting option of **4...d6**, protecting the e-pawn and therefore enabling ...♘d4 – an important positional resource we will encounter again in the course of this chapter. To see the potential behind this manoeuvre, the next game should act as an appetizer.

Game 69
D.Blair-G.Armani
Correspondence 2000

---

1 c4 ♘c6 2 ♘c3 e5 3 ♘f3 ♘f6 4 a3 d6

4...e4 is a move with an aggressive character and would be my first choice, if there had not been setbacks lately.

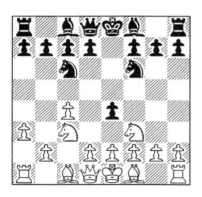

After 5 ♘g5 ♕e7 6 d3 exd3 7 e4! causes problems for Black. A.Beliavsky-M.Turov, Copenhagen 2002, continued 7...h6 8 ♘f3 d5 (if 8...♘xe4 9 ♘d5 ♕d8 10 ♗xd3 and White has more than adequate compensation for the pawn) 9 cxd5 ♘xe4 10 ♗e3 ♘xc3 11 bxc3 ♘e5 12 ♗xd3 ♘g4 13 0-0 ♘xe3 14

fxe3 ♗d7 (not 14...♕xe3+ 15 ♔h1 and Black is in danger) 15 e4 ♕c5+ 16 ♔h1 0-0-0 17 ♕b3 and Black had nothing to be glad about.

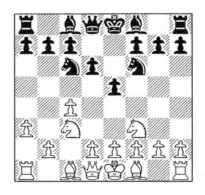

5 d3

White has various other ways to proceed:

a) 5 e3 reaches a position similar to that in Van Wely-Kasparov which we examined in the previous chapter (Game 65). Black should continue likewise with 5...g6, when White has to choose between two set-ups:

a1) 6 d4 exd4 7 exd4 ♗g7 is examined in the notes to Van Wely-Kasparov (via 3 e3 ♘f6 4 a3 g6 5 d4 exd4 6 exd4 ♗g7 7 ♘f3 d6).

a2) 6 d3 ♗g7 resembles a Closed Sicilian in which the white pieces are inexpertly placed. After 7 ♗e2 0-0 8 0-0 ♖e8 Black should seek to enforce ...e5-e4 to broaden the scope of his bishop on g7. By this he can get a comfortable game, for example 9 ♕c2 ♗f5 10 ♘d2 (10 e4 only weakens d4, which Black can immediately spring at with 10...♗g4) 10...a6 11 ♖b1 (the hasty 11 b4?! allows 11...e4! 12 d4 ♘xd4! 13 exd4 e3 14 ♗d3 ♗xd3 15 ♕xd3 exd2 16 ♗xd2 d5!, when the d4-pawn is a worthy target) 11...h5 12 b4 ♘h7, as in M.Gurevich-A.Karpov, Hilversum 1993, with attacking chances on the kingside.

b) 5 d4

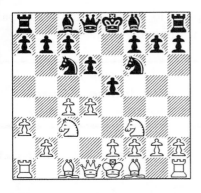

5...♗g4!? (5...exd4 is a bit too passive for my taste; after 6 ♘xd4 g6 7 ♗g5 ♗g7 8 e3 0-0 9 ♗e2 h6 10 ♗h4 ♘xd4 11 exd4 ♗f5 12 0-0 c6 13 g4 ♗e6 14 f4 White had a decent advantage in V.Korchnoi-E.Bacrot, Cannes 1996) 6 d5 ♘e7 7 e4 (if 7 g3 g6 8 ♗g2 ♗g7 9 ♘d2 ♕c8 10 h3 ♗d7 11 b4 a5 12 ♗b2 axb4 13 axb4 ♖xa1 14 ♕xa1 0-0 and Black was not worse in L.Marini-L.Schmid, correspondence 1954), when it looks like Black has a cramped position, but this can be proven wrong. After 7...♘g6 8 h3 ♗d7 9 ♗d3 ♗e7 10 ♘e2 (or 10 ♗e3 ♘h5 11 ♘e2 0-0 with good prospects on the kingside) 10...h6 11 g4?! ♘h7 12 ♘g3 ♘h4 13 ♘xh4 ♗xh4 14 ♗e3 ♗g5, Black reigned over the dark squares in J.Campeert-I.Schrancz, correspondence 1983.

c) Finally, 5 g3 is best met by 5...♗e6

6 d3 ♕d7 7 ♗g2 h6 8 e4 ♗h3 9 ♗xh3 ♕xh3 10 ♘d5 ♘xd5 11 cxd5 ♘e7 12 ♗e3 c6 13 dxc6 ♘xc6 14 ♕b3 ♕d7 and Black had no problems in S.Atalik-I.Miladinovic, Kastoria 1996.

5...♘d4!

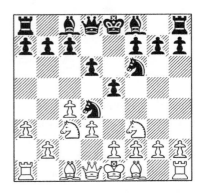

6 ♘d2 ♗g4 7 b4 ♗e7 8 h3 ♗h5

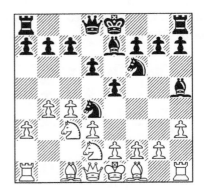

9 g4

Necessary for White to complete development, but it is also a further weakening.

Instead, 9 ♕a4+?! c6 10 e3? and then 10...♘e6 helped to ease the position in A.Chernin-A.Morozevich, Podolsk 1993. But following the spectacular 10...♘d5!! White is already lost.

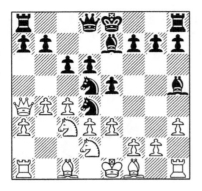

Here White has no time to play 11 ♗b2 due to 11...♘b6 trapping the queen; or if 11 ♘xd5, 11...b5 wins the queen again; while after 11 exd4 ♘xc3 12 ♕c2 exd4 Black went on to win in G.Chrestani-K.Krotofil, correspondence 1998.

9...♕g6 10 ♗g2 c6 11 ♗b2 ♘e6 12 b5 ♖c8 13 ♖b1 0-0 14 bxc6 bxc6 15 ♘f3 ♖b8 16 ♘h4 d5

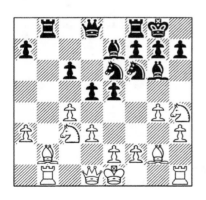

Black already has a significant advantage.

17 ♕a4 ♘f4 18 ♗f3 ♗xd3! 19 exd3 ♘xd3+ 20 ♔e2 ♖xb2+ 21 ♖xb2 ♘xb2 22 ♕xa7 ♘e4 23 ♘xe4 dxe4 24 ♗xe4 ♗xh4 0-1

White plays 4 d3

4 d3 is another way to lure Black into playing a reversed Sicilian. But instead of thinking about ...d5, Black turns his attention to the other central light square with **4...♗b4**, eventually trading his dark-squared bishop for the c3-knight in order to play ...e5-e4, and hoping to disrupt the white pawn structure in the process.

Game 70
A.Khalifman-A.Shirov
Moscow (rapid) 2002

---

1 c4 ♘c6 2 ♘c3 e5 3 ♘f3 ♘f6 4 d3 ♗b4

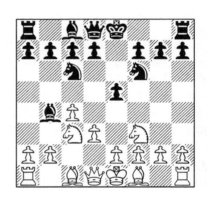

5 ♗d2

The only sensible way to react to Black's intentions.

5 e4 returns to the 4 e4 ♗b4 5 d3 of Rohde-Wolff (Game 68), while 5 e3?! simply invites Black to play 5...♗xc3+ 6 bxc3 e4?.

5 a3?! is treated similarly, but deserves a more detailed look: 5...♗xc3+ 6 bxc3 e4 7 ♘d2 (or 7 ♘d4 exd3 8 exd3 0-0 9 ♘xc6 dxc6 10 ♗e2 ♗f5 11 0-0 ♕d7

and Black looks towards a bright future) 7...d5 8 d4 e3! 9 fxe3 0-0 10 cxd5 ♘xd5 11 ♘f3 ♖e8 12 ♕d3 ♕e7 and Black had definite compensation for the pawn in T.Mahon-E.Jackson, New York 1924. The game continued 13 ♔f2 ♘f6 14 h3 ♘e4+ 15 ♔e1 ♕d6 16 ♘e5 ♖xe5! 17 dxe5 ♕xe5 18 ♕c2 ♗f5 19 ♕b3 ♕g3+ 20 ♔d1 ♘f2+ and White resigned.

5...0-0 6 g3

Instead:

a) 6 a3 is met by 6...♗xc3 7 ♗xc3 e4, and after 8 dxe4 (8 ♘d4?! exd3 9 ♕xd3 ♘e5 10 ♕c2 d5 11 cxd5 ♘xd5 12 0-0-0 ♘xc3 13 ♕xc3 ♕f6 was better for Black in S.Dyachkov-A.Berelovich, Russian Team Championship 1996) 8...♘xe4 9 ♖c1 d6 10 e3 ♘xc3 11 ♖xc3 ♕f6 12 ♗e2 ♗g4 13 0-0 ♖fe8 Black had equalized in P.Vernersson-Se.Ivanov, Stockholm 2001.

b) 6 e3 ♖e8 7 ♗e2 d6 8 0-0 a5! 9 b3 (9 a3?! allows Black to fix the queenside with 9...♗xc3 10 ♗xc3 a4) 9...♗g4 10 a3 ♗c5 11 ♕c2 h6! 12 ♖fd1 ♗h5 13 ♗e1 ♗g6 was level in L.Psakhis-V.Korchnoi, Dresden 1998.

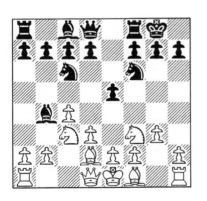

6...♖e8

The immediate 6...♗xc3 7 ♗xc3 e4 is

possible too. Marin claims an advantage for White after 8 dxe4 ♘xe4, but neither 9 ♕c2 ♕e7 10 ♗g2 ♘b4! 11 ♗xb4 ♕xb4+ nor 9 ♖c1 ♕e7 10 ♗g2 ♖e8 11 e3 d6 impresses me.

7 ♗g2 d6 8 0-0 h6 9 a3 ♗xc3 10 ♗xc3

10...e4

This thematic thrust equalizes, but now the game dries out rather quickly. 10...♗e6 is the more enterprising choice; for example, 11 ♖c1 ♕d7 12 ♖e1 ♗h3 13 ♗h1 ♘g4 14 d4 e4 15 d5 ♘e7 16 ♘h4 ♘f5 17 ♘xf5 ♕xf5 and Black had good attacking chances in D.Strauss-P.Littlewood, London 1979.

11 ♘d4 ♘xd4 12 ♗xd4 ♗f5 13 ♕d2 c5! 14 ♗c3 ♕e7 15 ♕f4 ♗g6 16 ♗xf6 ♕xf6 17 ♕xf6 gxf6 18 dxe4 ♗xe4 19 e3 a6 20 ♖fd1 ♗xg2 21 ♔xg2 ♖e6 22 a4 ♖c8 23 ♖a3 ♖c6 24 ♖b3 b6 25 ♖d5 ♖e4 26 ♖c3 b5 27 b3 ♔f8 28 f4 ♖e8 29 ♖h5 ♔g7 30 axb5 ½-½

White plays 4 e3

Among all the sensible fourth move options, **4 e3** is the second most popular, right after 4 g3. Compared to Game 64 in the previous chapter, White aims to play d2-d4 in favourable circumstances. Apposite to my recommendations from the previous games, **4...♗b4** is the move to be played here. In a way White has weakened his light squares by playing 4 e3, making a possible ...e5-e4 even more attractive. Now 5 d4 leads to a position already discussed, while the two main alternatives are 5 ♘d5 and 5 ♕c2. Regarding the former, the best reply to **5 ♘d5** is **5...e4**, gaining space and effectively forcing the white knight to retreat to g1. In addition to that, for the moment Black enjoys a certain lead in development, but he has to take care of his advanced e-pawn, as well as finding a place for his bishop to relocate. The position should be balanced, as you can see in the following game.

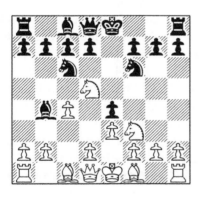

Game 71
J.Sunye Neto-
R.Martin del Campo
Linares, Mexico 1993

---

1 c4 ♘c6 2 ♘c3 e5 3 ♘f3 ♘f6 4 e3 ♗b4

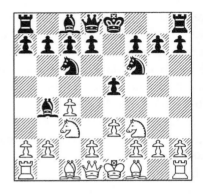

5 ♘d5

Besides this move, White has a few others at his disposal:

a) 5 ♕c2 (or 5 ♕b3) 5...♗xc3 6 ♕xc3 will be covered in the next two games.

b) 5 d4 exd4 6 exd4 d5 has already been dealt with elsewhere (see Game 64, note to Black's 6th move; while 7 cxd5 ♕xd5 transposes to Game 56).

c) 5 a3?!

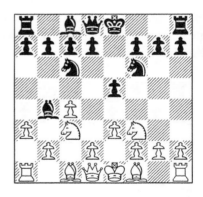

again leads to a worse position after 5...♗xc3 6 bxc3 e4. For example, 7 ♘d4 ♘e5 8 ♗e2 0-0 9 0-0 c5 10 ♘b3, and now after 10...d6 (rather than 10...b6 11 f4 exf3 12 gxf3 d6 13 d4 as in K.Vordank-A.Dessler, correspondence

1954) 11 f3 exf3 12 gxf3 ♗h3 13 ♖f2 ♖c8 White cannot play d2-d4 as he would lose the pawn on c4.

5...e4 6 ♘g1

Here 6 ♘xb4 looks natural and has to be investigated. After 6...♘xb4 White has two alternatives:

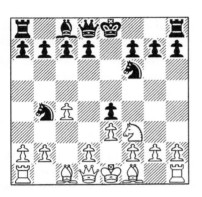

a) 7 ♘d4 c5! 8 ♘b3 (other moves are hardly better: 8 a3 ♘d3+ 9 ♗xd3 exd3 10 ♘f3 and now 10...d5! is good for Black; similarly 8 ♘c2 ♘d3+ 9 ♗xd3 exd3 10 ♘a3 d5, or 8 ♘b5 d5 9 cxd5 ♘fxd5, and once again ...♘d3+ is in the air) 8...d6 9 d4 ♗g4 10 ♕d2 (10 f3 is brutally countered by 10...exf3 11 gxf3 ♘e4!) 10...a5 11 a3 ♘c6 12 dxc5 dxc5 13 h3 (13 ♘xc5 ♕e7 14 ♘b3 0-0 gives Black good chances) 13...♕b6! 14 hxg4 ♕xb3 15 ♗e2 ♖d8 16 ♕c3 ♕xc3+ 17 bxc3 0-0 and White's position was plucked in G.Garcia Gonzales-R.Knaak, Leipzig 1973.

b) 7 a3 ♘c6 8 ♘d4?! (8 ♘g1 d5 9 d4 was played in L.Weglarz-A.Rotstein, Warsaw 1989, and now the simple 9...exd3 10 ♕xd3 ♘e5 11 ♕d4 ♘xc4 12 ♗xc4 dxc4 13 ♕xc4 0-0 gives Black a good game) 8...♘xd4 9 exd4 0-0 10 d3 ♖e8 11 ♗e3 d5! is also good for Black

after 12 ♗e2 (or 12 dxe4 ♘xe4 13 ♗e2 dxc4 14 ♗xc4 ♘d6 15 ♗d3 ♗f5, as in G.Carvalho-J. Sunye Neto, Cascavel 1996) 12...exd3 13 ♕xd3 dxc4 14 ♕xc4 ♗g4 as in L.Ehrlich-J.Barta, Brno 1937.

6...0-0 7 ♘e2 ♖e8 8 a3 ♗d6

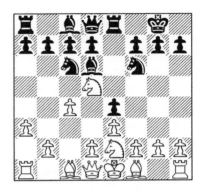

9 ♘ec3

Instead:

a) 9 ♘g3 is the other way to attack the e-pawn. Black should continue 9...b6 10 ♕c2 ♗b7 11 ♘xf6+ (if 11 ♗e2 b5!? 12 ♘xf6+ ♕xf6 13 cxb5 ♘e5 is interesting) 11...♕xf6 12 ♘xe4 ♕g6 13 d3 ♘e5 14 f3 (after 14 ♘xd6 cxd6! White is in a difficult position) 14...f5 15 ♘xd6 cxd6 16 ♕f2 d5 17 ♗e2 f4 18 e4 ♘xd3+! 19 ♗xd3 dxe4 20 ♗xe4 ♗xe4 21 fxe4 ♕xe4+ 22 ♔d1 ♕xc4 and Black had a devastating attack in M.Woerdemann-P.Rechmann, German League 1994.

b) 9 ♕c2 is also met by 9...b5! 10 ♘xf6+ ♕xf6 11 cxb5 ♘e5 and then 12 ♘g3 (or 12 ♕xe4 ♗b7! 13 ♕d4 a6 14 f4 ♕h4+ 15 ♘g3 ♘g4 16 bxa6 ♗c6 and Black had enough compensation for three (!) sacrificed pawns in M.Hochgraefe-P.Velicka, Hamburg 2000) 12...♗b7 13 ♘xe4 ♕g6 14 f3 (not

14 d3?! ♘xd3+ 15 ♗xd3 ♕xg2 16 ♖f1 ♗xe4 with a clear advantage in A.Gunnarsson-H.Stefansson, Icelandic Championship 1998; and 16 ♘f6+ gxf6 17 ♗xh7+ ♔h8 18 ♖f1 ♕xh2 is no better) 14...♘xf3+! 15 gxf3 ♖xe4 16 d3 (16 ♗d3 ♕g2 17 ♖f1 ♖h4 and 16 fxe4 ♗xe4 17 ♖g1 ♗xc2 18 ♖xg6 hxg6 are two more lines promising better chances for Black) 16...♖e5 17 e4 was played in K.Gasser-H.Grabher, Hohenems 1998; and now 17...♕f6, pointing the finger at the weak dark squares, would have given Black a nice game.

9...♗e5 10 d4 exd3 11 ♗xd3 d6

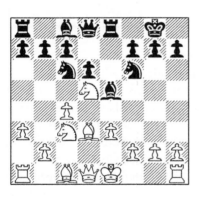

12 0-0

12 ♘xf6+ ♗xf6 13 ♘d5 ♘e5 14 ♗e2, from A.Greenfeld-A.Schenk, Lippstadt 2004, should have been answered by 14...c6 15 ♘xf6+ ♕xf6, intending ...♗e6 followed by ...d5 with equality.

12...♘xd5 13 ♘xd5 g6 14 f4 ♗g7 15 ♕c2 ♘e7 16 ♘xe7+ ♕xe7 17 ♗d2 f5

Having reorganized his forces effectively, Black has no problems.

18 ♖ae1 ♗d7 19 e4 ♗d4+ 20 ♔h1 ♕f6 21 b4 ♔h8 22 ♖e2 ♖e7 23 ♖fe1 ♖ae8 24 ♕d1 ½-½

Rather than 5 ♘d5, White more often prefers **5 ♕c2**, preventing Black from damaging the white pawn structure with 5...♗xc3. Nevertheless, **5...♗xc3** is still the right move! After **6 ♕xc3 ♕e7** the main idea of playing for ...e5-e4 is not new, but this line is actually one of the few examples where Black will play ...d7-d5 if he is put off implementing his first idea by a white d2-d3. One step at a time, though... what happens if White plays an immediate **7 d4**?

Game 72
T.Steinmetzer-W.Hobusch
Correspondence 1979

---

1 c4 ♘c6 2 ♘c3 e5 3 ♘f3 ♘f6 4 e3 ♗b4 5 ♕c2 ♗xc3 6 ♕xc3

6 bxc3?! cries out loud for the reply 6...e4. After 7 ♘g5 (if 7 ♘d4 ♘e5 8 f4 exf3 9 ♘xf3 ♘xf3+ 10 gxf3 0-0 followed by ...d7-d5 provides Black with an advantage due to his better pawn structure, while 8 ♗e2 d6 9 0-0 c5! 10 ♘b5 ♗f5 saw White totally surrounded in M.Schramm-G.Bagaturov, Bad Wildbad 2001) 7...♕e7 8 f3 exf3 9 ♘xf3 0-0 10 ♗e2 (10 d4 d5 is just bad, since White is left with a backward pawn on e3 and a bad bishop on c1) 10...d6 11 ♖b1 b6 12 0-0 ♘e5 13 d3 ♗g4 14 e4 ♘xf3+ 15 ♗xf3 ♗xf3 16 ♖xf3 ♘d7, Black had a good game in M.Suba-O.Korneev, La Coruna 1999.

6...♕e7 7 d4?!

7 ♗e2 and 7 d3 are examined in the next game.

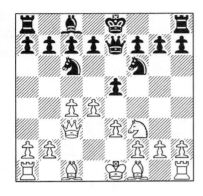

7...♘e4 8 ♕d3 exd4 9 ♘xd4 0-0!?

Black can force massive simplifications with 9...♘xd4 10 ♕xd4 ♕b4+ 11 ♗d2 ♕xd2+ 12 ♕xd2 ♘xd2 13 ♔xd2, but who wants that if you can successfully play aggressively instead?

10 ♗e2 ♕b4+ 11 ♔f1

Now 11 ♗d2? simply loses a pawn after 11...♕xb2.

11...♕e7 12 f3 f5! 13 ♕d1 ♘c5

White's inability to castle is only one thing that makes the black position much more likeable.

14 ♔f2 ♕h4+ 15 g3 ♕h3 16 ♕f1 ♕h5 17 ♕g2 d6 18 ♘xc6 bxc6 19 ♖e1 f4!?

Although this move is not entirely

correct, you have to give Black credit for his bold behaviour. Objectively though, 19...a5, securing the knight on c5, was preferable.

20 exf4

Not 20 gxf4? ♗h3 21 ♕g1 ♖f6 and the g-file is Black's road to success.

20...♗h3 21 ♕g1 ♖ae8 22 g4 ♕h6 23 f5

23 ♔g3! would have put Black to a serious test, but who would have the heart to play such a move during a serious game?

23...g5 24 ♗d2?

And here 24 ♕g3 was necessary to forestall ...♕h4+. Granted, that didn't seem like much of a threat, but...

24...♖xf5!

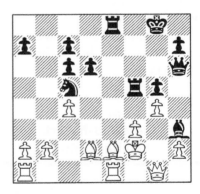

Now Black is on top again, since if 25 gxf5? ♕h4+ 26 ♕g3 ♕d4+ mates.

25 ♗f1 ♕h4+ 26 ♕g3 ♖xe1 27 ♖xe1 ♗xg4 28 ♕xh4 gxh4 29 ♖e3 ♗xf3 30 ♗h3

30 ♖xf3? ♘e4+ 31 ♔e3 ♖xf3+ 32 ♔xf3 ♘xd2+ 33 ♔f2 ♘xf1 34 ♔xf1 is obviously winning for Black.

30...♗g4+ 31 ♔g2 h5 32 ♖e7 ♘d3 33 ♗xg4 ♖f2+! 34 ♔g1 ♖xd2 35 ♗e6+ ♔f8 36 ♖xc7 ♖d1+ 37 ♔g2 ♘f4+ 0-1

OK, so the immediate 7 d4 doesn't pose too great a threat. A more cunning move is the innocuous-looking **7 ♗e2**. White ends the potential vis-à-vis of his king and the black queen down the e-file and now threatens to play 8 d4; for example 7...0-0?! 8 d4 exd4 9 ♘d4 and if now 9...♘e4, the white queen no longer has to remain in touch with the knight on d4.

Instead, Black should essay the more energetic **7...d5**. Normally I wouldn't recommend switching into a Open Sicilian-type position, but there are always exceptions to the rule. Here, Black can try to exploit the exposed position of the white queen, effectively gaining time to develop and organize play against White's backward d-pawn. A nice illustration can be seen in the following game by the British GM Nicholas Pert.

Game 73
C.McNab-N.Pert
Oakham 2000

---

1 c4 ♘c6 2 ♘c3 e5 3 ♘f3 ♘f6 4 e3 ♗b4 5 ♕c2 ♗xc3 6 ♕xc3 ♕e7 7 ♗e2

Instead:

a) 7 d3 is another of the cases where Black should accept the invitation to play a reversed Sicilian. After 7...d5 8 cxd5 ♘xd5 9 ♕c2 0-0 10 a3 a5! 11 b3 ♗g4 12 ♗e2 ♖ad8 13 0-0 f5 Black had a good game in A.Chernin-Zsu.Polgar, Budapest 1993.

b) 7 a3 d5 8 cxd5 ♘xd5 9 ♕b3 ♘b6 10 d3 0-0 11 ♗e2 a5 is similar to the text,

while after 8 d4 exd4 9 ♘xd4 ♘xd4 10 ♕xd4 Black can play 10...c5! 11 ♕h4 dxc4 12 ♗xc4 0-0 13 0-0 ♗e6 and White has problems finding something useful for his dark-squared bishop to do.

7...d5

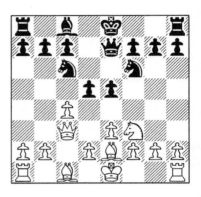

As noted above, 7...0-0?! is now inaccurate since the bishop on e2 prevents any of the actions from the previous game; after 8 d4 exd4 9 ♘xd4 ♘xd4 10 ♕xd4 White is just better.

8 cxd5

Now if 8 d4 exd4 9 ♘xd4 ♘xd4 10 ♕xd4 c5! 11 ♕h4 (or 11 ♕d1 dxc4 12 ♗xc4 ♕e4! 13 ♗b5+ ♗d7 14 ♗xd7+ ♘xd7 15 0-0 ♖d8 16 b3 0-0 17 ♗b2 ♘e5 18 ♕e2 ♘d3 with a clearly better position for Black in H.Teske-A.Baburin, German League 2000) 11...dxc4 12 ♗xc4 0-0 13 0-0 ♗e6 and we have the same position as after 7 a3 above, just with the pawn on a2 instead of a3.

Instead, 8 d3 0-0 9 0-0 e4 10 ♘d4 ♘e5 11 cxd5 exd3 12 ♗xd3 ♘xd5 13 ♕b3 ♘xd3 14 ♕xd3 c5 (14...♖d8 is more ambitious) 15 ♘f5 ♕e5 16 ♕xd5 led directly to a draw in A.Istratescu-I.Ivanisevic, Chania 2000.

8...♘xd5 9 ♕b3 ♘b6 10 0-0 0-0 11 d3 a5 12 ♗d2 a4 13 ♕c2 ♖d8 14 ♖fc1 ♗f5 15 e4

This is rather forced if White wants to keep hold of his d-pawn, but now d4 is incredibly weak.

15...♗g4 16 ♗e3 ♘d7 17 h3 ♗xf3 18 ♗xf3 ♘f8 19 ♕c4 ♘e6 20 ♗d1 ♘cd4

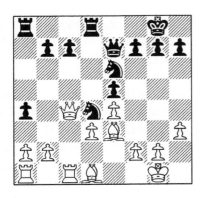

Black has managed to get a tight grip on d4 with his knights. In a higher sense, the position is already strategically won. The way the British grandmaster converts his advantage is very instructive.

21 ♔f1 c6 22 g3 ♕d6 23 ♗g4 g6 24 h4 ♔g7 25 ♗xe6 ♘xe6 26 ♖d1 ♘d4 27 ♗xd4 ♕xd4 28 ♕xd4 ♖xd4

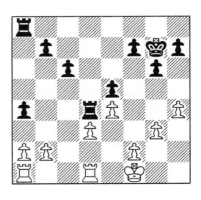

29 ♖ac1 f5 30 exf5 gxf5 31 ♔e2 ♔f6 32 ♖c4 ♖ad8 33 a3 ♔e6 34 ♖xd4 ♖xd4 35 ♖c1 ♔d5 36 h5 ♖g4 37 h6 f4 38 ♖c4 b5 39 ♖e4 ♖g6 40 gxf4 exf4 41 ♖xf4 ♖xh6 42 ♖f7 ♔e6 43 ♖c7 ♔d6 44 ♖f7 ♔e6 45 ♖c7 ♔d6 46 ♖f7 ♖h1 47 ♔d2 h5 48 ♖h7 h4 49 ♔c2 h3 50 ♖h6+ ♔d5 51 ♖h5+ ♔e6 52 ♖h6+ ♔d5 53 ♖h5+ ♔d6 54 ♖h6+ ♔d7 55 ♖h7+ ♔e8 56 ♔c3 c5 57 ♔d2 b4 58 ♔e2 h2 59 ♔f3 ♖b1 60 ♖xh2 ♖xb2 61 ♖h8+ ♔d7 62 ♖a8 b3 63 ♖xa4 ♖xf2+ 64 ♔xf2 b2 65 ♖c4 b1♕ 66 ♔e2 ♕b2+ 67 ♔d1 ♕xa3 68 ♔d2 ♔d6 69 ♔c2 ♕a1 70 ♔d2 ♔d5 71 ♖e4 ♕b2+ 72 ♔d1 ♕c3 73 ♔e2 ♕c2+ 74 ♔e3 ♕d1 75 ♖c4 ♕e1+ 76 ♔f3 ♕d2 0-1

White plays 4 g3

It is now time to deal with the absolute main line of the English Opening, **4 g3** in the Four Knights. As I pointed out in my introduction, White's main intention in the English is to get a grip on the central light squares, and by fianchettoing his king's bishop White is acting accordingly.

One could be tempted to continue

with 4...♗b4 again, but I feel that with a white bishop on the h1-a8 diagonal Black should not try to contest the light squares this time. I tried 4...♗c5 for a while, for positions similar to those in the previous chapter, but ultimately felt that things were not going my way. I needed something more aggressive.

Borrowing an idea from earlier on, **4...♘d4!?** is a move I quickly made friends with. The tactical justification is that 5 ♘xe5 allows Black a strong attack after 5...♕e7 6 f4 (surely not 6 ♘d3?? ♘f3 mate!) 6...d6 7 ♘d3 ♗f5, but the actual plan is to play ...c7-c6, when it is the white bishop that bites on granite this time. Although it is not played too frequently, 4...♘d4!? is my favourite, as I think that it allows Black to equalize comfortably.

Game 74
Kir.Georgiev-L.Van Wely
European Cup, Chalkidiki 2002

---

1 c4 ♘c6 2 ♘c3 e5 3 ♘f3 ♘c6 4 g3 ♘d4!?

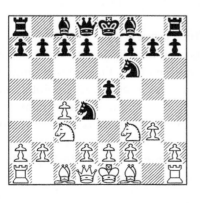

5 ♗g2

The most sensible answer. Other moves fail to impress:

a) 5 ♘xe5? ♕e7 is the tactical idea behind 4...♘d4. After 6 f4 (most certainly not 6 ♘d3?? ♘f3 mate) 6...d6 7 ♘d3 ♗f5 Black has a dangerous initiative for the pawn; for example, 8 e3 (if 8 ♔f2 c6 9 e3 ♗g4 10 ♕a4 ♘e4+ 11 ♘xe4 ♕xe4 12 ♖g1 ♕f3+ 13 ♔e1 h5! 14 ♘f2 ♖h6 with good attacking prospects, while 14 exd4 ♕e4+ 15 ♔f2 ♕xd4+ 16 ♔g2 ♕e4+ 17 ♔f2 ♕f3+ 18 ♔e1 ♖h6 just wins) 8...♗e4! 9 ♘xe4 ♕xe4 10 ♘f2 ♘c2+ 11 ♔e2 ♕g6 12 ♖b1 ♘xe3 13 ♕a4+ c6 14 d3 ♘xf1 15 ♔xf1 d5 with a clear advantage.

b) 5 ♘h4?! puts the knight on the rim for no reason, but it is reason enough for Black to strike in the centre with 5...d5!. Then 6 e3 ♘c6 7 cxd5 ♘xd5 8 d3 (8 ♗g2 neglects d3 and should be exploited by 8...♘db4; while after 8 a3 ♗e7 9 ♗g2 ♘xc3 10 bxc3 ♗xh4 11 gxh4 ♕xh4 Black was a pawn up for nothing in M.Pavlovic-S.Estremera Panos, Saint Vincent 2002; or if 9 ♘f3 ♘xc3 10 bxc3 e4 11 ♘d4 ♘e5 and the white position is a total wreck) 8...♗e7 9 ♘f3 0-0 10 ♗d2 (10 ♗g2?! ♘db4 11 ♔e2 ♗e6 12 ♘e1 ♕d7 13 a3 ♘d5 14 ♕c2 ♖ad8 was good for Black in V.Korchnoi-P.Svidler, Zürich 2001; while 10 ♗e2 faces 10...♗h3) 10...♘db4 11 ♕b1 ♗f5 12 ♘e4 (or 12 e4 ♗g4) 12...♗g4! 13 ♘g1 (a sad sight, but 13 ♗e2 allows 13...♘xd3+) 13...f5 14 ♘c3 f4! led to a massive attack in R.Slobodjan-J.Gustafsson, German Championship 2002.

c) 5 ♘xd4 exd4 is no challenge either. After 6 ♘b5 (6 ♘d5 ♘xd5 7 cxd5 ♗c5 8 ♕c2 ♕e7 9 ♗g2 0-0 10 0-0 d6 11 ♖e1 ♕f6 12 d3 ♗g4 13 a3 a5 14 b3 ♖ae8 was better for Black in J.Padreny Gutierrez-M.Illescas Cordoba, La Lira 1981) 6...♗c5 7 b4!? ♗xb4 8 ♘xd4 0-0 9 ♗g2 d5 10 cxd5 ♘xd5 11 ♗b2 ♘b6 12 ♖c1 c6 13 0-0 ♕g5 14 d3, now 14...♖e8 would have led to a comfortable game in A.Strikovic-M.Granados Gomez, Zaragoza 1997.

5...♘xf3+ 6 ♗xf3 ♗b4

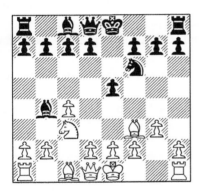

7 ♕b3

This is the right move if White wishes to fight for an advantage. Instead:

a) 7 0-0 0-0 8 d3 h6 9 ♗d2 c6 10 ♕a4 ♗e7 was simply equal in M.Gurevich-B.Avrukh, Antwerp 1999.

b) 7 d4 ♗xc3+ 8 bxc3 e4 9 ♗g2 h6! 10 ♕c2 (or 10 ♖b1 0-0 11 0-0 b6 12 ♕c2 ♗b7 13 d5 ♕e7 14 ♖d1 d6 15 ♖d4 ♖ae8 16 h3 ♗c8 when the e-pawn was the key to a good position for Black in R.Kerndl-A.Dunne, correspondence 1999) 10...♕e7 11 f3 (after 11 a4 d6 12 ♗a3 the bishop is thwarted by 12...c5)

11...b6 12 0-0 and a draw was agreed in B.Gulko-A.Chernin, FIDE World Championship, New Delhi 2000. If instead 12 fxe4?! ♗b7 13 d5 then 13...♕c5! 14 ♕d3 (or 14 e5 ♘g4) 14...♗a6 15 ♗e3 ♕xc4 16 ♕xc4 ♗xc4 is clearly better for Black.

c) The quiet 7 ♕c2 c6 8 0-0 0-0 was played in J.Timman-M.Tal, Tilburg 1980. After 9 d3 (unmindful play on the queenside, initiated by 9 a3 ♗e7 10 b4 d6 11 ♗b2, is best answered by a kingside attack; for example, 11...♗e6 12 d3 ♖c8 13 ♖fe1 ♕d7 14 e3 ♗h3 15 ♗h1 ♕g4! 16 ♕e2 ♕g6 17 ♘e4 ♘xe4 18 ♗xe4 f5 when Black had good attacking chances in U.Schumacher-H.Vitz, Troisdorf 1998) 9...♖e8 (or 9...h6 10 a3 ♗e7 11 e4 d6 12 b4 ♘h7 13 ♗g2 f5 as in R.Kasimdzhanov-J.Timman, Wijk aan Zee 1999) 10 ♗g5 h6 11 ♗xf6 ♕xf6 12 ♘e4 ♕g6 13 a3 ♗f8 14 c5 f5! 15 ♘d2 d5 16 cxd6 ♗xd6 17 ♘c4 ♗c7 Black was clearly better.

7...♗c5 8 d3 0-0

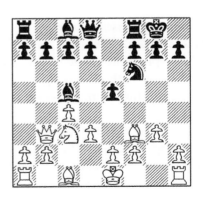

9 0-0

9 ♗g5 is not dangerous: 9...h6 10 ♗xf6 ♕xf6 11 ♘e4 ♕e7 12 ♘xc5 ♕xc5

13 0-0 d6 14 ♕c3 a5 and Black equalized in J.Timman-L.Portisch, Nice Olympiad 1974. Instead after 9 ♘a4 Black can play 9...♗e7 10 0-0 ♖e8 11 ♖d1 d6 12 ♘c3 ♗f8 13 ♕c2 c6, intending a later ...d6-d5, as in V.Tukmakov-M.Hebden, Hastings 1982/83.

9...c6

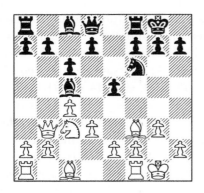

Diminishing the scope of the light-squared bishop, after which White has nothing.

10 ♗d2

10 ♗g5 h6 11 ♗xf6 ♕xf6 12 ♘e4 ♕e7 13 ♘xc5 ♕xc5 14 ♕c3 a5 is similar to Timman-Portisch above.

10...♖e8 11 ♗g2 ♗f8!

A prophylactic move. Black wants to play ...d6 without having to worry about his bishop being harassed by b2-b4.

11...♗b6 is another escape route for the bishop. L.Portisch-R.Hübner, Candidates match, Abano Therme 1980, continued 12 ♕c2 h6 13 ♘a4 ♗c7 14 ♖ac1 d6 15 b4 ♗d7 16 ♘c3 ♕c8 17 ♖fe1 ♗h3 18 ♗h1, and now Black could have played 18...♕f5 with chances on the kingside.

12 ♕a4 h6 13 ♖ac1 a6 14 ♘e4

Or 14 ♕b3 d6 15 ♗e3 ♕e7 16 ♘a4 ♗g4 17 ♖fe1 ♖ad8 18 h3 ♗e6 19 ♔h2 b5 20 ♘b6 and a draw was agreed in Z.Izoria-N.Pert, Hoogeveen 2003, although 20...d5 would have given Black a nice position.

14...♘xe4 15 ♗xe4

White has a slight advantage in space and the more active pieces, but Black's position is solid and without weaknesses.

15...d6 16 ♗a5 ♕g5 17 ♕b3 h5

17...f5!? 18 ♗g2 f4 is another way to proceed.

18 h4 ♕e7 19 ♕b6 g5!? 20 hxg5 ♕xg5 21 ♕e3

White had to take care of the threatened ...h5-h4.

21...♕xe3 22 fxe3 ♗h6 23 ♔f2 ♗g4 24 ♗f3 f5 25 ♖h1 ♔g7 26 ♖cf1

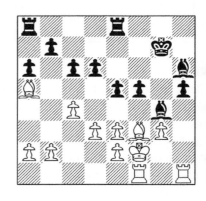

26...e4

There was nothing wrong with 26...♔g6, safely consolidating the position before making a move.

27 dxe4 fxe4 28 ♗xg4 hxg4 29 ♖h4 ♗g5?!

Here 29...♖f8+! 30 ♔g2 ♖xf1 31 ♔xf1

♖f8+ 32 ♔g2 ♔g6 33 ♖xg4+ ♔f5 34 ♖h4 ♗xe3 would have led to a slightly better endgame for Black. Whereas now it is Black who has to play very carefully, though his skilful play is rewarded with a draw in the end.

30 ♖xg4 ♔g6 31 ♔g2 ♖ac8 32 ♗c3 ♖e6 33 a4 ♖ce8 34 a5 ♖g8 35 ♖ff4 ♖ge8 36 ♔h3 ♖8e7 37 ♖f8 ♖e8 38 ♖ff4 ♖8e7 39 ♖f8 ♖e8 40 ♖f1 ♖8e7 41 ♖gf4!?

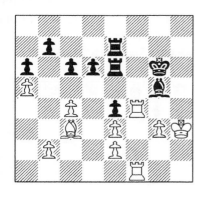

41...♗xf4 42 exf4 ♖h7+ 43 ♔g4 ♔f7 44 f5 ♖e8 45 ♔f4 e3! 46 g4 ♖h2 47 ♔f3 ♖g8 48 ♗e1 ♖gh8 49 g5 ♖h1 50 ♖xh1 ♖xh1 51 ♗c3 ♖f1+ 52 ♔e4 ♖f2 53 g6+ ♔f8 54 ♗d4 ♖xe2 55 ♗xe3 ♔g7 56 ♔f3 ♖c2 57 ♗d4+ ♔h6 58 ♗e3+ ♔g7 59 ♗d4+ ♔h6 60 ♗c3 ♖h2 61 ♔g3 ♖e2 62 ♔f3 ♖e8 63 ♗d2+ ♔h5 64 ♗e3 d5 65 cxd5 cxd5 66 b4 ♖d8 67 ♗c5 ♖e8 68 g7 ♖g8 69 f6 ♔g6 70 ♗e7 ♔f7 71 ♔f4 ♖c8 72 ♔e5 d4 73 ♔xd4 ♔e6 74 ♗f8 ♔f7 75 ♔d5 ♖c6 76 ♗e7 ♔g8 77 ♔e5 ♔f7 78 ♗d6 ♖c8 79 ♔f5 ♖d8 80 ♔e5 ♖c8 81 ♗c5 ♖c6 82 ♗e7 ♖e6+ 83 ♔d4 ♖c6 ½-½

White plays 4 d4

Although **4 d4** trails far behind 4 g3 in popularity, from my experience it has

to be considered the most dangerous line Black faces in the whole English Opening – not so much because of its theoretical value, but rather due to its practical problems. Agreed, after the continuation **4...exd4 5 ♘xd4 ♗b4 6 ♗g5 h6 7 ♗h4,**

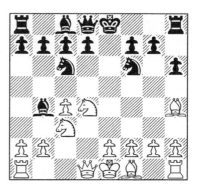

Black has many different options, but most of them require a high degree of knowledge, patience, discipline and positional understanding; things that few chess players can successfully combine.

Therefore I would like to introduce a more dynamic response. After **7...0-0 8 ♖c1 ♖e8 9 e3 ♘xd4 10 ♕xd4 c5!?,** followed by ...g7-g5 and ...d7-d5, Black may have scattered his pawn structure, but he gets adequate compensation in the form of active piece play.

> ### Game 75
> ### B.Gelfand-V.Korchnoi
> Groningen 1996

1 c4 ♘c6 2 ♘c3 e5 3 ♘f3 ♘f6 4 d4 exd4 5 ♘xd4 ♗b4

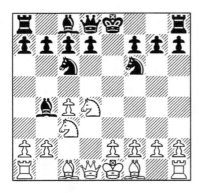

6 ♗g5

Alternatively:

a) 6 ♘xc6 is poor; after 6...♗xc3+ 7 bxc3 bxc6 8 ♗a3 d6 9 g3 0-0 10 ♗g2 ♕e8 11 0-0 ♖b8 12 ♕d3 ♗d7 13 ♖ab1 ♕e5 Black had the better prospects in the computer game Desp-Vchess, Austria (rapid) 2001.

b) 6 g3 is a popular alternative. Black should react aggressively with 6...♘e4!. Now 7 ♕d3 (7 ♘xc6 ♕f6? does not work this time because of 8 ♕d4, but 7...bxc6 8 ♕d4 ♘xc3 9 bxc3 ♗e7 10 ♗g2 0-0 is good for Black, who can attack the c-pawns with ...♗f6 and ...♗a6) 7...♘c5 8 ♕e3+ ♘e6 9 ♘xc6 (9 ♘xe6 dxe6 10 ♗g2 ♘d4! 11 ♕e4 f5 12 ♕d3 e5 led to a good game for Black in L.Karlsson-G.Bucciardini, correspondence 1997; while after 9 ♘c2 d5! 10 ♗g2 d4 11 ♕d2 ♗c5 12 ♘d5 ♘e5 13 b3, as in V.Chekhov-A.Kosikov, Daugavpils 1978, and now 13...c6, chasing the knight away, the position holds no worries for Black) 9...dxc6 10 a3 ♗c5 11 ♕f3 ♘d4 12 ♕e4+ ♗e6 13 ♗h3 was played in R.Brzezinski-K.Wojtczak, correspondence 1992, when 13...♘c2+!

14 ♕xc2 ♗xh3 would have given Black a big advantage.

6...h6 7 ♗h4 0-0 8 ♖c1

8 e3 should be met by 8...♗xc3+!? 9 bxc3 ♘e5. M.Hanauer-S.Reshevsky, US Championship, New York 1936, continued 10 ♗e2 ♘g6 11 ♗g3 (11 ♗xf6 ♕xf6 12 0-0 d6 13 ♖b1 ♕e7 14 ♗d3 c5! 15 ♘e2 b6 also led to a good game for Black in F.Sanz Alonso-M.Tal, Nice Olympiad 1974) 11...♘e4 12 ♕c2 ♖e8 13 0-0 d6 14 ♖ab1 c5! 15 ♘f3 b6 and Black was clearly better.

8...♖e8 9 e3 ♘xd4! 10 ♕xd4 c5!?

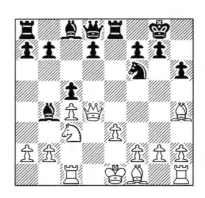

11 ♕d1

Instead:

a) 11 ♕d3 makes little difference, as 11...g5 12 ♗g3 d5 13 cxd5 ♕xd5 14 ♕xd5 would transpose to the text, or if 14 a3 ♗xc3+ 15 ♕xc3 ♘e4 16 ♕c2 ♗f5 17 ♗c4 ♕c6 and Black was not worse in B.Jobava-F.Vallejo Pons, European Team Championship, Plovdiv 2003.

b) 11 ♗xf6?? is refuted by 11...cxd4 12 ♗xd8 dxc3 13 bxc3 ♗a3.

c) 11 ♕d6!? seeks to disturb Black's development. I.Smirin-A.Onischuk, New York Open 1998, continued

11...♖e6 (11...g5 12 ♗g3 and then 12...♖e6 13 ♕d1 ♘e4 is a possible improvement) 12 ♕d1 ♕a5 13 ♗xf6 ♖xf6 14 a3 ♗xc3+ 15 ♖xc3 d6 16 ♗e2 ♗d7 17 ♗f3 ♖b8 18 0-0 b5 19 cxb5 and a draw was agreed.

11...g5 12 ♗g3 d5 13 cxd5 ♕xd5

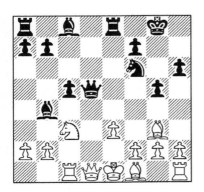

Black's scattered pawn structure is compensated by his piece activity. Black is OK.

14 ♕xd5

14 ♕a4?! ♖d8! 15 ♖d1 ♕xd1+ 16 ♕xd1 ♖xd1+ 17 ♔xd1 ♗e6 is not recommendable for White.

14...♘xd5 15 ♗b5 ♖d8 16 h4

Instead, 16 ♔e2 ♗xc3 17 bxc3 ♗e6 18 ♖hd1 ♘f6 19 ♖xd8+ ♖xd8 20 a3 ♘e4 was better for Black in C.Sega-I.Morovic Fernandez, Sao Paulo 2002 – especially as 21 ♗d3? ran into 21...♘xf2! 22 ♗xf2 ♗g4+ 23 ♔d2 c4 24 e4 ♖xd3+ 25 ♔c2 ♗d7! 26 ♗xa7 ♗c6 27 ♖e1 ♗a4+ 28 ♔b2 ♖d2+ 29 ♔b1 ♖xg2 and Black won quickly.

16...♗g4! 17 f3

17 hxg5?! leaves Black in better

shape after 17...♘xc3 18 bxc3 ♗xc3+ 19 ♔f1 ♗b2.

17...♗d7 18 ♗xd7 ♖xd7 19 hxg5 ♗xc3+ 20 bxc3 ♘xe3

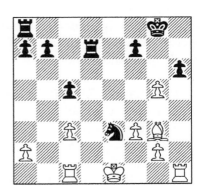

21 ♗f2

21 gxh6 ♖e8! 22 h7+ ♔h8 23 ♗f2 ♘xg2+ 24 ♔f1 ♘e3+ 25 ♗xe3 ♖xe3 26 ♔f2 ♖ee7 is nothing for Black to worry about either.

21...♘xg2+ 22 ♔f1 ♘f4 23 ♖xh6

If 23 gxh6 ♔h7 and the knight is of more use than the bishop.

23...♖d3 24 ♗xc5 ♖xf3+ 25 ♔g1 ♖e8

25...♖g3+ was also possible. After 26 ♔f2 ♖xg5 27 ♗d4 ♘g6 28 ♖ch1 ♔f8 White will have a hard time proving enough compensation for the pawn.

26 ♗xa7 ♘h3+ 27 ♔h1 ♘xg5 28 ♖b1 ♔g7 29 ♖h2 ♔g6 30 ♗d4

30 ♖xb7? is no good because of 30...♖e1+ 31 ♗g1 ♖g3 32 ♖g2 ♖h3+ 33 ♖h2 ♖xh2+ 34 ♔xh2 ♘f3+ 35 ♔g2 ♘xg1.

30...f6 31 a4 ½-½

Black still has the slightly better position.

Summary

The Four Knights is full of possibilities and provides White with a large variety of playable systems. Usually Black can employ similar plans against them; for example, playing for the control of the central light squares e4 and d5 with ...♗b4, and swapping the bishop for the white queen's knight (as in Games 68, 70-73 and 75). But there is also the dynamic resource ...♘d4, which allows Black either to create dangerous attacks (Game 69) or to make exonerating simplifications (Game 74). All in all, Black should not fear the English Four Knights.

1 c4 ♘c6 2 ♘c3 e5 3 ♘f3 ♘f6 (D) 4 e3

      4 e4 ♗b4 – *Game 68*

      4 a3 d6 – *Game 69*

      4 d3 ♗b4 – *Game 70*

      4 g3 ♘d4 (D) – *Game 74*

      4 d4 exd4 5 ♘xd4 ♗b4 – *Game 75*

4...♗b4 5 ♕c2

      5 ♘d5 e4 – *Game 71*

5...♗xc3 6 ♕xc3 ♕e7 (D) 7 ♗e2

      7 d4 ♘e4 – *Game 72*

7...d5 – *Game 73*

3...♘f6

4...♘d4

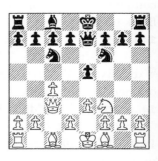

6...♕e7

Part Four

Black vs. 1 ♘f3: 1...♘c6

The variations arising from **1 ♘f3 ♘c6** shows how the different systems with 1...♘c6 are interlinked. As we have already treated 2 e4, 2 d4 and 2 c4 in the previous parts of this book, the only thing left to be examined is the so-called King's Indian Attack, **2 g3**. However, the 'Attack' doesn't quite live up to its name here, as in my recommended set-up with **2...e5 3 d3 d5 4 ♗g2 f6**, it is Black who attacks most of the time.

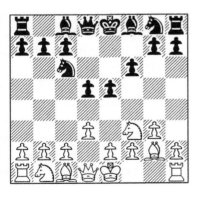

The formation Black adopts is often confused with the Sämisch Variation of the King's Indian Defence, but there is a key difference in that the black c-pawn still is on c7. As a result, the black centre is more stable and possible White attacks on the queenside are less efficient. This makes attacking on the kingside while castling queenside much more attractive.

If you want to make a comparison, the closest you could draw is a certain resemblance to a variation from the Pirc Defence (specifically that with ♗e3, f2-f3, ♕d2 etc). Therefore our current formation can be dangerous for White, as not everyone who plays the King's Indian Attack as White also has the Pirc Defence in his black repertoire. But even if that should be the case, Black still doesn't have much to worry about, as I would like to show you in our final chapter.

Chapter Fifteen

1 ♘f3 ♘c6

We are almost at the end of our journey through the realms of ...♘c6. As already mentioned in the introduction to the final part of this book on **1 ♘f3 ♘c6**, the remaining opening system to be examined is the King's Indian Attack. But as a little leaving present, I would like to look first at a game in which White plays **2 b3**.

White plays 2 b3

If anything, 2 b3 is a kind of improved Nimzo-Larsen Attack – although I find it hard to see what the exact improvement might be. Granted, Black cannot play ...c7-c5 anymore, but on the other hand, the white knight can now be harassed by the black e-pawn.

> ### Game 76
> **C.Bonnke-C.Wisnewski**
> Kiel (rapid) 2004

1 ♘f3 ♘c6 2 b3

2 d3 e5 usually transposes to systems already covered or to the KIA.

After 2 e3 Black should play 2...d5. Then 3 d4 transposes to Game 28, while 3 b3 is perhaps a better version of the text. Nevertheless, after 3...e5 4 ♗b2 (if 4 ♗b5 e4 5 ♘e5 ♕g5! 6 ♘xc6 ♕xg2 7 ♖f1 a6, the b3-pawn proves a hindrance after 8 ♗a4 ♗h3 9 ♕e2 b5 10 ♗xb5 axb5 11 ♕xb5 ♕xf1+ 12 ♕xf1 ♗xf1 13 ♔xf1 and Black has a winning material advantage; 5 ♘d4 ♕g5 6 ♘xc6 ♕xg2 is the same) 4...♗d6 (4...e4 was played in M.Basman-J.Nunn, London 1975, and while I wouldn't want to doubt such an authority as Nunn, I don't much like Black's position after 5 ♘d4 ♘xd4 6 ♗xd4 ♘f6 7 c4 dxc4 8 ♗xc4 ♗e7 9 0-0 0-0 10 f3 c5 11 ♗b2) 5 ♗b5 ♕e7 6 d4 e4 7 ♘e5 ♗xe5 8 dxe5 ♗e6 9 ♕d4 ♕g5 10 g3 ♘ge7 Black obtained a very good position in J.Fend-E.Arjmand, California 1993.

2...e5 3 ♗b2 e4 4 ♘d4

4 ♘e5?! was tried in I.Kaczmarek-U.Von Herman, German League 1995, but after 4...♕f6 5 ♘c4 (5 d4 would have been more to the point, although 5...♗b4+! 6 ♘d2 e3! 7 fxe3 ♘xe5 8 dxe5 ♕h4+ 9 g3 ♕e4 or 6 c3 ♘xe5 7 cxb4 ♘g4 is also better for Black) 5...♕e6 (funnily, after 5...♕d8 moves other than 6 ♘e5 seem to lead to a worse position as well) 6 e3 d5 the result of the opening is terrible for White.

4...♕f6 5 e3 ♗c5

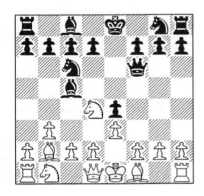

6 c3?

Now Black takes command. Instead, White should have played 6 ♘c3! (6 ♘b5!? ♕xb2 7 ♘1c3 ♘b4 8 ♖b1 ♕xc2 9 ♘xc7+ ♔d8 10 ♕h5 led to a

draw after 10...♘xa2 11 ♕xc5 ♘xc3 12 ♕f8+ ♔xc7 13 ♕c5+ ♔d8 in G.Timoscenko-Z.Topalovic, Opatija 2003, though Black might try 10...b6!?), when 6...♘xd4 7 ♘b5 (but not 7 ♘xe4? ♕g6 8 ♘xc5 ♘xc2+ and Black wins; while 7 ♘d5 ♕c6 8 exd4 ♕xd5 9 dxc5 ♘f6 is also good for Black) 7...♖b8 8 ♘xd4 ♘e7 is roughly equal, with an interesting struggle lying ahead.

6...♘e5 7 ♗e2 d5 8 ♘b5 ♗b6 9 ♕c2 c6 10 ♘d4 ♕g6 11 ♖g1 ♗g4 12 ♗f1 ♗d7 13 f4

Dropping a pawn, but the position was beyond repair anyway.

13...♗xd4 14 fxe5 ♗xe5 15 g3 ♘f6 16 c4 ♘g4 17 h3 ♘h2 18 ♗xe5 ♘f3+ 19 ♔f2 ♘xe5 20 ♔g2 ♘f3 21 ♖h1 ♘e1+ 0-1

White plays 2 g3

The King's Indian Attack is especially popular among players who dislike having to learn a load of theory – the first five to six moves at least are always the same, completely regardless of the black set-up, and even after that the plans and ideas are usually the same.

The set-up I am recommending is, in my opinion, the most reliable one to present White with a challenge, although the inferred black attack on the kingside is not often treated accordingly. Furthermore, White is not only threatened by danger on the kingside, as I would like to show you with our final game in this book.

Game 77
S.Martinsen-C.Wisnewski
Kiel 2004

---

1 ♘f3 ♘c6 2 g3 e5

3 d3

3 e4 ♘f6 4 ♘c3 (4 d3 was dealt with in Chapter 1 – see the notes to Game 2) actually transposes to the Glek Variation of the Four Knights. As a matter of principle Black should not switch to this area of the Open Games, but a certain amount of flexibility is nothing a chess player should be ashamed of, especially as this opening system is rather harmless. In my opinion, the most feasible plan for Black is 4...♗c5 5

♗g2 (evidently not 5 ♘xe5?? ♘xe5 6 d4 ♗xd4 7 ♕xd4 ♘f3+ and Black wins) 5...d6 6 d3 (6 0-0 a6 7 d3 is merely a transposition) 6...a6 (compare the black set-up with the one I recommended in Chapter 13 – it is just universal!) 7 0-0 ♗e6 8 ♗e3 ♗xe3 9 fxe3 ♘e7 10 h3 (or 10 ♘h4 ♕d7 11 ♕f3 0-0-0 12 d4 ♗h3 13 ♘f5 ♗xg2 14 ♔xg2 ♘xf5 15 ♕xf5 exd4 16 exd4 ♖he8 with equality in J.Smeets-L.Van Kooten, Dutch League 2000) 10...♘g6 11 ♕e1 c6 12 ♔h2 h6 13 a4 0-0 14 a5 d5 and Black equalized comfortably in R.Slobodjan-I.Sokolov, Nussloch 1996.

3...d5 4 ♗g2 f6!?

The calm 4...♘f6 is fine as well. After 5 0-0 ♗e7 White has to choose between the following moves:

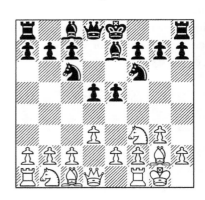

a) 6 c3 seeks to advance on the queenside, but Black can easily prevent this with 6...a5, when D.Langerak-M.Geenen, correspondence 1992, continued 7 ♘bd2 0-0 8 ♕c2 (or 8 e4 dxe4 9 dxe4 b6 10 ♖e1 ♗a6 11 ♗f1 ♗xf1 12 ♔xf1 a4 and Black successfully stopped any queenside ambitions White might have had in J.Maiwald-D.Werner,

German League 1997) 8...b6 9 b3 ♗b7 10 a3 ♖e8 11 ♗b2 e4! 12 dxe4 dxe4 13 ♘g5 e3 14 fxe3 h6 15 ♘ge4 ♘g4 and Black was better.

b) 6 a3 serves the same purpose, while leaving the door open to play c2-c4 at a later date. But this has to be considered carefully, as the game A.Miles-E.Michaelides, Lone Pine 1980, showed: 6...a5 7 b3 0-0 8 ♗b2?! e4 9 dxe4 ♘xe4 10 c4 dxc4 11 ♕c2 ♗f6! 12 bxc4 ♗f5 and White was in trouble.

c) 6 ♘bd2 is the typical set-up for the King's Indian Attack, but it failed to impress after 6...0-0 7 e4 dxe4 8 dxe4 ♗e6 9 b3 ♘d7 10 ♗b2 ♗f6 11 ♕e2 ♘b6 12 ♖fd1 ♕c8 13 ♘f1 ♖d8 in G.Emodi-J.Laszlo, Hajduboszormeny 1996.

d) Finally, we have 6 ♗g5!? which, with Black having already played ...♗e7, does not seem to make much sense.

But actually it does serve White's plan of fighting for control of d5. After 6...♗e6 7 ♘c3 0-0 8 e4 dxe4 (8...d4 9 ♘e2 h6 10 ♗d2 ♕d6 11 ♘e1 ♘d7 12 f4 f5 13 h3 fxe4 14 dxe4 a5 15 ♘d3 ♗c4 was unclear in J.Hickl-V.Hort, Dort-

mund 1989) 9 dxe4 h6 10 ♗xf6 ♗xf6 11 ♘d5 a draw was agreed in both R.Keene-A.Dückstein, Vienna 1972 and K.Hulak-J.Nunn, Reggio Emilia 1983/84. This position is one reason why I favour the text move.

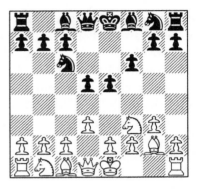

5 c3

The methodical 5 ♘bd2 ♗e6 6 e4 is best met by 6...dxe4 7 dxe4 ♕d7, followed by ..0-0-0, ...♗h3 and ...h7-h5 with an attack. Surprisingly, I have been unable to find any practical examples of this, besides a few non-essential blitz games I've played on the Internet. Nevertheless, I strongly urge you to try it!

5 0-0, on the other hand, is a move you will encounter more frequently. After 5...♗e6 the most probable line will be 6 e4 (6 ♘bd2 ♕d7 usually transposes above after e2-e4), when 6...dxe4 is playable, but the position after 7 dxe4 ♕xd1 8 ♖xd1 ♗c5 9 c3 ♘ge7 is a bit dull. Instead, 6...d4 leads to a good game for Black. The usual attacking scheme with ...0-0-0 followed by ...♗h3 and ...h7-h5-h4 is the idea, while if White challenges the centre

with 7 c3 Black can simply play 7...♕d7 8 cxd4 ♘xd4 9 ♘xd4 ♕xd4 10 ♕c2 0-0-0 and White will have problems with his backward d-pawn.

5...♗e6 6 b4 ♕d7 7 ♘bd2 ♗h3 8 ♗xh3

8 0-0?! castles right into the rising storm. Black should go for it with 8...h5 9 e4 dxe4 10 dxe4 0-0-0 when White has to be very careful. For example, 11 b5 ♘b8 12 ♕a4 h4 13 ♘xh4? (but grabbing the pawn with 13 ♗xh3 ♕xh3 14 ♕xa7 leaves Black with a dangerous attack after 14...hxg3 15 fxg3 ♘h6) 13...♖xh4! 14 gxh4 ♕g4 and mate next move. A motif worth remembering!

8...♕xh3

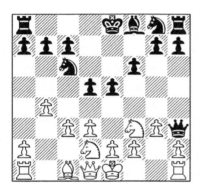

As I found out in my post-mortem analysis, we have now reached a variation of the Pirc Defence with revered colours (White wasted his extra move on 4 ♗g2). The fact that most White players are not Pirc experts should reassure you to play this system. And the fact that my opponent in this game actually was a Pirc expert and still did not get any advantage should reassure you even more.

9 b5 ♘d8 10 ♕b3 ♕d7 11 a4 ♘e6 12 ♗a3

White refuses to castle for the rest of the game, but even if he had castled short, Black would still have the better prospects. After Black castles queenside, the ensuing pawn race is not at all close, as Black can withstand the storm, while White cannot.

12...♗xa3 13 ♖xa3 ♘e7 14 ♕b4 c5 15 bxc6 ♘xc6 16 ♕b5 0-0-0 17 c4 a6 18 ♕b2 d4

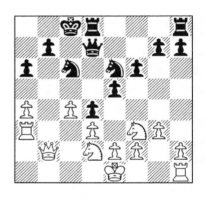

19 h4

Despite my last remark, it was now time for White to castle and at least try to generate some counterplay on the b-file. With the text move, White attempts to withstand the storm on the kingside, but then the attack comes from a different direction: in the centre.

19...♕e7 20 a5 f5 21 ♔f1 ♖hf8 22 ♔g2 ♘c5 23 ♖aa1 e4

Black is breaking through and White is getting crushed.

24 ♘e1 ♘e5 25 ♘b3 ♘e6 26 ♕d2 ♘g4 27 ♘c2 f4 28 dxe4 fxg3 29 fxg3 ♖f2+ 30 ♔g1 d3 31 ♘b4 ♘f4! 0-1

Summary

The 'improved' Nimzo-Larsen Attack from Game 76 can be hardly called an improvement, as with natural moves Black can hope for an advantage. More important are the discoveries in Game 77. By using the set-up advocated there, Black shouldn't be at all afraid to face the King's Indian Attack.

1 ♘f3 ♘c6 (D) **2 g3**

　　　　2 b3 e5 (D) – *Game 76*

2...e5 3 d3 d5 4 ♗g2 f6 (D) – *Game 77*

1...♘c6

2...e5

4...f6

Index of Complete Games

Alphabetical by Black Player

Nyholm.G-Alekhine.A, Stockholm 1912.. *193*
Stern.M-Alexopoulos.G, Somerset, USA 1985 .... *61*
Magerramov.E-Al Modiahki.M, Dubai 2000 .... *154*
Lopez Gracia.F-Ansola Marquinez.A, Zaragoza 1998.. *68*
Adianto.U-Arencibia.W, Cap d'Agde (rapid) 1998 .... *149*
Blair.D-Armani.G, Correspondence 2000... *240*
Serebro.A-Bairachny.R, Ukrainian Championship, Donetsk 1993.................... *218*
Bengsch.B-Becker.R, Kassel 1998... *54*
Dupre Guegan.M-Bergez.D, French League 1998..*56*
Farago.S-Bigaliev.R, Budapest 1996 .... *196*
Giardelli.S-Boissonet.C, Buenos Aires 1991.. *124*
Réti.R-Bogoljubow.E, German Championship, Kiel 1921 .... *186*
Grund.W-Broemmel.R, German League 2003..*24*
Ornstein.A-Brynell.S, Swedish Championship, Malmo 1986 .... *130*
Sulava.N-Brynell.S, European Team Championship, Plovdiv 2003 .... *104*
Schlindwein.R-Bukal Jr.V, Austrian League 2000 .... *96*
Etchegaray.P-Bukal Sr.V, Cannes 1997.. *159*
Dos Santos.F.J-Dolezal.C, Carilo 2005 .... *21*
Dorn.M-Flassig.D, Germany 2001 .... *128*
Socko.M-Foisor.C, Athens 2004.. *205*
Wiedner.R-Grabher.H, Austrian League 1996 .... *220*
Steinmetzer.T-Hobusch.W, Correspondence 1979.................................. *246*
Bunzmann.D-Hodgson.Ju, German League 1999 .... *229*
Nocci.R-Johnsen.K.H, Correspondence 2000.. *58*
Ter Minasjan.D-Jurkovic.H, Schwarzach 1999...................................... *102*

Autenrieth.M-Kabisch.T, West German Junior Ch'ships, Dortmund 1982....... *14*
Rotstein.J-Kalka.A, Essen 2000......................... *180*
Van Wely.L-Kasparov.G, Tilburg 1997 .... *226*
Sprenger.J-Keilhack.H, Correspondence 1996 .... *87*
Springer.O-Koenig.D, Passau 1999 .... *99*
Gelfand.B-Korchnoi.V, Groningen 1996...................... *253*
Klyuner.V-Koscielski.J, Duisburg 2000...................... *39*
Jovanic.O-Kovacevic.B, Zadar 2000........................ *111*
Koller.J-Lammers.M, German Junior Championships, Willingen 2004....... *16*
Meyer.M-Langrock.H, German League 1999..................... *162*
Sunye Neto.J-Martin del Campo.R, Linares, Mexico 1993 .... *244*
Drzemicki.D-Masternak.G, Slupsk 1992 .... *189*
Noakes.G-Menzel.T, Correspondence 1998 .... *35*
Schramm.B-Muehlig Versen.P, Schloss Schney 2002 .... *42*
Konopka.M-Muse.M, European Cup, Clichy 1995..................... *182*
Canal Oliveras.J-Narciso Dublan.M, Terrassa 1994.................... *29*
Rodriguez-Narciso Dublan.M, St Cugat 1993 .... *84*
Tarrasch.S-Nimzowitsch.A, Bad Kissingen 1928..................... *32*
McNab.C-Pert.N, Oakham 2000 .... *248*
Laurent.J-Popescu.D.D, Creon 1999....................... *135*
Tonning.E-Reefschläger.H, Gausdal 1995...................... *65*
Vujmilovic.N-Rumiancev.G, Pula 1990......................... *45*
Nemecek.P-Rybak.R, Correspondence 1999...................... *122*
Engqvist.T-Sadler.M, Isle of Man 1995...................... *141*
Eljanov.P-Sepman.Y, St Petersburg 1999..................... *132*
Khalifman.A-Shirov.A, Moscow (rapid) 2002....................... *242*
Razuvaev.Y-Skembris.S, Porto San Giorgio 1998 .... *115*
Spassov.L-Thiel.T, Badalona 1993 .... *107*
Myagmarsuren.L-Van Geet.D, World Student Team Ch'ship, Varna 1958....... *52*
Georgiev.Kir-Van Wely.L, European Cup, Chalkidiki 2002 .... *250*
Roskam.M-Vermeulen.W, Utrecht 2005 .... *224*
Schoebel.W-Vidonyak.R, Passau 1997 .... *170*
Bonnke.C-Wisnewski.C, Kiel (rapid) 2004.................... *258*
Degtiarev.E-Wisnewski.C, German Championship, Höckendorf 2004........... *175*
Grünberg.H-Wisnewski.C, German League 2002 .... *199*
Guddahl.V-Wisnewski.C, Oslo 2002 .... *117*
Homuth.M-Wisnewski.C, Luetjenburg 2003 .... *82*
Hort.V-Wisnewski.C, German Championship, Altenkirchen 2005.................. *119*
Justo.D-Wisnewski.C, Internet Chess Club (rapid) 2002.................... *151*
Korsus.B-Wisnewski.C, German League 2000...................... *146*

Kraemer.M-Wisnewski.C, Kiel 2003 .... *78*
Lamprecht.F-Wisnewski.C, German League 2005 .... *202*
Laqua.C-Wisnewski.C, German League 2006 .... *215*
Löffler.M-Wisnewski.C, Internet Chess Club (blitz) 2000............................ *190*
Martinsen.S-Wisnewski.C, Kiel 2004.. *260*
Plueg.A-Wisnewski.C, Hamburg 2003 .... *167*
Stanke.J-Wisnewski.C, Hamburg 2003 .... *233*
Redlicki.T-Wodzislawski.M, Malbork 2000.. *11*
Rohde.M-Wolff.P, Boston 1994 .... *237*
Jiganchine.R-Wright.S, Richmond, Canada 1999 .... *74*
Sokolov.I-Ye Rongguang, Antwerp 1997.. *164*
Gafner.E-Zolotukhin.V, Alushta 2005 .... *19*

Alphabetical by White Player

Adianto.U-Arencibia.W, Cap d'Agde (rapid) 1998 .... *149*
Autenrieth.M-Kabisch.T, West German Junior Ch'ships, Dortmund 1982....... *14*
Bengsch.B-Becker.R, Kassel 1998... *54*
Blair.D-Armani.G, Correspondence 2000.. *240*
Bonnke.C-Wisnewski.C, Kiel (rapid) 2004.. *258*
Bunzmann.D-Hodgson.Ju, German League 1999 .... *229*
Canal Oliveras.J-Narciso Dublan.M, Terrassa 1994............................... *29*
Degtiarev.E-Wisnewski.C, German Championship, Höckendorf 2004 .... *175*
Dorn.M-Flassig.D, Germany 2001 .... *128*
Dos Santos.F.J-Dolezal.C, Carilo 2005 .... *21*
Drzemicki.D-Masternak.G, Slupsk 1992 .... *189*
Dupre Guegan.M-Bergez.D, French League 1998....................................... *56*
Eljanov.P-Sepman.Y, St Petersburg 1999 .... *132*
Engqvist.T-Sadler.M, Isle of Man 1995.. *141*
Etchegaray.P-Bukal Sr.V, Cannes 1997.. *159*
Farago.S-Bigaliev.R, Budapest 1996 .... *196*
Gafner.E-Zolotukhin.V, Alushta 2005 .... *19*
Gelfand.B-Korchnoi.V, Groningen 1996.. *253*
Georgiev.Kir-Van Wely.L, European Cup, Chalkidiki 2002 .... *250*
Giardelli.S-Boissonet.C, Buenos Aires 1991.. *124*
Grünberg.H-Wisnewski.C, German League 2002 .... *199*
Grund.W-Broemmel.R, German League 2003... *24*
Guddahl.V-Wisnewski.C, Oslo 2002 .... *117*
Homuth.M-Wisnewski.C, Luetjenburg 2003 .... *82*
Hort.V-Wisnewski.C, German Championship, Altenkirchen 2005.................. *119*

Jiganchine.R-Wright.S, Richmond, Canada 1999 .... *74*
Jovanic.O-Kovacevic.B, Zadar 2000 .... *111*
Justo.D-Wisnewski.C, Internet Chess Club (rapid) 2002 .... *151*
Khalifman.A-Shirov.A, Moscow (rapid) 2002 .... *242*
Klyuner.V-Koscielski.J, Duisburg 2000 .... *39*
Koller.J-Lammers.M, German Junior Championships, Willingen 2004 .... *16*
Konopka.M-Muse.M, European Cup, Clichy 1995 .... *182*
Korsus.B-Wisnewski.C, German League 2000 .... *146*
Kraemer.M-Wisnewski.C, Kiel 2003 .... *78*
Lamprecht.F-Wisnewski.C, German League 2005 .... *202*
Laqua.C-Wisnewski.C, German League 2006 .... *215*
Laurent.J-Popescu.D.D, Creon 1999 .... *135*
Löffler.M-Wisnewski.C, Internet Chess Club (blitz) 2000 .... *190*
Lopez Gracia.F-Ansola Marquinez.A, Zaragoza 1998 .... *68*
Magerramov.E-Al Modiahki.M, Dubai 2000 .... *154*
Martinsen.S-Wisnewski.C, Kiel 2004 .... *260*
McNab.C-Pert.N, Oakham 2000 .... *248*
Meyer.M-Langrock.H, German League 1999 .... *162*
Myagmarsuren.L-Van Geet.D, World Student Team Ch'ship, Varna 1958 .... *52*
Nemecek.P-Rybak.R, Correspondence 1999 .... *122*
Noakes.G-Menzel.T, Correspondence 1998 .... *35*
Nocci.R-Johnsen.K.H, Correspondence 2000 .... *58*
Nyholm.G-Alekhine.A, Stockholm 1912 .... *193*
Ornstein.A-Brynell.S, Swedish Championship, Malmo 1986 .... *130*
Plueg.A-Wisnewski.C, Hamburg 2003 .... *167*
Razuvaev.Y-Skembris.S, Porto San Giorgio 1998 .... *115*
Redlicki.T-Wodzislawski.M, Malbork 2000 .... *11*
Réti.R-Bogoljubow.E, German Championship, Kiel 1921 .... *186*
Rodriguez-Narciso Dublan.M, St Cugat 1993 .... *84*
Rohde.M-Wolff.P, Boston 1994 .... *237*
Roskam.M-Vermeulen.W, Utrecht 2005 .... *224*
Rotstein.J-Kalka.A, Essen 2000 .... *180*
Schlindwein.R-Bukal Jr.V, Austrian League 2000 .... *96*
Schoebel.W-Vidonyak.R, Passau 1997 .... *170*
Schramm.B-Muehlig Versen.P, Schloss Schney 2002 .... *42*
Serebro.A-Bairachny.R, Ukrainian Championship, Donetsk 1993 .... *218*
Socko.M-Foisor.C, Athens 2004 .... *205*
Sokolov.I-Ye Rongguang, Antwerp 1997 .... *164*
Spassov.L-Thiel.T, Badalona 1993 .... *107*
Sprenger.J-Keilhack.H, Correspondence 1996 .... *87*

Springer.O-Koenig.D, Passau 1999 .... *99*
Stanke.J-Wisnewski.C, Hamburg 2003 .... *233*
Steinmetzer.T-Hobusch.W, Correspondence 1979 .... *246*
Stern.M-Alexopoulos.G, Somerset, USA 1985 .... *61*
Sulava.N-Brynell.S, European Team Championship, Plovdiv 2003 .... *104*
Sunye Neto.J-Martin del Campo.R, Linares, Mexico 1993 .... *244*
Tarrasch.S-Nimzowitsch.A, Bad Kissingen 1928 .... *32*
Ter Minasjan.D-Jurkovic.H, Schwarzach 1999 .... *102*
Tonning.E-Reefschläger.H, Gausdal 1995 .... *65*
Van Wely.L-Kasparov.G, Tilburg 1997 .... *226*
Vujmilovic.N-Rumiancev.G, Pula 1990 .... *45*
Wiedner.R-Grabher.H, Austrian League 1996 .... *220*